Encyclopedia of
U.S. Political History

Volume Editors

Volume One: Colonial Beginnings through Revolution, 1500 to 1783
Andrew W. Robertson
Lehman College and the Graduate Center of the City University of New York

Volume Two: The Early Republic, 1784 to 1840
Michael A. Morrison
Associate Professor of History, Purdue University

Volume Three: Expansion, Division, and Reconstruction, 1841 to 1877
William G. Shade
Distinguished Professor of History Emeritus, Lehigh University

Volume Four: From the Gilded Age through Age of Reform, 1878 to 1920
Robert D. Johnston
University of Illinois, Chicago

Volume Five: Prosperity, Depression, and War, 1921 to 1945
Robert H. Zieger
Distinguished Professor of History Emeritus, University of Florida

Volume Six: Postwar Consensus to Social Unrest, 1946 to 1975
Thomas S. Langston
Professor of Political Science, Tulane University

Volume Seven: The Clash of Conservatism and Liberalism, 1976 to Present
Richard M. Valelly
Claude C. Smith '14 Professor of Political Science, Swarthmore College

Editorial Consultants

Richard John, University of Illinois, Chicago

James Patterson, Brown University, Emeritus

Bruce Shulman, Boston University

ENCYCLOPEDIA OF U.S. POLITICAL HISTORY

VOLUME SEVEN
THE CLASH OF CONSERVATISM AND LIBERALISM, 1976 TO PRESENT

EDITOR
RICHARD M. VALELLY

CQ PRESS

A DIVISION OF SAGE
WASHINGTON, D.C.

CQ Press
2300 N Street, NW, Suite 800
Washington, D.C. 20037
Phone: 202-729-1900; toll-free, 1-866-4CQ-PRESS (1-866-427-7737)
Web: www.cqpress.com

Developed and produced by MTM Publishing, Inc.
New York, New York; www.mtmpublishing.com

President:	Valerie Tomaselli
Editor-in-Chief:	Eleanora von Dehsen
Project Editor:	Tim Anderson
Editorial and Production Associate:	Zach Gajewski
Design:	Annemarie Redmond Design
Maps and Charts:	Richard Garratt
Copyediting:	Carole Campbell, Peter Jaskowiak, Jason Miller
Fact Checking:	Robert Arlt, Jeff Galas, Mark LaFlaur, Jason Miller, Glenn E. Novak
Proofreading:	Susan Gamer, Carol Holmes, Jason Miller, Glenn E. Novak
Indexing:	AEIOU, Inc.

Cover design: Matthew Simmons, www.MyselfIncluded.com
Cover photo: President Barack Obama signs a proclamation celebrating the nineteenth anniversary of the Americans with Disabilities Act on July 24, 2009. (AP Images/Alex Brandon)

⊗ The paper used in this publication exceeds the requirements of the American National Standard for Information Sciences—Permanence of Paper for Printed Library Materials, ANSI Z39.48-1992.

Printed and bound in the United States of America

14 13 12 11 10   1 2 3 4 5

Library of Congress Cataloging-in-Publication Data

Encyclopedia of U.S. political history.
      p. cm.
      Includes bibliographical references and indexes.
      Contents: v. 1. Colonial beginnings through Revolution, 1500 to 1783 / editor, Andrew W. Robertson — v. 2. The early republic, 1784 to 1840 / editor, Michael A. Morrison — v. 3. Expansion, division, and Reconstruction, 1841 to 1877 / editor, William G. Shade — v. 4. From the gilded age through age of reform, 1878 to 1920 / editor, Robert D. Johnston — v. 5. Prosperity, Depression, and war, 1921 to 1945 / editor, Robert H. Zieger — v. 6. Postwar consensus to social unrest, 1946 to 1975 / editor, Thomas S. Langston — v. 7. The clash of conservatism and liberalism : 1976 to present / editor, Richard M. Valelly.
      ISBN 978-0-87289-320-7 (set : alk. paper) — ISBN 978-0-87289-312-2 (v. 1 : alk. paper) — ISBN 978-0-87289-313-9 (v. 2 : alk. paper) — ISBN 978-0-87289-314-6 (v. 3 : alk. paper) — ISBN 978-0-87289-315-3 (v. 4 : alk. paper) — ISBN 978-0-87289-316-0 (v. 5 : alk. paper) — ISBN 978-0-87289-317-7 (v. 6 : alk. paper) — ISBN 978-0-87289-318-4 (v. 7 : alk. paper) 1. United States—Politics and government—Encyclopedias. 2. Political science—United States—History—Encyclopedias. 3. Political culture—United States—History—Encyclopedias. I. Robertson, Andrew W. (Andrew Whitmore), 1951- II. Title.

E183.E53 2009
973.003—dc22
                                                                                                2010002253

Contents

Volume Seven
The Clash of Conservatism and Liberalism, 1976 to Present

List of Entries

Reader's Guide

African American Experience and Slavery

Volume One

African Americans, Free
Antislavery and Abolitionism
Slave Resistance and Rebellions
Slavery

Volume Two

Abolitionist Movement
African Americans, Free
American Anti-Slavery Society
American Colonization Society
Slave Resistance and Rebellions
Slavery

Volume Three

Abolitionist and Antislavery
    Movements
African Americans, Free
Amendment XIII
Amendment XIV
Amendment XV
Black Codes
Dred Scott Case
Emancipation Proclamation
Freedmen's Bureau
Fugitive Slave Act
Ku Klux Klan
Personal Liberty Laws
Pro-Slavery Argument
Reconstruction
Slavery

Volume Four

African Americans
Great Migration
Jim Crow
Lynching
National Association for the
    Advancement of Colored People
Plessy v. Ferguson

Volume Five

African Americans
Dyer Anti-Lynching Bill
Ku Klux Klan
National Association for the
    Advancement of Colored People
Smith v. Allwright

Volume Six

African Americans
Brown v. Board of Education of Topeka
Civil Rights Movement
Southern Christian Leadership
    Conference

Volume Seven

Affirmative Action
African Americans
Race

Civil Rights and Civil Liberties

(*See also* African American
Experience and Slavery; Women
and Women's Issues)

Volume One

Antislavery and Abolitionism
Religious Toleration
Suffrage
Zenger Trial

Volume Two

Abolitionist Movement
Alien and Sedition Acts
Civil Liberties
Civil Rights
Gag Rules
Indian Removals
Suffrage
Virginia Statute for Religious
    Freedom

Volume Three

Abolitionism and Antislavery
    Movements
Civil Rights and Civil Liberties
Milligan, Ex Parte
Personal Liberty Laws
Reconstruction
Woman Suffrage

Volume Four

Civil Liberties

Introduction

Since 1976, the two major American political parties have often been criticized for failing to find ways to achieve a broad national consensus. Such consensus has probably been impossible to achieve, however, given the contradictory impulses of the American public. For while they express a distrust of government, Americans also express economic anxiety and desire generous social policies from the very government that they claim to distrust. The result of these contradictory impulses has been an entrenched partisan debate over the federal government—over its size, its regulatory responsibilities, its spending, its revenue base, and its relationship to free market capitalism.

From the standpoint of democratic theory, the political parties have done exactly what they are supposed to do: promote national discussion until such time as a new consensus emerges in public opinion. This has often happened in American political development. The first great debate, of course, was over how to construct a national institutional order in the wake of the Revolutionary achievement of independence from Great Britain. Then came the debate over slavery, followed by the late nineteenth-century debates concerning national involvement in the politics of the former Confederate states, tariffs, whether to have a national monetary policy, and how to curb monopolies.

Viewed in historical perspective, one can see that the post-1976 debate over the role of government is only the latest in the American cycle of great debates. It is a debate that defined American politics from 1976 through the first decade of the twenty-first century, and that will likely define it for the foreseeable future. Disruptive and disturbing events such as the surprise attacks in New York, Washington, DC, and in the sky over Pennsylvania on September 11, 2001 have not altered the course of the debate.

A Public Divided

The persistence of the role-of-government standoff in the era after 1976 can be traced to three somewhat contradictory features of American public opinion. The first of these is the shift toward economic anxiety. Up until the mid-1970s, the public, when surveyed, never mentioned the state of the economy as its major worry, instead singling out either foreign policy or civil rights. After the mid-1970s, a large and permanent shift toward reported economic insecurity appeared.

Americans regularly call the United States the most prosperous country on the planet (though, in fact, Brunei and Singapore, among others, are far more prosperous). At the same time, Americans tell pollsters that they are very worried about their, and their country's, economic future—and they have been doing this since the mid-1970s.

Thus, in October 2002, a *Washington Post*/ABC News poll found that 75 percent of Americans were "very" or "somewhat" worried about the "direction of the nation's economy over the next few years." In January 2003, that figure was 67 percent, in late September 2008 it jumped to 79 percent, and by midsummer 2009 it was 77 percent. Citizens were also worried about their "own family's situation": in September 2008, 60 percent were "very" or "somewhat" worried; in midsummer 2009, 63 percent felt this way; and in mid-October 2009, 60 percent again had this same response.

But such surveys have been around for a generation. The University of Washington political scientist Mark Smith has underscored that from the late 1940s into the early 1970s, surveys of what the American public considered the "most important problem" rarely featured the economy. Only about 17 percent, at most, would name the economy, and respondents instead named such matters as foreign affairs or civil rights. But from the mid-1970s to the present, various aspects of the economy (e.g., inflation, trade competition, downsizing) were named "the most important problem" in 73 percent of such "most important problem" surveys. The American public, in short, sharply shifted toward a quite persistent and high level of anxiety about the economy.

Second, prior to the mid-1970s, the public reported very high levels of trust in government and in government officials. After the Vietnam debacle and the wrenching constitutional crisis of the Nixon administration, reported trust in government fell, and it never returned to the exceptionally high levels of the 1950s and 1960s.

The effort to measure public trust in government has been carried out since the mid-1960s by the American National Election Studies (ANES) at the University of Michigan. There are several questions that the ANES has asked, ranging from whether the respondent thinks that "you can trust the government in Washington to do what is right" (with answer choices being "just about always," "most of the time," or "only some of the time") to questions about government waste, whether government is run by a "a few big interests," and whether "people running the government are crooked." A composite index of responses to these questions devised by Vanderbilt University political scientist Marc Hetherington based on different survey items from the ANES shows that about half of the American public liked government in 1964, but that by 1976 only about 19 percent did. By 1980, that figure had rebounded to 31 percent, but it then dropped back again to 19 percent in 1994, followed by a rebound to about 30 percent by 2000. The bottom line: since the mid-1970s, public trust of government seems to have developed a "ceiling," as it were, of about 30 percent in the American National Election Studies trust index.

In the early 1990s, such distrust fed a major "deep pocket" independent candidacy by an amateur politician able to plausibly disassociate himself from government and to call for simple, compelling solutions to the "mess in Washington." The remarkably successful presidential candidacy of the Texas billionaire Ross Perot in 1992 plainly tapped

citizen distrust, as political scientists Ronald Rapoport and Walter Stone have shown in a study titled *Three's a Crowd* (2005).

One of Perot's leading themes was the lack of government accountability to the public. As he stated at one of the presidential debates, "We have to reform government." Thus, he called for term limits for elected public officials—a very popular idea that changed many state legislatures in the 1990s—on the theory that through the institution of term limits, government "won't be a lifetime career opportunity."

By mid-May 1992, Perot took the lead in public polls, with 33 percent of the public reporting that their first choice for the presidency was Perot; 28 percent saying they preferred the incumbent running for reelection, George H. W. Bush; and 24 percent expressing a preference for the Democrat Bill Clinton. By June 1992, Perot's lead had grown to 37 percent. In the end, Perot withdrew from the race. But his remarkable surge in the polls exposed just how receptive much of the public was to his antigovernment message.

Although it is often held that Perot's candidacy was simply a function of his enormous personal wealth (ironically the product of being a successful government contractor), Perot's candidacy was more remarkable for being a grass-roots phenomenon fed by self-starting organizations and activists that sprang up in response to the news that Perot was apparently taking a serious run at the presidency. Distrust of the federal government had a powerful effect in 1992.

The Perot mobilization also helped the Republican resurgence of 1994. A deep anti-Congress mood in the electorate, and the transfer to the Republican Party of much of the Perot base, benefited the Republican Party and ended 40 years of Democratic dominance of the U.S. House of Representatives—one of the longest periods of one-party control of a national legislature in the post–World War II period among all advanced industrial democracies.

In short, distrust of government has been a potent factor in American politics since the late 1970s. Such distrust has probably also affected citizen responses to policy questions. It was telling that an October 2009 NBC News survey on attitudes toward a government-run insurance option within the health insurance reform proposals showed quite different results depending on the wording of a question about the public option. One question asked, "In any health care proposal, how important do you feel it is to give people a choice of both a public plan administered by the federal government, and a private plan for their health insurance?" Of the survey sample of 1,009 adults, 72 percent said that it was "extremely or quite important" for people to have this choice. But an alternative wording appears to have tapped distrust of the government: "Would you favor or oppose creating a public health care plan administered by the federal government that would compete directly with private health insurance companies?" Only 48 percent of the survey supported the idea when phrased this way.

Similarly, as the noted pollster Andrew Kohut pointed out in mid-August 2009 the American public appeared to be balking "again at the prospect of health care reform" despite the priority of the issue during the 2008 presidential election campaign. (Kohut) This pattern was very striking from 1992 through 1994, when the public seemed very open to the idea of national health insurance, prompting the new president, Bill Clinton, to push hard for it. However, the more the public learned about national health insurance, and the more Republicans attacked it for raising the prospect of unwieldy bureaucratic regulation of personal health decisions, the more support for the idea of health insurance reform dropped. In contrast, in 1964 and 1965, when there was greater trust in government, support for Medicare never flagged in opinion polling.

From 1958 on, about 65 percent of Americans said they trusted the federal government. Thus in January 1965 a Gallup poll found that 63 percent of the public supported increased taxation to pay for compulsory health insurance for the elderly. In addition, the public favored—46 percent to 36 percent— a government plan paid for by increased Social Security taxes over the alternative of expanded private health insurance for the elderly.

Yet the recurring cycle of health care politics since 1976—which featured two great pushes by the Democratic Party for national health insurance—suggests that there has also been a third dimension of American public opinion. The public may balk once it learns the details, but in principle it has shown very strong support for social policies that, in the end, must come from government. Distrust of government has thus been coupled both to the American public's persistent sense of economic insecurity since the mid-1970s and to its support, in principle, for an activist federal government that addresses social policy problems and sustains existing and popular policy commitments, such as old-age income security and access by the elderly to health care.

A 1996 international survey, the Role of Government Survey of the International Social Survey Program, did show significant differences between the American public and Canadian or British citizens on whether, say, government should run hospitals. About 85 percent of the American public said that it was a government responsibility to care for the sick, while in Canada the figure was 94 percent and in the United Kingdom it was 99 percent. Two U.S. surveys in 2002 showed strong support for existing social policies, such as Social Security, and either high or very high levels of support for a range of policy proposals, including that government should provide the elderly with a decent standard of living, that there should be *more* spending on Social Security, and that there was *too little* spending on health. Support for more spending on public schools was also very high. Not all policies were popular, however. Practically no one advocated more spending on unemployment benefits in 2002, for example. On the other hand, in 2009, amid rising unemployment and in the midst of a severe recession, the liberal-leaning Center for American Progress reported polling results that showed 81 percent of the public supporting the extension of unemployment insurance benefits, while 74 percent supported direct government employment along the lines of the New Deal's Civilian Conservation Corps. Likewise, polls have consistently shown very high levels of public support for both the minimum wage and proposals to increase in the minimum wage.

By now the picture of paradox should be clear. The American public has become economically anxious and it strongly supports government-funded social policies—

as one would expect from an economically anxious public. But the American public also deeply distrusts the source of social policy and the remedy for economic insecurity—namely, the federal government.

The Role of the Political Parties

As a result of this paradoxical situation, there have been three interlocking types of politics since 1976. Distrust of the federal government has led to a politics of government bashing and tax resistance, while economic anxiety has led to both a politics of government remedy and a politics of "getting government off the backs of the people" so that they can handle their economic problems by themselves without help from a supposedly incompetent and potentially meddlesome government. Very high levels of support for strong labor market protections, assistance to the deserving poor, assistance to the elderly, and a variety of other social policy interventions have favored government activism that continues the legacies of the New Deal and the Great Society. The only exception has been "welfare," which the public does not like.

If a persistent debate rooted in the new structure of American public opinion was, in a sense, quite likely, there still had to be debaters who tapped the different parts of the public psyche. That role has been filled by party politicians who have come from the two stable political parties. One of these parties—the Republican Party—has become increasingly competitive. The growing parity of the national political parties was another major transformation in American politics after 1976.

In the late 1970s and the 1980s, more voters identified themselves as Democrats than as Republicans. From 1976 to 1982, according to the American National Election Studies, the percentage of the public that identified itself as Democratic ranged from 52 percent to 55 percent, with the corresponding Republican figures ranging from 32 percent to 33 percent. Then, in 1984, in the wake of the successful Republican administration of Ronald Reagan, the two levels began to converge, with 48 percent identifying as Democrats and 39 percent as Republicans. In 1988, the corresponding figures were 47 percent and 41 percent. In 1990 and 1992, Democratic identification rebounded some, but by 2004 it seemed to have settled back down

in the upper fortieth percentile, with Republican identifiers in the lower fortieth percentile. By 2008, there was a Democratic resurgence to about 50 percent of voters, with about 43 percent of voters identifying themselves as Republicans that year.

To be sure, it has been often remarked over the past generation that the number of "independents" has grown, and that independents now constitute a floating bloc of voters to whom politicians from the two major parties must cater. Certainly the Perot phenomenon and the arrival in the Senate of such independents as Bernard Sanders of Vermont and Joe Lieberman of Connecticut (despite the latter's presence on the Democratic presidential ticket in 2000) have shown that there is a strong potential for independent behavior among voters. Surveys show a growth in voter attraction to the idea of being independent.

On the other hand, partisan identification among citizens has also been a basic factor in American politics over the past generation. The American National Election Studies have shown that about 28 percent of the voting-age population, while initially calling themselves "independent," will, when pressed by a follow-up question about which party they feel closer to, identify with one or the other of the two parties. Only about 11 percent of the voting-age population in 2008 was made up of "pure independents." The percentage of voters in 2008 who were "pure independents" was 7 percent, a large decrease from the figure for the voting-age population—which suggests that even "pure independents" divide along partisan lines once they are in the polling booth and are not offered an attractive or viable independent candidacy.

In short, the public has remained partisan—and partisanship among the public, when the choices on offer are partisan choices, has become increasingly balanced between the two parties. Moreover, a very consequential sectional shift in partisan allegiance has occurred in the former Confederate states.

In the late 1970s, over half of Southerners identified themselves as Democrats. By the early twenty-first century, however, that percentage had shrunk, particularly among white Southerners, to less than half. As recently as 1990, as the political scientists Danny Hayes and Seth McKee have shown,

Republicans held less than 20 percent of all statewide political offices in the South. By halfway through the second administration of Pres. George W. Bush, however, they held a little more than half of all statewide offices. Moreover, once in office, Republican incumbents running for reelection—such as governors and U.S. senators—win overwhelmingly. These facts underscore that the South is now a stronghold of the Republican Party. In the late 1970s, only about 25 percent of U.S. House seats in the South were held by Republicans. By the early twenty-first century, that percentage had climbed to well over half.

Southern Republicans are, moreover, particularly receptive to antigovernment themes. In a typical statement, an Alabama Republican Web site (accessed in mid-November 2009) stated that conservative principles included such statements as: "I believe government must practice fiscal responsibility and must limit taxes to levels necessary to carry out constitutionally granted duties of government," and "I believe the proper role of government is to provide for the people only those critical functions that cannot be performed by individuals or private organizations." The conservatism of white Republican Southerners has infused the national party. George W. Bush was a conservative and a very polarizing president, in large part because he was a Southern Republican. The Republican congressional revolution of 1994 was led by a talented, conservative, and highly ideological Southern Republican, Newt Gingrich.

The South has, historically, been a one-party region of the country, except for rare periods of two-party competition, such as during Reconstruction (1865–1890). Although it has not become a "solid Republican South," it has certainly become a region in which one party is dominant, the Republican Party. Now that the G.O.P. has become dominant in the region, with enormously deep support among white Southerners, Southern Republicans face little pressure to moderate their strongly conservative ideological stances.

To sum up, the structure of public opinion and the competitiveness of party politics have come to "fit" each other. In a context of growing parity, politicians in both parties have sought to find ways to exploit public opinion to their advantage. The two major political parties have responded to the rich opportunities for conflict and division that are inherent in the different dimensions of American public opinion. On the one hand, government-bashing politics rests on both a broad distrust of government and economic insecurity. The Republican Party has repeatedly pictured the government as a source of economic insecurity. Fuelled by a conservative Southern base, Republicans have been able to offer a strong ideological contrast to the Democratic Party nationally. On the other hand, Democratic politicians eager to address policy problems have been able to tap the general social-policy liberalism of the public across a range of policy questions, even though that approach has not been a particularly strong sell for them in the South.

The Emergence and Evolution of the Role-of-Government Debate

It is also important to see *how* national politicians helped to fit party competition and conflicted public opinion together. The beginning of the great post-1976 role-of-government debate can in fact be traced to Pres. Jimmy Carter. One of Carter's most famous acts as president was to suggest to Americans—in what is known as his "malaise speech," televised on July 15, 1979—that the country was experiencing a crisis of confidence and purpose. The suggestion cried out for a response, which came from one of the great political entrepreneurs of American history, Ronald Reagan.

In his July 17, 1980, speech accepting the nomination of the Republican Party for the presidency, Reagan stated, "I believe it is clear our federal government is overgrown and overweight. Indeed, it is time for our government to go on a diet." Shortly afterward, at his first inaugural, in 1981, Reagan issued a remarkable call to Americans to think long and hard about the proper role of government: "In this present crisis, government is not the solution to our problem; government is the problem. . . . It is no coincidence that our present troubles parallel and are proportionate to the intervention and intrusion in our lives that result from unnecessary and excessive growth of government."

There was a ringing Jacksonian quality to Reagan's call. Andrew Jackson sought to scale back the national government, making the Bank of the United States a symbol of overgrown federal power. Reagan's targets were different: they included social policies and New Deal legacies such as Social Security. Reagan did not succeed in retrenching Social Security; in fact, he reformed it. But his Jacksonian call to scaling back the federal government was later echoed by Pres. George W. Bush, who, after his 2004 election, pushed hard—if quite unsuccessfully—for the privatization of Social Security.

Undergirding the Reagan Revolution's call to a new sense of national purpose was a highly experimental, and often derided, understanding of political economy: supply-side economics. Herbert Stein, an economist and advisor to Pres. Richard Nixon, called it the "economics of joy." Less charitably, Reagan's vice president, George H. W. Bush, when he was running against Reagan in the Republican presidential primaries of 1980, called it "voodoo economics."

A simple and compelling trade-off—captured by the Laffer Curve, named after the supply-side economist Arthur Laffer—was at the heart of the supply-side economics that Reagan strongly espoused. Picture a two-dimensional plot with two axes, X and Y, at perpendicular angles. One axis (it does not matter which) is labeled "revenues" and the other is labeled "tax rates," with government revenues running from 0 on up on the "revenues" axis, and tax rates running from 0 to the confiscatory level of 100 percent on the "rates" axis. Arthur Laffer proposed a curve with an optimal zone of taxation located at low taxes and high revenues. The curve implied that government would receive more revenue if it cut taxes.

This message of supply-side economics coincided, it happened, with the property tax revolts of the late 1970s. As Stephen Moore of the libertarian Cato Institute wrote in 1998, looking back on what he had seen:

> *The conservative, anti-big-government tide in America began . . . with the passage of taxpayer advocate Howard Jarvis's Proposition 13 in California. Proposition 13 was a political earthquake whose jolt was felt not just in Sacramento but all across the nation, including Washington, D.C. Jarvis's initiative to cut California's notoriously high property taxes by 30 percent and then cap the rate of increase in the future was the prelude to the Reagan income tax cuts in 1981. It also incited a nationwide tax revolt at the state and local levels. Within five years of Proposition 13's passage, nearly half the states strapped a similar straitjacket on politicians' tax-raising capabilities.*

In the late 1970s, Americans were indeed reacting to actual, not imagined, increases in their tax burden. Before the 1970s, politicians hardly mentioned taxes, as the MIT political scientist Andrea Campbell has shown. But the tax burden had increased in real terms by the mid-1970s, driven by increases in payroll, state income, and local property taxes. Also, as inflation lifted incomes upward, many found themselves in federal income tax brackets once reserved for far richer people. By the late 1970s, a majority of Americans believed that they were paying too much in taxes.

In this context, the message of supply-side economics was certain to resonate. Government was probably taxing on the wrong side of the Laffer Curve (closer toward the 100 percent endpoint on the "rates" axis), and thus getting less revenue than it would receive if government cut taxes *back* toward the ascending side of the curve. Why would cutting taxes generate higher revenues, if not in the short run then certainly in the medium or long run? The belief behind this theory was that cuts in taxes would lead to an increased supply of work effort and entrepreneurial innovation from workers and investors, causing broad economic growth, which in turn would result in higher revenues.

The Republican Party, led by Reagan, thus committed itself to an avowedly experimental but nonetheless promising program of tax cuts to encourage economic actors to "supply" effort and entrepreneurship. That program would be coupled to cuts in welfare programs that encouraged dependency and thus interfered with the effort-releasing element of supply-side economics.

The ideas of supply-side economics and ending welfare dependency brilliantly combined a promise of a better future, a story about the need for government to shrink, and a portrait of an American public eager to release its economic energies, wean itself from government programs, and put the country on the road to greater prosperity. Small wonder that Stein called it the "economics of joy."

The practical politics of the Republican Party since the Reagan Revolution has, to be sure, frequently varied from its ideological commitment to supply-side economics. Despite the Republican Party's new approach to fiscal balance, which has been to portray fiscal imbalance as a problem which disappears if taxes are cut sharply, both Ronald Reagan and his successor, George H. W. Bush, presided over tax increases, in the early 1980s and in 1990.

Also, Republicans have hardly been as hostile to social policies and welfare as they have often been depicted as being. Medicaid, which provides means-tested medical care in cooperation with state governments, has grown enormously since the Reagan Revolution. President Reagan presided over a reform of Social Security that put it on much sounder footing. During the administration of Pres. George H. W. Bush, the Republican Party pushed for the Americans with Disabilities Act of 1990. Congressional Republicans also pushed for the Child Tax Credit in the late 1990s. During the administrations of George W. Bush, the Republican Party pushed for two major expansions of government: the No Child Left Behind Act of 2001, which set federal standards for local schools, and the Medicare Modernization Act of 2003,which promised a generous new prescription drug program for the elderly and went into effect in 2006.

But a new political economic formula could be discerned in the enormous impact of the Reagan Revolution on the Republican Party: indifference to fiscal imbalance as an immediate problem (since the answer to deficits was actually to cut taxes further), a certainty that tax cuts are a sovereign remedy for addressing the economic insecurity of Americans, and a rhetoric of concern over the size and scope of government and the dependency-creating interference of "welfare" that taps into popular distrust of government and is amplified into government bashing by Republican political activists and, sometimes, Republican officeholders. This new formula has defined the Republican Party for a generation.

The policy correlates of this formula, both nationally and in state government, have been tax cuts and strident opposition to any tax increases. The Economic Recovery Tax Act of 1981, strongly promoted by President Reagan, was easily the largest tax cut that had ever been enacted in American history up to that time. Under Pres. George W. Bush, there were two additional tax cuts. The Economic Growth and Tax Relief Reconciliation Act of 2001 lowered tax rates, provided a $300 rebate to millions of taxpayers, increased a child tax credit dating to the Clinton presidency and the Gingrich revolution in Congress, lowered the rate on dividend income, increased real estate depreciation, lowered the capital gains tax, set the estate tax on a course toward temporary repeal in 2010, and created generous incentives for private retirement income planning. The Jobs and Growth Tax Relief Reconciliation Act of 2003 accelerated the phase-ins of several of the 2001 changes and further lowered taxes on capital gains and dividend income.

Looking back toward 1980 and the rise of Reagan, one can see that in the years since Reagan's election the Republican Party has reorganized itself around a "starve the beast" formula for economic policy—the "beast" being the national government and its revenue base. This kind of government-bashing politics rests on both a broad distrust of government and economic insecurity. The Republican Party portrays the federal government as a source of economic insecurity, not as a source of answers to economic insecurity.

Among Republican voters, these sorts of themes have taken strong hold. In late May 2009, a survey by the Pew Research Center for the People and the Press found that 72 percent of respondents who identified themselves as Republicans agreed with the statement that "the federal government controls too much of our daily lives," while 77 percent of conservative Republicans and 67 percent of moderate to liberal Republicans thought that "when something is run by the government it is usually inefficient and wasteful." Likewise, 75 percent of Republicans thought that "government regulation of business does more harm than good." Republicans also disliked social policies. Just 29 percent of Republicans thought that government "should help more needy people, even if it means debt"; and just under half of Republicans agreed that government should "guarantee everybody enough to eat and a place to sleep" and that it was a "government responsibility to care for those who can't care for themselves."

From Carter to Obama: The Party of Liberalism and Activist National Government

Democrats have offered a clear alternative to the Republican approach to political economy. There has been a continuing Democratic commitment to activist government, with an emphasis on low unemployment, the labor market, and more generous social policies. Since 1976, this approach has been particularly evident in Democratic pushes for national health insurance.

During the administration of Pres. Jimmy Carter, Democrats in Congress sought, for example, to respond to the effects of inflation on the minimum wage by indexing the value of the federal minimum wage to the rate of inflation. They ultimately failed at this in 1977, but Democrats have since continued to push for adjustments to the federal minimum wage, not least because increases in the minimum wage are enormously popular, notwithstanding the beliefs of many (though not all) reputable economists that the minimum wage increases unemployment. In 2004, for instance, Democratic presidential candidate John Kerry advocated a significant increase in the minimum wage. Such continuing Democratic commitment to this policy has encouraged inflation indexing of minimum wage increases, or inflation indexing of minimum wages, in a total of 24 states.

To be sure, Democrats twice forcefully responded to the relative indifference of Republicans to fiscal imbalance. Rather surprisingly, the Eisenhower-era proclivity of the Republican Party for balancing the budget migrated into the Democratic Party halfway through the Reagan presidency. In 1984, Democratic presidential candidate Walter Mondale responded to the Reagan deficits by campaigning on a tax increase to close the deficit. Also, early in the Clinton administration, President Clinton and congressional Democrats pushed through a tax increase and embarked on a continuation of the deficit control that Democrats and Pres. George H. W. Bush had agreed to in the Omnibus Budget Reconciliation Act of 1990.

Then, too, President Clinton cooperated with a revitalized congressional Republican Party under Speaker Newt Gingrich—the first Republican Speaker of the House since Speaker Joseph Martin (1953–1955)—to "end welfare as we know it" in the 1996 Personal Responsibility and Work Opportunity Reconciliation Act. This landmark statute ended 60 years of open-ended federal and state support for "welfare" in the form of cash grants to typically single-mother families in which the mother did not have a steady work history, replacing the Aid to Families with Dependent Children (AFDC) program with another called Temporary Assistance for Needy Families (TANF).

Yet, since the administration of Pres. Jimmy Carter, there have been very strong efforts during periods of unified Democratic control of national government to develop generous social policies and to provide macroeconomically assertive national government. The Clinton presidency saw an intense effort to expand the scope of employer-provided health insurance, to "insure the uninsured," and to publicly provide health insurance to those who were not covered by Medicaid but were prone to bouts of unemployment and, when work was available, to have only low-wage work. Although that effort famously "boomeranged" on Clinton and the Democrats (to use an apt metaphor devised by the Harvard social policy scholar Theda Skocpol), it set the stage for enormous activism during the next moment of unified Democratic control of Congress and the White House, which came in 2009, under the Obama administration. Another major innovation of the Clinton presidency was an expansion of the Earned Income Tax Credit (EITC). The tax credit dates to 1975, and today it reduces the amount of income tax that low-wage "working poor" Americans pay. In 2003, as the College of William and Mary policy scholar Chris Howard has shown, the EITC lowered the tax of the average eligible family (the credit "phased out" that year at $25,000) to zero, and it generated a refund check of $1,600 to claimants. Clinton and the Democrats pushed in 1993 to make the credit available to working poor adults without children, to increase benefits beyond inflation, and to raise the eligibility level. A year later, the number of families receiving the EITC had grown by 25 percent and the cost of the program had shot up by 35 percent. Eventually, the real (inflation-adjusted) value of the credit had about doubled. In 1990, the program cost about $10 billion (in 2000 dollars), and in 2000 it cost $32 billion.

Such an expansion of the EITC was sufficiently forceful that it had a distinct impact on public opinion. In 2003, the Kaiser Family Foundation, National Public Radio, and the Kennedy School of Government released the results of their joint Survey of Americans Views on Taxes, which found that 61 percent of the public had heard of the term "earned income tax credit" and knew what it meant. Just as Republican policies—such as the prescription drug benefit of 2003, which went into effect in 2006—have impacted public opinion, so too have Democratic policy innovations changed the contours of public opinion.

But reconfiguring public opinion has hardly been the motivation for Democratic policy activism. Republicans have consciously sought to affect public opinion—and the data from 2009 concerning Republican voters' policy views suggest that they have succeeded. The Democrats' motivation appears to have been based on a different view of historic purpose: fulfillment and extension of a legacy.

No politician was better at capturing this sense of fulfilling permanent commitments to social policy than Sen. Edward M. Kennedy (D–MA). Kennedy was masterfully pragmatic, but his pragmatism was always apparently guided by an historicist sense of delivering on New Deal and Great Society dreams whenever possible. Thus, when the U.S. House passed a reform of health insurance in early November 2009, the Democratic Speaker of the House, Nancy Pelosi, among other leading Democrats, placed the House passage in the context of twentieth-century efforts to develop federal social policies: "It is very humbling to stand here at a time when we can associate ourselves with the work of those who passed Social Security, those who passed Medicare, and now we will pass health care reform." Interestingly, Pelosi switched to invoking the memory of Senator Kennedy, saying, "I couldn't help but think of Senator Kennedy. Senator Kennedy called passing health care 'the great unfinished business of our country.'"

But the push for health insurance reform was hardly the only social policy innovation of 2009. The 2009 "stimulus package," enacted to combat the effects of a deep recession begun in 2007, was laced with social policy changes. It subsidized a program through which unemployed citizens can provide for their own health coverage; it boosted the Child Tax Credit (initially a Republican policy to be sure); it provided $2 billion for the Child Care and Development Block Grant, $1 billion for Head Start, and $1.1 billion for Early Head Start; it had a $20 billion increase for the Supplemental Nutrition Assistance Program (SNAP), formerly known as Food Stamps, as well as funding for food banks and the Special Supplemental Nutrition Program for Women, Infants, and Children (WIC); it had an increase of $25 per week for unemployment insurance recipients and incentives for states to expand unemployment insurance eligibility; and it contained an extra $250 payment to Social Security and Supplemental Security Income beneficiaries.

In fact, if one accessed the White House website in early November 2009, one found a long list of legislative accomplishments. The first legislation that President Obama signed, on January 29, 2009, was the Lilly Ledbetter Fair Pay Act, an override by the Democratic Party of a Supreme Court decision adversely affecting the rights of women for equal pay for equal work. On February 4, the second piece of legislation President Obama signed was the Children's Health Insurance Program Reauthorization Act, which increased coverage under the State Children's Health Insurance Program. The White House Web site clearly connoted activist government.

In short, even as the Republican Party grew stronger after 1976, and as it sounded antigovernment, tax-cutting, and deregulatory themes, the Democratic Party remained committed to activism. To be sure, in January 1996, Pres. Bill Clinton said in a radio address that the "era of big government was over." But the Democratic Party's commitment to big government emerged strongly and forcefully under Barack Obama.

Moreover, the commitments of the Democratic Party to activist government seemed entrenched among citizens who identified themselves as Democrats. A Pew Research Center report, "Trends in Political Attitudes and Core Values: 1987-2009," released in late May 2009, found that 65 percent of Democrats agreed that "the government should help more needy people even if it means going deeper into debt," while 79 percent thought that the government should guarantee every citizen enough to eat and a place to sleep. Support for labor unions among Democratic respondents was 80 percent, and support for "stricter laws . . . to protect the environment" was close to 100 percent among Democrats. The Democratic Party's activism seemed matched by the activism of its electoral base.

Hardwired into American Politics

All of these trends suggest that the post-1976 role-of-government debate has become hardwired into national politics—indeed, it has also increasingly affected state politics. During the state budget crises of 2009, the push for tax increases was met by Republican hostility in many states, leading to a partial shutdown of governmental functions in California and, in Pennsylvania, temporary suspension of day care funds until compromises could be reached.

Republicans have actively sought to create political contexts in which their approach to the role-of-government debate can be showcased to their advantage. For example, a key feature of the tax cuts that President Bush pushed for in 2001 and 2003 is that they would "sunset." These tax cuts increased the deficit, but deficit control has now been built into the rules of congressional budgeting—though in a way that permits short-term deficit increases if they are "paid for" over a 10-year period and if the provisions that cause them eventually expire. Thus, the debate over supply-side economics was guaranteed to return to center stage no later than midway through the Obama administration. The two parties were, in effect, required in advance to debate supply-side economics.

Even had the Bush tax cuts of 2001 and 2003 not been structured in a way certain to subsequently stage a national debate about the size of government, the fiscal imbalance bequeathed by the Bush administration, coupled with the outsized government spending of the Obama administration, also hardwired the size-of-government debate into American politics. The Clinton presidency was proud of the fiscal balance it achieved by 2000. But the tax cuts of the presidency of George W. Bush, the generosity of Bush's new prescription drug benefit for senior citizens, and the off-budget but nonetheless massive military spending of the Iraq and Afghan wars placed a considerable potential claim on taxpayers. The deficit spending of the Obama administration has done the same. Clinton may have thought that he was assuring the future of social-policy activism by taking taxation off the table through his efforts to balance the budget. In fact, budget balance seemed so stable that there was at one time real concern about whether the market in Treasury securities—and thus a policy instrument for the Federal Reserve—would disappear. If the Fed cannot buy or sell Treasury securities it cannot after all affect the cost of credit.

But Clinton's successors, Bush and Obama, undertook initiatives that have guaranteed a continuing size-of-government debate. In 2009, the U.S. federal deficit was larger than the gross domestic product (GDP) of all but a handful of other countries in the world. The debt-to-GDP ratio of the United States appeared poised to be larger, and remain larger, than it had been since the early 1980s. Moreover, such inherited commitments as Medicare seemed certain to become fiscally pressing. Medicare's impending insolvency cast a little-remarked upon but deepening shadow over the emerging fiscal crisis of the twenty-first century, while the 50 states experienced severe fiscal pressures in 2009 and 2010.

In 2009, however, the Democrats showed little hesitation in reaching for highly activist approaches to government. No one struck a more activist tone than America's first African American president, Barack Obama. The size of his agenda in 2009—combating the recession, responding to climate change, more generous social policies, reforming unregulated finance, spurring industrial innovation through the development of "green manufacturing"—spoke volumes.

But Obama himself was as full-throated as his agenda. At a construction site in Fairfax County, Virginia, being funded by the American Recovery and Reinvestment Act of 2009 (known as the "Stimulus Bill"), President Obama sounded much like Pres. Lyndon Johnson or Pres. Harry Truman as he referenced "8,000 highway projects that have been approved under the Recovery Act across this country . . . as part of the largest investment in the nation's infrastructure since President Eisenhower built the Interstate Highway System back in the 1950s."

To be sure, in a nod to the distrust that Americans show pollsters when asked about government waste and inefficiency, President Obama noted, "because so many of these projects are being managed well—and I want to thank the team that's been working so hard out here—these projects are coming in, on average, 10 to 20 percent under budget." But then the president tacked back toward classic Democratic Party governmental activism, ticking off facts and figures: "unemployment insurance for 12 million Americans . . . COBRA 65 percent cheaper . . . emergency relief to more than 1 million seniors . . . 30,000 loans to small businesses across America . . ." His restlessness was palpable: "We're moving forward on a number of different economic fronts. . . . That's what we committed ourselves to doing when I took office; we are moving forward."

Even as the Republican Party has repeatedly returned to a rhetoric of small government, Democrats have repeatedly sought to tap into the persistent economic anxieties of the American public and connect them to the surprising extent of support for generous policies—surprising, that is, in light of the low levels of trust in government and the great public sensitivity to tax burdens. As Robert Pear, the *New York Times* correspondent whose beat for a quarter of a century has been the politics of social policy, reported in late October 2009, "many Congressional Democrats" had come to the "conclusion . . . that economic insecurity and high unemployment stoke public support for their proposals to guarantee insurance for millions of Americans," referring here to health insurance.

At the same time, congressional Republicans were actively sponsoring protests against big government. In the fall of 2009, the conservative representative Michele Bachmann of Minnesota led dozens of her House Republican colleagues in protests on the steps of the Capitol. In a fiery press release, she assailed the Democrats' push for health reform, calling it "gangster government at its worst." Much remarked, in fact, was this sort of move to the right, and away from the center, that occurred within the Republican Party in response to the first instance of unified Democratic control of national government since the first Clinton administration.

In short, in 2009, the great role-of-government debate under way since the mid-1970s showed no sign of letting up. The two parties were far apart—but then so were Americans. It has been an era, indeed, of dissensus and conflict. The looming fiscal crises of national and state governments foreshadowed either a resolution of the debate—or increased division.

The Great Role-of-Government Debate in Historical Perspective

Democratic political systems are built, in part, around conflict and debate. Professional politicians fish out issues to differentiate themselves. Since 1976, the Democratic and Republicans parties have developed an enduring discussion that taps the contradictory impulses of the American public: distrust of government, economic anxiety, and a desire for generous policies from the very government that the public distrusts.

Actions by the major parties to promote a national discussion—at least until such time as a consensus or a resolution somehow emerges—have often occurred in American political development. America's first great debate—between Federalists and Antifederalists—focused on how to construct a new national institutional order in the wake of the Revolutionary achievement of national self-determination. A second great debate emerged in the late 1850s: the debate over slavery. Its greatest symbol is the series of Lincoln-Douglas debates. The late nineteenth century saw interparty debates concerning national involvement in the politics of the former Confederate states, tariffs, whether to have a national monetary policy, and how to curb private monopolies—conflicts that led to the development of independent regulatory agencies for managing interstate commerce and transportation and a central bank in the form of the Federal Reserve. The post-1976 role-of-government debate renews this American cycle of great debates. As with the previous debates, it has been dramatic, and even strident.

Bibliography and Further Reading

Bartels, Larry. *Unequal Democracy: The Political Economy of the New Gilded Age.* New York: Russell Sage Foundation; Princeton, NJ: Princeton University Press, 2008.

Brooks, Clem, and Jeff Manza. *Why Welfare States Persist: The Importance of Public Opinion in Democracies.* Chicago: University of Chicago Press, 2007.

Campbell, Andrea Louise. "What Americans Think of Taxes." In *The New Fiscal Sociology: Taxation in Comparative and Historical Perspective,* edited by Isaac William Martin, Ajay K. Mehrotra, and Monica Prasad, 48–67. Cambridge: Cambridge University Press, 2009.

Fiorina, Morris. *Culture War? The Myth of a Polarized America.* With Samuel J. Abrams and Jeremy Pope. New York: Pearson Longman, 2005.

Gelman, Andrew, et al. *Red State, Blue State, Rich State, Poor State: Why Americans Vote The Way They Do.* Princeton, NJ: Princeton University Press, 2008.

Hacker, Jacob S. "Policy Drift: The Hidden Politics of U.S. Welfare State Retrenchment." In *Beyond Continuity: Institutional Change in Advanced Political Economies,* edited by Wolfgang Streeck and Kathleen Thelen, 40–82. Oxford: Oxford University Press, 2005.

Hayes, Danny. "Has Television Personalized Voting Behavior?" *Political Behavior* 31, no. 2 (June 2009): 231–260.

Hayes, Danny, and Seth McKee. "Toward a One-Party South?" *American Politics Research* 36, no. 1 (January 2008): 3–32.

Hetherington, Marc J. *Why Trust Matters: Declining Political Trust and the Demise of American Liberalism.* Princeton, NJ: Princeton University Press, 2005.

Howard, Christopher. *The Welfare State Nobody Knows: Debunking Myths About U.S. Social Policy.* Princeton, NJ: Princeton University Press, 2007.

Kohut, Andrew. "Would Americans Welcome Medicare if It Were Being Proposed in 2009?" Pew Research Center Publications, August 19, 2009.

Levendusky, Matthew. *The Partisan Sort: How Liberals Became Democrats and Conservatives Became Republicans.* Chicago: University of Chicago Press, 2009.

McCarty, Nolan, Keith Poole, and Howard Rosenthal. *Polarized America: The Dance of Ideology and Unequal Riches.* Cambridge, MA: MIT Press, 2006.

Moore, Stephen. "Proposition 13 Then, Now, and Forever." http://www.cato.org/pub_display.php?pub_id=5682 (accessed November 22, 2009).

Pear, Robert. "Democrats See Positive In A Bad Economy." *New York Times,* October 24, 2009, p. A22.

Pierson, Paul, and Theda Skocpol, eds. *The Transformation of American Politics: Activist Government and the Rise of Conservatism.* Princeton, NJ: Princeton University Press, 2007.

Rapoport, Ronald B., and Walter J. Stone. *Three's A Crowd: The Dynamic of Third Parties, Ross Perot, and Republican Resurgence.* Ann Arbor: University of Michigan Press, 2005.

Shafer Byron E., and Richard Johnston. *The End of Southern Exceptionalism: Class, Race, and Partisan Change in the Postwar South.* Cambridge, MA: Harvard University Press, 2006.

Shoch, James. "Bringing Public Opinion and Electoral Politics Back In: Explaining the Fate of 'Clintonomics' and Its Contemporary Relevance." *Politics and Society* 36, no. 1 (March 2008): 89-130

Skocpol, Theda. *Boomerang: Clinton's Health Security Effort and the Turn against Government in U.S. Politics.* New York W. W. Norton, 1996.

Smith, Mark A. *The Right Talk: How Conservatives Transformed the Great Society into the Economic Society.* Princeton, NJ: Princeton University Press, 2007.

Richard M. Valelly

ABORTION

Abortion policy—the conditions under which women can legally terminate pregnancy—has generated one of the most contentious and long-standing debates of contemporary U.S. politics. In *Roe v. Wade*, 410 U.S. 113 (1973), the U.S. Supreme Court declared that a woman's right to privacy was broad enough to encompass the decision to terminate her pregnancy. Rather than resolving the conflict, however, *Roe* created a firestorm permeating policymaking and political institutions at all levels. Abortion policy became the focal point of a pitched battle over the status of women and values in the late twentieth century; as these policy differences became organized into politics, they converged with the rise of the Christian Right and a constellation of related interest groups, rebirth of the Republican Party, and polarization of party politics. *Roe* legalized abortion, but the issue's politicization created policies that limited accessibility to the procedure, especially for women of limited means.

U.S. Abortion Policy before *Roe*

Under common law, abortion early in pregnancy was not a crime. Only after quickening (detection of fetal movement) was abortion deemed illegal. Common law tradition was followed until the late nineteenth century when state legislatures, prompted by a physicians' crusade, criminalized abortion throughout pregnancy, except to save the life of the mother. "Regular" physicians (those trained in medical schools) hoped to

drive their competition ("irregulars"—homeopaths, midwives) out of business by criminalizing a lucrative part of the irregulars' trade.

Abortion remained out of public purview until the late-1950s, when public health professionals, doctors, and lawyers advocated for abortions in cases of rape, incest, and gross fetal abnormality. In 1967, Colorado, North Carolina, and California became the first states to substantially relax their abortion statutes; by 1970, 13 other states passed reform-oriented legislation. Women's rights organizations formed during the mid-1960s called for repeal, not reform, of abortion laws. It was in this milieu that the National Association for the Repeal of Abortion Laws (NARAL) emerged. Four states—Washington, Alaska, Hawaii, and New York—would decriminalize abortion before *Roe*.

Abortion-rights advocates did not limit attacks against abortion laws to state legislatures. They launched constitutional challenges in state and federal courts, with the result that numerous state laws were deemed invalid under various constitutional arguments. The right to privacy—to make life's most important decisions unfettered by governmental interference—emerged as an especially fruitful approach given the Court's decision in *Griswold v. Connecticut*, 381 U.S. 479 (1965), which struck down Connecticut's ban on dispensing contraceptives to married couples. Ultimately, the judicial strategy would lead to *Roe*, which declared Texas's abortion statute an unconstitutional violation of the right to privacy.

1973–1983: Backlash

Roe's sweeping pronouncement invalidated abortion statutes in nearly all states. Moreover, it ensured a significant role for the federal courts in determining abortion policy. In Congress, numerous versions of a Human Life Amendment (HLA) designed to overturn *Roe* were introduced. The HLA remained on the congressional agenda until 1983, when it was defeated in the Senate. Anti-abortion forces, however, won a significant victory in 1976 when Congress restricted funding for abortions under the Medicaid program to those cases in which the mother's life was at risk. Public funding of abortion generated three significant Supreme Court cases, culminating in *Harris v. McRae*, 448 U.S. 297 (1980), which upheld congressional funding restrictions. Though *Harris* quelled the debate in Washington, it did little to stop the fury in the states, where public funding debates produced battles that pitted governors and state supreme courts against legislatures. Public funding also was a staple item on the ballot in states that permitted initiatives and referenda. In 2008, only 17 states funded most abortions for indigent women.

In the wake of *Roe*, state legislators in jurisdictions hostile to the ruling (e.g., Missouri, Utah, North Dakota, and Pennsylvania) wrote highly restrictive laws that tested *Roe*'s limits. These laws required spousal or (in the case of minors) parental consent; banned abortions in public facilities; and prohibited saline abortions, the most common method for performing second-trimester procedures. Abortion-rights organizations challenged these laws, and Supreme Court decisions such as *Planned Parenthood of Central Missouri v. Danforth*, 428 U.S. 52 (1976) and *Bellotti v. Baird*, 428 U.S. 132 (1976) struck down the new regulations, or in the case of minors suggested there was a diminished right to privacy but one that nonetheless required protection. Undaunted, antiabortion legislators and advocacy groups introduced items in sympathetic state legislatures concerning parental involvement and informed consent laws that mandated information be given to women before obtaining an abortion. Informed consent laws were coupled with waiting periods, which were nullified on privacy grounds by the Supreme Court in *Akron v. Akron Center for Reproductive Health*, 462 U.S. 416 (1983).

Although anti-abortion forces had little to show 10 years after *Roe* in terms of changes in abortion policy, they were beginning to wield political clout. The midterm elections of 1978 showed the power of single-issue antiabortion voters, who played an important role in defeating abortion-rights Senators Dick Clark (D–IA) and Thomas McIntyre (D–NH). Similarly, antiabortion strategists were credited for the defeats of four abortion-rights senators in 1980, and antiabortion voters also played an important role in the 1980 presidential election of Ronald Reagan.

The late 1970s and early 1980s represented the rise of the New Christian Right. The marriage of abortion with larger conservative and New Christian Right concerns—school prayer, scientific creationism, gun control, gay rights, and the Equal Rights Amendment, among others—gave abortion a wider audience than ever. The politicization of abortion in the late 1970s and early 1980s added much stronger antiabortion language to the Republican Party's platform, including the goal of appointing antiabortion judges to the federal bench. The influx of moral conservatives into the political process augured well for the Republican Party, which was attempting to exploit issues that would lure socially conservative voters (including Roman Catholics and evangelical Protestants) away from the Democratic Party. The antiabortion movement's agenda, which the Roman Catholic hierarchy had assisted in founding, was increasingly supplanted by conservative Protestants whose leaders sought to reshape the movement and broaden its goals; abortion became indicative of a decline in the family—a more powerful condensational symbol than rights for the unborn alone. Abortion was the focal point for a divide in American society between traditionalists and modernists; it became a battle over the definition of the American family and a woman's place in it. And abortion was central to two important emerging social movements—feminism and the New Christian Right.

1984–1992: Rightward Drift in the Federal Courts

Dramatic changes in abortion policy did not occur at the national level during the 1980s. Far more important than policy considerations were political ones:

abortion was more fully incorporated into partisan politics, with Republicans siding with the antiabortion forces and Democrats with the abortion-rights community. As a result, President Reagan's nominations to the federal judiciary, particularly to the U.S. Supreme Court, signaled a rightward shift in abortion jurisprudence as supporters of *Roe* retired and were replaced by those skeptical of or hostile to the decision.

The changing complexion of the Court was seen most dramatically in *Thornburgh v. American College of Obstetricians and Gynecologists*, 476 U.S. 747 (1986), *Webster v. Reproductive Health Services*, 492 U.S. 490 (1989), and *Planned Parenthood of Southeastern Pennsylvania v. Casey*, 505 U.S, 833 (1992). In *Thornburgh*, a 5–4 Court struck down most of Pennsylvania's strict regulations on informed consent and record keeping. In 1989, when the Court considered *Webster*, President Reagan had appointed two new justices, Antonin Scalia and Anthony Kennedy. A reconstituted court upheld Missouri's regulations (restrictions on performance of abortions by public employees and in public facilities, as well as testing for fetal viability for women 20 or more weeks pregnant) in *Webster*, but it did not abandon the *Roe* framework. The Court's composition changed again when the nominees of Pres. George H. W. Bush, David Souter and Clarence Thomas, were confirmed in 1990 and 1991, respectively. The *Casey* court heard a challenge to Pennsylvania's abortion law (spousal notification, reporting requirements, parental consent, and informed consent). It announced the adoption of the undue burden standard as the new framework under which abortion regulations would be evaluated. Using this standard, the Court found all of Pennsylvania's regulations constitutional, except spousal notification.

Numerous antiabortion activists and organizations no longer countenanced the slow, arduous process of undoing *Roe*. They chose instead to engage in direct-action techniques such as blocking clinic access and picketing the homes of doctors who performed abortions. Direct-action tactics rose significantly after 1983 and became associated with the Pro-Life Action League, led by Joseph Scheidler, and Operation Rescue, led by Randall Terry.

1993–Present: Ascendancy of the Antiabortion Movement

Abortion-rights advocates hailed Pres. Bill Clinton's 1992 election and moved to enact their agenda in Congress. Though President Clinton's election did lead to the 1994 passage of the Freedom of Access to Clinics Entrances law, making it a federal crime to block entrances to abortion clinics, the abortion-rights community overreached during 1993–1994 in its attempt to pass the Freedom of Choice Act (FOCA), which would have written abortion rights into federal law. That failing effort reenergized the antiabortion community. The fight against FOCA paved the way for the Partial Birth Abortion Act, which banned the D&X procedure (the so-called partial-birth abortion) used to perform late-term abortions, to become law when Republicans took control of Congress in 1995. The legislation failed, however, because Congress could not override President Clinton's vetoes.

The election of Pres. George W. Bush buoyed antiabortion organizations, as did the fact that members of Congress were increasingly ideological, including their commitment to the antiabortion position. As a result, Congress did pass the Partial Birth Abortion Act in 2003 and the Unborn Victims of Violence Law in 2004, and President Bush signed both into law. The Unborn Victims law established legal status for the fetus by permitting charges to be filed on behalf of the fetus when a pregnant woman was assaulted or murdered.

After 1993, state legislatures were enacting informed consent and parental involvement statutes, as well as provisions that strictly regulated abortion clinics. For example, in 2006, South Dakota's legislature banned abortions except to save the mother's life, but the law was subjected to a referendum vote and was defeated by voters later that year. Federal courts employing the undue burden standard announced in *Casey* upheld most regulations. In states with strong privacy protections (Florida, California), however, the Courts invalidated a variety of abortion regulations under state constitutional provisions.

George W. Bush further solidified the conservative majority on the U.S. Supreme Court through his appointments of Chief Justice John Roberts and Justice

Samuel Alito in 2005. The influence of Justice Alito (Justice Sandra Day O'Connor's replacement) was especially apparent when he voted in the five-person majority upholding the congressional ban on partial-birth abortion in *Gonzales v. Carhart*, 550 U.S. 124 (2007). In a similar case, *Stenberg v. Carhart*, 530 U.S. 914 (2000), challenging a state partial-birth abortion law, the Court struck Nebraska's law in which Justice O'Connor was in the five-person majority. As of 2009, the future of *Roe* appears tenuous, especially since its supporters on the high court are nearing retirement.

During this period, the long-term effects of anti-abortion organizing have resulted both in fewer abortions and abortion clinics, along with the continuing marginalization of the abortion procedure (not covered by insurance, not publicly funded by most states, not part of most OB-GYN practices, not taught in medical schools). Abortion remains legal throughout the nation, but access to it, especially by poor, rural, and young women, presents many challenges.

Since the mid-1970s, cleavages in American politics have come to focus on cultural issues to a greater degree than have economic or class divisions, which characterized much of American political history. The rise of the culture war centers on several issues, the most iconic of which is abortion, and the watershed event is the U.S. Supreme Court's decision in *Roe*. This so-called culture war has led to the realignment of American politics along red (religiously devout and socially conservative) and blue (religiously skeptical and socially liberal) lines. This political realignment has occurred concomitantly with an increase in political polarization in Congress and state legislatures where there are few incentives to compromise and every reason to push deep red or deep blue political agendas. Profound partisan divides are especially evi-

dent in the selection of judges, given the importance that the judiciary has played in setting policy on cultural issues, most notably abortion. Whatever the future may portend for the culture wars as a result of the 2008 presidential election, it is certain that abortion will continue to play a prominent role.

Bibliography and Further Reading

Garrow, David J. *Liberty and Sexuality: The Right to Privacy and the Making of Roe v. Wade*. New York: Macmillan, 1994.

Gorney, Cynthia. *Articles of Faith: A Frontline History of the Abortion Wars*. New York: Simon & Schuster, 1998.

Risen, James, and Judy L. Thomas. *Wrath of Angels: The American Abortion War*. New York: Basic Books, 1998.

Rose, Melody. *Safe, Legal, and Unavailable: Abortion Politics in the United States*. Washington, D.C.: CQ Press, 2007.

Rosenberg, Gerald N. *The Hollow Hope: Can Courts Bring About Social Change?* Chicago: University of Chicago Press, 1991.

Saletan, William. *Bearing Right: How Conservatives Won the Abortion War*. Berkeley: University of California Press, 2003.

Silverstein, Helena. *Girls on the Stand: How Courts Fail Pregnant Minors*. New York: New York University Press, 2007.

Schroedel, Jean Reith. *Is the Fetus a Person? A Comparison of Policies across the Fifty States*. Ithaca, NY: Cornell University Press, 2000.

Glen A. Halva-Neubauer

AFFIRMATIVE ACTION

Affirmative action refers to a program of legislative instruments that mandate the consideration of the race or gender of applicants in the making of employment or school admissions decisions, or in the awarding of government contracts. Affirmative action programs began with the federal government in the 1960s as a result of arguments that the mere passage of civil rights legislation would not bring about the end of historical inequities resulting from years of racial segregation or sex discrimination. Throughout its history, affirmative action has itself been controversial, and it has often been left to the nation's highest court to determine whether the Constitution under any circumstances permits the use of race or gender for remedial purposes to abate discrimination or bars its use for any purpose.

Constitutional and Historical Background

Racial discrimination is a problem as old as the republic itself. The Civil War and the Emancipation Proclamation freed African Americans from slavery, and the passage of Amendments XIII, XIV, and XV after the Civil War, along with the 1866 Civil Rights Act, was meant to grant them the same rights as whites. What progress was made in the years immediately following the war, however, came to a stop in 1877 with the end of federal Reconstruction in the South and the beginning of a new era of racial discrimination. The Ku Klan Klan's cross burnings and lynchings intimidated blacks. Jim Crow laws passed in the South undid civil rights for African-Americans, and the Supreme Court's decision in *Plessy v. Ferguson*, 163 U.S. 537 (1896) upheld the concept of "separate but equal," ensuring its use as a tool of discrimination for the next half century.

During the first half of the twentieth century, civil rights organizations such as the National Association for the Advancement of Colored People (NAACP) challenged "separate but equal" and other racially discriminatory laws in court. Finally, in the landmark 1954 case of *Brown v. Board of Education of Topeka, Kansas*, 347 U.S. 43 (1954), Thurgood Marshall, serving as the NAACP's attorney, successfully argued that the separate-but-equal doctrine could not, in any meaningful constitutional sense, apply to the arena of public education. It was as a result of these efforts—as well as those of many other citizens and groups—that the U.S. Congress was moved to pass the 1964 Civil Rights Act and other legislation that banned discrimination on the basis of race, national origin, and sex. The legal equality of African Americans appeared to have been secured.

The Emergence of Affirmative Action

Affirmative action arose out of the context of the civil rights movements of the 1950s and 1960s. Dismantling separate but equal in *Brown* and making most forms of employment discrimination illegal under the Civil Rights Act of 1964 was not enough to achieve racial equality according to some in government. But even outlawing discrimination, some argued, was not enough. Mere legal or de jure equality would not overcome the effects of past or de facto discrimination. Other measures were also needed. Presidents John Kennedy and Lyndon Johnson took these initial steps in presidential Executive Orders 10925 and 11246. The former, issued by Kennedy in 1961, prohibited discrimination in the executive branch and urged what it called "affirmative action" to diversify the federal workforce. However, this "affirmative action" did not call for any specific steps by which to reach out and recruit women or people of color. Executive Order 11246, issued by President Johnson in 1965, called for efforts to diversify the workforce by reaching out to women and individuals of color; however, even it fell short of suggesting concrete plans to hire women and minorities. Nevertheless, it is out of these executive orders that the concept of affirmative action evolved. The original notion of affirmative action was thus both nondiscrimination and an effort to increase the hiring and recruitment rates of blacks and other people of color and, eventually, women. Such abstract efforts at remediation were soon to give way to more concrete plans of action.

Under Pres. Richard Nixon, affirmative action programs were extended to include unions and companies that received federal contracts. However, these programs also required, for example, that minority or women's business enterprises be given special consideration when competing for government contracts. In 1972, the Office of Federal Contract Compliance began to gather data on the racial make up of vendors to determine whether they were complying with federal executive orders. The office wanted to ensure that companies that did business with the federal government did not discriminate and were in fact making efforts to diversify their workforce. The information gathered from these vendors would also be used to construct remedies. One of these was an effort to ensure that the racial or ethnic origin of prospective employees, applicants, and candidates was used as a positive consideration during the hiring or selection process. In the meantime, educational institutions began to consider race and gender in admissions decisions. In some cases, race was used as merely one of several other characteristics, while in others quotas were initiated in which the race of an applicant was employed as a single factor.

The Supreme Court and Affirmative Action

Affirmative action proved to be controversial. Although some argued that such programs were a necessary and permissible means of overturning past injustices, others

Allan Bakke leaves class after his first day at the University of California Davis Medical School on September 25, 1978, accompanied by plainclothes security officers helping him through the crowd of reporters and photographers. In *Regents of the University of California v. Bakke*, the Supreme Court ruled 5–4 that the use of a separate admissions policy for people of color for the medical school at UC-Davis violated Bakke's civil rights. Although the Court also held in the same case that Amendment XIV permitted the use of race in school admissions to promote diversity, from the 1980s onward it would become increasingly hostile toward affirmative action policies. (Bettmann/Corbis)

contended that that the use of race for any purpose violated Amendment XIV's equal protection clause. Still others contended that these programs in fact amounted to a form of reverse discrimination against whites. Not surprisingly, the politics of affirmative action pushed some to challenge its constitutionality in court. In *Regents of the University of California v. Bakke*, 438 U.S. 265 (1978), the Supreme Court under Chief Justice Warren Burger upheld the use of affirmative action in school admissions policies. The opinion was controversial and it divided liberal justices from the new, more conservative ones appointed by President Nixon.

At issue in the *Bakke* case was the question of whether a separate admissions policy for people of color for the medical school at the University of California at Davis served to discriminate against Allan Bakke, a white applicant, violating his civil rights under Amendment XIV. In a 5–4 ruling, the Court agreed that it did. Five justices held that Davis could not use a separate admissions policy based on race because to do so amounted to the use of a constitutionally impermissible quota. However, five Justices also ruled that there were some situations in which race could be used in admissions decisions. Lewis Powell, writing a separate concurrence in a Court otherwise split 4–4 (four justices upholding the Davis plan and four rejecting it), held that Amendment XIV permitted the use of race in school admissions in order to promote diversity. However, race could only be used as one of several criteria.

After *Bakke*, the Supreme Court remained at the center of the affirmative action controversy. In *United Steelworkers v. Weber*, 443 U.S. 193 (1979), the Court permitted the voluntary use of affirmative action in employment. In *Fullilove v. Klutznick*, 448 U.S. 448 (1980), it upheld federal programs that set aside money for minority business enterprises. In *Johnson v. Santa Clara County*, 480 U.S. 616 (1987), the Court upheld a gender-based affirmative action hiring program, and in *Metro Broadcasting v. Federal Communications Commission*, 497 U.S. 547 (1990) it permitted the use of race in the awarding of broadcast licenses.

In the 1980s, the Rehnquist Court proved less supportive of affirmative action than had the Burger Court. An increasing majority of the justices preferred nominal color-blind approaches, arguing that the

AFRICAN AMERICANS

Constitution did not permit the use of race either for discriminatory or remedial purposes. Thus, in four cases in 1989, the Court made it more difficult for employees to sue for racial discrimination. In response, Congress passed the 1991 Civil Rights Act clarifying and expanding employee rights. Then, in *Adarand Constructors v. Peña*, 515 U.S. 200 (1995), the Court invalidated a program using racial preferences when awarding federal contracts. The decision effectively overturned *Metro Broadcasting*, bringing nearly to an end programs that considered race when awarding government contracts and licenses. Many thought it the end of affirmative action programs.

However, in *Grutter v. Bollinger*, 539 U.S. 306 (2003), the Supreme Court ruled constitutional the University of Michigan Law School's admissions program that was meant to ensure the matriculation of a "critical mass" of minority students. The Court again accepted diversity as a reason for schools to consider race as one of several factors when making admissions decisions. But in writing for the Court, Justice O'Connor indicated hope that in 25 years affirmative action would no longer be needed. Adding to the confusion, the Court invalidated what it perceived to be a racial quota system in the undergraduate admissions policy of the same university. Paired with *Grutter*, that case, *Gratz v. Bollinger*, 539 U.S. 244 (2003), sent a mixed message on race.

Changes at the Supreme Court again affected the fate of affirmative action when in 2005 John Roberts became chief justice and in 2006 Samuel Alito replaced Sandra Day O'Connor. In *Parents Involved in Community Schools v. Seattle School District*, 551 U.S. ___ (2007) and *Meredith v. Jefferson*, 551 U.S. 701 (2007), the Supreme Court ruled unconstitutional the use of race in the assigning of students to specific schools. Some legal scholars interpreted these decisions as prohibiting all use of race and gender in employment and school admissions decisions. A more conservative Court was proving increasingly hostile to affirmative action programs.

Affirmative action programs have sought to address the residual problems of slavery and racial and gender discrimination in the United States that civil rights legislation has been unable to address. Their

RELATED ENTRIES

THIS VOLUME
Supreme Court and the Judiciary

development and use grew out of the context of the civil rights protests of the 1960s and 1970s. The use of race or gender for remedial purposes in affirmative action has been a controversial political and constitutional issue in the United States since the 1960s. Supporters of affirmative action see its use as necessary to overcome past discrimination. Opponents contend that any use of race or gender violates the Constitution and that the only way to overcome discrimination is to ban it.

Bibliography and Further Reading

Anderson, Terry H. *The Pursuit of Fairness: A History of Affirmative Action*. New York: Oxford University Press, 2005.

Du Bois, W. E. B. *The Souls of Black Folk*. Chicago: A. C. McClurg & Co, 1903.

Kellough, J. Edward. *Understanding Affirmative Action: Politics, Discrimination, and the Search for Justice*. Washington, D.C.: Georgetown University Press, 2006.

Myrdal, Gunner. *An American Dilemma: The Negro Problem and American Democracy*. New Brunswick, NJ: Transaction Publishers, 1996.

Spann, Girardeau. *The Law of Affirmative Action: Twenty-Five Years of Supreme Court Decisions on Race and Remedies*. New York: New York University Press, 2000.

Yuill, Kevin L. *Richard Nixon and the Rise of Affirmative Action: The Pursuit of Racial Equality in an Era of Limits*. Lanham, MD: Rowman & Littlefield, 2006.

David Schultz

AFRICAN AMERICANS

In the wake of the civil rights movement and the multiple social movements of the postwar period, African Americans' political participation increased exponentially. With the legal vestiges of slavery and Jim Crow eradicated, African Americans could vote and hold a greater range of jobs than ever before. Black Americans were visible in government positions—elected and appointed—sports, the media, the suburbs, and the middle class. With these changes came political power and influence as well as an increased living standard for many individuals. Yet racism and inequality were still prevalent. Deindustrialization, a process during which large scale industrial production relocated away from Northern and Midwestern cities, left many African Americans trapped in rapidly declining urban areas where the tax base and job prospects were vanishing with few options to improve their situation. At the same time, a conservative backlash succeeded in stalling and, in same cases, pushing back efforts to compensate for the structural inequalities resulting from centuries of racism. Finally, crime and a rising prison population formed one of the greatest political challenges facing African Americans at the end of the century.

The Civil Rights Movement: A Thing of the Past?

By 1975, the key events commonly associated with the civil rights movement had passed and most of the leading organizations were shrinking in size and activity, if not disbanding altogether. Nonetheless, legacies of the movement were apparent throughout American politics. Political activism continued in myriad forms, particularly through cultural politics and supporting African, South Asian, Middle Eastern, and South American anti-colonial movements. Expressions of black pride persisted into the late 1970s as young African Americans embraced African history and culture, ranging from taking classes in newly created black studies departments to wearing their hair natural as a political statement. The use of cultural expression to claim a political voice was a strategy that African Americans continued to wield in subsequent decades, particularly in the 1980s and 1990s with the development of rap music and hip-hop culture.

Anticolonial movements formed another focus for African American political involvement. Blacks continued to support nonwhite colonial subjects, such as those in Southern Rhodesia, now Zimbabwe, and Algeria in their struggles for self-determination, as well as participating in an international antiapartheid movement. Activists pushed the U.S. government to create a foreign policy that supported decolonization and condemned racist governments, particularly that in South Africa. Through these movements, African Americans formed connections with an international African Diaspora—alliances that built on previous pan-African efforts—while also claiming space within the American political culture.

The substantial increase in African American participation in mainstream politics through voting and as elected officials was perhaps the most visible legacy of the civil rights movement. By 1975, the movement had eradicated all of the legal barriers preventing African American political participation. As a result, the number of black elected officials skyrocketed in the last third of the century, increasing sixfold between 1970 and 2000. By 1999, African Americans held 9 percent of U.S. House seats and most of the nation's largest cities had elected at least one black mayor. Despite these gains, African Americans remained underrepresented at the state and county levels of government—for example, as sheriffs and county officials and on school boards—as well as in the U.S. Senate and in governors' offices. Additionally, voter registration and actual voting rates nearly equalized with whites. In the mid 1970s, the gap between black and white registration hovered around 9 percentage points and the gap in voting rates at around 12 percentage points. By 2004, however, that gap had narrowed to approximately 3.5 percentage points. Throughout the period, politicians of any race and party had to respond to African American voters; however, blacks continued to vote primarily Democratic.

The trends following the civil rights movement were not entirely positive, however. By 1975, a conservative backlash had slowed racial progress, and white anxiety about racial changes coalesced in an antibusing movement that impeded attempts at meaningful school desegregation. In the early 1970s, Southern schools finally capitulated to the court-ordered desegregation that had issued from the Supreme Court's holding in *Brown v. Board of Education of Topeka, Kansas*, 347 U.S. 43 (1954). By the end of the decade, they were the least segregated schools in the nation. De facto segregation continued to afflict Northern schools, on the other hand, leading to a series of court orders mandating that school districts achieve a better racial balance. By 1979, estimates suggested that these orders affected nearly 30 percent of public school children. White parents quickly demonstrated the depth of Northern racism by organizing to protest busing, moving to the suburbs, or sending their children to private schools. In Boston, a federal judge ruled that the schools were unconstitutionally segregated and ordered the school system to bus students to schools outside their neighborhoods to remedy the problem. Hostility was so intense that white crowds greeted black students with violence when court-ordered busing began. In the face of such antagonism, some black parents quickly began to question the advantages of racially balanced schools, and urban politicians looked for other solutions to segregation. By the early 1980s, the controversy had subsided, though in some part because white flight had left most of the largest urban school districts with a poor and black majority.

Affirmative action programs were a longer-lived legacy of the Civil Rights era. Widespread affirmative action began in the early 1970s and with it came immediate controversy. Not a few believed that affirmative action, designed to level the playing field for blacks and other oppressed groups, instead gave an unfair advantage to minority applicants whose exposure to sexism or racism was not sufficiently deleterious to merit the institutionalized advantage—most women and blacks benefiting from the programs were among the most educated and least obviously harmed by oppression. They also claimed that such programs punished well-qualified candidates for being white. In 1978 the Supreme Court ruled in *Regents of the University of California v. Bakke*, 438 U.S. 265 that simple quota systems were unconstitutional, but in a concurring opinion, Justice Lewis Powell declared that race could be used as one factor in admissions decisions. Affirmative action programs flourished in the decades following the decision, until debates resurfaced in the late 1990s. In 2003, the court clearly upheld Powell's position in *Grutter v. Bollinger*, 539 U.S. 306. The case challenged the University of Michigan Law School admissions policy that considered race as one factor among many. The court held that the school could legally pursue a "compelling interest" in a diverse student body. The majority opinion suggested that such race-based considerations should be unnecessary within a few decades, but at least temporarily reaffirmed their legitimacy.

Stagflation and the Urban Crisis

The late 1970s was a time of economic hardship for much of the nation, but predominantly African American urban areas faced particular peril. By the end of the decade, city dwellers confronted an "urban crisis" consisting of declining industry, job options, and tax revenues that continued for years. African Americans, who made up increasing percentages of urban populations, were disproportionately affected by this crisis. In Detroit, for instance, blacks made up 9.2 percent of the population in 1940, 16.2 percent in 1950, and 43.6 percent by 1980. Even though the rising black middle class joined the trend toward suburbanization in large numbers during this period, by 1990 African Americans made up 31 percent of the population in America's 10 largest cities. Furthermore, regardless of their numbers, African Americans were frequently among the poorest urbanites. In Chicago in 1980, the median income in predominantly white wards was $24,535, but only $14,796 in black ones.

Cities faced a host of problems beginning in the late 1970s. In addition to the tension relating to busing, Americans were generally anxious about the quality of public schools. Although some of this anxiety may have been unfounded—much evidence exists that public schooling was improving during this period—educational opportunity and achievement did vary greatly depending on one's racial and socioeconomic group. Throughout the last quarter of the twentieth century and into the twenty-first, urban school systems were by far the most poorly funded and underachieving. Crime rates increased during the same period, peaking in the late 1970s and early 1980s. Although the cause of this increase was difficult to accurately determine, it was likely tied to an increase in drug use, related gang conflicts, pervasive poverty, and growing economic inequality. Again, these problems affected African Americans disproportionately. Black men were six times more likely to commit murder than were white men, and homicide quickly became the leading cause of death among young black men. Finally, cities frequently found it difficult to provide basic maintenance and services to residents.

The greatest problem facing urban areas and a basic cause of all of these issues was a lack of funds. Throughout the postwar period, the tax base of urban areas saw a steady decline, leaving cities with fewer resources and more people in need. The mass influx of poor whites and blacks in pursuit of industrial jobs crowded cities during the 1950s and 1960s. At the same time, the middle class overwhelmingly fled the cities for the suburbs. Between 1975 and 1995, the percentage of urbanites remained steady at around 31 percent of the total U.S. population, but tax revenue decreased due to declining incomes. With the same number of people to serve but less money to serve them with, cities struggled to provide for the needs of their inhabitants. Moreover, in addition to the middle-class flight, the American economy as a whole was in crisis. Stagflation—economic stagnation and inflation—left many Americans without jobs or sufficient income. Furthermore, businesses were rapidly leaving urban areas. Industry left for locations in the suburbs, South, and West, which had lower taxes and cheaper labor. At the same time, overseas competition and increasing mechanization constrained American industry as a whole. Deindustrialization and stagflation further depleted the urban tax base and decreased job opportunities. African Americans had found opportunity in industrial jobs during the previous decades, but frequently still occupied the lower rungs of the economy, making them the first to suffer in tough times. Together, the declining health of American cities, fewer jobs, and poor schools made it harder for African Americans who grew up in these urban environments to ever leave them, creating a cycle of poverty. The stereotype of poor blacks choosing to live on welfare proliferated, furthering the political marginalization of these urbanites. What progress there was was uneven: cities such as New York and Chicago improved significantly toward the end of the century, while others like Detroit and St. Louis continued to suffer.

The urban crisis had some positive effects on African Americans' political participation, even as it posed a number of challenges. Within the cities themselves, poor African Americans had greater political power than they tended to have elsewhere, and black elected officials quickly became common in the political landscape. By the mid-1970s, several major U.S. cities had African American mayors, including Detroit, Cleveland, and Atlanta. Moreover, greater voting numbers meant that anyone running for city office had to respond to black concerns. As significant as such political progress was, the reality was that city governments were limited in their political power and national influence. The fiscal crises facing these urban areas meant that even those in power had a limited ability to make changes and improve the lives of their fellow residents. Furthermore, the troubled state of American cities harmed black politics on a federal level. The persistence of urban problems quickly led federal politicians to lay blame on the urbanites themselves, creating new or reinvigorating old negative racial stereotypes in the decades to come.

A Color-Blind Society?

Ronald Reagan's election in 1980 represented a triumph for Conservatives but was generally considered a setback for African Americans' political interests (black approval ratings of Reagan tended to be more than 30 percentage points lower than that among whites throughout his terms). The administration quickly signaled its approach to civil rights through the key political and judicial appointment of individuals hostile to civil rights leaders. Reagan repeatedly opposed civil rights legislation and even attempted to weaken the Voting Rights Act of 1965, before realizing the extent to which Congress supported it. Reagan claimed he wanted a "color-blind" society that gave everyone an equal opportunity to succeed in a free marketplace. These views had important long-term implications. Reagan's judicial appointments would remain on the bench for the foreseeable future, and his policies furthered the idea that providing equal opportunity was sufficient to allow racial equality to take hold in American politics.

Reagan's tax policies demonstrated the clearly unequal results of these polices, however. Isolating the effects of supply side economics, including significant tax cuts for the wealthy, is difficult; continued deindustrialization and an increasingly competitive labor market combined to exacerbate economic hardship for impoverished minorities. Nonetheless, the Reagan tax cuts benefited the wealthy while the bottom 50 percent saw tax increases. Furthermore, the confluence of the aforementioned factors meant that, during the 1980s, the after-tax income of the top 1 percent of the population increased while that of the bottom fifth decreased by 10 percent. In 1990, blacks at the bottom of the economic scale were worse off in relation to whites than at any time since the 1950s.

Equally problematic was that Reagan's "color-blind" political rhetoric was clearly racially coded, a sub rosa political racism that harked back to Richard Nixon's law and order campaigns but that reached a new height in the 1980s and continued to plague American political culture through the end of the century. One of the clearest examples of this came during the 1988 presidential election. Vice Pres. George H. W. Bush's advisors developed a damning campaign issue that connected the Democratic presidential candidate, Michael Dukakis, to racialized crime—crime that the campaign and consequently observers infused with racial overtones. Bush's advisors criticized Massachusetts's policy of allowing prisoners to take occasional furloughs. Though such policies were relatively common, Bush and his advisors focused on Willie Horton, a felon who, while on furlough during Dukakis's governorship, had murdered a man and raped his fiancée. Horton's race was not mentioned, but advertisements broadcast pictures of him as an ominous black man, reinforcing a clear link between criminality and black men without expressly stating it. Democrats charged racism, but the issue provided an important boost for Bush's candidacy and demonstrated the extent to which Americans associated blacks with criminality.

Crime and Imprisonment

Indeed, crime proved to be one of the most difficult problems facing African Americans and politicians throughout the period and became a focus in the 1990s. Violent crime rates as a whole grew in the United States during the late 1970s, but declined in the late 1990s. Gang conflict and drug trafficking also expanded, further taxing law enforcement and politicians. By the mid-1990s, drug and alcohol offenses accounted for 34 percent of new prisoners, an increase of over 20 percent since 1970. Homicide and other violent crime rates generally increased from the mid-1970s through the early 1990s (with a short-lived decrease in the 1980s) before dropping off in the mid 1990s. Rates varied significantly across the nation and across demographic groups, however. Blacks were eight times more likely to be involved in a murder, as either a victim or perpetrator, than were whites. Young African American men were the most commonly involved group.

Although the problem was most prevalent in urban areas, the proper response to high crime rates was a question of national debate. Politicians at all levels worked to enact laws to fight crime and assure Americans that the streets were safe. Most liberals, including many African Americans, believed poverty, limited job opportunities, and poor schools to be at the root of urban crime and drug use, but such problems were extremely difficult to remedy and necessitated large amounts of money and effort before reductions could be expected to occur.

Conservatives, who dominated national politics for much of the period, offered alternative solutions. Through "color-blind" rhetoric and a renewed emphasis on American individualism, they suggested that criminals and drug users, whom they racialized as black, only had themselves to blame and that the real focus should be on protecting the rest of the country. Consequently, between 1970 and 2000, cities and states cracked down on crime. Conviction rates and sentence lengths increased; the prison population increased fivefold. During the 1990s, the height of the crackdown, the length of the average sentence increased by 13 percent. These changes had profound effects on black men. At the dawn of the twenty-first century, 12 percent of black men between the ages of 20 and 34 were in prison, but only 1.6 percent of the same group of whites. African Americans made up 46 percent of all inmates, but only 12.3 percent of the population. Furthermore, expanding police forces and prison populations were extremely expensive and funneled money away from other uses, such as schools, infrastructure, and health care, all of which urban black communities desperately needed.

The combination of high crime, victim, and incarceration rates made crime an important issue for black activists. Frustration with racial profiling and police brutality associated with this crackdown combined with other urban problems, leading to racialized urban riots during the 1990s, most famously in Los Angeles in 1992. In addition to elected officials' continued debate over how to best lower crime rates and prison populations, small movements aimed at reforming the prison system blossomed in the 1990s and have continued into the early twenty-first century. In some inner-city areas, African Americans joined with other minorities to fight crime within their own communities rather than rely on police who tended to criminalize the entire population in a system of racial profiling. This sort of grassroots activism provided one alternative method of political participation, but has yet to become a widespread movement or make significant changes in the justice system.

Despite these continued challenges, there were many positive increases in African American political participation at the dawn of the twenty-first century. The economic boom of the 1990s significantly increased the number and income of the black middle class and decreased the poverty rate. In 2000, the median income for black households was 69 percent of that of whites', compared to only 60 percent in 1990, and black poverty rates had decreased from 31.9 percent to 22 percent. At the same time, the numbers of black elected officials continued to increase. Both of these changes represented greater, although not complete, equality in political participation and quality of life for African Americans. The 2008 presidential election demonstrated the extent to which American politics had opened to African Americans and represented a triumph in the long struggle for civil rights. The election of an African American man, Barack Obama, to the office of the presidency of the United States was widely hailed as a historic victory for all African Americans and for the United States as a whole.

From the mid-1970s on, African American political participation steadily increased. The civil rights movement had eradicated legal barriers to political participation and blacks increased their political power both through voting influence and by running for elective office themselves. Nonetheless, they still face myriad political challenges, most notably unequal schooling, an urban crisis, and high crime and incarceration rates. The 1980s and the national triumph of conservative politics in Reagan's election posed particular difficulties for rights-conscious African American politicians and activists. Affirmative action continued, however, as did economic gains, leading to greater equality by the end of the century. Full equality has yet to come, but the election of Barack Obama demonstrated the extent to which American politics have opened to blacks in the late twentieth and early twenty-first centuries.

Bibliography and Further Reading

Anderson, Terry H. *The Pursuit of Fairness: A History of Affirmative Action.* New York: Oxford University Press, 2005.

Barker, Lucius J., Mark H. Jones, and Katherine Tate, eds. *African-Americans and the American Political System,* 4th edition. Upper Saddle River, NJ: Prentice-Hall, 1999.

Carter, Dan T. *From George Wallace to Newt Gingrich: Race in the Conservative Counterrevolution 1963–1994.* Baton Rouge: Louisiana State University Press, 1996.

Hacker, Andrew. *Two Nations: Black and White, Separate, Hostile, Unequal.* New York: Scribner's, 2003.

Lassiter, Matthew. *The Silent Majority: Suburban Politics in the Sunbelt South.* Princeton, NJ: Princeton University Press, 2007.

Preston, Michael B., Jr., Lenneal J. Henderson, and Paul L. Puryear, eds. *The New Black Politics: The Search for Political Power.* New York: Longman, 1987.

Sugrue, Thomas. *The Origins of the Urban Crisis: Race and Inequality in Postwar Detroit.* Princeton, NJ: Princeton University Press, 2005.

Christine M. Lamberson

AIDS

See HIV/AIDS

AMENDMENT XXVII

Amendment XXVII to the Constitution—currently the last amendment to the Constitution—is commonly known as the Congressional Pay Raise Amendment. Ratified in 1992, it clearly implies that members of Congress cannot vote themselves pay raises unless they are willing to defend the raise to their constituents: "No law, varying the compensation for the services of the Senators and Representatives, shall take effect, until an election of Representatives shall have intervened." But the amendment is actually a dead letter because congressional salary increases happen automatically as cost-of-living adjustments.

So far, though, no one has brought the contradiction between Amendment XXVII and Congress's practice to the courts—and members of Congress are probably quite happy with that state of affairs. Like everyone else, they need regular pay raises. But pay raises for members of Congress are extremely unpopular. Indeed, Amendment XXVII was added to the Constitution without the support of the leadership of either the House or the Senate. The Archivist of the United States added it on his own authority. But no one in Congress dared to seriously protest. Originally proposed over two centuries before its ratification, the addition of Amendment XXVII to the Constitution is in large measure the astonishing story of a college student publicizing an amendment that first was devised by none other than James Madison.

When the original Constitution of 1787 was ratified, it became clear to James Madison that the document needed a little help in order to become more popular. The opponents of the Constitution—known as the Antifederalists—had protested the Constitution as an undesirable concentration of political power in a new national government. Although the Constitution went into effect when a majority of 9 of the 13 original states ratified it, its ratification was accompanied by around two hundred formal resolutions from state legislatures for its amendment and change. Among these resolutions was the idea behind Amendment XXVII.

James Madison took 12 of the resolutions and reworked them into a package of amendments to be proposed to the states. Madison thought that three-fourths of the states would quickly ratify them. In other words, when Congress reported what became the Bill of Rights, it also reported two other amendments: one that would have rapidly expanded the size of the House as the population of the United States grew, and a second regulating congressional salaries. But neither of these amendments was ratified; only the third through twelfth proposals were ratified, creating what we now call the Bill of Rights. In 1873 the Ohio legislature ratified the pay raise amendment as a protest against a very unpopular and quite large congressional pay increase—but that was simply a symbolic gesture. In fact, later, in a 1921 decision, the Supreme Court said that the amendment was basically dead.

Then in 1982, a University of Texas undergraduate, Gregory Watson, discovered the amendment while doing research for one of his classes in political science. Excited by the idea that the amendment might still be ratified, he wrote a paper about it. Watson then began a one-man crusade to get state legislatures to ratify the pay raise amendment. In 1982 Watson thought that only Ohio (which ratified it in 1873) and the 6 states which ratified it between 1789 and 1791 (Delaware, Maryland, North Carolina, South Carolina, Vermont, and Virginia) had ratified the amendment, and that he needed to get another 31 states to ratify. He soon discovered that Wyoming had ratified it in 1977 (in protest over a congressional pay increase), but that still left 30 states to round up.

Watson's success over the course of just a decade in persuading 30 other legislatures to also ratify the congressional salary amendment is a testament to what one citizen can do. But it also reflects the deep unpopularity of congressional pay raises—indeed, of the idea that legislators are full-time professional politicians and not amateurs or citizen-legislators uninterested in taking salaries. Whether the Amendment will someday be enforced by the courts is an open question that is something of a ticking time bomb for Congress.

Bibliography and Further Reading

Bernstein, Richard B. "The Sleeper Wakes: The History and Legacy of the Twenty-Seventh Amendment." *Fordham Law Review* 61 (December 1992): 497–557.

Dean, John W. "The Telling Tale of the Twenty-Seventh Amendment: A Sleeping Amendment Concerning Congressional Pay Compensation Is Later Revived." *Find Law*, September 27, 2002.

Richard M. Valelly

AMERICAN INDIANS

The 1975 Indian Self-Determination and Education Assistance Act initiated a new era for American Indian tribes. With its passage, the locus of power shifted from the federal government to the 556 federally recognized Indian tribes. In the ensuing years, tribes have used their newfound political power and autonomy to assert control over their natural resources, protect tribal cultural resources, and improve reservation economies. Significant claims for water, hunting, and fishing rights, the expansion of tribal gaming enterprises, tax and trust issues, and voting rights dominated the political landscape, often pitting tribes against local and state officials and creating a political backlash among some non-Indian interests.

Sovereignty and the Federal Trust Responsibility

Since the founding of the United States, Indian tribes have had an exclusive relationship with the federal government, which lies beyond the direct control of state and local governments. The federal government, as a result of numerous treaties, statutes, and negotiated agreements, has a "trust responsibility" to Indian people to provide services, support, and legal protection. This responsibility is administered primarily through the Department of Interior's Bureau of Indian Affairs (BIA); however, Indian programs are found throughout the federal bureaucracy. The trust responsibility is at the heart of the federal government's relationship to tribes; according to the 1977 American Indian Policy Review Commission, the trust doctrine is designed to ensure the survival and enhance the welfare of Indian people, including the protection of their resources and the improvement of their standard of living.

Aboriginal title, an estimated 400 treaties signed over the last 200 years, and numerous statutes gave Indian tribes a unique but limited sovereign status, providing tribes with the ability to govern themselves, but within certain confines established by Congress and the U. S. Supreme Court. The law professor Charles Wilkinson described this as "measured sovereignty" (Wilkinson 1987), and the Supreme Court, in *Oliphant v. Suquamish*, 435 U.S. 191 (1978), described it as a "quasi-sovereign" status. But despite its limits, tribal sovereignty provided tribes with a great degree of freedom in managing their own affairs.

Federal Indian policy in the twenty-first century was also shaped by two federal laws. The 1934 Indian Reorganization Act (IRA) gave Indian tribes the right to set up their own governments. The 1975 Indian Self-Determination and Education Assistance Act clarified the federal trust relationship and endorsed tribal self-government. As a result, Indian reservations developed their own complex governing systems, including elected officials, tribal court systems, and administrative bureaucracy.

The policy of self-determination was buttressed by a corollary policy that described the relationship between tribes and other layers of government—federal, state, and local—as a government-to-government relationship. At the federal level, Pres. Bill Clinton made this the official policy for all executive departments in 1994. The policy was reiterated by Pres. George W. Bush in 2004. Several state governments followed suit and signed government-to-government agreements with tribes within their borders. The state of Washington, for example, instituted an unambiguous policy in support of such a relationship.

The federal government also recognized the need to consult with tribes on all issues that affect reservation lands, resources, and tribal members. In 1993, President Clinton made this a legal requirement for all federal agencies. Following this order, federal agencies developed their own official policies to consult directly with tribal governments.

Nonetheless, despite—or perhaps because of—the welter of legislation, litigation, and executive orders, the exact relationship between tribes, the federal government, and state governments remained inconsistent, even sharply contested. The relationship between tribes and local governments, especially in regard to service delivery, was particularly unclear and problematic. There was a nearly constant clamor from states, local governments, private citizens, and some elements in the federal government to reduce or eliminate tribal sovereignty and gain control over Indian natural resources and governing power. Tribes resisted this fiercely, meeting with success on many fronts, but occasionally experiencing setbacks. Although this struggle was multifaceted, three important issues illustrate the complexity and changing nature of tribal sovereignty and the role of American Indians in contemporary society: control over natural resources, gaming, and voting rights.

Natural Resources

In addition to owning 66 million acres of land in the lower 48 states and 44 million acres in Alaska, by the twenty-first century tribes had legal access, usufructuary rights, and private title to millions of additional acres. According to a Native American Fish and Wildlife Society estimate, tribes had either partial or complete control over 140,625 square miles. According to the Indian Data Center, Indian reservations contain 44 million acres of grazing land, 5.3 million acres of commercial forest, 2.5 million acres of farmland, 4 percent of U.S. oil and gas reserves, 40 percent of known uranium deposits, and 30 percent of Western coal.

Tribes had a long and often troubled relationship with the non-Indian private companies and individuals who bought, leased, or exploited their resources. Often, the conflicts between these entities and tribal governments were exacerbated by incompetent and sometimes dishonest federal trust administration. In 1996, the Department of the Interior was sued in a class action, led by the Blackfeet tribal member Elouise Cobell, for losing millions of dollars in trust assets that were due to tribal members.

Beginning in the 1980s, much of the controversy over Indian resources focused on water rights and water development. Until then, Western water development occurred without regard to its impact on Indian reservations. Many water development projects diverted water away from Indian reservations. Indeed, just such a situation went before the Supreme Court in a case that became the foundation of modern Indian water rights. In 1908, in *U.S. v. Winters*, 207 U.S. 564, the Supreme Court held that Indian reservations have a right to sufficient water to meet the needs for which the reservation was created. This doctrine of federally reserved water rights proved to be extremely contentious, pitting Indian tribes against local citizens, the Bureau of Reclamation, and the U.S. Army Corps of Engineers.

After years of nearly endless litigation over the claims of the defendant in the *Winters* case (Henry Winters was one of many non-Indian farmers who wanted the same water in the Milk River as the Fort Belknap Indian Reservation), the federal government began negotiating with tribes in the early 1980s as an alternative way to resolve water rights claims and meet the needs of both tribes and non-Indians. This policy resulted in approximately 20 completed settlements, with at least that number in further negotiation.

Though negotiated settlements did not solve all of the conflicts over water, they were successful in reducing tensions and funneling money to problem areas. The 2004 Arizona Water Settlements Act was a case-in-point. It was enormously complicated and involved literally hundreds of stakeholders and the water rights of two tribes. It clearly illustrates the difficulty in reaching any agreement when water is in short supply and the parties have been in conflict for many decades. As with other natural resources on Indian reservations, control over access to water became a significant point of contention. As resources grew scarcer amid greater demand, such conflicts threatened to intensify.

Gaming

In the late 1970s, some tribes began experimenting with various types of gambling, usually focusing on simple games such as bingo. Most state officials assumed that tribes had to comply with state gaming laws, but this notion violated the long-standing policy of tribal sovereignty and immunity from state law. In 1979, the Seminole Tribe of Florida undertook a test case, purposefully violating state law in the operation of their bingo parlor. Local officials arrested tribal officials, who then sued on the grounds that Indians on the reservation did not have to comply with state laws. In *Seminole Tribe v. Butterworth* (1979), a federal district court found in the tribe's favor, noting that Indian Nations had long governed themselves, free of state control.

The ruling touched off a fierce debate. States clamored for control of Indian gaming, while Indian tribes suddenly saw a new potential for increasing tribal revenues. The BIA made several attempts to regulate Indian gaming, satisfying no one. By 1986, 108 tribes had established some sort of gaming activities on their tribal lands. In 1984 and again in 1986, Congress held hearings on this newfound, contentious source of wealth. In 1985, the gaming tribes formed the National Indian Gaming Association to protect their operations. In 1987, in *California v.*

Cabazon Band of Mission Indians, 480 U.S. 202, the Supreme Court upheld the tribe's right to self-government, including their right to operate a bingo parlor without regard to state law.

Such court cases and political maneuvering ultimately led to the passage of the Indian Gaming Regulatory Act (IGRA) in 1988. IGRA was compromise legislation that introduced new controls over Indian gaming and tied it to the level of gaming allowed under state law, but nevertheless resulted in a dramatic expansion of Indian gaming. The act established the National Indian Gaming Commission to regulate tribal gaming, and set up three different categories of gambling. (Class III, what is usually referred to as casino-style gaming, is the economic mainstay of most Indian gaming establishments.) The act also required tribes and states to work out a compact to regulate gaming in that state.

By the beginning of the twenty-first century, Indian gaming had become hugely successful, with annual revenues of $26 billion in 2007, and an additional $3.3 billion in revenues from associated entertainment and hospitality services. By 2007, the National Indian Gaming Association had 184 tribal members and 190 associate members. In 2007, 225 tribes in 28 states had established some kind of gaming activities.

Gaming, however, did not make Indians rich. Some tribes, most notably the Pequot in Connecticut, were wildly successful, but most tribal gaming enterprises were fairly modest, and many tribes had no gaming whatsoever (two states, Utah and Hawaii, do not allow any type of gambling). Moreover, with so much money at stake, conflict over gaming policy was inevitable. In 2007, some conservative members of Congress introduced legislation clearly designed to thwart some forms of Indian gaming. One bill would have prohibited the Department of the Interior from spending money to review pending tribal gaming applications, which were required under IGRA. Another bill would have imposed a two-year moratorium on new tribal-state gaming compacts, and another tried to have tribes classified as corporations under the Federal Election Campaign Act, which would have made it illegal for tribes to make campaign contributions. Because of intensive lobbying by tribes, all of these bills failed, but they pointed to the endurance of Indian gaming as a salient issue.

Indian Voting

American Indians, like other minorities, faced a long and difficult struggle to gain the right to vote. To attain the franchise, Indians had first to establish themselves as citizens—a status denied many of them until the passage of the Indian Citizenship Act in 1924. This act did not, however, automatically result in the right to vote. Rather, many Western states used a variety of stratagems to prevent Indians from voting, ranging from residency requirements, to state constitutional limitations, to the claim that because Indians did not pay taxes they therefore could not vote.

Indians could, of course, vote in tribal elections, but there was considerable resistance to Indians voting in state and local, and even federal, elections. Much of the effort directed at preventing Indians from voting in a meaningful way paralleled the efforts made by white racists in the American South to prevent blacks from voting. In response to the antivoting measures in the South, the U.S. Congress passed the Voting Rights Act in 1965. This act was repeatedly reauthorized over the years.

In the early years of its passage, nearly all of the lawsuits under the act were filed on behalf of black plaintiffs, but since the 1980s, numerous cases have involved Indian plaintiffs. Since the 1940s, there were a total of 75 voting rights cases in Indian country, nearly all of them filed under the Voting Rights Act. Of these, the Indian plaintiffs prevailed, either through court victory or settlement, in 70.

In the 1990s, Indians began to use their newfound electoral power. Historically, Indian registration and voting in non-tribal elections was abysmally low, but by 2000, tribes were making systematic efforts to register their members and get them to the polls. As a result, Indian voters played a pivotal role in some close elections. In 2000, in the Washington U.S. Senate race, Indian voters came out strongly for Democratic challenger Maria Cantwell, who was running against the Republican incumbent, Sen. Slade Gorton. Gorton was widely perceived as anti-Indian, so Indian voters had a strong incentive to get involved in the electoral process. In the end, they helped tip the scales in favor of Cantwell. Indian voters played a pivotal role in South Dakota in 2002, when they turned out in unprecedented numbers for Democratic senator Tim Johnson; he won reelection in a very close race, which would not have been possible without a strong bloc vote from Indians. Janet Napolitano, the governor of Arizona, also credited her victory in 2002 to a strong Indian vote.

The effort to register Indian voters was aided immensely by the National Congress of American Indians (NCAI), which began a "Native Vote" campaign in 2004. A pan-Indian advocacy organization based in Washington, D.C., NCAI lobbied on behalf of Indian interests and assisted Indian nations in various political and legal efforts. Its "Native Vote 2008" campaign consisted of several programs, including a voter registration drive, voter education, a program to protect Indians when they go to the polls, and an election-day "get-out-the-Native-vote" campaign.

The right of Indians to vote in state and local elections remains contested, but it is clear that Indians are realizing their power at the ballot box and will continue to increase their political activity. In addition to voting, Indian people became increasingly engaged in other forms of participation, including running for office, making campaign donations (especially the gaming tribes), and lobbying.

Indian people have faced formidable odds in their struggle to retain their independence, their lands, and their culture. Indian policy today is arcane, complex beyond sensibility, and often contradictory. But Indian tribes continue to make progress in controlling their own destiny, improving their economic condition, and protecting their remaining land and resources. Growing conflicts over the West's water supply, contention over the expansion of Indian gaming, and the nature of the federal trust responsibility dominated Indian policy in the early part of the twenty-first century. In addition, tribes fought hard against efforts to reduce federal spending for Indian programs. Indians used their newfound power at the ballot box to gain concessions from non-Indian governments, and used their newfound wealth from gaming and natural resources to improve the lives of their people.

Bibliography and Further Reading

Clow, Richmond, and Imre Sutton, eds. *Trusteeship in Change: Toward Tribal Autonomy in Resource*

Management. Boulder: University Press of Colorado, 2001.

Colby, Bonnie, John Thorson, and Sarah Britton. *Negotiating Tribal Water Rights: Fulfilling Promises in the Arid West.* Tucson: University of Arizona Press, 2005.

McCool, Daniel. *Native Waters: Contemporary Indian Water Settlements and the Second Treaty Era.* Tucson: University of Arizona Press, 2002.

McCool, Daniel, Susan Olson, and Jennifer Robinson. *Native Vote: American Indians, the Voting Rights Act, and the Right to Vote.* New York: Cambridge University Press, 2006.

O'Brien, Sharon. *American Indian Tribal Governments.* Norman: University of Oklahoma Press, 1989.

Wilkins, David, and K. Tsianina Lomawaima. *Uneven Ground: American Indian Sovereignty and Federal Law.* Norman: University of Oklahoma Press, 2001.

Wilkinson, Charles. *American Indians, Time, and the Law.* New Haven, CT: Yale University Press, 1987.

———. *Blood Struggle: The Rise of Modern Indian Nations.* New York: W. W. Norton, 2005.

Daniel McCool

ASIAN AMERICANS

Following the lifting of immigration restrictions in 1965, the number of Asian immigrants in the United States increased dramatically, simultaneously increasing the visibility, diversity, and political power of the group. This change, along with a general decrease in racial discrimination, allowed Asian Americans to participate fully in American social, economic, and political life. This participation was uneven, however, as some groups, particularly East and South Asian immigrants and American-born Asian Americans, tended to have higher education levels and excelled economically, while those immigrants from Southeast Asia were more frequently refugees, who struggled more acutely for economic and political success.

Asian American Activism

The late 1960s saw the rise of several movements against racism stemming from the Black Power movement. The Asian American movement, which began at the height of the antiwar and Black Power movements, marked the first attempt by several Asian nationalities to forge a unified identity and fight for political rights and empowerment. Though the movement had reached its peak and was beginning to disintegrate by 1975, it nonetheless provides an important starting point for understanding Asian Americans' political involvement in the period that followed.

The movement was instrumental in the creation of "Asian American" as an identity and political category, a category that framed the political life of these Americans for decades to come. Initially, the Asian American movement consisted largely of people of Chinese, Japanese, and Filipino descent—a varied, but limited group. In the 1970s and beyond, however, the amount and diversity of Asian immigration increased dramatically. This diversity, which included immigrants not only from different nations but also from different economic and educational backgrounds, made sustaining a unified identity and movement all the more difficult. By the late 1970s and early 1980s, the challenge of creating a pan-ethnic movement with a cohesive agenda joined with an economic recession and a national conservative backlash against all movements for racial equality to decrease the national prominence of the movement. Nonetheless, grassroots activism within the frame of a pan-Asian American identity continued throughout the next several decades. Finally, even as fissures lingered, at the close of the twentieth century and dawn of the twenty-first, efforts to create a cooperative, if not unified, group continued, particularly in the arena of electoral politics where some collaboration could significantly increase Asian Americans' political power.

This inclusive Asian American category would also frame dominant white public perceptions and stereotypes of Asian Americans, a crucial factor in determining the nature and persistence of challenges facing the group. The pan-ethnic categorization has frequently allowed politicians to elide the real differences between multiple immigrant groups and ethnicities. This tendency has also allowed the visible success of certain individual Asian Americans to transform into a broad stereotype of the "model minority," thereby allowing some observers to more easily overlook the real problems and challenges facing other Asian Americans. Further complicating matters is that the reaction of the dominant culture to Asian Americans and Asian American issues is often shaped by current foreign policy and global relationships. Even as these conflicts have been nationally specific, such as Japanese Internment, white Americans' frequent conflation of Asian nationalities resulted in discrimination across nationalities, a tendency typified in the 1982 murder of a Chinese American student in Detroit in reaction to a wave of anti-Japanese sentiment. Such conflations further reinforced the necessity of "Asian American" as a political category.

By 1975, Asian American activism in combination with changes in immigration laws—which permitted larger numbers of Asian immigrants and, starting in the late 1940s and early 1950s (depending on the country of origin), allowed Asian Americans to become naturalized citizens—enabled Asian Americans to participate fully in American electoral politics. More and more Asian Americans became American citizens and voters. Despite this fact, the image of Asian Americans as foreigners lingered among white Americans, an image reinforced by the presence of large numbers of recent immigrants. Even though this stereotype did not exclude Asian Americans from electoral politics, it ensured that they remained outsiders within the political system and necessitated the continuation of Asian American activism.

Refugees and New Immigration

Immediately following the passage of the Immigration and Nationality Act of 1965, which eradicated the national-origins quota system that had been in place since 1924, the influx of Asian immigrants increased dramatically. Initially, the law encouraged the immigration of the family members of earlier immigrants, as well as of professionals. Consequently, in the years between 1965 and 1975, the new immigration act dramatically increased the numbers of Chinese and Filipino Americans, already well represented within Asian American populations, and created new populations of professional Korean and Indian immigrants. Between 1970 and 1980, the population of Chinese Americans rose 85 percent; the population of Filipinos increased by over 126 percent; and that of Korean immigrants by 407 percent. Beginning in 1975, these growth rates slowed as Congress, reacting to a weakening economy, restricted the numbers of professionals and workers who could enter the United States. Asian professionals would continue to immigrate to the United States, though in smaller numbers.

With these changes, the character of Asian immigration shifted to a greater representation of refugees. The Vietnam War and its extension into Cambodia and Laos created profound disruption within Southeast Asia, resulting in large numbers of refugees fleeing to the United States. A small number of Vietnamese had immigrated following the fall of French colonialism in 1954. Much greater numbers arrived following the fall of South Vietnam and the final withdrawal of all American soldiers in 1975. In that year alone, 130,000 Southeast Asian refugees arrived in the United States. These refugees included large proportions of well-educated, prosperous families, consisting of South Vietnamese military personnel, other active supporters of U.S. involvement during the war, and business classes who feared their fate under communist rule. Many of these refugees came from Saigon and spoke English well, facilitating their political and economic participation in their new home.

In the years following the implementation of communist governance, another wave of refugees made their way to the United States, and by 1986 approximately 425,000 Vietnamese had emigrated. These later refugees arrived under much more difficult circumstances, however. Some were educated professionals, but most were farmers or workers from rural areas and few of them spoke English. Many were ethnically Chinese and had experienced discrimination for decades in Vietnamese society, but found the oppression more severe after 1975. Moreover, these immigrants illegally escaped Vietnam by boat, floated to Thailand in a journey plagued by pirates as well as natural hardships, and then spent months if not years in crowded refugee camps before coming to the United States. Consequently, they were generally poor and ill-equipped to quickly assimilate and thrive economically or politically in American society.

Refugees also came to the United States from Cambodia and Laos under similar circumstances. American bombing extended the Vietnam War into both countries, leading to political instability and, after American withdrawal, a shift in political regime. As in Vietnam, those individuals who had supported the United States were forced to flee or face persecution. In Laos, large numbers of ethnic Hmong and other Laotians helped the U.S. military and consequently fled in the late 1970s. They continued to immigrate to the United States via Thailand throughout the 1980s and 1990s. By 1990, 149,014 Lao, 147,411 Cambodians, and 90,082 Hmong refugees lived in the United States.

This new group of refugees had vastly different experiences and faced a new set of political challenges. Their increasing diversity rendered a unified Asian American political identity ever more elusive. Furthermore, these Asian Americans faced extreme difficulties gaining the language skills and education necessary to find sufficient employment to support their families. These barriers to employment, along with their recent immigrant status, made active political participation yet more difficult, if not impossible. During the 1980s, public anxiety about the high number of refugees on public assistance led government officials to decrease the amount available to refugees and to instead emphasize job and language training courses. Even as this training was essential in the long term, the new programs frequently expected immigrants to find jobs more quickly than they could reasonably be expected to learn the skills necessary to secure anything but the lowest-paying employment. Without language skills or other resources, it was difficult for these immigrants to represent their interests within American politics. According to the 1990 U.S. census, poverty levels ranged from 25.7 percent among Vietnamese to 63.6 percent among Hmong refugees. These numbers reiterate the nature and scope of the economic challenges facing these refugee populations.

The 1980s: A Decade of Contradictions

The 1980s was a decade of sharp contrasts for more established Asian Americans, particularly Chinese and

Japanese Americans, as stereotypes cast them simultaneously as economic threats and a model minority.

In the late 1970s and early 1980s, deindustrialization plagued American cities, leaving many workers without jobs. The U.S. economy was quickly shifting to one based on consumer services, while large industries were declining or moving overseas. In contrast, the Japanese economy, including auto manufacturers and electronics industries, was booming. The contrast revived old fears of the "Yellow Peril." White Americans—workers and some politicians alike—blamed the Japanese for the declining fortunes of American cities and workers, and painted an image of mass Asian immigration depressing American wages and Asian capital taking over U.S. industry. These fears led to new outbursts of racism toward Japanese Americans, even though most Japanese Americans at this time were American-born and were certainly not directly connected to the structural changes affecting the American economy. Nonetheless, this perception caused anti-Asian violence, which came to national attention in 1982. Two white autoworkers in Detroit clubbed Vincent Chin, a Chinese American, to death, thinking he was Japanese and therefore somehow to blame for recent layoffs. A local jury found the men guilty of manslaughter, not murder, and sentenced them to probation. The case renewed Asian American alliances and activism against violence and for equal justice. Despite these efforts, white public anxiety about Japanese wealth persisted into the next decade as Japanese businesses bought a range of American properties and companies.

Despite this negative image, Japanese Americans did achieve an important political goal through the Redress Movement. The development, which began immediately following World War II but gained significant new strength following the Asian American movement of the 1960s, focused on gaining not only economic compensation but also official acknowledgement of the injustice of Japanese internment during the war. In 1988, persistent lobbying and organization finally pushed Congress to pass and Ronald Reagan to sign the Japanese-American Redress Act. The act included an official admission of wrongdoing and provided for reparations to be paid to the survivors of internment and to some others' heirs. The measure was an important political victory for Japanese Americans specifically and for Asian American activism more generally.

Seemingly in contrast to fears of a Yellow Peril, the 1980s saw the solidification of the model minority stereotype. The term "model minority" originally appeared in 1966 in relation to Japanese Americans and became particularly common in American media during the early 1980s when it was used to refer to Asian Americans generally and most frequently to Chinese or Japanese Americans. The image quickly spread from the media to the political realm: even Ronald Reagan congratulated Asian Americans for their tendency to excel and achieve the "American dream." This image stemmed from the real educational, economic, and political successes of a large group of Asian Americans, but was hardly representative of everyone. Moreover, even as the image celebrated some Asian Americans' achievements, it also delegitimized the problems facing others and the continued discrimination of certain minority groups. This political rhetoric, which continues in the early twenty-first century, was sometimes used as an excuse to avoid or oppose systematic programs to alleviate the poverty or employment discrimination facing some Asian Americans, such as the refugee populations and poorer East-Asian immigrants, and African Americans. Consequently, the model minority myth has played a mixed role in Asian-American politics, recognizing and celebrating educated Asian Americans as full, productive participants in American society, even as it perpetuates the exclusion of the less educated and poor.

1992 Los Angeles Riots

The 1992 Los Angeles riots erupted in response to police brutality, persistent unemployment, and poverty in Los Angeles's African American community. The resulting looting and property damage targeted not just whites but also Korean American merchants, whom some rioters saw as wealthy representatives of racial oppression and as rude and racist themselves. For their part, the Korean Americans saw themselves as barely making a living in American society. The riots brought to light the multiracial nature of American politics at the close of the twentieth century and also demonstrated the liminal political space occupied by Asian Americans. Korean Americans were much better off economically than the African Americans of the area, but also were similarly exposed to racism and stereotypes. Korean Americans argued that they deserved compensation for their losses in the riots, but a larger political climate of white conservatism prevented national sympathy and, locally, they did not possess the political power necessary to demand redress. Along with new Latino immigrants, Asian Americans had vied for political representation in local elective bodies, but African Americans tended to see these newer immigrants as impinging on gains made during the Civil Rights Movement. Cultural misunderstandings between Korean Americans and African Americans only deepened this political conflict and contributed to the tensions brought to the surface during the riots. Together, the complexity of the politics surrounding the riots show the precarious position of Asian Americans between complete acceptance and the most acute discrimination. Finally, the incident again highlights the diversity within the category of Asian American as Korean Americans expressed disappointment in the failure of a larger Asian American community to rally to their political defense, partially due to their perceived complicity in the tensions leading to the riots.

Electoral Politics

In 2000, 10.1 million people (3.6 percent of the U.S. population) identified themselves as Asian American, and nearly half that number, 5 million, was born in Asia (a significant increase from 1970, which found eight hundred thousand Asian-born immigrants living in the United States). During the 1990s and early twenty-first century, Asian immigration again included a greater proportion of highly educated professionals from East and South Asia. As a result, in 2004, according to the U.S. Census Bureau, the median household income of Asian Americans was $57,518, the highest of any racial group. This number indicates prosperity for many Asian Americans, though ethnic variations persisted.

In the early twenty-first century, Asian American citizens have high voter turnout rates, although, like those of other racial groups, these rates vary with education and income level. Reflecting the diversity of the group discussed throughout this essay, Asian

RELATED ENTRIES

THIS VOLUME
Immigration

OTHER VOLUMES
Asian Americans (vols. 4–6)

Americans do not form a unified voting bloc. Their party affiliation varies regionally and across ethnicities. The most salient voting patterns are Asian Americans' consistent support for Asian American candidates of either major party. Nonetheless, Asian American office holding continues to be small on a national level. The numbers are increasing, however, toward being representative of the population. In 2009, two senate members and eight congressional representatives were Asian American or claimed some Asian American heritage. On the state and local level, Asian Americans have been more successful, particularly in states like Hawaii and California with particularly large Asian American populations.

Over the last quarter of the twentieth century and into the twenty-first, the drastic increase in the size of the Asian American population has necessitated an increased political role for the group, even as that role has always been multifaceted and contradictory. High voting rates have given Asian Americans a particularly important role in elective politics; however, this participation has only recently resulted in significant numbers of Asian American officeholders. Images of the group as either a model minority or a threat have played, and continue to play, a particularly large role in shaping national political agendas and rhetoric. Finally, as the Asian American population continues to increase, the group's participation in electoral politics is bound to grow as well.

Bibliography and Further Reading

Chan, Sucheng. *Asian Americans: An Interpretive History.* Boston: Twayne, 1991.

Chang, Gordon H., ed. *Asian Americans and Politics: Perspectives, Experiences, Prospects.* Stanford, CA: Stanford University Press, 2001.

Creef, Elena Tajima. *Imaging Japanese America: The Visual Construction of Citizenship, Nation, and the Body.* New York: New York University Press, 2004.

Hein, Jeremy. *From Vietnam, Laos, and Cambodia: A Refugee Experience in the United States.* New York: Twayne, 1995.

Lien, Pei-te. *The Making of Asian America through Political Participation.* Philadelphia: Temple University Press, 2001.

Nakanishi, Dan T., and James S. Lai, eds. *Asian American Politics: Law, Participation, and Policy.* New York: Rowman & Littlefield, 2003.

Takaki, Ronald. *Strangers from a Different Shore: A History of Asian Americans.* Boston: Little, Brown, 1998.

Christine M. Lamberson

BURGER, WARREN EARL

1907–1995

Fifteenth Chief Justice of the
United States

Appointed by Pres. Richard Nixon to replace Chief
Justice Earl Warren in 1969, Burger carried the hopes
of political conservatives for a counter-revolution at the
nation's highest court that would reverse the perceived
excesses of the liberal Warren Court. Although scholars
disagree on the legacy of the Burger Court, one can say
that the counter-revolution never occurred. Instead,
the Burger Court expanded constitutional protections
in some crucial areas, most notably in reproductive
rights, in *Roe* v. *Wade*, 410 U.S. 113 (1973), and in
gender discrimination. Personally, Burger won praise
as an energetic judicial administrator of the federal
courts and for his leadership as Chairman of the
Commission on the Bicentennial of the Constitution.
However, he was criticized as an ineffective leader of
the Supreme Court and an uninspired and at times
inconsistent jurist. Upon Burger's retirement in
1986, Ronald Reagan elevated Justice William
Rehnquist as his replacement.

From Loyal Republican to Chief Justice

Born in St. Paul, Minnesota, Warren Burger attended
night classes at the University of Minnesota and
received his J.D. from St. Paul College of Law in 1931.

A lifelong Republican of some prominence in
Minnesota politics, Burger organized Harold Stassen's
successful 1938 campaign for governor and unsuccessful bid for the Republican presidential nomination
in 1952. Burger was central to the decision at the
Republican Convention to shift Stassen support to
Dwight Eisenhower to ensure a first-ballot nomination. Burger's support for Eisenhower earned him a
position as assistant attorney general in the Eisenhower
Department of Justice as head of its Civil Division,
where in 1955 he gained public attention by defending
the government's dismissal of John Peters for disloyalty
after Solicitor Gen. Simon Sobeloff refused to do so. In
1955, Eisenhower named Burger to the U.S. Court of
Appeals for the District of Columbia Circuit, where he
was an outspoken critic of the Supreme Court's liberal
majority, especially on criminal justice issues. President
Nixon, who had been elected on a law-and-order platform in 1968, saw Burger as a natural choice to replace
the liberal Chief Justice Earl Warren. Nixon held high
hopes that his strict constructionist appointee Burger
would bring about a conservative realignment on the
Supreme Court. Burger was confirmed on a 74–3
Senate vote and was sworn in on June 23, 1969.

Leader of the Supreme Court

Burger inherited a Court with a pronounced liberal
bent. Within two years of Burger's appointment, however, the Court's composition had changed dramatically, and it was expected that Nixon's appointees—

justices Harry Blackmun, Lewis Powell, William Rehnquist, and Burger—would produce a noticeable shift to the right in the Court's jurisprudence.

Buffeted by the ideological cross-currents prevailing at the Court in the early 1970s, Burger never established himself as a strong judicial leader in the way his predecessor had. Partly this was a result of the increasingly fractured ideological composition of the Court; however, commentators generally agree that Burger himself contributed to the sometimes-tumultuous conditions prevailing within the Court. Journalists Bob Woodward and Scott Armstrong's *The Brethren*, publicized as an inside account of the Court during Burger's first five terms as Chief, depicts Burger as deceptive and manipulative in the use of his authority to assign the Court's opinion in cases in which he was in the majority. Other complaints aired against Burger include his occasional practice of listing controversial cases for reargument, a tactic often perceived as a deliberate and cynical delay of rulings with which Burger disagreed.

Scholars also criticized Burger's drafting skills; on one notable occasion, the Watergate tapes case (*United States* v. *Nixon*, 418 U.S. 683 [1974]), Burger's draftsmanship of the opinion for the Court resulted in a humiliating rewrite by several members of the majority. Many of these complaints were amplified in later accounts of the Burger Court, and confirmed in the papers of justices who later retired. By most measures, then, Warren Burger was not a success in his role as first among equals at the nation's highest court; his attempts to use his position's power to influence the results of cases before the Court often had the perverse effect of provoking his colleagues to abandon his views.

Criminal Procedures and Rights

In the doctrinal area of criminal procedure, Burger frequently voted to roll back protections for suspects and defendants. The most notable criminal procedure opinion contributed by Burger was *Nix* v. *Williams*, 467 U.S. 431 (1984), in which he spoke for the majority to establish the "inevitable discovery" exception to the exclusionary rule, holding that in situations in which unlawfully obtained evidence would inevitably have been uncovered through the lawful course of police investigatory work, there was no basis for excluding that evidence. Yet, although he was a noted critic of the landmark *Miranda* v. *Arizona*, 384 U.S. 436 (1966) decision, requiring that criminal suspects be advised of their rights prior to interrogation, Burger eventually made his peace with the decision's place in American society and did not seek to have it overruled.

The constitutionality of the death penalty under Amendment VIII's Cruel and Unusual Punishment Clause was a hotly contested issue throughout the Burger years. In 1972, the Court halted all pending executions in *Furman* v. *Georgia*, 408 U.S. 238 (1972). Burger dissented, taking issue with both the absolutist position that the death penalty was per se cruel and unusual punishment and with moderates' concern that capital sentencing schemes were excessively arbitrary. *Gregg* v. *Georgia*, 428 U.S. 153 (1976) upheld the constitutionality of a new generation of capital sentencing statutes passed in response to the *Furman* moratorium. In *Gregg*, Burger joined a concurrence by Byron White which argued that aggravating and mitigating factors had cured the sentencing scheme of the arbitrariness found in pre-*Furman* sentencing regimes.

First Amendment

Burger had the most impact on First Amendment doctrine in the application of Amendment I's requirement that the government should not establish religion and in obscenity cases. He authored the majority opinion in *Lemon* v. *Kurtzman*, 403 U.S. 602 (1971), which established the important tripartite *Lemon* test for determining whether legislation and government actions violate the Establishment Clause. To pass constitutional muster under the *Lemon* test, a statute or government action must have the following qualities: 1) it must have a primarily secular purpose; 2) its primary effect must be one that neither advances nor inhibits religion; and 3) it must not foster an excessive government entanglement with religion. The *Lemon* test was the standard in Establishment Clause cases until several justices in *Lee v. Weisman*, 505 U.S. 577 (1992) sought to replace the *Lemon* test with a weaker standard which emphasized that government not be overly coercive on citizens when it allowed prayer, such as at school graduation. Although it has never been officially overruled, the *Lemon* test began to encounter increasingly strident criticism from various conservative justices. Burger himself generally dissented from rulings that invalidated government actions on Establishment Clause grounds.

Burger led the Court's effort to restructure obscenity law after a decade in which the justices had decided what was legally obscene on a case-by-case basis. His majority opinion in *Miller* v. *California*, 413 U.S. 15 (1973) established the three-part obscenity test that is, in modified form, still in effect today; a critical component of the *Miller* test is its explicit reliance on local community standards, which allows for different obscenity standards in different jurisdictions. The application of this test has been quite inconsistent and difficult, especially in cases since 1997 involving the regulation of pornographic and indecent speech on the Internet.

Privacy and Abortion Rights

Burger joined his conservative colleagues to limit the expansion of the right to privacy. Although Burger concurred in the judgment in the landmark decision in *Roe* v. *Wade*, 410 U.S. 113 (1973), which held that the right of privacy established in *Griswold v. Connecticut*, 381 U.S. 479 (1965) extended to a woman's decision to terminate her pregnancy, he rarely voted to invalidate any substantive abortion restrictions in the years following *Roe*, and some of his colleagues suspected him of joining the majority only in order to control the opinion assignment. A notable opinion in the privacy context was his concurrence in *Bowers* v. *Hardwick*, 478 U.S. 186 (1986), in which Burger suggested that proscriptions of homosexual conduct were inherent in the values of "Western civilization." It is rare for the Court to rebuke dicta, especially in a concurring opinion; however, this contention was specifically rebuked in the majority opinion in *Lawrence* v. *Texas*, 539 U.S. 558 (2003), which overruled *Bowers* and established the right of privacy for gay men and lesbians with regard to non-procreative sex, such as sodomy.

Civil Rights

Burger's record on civil rights was neither consistently conservative nor liberal, and his approach to constitutional and statutory questions of race was dependent on factors such as the governmental entity involved and the existence of a specific history of discrimination in the context of a given case. Burger wrote for a unanimous majority in *Swann* v. *Charlotte-Mecklenburg Board of Education*, 402 U.S. 1 (1971), allowing federal courts to use busing to achieve desegregation, but later restricted *Swann*'s impact by writing for a fragmented majority in *Milliken* v. *Bradley*, 418 U.S. 717 (1974), which refused to sanction broad inter-district busing plans.

In the context of federal civil rights statutory law, his opinion in *Fullilove* v. *Klutznick*, 448 U.S. 448 (1980) approved a remedial set-aside program authorized by Congress to ensure greater minority business participation in public works projects. In *Griggs* v. *Duke Power Co.*, 401 U.S. 424 (1971), he wrote for a majority in interpreting Title VII of the Civil Rights Act of 1964 not to require proof of discriminatory intent to sustain a claim of employment discrimination, but rather to require only a finding of disparate impact, a less difficult way to demonstrate discrimination.

In the landmark *Regents of the University of California* v. *Bakke*, 438 U.S. 265 (1978) affirmative action case, Burger joined Justice Stevens' partial dissent, which argued against racial preferences intended to account for the effects of past discrimination in higher education.

Outside of the context of race, Burger authored the majority opinion in *Reed* v. *Reed*, 404 U.S. 71 (1971), the first Supreme Court case to strike down a statute on Equal Protection grounds for discriminating on the basis of gender. He dissented, however, from *Craig* v. *Boren*, 429 U.S. 190 (1976), which heightened the standard of review for laws discriminating on the basis of gender.

Separation of Powers

In the area of separation of powers, Burger was generally deferential to claims of executive authority, and the opinion he delivered in *United States* v. *Nixon*, 418 U.S. 683 (1974) was a landmark, supporting executive power even as it placed restraints on the president's authority to shield himself from an ongoing criminal investigation. His other notable separation of powers opinion was *INS* v. *Chadha*, 462 U.S. 919 (1983), which invalidated "legislative veto" provisions in hundreds of federal statutes. Legislative veto provisions allowed the House or the Senate alone to veto government decisions of an executive nature. In this case, by voice-vote the House of Representatives rejected the INS decision to allow Jagdish Chadha, a foreign exchange student, to stay in the United States. Burger noted that legislative vetoes were violative of the bicameral and present-ment clauses of the Constitution which require all legislation to be passed by both branches of Congress and presented to the president for possible veto. Many scholars criticize Burger for being too formal and not minimalist enough in his separation of pow-ers opinions. In *INS*, Burger was criticized for failing to have courts consider the constitutionality of each law which included a legislative veto, one at a time, based on policy area, history, and whether it required one and two-house approval.

Judicial Administrator and Innovator

Burger was vigorous and more successful in executing his duties as administrative head of the federal judici-ary. He successfully advocated the creation of the National Center for State Courts and a subsidiary institution, the Institute for Court Management. Both organizations have served important functions in cen-tralizing and standardizing knowledge about judicial systems both in the United States and abroad. He was an advocate for new alternative dispute-resolution procedures as options parties could pursue rather than litigation. Within the Supreme Court itself, he expanded and modernized the Court's administrative staff and introduced new technologies. He lobbied Congress for the creation of a national court of appeals whose primary responsibility would be the resolution of circuit splits, leaving the Supreme Court free to select cases worthy of its limited resources. In this lat-ter effort, he was unsuccessful, but the elimination of

most of the remaining vestiges of the Supreme Court's mandatory jurisdiction in the late 1980s accomplished some of the goals Burger had in mind in proposing the national appeals court. Historians generally agree that Burger was one of the most enthusiastic judicial administrators to ever hold the office of chief justice, and his achievements in this area were substantial.

Burger retired on September 26, 1986 to over-see the official preparations for the celebration of the Constitution's bicentennial in 1987. Ronald Reagan named Justice Rehnquist as his replacement. Burger published a book in 1995, *It Is So Ordered: A Constitution Unfolds*, an account of notable cases from the Court's history that skirted most of the Court's modern controversies. He died in 1995 at the age of 87.

Conclusion

The ways in which Burger used the prerogatives of his office were controversial throughout his tenure, and later assessments have generally concluded that he was not an effective leader of the Court. What is striking about the Burger Court is that, during an era of increasing political conservatism and multiple Republican appointments to the high bench, it con-sistently refused to attack Warren Court landmarks head-on, and actually was quite activist and rights-expansive in several doctrinal areas, including repro-ductive rights, gender discrimination, and affirmative action, foci of social action politics in the 1960s and 1970s. The extent to which a man who gives his name to a judicial era influenced its doctrinal developments is difficult to pinpoint, but it seems fair to say that Burger was generally not a leader in the Burger Court era's doctrinal expansions; in some cases, he actively resisted them. He will not be remembered as a great chief justice; however, his more active efforts, as com-pared to prior chief justices, to foster better adminis-tration of federal and state courts have become a model followed by his successors.

Bibliography and Further Readings

Blasi, Vincent, ed. *The Burger Court: The Counter-Revolution That Wasn't*. New Haven, CT: Yale University Press, 1983.

Kahn, Ronald. *The Supreme Court and Constitutional Theory, 1953-1993.* Lawrence: University Press of Kansas, 1994.

Lamb, Charles M. "Chief Justice Warren E. Burger: A Conservative Chief for Conservative Times." In *The Burger Court, Political and Judicial Profiles*, edited by Charles M. Lamb and Stephen C. Halpern. Urbana and Chicago: University of Illinois Press, 1991.

Maltz, Earl M. *The Chief Justiceship of Warren Burger, 1969-1986.* Columbia: University of South Carolina Press, 2000.

Woodward, Bob, and Scott Armstrong. *The Brethren.* New York: Simon and Shuster, 1979.

Schwartz, Bernard. *The Ascent of Pragmatism: The Burger Court in Action.* New York: Addison-Wesley Publishing, 1990.

Ronald Kahn

BUSH, GEORGE H. W.

1924–
Forty-first President of the United States

Foreign relations were a major concern of every Cold War–era president, and this was especially true in the presidency of George Herbert Walker Bush. It was during the Bush administration (1989–1993) that the Berlin Wall fell, the Warsaw Pact dissolved, Germany was reunified, and the Soviet Union ceased to exist. Unfortunately for his administration, Bush's success in foreign policy was not mirrored in his domestic agenda. Operating under a huge national debt, caused in large part by the economic policies of Ronald Reagan, Bush failed to take bold action as the nation slid into a recession. Although the "peace dividend" from the end of the Cold War would ensure that the last decade of the twentieth century was a prosperous one for the United States, it did not happen in time to save Bush in his 1992 reelection bid.

Early Career
The son of a successful businessman and later senator, Bush was born into affluence in Massachusetts.

Although he had already been accepted to Yale University, Bush felt compelled to serve his country in World War II. He enlisted in the navy on his eighteenth birthday, serving in the Pacific as a pilot and earning the Distinguished Flying Cross. After the war, he took a degree in economics from Yale before beginning a successful business career in the oil fields of Texas.

Bush's political career was heavily influenced by his father's 1952 election as a U.S. senator from Connecticut. In 1964, he mounted his own Senate campaign in Texas, only to go down to defeat. He ran successfully in 1966 for a House seat and served two terms before making another unsuccessful bid for the Senate in 1970. Not long after, Pres. Richard Nixon tapped him as ambassador to the United Nations. In 1972, Bush became head of the Republican National Committee (RNC), providing leadership during the difficult Watergate crisis. The new president, Gerald Ford, appointed him as the American envoy to the People's Republic of China, a position Bush had requested after Ford had offered ambassadorships to Britain or France. In 1975, he returned to the United States as Director of Central Intelligence (DCI) with a mandate to clean house at the CIA after that agency suffered through a series of investigations and accusations of alleged domestic abuse.

With Jimmy Carter's presidential victory in 1976 and Bush's subsequent dismissal as DCI, Bush found himself in the private sector. This would be short-lived as Bush quickly began fundraising for a presidential run in 1980. After Bush's win in the Iowa caucuses, it appeared that the contest between Bush and Ronald Reagan for the Republican nomination would be close. However, after a brilliant performance in a debate in Nashua, New Hampshire, Reagan won the state in impressive fashion and dominated the remainder of the primary season. Needing to balance his ticket with a moderate, the conservative Reagan turned to Bush after deciding against the idea of a possible "dream-ticket" with Gerald Ford. The Reagan/Bush ticket dominated Carter in the fall election, beginning what would come to be known as the Reagan Revolution.

Reagan's Loyal Vice-President and the 1988 Election

With a conviction greater than perhaps any vice president in history, George Bush believed that his primary role was to be absolutely loyal to the president. Reagan knew that he could trust Bush completely without fear of leaks to the press or public disagreements over policy. Add to this that Bush had substantially more foreign policy experience than Reagan, and it is easy to see why Reagan encouraged Bush's counsel on foreign affairs. As a result, Bush was deeply involved in foreign policy discussions concerning the Soviet Union during the Reagan presidency.

Bush's quiet loyalty did have a cost: continued questions of Bush's role in the Iran-Contra Affair began to mount as the vice president prepared for his own presidential run in 1988. The scandal involved the Reagan administration's financial support of a right-wing guerilla group (the *contras*) in Nicaragua with profits from the illegal sale of weapons to Iran. Ever since the scandal became public in 1986, Bush had refused to provide a full accounting of his role in the clandestine operation. The problem with the Iran-Contra Affair for Bush was that his claim that he was "out of the loop" raised questions regarding his experience in intelligence and diplomacy, his loyal service to Reagan, and his concern for ethics in government—his greatest assets. During the primary season, Kansas senator Bob Dole hammered Bush on his role in Iran-Contra. Along with New York congressman Jack Kemp and the Rev. Pat Robertson, Dole looked to be a formidable challenge to Bush for the Republican nomination, with each candidate trying to emphasize a connection to Reagan-style conservatism. Although Dole won the Iowa caucuses, Bush was able to regroup and take the New Hampshire primary with help from New Hampshire governor John Sununu.

Bush emerged from the bruising primary campaign; however, the situation looked bleak for Bush as the Democratic nominee, Massachusetts governor Michael Dukakis, built a double-digit lead in the polls heading in to the party conventions. Ironically, Bush would find help from the left when Democratic presidential-hopeful Al Gore attacked Dukakis on Massachusetts' record of permitting "weekend passes"

for convicted first-degree murderers who were serving life sentences without possibility of parole. Bush's staff seized on this story to paint Dukakis as soft on crime and destroy his lead. From that point, the Bush campaign emphasized Dukakis' support of high taxes and increased federal spending, lack of support for defense, support for abortion, attempt to "disarm the state" through gun control, and his veto of a Massachusetts' law that required teachers to lead students in the daily reciting of the Pledge of Allegiance.

The negative campaigning worked: Bush won the 1988 election and became the forty-first president of the United States. Though the comeback was impressive, Bush entered his presidency with no clear agenda on how to correct the domestic policy problems that had been created by the deficit spending of the Reagan years. With Democrats achieving net gains in both houses of Congress, governors' offices, and state legislatures, Bush would have little chance of forwarding a domestic agenda, even if he had one. Bush turned to an area where he would have greater freedom and an area where he had considerable expertise. Along with his inner circle of Sec. of State James Baker III and National Security Advisor Brent Scowcroft, Bush would direct most of his energies to foreign policy.

President Bush and the End of the Cold War

During the first few months of his presidency, Bush conducted a comprehensive review of U.S. policy toward the Soviet Union. The press interpreted "the pause" as another sign of Bush's lack of vision. In 1988–1989, as the United States entered a critical period of foreign policy, many pundits wondered whether Bush was the right man to replace Reagan. For his part, Bush had to prove to a press accustomed to the public, charismatic styles of Ronald Reagan and Soviet leader Mikhail Gorbachev that his private, quiet style of diplomacy could be effective. He spent the summer of 1989 focusing on the changes that were taking place in Central and Eastern Europe and hoping to encourage an incremental reform not threatening to the Soviets. On November 9, 1989, Bush received news of the fall of the Berlin Wall with much personal pleasure. In public, however, he urged caution. He feared that a Western celebration of the

Wall's collapse might encourage a backlash by hard-liners in East Berlin and Moscow.

In December 1989, during a historic meeting in Malta, Bush sought to test the intentions of the Soviet Union, to move beyond the Containment Doctrine that had dominated U.S. Cold War policy, and to establish a new relationship with the Soviet Union. George Bush's quiet style achieved what he most wanted—the peaceful transfer of power in Eastern Europe. President Bush used the new U.S.-Soviet relationship that he had forged at Malta to gain Soviet acceptance of a unified Germany within NATO. This acceptance occurred over a period of months involving private meetings, letters, and telephone conversations between leaders from both the East and West. Bush used personal diplomacy to achieve what had seemed unthinkable: convincing the Soviet Union to allow a unified Germany to remain in NATO. The reunification of Germany within NATO, in conjunction with the withdrawal of Soviet troops in Eastern Europe, marked the end of the division of Europe and with it an important step toward ending the Cold War.

The Persian Gulf War, 1990–1991

In the fall of 1990 and spring of 1991, the reunification of Germany was finalized; relations between the United States and the Soviet Union were continuing to improve; and by the end of 1991, the Soviet Union would cease to exist. It was against this backdrop that President Bush confronted Iraq's aggression in what many of his administration viewed as the first real crisis of the post–Cold War era and a difficult test of the newfound U.S.-Soviet relationship.

On August 2, 1990, Iraq invaded the oil-rich country of Kuwait. Heavily in debt, Iraq's leader Saddam Hussein was using the fourth largest military in the world to make a move for hegemony in the region and to take a leading role in the Organization of Petroleum Exporting Countries (OPEC) and the Arab world. On August 8, 1990, Bush announced that he was sending U.S. troops to Saudi Arabia, an operation dubbed Desert Shield. The Bush administration also asked the United Nations Security Council to push through a series of resolutions to condemn the Iraqi invasion and to demand that Iraq withdraw immediately and uncon-

ditionally. After the January 15, 1991, deadline set by UN Resolution 678, which authorized coalition forces to use "all necessary means" to remove Iraqi troops from Kuwait, Operation Desert Shield became Operation Desert Storm. Five and a half week's of air bombardment were followed by a land war that lasted exactly 100 hours.

The war was concluded on February 27, 1991, after President Bush announced in a televised address from the Oval Office an end to all Allied offensive combat operations. But several issues would prove controversial and begin to tarnish the luster of the victory. Convinced that the land campaign had run its course and concerned over excessive carnage and the needless killing of retreating Iraqis, Bush ended the war without pushing toward Baghdad. Saddam Hussein had been severely weakened but not vanquished; however, Bush had succeeded in building a coalition that did not mirror the old Cold War rivalries. In the process, he offered the first glimpse of the leadership burden that the United States would be forced to take in a world in which it was quickly becoming the lone superpower.

The Collapse of the Soviet Union

The new U.S.-Soviet relationship that was evident during the Persian Gulf War was jeopardized in August 1991 as a coup attempt sought to remove Gorbachev from power. The Bush administration had always been worried about hard-line Communists in Moscow. Indeed, one reason that the Bush administration had been slow to embrace Gorbachev was an uncertainty as to whether he would remain in power. Although the coup failed and Gorbachev returned to power, it accelerated the rise of Russian president Boris Yeltsin and the demise of Gorbachev and the Soviet Union. Gorbachev relinquished his duties as president and the USSR came to an end on December 25, 1991. During the collapse of the Soviet Union, Bush played a pivotal role in the peaceful transition of power between Gorbachev and Yeltsin.

Domestic Problems

During his 1988 campaign, Bush promised social and economic conservatives that he would continue many of Reagan's policies. In his convention acceptance speech, Bush had famously said "Read my lips: no new taxes" as a way to assure conservatives that they could trust him just as they had Reagan. Although this unabashed courting of the conservative vote helped him to win the presidency, Bush found that it was a promise he could not keep as he struggled to deal with the long-term economic problems created by Reagan's policies.

Bush's first crisis was a savings and loan (S&L) scandal caused by Reagan's bank deregulation policies. Lacking the protections afforded by government oversight, millions of Americans lost their savings in high-risk investments made by some S&Ls. Bush developed a solution that would allow depositors to be reimbursed for their lost savings, but the price tag for this program only added to the huge national debt that Bush had inherited. Bush was already paying the political price for Reagan's dramatic increase in defense spending and tax cuts; now he had to deal with payouts to fix the problems associated with deregulation. In 1990, Bush and Congress agreed on a budget that would reduce military spending and raise taxes, thus breaking Bush's famous campaign pledge. It was not enough, and the nation slid into a lingering recession.

Operating with a huge national debt and a Congress controlled by the Democrats, Bush had limited options when it came to his domestic agenda. He did enjoy some minor successes in domestic policy, such as the passage of a clean air bill and legislation to help disabled Americans, an improved immigration bill, and the first steps toward a North American Free Trade Agreement (NAFTA). Few of his domestic programs, however, had significant amounts of government money attached. Bush struggled to articulate a domestic agenda that would not add to the budget deficit. Adding to his lack of vision in domestic affairs was the simple fact that he preferred foreign

policy. With so many monumental world events occurring during the first three years of his presidency, it was easy for Bush to justify delegating domestic responsibilities to others. This lack of leadership would cost him dearly in his reelection bid.

The 1992 Election

The concept of George Bush as an excellent president with regard to foreign policy and a poor president in regard to domestic policy seems to have been prevalent by the start of his 1992 reelection campaign. Faced with a Democratic Congress, hamstrung by a soaring federal deficit, and lacking a vision for a domestic agenda, Bush was not able to form a cohesive list of domestic accomplishments. Already reeling from his flip-flop on taxes, an uproar over NAFTA negotiations, and his adamant assertion that the economy did not need to be fixed, Bush lost his reelection bid to Arkansas governor Bill Clinton.

Despite Bush's foreign policy success, the main issue in the election was the economy. Even as most Americans felt the effects of a lingering recession, Bush repeatedly defended his inaction by promising that the economy would soon turn around, as the peace dividend from the end of the Cold War would bring prosperity. Most Americans, however, were not willing to wait. They decried the gridlock in Washington and the seemingly lethargic reaction by President Bush. The grassroots candidacy of Texas billionaire Ross Perot illustrated the widespread discontent with the Washington establishment. In the end, Bush could not imagine that the American people would turn to an unproven Democrat rather than reward him for his foreign-policy accomplishments. His poorly run reelection campaign, which included rather disastrous debate performances, floundered as the public mood focused on the faltering economy and Bush's lack of vision for domestic changes. Despite Bush's impressive foreign-policy record, the end of the Cold War had convinced many Americans that foreign-policy expertise was no longer needed as much as domestic-policy experience.

George H. W. Bush was president at a time when the United States needed a capable foreign policy leader. As such, he led a transition from the Cold War to a post–Cold War world in which the United States was the lone superpower. His management of the end of the Cold War, as well as the Persian Gulf War, established Bush as one of the most successful foreign policy presidents in the history of the United States. His inability to effectively deal with the lingering costs of Reagan's economic policies, however, led to a lingering economic recession and an inability, or unwillingness, to forge a successful domestic agenda.

Bibliography and Further Reading

Atkinson, Rick. *Crusade: The Untold Story of the Persian Gulf War.* Boston: Houghton Mifflin, 1993.

Baker, James A., III, with Thomas M. DeFrank. *The Politics of Diplomacy: Revolution,* War & *Peace, 1989–1992.* New York: Putnam's Sons, 1995.

Barilleaux, Ryan K., and Mark J. Rozell. *Power and Prudence: The Presidency of George H. W. Bush.* College Station: Texas A&M University Press, 2004.

Bush, George. *All the Best, George Bush: My Life in Letters and Other Writings.* New York: Scribner, 1999.

Bush, George and Brent Scowcroft. *A World Transformed.* New York: Alfred A. Knopf, 1998.

Fitzwater, Marlin. *Call the Briefing! Bush and Reagan, Sam and Helen: A Decade With Presidents and the Press.* New York: Times Books, 1995.

Greene, John Robert. *The Presidency of George Bush.* Lawrence: University Press of Kansas, 2000.

Maynard, Christopher. *Out of the Shadow: George H. W. Bush and the End of the Cold War.* College Station: Texas A&M University Press, 2008.

Parmet, Herbert S. *George Bush: The Life of a Lone Star Yankee.* New York: Scribner, 1997.

Christopher Maynard

BUSH, GEORGE W.

born 1946
Forty-third President of the United States

Although he was elected primarily on a domestic agenda, George W. Bush would spend much of his presidency focused on foreign policy and national security issues, waging a war against terrorism following the al Qaeda attacks of September 11, 2001. A massive reorganization of homeland security and intelligence gathering followed, along with a shift toward preemptive war abroad as a means of preventing further terrorist attacks from occurring on U.S. soil. This led to a war in Afghanistan to oust al Qaeda forces and remove the Taliban regime and, more controversially, to an invasion of Iraq to topple Saddam Hussein, whose government was declared by the Bush administration to be a state sponsor of international terrorism. Despite the focus on national security, Bush would be responsible for a dramatic shift to an unorthodox conservatism, what he termed "compassionate conservatism," that utilized high levels of government spending to achieve what Bush claimed were conservative results. After the country slipped into recession during his second term, Bush finished his presidency with dismal public job approval ratings.

Early Career

Born in New Haven, Connecticut, George Walker Bush was the eldest son of George Herbert Walker Bush (the forty-first president of the United States) and Barbara Bush. Eager to begin a successful business career in the oil fields of Texas, Bush's father moved the family to Midland, Texas. After spending most of his childhood in Midland and Houston, Bush followed in his father's footsteps by attending boarding school at Phillips Academy in Andover, Massachusetts, and then studying at Yale University, from which he received an undergraduate degree in history in 1968. During the Vietnam War, Bush remained in the United States and served as a pilot in the Texas Air National Guard from 1968 until 1973 before receiving a discharge to attend graduate school. In 1975, he received an M.B.A. from Harvard University and subsequently returned to west Texas to work in the oil industry. In 1978, he ran as a Republican candidate for the U.S. House of Representatives. Although he lost that campaign, Bush remained tied to politics through his father; the elder Bush became vice president after Ronald Reagan's 1980 election to the presidency. After serving on his father's successful presidential campaign in

1988, Bush moved to Dallas and became co-owner and managing partner of the Texas Rangers baseball franchise. Using the heightened media exposure of owning a professional sports team, he mounted a successful challenge to Texas governor Ann Richards in 1994. As governor, Bush was heralded for his bipartisanship, eagerly working with Democrats in the state legislature. His overwhelming reelection in 1998 (with close to 70 percent of the vote) positioned him as a strong candidate for the presidency in 2000.

2000 Election

Bush's father had lost to Bill Clinton in the 1992 presidential election; now Bush faced Clinton's vice president, Al Gore, in what proved to be a close election with a controversial finish. From the start, Bush faced a difficult challenge; Gore represented the incumbent administration during a time of relative prosperity and had far more political experience. But Gore's bland campaign, Bush's better-than-expected performance in presidential debates, and a slowing economy helped create one of the closest elections in American history. Although Bush did not win the popular vote, he did capture the electoral vote, which included a narrow win in Florida that took more than a month of legal wrangling to decide. When the U.S. Supreme Court, in a 5–4 vote, ordered a stop to the partial recount of the vote in Florida, Bush was left to begin his presidency with a significant portion of the population viewing his victory as illegitimate.

Domestic Priorities

Throughout the campaign Bush had billed himself as a "compassionate conservative." This label, along with narrow Republican majorities in Congress, had given Democrats reason to expect that Bush would be a national-unity president and work with them much as he had worked with Democrats in the Texas legislature. His agenda included tax cuts, Social Security and Medicare reform, conservative judicial nominees, aid to faith-based organizations, and education reform. The promise of bipartisanship seemed to be in full force at the beginning of his presidency as Bush joined with Massachusetts senator Edward Kennedy to pass No Child Left Behind (NCLB, 2001), an educational

reform law designed to narrow the achievement gap in student performance, hold failing public schools accountable, and ensure that teachers would be highly qualified in their content area. Although some critics argued that it provided inadequate funding, inordinate reliance on standardized testing, and too much federal intrusion into state education, NCLB contained provisions favored by both Democrats and Republicans. This cooperation had also been seen earlier in 2001 when Bush was willing to negotiate the amount and terms of his proposed tax cut. After calling for a $1.6 trillion tax cut over a ten-year period, Bush negotiated a $1.35 trillion tax cut in an agreement that was reached by uniting congressional Republicans, but also by bringing in a handful of Democrats.

What shattered the initial optimism of bipartisanship was Bush's aggressive push for what he called an "Ownership Society," which argued that personal welfare was directly related to a person's ability to control his or her own life rather than rely on government regulations and transfer payments. Bush thought that individuals should have control of their children's education, control over personal health care, and control over their retirement savings. In the field of health care, Bush pushed for a voluntary Medicare prescription drug benefit and other sweeping reforms found in the Medicare Modernization Act (2003), which was lambasted by some Republicans as too expensive.

In a style that was, according to one Bush admirer, Fred Barnes, "brisk, confident, and uncompromising," Bush forwarded his reforms despite growing criticism. (200) Many Democrats, as well as members of the media, interpreted this confident and determined style as arrogance. For their part, many conservative Republicans were alarmed that Bush's reforms would cost a considerable amount of money. Bush, however, was not a traditional small-government conservative; he believed in an activist federal government that could focus on conservative goals, such as individual choice, without necessarily following conservative methods. To the alarm of many conservatives, this would result in a larger federal government costing billions in taxpayer dollars. In 2001, Bush pushed through legislation to provide federal funds to "faith-based" charities, thereby targeting federal dollars for social services for the poor without the government directly administering the benefits. In 2002, Bush gained approval for a second major tax cut, this time for $350 billion. In his second term, Bush proposed a complete overhaul of Social Security that would have given people the choice of having a private retirement savings account or staying in the current system. This proved too controversial and unpopular. Democrats strongly resisted any changes to the program and many Republicans were alarmed at the cost involved in completing a transition to a private system. Bush also attempted sweeping immigration reforms; but again the effort proved too controversial, especially among members of his own party, many of whom considered Bush's approach (which included a provision for amnesty) too lenient. A second major domestic initiative went down to defeat.

War on Terrorism

In 2001, George W. Bush returned many familiar faces to foreign policy, including Vice Pres. Dick Cheney, Sec. of State Colin Powell, and National Security Advisor Condoleezza Rice. Each had played important roles in the elder Bush's administration, yet none had been as vital to the foreign-policy apparatus as they would this time around. George H. W. Bush, Brent Scowcroft, and James Baker had served as the senior decision makers of the earlier administration, directing foreign policy with a top-down approach. Lacking the experience and foreign-policy expertise of his father, George W. Bush would rely more on his advisors, particularly Rice, who began tutoring him on foreign policy during his successful campaign for the presidency. Criticizing Clinton's failure to form an "articulated 'national interest'," Rice rejected "assertive multilateralism" and preferred to concentrate on traditional big power relationships, particularly with Russia and China, to reassert American self-interests. (Rice 45–62) Yet throughout most of 2001, there was still no clear foreign policy doctrine for the new Bush administration and its unilateral approach would be implemented in much the same case-by-case, "crisis-by-crisis" basis that Rice had chided the Clinton administration for during the 2000 election. Foreign policy was not a major focus, however, during the first year of his presidency, and Bush largely focused his attentions on achieving his domestic agenda.

The trajectory of the Bush administration was unalterably changed on September 11, 2001, when terrorists hijacked four commercial passenger planes, crashing two of them into the twin towers of the World Trade Center in New York City and one of them into the Pentagon in Washington, D.C. The fourth plane crashed into an empty field in Pennsylvania, perhaps after its passengers disrupted the terrorists' plans. Bush would set the priority of re-exerting American hegemony abroad; the Bush Doctrine called for military preemption against emergent threats. Bush's reductive rhetoric would echo Ronald Reagan's moralistic view of good versus evil, as would his muscular responses to what he deemed to be threats by "the evildoers." The attacks had been planned by a militant Islamist, Osama Bin Laden, who operated a terrorist network known as al Qaeda, which was partially based in Afghanistan. When Afghanistan's ruling Taliban regime refused to fully cooperate in capturing bin Laden, Bush responded with U.N.-sanctioned air strikes that quickly toppled the regime. Though Bin Laden escaped, many of al Qaeda's leaders were captured and their global terror network disrupted. Bush's popularity soared, and Republicans swept to victory in the midterm elections of 2002.

Homeland Security

In the month after the 9/11 attacks, the Bush administration sent to Congress the USA PATRIOT Act, which expanded the powers of the FBI and other law-enforcement agencies regarding search and surveillance powers. Roundly criticized by civil liberty groups, the act allowed federal agents to arrest and hold suspects without charges, evidence, or legal counsel. Despite concerns over the violation of basic constitutional and political rights, Congress overwhelmingly reauthorized the Patriot Act in 2006. In 2002, Bush sent a plan to Congress to form a Department of Homeland Security that would be housed in the executive branch and be responsible for thwarting future terrorist attacks on American soil. Tighter airport security was the most visible sign of an overall effort to strengthen American boarders and prevent future attacks.

As the global war on terror continued, captured Taliban and al Qaeda members began to be interrogated at the U.S. naval base in Guantánamo Bay, Cuba. The Bush administration argued that constitutional protections did not apply to these prisoners, nor did the Geneva Conventions regarding the treatment of prisoners of war because they were "unlawful enemy combatants." A debate emerged over the methods that the CIA and other groups were using to elicit information from detainees. The government confirmed that some detainees had been subjected to "enhanced interrogation techniques," including waterboarding (simulated drowning), that were considered torture under international law. The administration was further embarrassed by the publication of photographs of Abu Ghraib prison in Iraq clearly showing the abusive treatment of prisoners by American soldiers. Despite continued objections, the administration never backed away from its public stance that many of the steps undertaken were necessary to stop terrorist attacks; the Bush administration would point to the lack of terrorist attacks on the United States in the years following 9/11 as proof of the effectiveness of its policies.

War in Iraq

In his 2002 State of the Union address, Bush had referred to an "axis of evil" consisting of North Korea, Iran, and Iraq. Bush felt that Iraq was of particular importance and had to be included in any global war against terrorism because intelligence reports indicated that Iraq possessed the potential to produce chemical, biological, or nuclear weapons. Worse yet, intelligence reports indicated that Saddam Hussein had been secretly amassing large amounts of these so-called weapons of mass destruction (WMD). Although these reports would later be shown to be inaccurate, the Bush administration concluded that regime change in Iraq would help further the goal of weakening the terrorist threat and launched Operation Iraqi Freedom in 2003. In the build-up to military action, key Bush administration officials made the case for war in a series of hawkish speeches, culminating in President Bush's State of the Union address in January 2003 and Sec. of State Colin Powell's presentation to the United Nations in February 2003. Unlike his father, George W. Bush did not work to garner the same level of consensus among a broad coalition, preferring to act in a more unilateral manner in what Bush called the "coalition of the willing," which included countries who supported military action against Iraq even with the absence of a United Nations Security Council agreement. Despite disagreement within the world community concerning the validity of the invasion, Saddam Hussein was quickly ousted from power by a U.S.-British invasion force, and the Bush administration was left to begin the more difficult task of creating a provisional government and reconstructing the economy and security of the conquered nation.

2004 Election

Bush ran for re-election in 2004 against Democratic senator John Kerry of Massachusetts. The 9/11 attacks and subsequent war on terrorism had brought national security to the political forefront for the first time since the end of the Cold War. Bush's father had lost his 1992 reelection bid in part because voters viewed domestic affairs as more important than foreign ones. The climate in 2004, however, was quite different, and voters, who according to exit polls viewed Bush as a stronger leader than Kerry, handed the sitting president a victory. Even though Bush's approval numbers were beginning to sag as the situation in Iraq became more troubled, his campaign was able to portray the president as the best man to stop future terrorist attacks, painting his opponent, Senator Kerry, as a "flip-flopper" who voted for the war and subsequently voted not to fund it and, thus, could not be trusted to keep the nation safe. Bush's electoral support was short-lived, and his approval ratings steadily declined after his reelection victory.

A Difficult Second Administration

Although his popularity had remained strong for most of his first term, Bush's approval ratings would slide to near record lows by the end of his second. Continued problems in Iraq would contribute to his sinking popularity. As American casualties continued to mount, criticism of Bush's handling of the war would steadily increase and lead to declining public approval. One issue that garnered considerable criticism was the failure of U.S. forces to find the active production facilities or stockpiles of weapons of mass destruction in Iraq that Bush had used in his argument leading up to the invasion. Critics also pointed to the Bush administration's claimed connection between Iraq and al Qaeda. By 2005, opinion polls in the United States clearly showed a belief that the ouster of Saddam Hussein had not been worth the tremendous cost in lives and taxpayer dollars. Adding to the financial burden was the decision made by Bush that the rebuilding of Iraq would be financed with U.S. grants, not loans. By the end of the Bush administration, the situation in Iraq was improved, with democratic elections, a new Iraqi constitution, and a commitment to withdraw U.S. troops from Iraq by 2011. Still, American doubts remained as to the validity of the invasion and subsequent occupation.

Criticism over the administration's handling of the devastation caused to New Orleans and the Gulf Coast by Hurricane Katrina in August 2005 would also contribute to Bush's eroding popularity. In the 2006 midterm elections, Democrats seized both houses of Congress. Even as the situation in Iraq began to improve, Democratic control of Congress and Republican candidates—particularly those running for reelection in 2008—choosing to distance themselves from Bush's poor job approval rating would make it difficult for the president to pursue an aggressive domestic agenda. Despite these setbacks, Bush was able to achieve victories with his appointments of John Roberts Jr. (confirmed as chief justice in 2005), and Samuel Alito Jr. (confirmed in 2006) to the Supreme Court. The major concern in the final years of his presidency, however, was the failing economy. Massive military spending, large tax cuts, and slow economic growth combined to create a deep recession. Mortgage defaults, soaring energy costs, and a severe credit crisis led to a string of bankruptcies and a controversial plan to "bailout" both the financial and American automobile industries to the tune of more than $700 billion in government-secured loans. These steps, taken by the lame-duck president and lame-duck Congress, were greeted by the public with skepticism and a long-term approach

President George W. Bush addresses the press on May 1, 2006, concerning the recent trip to Iraq made by Sec. of Defense Donald Rumsfeld (left) and Sec. of State Condoleezza Rice (right). Three years after the landmark speech he gave on an aircraft carrier beneath a banner hailing 'Mission Accomplished' in Iraq, the president declared that the situation in the war-torn country was improving and moving toward security and democracy. Continued doubts about the decision to go into Iraq, however, in addition to the botched federal response to Hurricane Katrina, would lead to the Democrats seizing control of both houses of Congress in the 2006 midterm elections and the continued erosion of Bush's public approval rating. (Paul J. Richards/AFP/Getty Images)

to the recession would be left to the incoming administration of president-elect Barack Obama. Bush left office with some of the lowest public approval ratings of any American president, yet maintained the characteristically defiant confidence that so infuriated his critics throughout his presidency.

Bush was a bold leader who prided himself on his ability as a problem-solver, had an affinity for grand proposals, and detested what he termed the "small ball" politics of the Clinton administration. The price of his boldness, however, was often partisan squabbles, dramatic swings in his approval ratings, and intense criticism from both conservatives, who thought many of his programs were too expensive and unnecessarily increased the size of government, and liberals, who thought many of Bush's programs were just plain wrong and the way he presented them arrogant. In the aftermath of the September 11, 2001, attacks, Bush emerged as a forceful commander-in-chief and his poll numbers reached historic heights. He pushed a worldwide crusade for democracy, assuming that was the only way to prevent terrorism. An invasion of Afghanistan to destroy the power of the Taliban and root out leaders of al Qaeda was deemed a success. A subsequent invasion of Iraq proved more complex and controversial, with American casualties exceeding four thousand by the end of his presidency. In the Middle East, Bush's father had chosen stability over democracy; George W. Bush had faith that building democratic institutions would be the proper course for the long term. His new strategic doctrine of preemption, although not without historical precedent, did change the direction of American foreign policy and how the country was perceived abroad, causing much of the world to develop unfavorable opinions concerning the United States in general and of President Bush in particular. His skepticism of multilateral organizations was also a break from both the Clinton administration and that of his father. Although he had set out in his presidency to solve a litany of domestic issues, the war on terrorism would come to dominate all other issues. It was not until the final years of his presidency, when a deepening economic recession focused the nation's attention on domestic issues, that Bush began to move away from his role as a wartime president.

Bibliography and Further Reading

Baker, James A., III, and Lee H. Hamilton, Co-Chairs. *The Iraq Study Group Report: The Way Forward—A New Approach.* New York: Vintage Books, 2006.

Barnes, Fred. *Rebel-in-Chief: Inside the Bold and Controversial Presidency of George W. Bush.* New York: Three Rivers Press, 2006.

Brzezinski, Zbigniew. *Second Chance: Three American Presidents and the Crisis of American Superpower.* New York: Basic Books, 2007.

Campbell, Colin, Bert A. Rockman, and Andrew Rudalevige, eds. *The George W. Bush Legacy.* Washington, D.C.: Congressional Quarterly Press, 2007.

Draper, Robert. *Dead Certain: The Presidency of George W. Bush.* New York: Simon & Schuster, 2007.

Edwards, George C., and Desmond S. King, eds. *The Polarized Presidency of George W. Bush.* New York: Oxford University Press, 2007.

Gaddis, John Lewis. *Surprise, Security, and the American Experience.* Cambridge: Harvard University Press, 2004.

Greenstein, Fred I., ed. *The George W. Bush Presidency: An Early Assessment.* Baltimore, MD: Johns Hopkins University Press, 2003.

Rice, Condoleezza. "Promoting the National Interest." *Foreign Affairs* 79 (January-February 2000): 45–62.

Christopher Maynard

Cable Television and Talk Radio

In the nineteenth and early twentieth centuries, Americans received their news from scores of small partisan newspapers, most of which depended on party patronage for the printing of government notices and election ballots. Urbanization, however, created the modern nonpartisan newspaper, which could survive on advertising and a paid subscription base. As a result, in the twentieth century news media became more nonpartisan and professionalized, a trend furthered by government regulations requiring broadcast media to assume a nominally neutral stance. The rise of the Cable News Network (CNN) in the 1980s and the subsequent politicization of the cable news environment, along with the explosion of talk radio in the 1990s, made journalistic objectivity less relevant. The news media became far less "professional" and more openly partisan and opinionated—re-creating the stridency and bombast of the nineteenth-century press.

Cable Television

The wealthy entrepreneur Ted Turner led the cable television communications revolution, launching CNN on June 1, 1980, with a 24-hour news format designed to present viewers with complete, in-depth news from around the world. However, CNN experienced difficulty breaking the hold that network news broadcasts held on national viewership until the 1990–1991 Persian Gulf War, when the cable source emerged as America's preeminent news outlet. Taking advantage of the network's continuous coverage and 24-hour live feed, viewers chose CNN over the traditional networks' more limited daily news cycle.

Challengers to CNN were now inevitable, and a number of them arose during the mid-1990s, fracturing and polarizing the cable news viewership. MSNBC, a joint venture of the Microsoft corporation and the National Broadcasting Company (NBC), launched on July 15, 1996, with a schedule that combined newscasts with feature programs. The network sought to capitalize upon the Internet revolution in communication by integrating the World Wide Web and television into one news source. The viewing experience was interactive as MSNBC listed hosts' e-mail addresses and encouraged viewers to submit questions, comments, and instant feedback. The Fox News Channel launched on October 7, 1996, as the conservative counterbalance to the "liberal" mainstream news media. For the next few years, CNN won the ratings wars, with MSNBC and Fox News battling for second. The Australian-born media mogul Rupert Murdoch helped move Fox firmly into second place by garnering a loyal following for Fox among partisan conservatives, many of whom came to Fox via conservative talk radio programs. Fox News surpassed CNN in viewership in the wake of the September 11, 2001, attacks as viewers sought pro-American certainty in their news. In 2007–2008, however, MSNBC surged as the liberal antidote to Fox News by promoting progressive hosts.

In response to the growth of cable news networks, some argued that their capacity to transmit dramatic stories and images and air them repeatedly gave the networks the ability to shape the domestic and foreign policy agenda. This so-called CNN Effect forced elected officials to react quickly to the events highlighted by the cable networks, even if it helped to confirm pre-existing policy decisions as well as to precipitate them.

On occasion, cable news had a significant influence on the domestic political scene. On election night 2000, Fox News helped shape the national response to the disputed presidential contest. That evening John Ellis—then-Gov. George W. Bush's first cousin and a Fox News election projections expert—made the premature call that his cousin had won the state of Florida and thus the presidency. Other news outlets followed Fox's lead, cementing the image of Bush as president-elect. News networks retracted that projection in the early morning hours and deemed the race too close to call. Vice Pres. Al Gore as loser began to harden. Five years later, the cable news coverage of the Hurricane Katrina catastrophe proved devastating to the Bush presidency, as cable networks showed the administration's bungled handling of the disaster's aftermath.

The 24-hour news format had a significant effect, too, on television journalism, with critics charging that journalistic standards were suffering under the growing competition to be first rather than best and that cable was creating tabloid TV in an effort to keep up ratings and advertising revenue. Moreover, cable news moved away from CNN's early attempts at objective, complete coverage, instead placing a high premium on instant opinions and unverified assertions such as the infamous "War on Christmas" promoted by Fox News. By the end of the first decade of the twenty-first century, viewers on the political right and left watched cable news to have their viewpoints reinforced rather than challenged. For many, "cable news" became derisive cultural shorthand for opinion-based, myopic, personality-driven programming.

Talk Radio

In 1987, during the Reagan era, the Federal Communications Commission abolished the Fairness Doctrine that had stipulated that holders of public broadcasting licenses must present both sides of controversial issues in a balanced manner. The result was a wave of partisan political commentary. Perhaps chief among these was *The Rush Limbaugh Show*, which debuted nationally on August 1, 1988. The acerbic, hyper-conservative Limbaugh's political clout dramatically increased from the late 1980s through the mid-1990s, by which time he broadcast to over 650 stations nationally with nearly 20 million listeners per week. As a voice for movement conservatives, he helped the Republican Party regain control of the House of Representatives for the first time in 40 years. But he was not alone. Between 1985 and 1995, the number of American talk-radio shows jumped from 200 to 1,000. Limbaugh spawned imitators such as Michael Savage, Sean Hannity, and Laura Ingraham.

Limbaugh and his conservative colleagues became a powerful force in politics in the 1990s and 2000s. In 1993, Limbaugh helped block Clinton's job stimulus package, quashed an attempt for the federal government to certify home-school teachers, and halted the administration's attempt to reinstate the Fairness Doctrine. House Republican Whip Newt Gingrich regularly consulted him in 1993 and 1994. Limbaugh's popularity allowed him to claim credit for the 1994 Republican Revolution. Following the Republican defeat in the 2008 presidential election, conservative Republicans again began relying on Limbaugh to lead their party against Democratic president Barack Obama. Some in the Republican establishment who tried to distance themselves from the controversial Limbaugh found themselves under attack from movement conservatives, and critics were often forced to issue apologies for their anti-Limbaugh comments.

Liberals began imitating the conservative talk radio format in 2004 with the launching of Air America Radio. In contrast to the political right, however, Americans on the left had difficulty succeeding in partisan radio. They lacked the homogeneity between host and audience possessed by conservatives on talk radio. Al Franken, a comedian and writer who had appeared on the television show *Saturday Night Live*, hosted the flagship show on Air America Radio, but left the network in 2007 to run for U.S. Senate in Minnesota. The network rose and fell quickly. Though launched to great fanfare, by 2006 it had filed for bankruptcy. After its sale, a lower profile version of Air America remained. Listeners on the political left did not have an appetite for shrill polemics on the radio, instead holding sway on the Internet.

Bibliography and Further Readings

Ammon, Royce J. *Global Television and the Shaping of World Politics.* Jefferson, NC: McFarland and Co., 2001.

Collins, Scott. *Crazy Like a Fox.* New York: Penguin Group, 2004.

Joshi, S.T. *The Angry Right.* Amherst, NY: Prometheus Book, 2006.

Nimmon, Dan, and Chevelle Newsome. *Political Commentators in the United States in the 20th Century.* Westport, CT: Greenwood Press, 1997.

Robinson, Piers. *The CNN Effect.* New York: Routledge, 2002.

Schonfeld, Reese. *Me and Ted Against the World.* New York: HarperCollins, 2001.

Streitmatter, Rodger. *Mightier than the Sword.* Boulder, CO: Westview Press, 1997.

Jon R. Peterson

CAMPAIGN FINANCE REFORM

Campaign finance reform refers to proposed changes in two kinds of laws: statutes governing the amounts of money that political candidates or parties may receive from individuals or organizations, and measures regulating the cumulative amounts that individuals or organizations can donate. Proposals have also sought to define or redefine *who is eligible* to make political contributions and *what sorts of activities* constitute in-kind contributions. Campaign finance reform was a major issue in congressional and presidential elections during the 1990s and 2000s. The most prominent campaign finance reform proposals were associated with legislation first introduced in the Senate by senators John McCain (R–AZ) and Russell Feingold (D–WI) in 1995.

These proposals are part of a larger history. There have been two major periods of campaign finance reform in the past century—the proposals that led to the Federal Election Campaign Act (FECA) of 1971 and its subsequent amendments, and the most recent era, in which dissatisfaction with the FECA regime led to the enactment of a variant of the McCain-Feingold legislation in the form of the Bipartisan Campaign Reform Act (BCRA) of 2002.

The Federal Election Campaign Act

Campaign finance laws before FECA generally focused not on the recipients of contributions but on those who made them. During the first half of the twentieth century, laws were passed prohibiting direct contributions from corporations, labor unions, and federal employees. Political Action Committees (PACs) were set up by corporations and unions as a means of soliciting individual contributions that could then be donated to politicians or spent independently.

The FECA of 1971, and its subsequent 1974 and 1979 amendments, established limits on candidate spending; on the contributions of individuals and PACs to candidates, parties, or political committees; and on the amount of money candidates could spend on their own campaigns. It also established an oversight body, the Federal Election Commission (FEC) to enforce campaign finance laws. Another campaign finance bill of the time, the Revenue Act of 1971, established a voluntary public funding system for presidential candidates and a voluntary income tax checkoff to support this system.

In its 1976 *Buckley v. Valeo*, 424 U.S. 1 decision, the Supreme Court ruled that restrictions on candidate spending and candidate self-financing violated the First Amendment. The Court nonetheless allowed the limits on spending in presidential campaigns to stand because these limits were contingent on receipt of public funds. The Court also upheld the individual and PAC contribution limits. Under FECA, individuals could contribute no more than $1,000 to a candidate, $5,000 to a PAC, or $20,000 to a party. The total individual donor limit was $25,000. PACs were limited to contributing no more than $5,000 to a candidate but had no aggregate limit.

It has been argued that FECA led to a proliferation of PACs and that it increased the percentage of congressional candidate funds raised from PACs. The number of registered PACs grew from approximately 600 in 1974 to over 4,000 by 1984. FECA also, however, reduced the influence that any individual donor or organization could have over congressional candidates because no candidate would be reliant upon any one individual donor or PAC. At the presidential level, FECA's public matching funds also encouraged candidates to voluntarily limit their spending. All major party nominees accepted matching funds, and their corresponding limits, from 1976 through 1996, as did virtually all qualifying, unsuccessful primary candidates. All major party nominees also accepted FECA's general election flat grant—and corresponding prohibition on raising any money for the general election—until Barack Obama's 2008 campaign. This ensured equal funding of major party candidates in all general elections from 1976 through 2004.

The Bipartisan Campaign Reform Act

By the 1990s, however, two developments had begun to weaken the FECA regime. First, although corporations and labor unions could not contribute directly to candidates, FECA did not prohibit them from contributing to political parties as long as this money was used for "party building" activities, and not to directly advocate for the election or defeat of a candidate. During the 1990s, parties began to solicit such "soft money" donations from corporations, labor unions, and wealthy individuals. Second, advocacy groups also increased their spending on so-called issue advocacy or electioneering advertisements. Like soft money expenditures, these ads also could not directly advocate for or against a candidate, but many of them left viewers with a clear impression of which candidates the group favored or opposed—for instance, by harshly criticizing a candidate's position on an issue and then exhorting viewers to call that candidate to express their views on the matter.

The original McCain-Feingold campaign finance reform bill predated these developments somewhat, but over the course of the 1990s the bill was changed to incorporate responses to both of these developments, and it therefore became the primary focus of the campaign finance reform debate. The most com-prehensive early version of the bill, introduced in 1997, called for a system of advertising vouchers to be provided to congressional candidates who adhered to voluntary spending limits, for greater limitation of PAC contributions, and for a ban on soft money contributions. An amendment initially proposed by senators Olympia Snowe (R–ME) and James Jeffords (R–VT) called for limitations on issue advocacy advertising by outside groups. In subsequent congresses, the voucher system and the PAC limitations were dropped and the bill became more about soft money and issue advocacy.

Although the House companion bill to McCain-Feingold, known as the Shays-Meehan bill, narrowly passed in the House of Representatives in 1998 and 2000, McCain and Feingold were unable to gain enough votes to invoke cloture in the Senate until 2002. The bill eventually passed both houses in 2002, and became known as the Bipartisan Campaign Reform Act, or BCRA. BCRA had two major components. First, it prohibited soft money contributions entirely at the federal level. Second, it imposed restrictions on "electioneering" advertisements; these restrictions prohibit organizations that receive corporate or labor funding from broadcasting advertisements that refer to a candidate for election within 30 days of that candidate's primary election or 60 days of the general election, although PAC money could be used. BCRA also doubled limits on individual contributions to candidates, raised limits on individual contribution to parties to $25,000, and raised the aggregate contribution limit to $95,000. All of these hard money limits were indexed to inflation. Limits on contributions to and from PACs were unchanged. BCRA took effect the day after the 2002 election. Initially, the Supreme Court in *McConnell v. FEC*, 540 U.S. 93 (2003) upheld all of the major provisions of BCRA—but after Pres. George W. Bush appointed a new chief justice, John Roberts, and a new associate justice, Samuel Alito, the Court, in *Federal Election Commission v. Wisconsin Right to Life, Inc.*, 551 U.S. 449 (2007), struck down in part the limitation on advocacy expenditures and advertising on free speech grounds. As of late 2009, the court was considering a broader challenge to the advertising restrictions in the

Citizens United v. Federal Election Commission case. There is the potential that the court could take further steps to do away with limitations on advertising by groups, corporations, and labor unions.

Consequences of the Bipartisan Campaign Reform Act

Some analyses of campaign finance distinguish between money that is voluntarily "pushed" into campaigns by enthusiastic donors and money that is "pulled" into the system, often from reluctant donors, through the solicitations of candidates. Even before the passage of BCRA, many corporations had begun to report that they were frustrated with the pressure put on them by the parties to make soft money contributions. As a consequence of BCRA's prohibition on soft money, political expenditures by many corporations, particularly publicly held corporations, declined substantially in 2004 and 2006—evidence that these were "pulled" contributions. Individual donors, including some prominent business leaders, who still wanted to "push" money into the system could do so by giving to "527" organizations—groups that, because they were not organized as PACs or as political committees, were still able to raise money in unlimited sums for the purpose of non-candidate-specific advertising, voter mobilization, and voter registration. Although 527 organizations raised over $400 million in 2004, their fund-raising did not come close to matching the soft money receipts of the parties in 2000.

BCRA's advertising restrictions prohibited the sorts of multi-million dollar campaigns waged by business, labor, and advocacy groups in the late 1990s, 2000, and 2002. By 2002, however, many of these groups had already begun to reduce their spending on television advertising; the television market had become too fragmented for the ads to be as effective as they once had been, and groups had begun to redirect their money toward face-to-face communication with members or employees, and toward communicating via the Internet. BCRA did not restrict Internet communication at all, a fact that likely will further dilute the effectiveness of its advertising restrictions in years to come.

Other Campaign Finance Reform Proposals

Following the enactment of BCRA, several smaller campaign finance reform proposals gained prominence at the federal level. Most notable among these were proposals for overhaul of the presidential public financing system. Under FECA, presidential primary candidates who agreed to limit their spending according to overall and state-by-state limits would receive federal matching funds for the first $250 of each individual contribution. Candidates also would receive a flat grant (and hence would not raise money at all) during the general election. The maximum amount for primaries was set at $10 million for the 1976 election and had risen to $45 million by 2004; the amount of the general election grant had risen from $20 million to $74 million. Almost all major-party candidates adhered to the primary limits from 1976 to 1996, and all major-party candidates have accepted the general election flat grant. In 2000, George W. Bush declined to limit his primary spending, and in 2004, Bush, John Kerry, and Howard Dean declined the primary matching funds, and Kerry speculated about declining the general election flat grant as well. In 2008, all of the major party candidates devised finance strategies that presumed their opting-out of the public finance system.

Because of the dramatic increase in spending in 2004 and 2008 by candidates of both parties, many reform advocates have proposed either changing the matching fund provisions—by, for instance, raising the limit, raising the amount of the match from one-to-one to three-to-one or four-to-one—and others have called for doing away with the public financing system entirely. An added concern for many reform proponents is that the funds for this system have come from a voluntary tax check-off, and the amount available from this tax check-off has nearly become insufficient for candidates' needs. What can safely be said is that public financing of presidential campaigns effectively collapsed between 2004 and 2008.

A final set of campaign finance reform initiatives has come from the states. Currently, 6 states (Arizona, Connecticut, Hawaii, Maine, Minnesota, and Wisconsin) provide some form of public financing to candidates, and 11 states use a tax check-off to provide funds to state parties. Following the Supreme

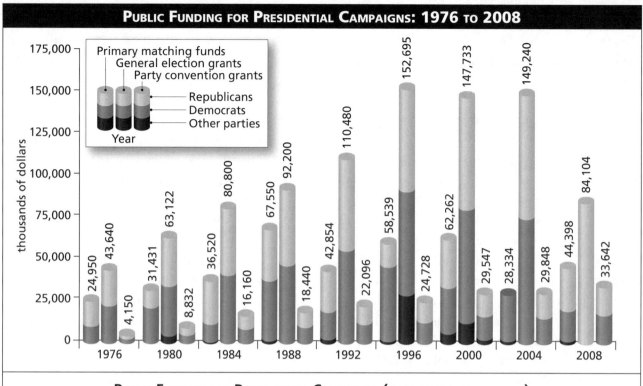

PUBLIC FUNDING FOR PRESIDENTIAL CAMPAIGNS: 1976 TO 2008

PUBLIC FUNDING FOR PRESIDENTIAL CAMPAIGNS (THOUSANDS OF DOLLARS)

	1976	1980	1984	1988	1992	1996	2000	2004	2008
Primary matching funds									
Republicans	9,746	20,760	10,100	35,496	15,859	43,997	26,962	0	17,528
Democrats	15,204	10,671	26,226	31,115	24,629	14,037	29,367	27,442	25,989
Other parties	0	0	194	939	2,366	505	5,933	892	881
Total	24,950	31,431	36,520	67,550	42,854	58,539	62,262	28334	44,398
General election grants									
Republicans	21,820	29,440	40,400	46,100	55,240	61,820	67,560	74,620	84,104
Democrats	21,820	29,440	40,400	46,100	55,240	61,820	67,560	74,620	0
Other parties	0	4,242	0	0	0	29,055	12,613	0	0
Total	43,640	63,122	80,800	92,200	110,480	152,695	147,733	149,240	84,104
Party convention grants									
Republicans	1,964	4,416	8,080	9,220	11,048	12,364	13,512	14,924	16,821
Democrats	2,186	4,416	8,080	9,220	11,048	12,364	13,512	14,924	16,821
Other parties	0	0	0	0	0	0	2,523	0	0
Total	4,150	8,832	16,160	18,440	22,096	24,728	29,547	29,848	33,642
Total public funding	72,739	103,386	133,479	178,190	175,430	235,962	239,542	207,422	138,753

Source: Federal Election Commission, "Presidential Election Campaign Fund (PECF): The Bottom Line," 2009.
Available online from http://www.fec.gov/press/bkgnd/ fund.shtml.
Notes: Due to rounding, total public funding may not equal the total of all grants and funds.

All major party presidential candidates accepted the Federal Election Campaign Act's general election grants in all general elections from 1976 to 2004, ensuring equal funding for each contender. In 2008, however, then-Sen. Barack Obama chose not to accept public funding, which allowed him to raise more money than his opponent, Sen. John McCain.

Court's *Nixon v. Shrink Missouri Government PAC*, 528 U.S. 377 (2000) decision, states are permitted to limit expenditures in legislative or statewide races. Though there has been debate over the relevance of these state laws to federal campaigns, many reform groups have increased their attention to reform at the state level, where the Supreme Court's *Buckley v. Valeo* decision plays less of a role in dictating policy.

The purported aims of campaign finance reform vary. Historically, many changes in campaign finance law have aimed at increased transparency in the political system. Even opponents of FECA and BCRA have argued in favor of making campaign finance visible to the public, and even in states where few restrictions have been placed on campaign funding, Web sites often provide information to the public on candidates' finances. A second goal for many reformers has been reducing corruption or reducing the appearance of corruption. Many advocacy groups have also referred to the role of major contributors in the political system, and some have argued that reducing the cost of campaigns may encourage different types of candidates to run for office. Public opinion surveys frequently show that few Americans rank campaign finance as a high priority, but majorities do support greater regulation of campaigns and increased disclosure of campaign contributions. A frequently discussed argument about campaign finance is the "hydraulic theory," which holds that campaign finance reform will be a recurring issue because money will always find its way into the system. Regardless of the veracity of this theory, campaign finance reform has been a recurring issue in American politics and will likely continue to reappear at regular intervals.

Bibliography and Further Reading

Corrado, Anthony, Thomas E. Mann, Daniel Ortiz, and Trevor Potter. *The New Campaign Finance Sourcebook.* Washington, D.C.: Brookings Institution, 2004.

Drew, Elizabeth. *The Corruption of American Politics.* New York: Overlook Press, 1999.

Gross, Donald A., and Robert K. Goidel. *The States of Campaign Finance Reform.* Columbus: Ohio State University Press, 2003.

Magleby, David B., and J. Quin Monson, eds. *The Last Hurrah.* Washington, DC: Brookings Institution, 2003.

Malbin, Michael J., ed. *The Election after Reform: Money, Politics, and the Bipartisan Campaign Reform Act.* Lanham, MD: Rowman & Littlefield, 2005.

Sorauf, Frank J. *Inside Campaign Finance: Myths and Realities.* New Haven, CT: Yale University Press, 1994.

Robert G. Boatright

RELATED ENTRIES
THIS VOLUME
Political Action Committees
OTHER VOLUMES
Campaign Finance Reform (vol. 6)

CAPITAL PUNISHMENT

Capital punishment—the state-sanctioned use of execution as a punishment for crimes—has a long history in the United States. Its use has raised constitutional questions under Amendment VIII's cruel and unusual punishment clause and Amendment XIV's due process clause. Though some forms or uses of the death penalty have been invalidated as unconstitutional, a majority of the Supreme Court has never ruled that the imposition of capital punishment itself is cruel and unusual or unconstitutional, per se.

Since the 1970s, there have been three waves of litigation involving capital punishment. The first of these challenged the use of the death penalty for a variety of crimes, which led to a ban on its use for some crimes and which produced a moratorium on executions until 1975. Since 1975, a second wave of litigation has resulted in the reinstatement of capital punishment for murder, subject to strict constitutional and procedural limits. Finally, a third wave of litigation has challenged specific uses of death as a form of punishment for minors or those who are intellectually disabled. Death penalty opponents have also used DNA evidence to question the guilt of many individuals sentenced to death, and have disputed the constitutionality of some of the technologies and methods used to execute.

Legal and Political History

At the time of the framing of the Constitution and the writing of Amendment VIII, scores of crimes were punishable by death, including murder, rape, robbery, and arson. Common forms of execution included firing squads and hanging. Capital punishment was employed as a punishment, in part, because prisons and incarceration were uncommon until the nineteenth century. As prisons emerged as an alternative form of punishment, the number of crimes punishable by death decreased.

After the Civil War, capital punishment was challenged under Amendment VIII. In *Wilkerson v. Utah*, 99 U.S. 130 (1878), the U.S. Supreme Court found that death by firing squad did not violate Amendment VIII. Then in *In re Kemmler*, 136 U.S. 436 (1890) the Court ruled that the recently invented method of execution—electrocution—that was being used in New York State did not violate Amendment VIII because it would "produce immediate and painless death." The Court also ruled that Amendment VIII did not apply to the states but only to the federal government. However, in *Robinson v. California*, 370 U.S. 660 (1962), the Court reversed itself, holding that the cruel and unusual punishment clause was incorporated through the due process clause of Amendment XIV to apply to states. Finally, in 1947 the Court ruled in *Louisiana ex rel. Francis v. Resweber*, 329 U.S. 459 (1947) that it was not unconstitutional to subject a condemned prisoner, Willie Francis, to execution a second time after the first effort to electrocute him had failed.

Challenging Capital Punishment

Though execution was used through the 1960s and 1970s, public support for it declined and changes in the public's ideas about how prisoners ought to be treated led to a reevaluation of capital punishment. The Supreme Court in *Trop v. Dulles*, 356 U.S. 86 (1958) recognized these changes and proposed a rule for determining whether a punishment violated Amendment VIII: "The Amendment must draw its meaning from the evolving standards of decency that mark the progress of a maturing society." This evolving standards-of-decency rule has been important in death penalty cases and other evaluations of punishment since 1958.

Beginning in the 1970s, opponents of capital punishment challenged its use both substantively as a violation of the cruel and unusual punishment clause of Amendment VIII, and as arbitrary and capricious under the due process clause of Amendment XIV. In *Furman v. Georgia*, 408 U.S. 238 (1972), the Court struck down a Georgia death penalty law along with those in several other states. The justices did so mostly on due process grounds, finding either that juries had too much discretion in imposing the sentence or that capital punishment was imposed in ways that

were disproportionately inflicted upon people of color. Two justices, Thurgood Marshall and William Brennan, used the *Trop* standard to invalidate the death penalty as a cruel and unusual punishment.

But rising crime rates in the United States led to increased support for capital punishment, and after *Furman* states reenacted death penalty laws. In *Gregg v. Georgia*, 428 U.S. 153 (1976), the Court upheld a Georgia death penalty statute after the state created a new system for imposing capital punishment. Under this system, there would first be a phase of a trial to determine guilt or innocence. If the accused was convicted, a punishment phase would ask jurors to consider whether death was warranted based upon a list of legislatively designed aggravating or mitigating factors surrounding the crime or the defendant.

Challenges to capital punishment based on race were raised in *McCleskey v. Kemp*, 481 U.S. 279 (1987). The challenges were premised upon a study done by a famous criminologist, David Baldus. The Baldus report demonstrated that the killer of a white person was four times more likely to receive a death sentence than was someone who murdered a black person. This report was used in *McCleskey* to argue that the death penalty was constitutionally biased against some individuals and therefore violated the equal protection clause. The Court rejected this claim, stating that unless one could show that race was a factor in a specific case, aggregate statistics such as those found in the Baldus report could not be used to invalidate the use of the death penalty.

Other challenges to capital punishment came in *Stanford v. Kentucky*, 492 U.S. 361 (1989), in which the Court ruled that it was constitutional to execute minors over the age of 15, and in *Penry v. Lynaugh*, 492 U.S. 302 (1989), in which it ruled that it was not unconstitutional to execute individuals who were intellectually disabled. However, in *Roper v. Simmons*, 543 U.S. 551 (2005), the Court overruled itself in *Stanford* and held that the death penalty for individuals under the age of 18 was cruel and unusual, and in *Atkins v. Virginia*, 536 U.S. 304 (2002) the Court found that executing the mentally retarded was also a violation of Amendment VIII. In addition, in *Coker v. Georgia*, 433 U.S. 584 (1977), the Court found the use of the death penalty to punish someone who had raped an adult women to be cruel and unusual. In *Eberheart v. Georgia*, 433 U.S. 917 (1977), the use of the death penalty was invalidated for kidnapping.

Despite these decisions and others that have questioned the use of capital punishment on procedural grounds, the Court has not been willing to strike down capital punishment across the board as unconstitutional. In *Herrera v. Collins*, 506 U.S. 390 (1993), the Court found that executing individuals who had been legally convicted and sentenced to death but who nonetheless claimed that they were "factually innocent" (that in fact they really did not commit the crime and were not just pleading innocence) did not violate the Constitution. In *Baze and Bowling v. Rees*, 553 U.S. ___ (2008), the Supreme Court rejected claims that the use of lethal injection was a form of cruel and unusual punishment. This form of punishment began in Texas in 1982 and supporters claimed that it did not inflict pain. Challengers in *Baze* sought to argue that there was evidence that the drug mixture used to execute did allow for the possibility of pain, but the Court rejected these assertions, citing a lack of supporting evidence. In that decision, Justice John Paul Stevens became only the fourth Supreme Court justice—joining Brennan, Marshall, and William Blackmun—to determine that all forms of the death penalty violated Amendment VIII.

Continuing Issues

Two issues, race and innocence, continue to affect questions surrounding capital punishment. Questions about racial bias and the death penalty were raised in the Baldus study and were generally ignored in the *McCleskey* opinion. But additional studies indicate that racial bias continues to be a problem in the imposition of the death penalty. A 1990 General Accounting Office (GAO) study found that the race of the victim continued to be a major factor influencing the imposition of capital punishment. Specifically, when the murder victim was white, the accused was much more likely to be charged with capital murder or to receive the death penalty than when the victim was a member of a different racial group. However, despite GAO

RELATED ENTRIES

THIS VOLUME
Supreme Court and the Judiciary

and other studies documenting the racial bias in capital punishment, there is little indication at present that the Supreme Court is willing to revisit its *McCleskey* precedent.

The increased use and availability of DNA and other forensic evidence has also made it possible for opponents to attack the death penalty by demonstrating that some individuals convicted of murder and sentenced to death were actually innocent. The Innocence Project, founded in 1992, has used DNA evidence to overturn the conviction of more than two hundred individuals falsely convicted of crimes. Many of these individuals were on death row. The American Civil Liberties Union (ACLU) claims that since 1973 at least 129 death row inmates have been set free because they were later proved to be innocent. The Death Penalty Information Center estimates this false conviction number to be 130 individuals as of 2008. The ACLU also claims that at least seven factually innocent individuals have been executed. In 2003, Illinois governor George Ryan commuted the sentences of all 167 individuals on death row in that state. He did so after DNA evidence revealed several individuals facing the death penalty in that state had been falsely convicted, and because of concerns that others might also have been wrongly convicted.

As of 2008, over 35 states and the federal government continue to use capital punishment. Some claim that its use is either an effective deterrent or a fitting punishment to some crimes. Others see it as ineffective as a deterrent or that it is unconstitutional as either cruel and unusual or administered in an arbitrary and capricious fashion. But for a few exceptions, the Court appears to give wide latitude to legislatures to decide what punishments are appropriate, and public support for capital punishment persists.

Bibliography and Further Reading

Amar, Akhil Reed. *The Constitution and Criminal Procedure*. New Haven, CT: Yale University Press, 1997.

Bedau, Hugo Adam, and Paul G. Cassell, eds. *Debating the Death Penalty: Should American Have Capital Punishment? The Experts on Both Sides Make Their Best Case*. New York: Oxford University Press, 2004.

Bohm, Robert M. *Death Quest II: An Introduction to the Theory and Practice of Capital Punishment in the United States*. New York: Lexis-Nexis, 2005.

LaFave, Wayne R, Jerold H. Israel, and Nancy J. King. *Criminal Procedure*. St. Paul, MN: Thomson/West, 2004.

David Schultz

CARTER, JIMMY

born 1924
Thirty-ninth President of the
United States

Thirty-ninth president of the United States, Nobel Peace Prize recipient, and human rights activist, James (Jimmy) Earl Carter Jr., helped to shape post-Watergate politics and define post–New Deal liberalism. Though his one-term presidency was marred by foreign policy crises and a tumultuous economy, Carter's post-presidential career has rendered him a revered citizen of the world.

Early Life
Born October 1, 1924, in Plains, Georgia, Carter earned his bachelor's degree from the U.S. Naval Academy in 1946 but left the service in 1953 and moved home to revive the family's flagging business interests, peanut farm, and warehouse. After turning the family business around, Carter plunged into the wider world of public service, serving two terms in the state senate before running unsuccessfully for governor in 1966. Though he emerged from obscurity to nearly defeat two well-known opponents, the near miss devastated him. Between 1966 and 1970, Carter underwent a spiritual transformation in which he fully embraced his evangelical Baptist faith and became "born again." In 1970, he captured the governorship where he displayed the hardnosed, ambitious, and self-righteous tendencies that came to define his unique political style. By late 1972, Carter had begun thinking about a run for the White House.

Presidential Campaign
Though Carter and his cadre of supporters, affectionately dubbed the "Peanut Brigade," had virtually no national political experience, the early 1970s proved to be an ideal time for political novices to leap into a presidential run. Following the tumultuous 1968 Democratic Convention, party bosses ceded control of the nominating process to primary voters and caucusgoers. Understanding an "outsider" with a small core of dedicated activists could win the Iowa caucus and New Hampshire primary, attract media attention, and race to victory, Carter began running for the 1976 nomination in late 1972. Adding to his chances was Richard Nixon's Watergate scandal and the fallout from the social tumult of the 1960s, which created a national mood matching Carter's populist "Washington outsider" campaign. Indeed, Carter's strategy so successfully fit the national mood that it became the model for most post-Watergate presidential aspirants.

Armed with a coherent strategy and an understanding of the national political environment, Carter spent three years building an organization, fund-raising, and gaining much-needed media exposure. Similar to what he had done during his gubernatorial race, Carter avoided specific policies while campaigning, preferring to use his charm, integrity, and sincerity as selling points. On the trail in relatively small and rural states like Iowa, Oklahoma, Maine, and Alaska, Carter established a rapport with voters that translated into a string of early victories and strong showings that served to create the intense media coverage necessary for a relative unknown to remain competitive in big states. The nature of a divided and crowded Democratic field—combined with Carter's personal charm, unusual biography, and understanding of the national mood—propelled him to the nomination.

As the Democratic standard-bearer, Carter faced a caretaker incumbent in Pres. Gerald Ford. Despite an enormous early lead in the polls, Carter committed a number of costly mistakes that led to a close race. The candidate's admission that he had "committed adultery in my heart many times" in an interview with

Playboy as well as his contradictory promises to reduce budget deficits while enacting significant social welfare programs enabled the Republicans to make a race of it. (Scheer 63–68)

It was President Ford, however, who committed the fatal mistake in the 1976 campaign. At the height of the hotly tested contest and during a televised debate, Ford claimed, "there is no Soviet domination of Eastern Europe." With Carter's mistakes obscured by the president's televised foreign policy gaffe, the challenger reversed his plummeting poll numbers.

Carter's appeal to organized labor, Southern white evangelicals, African Americans, and middle-class and educated liberals proved the difference in a razor-thin election. Winning every state in the former Confederacy, except Virginia, along with the Northern industrial states of Pennsylvania, New York, Ohio, Minnesota, and Wisconsin, Carter captured a 50.1 percent–48 percent victory in the popular vote and a 297–240 Electoral College squeaker.

The Presidency

The mid-1970s presented enormous domestic and foreign policy challenges. The combination of Vietnam War–related spending, increased social welfare expenditures, untimely tax cuts, and an Arab oil embargo had pummeled the American economy. By 1977, the U.S. economy was dogged by stagflation, a combination of high unemployment and inflation, a condition that economists had believed impossible. As if dealing with a troubled economy were not enough, Carter also faced significant foreign policy issues. Though Richard Nixon's policy of détente had successfully relaxed tensions with the Soviet Union during the early to mid 1970s, the strategy collapsed under Carter's watch. In addition, the president dealt with an increasingly turbulent Middle East, a condition highlighted by the 1979 Iranian Revolution.

In addition to these significant policy challenges, profound demographic changes had produced a population shift from the Northeast to the "Sunbelt" that fundamentally altered American politics. Consequently, the Roosevelt coalition that had dominated American political life since the Great Depression had come undone. Made up of Northern industrial states and

organized labor, the white South, and African Americans, the pieces and parts of the Roosevelt coalition had either lost their electoral clout, as was the case with organized labor, or were gravitating away from the Democrats, as happened in the white South.

This seismic shift presented Carter with a different political world than that encountered by his Democratic predecessors. Thus, the amalgamation of a turbulent economy, assorted foreign policy crises, and a changed political environment severely limited Carter's chances for success.

Domestic Policy Overview

Carter entered office without a coherent domestic program. He called for balanced budgets but also promised expansive and expensive social welfare programs such as national health insurance. Once in office, Carter came to see inflation and government excess as a significant national problem and shelved jobs programs and social welfare spending in favor of reducing government expenditures. Though congressional liberals balked mightily at the president's priorities, more than anything it was Carter's eye for minutiae and calls for "comprehensive" fixes that killed his domestic agenda. Because omnibus legislation creates more opposition than does incremental reform, Carter's "comprehensive" welfare reform and energy plan raised public expectations while also creating additional congressional opposition. Thus, even when Congress passed some of the energy plan, the president had unnecessarily expended precious political capital.

Ignoring the pleas of congressional leaders to limit his priorities and the scope of his legislation, Carter instead called for comprehensive welfare reform, governmental reorganization, and the creation of cabinet-level departments of Energy and Education. By pushing such big legislative items all at once, the president created a congressional logjam. With legislators alternately overworked and angry, Carter's welfare reform bill died in Congress.

In welfare reform, Carter had promised to make all recipients find work in return for government aid. The president could not even forge an agreement within his own Cabinet on the issue, and the plan died a quiet death before Carter's first year in office was complete. Though Carter eventually passed an energy plan, which presciently funded alternative energies, the combination of an overstuffed legislative agenda and a combative Congress caused the president's ambitious package to fail.

Although the president was eventually successful in overseeing the creation of departments of Energy and Education, passed his government reorganization plan, and pushed unpopular budgets through Congress, the bumbling manner in which they were passed, coupled with his high-profile legislative failures, established a lasting image of a feckless and bumbling chief executive.

Foreign Policy

If anything, the Carter administration's foreign policy was even messier and more confused than its domestic agenda. To be fair, the president took office at a time when congressional support for détente had flagged and the U.S.S.R. was actively supporting communist insurgencies and governments across Africa and Central Asia. The turbulent nature of the times notwithstanding, the president's inability to formulate a consistent foreign policy badly hamstrung the administration.

Carter had entered office promising to make "human rights" the cornerstone of his administration's foreign policy. Though this commitment made for a wonderful campaign applause-line, the geopolitical realities of the Cold War rendered the promise difficult, if not impossible, to keep. Consequently, when the United Sates made positive overtures to a nation with a poor human rights record, such as China, Carter's own lofty pronouncements exposed him to calls of "hypocrisy."

Similar to that of every other president during the Cold War, Carter's foreign policy was inevitably defined by U.S.-Soviet relations. A combination of the president's inexperience in foreign policy and the rapidly changing international environment made for erratic strategy. Indeed, Carter's primary foreign policy advisors, Sec. of State Cyrus Vance and National Security Advisor Zbigniew Brzezinski, were emblematic of the administration's seemingly schizophrenic policy. Until he abruptly resigned in 1980, Vance

sought to maintain détente, even as Brzezinski urged a hard line. Consequently, from 1977 through early 1980, Carter's foreign policy drifted.

By the time of the Carter administration, the Middle East had become an increasingly strategic point in the Cold War and in the global economy even as it grew less politically and culturally stable. Following American assistance to Israel during the 1973 Yom Kippur War, Arab states had imposed an oil embargo against the United States and Western Europe. The consequent spike in oil prices, gasoline shortages, and inflationary pressures transformed the Arab-Israeli conflict into a matter of national security.

Foreshadowing Carter's post-presidential career was his administration's one shining foreign policy success, the 1978 Camp David Accords. The task of personally negotiating the first peace agreement between Israel and Egypt played to Carter's considerable strengths. Using his personal charm, tenacity, and unshakeable belief in his own righteousness, Carter brokered a peace agreement between Egypt's Anwar Sadat and Israel's Menachem Begin. The Camp David Accords represent a significant milestone, but the turbulent Middle East eventually consumed Carter's presidency.

The Malaise Speech

Despite the president's austere budgets, "stagflation" continued to plague the American and world economy. In conjunction with stagflation was yet another "oil shock." The 1979 Iranian Revolution and subsequent "oil crisis" sent energy prices upward and resulted in severe gasoline shortages. On July 15, 1979, Carter responded to the crisis by delivering what is considered the most important speech of his presidency. More sermon than a traditional speech, Carter blamed the nation's problems on a "crisis of confidence" and urged Americans to look inward to alter the nation's economic and social ills. Though Carter never used the term "malaise," his dour tone led observers to give the speech its moniker. At first, the address received high marks from observers and the public but when Carter inexplicably fired four Cabinet secretaries days later, the "malaise speech" became a symbol of a listless and directionless administration.

The Final Year: 1980

It was the Soviet invasion of Afghanistan, on Christmas Day 1979, which finally forced the president to create a coherent foreign policy, dubbed the Carter Doctrine. Because the administration believed the Soviet incursion into Central Asia was an initial move toward the Persian Gulf, the Carter Doctrine claimed Soviet hegemony in the Persian Gulf represented a threat to U.S. national security. The Carter Doctrine led to increased defense spending and marked the official demise of détente and the return of the Cold War.

Though the president had forged a decisive foreign policy, events—specifically the Iranian hostage crisis—engulfed the administration for the duration of Carter's tenure. Because of America's prior close relationship with Iran's strongman Shah Mohammed Reza Pahlavi, when Islamic radicals overthrew the shah in 1979, they directed their venom at the United States. This turmoil turned for the worse when the formerly exiled cleric Ayatollah Khomeini, who had returned to Iran in early 1979, pushed young militants to seize the American embassy in Tehran and hold 52 hostages (on November 4, 1979).

Carter made the release of what became 53 American hostages his highest priority. Though his efforts to secure the hostages' release temporarily lifted his public approval numbers, as the crisis dragged on for weeks and months, the public gradually turned against him. The hostage crisis and spiraling energy prices sent inflation and unemployment rates surging. Carter's newly appointed Federal Reserve Chairman, Paul Volcker, opted to squash inflation by imposing high interest rates, which in early 1981 peaked at 21.5 percent. Though Volcker's policy effectively demolished inflation and ended stagflation by late 1983, Carter was left to face a reelection campaign saddled with a troubled economy, a foreign policy crisis, and a Democratic primary challenger in the person of Sen. Edward (Ted) Kennedy.

The 1980 Election

Kennedy underperformed in the Democratic primaries and never came close to actually winning the nomination. The senator's challenge, however, further weakened an already diminished incumbent.

Adding insult to injury, Kennedy took what became his quixotic fight for the nomination all the way to the 1980 Democratic Convention. There, as the keynote speaker, Kennedy gave what many consider the finest speech of his political career. Unfortunately for Carter, the speech was not a ringing endorsement of the president so much as a defense of Kennedy's liberal ideals.

Despite the avalanche of unrelenting bad news, in the weeks prior to the 1980 election the polls revealed a dead heat between Carter and his Republican rival Ronald Reagan. Further complicating an already jumbled and confusing political season was Rep. John Anderson's third-party candidacy. Due to his frank rebuke of Reagan's social conservatism and Carter's ineptitude, the otherwise obscure Illinois Republican drew support from moderate "Rockefeller Republicans" and disaffected liberals. In the weeks and months prior to election day, Carter's reelection hopes hung on lingering questions of Ronald Reagan's temperament and conservative philosophy. From railing against Social Security and literally blaming air pollution on trees, Reagan had earned a reputation as an eloquent speaker given to bombast.

One week before the election, Reagan and Carter squared-off in their only televised debate. Reagan's cool, calm demeanor largely negated voters' fears. What followed was an electoral rout. Though Reagan only won 50.8 percent of the popular vote, he captured nearly 500 votes in the Electoral College. His resounding victory not only represented the voters' repudiation of Carter but by winning votes across the deep South and Northern industrial states it also signaled the death knell for Franklin Roosevelt's New Deal coalition. Reagan's victory effectively signaled an electoral realignment and made conservative Republicans dominant for a generation.

Though Carter's presidency was largely defined by failure, he did realize a number of signature legislative and institutional achievements. After shepherding the controversial Panama Canal Treaty through the Senate in 1978, ceding eventual control over the canal to the Panamanian government, in 1979 he officially recognized the People's Republic of China, ending nearly three decades of diplomatic wrangling. In the weeks after his loss to Reagan, he signed what was one of the most significant pieces of environmental legislation in American history, the National Interest Lands Conservation Act. The legislation designated over 100 million acres in Alaska as protected federal reserves, of which 27.47 million acres were designated as wilderness. In addition to this legislation, Carter helped revolutionize the office of the vice presidency. Prior to the Carter administration, the vice president's office was largely ceremonial. Rather than stick with this model, Carter gave Walter Mondale considerable influence and wide latitude over policy decisions, a turnabout and example his successors have followed.

After losing the White House at the age of 56, Carter transformed the post-presidency. Prior to Carter, most ex-presidents remained aloof from national and international politics. After penning an unusually frank and absorbing presidential memoir, *Keeping Faith*, he used the Carter Center as an institutional base of operations. Combining its namesake's fundraising acumen, personal charm, and humanitarian goals, the Carter Center became a significant nongovernmental organization helping to mediate conflicts and oversee elections across the globe. Through his work at the Carter Center, the president became so associated with democracy and human rights that the Nobel Committee awarded him the 2002 Nobel Peace Prize.

Though it involved more calamities than success, the Carter presidency represents a transition between two political eras, and Carter himself transformed the vice presidency and post-presidency.

Bibliography and Further Reading

Bourne, Peter. *Jimmy Carter: A Comprehensive Biography from Plains to Post-Presidency.* New York: Scribners, 1997.

Brinkley, Douglas. *The Unfinished Presidency: Jimmy Carter's Journey beyond the White House.* New York: Viking, 1998.

Carter, Jimmy. *Turning Point: A Candidate, a State, and a Nation Come of Age.* New York: Times Books, 1992.

Fink, Gary, and Hugh Davis Graham, eds. *The Carter Presidency: Policy Choices in the Post–New Deal Era.* Lawrence: University Press of Kansas, 1998.

Kaufman, Burton, *The Presidency of James Earl Carter, Jr.* Lawrence: University of Kansas Press, 2006.

Scheer. Robert. "The Playboy Interview: Jimmy Carter." *Playboy*, November 1976: 63–86.

Stroud, Kandy. *How Jimmy Won: The Victory Campaign from Plains to the White House.* New York: William Morrow, 1977.

Jeffrey Bloodworth

CENTRAL INTELLIGENCE AGENCY

The year 1976 marked a turning point for the Central Intelligence Agency (CIA), not so much for the functions it carried out (intelligence collection, analysis, and covert operations) but rather in terms of the domestic political environment in which it operated. No longer would the CIA function under a veil of secrecy, nor would its actions be seen as nonpolitical or above politics. Indeed, from this point forward, the CIA would become an institution that was frequently in the public eye, viewed by many as a threat to American national security rather than an instrument for promoting it.

Advent of Congressional Oversight

Precipitating this transformation was a December 1974 article in the *New York Times* detailing extensive—and illegal—domestic activities such as wiretappings, break-ins, and mail openings by the CIA. Though many of these actions were related to the Vietnam War and those who opposed U.S. participation in it, others dated back to the 1950s. The list of transgressions published by the *Times* was actually the result of an in-house CIA study, nicknamed the "family jewels" report, which had been ordered by Director of Central Intelligence (DCI) James Schlesinger and completed by his successor, William Colby.

In response to the resulting furor, in 1975 Pres. Gerald Ford established a committee chaired by Vice

Pres. Nelson Rockefeller to investigate the CIA's behavior. Both houses of Congress likewise established special committees to investigate, though the Senate's committee was the more prominent of the two. In that chamber, the Church Committee—so named after its chairperson, Sen. Frank Church (D–ID)—opened its investigations in January 1975, concentrating its efforts on uncovering questionable CIA activities. Among its most stunning revelations was the existence of a program designed to remove Salvadore Allende from power in Chile, and unsuccessful assassination plots against Fidel Castro in Cuba and against other foreign leaders.

One of the assumptions of the Church Committee was that the CIA had been, in the words of its chair, "a rogue elephant" running around the world out of control. In fact, the opposite proved to be the case. The committee concluded that "presidents and administrations have made excessive . . . use of covert action." It documented that 81 projects were approved by the Director of Central Intelligence between 1949 and 1952, and that this number grew to 163 during the Kennedy administration and 142 in the Johnson administration.

Seeking to strengthen oversight of the CIA, the Church Committee recommended two steps. First, each house should establish permanent intelligence oversight committees, rather than rely upon the current system of oversight by subcommittees of the Appropriations and Armed Services committees. Second, a legislative charter should be written to clearly establish what behavior was permissible for the agency and what was not. Without such a charter, the intelligence community would continue to be governed solely by largely secret orders and directives coming from the executive branch. The first goal was quickly realized as each house set up permanent Select Committees on Intelligence. The second was not; efforts toward it bogged down during the Carter administration and were not resurrected. Still, the principle of legislative oversight was firmly established. The Senate created a permanent intelligence committee in 1976, and the House followed suit in 1977. At first, congressional oversight was conducted largely in a nonpartisan manner, but as what was once a somewhat broader public consensus over the purposes of American foreign policy frayed and more and more political backbiting took place in the halls of Congress, intelligence oversight also became increasingly partisan in its tone.

Presidents countered Congress's effort by moving to increase their control over the CIA through the power of appointment. In the aftermath of the Church Committee hearings, Directors of Central Intelligence—even those with backgrounds in intelligence such as William Casey (1981–1997), George Tenet (1997–2004), and Porter J. Goss (2004–2005)—tended to adopt roles that emphasized responsiveness to the president over loyalty to the CIA itself. The questioning of intelligence began with the A Team–B Team exercise organized during the Ford administration, during which conservative critics of détente and opponents of CIA estimates of Soviet military power from outside the government were organized into a competing analytic team to challenge the CIA's conclusions. Defenders of the exercise asserted that such competitive analysis improved the overall quality of intelligence. Detractors argued that it opened the door to the politicization of intelligence and the tendency for policy makers to "cherry-pick" intelligence to support their preferred policy objectives.

Renewal of Covert Operations

In this new political environment, CIA covert actions rarely remained covert. They did not end, however. Upon assuming the presidency in 1981, Ronald Reagan signaled a willingness to engage the Soviet Union in a new round of Cold War confrontations. His administration chose Central America as its battleground: El Salvador and Nicaragua became test cases for what would become known as the Reagan Doctrine. Unlike previous presidential foreign policy doctrines that emphasized the need to defend freedom and democracy from communist aggression, the Reagan Doctrine asserted that the United States had a responsibility to actively work to remove communist regimes from power. To this end, in November 1981 Reagan signed Presidential Directive 17 calling for the creation and secret funding of an anti-Sandinista guerilla force in Nicaragua that would become known as the Contras. This force was to target the Cuban presence in Nicaragua responsible for training and aiding the left wing FMLN (Farabundo Marti National Liberation Front) in neighboring El Salvador that was challenging the pro-American government there. In early 1982, buoyed by some early successes, the Reagan administration expanded the goals of the Contras to include bringing down the Sandinista government. Accordingly, the CIA stepped up its covert action program. Its contacts bombed an airport in Nicaragua in 1983 (just as two U.S. senators were landing there), mined harbors in 1984, and distributed psychological warfare pamphlets that could be read as advocating assassination.

From the outset, Congress was skeptical of the Reagan administration's Contra policy and sought to restrict how it could spend funds to achieve its goals. The instrument it chose was the Boland Amendment to the Defense Appropriations Act of 1983. Sponsored by Rep. Edward Boland (D–MA), the amendment prohibited the use of U.S. funds to overthrow the Sandinista Nicaraguan government. The appropriations act was signed into law by President Reagan on December 21, 1982. Boland Amendment restrictions were attached to subsequent House appropriations bills that also became law. The Senate also acted to curb the administration's Contra policy. It reacted angrily to having been kept in the dark about the mining of harbors. Widespread human rights violations attributed to the Contras also sparked congressional opposition. After information about the CIA's psychological warfare manuals became public, the Senate passed another Boland Amendment, which terminated all aid to the Contras effective October 1, 1984.

Following Reagan's reelection, his administration sought to expand the war in Nicaragua in spite of congressional opposition. A plan was devised under the direction of the National Security Council and Lt. Col. Oliver North to circumvent Congress. Funds from allies were solicited: Saudi Arabia ($32 million), the Sultan of Brunei ($10 million), and Taiwan ($2 million) all came forward with money. The administration also secretly sold weapons to moderates in Iran in the dual hope of bringing about the release of

Americans held hostage in Lebanon and using the money from the weapons sales to fund the Contras.

In November 1986, the existence of the plan to sell weapons to Iran became public. Reagan denied that the sale was part of a hostage exchange agreement and established a three-person commission chaired by former Sen. John Tower (R–TX) to examine the Iran-Contra issue and more generally the strengths and weaknesses of the National Security Council system. The commission's report was published in 1987 and concluded that Reagan did not have any knowledge of the program or plans to divert funds to the Contras.

The CIA also played a central role in Reagan's response to the 1979 Soviet invasion of Afghanistan. Rather than acquiesce to the occupation or send in U.S. military forces, Reagan instead adopted a strategy of using the CIA to support anti-Soviet guerillas known as the Mujahideen. American military aid to the Mujahideen rose from $120 million in 1984 to $630 million in 1987, bringing the accumulated total of U.S. military aid to $2.1 billion. Additional U.S. aid was funneled through allies such as Saudi Arabia, China, and Pakistan. Pakistan was a key player, acting as conduit for U.S. arms, a recruiting ground for the Mujahideen, and the destination of some 3.5 million Afghan refugees.

CIA covert action programs did not end with the Reagan administration or the Cold War. One of the most notable post–Cold War covert operations took place in Iraq. Between 1992 and 1996, the CIA sought to remove Saddam Hussein from power by encouraging a military coup and reducing the Iraqi leader's control over the country's outlying regions. The estimated cost of this program was $100 million, though ultimately little was accomplished. Opposition leaders fell prey to political squabbling, and Hussein moved aggressively against them, executing more than one hundred dissidents and disloyal military officers. A similar scenario took place in Serbia in 1998–1999 when the presidential administration of Bill Clinton sought to unseat the Serb leader Slobodan Milosevic. The local opposition was divided, had no real plan, and had been infiltrated by Milosevic's agents.

Another failed covert action involved efforts by the CIA to capture the Saudi terrorist Osama bin

Laden. By 1996, evidence of bin Laden's involvement in terrorist attacks against the United States had led to the creation of a special bin Laden unit. The earliest efforts to capture him can be dated to 1997 and involved the recruitment of a family-based team of Afghan tribal members. A second pre–9/11 effort to capture bin Laden, called JAWBREAKER-5 and set in motion in 1999, involved the recruitment of Ahmed Shah Massoud, the guerilla commander of the Northern Alliance, a coalition of anti-Taliban guerilla organizations that operated in Northern Afghanistan, and who had long worked with the CIA against the Soviet Union. As with the first plan, nothing came of this effort. The CIA would turn again to the Northern Alliance after the terrorist attacks of September 11, 2001, for help in trying to find bin Laden and to bring down Afghanistan's Taliban government.

The Post–Cold War Era Begins

Although the end of the Cold War in 1991 did not bring with it an end to CIA covert action programs, it did present the CIA with two major challenges. First, the Agency's failure to predict the fall of the Soviet Union led some policy makers, most notably Sen. Daniel Patrick Moynihan (D–NY), to call for the CIA's dissolution. Responding to these concerns on November 15, 1991, Pres. George H. W. Bush issued National Security Review 29 calling for a top-to-bottom examination of the mission, roles, and priorities of the intelligence community This review led to a subsequent National Security Directive that divided post–Cold War security threats into four levels of priority.

Second, and even more damaging to the CIA's political standing in Washington, was the revelation that the agency had repeatedly been penetrated by Soviet agents during the Cold War. The most significant case involved Aldrich Ames, a CIA officer who was arrested on February 21, 1994, on the eve of a trip to Moscow. Ames had begun spying for the Soviet Union in 1985. Published reports suggest that Ames may have compromised the identities of as many as fifty U.S. intelligence operatives, services for which it is estimated he reportedly received in excess of $2 million. His case brought on a wave of investigations into

the operation of the CIA, including one by the Senate Select Committee on Intelligence. Among the conclusions reached by this report and others was that the security problems at the CIA were deep-seated and pervasive. Congress called for stronger action by the Director of Central Intelligence to deal with suspicious cases of counterintelligence.

September 11 and Beyond

The September 11, 2001, terrorist attacks on the Pentagon and the World Trade Center were widely characterized as a second Pearl Harbor, and the CIA's failure to anticipate them was seen as an intelligence failure of the greatest magnitude. Blame was placed on its intelligence-collection capabilities, especially its lack of reliable human intelligence, as well as its tendency to "stovepipe" information—that is, the institutional habit of shuttling information "up and down" the intelligence community rather than across it to other agencies, which might in turn make better use of it. Also called into question was the agency's analysis, which critics characterized as marked by groupthink and a lack of imagination, and its failure to cooperate fully with the FBI and other members of the intelligence community.

In the aftermath of the attacks, Congress quickly pressed for the creation of an independent panel to review the performance of intelligence agencies. Though Pres. George W. Bush initially opposed the creation of this body for fear that its recommendations would impinge on presidential power, he later bowed to political pressure and established the 9/11 Commission chaired by former Republican New Jersey governor Thomas Kean and former Democratic Indiana representative Lee Hamilton, who had chaired the House committees on foreign affairs and intelligence. Included in the commission's recommendations (published in July 2004) were the creation of a new national terrorism center and the establishment of a cabinet-level post of Director of National Intelligence to oversee the CIA, FBI, and other intelligence agencies. Support was strong in Congress for such reforms but they were opposed within the Executive Branch. The CIA called them unnecessary and the Defense Department feared that it would lose budgetary control over military intelligence matters and over the operation of defense intelligence agencies. (An estimated 80 to 90 percent of the intelligence budget is allocated to Pentagon intelligence units.)

Not long after the 9/11 Commission issued its findings, in 2004 CIA analytical efforts came in for a second round of criticism following the revelation that no weapons of mass destruction (WMD) were found in Iraq. Saddam Hussein's possession of WMDs had been presented by the Bush administration as a primary justification for launching of the Iraq War. The Robb-Silberman Study (formally the Commission on the Intelligence Capabilities of the United States Regarding Weapons of Mass Destruction) laid blame on the analytic undertakings of the CIA and echoed calls for the reorganization of the intelligence community and the creation of the position of Director of National Intelligence.

Under pressure to act and in the middle of a close election campaign, a reluctant George W. Bush endorsed the concept of a White House–based national intelligence director in August. The position was officially created in December 2004 with the signing of the Intelligence Reform and Terrorism Prevention Act. Under that law, the Director of National Intelligence (DNI) was identified as the president's chief advisor on intelligence matters and primary briefer on intelligence matters, but the DNI did not obtain the budgetary power over other members of the intelligence community, most notably those located in the Defense Department, that reformers argued was necessary if the intelligence community was to become anything other than a loose confederation of intelligence agencies.

Though post–September 11 CIA operations in Afghanistan enjoyed widespread public support, the same could not be said of other aspects of the CIA's involvement in the global war against terrorism. Of particular concern were CIA renditions, the forcible abduction and transport of suspected terrorist to non-U.S. prisons for what the administration regarded as interrogation but that under international law is defined as torture. Interrogation techniques included waterboarding, in which the suspect is made to feel that he or she is drowning through the actions of an intelligence agent. In 2006, CIA Director Michael Hayden banned the use of waterboarding in CIA interrogations, but the controversy continued largely because, though in July 2007 George W. Bush signed an executive order banning torture during interrogations, the administration left open the possibility that waterboarding could be used under certain circumstances.

Since 1976, the CIA has found itself operating in an environment quite different from that which characterized its first decades of existence. At home, setting and overseeing intelligence policy is no longer seen as solely the prerogative of the president. Congress now claims a role and public scrutiny through the media has increased. Abroad, the CIA no longer has one major hostile enemy of long standing to spy upon and conduct covert operations. Rather, the Agency faces an uncertain world where threats can come from many different and often unexpected directions. These domestic and global changes have transformed the CIA from a highly secret organization into a lightning rod for public debate about the proper content and direction of U.S. foreign policy.

Bibliography and Further Reading

Betts, Richard. *Enemies of Intelligence: Knowledge and Power in American National Security.* New York: Columbia University Press, 2008.

Coll, Steven. *Ghost Wars.* New York: Penguin, 2004.

Immerman, Richard. *The CIA in Guatemala.* Austin: University of Texas Press, 1982.

Johnson, Loch K. *A Season of Inquiry.* Lexington: University Press of Kentucky, 1985.

Lowenthal, Mark. *Intelligence from Secrets to Policy.* Washington, D.C.: Congressional Quarterly Press, 2006.

Richelson, Jeffrey. *The U.S. Intelligence Community.* Philadelphia: Westview, 2008.

Tenet, George. *At the Center of the Storm: My Years at the CIA.* New York: HarperCollins, 2007.

United States Congress, Senate. Select Committee on Intelligence. "An Assessment of the Aldrich H. Ames Espionage Case and Its Implications for U.S Intelligence." Washington, D.C.: Government Printing Office, 1994.

United States Congress. Senate. Select Committee to Study Governmental Operations with Respect to Intelligence Activities. "Church Report: Covert Action in Chile 1963–1973." Washington, D.C.: Government Printing Office, 1975. Available at http://foia.state.gov/Reports/ChurchReport.asp

Wise, David. *Nightmover: How Aldrich Ames Sold the CIA to the KGB for $4.6 Million*. New York: HarperCollins, 1995.

Glenn Hastedt

CHENEY, DICK

born 1941
Forty-sixth Vice President of the United States

Traditionally, the vice presidency is seen as an unimportant and obscure job tantamount to "a pitcher of warm spit." (Quoted in Dorman 6-7) However, this standard view, espoused by John Nance Garner, Franklin Roosevelt's first vice president, did not account for Dick Cheney's two terms in the office. A Republican from Wyoming, Cheney was vice president from 2001 to 2009 in the presidential administration of George W. Bush. He is considered not only the most powerful vice president in American history but also among the most controversial.

A Quick Rise in Washington

A consummate Washington insider, Cheney served in a number of public capacities prior to becoming vice president. Among other things, he was Pres. Gerald Ford's chief of staff, a U.S. representative, and secretary of defense under Pres. George H. W. Bush (1989–1993).

Cheney's political career began in 1969 when he took a leave of absence from doctoral studies at the University of Wisconsin to accept a congressional fellowship. While working in Rep. Bill Steiger's (R–WI) office,

Cheney became immersed in antipoverty policy. His expertise caught the eye of President Ford's new director of the Office of Economic Opportunity, Donald Rumsfeld. When Cheney's one-year fellowship ended, he chose to accept a full-time position with Rumsfeld instead of returning to his studies in Wisconsin.

Over the next 30 years, the two men would cross paths multiple times while ascending to the upper echelons of American government. After holding a number of jobs in the Ford administration, Cheney was promoted to his first highly visible post as White House chief of staff in 1975 after Rumsfeld resigned that position to become secretary of defense. In addition to his White House duties, Cheney also ran Ford's unsuccessful reelection campaign in 1976 against Democrat Jimmy Carter. Two years later, Cheney was elected to the U.S. House of Representatives from Wyoming. In six terms on Capitol Hill, he served as chair of the Republican Policy Committee, chair of the House Republican Conference, and House minority whip. Cheney left Congress to become secretary of defense under the first President Bush in 1989. During his four years at the Pentagon, Cheney oversaw the U.S. invasion of Panama to depose the military dictator Manuel Noriega as well as the Persian Gulf War.

When Bush was defeated by Bill Clinton in 1992, Cheney left public service to work in the private sector. His most notable position outside government was his five-year stint as CEO of the energy company Halliburton. But in the summer of 2000, Cheney had an opportunity to return to Washington when presidential nominee (and son of the former president) George W. Bush asked him to join the Republican ticket. Cheney's history at Halliburton—and his continued deferred compensation and stock awards—became controversial when he became involved in energy policy and related issues as vice president.

Vice President

When Pres. William McKinley offered then-New York governor Theodore Roosevelt the number two slot on his 1900 Republican ticket, Roosevelt worried that the office would be "an irksome, wearisome place where I could do nothing." (Roosevelt 1159) The former Rough Rider had good reason to worry: short of assuming the presidency for a dead or resigned boss (as Roosevelt ultimately did), the vice president had held a uniquely inconsequential post in presidential administrations throughout American political history. Cheney's tenure, however, has forced scholars to reassess the office. Though other recent vice presidents—starting with Jimmy Carter's second-in-command, Walter Mondale—had expanded the traditional role of the vice presidency, none amassed as much influence, praise, and scorn as Cheney.

Cheney returned to public life in the summer of 2000 when he accepted the offer to be George W. Bush's running mate. (His appointment came after Cheney led the search committee tasked with vetting Bush's potential vice presidents.) In the weeks of litigation following the contested election, Cheney helped organize a government-in-waiting. His influence was immediately evident when his preferred secretary of defense, Rumsfeld, ultimately won Bush's nomination to the Pentagon post.

Beginning with these early staffing victories, Cheney's presence was widely felt throughout his eight years in office, earning him undisputed claim to the title of the most powerful vice president ever. Cheney established a separate center of authority within the administration, complete with its own resources and an extensive staff. His close personal relationship with the president also allowed him to play a critical role in the development of a wide range of policy issues. In the domestic realm, the vice president led the National Energy Policy Development Group, oversaw new national policies to protect the country from weapons of mass destruction, and helped develop and ensure passage of Bush's tax cuts. In these roles, Cheney was widely seen as staking out a strongly conservative position and effectively shaping policies to that end. In the debate over taxes, for instance, Cheney forcefully and successfully argued for a broad set of tax cuts that would benefit all Americans, including the wealthy, and opposed efforts by Cabinet officials and Federal Reserve Chairman Alan Greenspan to implement more modest reductions.

Cheney was also a forceful advocate for expanding the powers of the presidency. According to

Cheney, reverberations from the Vietnam War and the Watergate scandal led to severe restrictions on presidential power. This process culminated in the 1973 War Powers Act, a controversial law—which Cheney asserted was unconstitutional—that sought to limit the president's ability to use military force. The vice president attempted to continue the gradual trend since that time of reestablishing expansive presidential power, particularly with regard to the president's role as commander in chief. Cheney also cited presidential prerogative in refusing to give Congress certain documents or permit some White House officials to testify in front of congressional committees.

Yet his most profound influence was evident in foreign policy. Indeed, Cheney was credited with—or just as often, condemned for—engineering everything from the hunt for the terrorist mastermind Osama bin Laden to the Iraq War to the procedures for detaining and allegedly torturing terror suspects. Much of the acclaim or disdain, depending on one's perspective, is warranted. Cheney's unique position within the administration allowed him unprecedented power to shape American foreign policy.

The vice president was at the center of the planning for the War on Terror and the Iraq War. Within the administration, he, along with Rumsfeld, was a strong advocate for aggressive military policies in Afghanistan and Iraq. Cheney's hawkish posture occasionally brought him into conflict with other top administration officials, including Sec. of State Colin Powell and National Security Advisor and later Sec. of State Condoleezza Rice. In addition, he played a key role in making the public argument for the Administration's policies. Cheney's repeated assertions of a connection between Osama bin Laden's al Qaeda network and Saddam Hussein's regime in Iraq prior to the invasion of that country was particularly vexing to his critics. The vice president is also remembered by his detractors for persistently alleging that Iraq possessed weapons of mass destruction, a charge that turned out to be unfounded.

A related controversy surrounded the treatment of suspected terrorists captured in various countries throughout the world. Following the September 11, 2001, attacks, the Bush administration revised certain policies dealing with these individuals. Critics alleged the new policies for treating and interrogating prisoners were tantamount to torture, or allowed torture under the cover of law. A technique known as waterboarding was specifically cited and turned into a public controversy. During a radio interview, Cheney endorsed the technique, calling it a "no brainer." Addressing the issue again shortly before he left office, Cheney acknowledged its use and reiterated his support of it.

Cheney's power and influence were diminished, at least temporarily, by a serious scandal. What is known as the Plame Affair began when Valerie Plame's status as a CIA operative was revealed to the public by the newspaper columnist Robert Novak. Though the leak came from a top State Department official, one of Cheney's closest assistants, I. Lewis "Scooter" Libby, was convicted of perjury and obstruction of justice as part of an effort to cover up the incident during a federal probe. Cheney was never implicated in the cover-up attempt, but his close relationship with Libby was damaging to the vice president's public persona. President Bush later commuted Libby's 30-month prison sentence but chose not to issue a pardon despite repeated requests from Cheney, who maintained that his former associate was the "victim of a serious miscarriage of justice." (Quoted in Hayes, 2009)

Vice Presidential Power and the Source of Cheney's Influence

Cheney's power was informal in nature. His official position contained no prescribed authority that allowed him to exert such influence. Decades ago, the scholar Richard Neustadt's key insight into the modern presidency was that the office's real power lies in a president's ability to persuade, rather than in the power to give orders stemming from the Constitution's assignment of formal powers. The best and most effective presidents persuaded key political actors to do what the presidents wanted instead of forcing them to act through the executive branch's formal power structure. Cheney's influence stemmed from the same kind of informal power source. For the vice presidency, this kind of informal power is critical because the office itself has few formal powers. In Cheney's case, his influence was tied to the trust President Bush placed in him.

RELATED ENTRIES

THIS VOLUME
Bush, George W.; Iraq War; War on Terror

This unique level of trust, in turn, was rooted largely in a long-standing relationship dating back to the George H. W. Bush presidency and Cheney's lack of personal political ambition. The vice president repeatedly and consistently said that he had no intention of running for president in 2008 and that his only concern was serving President Bush. Cheney also said that he was not worried about his own popularity among the American people. His lack of concern in this area was fortunate, because he maintained a historically low public approval rating throughout his final years in office.

There are indications that the relationship soured and that Cheney's influence diminished at some point during Bush's second term. One aide familiar with the situation told a reporter that the relationship "isn't what it was" and that "it's been a long, long time since I've heard the President say, 'Run that by the Vice President's office.' You used to hear that all the time." (Quoted in Rutenberg and Becker) Bush's refusal to pardon Libby during his final days in office reportedly left Cheney furious and was a further indication of tension after what had been a remarkably close bond.

Nonetheless, for a president known to prize loyalty, Cheney's lack of presidential ambition was highly attractive. Vice presidents who have eyes on occupying the Oval Office themselves often have split loyalties—both to the president and to their own long-term political interests. Cheney had no such distractions, which allowed him to gain Bush's confidence and play a central role in his administration.

Bibliography and Further Reading

Dorman, Michael. *The Second Man: The Changing Role of the Vice Presidency.* New York: Delacorte Press, 1964.

Dubose, Lou, and Jake Bernstein. *Vice: Dick Cheney and the Hijacking of the American Presidency.* New York: Random House, 2006.

Edwards, George C., and Lawrence R. Jacobs. "The New Vice Presidency: Institutions and Politics." *Presidential Studies Quarterly* 38, no. 3 (2008): 369–373.

Gellman, Barton. *Angler: The Cheney Vice Presidency*. New York: Penguin Press, 2008.

Goldstein, Joel K. "The Rising Power of the Modern Vice Presidency." *Presidential Studies Quarterly* 38, no. 3 (2008): 374–389.

Hayes, Stephen F. "Cheney Speaks Out on Libby." *The Weekly Standard*, 22 Jan. 2009. http://www.weeklystandard.com/Content/Public/Articles/000/000/016/044cbxcp.asp.

———. *Cheney: The Untold Story of America's Most Powerful and Controversial Vice President*. New York: HarperCollins, 2007.

Montgomery, Bruce P. "Congressional Oversight: Vice President Richard B. Cheney's Executive Branch Triumph." *Political Science Quarterly* 120, no. 4 (2005): 581–617.

Nichols, John. *The Rise and Rise of Richard B. Cheney*. New York: New Press, 2005.

Roosevelt, Theodore. "To Benjamin Barker Odell." *The Letters of Theodore Roosevelt*, Volume II: *The Years of Preparation, 1898-1900*, Elting E. Morison, ed. Cambridge, MA: Harvard University Press, 1951, 1159.

Rutenberg, Jim, and Jo Becker. "Aides Say No Pardon for Libby Irked Cheney." *New York Times* 17 Feb. 2009, A14.

Robert P. Saldin

CIVIL LIBERTIES

Since the mid-1970s, the state of civil liberties in the United States might be thought of as a dialogue between the Republican appointees who have dominated the High Court since the election of Richard Nixon (a dominance reinforced by subsequent Republican presidents) and the civil liberties precedents set during the Court's Warren era. Many have predicted that the Burger, Rehnquist, and Roberts Courts would usher in a counter-revolution in civil liberties law. In a much-discussed "counter-revolution that wasn't," however, the Court has mostly ratified and modified—and not repudiated—the Warren-era civil liberties precedents. In a few areas, it has even, unexpectedly, extended them.

Freedom of Expression

The Burger and Rehnquist Courts accepted the general contours of the Warren Court's free expression precedent, though they modified it incrementally to allow government greater powers to regulate sexually explicit speech in the interest of protecting children and preserving public decency. For example, in *Miller v. California*, 413 U.S. 15 (1973), the young Burger Court continued to hold "softcore" pornography to be constitutionally protected, but gave local communities greater powers to regulate "hardcore" obscenity. Some years later, in *FCC v. Pacifica Foundation*, 438 U.S. 726 (1978), the Court held that the Federal Communications Commission could not issue a blanket ban on sexually explicit speech on radio or television but that the commission had broad authority to regulate it during hours when there is a reasonable risk that children will be listening or watching. In *Reno v. ACLU*, 521 U.S. 844 (1997), the Rehnquist Court ruled that the Internet should be afforded broad free speech protections, but its determination in *United States v. American Library Association*, 539 U.S. 194 (2003) stated that, as a condition of their receiving public funds, the federal government could require public libraries to install filtering software to protect children from sexually explicit materials. It also gave municipalities broader leeway to regulate sexually explicit performances through zoning (*City of Renton v. Playtime Theatres*, 475 U.S. 41 [1986]) and restrictions against public nudity (*Barnes v. Glen Theatre*, 501 U.S. 560 [1991]; *Erie v. Pap's A.M.*, 529 U.S. 277 [2000]).

The Right to Privacy

Reflecting its roots in the more moderate pre-Reagan Republican Party, as well as the arguments advanced by the feminist movement in its 1970s heyday, the Burger Court aggressively extended the scope of the "right to privacy" first enunciated by the Warren Court in *Griswold v. Connecticut*, 381 U.S. 479 (1965), a case overturning a state ban on the use of contraception by married couples. The Burger Court held the right, first, to be equally applicable to unmarried couples (*Eisenstadt v. Baird*, 405 U.S. 438 [1972]), and, second, to cover a woman's right to choose abortion (*Roe v. Wade*, 410 U.S. 113 [1973]). One of the most politically significant decisions in the Court's history, *Roe* ignited a powerful right-to-life movement that soon wrested control of the Republican Party away from the moderates and moved it increasingly to the right. Although the Rehnquist Court, in a series of sharply divided opinions, approved increasingly stringent abortion regulations (requiring, for example, waiting periods and parental notification by minors), several subsequent Republican appointees to the Court nevertheless insisted on the continuing viability of the abortion right (*Planned Parenthood of Southeastern Pennsylvania v. Casey*, 505 U.S. 833 [1992]), thus infuriating many conservatives in the new Republican Party. Since then, the party has moved even more aggressively to vet future judicial nominees for pro-life positions (or philosophies of constitutional interpretation that signal a commitment to them, like "originalism," ostensibly entailing a commitment to reading the Constitution in light of its original eighteenth-century meaning). Although Republican appointments to the early Roberts Court, justices John Roberts and Samuel Alito, declared their fidelity to a constitutional privacy right, they demurred on whether they would apply that right to abortion.

In *Bowers v. Hardwick*, 478 U.S. 186 (1986), the Burger Court rejected a claim that same-sex sexual intimacy was a constitutionally protected privacy right. Later, however, with the help of the same moderate Republican justices who voted to sustain *Roe* (justices Sandra Day O'Connor, Anthony Kennedy, and David Souter) and both of Democrat Bill Clinton's appointees (justices Ruth Bader Ginsburg and Stephen Breyer), the Rehnquist Court overruled that earlier decision in *Lawrence v. Texas*, 539 U.S. 558 (2003)—this time, not on the grounds of privacy but rather as a matter of due process "liberty." Concurrently, as medical technology advances, the Court has more frequently been asked to weigh in on whether there is a due process liberty right to end a life, either through refusing life-sustaining treatment or through physician-assisted suicide. As with abortion and gay rights, a position against such a right is one of the litmus test issues for Republican social conservatives. To date, the Court has refused to accord constitutional recognition to such a right.

Non-Establishment of Religion and Religious Liberty

Yet another area in which the Burger Court sparked the ire of social conservatives was in its Establishment Clause decisions involving Amendment I's requirement that "Congress shall make no law respecting an establishment of religion." Building on strands of earlier liberal precedent dating back to the 1940s, the Burger Court's *Lemon v. Kurtzman*, 403 U.S. 602 (1971) set the landmark test for Establishment Clause violations. The "Lemon Test" requires that, to avoid running afoul of Amendment I, government action 1) must have a secular purpose; 2) must neither advance nor inhibit religion; and 3) must not foster excessive entanglement between government and religion. Burger Court decisions were solicitous of claims by religious groups that they should not be discriminated against in public settings. For example, *Widmar v. Vincent*, 454 U.S. 263 (1981) held that student religious groups at a public university must be given the same access to meeting spaces as the campus's secular groups. At the same time, many Burger Court Establishment Clause decisions policed church-state boundaries fairly aggressively, adopting a "strict separationist" framework for constitutional analysis. The Court's strict separationism thus became a rallying cry for religious conservatives who called on Republican presidents and senators to appoint judges who would reject the prevailing strict separationist doctrine.

The Rehnquist Court, however, was conflicted in its Establishment Clause decisions. A number of them hewed to strict separationism. *Lee v. Wiseman*, 505 U.S. 577 (1992), for example, struck down as unconstitutional a public school graduation prayer delivered by a clergyman. *Santa Fe Independent School District v. Doe*, 530 U.S. 290 (2000) voided a school-sponsored prayer at a public high school football game. Nevertheless, during the Rehnquist years there was a discernible shift away from strict separationism in favor of an "accommodationism" that was more solicitous of the claims of religion. *Agostini v. Felton*, 521 U.S. 203 (1997), for example, overruled a late Burger Court decision forbidding public school teachers from teaching remedial classes in secular subjects in religious schools. *Rosenberger v. Rector and Visitors of the*

University of Virginia, 515 U.S. 819 (1995) held that a public university's refusal to provide funding for a student-run evangelical Christian magazine when it readily funded a wide range of student publications from diverse perspectives unconstitutionally infringed on the free speech rights of religious students. *Zelman v. Simmons-Harris*, 536 U.S. 639 (2002) approved the constitutionality of a Cleveland school voucher program that allowed vouchers to be used at (secular) public and religious schools alike—a major pillar of the Republican Party's education reform plank.

Some efforts were made on the Rehnquist (and late-Burger) Court to fashion alternatives to the Lemon Test. Justice O'Connor advanced an "endorsement test" to gauge whether the government impermissibly endorses religion, and thus conveys to outsiders a sense that they are "not full members of the political community." (*Lynch v. Donnelly*, 465 U.S. 668 [1984]) Justices Kennedy and Scalia each intimated that it would be better to ask instead whether an individual was coerced into agreement with or participation in religious exercises. Those justices, however, disagreed vehemently over what would count as "coercion." Justice Kennedy evinced considerable sympathy for claims of "psychological" coercion, while Justice Scalia insisted that any such coercion amount to "hard" legal or physical compulsion. At the twenty-first century's outset, this area of the law remained seriously confused, with an array of Establishment Clause tests jockeying for preeminence. As a pair of cases—*McCreary County v. ACLU*, 545 U.S. 844 (2005); *Van Orden v. Perry*, 545 U.S. 677 (2005)—concerning the display of the Ten Commandments on public property attested, Establishment Clause controversies had become an important part of the partisan, and symbolic, politics of the early twenty-first century.

In free exercise cases, the Rehnquist Court insisted that ordinances not specifically target religious practices. So, for example, in *Church of Lukami Babalu Aye v. Hialeah*, 508 U.S. 520 (1993), the Court struck down a municipal ban on animal sacrifices undertaken as part of religious rituals but, by the law's terms, not otherwise. In *Employment Division v. Smith*, 494 U.S. 872 (1990), however, the Court upheld the power of governments to apply "neutral law[s] of general applicability" across the board (here, a law criminalizing the use of the hallucinogenic drug peyote), even if those laws imposed incidental burdens on the religious practices of some (in this case, members of the Native American Church). The *Smith* decision became a rallying cry for many religious conservatives, and Congress attempted to overturn it with the Religious Freedom Restoration Act (RFRA) of 1993. A powerful Supreme Court jealous of its prerogatives to determine constitutional meaning, however, voided RFRA (in *Boerne v. Flores*, 521 U.S. 507 [1997]) as having exceeded Congress's constitutional powers.

Criminal Procedure

Crime, drug use, and social disorder became major political issues in the 1970s. Inspired by gross instances of police brutality—often directed toward racial minorities—between the 1930s and the 1970s, the Court, at the urging of civil rights and civil liberties groups like the NAACP and the ACLU, instituted reforms in constitutional criminal process doctrine. In the context of the social breakdown and disorder of the 1970s, however, these reforms were targeted by conservatives, who accused the Court of tying the hands of law enforcement, and with a pervasive hostility to the police. The deeply divided early Burger Court's decision in *Furman v. Georgia*, 408 U.S. 238 (1972) holding that the death penalty (as then administered) was so arbitrary as to amount to cruel and unusual punishment whipped up a firestorm of outrage. In an immediate popular backlash against the decision, more than two-thirds of the states passed reformed death penalty statutes, which the Supreme Court subsequently upheld in *Gregg v. Georgia*, 428 U.S. 153 (1976). The pro-death penalty trend on the Court has held ever since, with Congress and Chief Justice Rehnquist laboring to limit the annual flood of habeas corpus appeals to the Court. From time to time, however, a closely divided Court—influenced by declining crime rates, transnational human rights group lobbying, and a spate of high-profile exonerations of convicted murderers through the admission of new DNA evidence—has placed some limits on capital punishment. In *Roper v. Simmons*, 543 U.S. 551 (2005), for example, the

Court voted 5–4 to bar the execution of the intellectually disabled.

Buttressed by its law-and-order appointees, the Burger and Rehnquist Courts forged an array of exceptions to the exclusionary rule, allowing greater use in court of illegally seized evidence. The Court has also adjusted Amendment IV search-and-seizure doctrine to provide more authority to the police. In this area, as in others, though, it has demurred from the opportunity to repudiate the core of the Warren era's criminal procedure precedent.

National Security and Civil Liberties

A host of distinctive civil liberties issues involving government surveillance and personal privacy; freedom of the press and association; and the appropriate procedural requirements for trials, detentions, and deportations are raised at times when the nation's security is threatened. One of the traditional marks of constitutional conservatism is its willingness to defer to the executive when he justifies his actions on national (and domestic) security grounds. The Burger Court, buttressed by a series of Nixon administration appointments, was traditionally conservative in this sense, refusing, for example, in *Branzburg v. Hayes*, 408 U.S. 665 (1972) to recognize a right of reporters to uphold the confidentiality of their sources when testifying in Court. The widespread abuses of the Nixon administration (for which the president was forced to resign), however, led the Congress to impose an array of statutory restrictions on the government's domestic surveillance powers (and led most of the states to pass laws providing a confidentiality privilege for reporters). After the most deadly foreign attack on U.S. soil in history on September 11, 2001, though, Congress relaxed many of these restrictions, and for the first time since the 1970s the president began once again to assert his claim to enhanced national security powers in a time of war.

As the immediacy of the threat subsided, however, and as warrantless wiretapping and abuses of prisoners of the "war on terror" held in Abu Ghraib, Iraq, and Guantanamo Bay, Cuba, came to light, the Court became increasingly aggressive about enforcing civil liberties. Acting pursuant to writs of habeas cor-

pus filed by Guantanamo prisoners, for example, the Court in *Hamdi v. Rumsfeld*, 542 U.S. 547 (2004); *Hamdan v. Rumsfeld*, 548 U.S. 557 (2006); and *Boumediene v. Bush*, 553 U.S. ___ (2008) aggressively asserted its authority to supervise the treatment and trial of detainees.

The Civil Libertarian Legacy and America's Future

The story of the trajectory of civil liberties doctrine on the Supreme Court since the 1970s has been one of how ostensibly conservative justices appointed in the wake of the Warren era grappled with the legacy of the mid–twentieth century civil libertarianism. The doctrinal legacy of the new constitutional conservatism for civil liberties has been complicated. In a reflection of the depth of the cultural and institutional changes wrought by the twentieth-century rights revolution, the conservative appointees to the Court have left most of the architecture of the liberal civil liberties jurisprudence intact. They have, however, refused to extend that doctrine in some areas, and trimmed it back in others, correcting (as they see it) for some of its more antisocial excesses.

Implicitly accepting the civil libertarian premise that basic rights are best protected by powerful, assertive courts, some contemporary conservatives have positioned themselves, not as fighting for a doctrinal counter-revolution but rather as civil liberties proponents. These litigious, rights-wielding conservatives understand themselves as fighting for the kinds of civil liberties that ideological blinders led liberals to either ignore or oppose—such as religious liberty, property rights (pursuant to the Amendment V takings clause—see, for example, *Kelo v. New London*, 545 U.S. 469 [2005]), Amendment II rights to keep and bear arms (see *District of Columbia v. Heller*, 554 U.S.—(2008), free speech (in contexts de-emphasized by liberals, such as sexual harassment law and campaign speech), and full jury trial rights. Other contemporary conservatives were proudly reactionary in their constitutional visions, insisting that the nation return to pre–New Deal—indeed, pre–Civil War—understandings of federalism, the separation of powers, and civil liberties. This latter group of conservatives, however,

Tushnet, Mark V. *A Court Divided: The Rehnquist Court and the Future of Constitutional Law*. New York: W. W. Norton, 2005.

Woodward, Bob, and Scott Armstrong. *The Brethren: Inside the Supreme Court*. New York: Simon & Schuster, 2005.

Kenneth I. Kersch

proved more prominent in the intellectual sense than in the practical.

Conservative efforts notwithstanding, the trajectory of civil liberties law from the 1970s has suggested that you can't go home again. The civil libertarian triumphs of mid–twentieth century liberalism are bound inextricably in the national memory to the social movements and cultural shifts that spawned them: the civil rights and anti-war movements, the sexual revolution, a cresting religious pluralism, and a modernist suspicion of authority. Moreover, these triumphs have become central to the nation's understanding of itself and its constitutionally guaranteed liberties. Waxing in influence from Nixon through George W. Bush, conservatives succeeded in trimming certain doctrinal excesses. They were, however, unable to turn mid–twentieth century civil liberties law in a radically different direction.

Bibliography and Further Reading

Blasi, Vincent, ed. *The Burger Court: The Counterrevolution That Wasn't*. New Haven, CT: Yale University Press, 1983.

Kahn, Ronald. *The Supreme Court and Constitutional Theory, 1953–1993*. Lawrence: University Press of Kansas, 1994.

Keck, Thomas M. *The Most Activist Supreme Court in History: The Road to Modern Judicial Conservatism*. Chicago: University of Chicago Press, 2004.

Klarman, Michael J. "Rethinking the Civil Rights and Civil Liberties Revolutions." *Virginia Law Review* 82, no. 1 (1996): 1–67.

Maltz, Earl. *The Chief Justiceship of Warren Burger, 1969–1986*. Columbia: University of South Carolina Press, 2000.

Powe, Lucas A., Jr., *The Warren Court and American Politics*. Cambridg, MA: The Belknap Press of Harvard University Press, 2000.

CIVIL RIGHTS

The term *civil rights* refers to legal protections against discrimination at the hands of the government or private parties. Such laws generally aim to prevent individuals from facing discrimination in voting, employment, housing, and in the use of public accommodations such as buses or restaurants. There are two civil rights eras in American history. The first dates from after the Civil War in 1865 until the end of Reconstruction in 1877. The second began during the 1950s as a result of civil rights demonstrations led by individuals such as Martin Luther King Jr. Civil rights laws in the United States have historically protected blacks from discrimination. Subsequently, since the 1970s, women, other people of color, and gays, lesbians, bisexuals, and transsexuals have increasingly benefited from expanded civil rights protections.

The First Civil Rights Era

The first civil rights era in American history began when blacks were freed from slavery though the adoption of Amendment XIII after the Civil War. The Reconstruction Congress passed the 1866 Civil Rights Act to protect the rights of freed slaves. This act prohibited discrimination against blacks by the government or by private parties in many areas, such as in employment. Because of concerns that Congress lacked the authority to prohibit private discrimination as described in the 1866 Civil Rights Act, the federal legislature soon moved to pass Amendments XIV (1868) and XV (1870). Sections 5 and 2, respectively, of these Amendments declared that Congress had the power to enforce these articles by appropriate legislation).

These enforcement provisions appeared to grant Congress the authority it needed to adopt civil rights legislation. In addition to these Amendments and the

1866 Act, Congress also adopted other legislation to protect civil rights during Reconstruction. For example, the Civil Rights Act of 1871, otherwise known as the Klan Act, was meant to give the freed slaves legal remedies to protect themselves from violence committed by the Ku Klux Klan. The most important part of the Act—Title 42, United States Code 1983—remains in force even today to protect individual civil rights.

Yet not all of the civil rights legislation passed by the Reconstruction Congress remained intact. In the *Civil Rights Cases*, 109 U.S. 3 (1883), the Supreme Court ruled that despite the enforcement language of Amendment XIV, Congress lacked the constitutional authority to ban private discrimination. This decision, along with the end of Reconstruction in 1877 and the removal of federal troops from the South, brought an end to the first civil rights era.

The Second Civil Rights Era

The impetus behind the second civil rights era can be attributed to three events. First, in 1948 Pres. Harry Truman issued Executive Order 9981 desegregating the U.S. armed forces. Second, as part of an effort to overturn *Plessy v. Ferguson*, 163 U.S. 537 (1896) and the separate-but-equal doctrine, the National Association for the Advancement of Colored People (NAACP) was formed in 1909. Representing the NAACP, future Supreme Court Justice Thurgood Marshall successfully argued for the overturning of separate-but-equal in *Brown v. Board of Education*, 347 U.S. 483 (1954). Third, and perhaps most important, in 1955 in Montgomery, Alabama, Rosa Parks, an African American woman, refused to give up her seat on a city bus to a white passenger, as she was required to do by law. Her civil disobedience, along with the resulting Montgomery Bus Boycott, was the main inspiration for Martin Luther King Jr. and the emergence of a modern civil rights movement. In response, Congress passed the 1957 Civil Rights Act, which aimed at strengthening the voting rights of African Americans. Passage of the 1964 Civil Rights Act, especially Title VII, further expanded civil rights. This act, like its 1866 predecessor, barred private discrimination, but it also extended its protections to include women and other people of color.

Following passage of the 1964 Civil Rights Act, Congress adopted the Voting Rights Act of 1965 in order to strengthen the ability of blacks to register and vote. The adoption of Amendment XXIV in 1964 barred poll taxes and other legislation aimed at discrimination—in housing, for example.

The Transformation of the Second Civil Rights Era

Beginning in the 1970s, the second civil rights era in American history changed in two profound ways. First, though the focus on civil rights had heretofore mainly been on African Americans, now other people of color, women, and (soon) gays, lesbians, bisexuals, and transsexuals increasingly sought the protection of antidiscrimination laws. Second, a backlash against civil rights laws, especially regarding affirmative action, emerged to become a contentious social, political, and legal issue.

The 1964 Civil Rights Act also extended protection against discrimination based on "sex." Beginning in the 1970s, those who sought to eradicate sex discrimination used this law and Amendment XIV's Equal Protection Clause to protect the civil rights of women. In cases such as *Reed v. Reed*, 404 U.S. 1 (1971) and *Frontiero v. Richardson*, 411 U.S. 677 (1973), the Supreme Court struck down laws treating women differently from men when it came to assigning the former as estate administrators or to receiving military benefits. In 1978, Congress amended the 1964 Civil Rights Act with the Pregnancy Discrimination Act, making it illegal for companies with 15 or more employees to discriminate against women who are pregnant. The 1978 act overturned *General Electric v. Gilbert*, 429 U.S. 125 (1976), which had ruled that pregnancy was not protected under the original 1964 law. In *Meritor Savings Bank v. Vinson*, 477 U.S. 57 (1986), the Court extended the scope of the 1964 Civil Rights Act by declaring sexual harassment to be a form of sex discrimination. In the Civil Rights Act of 1991, Congress enacted legislation to make it easier to prove employment discrimination, thus overturning numerous earlier Supreme Court decisions.

In addition to the extension of civil rights protections to women, Congress also moved to protect other people of color. For example, the 1975 amendments to the 1965 Voting Rights Act added language meant to address discrimination against Hispanics, Asian Americans, and American Indians. These provisions have also been used to protect other minority language groups against discrimination. In the Americans with Disabilities Act of 1990, Congress adopted legislation to protect the civil rights of individuals with physical disabilities.

Though many civil rights laws were extended to protect women and other groups, there was concern among some in government and among activists that the mere adoption of antidiscrimination laws would not be enough to achieve equality. Other efforts were needed. In 1961, Pres. John Kennedy issued presidential Executive Order 10925 banning discrimination in the executive branch and urging "affirmative action" to diversify the federal workforce. Executive Order 11246, issued by Pres. Lyndon Johnson in 1965, reinforced this order and again called for steps to diversify the workforce by reaching out to women and individuals of color.

Beginning in the 1970s, the expansion of affirmative action programs meant that race and gender would be increasingly used by schools and employers engaged in making admissions and hiring decisions. Some argued that the use of race, for example, was necessary to overcome past discrimination. Others asserted this was itself a form of discrimination. Such divergent views often resulted in yet more confusion. For example, in *Regents of the University of California v. Bakke*, 438 U.S. 265 (1978), the Court upheld the use of affirmative action in the school's admissions policies while also holding that the school's program overstepped constitutional bounds by placing too much emphasis on the single characteristic of race. No one majority opinion was authored. Justice Lewis Powell, writing a separate concurrence in a Court otherwise split 4–4, held that Amendment XIV permitted the use of race in school admissions in order to promote diversity. In *United Steelworkers v. Weber*, 443 U.S. 193 (1979), the Court upheld the voluntary use of affirmative action in employment, and in *Fullilove v. Klutznick*, 448 U.S. 448 (1980), the Court permitted federal programs setting aside

money for minority business enterprises. In *Johnson v. Santa Clara County*, 480 U.S. 616 (1987), it upheld a gender-based affirmative action hiring program. In *Metro Broadcasting v. Federal Communications Commission*, 497 U.S. 547 (1990), the Court upheld the use of race in the awarding of broadcast licenses.

But changes in the composition of the Court produced decisions more critical of affirmative action. In *Adarand Constructors v. Peña*, 515 U.S. 200 (1995), the Court invalidated a set-aside program using racial preferences when awarding federal contracts. The decision overturned *Metro Broadcasting*. In *Grutter v. Bollinger*, 539 U.S. 306 (2003), the Court upheld a law school admissions program that was narrowly tailored to ensure a "critical mass" of minority students at the school. Yet in a companion case challenging the University of Michigan's undergraduate admissions policy, the Court invalidated the policy in *Gratz v. Bollinger*, 539 U.S. 244 (2003), claiming it involved a more rigid use of race that was the type of quota the Court had struck down in *Bakke*. Moreover, in *Parents Involved in Community Schools v. Seattle School District No. 1*, 551 U.S. ___ (2007), decided with *Meredith v. Jefferson*, 551 U.S. ___ (2007) the Supreme Court invalidated the use of race in school assignments. Overall, these more recent affirmative action decisions question how far the Supreme Court and the law will go in permitting race to be used to remedy past discrimination. For some critics, decisions such as these suggest that the second civil rights era has come to an end. Others who defend them claim that the law is simply seeking a "color-blind" approach to enforcing the law.

Sexual Orientation and Civil Rights

Perhaps the most significant transformation in the civil rights movement has come in terms of the battle for equality for gays, lesbians, bisexuals, and transsexuals. Beginning with a police raid in June 1969 on the the Stonewall Inn, a gay bar in New York City, and the riots that grew out of it, civil rights became the focus for many in the Gay, Lesbian, Bisexual, and Transgender (GLBT) community.

In *Bowers v. Hardwick*, 478 U.S. 186 (1986), the Supreme Court ruled that laws criminalizing consensual sodomy with members of the same sex but not members of the opposite sex were constitutional. Many in the GLBT community considered this decision equivalent to the 1896 Supreme Court decision in *Plessy v. Ferguson*. However, the courts since the *Bowers* decision had gradually whittled away at many of the discriminatory laws aimed at GLBT people. In *Romer v. Evans*, 517 U.S. 630 (1996), for example, the Court struck down a state ballot initiative that would have prevented cities in Colorado from adopting laws to ban discrimination against gays and lesbians. In *Lawrence v. Texas*, 539 U.S. 558 (2003), the Court overturned its *Bowers* decision. Perhaps the most significant battle for civil rights for the GLBT community has come in terms of securing the right for same-sex couples to marry. In *Baker v. Nelson*, 291 Minn. 310, 191 N.W.2d 185 (1971), a same-sex couple argued that Minnesota marriage laws did not prevent them from marrying. The Court disagreed. However, 20 years later the courts began to look at the issue differently. In *Baehr v. Lewin*, 852 P.2d 44 (Haw, 1993), the Hawaiian Supreme Court used its state constitution to rule that precluding gays and lesbians from marrying violated its equal protection clause. However, in 1998 the state constitution was amended to overturn that decision.

Growing fear that some legislature or state court would repeat the actions of the Hawaiian supreme court led Congress in 1996 to pass the Defense of Marriage Act (DOMA). DOMA specified that no state could be forced to honor the marriage standards of any other, as would normally be required under the Constitution's Full Faith and Credit Clause. Many states adopted their own versions of DOMA or otherwise moved to legislate against gay marriage. For example, when in *Baker v. Vermont*, 744 A.2d. 864 (VT. 1993), the Vermont supreme court struck down laws that denied same-sex couples the same benefits as married heterosexual couples, the state legislature created "civil unions," thus allowing same-sex couples to register and secure many of the benefits of marriage while also denying them the official recognition of marriage. GLBT activists considered this an inferior status and continued to litigate the issue.

In Massachusetts in *Goodrich v. Department of Public Health*, 798 N.E. 2d. 941 (Mass. 2003), the state supreme court struck down laws preventing gays and lesbians from marrying. This decision prompted many states to amend their constitutions to ban same-sex marriage. California became the second state to legalize same-sex marriages, when in spring 2008 the California supreme court invoked the state constitution to strike down the ban on gay marriage. Several thousand same-sex couples rushed to marry, only to see voters overturn the court's decision by ballot initiative in November 2008. Challenges to that ballot proposition leave the status of it and same-sex marriage in California in question. The third state to legalize same-sex marriage through court decision was Connecticut. In *Kerrigan v. Commissioner of Public Health*, 957 A.2d 407 (Conn. 2008), the Connecticut supreme court struck down the ban on same-sex marriage. Iowa legalized same-sex marriage in April 2009. Other states have since passed legislation allowing for civil unions, such as New Jersey, or are considering legalizing same-sex marriages, such as New York.

The GLBT community has fought to extend its civil rights in other areas as well. For example, in November 2008, the Florida supreme court struck down as unconstitutional a state law banning same-sex couples from adopting children. Overall, GLBT advocates have successfully used the strategies of the first two civil rights eras to pursue their cause.

Civil rights laws have been adopted in two historic periods in the United States in order to address discrimination against women and people of color. In recent years, these laws have also been extended to members of the GLBT community. The purpose of these laws is to protect voting, employment, and other rights and ensure that members of groups historically discriminated against are treated the same as others who are considered part of the majority. Although there is no doubt that significant progress has been made to address many civil rights issues, discrimination still exists and advocates for different groups continue to call for more federal or state laws to protect their constituents.

Bibliography and Further Reading

Babst, Gordon A. *Liberal Constitutionalism, Marriage, and Sexual Orientation: A Contemporary Case for Dis-Establishment*. New York: Peter Lang, 2002.

Foner, Eric. *Reconstruction: America's Unfinished Revolution, 1863–1877*. New York: Harper & Row, 1988.

Gerstmann, Evan. *Same-Sex Marriage and the Constitution*. Cambridge, MA: Cambridge University Press, 2004.

Kluger, Richard. *Simple Justice: The History of* Brown v. Board of Education *and Black America's Struggle for Equality*. New York: Vintage, 2004.

Landsberg, Brian K. *Enforcing Civil Rights: Race, Discrimination, and the Department of Justice*. Lawrence: University Press of Kansas, 1997.

Skrentny, John. *The Minority Rights Revolution*. Cambridge, MA: Harvard University Press, 2003.

Spann, Girardeau. *The Law of Affirmative Action: Twenty-Five Years of Supreme Court Decisions on Race and Remedies*. New York: New York University Press, 2000.

Williams, Juan, and Julian Bond. *Eyes on the Prize: America's Civil Rights Years, 1954–1965*. New York: Penguin Books, 1988.

Woodward, C. Vann. *The Strange Career of Jim Crow*. New York: Oxford University Press, 2001.

David Schultz

CLIMATE CHANGE

The problem of human-induced climate change might be the most significant and vexing environmental issue of the twenty-first century. Climate change has proved especially troubling for the United States, which once prided itself on being a global leader in environmental protection policies but is by much of the world considered a laggard on this issue. Though the United States produces close to a quarter of the world's greenhouse gas emissions, it has failed to ratify the 1997 Kyoto Protocol to the United Nations Framework Convention on Climate Change, and as of early 2009 has yet to take significant federal action to reduce domestic greenhouse gas emissions. The most notable policy progress in the United States has occurred in the states, many of which are embracing innovative solutions to the problem. Without federal involvement, however, the effect of such actions will be limited.

Political and Policy History

Although the problem of global warming was hypothesized by the scientific community in the nineteenth century, the U.S. Congress did not give it any official attention until the late 1970s, when Rep. Al Gore (D–TN) held the first congressional hearing on climate change. A decade passed before Congress revisited the issue in a serious way, proposing legislation and holding hearings during the hot summer of 1988, one that brought dramatic droughts, forest fires, and floods. Senator Tim Wirth (D–CO) led the effort and invited Dr. James Hansen, director of NASA's Goddard Institute for Space Studies, to testify before the U.S. Senate in what proved to be a critical event for attracting media, scientific, and public attention to the issue. Hansen boldly stated that he was "99 percent" certain that the world was warming and it was most likely due to human activity. Critics within the scientific community claimed that his statement was too strong, and the subsequent scientific debate led to the formation of the United Nation's Intergovernmental Panel on Climate Change (IPCC) later that year. The panel brought together the top climatic scientists in the world and since its inception has provided vital information to policy makers on the scientific basis of climate change, likely impacts, and possible policy responses.

The IPCC's first assessment report, published in 1990, was critical to the convening and signing of the U.N. Framework Convention on Climate Change (UNFCCC) at the 1992 Earth Summit in Rio de Janeiro, Brazil. President George H. W. Bush signed the document along with more than 150 other nations, but the United States had insisted that the UNFCCC include only voluntary targets and timetables for reducing greenhouse gases. Despite its weaknesses, the UNFCCC established a structure for creating a stronger climate change treaty, and after several years of meetings, agreement was reached in Kyoto, Japan, to commit to mandatory emissions reductions. The 1997

Kyoto Protocol committed industrialized countries to decrease their emissions of greenhouse gases by an average of about 5 percent below 1990 levels by 2012. The United States agreed to a 7 percent reduction, but Pres. Bill Clinton never asked the U.S. Senate to ratify the treaty, fearing that both Republicans and Democrats would soundly reject the agreement. Politicians from coal-rich states were the most vocal opponents, but they found plenty of allies, including supporters of the automobile companies and other industries that stood to lose if Kyoto went into effect.

In 2000, George W. Bush ran for the U.S. presidency pledging to cut carbon dioxide emissions, and skeptics were relatively pleased when he chose Christine Todd Whitman to head the Environmental Protection Agency. Whitman had been governor of New Jersey and was known for improving that state's environmental record and strengthening its conservation policy. Hopes that the new administration would follow through on its climate promises, however, were dashed when President Bush surprised the international community by publicly rejecting the Kyoto Protocol and removing the United States from global negotiations. Bush cited concerns about the economic consequences were the United States to cut its emissions and raised questions about the logic and fairness of excluding large nations like China and India from any binding targets. President Bush instead called for voluntary efforts to reduce U.S. greenhouse gas emissions.

Since 2006, pressure has been mounting for the United States to move beyond voluntary measures and toward a regulatory regime that would mandate reductions in greenhouse gas emissions. Al Gore's documentary *An Inconvenient Truth* (2006) helped to turn up the volume on the issue of climate change, and the IPCC's Fourth Assessment Report used strong language to convey the idea that the problem was both real and urgent. During the One Hundred Tenth Congress, proposed legislation on climate change was introduced at a faster pace than in any previous Congress, reflecting the growing public and political attention to the issue and the desire of some industries to obtain more regulatory certainty.

Despite Congress's growing attention to the problem, however, the federal government has been slow to respond to climate change. The lack of national political action has been aided by the perception of scientific uncertainty about whether and to what extent humans are causing a rise in global temperatures. Starting in the 1990s, several industries whose activities would be subject to regulation under a climate change law launched campaigns to discredit global warming science. For example, in 2004, the oil company Exxon Mobil sponsored a series of advertisements on the editorial page of the *New York Times* to urge caution in responding to climate change, given what it claimed was lingering scientific uncertainty about both causes and effects. Conservative policy think tanks including the American Enterprise Institute and the George Marshall Institute also raised doubts by highlighting the views of a small minority of scientists who disagreed with the mainstream.

Climate change skeptics found a friend in the Bush administration, which was accused of suppressing scientific information on global warming and interfering in the activities of agency scientists, including James Hansen, who spoke about the need for mandatory reductions of greenhouse gases. In a 2007 congressional hearing on the matter, several witnesses testified that the administration had downplayed, edited, and suppressed government reports and research, controlled media access to agency scientists, and engaged in other means of political interference.

The media added to the perception of scientific uncertainty in the 1990s by giving roughly equal time to the idea that humans are responsible for climate change and to the notion that natural fluctuations in the earth's temperature are to blame for recent warming trends. More recently, media attention has better reflected scientific consensus on the issue. But though the majority of Americans now believe climate change is real and is caused by humans, less than half believe there is consensus within the scientific community. And when the public is exposed to claims of scientific uncertainty, it is less likely to support immediate actions to combat global warming. To make matters worse, Americans believe that solutions to climate change will be costly and painful, which also decreases support for action. The greatest barrier to action on global warming, though, has been the lack of salience, or a sense of urgency: rarely do Americans list climate change as one of the top problems facing the country. Other problems, like the economy, national security, and health care, routinely generate more public concern.

The 2008 presidential campaign and the election of Barack Obama gave renewed hope that the United States would pass major climate change legislation in the near future. The 2008 campaign was notable for the fact that both John McCain, the Republican presidential nominee, and Barack Obama believed that global warming was both real and urgent. Both candidates supported deep cuts in greenhouse gases by mid-century and thus represented a significant break from the Bush administration. Some fear, though, that the global economic recession will delay or weaken efforts to enact aggressive climate change legislation. More hopeful signs come from President Obama, whose appointments to key environmental posts in his administration and his rhetoric about creating a new green economy suggest that he plans to move forward with his campaign promises.

State Action

Several U.S. states have been busy taking measures into their own hands, acting both unilaterally and cooperatively to combat climate change. For example, in 2003 states in the Northeast and Mid-Atlantic formed the Regional Greenhouse Gas Initiative, which commits participants to reduce greenhouse gas emissions from electric power generators through a multi-state "cap and trade" program. About half the states have enacted "renewable portfolio standards" that require states to purchase a certain percentage of their electricity from renewable sources like wind, solar, and hydropower by a particular date. Some states have gone further by pledging to reduce the state's aggregate emissions and setting binding targets and timetables. In 2007, New Jersey became the first state to mandate emissions cuts of 80 percent below 1990 levels by 2050.

States have also tried through litigation to pressure the federal government to regulate carbon diox-

ide emissions In a high-profile lawsuit (*Massachusetts v. EPA*, 549 U.S. 497 [2007]), Massachusetts and 11 other states sued the Environmental Protection Agency for its failure to regulate carbon dioxide under the Clean Air Act. The Supreme Court found in favor of the states, prompting speculation about the fate of other climate change litigation working its way through the court system. Additional lawsuits take direct aim at car manufacturers and utility companies for causing harm to states because of their contributions to climate change.

The actions of the states suggest that the American political system is dynamic and capable of instituting change even when some institutions and levels of government are sluggish to respond to emerging problems. The outcome of all this activity, however, remains to be seen. Most analysts suggest that the federal government must take a leadership role; this is especially important when considering the need for ongoing international cooperation and commitment to combat a global problem of enormous proportions.

Policy Responses

As the debate over global warming moved from whether climate change was in fact happening to what could be done about it, attention has focused on potential solutions and the overall design of climate change policy. Many policy makers have expressed support for a cap-and-trade program, wherein the government would set an overall limit on greenhouse gas emissions, issue permits to emitting industries, and then allow these industries to trade permits on the open market. Proponents of cap-and-trade insist that this is the most efficient way to achieve greenhouse gas reductions, as it would allow industries with high reduction potential to sell excess permits to industries that find it more difficult and expensive to reduce emissions. In other words, a cap-and-trade program would set emissions limits, but not dictate the means of emissions control. Several large industries have teamed up with mainstream environmental groups in the U.S. Climate Action Partnership to lobby Congress and the administration to adopt a cap-and-trade program and cut greenhouse gases. Though these alliances indicate a growing acceptance by industry of the inevitability of climate change regulations and a possible end to policy gridlock, debate will no doubt continue as legislative details are worked out. For example, there is still the question as to whether the government should auction the permits, thus generating billions of dollars in government revenue, or distribute them for free (as is preferred by industry). And debate is already raging about various carbon-free energy technologies, with the most heated being the debate over nuclear energy.

Bibliography and Further Reading

DiMento, Joseph F. C., and Pamela Doughman, eds. *Climate Change: What It Means for Us, Our Children, and Our Grandchildren.* Cambridge, MA: MIT Press, 2007.

Flannery, Tim. *The Weather Makers: How Man Is Changing the Climate and What It Means for Life on Earth.* New York: Grove Press, 2005.

Hempel, Lamont C. "Climate Policy on the Installment Plan." In *Environmental Policy: New Directions for the Twenty-First Century,* edited by Norman J. Vig and Michael E. Kraft, 288–310. Washington, D.C.: CQ Press, 2006.

Kolbert, Elizabeth. *Field Notes on a Catastrophe: Man, Nature, and Climate Change.* New York: Bloomsbury Publishers, 2006.

Rabe, Barry G. *Statehouse and Greenhouse: The Emerging Politics of American Climate Change Policy.* Washington, D.C.: Brookings Institution Press, 2004.

Sarah B. Pralle

CLINTON, BILL

born 1946
Forty-second President of the United States

William Jefferson "Bill" Clinton was the first member of the "baby boomer" generation (those born after World War II) to serve as president. Elected in what was primarily a conservative and Republican era, Clinton governed from the center. Domestically, he placed a premium on balanced budgets and free trade. Internationally, Clinton extended NATO's reach to include former satellites of the Soviet Union, attempted "nation building" in developing nations, halted ethnic cleansing (that is, genocide) in the former Yugoslavia, and promoted peace in Ireland and the Middle East. He was the second president to be both impeached and acquitted.

Early Life

Clinton was both on August 19, 1946, in Hope, Arkansas. His father, William Jefferson Blythe Jr. died in a car accident three months before Clinton's birth. Clinton's mother, the former Virginia Dell Cassidy, subsequently married Roger Clinton, whose family owned and operated a car dealership in Hot Springs, Arkansas. When he was 14, Clinton took his stepfather's surname.

Through his participation in the American Legion's Boys State and Boys Nation, Clinton met Pres. John F. Kennedy on a visit to the nation's capital. Twenty-nine years later, the 1992 Democratic National Convention that nominated Clinton aired footage of the 16-year-old Bill Clinton elbowing his way past colleagues to shake JFK's hand. Clinton went on to attend Georgetown University. In the summer of his senior year, he interned for Arkansas senator J. William Fulbright, then chairman of the Senate Foreign Relations Committee.

After graduating in 1968, Clinton won a Rhodes scholarship to Oxford University. He traveled widely, played rugby, developed an interest in German, and demonstrated against the Vietnam War. He also forged lifelong friendships with several fellow Rhodes scholars, who would prove helpful to his subsequent career. Some subsequently served in his presidential administration.

Expecting to be drafted to fight in Vietnam, Clinton arranged to join the Arkansas National Guard but declined induction when he learned that his odds of being drafted were minimal. He enrolled at Yale Law School, dabbled in Connecticut political campaigns, and directed George McGovern's 1972 presidential campaign in Texas. He took his JD degree in 1973.

Career in Arkansas Politics

Later that same year, Clinton accepted a teaching post at the University of Arkansas Law School. In 1974, hoping to benefit from the toll the Watergate scandal promised to take on Republican candidates, Clinton challenged incumbent congressman John Paul Hammerschmidt. He lost 52–48 percent. In 1976, Clinton easily obtained the Democratic nomination for attorney general of Arkansas and was elected at the age of 30. The previous year, he had wed his long-time girlfriend, Hillary Rodham. Two years later, he was elected governor of Arkansas.

Of the six two-year terms he would serve as governor, Clinton's first proved the most turbulent. He pressed for education reform and road repairs. To help fund such initiatives, he imposed what proved to be an unpopular motor-vehicles tax. Clinton lost his first bid for reelection during the Reagan landslide of 1980. He spent the next two years plotting his political come-back. Voters returned Clinton to the governorship in 1982, and there he would remain for a decade. Back in office, he resumed his efforts to improve Arkansas schools, insisting on higher standards for teachers and better performance by students. He worked to improve the state's business climate through favorable tax and regulatory policies designed to attract new businesses.

Clinton became the prototype of the "New Democrat," a member of that party who, though moderate or liberal on social policy, took a more conservative view on taxes, crime, government spending, and national security. In 1986, Clinton used his chairmanship of the National Governors Conference to showcase his ideas on education and welfare reform and to press for a greater role for the states in the development of national policy on those issues. In 1990, he assumed the leadership of the Democratic Leadership Council (DLC), an organization committed to moving the Democratic Party to the political center.

Clinton considered running for president in 1988, but deferred to Michael Dukakis. His speech on Dukakis's behalf at the Democratic National Convention was one of the least successful of his career. (Delegates cheered him the loudest when he noted that he was nearing the end of his remarks.) After pledging that he would not run for president if he won reelection in 1990, Clinton reversed himself and declared for the nation's highest office months after winning his last gubernatorial campaign.

Clinton Becomes President

Having placed third in the Iowa caucuses, Clinton confounded his detractors when he finished second in the New Hampshire primary on February 18, 1992. For weeks prior to the primary, Clinton was weighed down by allegations of an extramarital affair and by assertions that he had been less than forthcoming in explaining how he had avoided military service during the Vietnam War. In a joint interview on *60 Minutes*, Bill and Hillary Clinton denied the affair, while Clinton admitted to having had "troubles" in his marriage. After praising his wife's achievements, Clinton invited viewers to "buy one, get one free." Pundits subsequently proclaimed Clinton's come-from-behind second-place finish, eight points behind Massachusetts senator Paul Tsongas, the equivalent of victory. Clinton dubbed himself the "comeback kid." After winning a string of other primaries, Clinton seized the New York primary in April and emerged as the presumptive party favorite.

With Tennessee senator Al Gore as his running mate, Clinton won 43 percent of the popular vote against incumbent president George H. W. Bush, who received 37.4 percent, and independent candidate Ross Perot, who received 18.9 percent. In the Electoral College, Clinton received 370 votes to Bush's 168. Clinton's promise to "focus on the economy like a laser beam" resonated with voters weary with an unemployment rate that remained stubbornly high for more than a year after the July 1990–March 1991 recession had ended. ("It's the economy, stupid," proclaimed a much-quoted sign that adorned a wall in Clinton's headquarters.) Clinton also benefited from Perot's appeal to middle-class and Republican voters, concerned about mounting federal budget deficits. Bush suffered from the prevailing sentiment that he was primarily interested in foreign policy and was "out of touch" domestically. Many conservatives deserted Bush after he reneged on his 1988 pledge not to raise taxes.

Domestic Policies

Clinton took office determined to press ahead with his New Democrat agenda, which included deficit reduction, free trade, and health care reform. He was immediately distracted, however, by events he had not anticipated. Soon after his election, Clinton became embroiled in controversy with the military establishment and members of Congress over whether gays and lesbians should be allowed to serve openly in the armed forces. Eventually, Clinton agreed to what became the "Don't Ask, Don't Tell" compromise. Meanwhile, insufficient vetting during his transition forced two successive nominees for attorney general to withdraw their names from consideration.

Clinton and his advisors also displayed indecision as to their priorities. With economists forecasting federal budget deficits well into the future, they resolved to address fiscal issues first. Clinton reasoned that lower interest rates would encourage business investment in new industries and create high-paying jobs. He hoped that his deficit-reduction package would cut interest rates by curbing the federal demand for credit. To reduce federal budget deficits, Clinton initially relied mainly on higher taxes and lower defense spending. In the Omnibus Budget Reconciliation Act of 1993, Clinton won congressional approval for increasing the top federal income tax rate for individuals from 31 percent to 39.6 percent, raising the corporate income tax rate by one percentage point, repealing the earnings cap on the Medicare payroll tax, increasing the taxable portion of Social Security benefits, and increasing the gas tax by 4.3 cents per gallon. Clinton provided some additional benefits to low-income families through an expansion of the earned income tax credit.

Though Wall Street reacted favorably, Clinton's centrist agenda found its share of detractors. Unwilling to go along with the tax increases, Republicans unanimously opposed the bill. Unhappy at the prospect of spending restraint, some liberal Democrats also balked. The act passed both the House (219 to 213) and the Senate (by one vote), with Vice President Gore casting the tie-breaking vote.

Clinton reached common ground with Republicans in order to pass the North American Free Trade Agreement (NAFTA), a Reagan-inspired idea that would eliminate tariffs on goods made and sold throughout North America. Though popular among New Democrats because it lowered business costs and

consumer prices, labor unions and environmental groups were opposed, fearing that NAFTA would drive down wages and erode environmental safeguards. With 156 Democrats, 43 Republicans, and 1 Independent opposing NAFTA and 102 Democrats and 132 Republicans favoring it, the measure passed the House 234–200. Pressure from the New Democratic president proved essential to its success. In the Senate, NAFTA passed by 61–38.

A year later, Clinton also won congressional approval for the Uruguay Round Agreements. This eighth in a series of multilateral trade liberalization agreements since World War II created the World Trade Organization (WTO), reduced tariffs on non-agricultural goods by an average of 40 percent in the United States and other WTO member-countries, expanded the scope of trade liberalization to for the first time include agricultural goods and services, and established a Dispute Settlement Mechanism to resolve trade disputes among WTO members. In effect, the Uruguay Round Agreements were the largest single tax cut that had occurred up to that time.

During his first year in office, Clinton signed the Family and Medical Leave Act, mandating that large employers grant leaves of absence to employees who wished to spend time caring for small children and sick relatives. Later in his first year, he approved the "Brady Bill" (named for Pres. Ronald Reagan's press secretary, James Brady, who was seriously wounded, along with the president, during an assassination attempt), requiring a five-day waiting period for handgun purchases. Clinton also won passage of AmeriCorps, a program that provides funds for the training, recruitment, and placing of community volunteers. Analysts saw all these measures as attempts by Clinton to assuage liberal elements within his electoral coalition who were less than enthusiastic about his deficit-reduction and free-trade initiatives.

At the outset of his presidency, Clinton put the First Lady in charge of a task force he charged with devising a plan to provide universal health coverage. The group immediately came under fire for holding secret meetings and for not identifying all of its members. In a message to a special session of Congress on September 22, 1993, Clinton presented its recommendations. Its central component was to mandate employers to provide health insurance through tightly regulated HMOs. The insurance industry mounted a highly effective campaign against this proposal with television advertisements that featured a fictitious couple, "Harry and Louise," struggling to make sense of the complicated plan. Several congressional committees, each having jurisdiction over parts of the more than 1,000-page bill, gave the plan a cool reception. The proposal never came to a vote. Clinton had better luck winning passage of his anti-crime package, which funded the hiring of an additional 100,000 local police officers.

Early Scandals

Multiple allegations of corruption and conflicts of interest plagued Bill and Hillary Clinton throughout Clinton's presidency. The list of asserted wrongdoings revolved around the nature of the First Lady's association with the Rose Law firm in Little Rock that handled state business; the Clintons' participation in the Whitewater Development Corporation, a failed real estate operation in which federal funds had been invested; improper firings of personnel in the White House travel office ("travelgate"); and the improper gathering and perusal of FBI files concerning security investigations of people in prior (Republican) administrations ("filegate"). Clinton asked his attorney general, Janet Reno, to appoint independent counsel to investigate. A series of investigations failed to find evidence of wrongdoing on the Clintons' part in these episodes.

The Gingrich Revolution and Clinton's Second Term

In 1994, Republicans for the first time in 40 years won control of both Houses of Congress. Their success stemmed in part from public disapproval of the Clintons' health care proposals, press coverage of the scandals swirling around the president, his failure to keep his pledge not to raise taxes on the middle class, and a series of misdeeds by Democratic members of Congress (including irregularities in the bank and post office maintained for House members).

In planning their moves, however, the Republican leadership misjudged the nature of its opposition and overreached. In spite of their tremendous gains (54

seats in the House and 8 in the Senate), Republican majorities were narrow, controlling the House by an average of 26 seats and the Senate by an average of 8 seats. Nevertheless, they proceeded on the assumption that Clinton would accede to the cuts they planned to make in spending and taxes. Clinton's veto of two successive budgets and Congress's failure to pass continuing resolutions to keep the government functioning while the executive and legislative branches resolved their differences resulted in two government shutdowns of non-essential services from November 14 to November 19, 1995, and from December 16, 1995, to January 6, 1996.

Clinton had also gone into the budget negotiations with improved public standing, the result of the empathy he showed the families of victims of the Oklahoma City bombing, an act perpetrated by domestic terrorists that took the lives of 168 and wounded hundreds. Throughout the budgetary impasse, Clinton maintained that, though he was open to some spending and tax cuts, he would veto cutbacks that eroded funding for education, the environment, and Medicare and Social Security. Clinton's embrace of four programs he knew to be popular with swing voters, coupled with Republican blunders (such as House Speaker Newt Gingrich's public complaint that Clinton had snubbed him by once forcing him to exit from the rear of Air Force One after returning from an official visit), gave Clinton the edge in public opinion.

Though Clinton won the first round with the G.O.P. on spending priorities, once the government had reopened, he and they saw a common interest in working together. Because both sides were willing to compromise, real outlays for domestic discretionary spending fell by an average of 0.6 percent per year during the last six years of Clinton's presidency. Clinton, thus, left office with a budget surplus of $128 billion.

The two sides also drew closer together on welfare reform. As a presidential candidate, Clinton had promised to "end welfare as we know it." Yet as president, anxious to dissuade liberals within his party from mounting a primary challenge to his renomination, Clinton twice vetoed bills that would have reformed Aid to Families with Dependent Children (AFDC) and reduced welfare outlays. On August 22, 1996, after his renomination was assured, Clinton reversed course and signed the Personal Responsibility and Work Opportunity Reconciliation Act of 1996. This act abolished two entitlements, including AFDC, replaced them with a block grant to states, imposed minimum work and training requirements, and limited lifetime benefits to 60 months. Predicting dire consequences, three Clinton advisors resigned in protest. Yet a decade later, Clinton noted that welfare rolls had plummeted from 12.2 million in 1996 to 4.5 million in 2006 and that 60 percent of single heads of households, once on welfare, had found work.

Commentators openly speculated that Clinton and the Republican congressional leaders saw it in their mutual interest to demonstrate a capacity to work together in order to remain in power. In 1996, Clinton defeated the Republican Bob Dole, carrying 49.2 percent of the vote to Dole's 40.7 percent. In the Electoral College, Clinton prevailed 379–159. The campaign was largely a lackluster affair in which the still youthful Clinton pledged that he would metaphorically "build a bridge" to the twenty-first century. His promise began as a retort to the 73-year-old Dole's assertion that he wanted to "build a bridge to the past."

Beginning his second term facing a Republican rather than a Democratic Congress, Clinton approved many of the Republican-sponsored tax measures he had vetoed 18 months earlier. Among the reasons

President Bill Clinton directs a national forum on welfare on August 3, 1999, in Chicago, where he listens to former welfare recipients who have since found employment. Campaigning as a "New Democrat" in 1992, Clinton had promised to "end welfare as we know it," but it was only after securing his own renomination in August 1996 that he signed the bipartisan Personal Responsibility and Work Opportunity Reconciliation Act. Clinton's signing of this bill, which alienated him from some in his own administration, exemplified his fiscally centrist approach to governing. (Paul J. Richards/AFP/Getty Images)

Clinton gave for these policy reversals (other than changed political realities) was that the movement of the federal budget from deficit into surplus made tax cuts affordable. He signed bills that reduced the maximum tax rate on capital gains from 28 to 20 percent, instituted a $500 child tax credit for middle-income families, and increased the estate tax exemption to $1 million. Many expected Clinton to make entitlement reform a hallmark of his second term as he had welfare reform in the first. Though as a candidate for reelection Clinton had promised to reform Social Security, once back in office he left the issue to his successors.

Foreign Policy and National Security

The first president to take office in the aftermath of the Cold War, Clinton was bereft of an overall strategy for engaging other great powers. Outside of trade liberalization, Clinton confined most of his efforts internationally to putting out small brush fires. The supply of these was considerable.

Early in his term, Clinton tried and failed to bring democracy and stability to two failed states. In Somalia, he expanded the mission that his predecessor had set for U.S. troops from the mere keeping of order to one of nation building. After one side in Somalia's ongoing civil war downed a series of American helicopters and dragged the bodies of slain soldiers through the streets, Clinton removed all U.S. troops. He sent U.S. troops to Haiti to return to office an elected president who had been ousted in a coup only to find that the man on whose behalf he intervened refused to vacate his office when his legal term expired.

Clinton forged a cooperative relationship with Boris Yeltsin, the first democratically elected president of Russia, and used the goodwill that existed between the two countries to shepherd new democracies in Central and Eastern Europe, once part of the Soviet bloc, into NATO. Standing down congressional opponents who maintained that intervention in internal warfare in the former Yugoslavia was not in the interests of the United States, Clinton ordered bombing missions and followed up by sending ground forces to Bosnia in order to stop the ethnic cleansing of the Muslim minority by forces loyal to Serbian leader Slobodan Milosevic. Anticipating that the Soviet

Union would exercise its veto in the Security Council to block the United Nations from acting against its historical ally, Clinton took the unusual step of acting through NATO. Clinton tried this approach a second time when he ordered U.S. bombers to destroy targets in Kosovo, another Yugoslav province, as a means of preventing further atrocities against the ethnic Albanian minority. U.N. peacekeepers eventually restored order. Clinton stated that among his major regrets was his failure to do more to stop genocide in Rwanda.

Clinton used his office and popularity abroad to broker a peaceful end to the fighting between Protestants and Catholics in Northern Ireland. In the waning days of his administration, he came close to achieving a peace accord between Israelis and Palestinians.

During Clinton's presidency, terrorist networks struck targets in the United States and attacked its citizens abroad. They set off a bomb at the World Trade Center in New York in 1993 and attacked the Khobar Towers housing complex in Saudi America in 1996, killing 19 American military personnel. Terrorists also perpetrated attacks on two American embassies in Africa in 1998, killing hundreds; and on the U.S.S. *Cole*, docked in Yemen, in 2000, taking the lives of 17 U.S. sailors. Subsequent investigations, including that of the 9/11 Commission, found the Clinton administration's response either insufficient or ineffective.

Impeachment and Acquittal

Early in 1998, the media reported that Clinton had been conducting a furtive relationship with a White House intern, Monica Lewinsky. Clinton and his aides repeatedly denied the allegations. In response to reports that the president had lied about the nature of the relationship in a sworn deposition and again in testimony before a grand jury in a civil sexual harassment suit, Attorney Gen. Janet Reno asked Independent Counsel Kenneth Starr, already investigating the Whitewater episode, to look into the question of whether Clinton committed perjury.

Faced with evidence that Clinton had, in fact, lied to the grand jury, the lame-duck House voted two articles of impeachment against him. The Senate voted 55–45 to acquit Clinton of the perjury charge. It split 50–50 over whether he had obstructed justice, well short of the two-thirds necessary to convict.

Pardons

On his last day in office, Clinton issued 140 pardons and several commutations of sentences. The most controversial of these actions was his pardoning of Marc Rich, a commodities trader who had been indicted for tax evasion and illegal trading with Iran and who had fled the United States. Rich's former wife had donated heavily to the Clinton presidential library. Clinton also pardoned two people who had paid Hillary Clinton's brother for intervening on their behalf, and 16 members of the FALN, a Puerto Rican nationalist group that had carried out 120 bombings in the United States.

After the Presidency

In addition to establishing a presidential library and an accompanying public policy school, Clinton, through the foundation that bears his name, funds multiple efforts to make treatment of HIV and AIDS more affordable for millions of people across several continents. The Clinton Global Initiative, operating under the foundation, works to improve the quality of public health, reduce poverty, and resolve ethnic conflicts worldwide. Along with fellow former president George H. W. Bush, Clinton raised substantial sums of money to assist victims of the devastating tsunami that struck Indonesia in 2004 and residents of New Orleans in the aftermath of the 2005 Hurricane Katrina catastrophe.

Bill Clinton's presidency marked a period of transition. He served in the interval between the Cold War and what has become a struggle against international terrorism, waged by forces aligned with no particular nation or by rogue states. In his time, Clinton demonstrated that, after suffering three landslide defeats, the Democratic Party could be trusted to govern. He shed it of its reputation for bloated budgets, wasteful spending, and disregard of middle-class concerns. He also demonstrated that the United States could be a force for good in the world, without embarking on prolonged, unsustainable, and costly wars. Clinton tried but failed to

RELATED ENTRIES

THIS VOLUME
Clinton, Hillary Rodham; Democratic Party; Election of 1992; Impeachment of Bill Clinton; Presidency

develop a coherent and effective strategy to deter attacks upon American soil of the kind that transpired nine months after he left office.

Bibliography and Further Reading

Branch, Taylor. *The Clinton Tapes*. New York: Simon & Schuster, 2009.

Clinton, William Jefferson. *My Life*. New York: Vintage, 2005.

Dickenson, Matthew. "Bill Clinton." In *The American Presidency*, edited by Alan Brinkley and Davis Dyer, 499–529. Boston: Mariner Books, 2004.

Drew, Elizabeth. *On the Edge: The Clinton Presidency*. New York: Simon & Schuster, 1994.

Gillon, Steven M. *The Pact: Bill Clinton, Newt Gingrich, and the Rivalry that Defined a Generation*. New York: Oxford University Press, 2008.

Hamilton, Nigel. *Bill Clinton: Mastering the Presidency*. New York: Random House, 2003.

Harris, John F. *The Survivor: Bill Clinton in the White House*. New York: Random House, 2005.

Klein Joe. *The Natural: The Misunderstood Presidency of Bill Clinton*. New York: Broadway, 2003.

Maraniss, David. *First in His Class: A Biography of Bill Clinton*. New York: Simon & Schuster, 1996.

Stephanopoulos, George. *All Too Human: A Political Education*. Thorndike, ME: Thorndike Press, 1999.

Woodward, Bob. *The Choice*. New York: Simon & Schuster, 1999.

Alvin S. Felzenberg

CLINTON, HILLARY RODHAM

born 1947
First Lady, U.S. Senator, and Secretary of State

Hillary Rodham Clinton has risen higher than any other woman in American politics and has come to symbolize, for many women, the possibility of political equality. At a time of conservative ascendancy, she provided a powerful voice for governmental and social activism in health care, business regulation, and other areas. She played a major role in the administration of her husband, Pres. William Jefferson Clinton, including its controversies and its efforts to balance the liberal and moderate wings of the Democratic Party. An influential champion of the rights of women, she suffered personally as a result of her husband's infidelity and impeachment, but emerged politically strengthened to become the first female senator from New York. With Barack Obama, she gave Democratic primary voters a choice of historic firsts in 2008, and her support helped to secure the election of the nation's first African American president. In January 2009, President Obama appointed her secretary of state.

Early Life

Hillary Diane Rodham won her first election—as patrol captain in sixth grade—because of her reputation for standing up to her school's "most incorrigible" boys. (Clinton 12) Her parents had strong interests in politics and world affairs: her father, Hugh Rodham, espoused individual responsibility and initiative while her mother, Dorothy Howell Rodham, inculcated in her a concern for the needy and friendless. The future First Lady's political outlook was further shaped by a traditional Methodist insistence on improving the world and strong role models among her extended family and teachers.

Coming of age at the cusp of the turbulent 1960s, she took advantage of opportunities while still in high school to hear Martin Luther King Jr., Sen. Barry Goldwater, and the social activist Saul Alinsky. She campaigned for Goldwater in the 1964 presidential election.

From Goldwater to McCarthy

Enrolling at Wellesley College a year later, she was elected president of the campus Young Republicans. By 1968, her political outlook had changed enough that she campaigned for the liberal icon Eugene McCarthy in the Democratic presidential primaries. Her classmates and the Wellesley administration chose her to

make the college's first-ever student commencement speech. She attracted national media attention with remarks on student activism that were seen as a younger generation's dismissiveness toward authority, in this instance represented by her fellow speaker Sen. Edward Brooke of Massachusetts. She graduated from Yale Law School in 1973.

Working with organizations such as the American Civil Liberties Union (ACLU) and Children's Defense Fund during and after law school, she sought to advance social change in a variety of areas, including the legal rights of children. Such contacts led to a position on the staff of the House Judiciary Committee as it prepared the articles of impeachment against Pres. Richard Nixon, and to Pres. Jimmy Carter's naming her the first female chair of the Legal Services Corporation in 1978.

Having met at Yale, she and Bill Clinton married on October 11, 1975, while both were teaching law at the University of Arkansas in Fayetteville. As attorney general and later 12-year governor of Arkansas, Bill Clinton rose to become a leader of the moderate movement in the national Democratic Party. His wife played an important role in education reform and other policies, appointments, and political strategy both in Arkansas and in Washington. The two made an effective team; both were deeply interested in the details of policies that would expand and use the power of government to change society. Her discipline complemented the future president's keen political sense, and Democrats who saw Bill Clinton as too centrist could take comfort in her clearer embrace of left-leaning causes. The partnership would remain intact and effective despite periodic crises relating to his involvement with other women. When reports of Bill Clinton's marital infidelity threatened to derail his 1992 presidential campaign, Hillary Clinton's continued support helped her husband win the presidency in November.

The Most Influential First Lady

More than any other First Lady, Clinton was an influential voice in the administration's policy and personnel decisions. Though Edith Wilson had controlled most access to her husband, Pres. Woodrow Wilson, after his stroke, her influence lasted only eighteen months, and she served more as gatekeeper than decision maker. Eleanor Roosevelt influenced her husband, Pres. Franklin Delano Roosevelt, in numerous ways but did not carry the breadth of authority that Hillary Clinton did.

In early 1993, Hillary Clinton's role in deciding top-level appointments such as attorney general contributed to early controversies for the new administration when potential nominees had to withdraw for personal reasons. She then led the new president's efforts to establish a national health care plan that would have guaranteed coverage to all Americans and expanded the federal government's control over the health care sector. That initiative proved a political disaster, as critics and political opponents argued that proposed reliance on managed-care organizations would limit individuals' choices in health care and a mandate for coverage by employers would hamper economic growth. The Clinton initiative's failure contributed to the unexpected Republican takeover of the House of Representatives in the 1994 mid-term elections.

The Clintons' joint investments in a failed land development business, and Hillary Clinton's work for the politically connected Rose Law Firm in Arkansas, led to federal investigations both by independent federal prosecutors and by Congress. While those investigations produced no substantive charges, one probe resulted in her husband's sworn statements that a succeeding independent counsel and the House Judiciary Committee later declared to be perjury, leading to his impeachment in 1998. Responding to evidence that President Clinton had a sexual relationship with a young White House intern, the First Lady ascribed criticisms to a "vast right-wing conspiracy" that sought to drive her husband from office. Though these and other controversies contributed to political polarization in Washington and across the country, her popularity among liberal voters likely also played a role in the 1996 victory that made President Clinton the first Democrat since Franklin Delano Roosevelt to win reelection to the White House.

Though a variety of human-rights issues have driven her efforts, the cause of women's rights has been most prominent. In an address to the United Nations'

Fourth World Conference on Women in Beijing in September 1995, she criticized practices such as the killing of baby girls and the selling of girls into prostitution. Her admonition in that address that "Human rights are women's rights, and women's rights are human rights" has been cited widely in campaigns for women's political advancement internationally.

To the Senate, and to the Center

Although no First Lady had ever run for office and no woman had won a statewide election in New York, party leaders urged her to seek Daniel Patrick Moynihan's Senate seat after he announced plans for retirement in 2000. Benefiting from an ineffective campaign by her Republican opponent, Rick Lazio, she won 55–43 percent, faring well in suburban and upstate New York, centers of Republican strength. In 2006, she won reelection easily over weak opposition, taking 67 percent of the vote.

In the Senate, Clinton quickly earned a reputation for deference to more senior senators and for close attention to New York's more moderate-to-conservative upstate region. She worked with Republicans frequently—for example, with the conservative congressman Tom DeLay on care for foster children—yet she always maintained a strong Democratic voting record, with *Congressional Quarterly* party unity ratings in the mid- to high 90s. She consistently opposed the Bush administration in areas ranging from taxes to abortion rights, and referred to Pres. George W. Bush's domestic agenda as a "radical" effort to reverse the New Deal. Yet, as a member of the Senate Armed Services Committee, she supported much of the Bush administration's domestic and international response to the September 2001 terrorist attacks. In 2002, calling Iraqi President Saddam Hussein a potential threat, she voted in favor of a resolution empowering Pres. George W. Bush to take action against the Iraqi leader. She later criticized the management of the war, but Barack Obama and other opponents in the 2008 Democratic presidential primaries used her initial support to stir resentment from increasingly antiwar voters.

Given her wide visibility and popularity among female and liberal voters, the 2008 presidential primary

RELATED ENTRIES

THIS VOLUME
Clinton, Bill; Democratic Party; Election of 2008; Obama, Barack

campaign began with her as the first woman to be the early favorite—indeed, widely considered the presumptive nominee—of a major political party. Her early support of what had become a highly unpopular war, lingering distaste for various aspects of her husband's administration, a sometimes weak campaign, and Obama's sheer inspirational power sent more voters to the lesser-known candidate. Democratic primary voters' rejection of her in favor of a relatively inexperienced rival demonstrated the resurgence of a left-wing base that had been largely pushed aside during the successes of the Clinton administration as well as Obama's ability to reach out to African American and young voters. Her appointment as secretary of state in 2009 gave her a worldwide platform, although the Obama administration dispersed some important foreign-policy responsibilities to other high-level officials.

Hillary Rodham Clinton's career reflects a clear ideology—a belief in government's ability to bring dramatic improvements in social conditions—along with evolving understanding that many Americans distrust ideology and that the U.S. system of government can only change so far, so fast. Though her husband succeeded in pulling the Democratic Party toward the center, and the president whom she served as secretary of state has sought to move the nation back in the direction of more active government, Hillary Rodham Clinton's own political dreams remain not only unfulfilled but also in many ways unknown. Her unsurpassed star power, particularly among many women voters, make her a continuing force in American politics.

Bibliography and Further Reading

Bernstein, Carl. *A Woman in Charge: The Life of Hillary Rodham Clinton*. New York: Alfred A. Knopf, 2007.

Clinton, Hillary Rodham. *Living History*. New York: Simon & Schuster, 2003.

Gerth, Jeff, and Don Van Natta, Jr. *Her Way: The Hopes and Ambitions of Hillary Rodham Clinton*. New York: Little, Brown, 2007.

Milton, Joyce. *The First Partner: Hillary Rodham Clinton*. New York: William Morrow, 1999.

Tomasky, Michael. *Hillary's Turn: Inside Her Improbable, Victorious Senate Campaign*. New York: Simon & Schuster, 2001.

Robert B. Ward

COLD WAR, END OF

From 1985 to 1988, the Cold War began to thaw as the United States and the Soviet Union began negotiations to move away from heated rhetoric and nuclear arms buildup. Starting in 1989, newly elected president George H. W. Bush sought to move beyond the strategy of containment and seek the peaceful transfer of power in Eastern Europe. It was during Bush's administration that the Cold War ended, Germany was reunified, the Soviet Union collapsed, and the former Soviet Bloc countries began the transition to democracy and market economies.

Reagan and Gorbachev: The Cold War Thaws, 1985–1988

Selected as general secretary of the Communist Party in 1985, Mikhail Gorbachev represented a new generation of Soviet leaders. He sought to improve East-West foreign relations in order to free his energies and financial resources so that he could instead address pressing domestic problems. It was clear to Gorbachev that the stagnant Soviet economy could not continue to keep pace with U.S. defense spending. Meanwhile, and despite his administration's focus on heightened defense spending and stern rhetoric about the Soviet Union as "an evil empire," Pres. Ronald Reagan was determined to reach an arms control agreement with the Soviets. After his reelection in 1984, Reagan began making efforts to ease U.S.-Soviet tensions. At the 1985 Geneva Summit, Reagan and Gorbachev met and signed several cultural and scientific agreements and initiated arms limitation talks that eventually resulted in the Intermediate-Range Nuclear Forces (INF) Treaty of 1987, which eliminated intermediate-range nuclear forces and signaled the first step toward the eventual end of the arms race. Although the U.S.-Soviet relationship encountered a serious setback as the 1986 Reykjavik Summit ended with disagreement over Reagan's refusal to shelve his Strategic Defense Initiative (SDI), several actions by Gorbachev, including Soviet withdrawal from Afghanistan in 1988, indicated that there was still a chance for the Cold War to come to a peaceful conclusion.

Bush and Gorbachev: The End of the Cold War, 1988–1991

President Bush did not merely continue down the foreign policy path set by Reagan. Instead, he sought to shift the focus from arms control and decided to conduct a comprehensive review of U.S. policy toward the Soviet Union before any new agreements would be reached. Labeled "the pause" by some critics, the lengthy policy review ended with Bush's announcement of a new initiative to move beyond containment of Soviet expansionism. To that end, the president spent most of the summer of 1989 addressing the changes that were taking place in Central and Eastern Europe. Gorbachev had renounced the Brezhnev Doctrine, which provided the Soviet Union a rationale for intervening in the affairs of socialist countries. Now, Eastern European countries began to tentatively explore political changes. Worried that dramatic changes would lead to chaos and possibly a Soviet backlash, Bush did not urge ferment in Eastern Europe. Instead, he encouraged incremental reform at a pace not threatening to the Soviets. On November 9, 1989, East Germany relaxed its border-control policy with West Germany, thus allowing East German citizens to travel back and forth to the West. Crowds began to form along the Berlin Wall and, after an initial period of confusion, people began to pour into West Berlin. Though Bush received news of the fall of the Berlin Wall with much personal pleasure, in public he expressed caution. He feared that a Western celebration of the wall's collapse might encourage a backlash by hard-liners in East Berlin and Moscow. In December 1989, during a historic meeting in Malta, Bush sought to make sure that the Soviet Union was indeed committed to building cooperation rather than

in continuing confrontation. Bush used the new U.S.-Soviet relationship that he had forged at Malta to gain Soviet acceptance of a unified Germany within NATO. The reunification of Germany within NATO, in conjunction with the withdrawal of Soviet troops in Eastern Europe, marked the end of the division of Europe and, arguably, the Cold War.

The Collapse of the Soviet Union

The new relationship between the United States and the Soviet Union was evident during the Persian Gulf War (1990–1991) when the Bush administration was able to garner Soviet support for U.N. resolutions against Iraq. This relationship was jeopardized in August 1991 as a coup attempt led by hard-liners sought to remove Gorbachev from power. The coup collapsed, thanks to determined maneuverings of Russian president Boris Yeltsin, who organized protest demonstrations and declared the coup illegal, and Bush, who orchestrated international pressure against the coup leaders and called for a restoration of the legitimate government. Although Gorbachev resumed control of the Soviet Union, his power continued to weaken over the next several months as Yeltsin argued that the republics should have greater autonomy. Only after Yeltsin and other republic leaders reached agreement on a commonwealth of fully independent countries and called Bush to ask for his support did Yeltsin call Gorbachev to inform him of what had been decided. A furious Gorbachev relinquished his duties as president and the U.S.S.R. came to an end on December 25, 1991.

Although the end of the Cold War was seen by most U.S. political leaders as a triumph, the future became less certain. What became increasingly more likely was that there were not going to be any easy answers, no grand strategy, no further counting "on power and legitimacy to preserve traditional stability." (Brzezinski 179) For political leaders who had been hard-wired for the bipolar world of Cold War strategy, the new complexities and realities of a multipolar world proved difficult to grasp. This uncertainty became evident as Pres. Bill Clinton and then Pres. George W. Bush pondered how to react to terrorists that acted on behalf of no state, but rather in support of a militant anti-Americanism infused with religious zeal. The only post–Cold War certitude was the existence of revived political debates about America's world role.

Bibliography and Further Reading

Baker, James A., III, with Thomas M. DeFrank. *The Politics of Diplomacy: Revolution, War & Peace, 1989–1992.* New York: Putnam's, 1995.

Brzezinski, Zbigniew. *Second Chance: Three American Presidents and the Crisis of American Superpower.* New York: Basic Books, 2007.

Bush, George, and Brent Scowcroft. *A World Transformed.* New York: Alfred A. Knopf, 1998.

Matlock, Jack F. *Reagan and Gorbachev: How the Cold War Ended.* New York: Random House, 2004.

Maynard, Christopher. *Out of the Shadow: George H. W. Bush and the End of the Cold War.* College Station: Texas A&M University Press, 2008.

Oberdorfer, Don. *From the Cold War to a New Era: The United States and the Soviet Union, 1983–1991.* Baltimore, MD: Johns Hopkins University Press, 1998.

Zelikow, Philip, and Condoleezza Rice. *Germany Unified and Europe Transformed: A Study in Statecraft.* Cambridge, MA: Harvard University Press, 1995.

Christopher Maynard

CONGRESS

The U.S. Congress in the mid-1970s underwent tremendous transformation and reform. The institution experienced some changes in the partisan control of its chambers, switching several times into the first decade of the twenty-first century. This "post-reform Congress"—as Congress after the early-1970s is sometimes referred to—was transitioning from control over its legislative agenda by conservative committee chairs, mainly from Southern states, to a period during which power was diffused both to more junior rank-and-file lawmakers and to party leaders. All the while, Congress was struggling to maintain its influence over the legislative agenda with presidents that were, for most of the period, of the opposing party.

Elections and the Composition of Congress

By the mid-1970s, Congress had reached the end of what had been a fairly lengthy process of internal and external reorganization. Building off the liberal political mood of the late 1960s and early 1970s, Democrats were able to erect sizeable majorities in both chambers through the end of the decade. However, dissatisfaction with Pres. Jimmy Carter's legislative record, poor economic conditions, and the Iran hostage crisis resulted in the Democratic Party losing control of both the presidency and the Senate in the 1980 election. This ushered in a rare instance of split partisan control of the two chambers of Congress. Following the relatively common occurrence of a backlash to the president's party in midterm elections, Republican Pres. Ronald Reagan lost his majority in the Senate during the 1986 elections, and Democrats would retain control of both chambers throughout George H. W. Bush's presidency. Two tumultuous years in Congress started the Clinton presidency, which along with a number of well-publicized scandals involving Democrats helped to bring about the simultaneous takeover of both chambers by the G.O.P. after the 1994 election. Republican control of Congress existed with only a brief interruption in 2001–2002 in the Senate, until the 2006 election when Democrats won majorities in both chambers and significantly widened those majorities on the coattails of Barack Obama's election in 2008. With Sen. Arlen Specter switching his party affiliation from Republican to Democratic in the spring of 2009, and the settlement of the close Senate race in Minnesota, Democrats enjoyed a filibuster-proof majority of 60 lawmakers.

However, shifts in majority control of Congress are only a piece of the partisan story. In the late twentieth and early twenty-first centuries, Congress was increasingly being defined by the growing ideological gulf between the members of the two parties. This ideological polarization was in part a result of the gradual disappearance of moderate elements in both political parties. Slowly, the number of congressional seats held by Democrats in almost every Southern state—as of 1951, Democrats controlled 98 percent of House seats and 100 percent of Senate seats in the South—were being turned over to either conservative Republicans, who had found a new footing among like-minded voters, or to more liberal, often African American, Democrats. Reagan's election in 1980 propelled an expansion of conservative Republicans in Congress that culminated with the enormous strides that Rep. Newt Gingrich (R–GA) fostered in Southern congressional districts to engineer majority control of Congress in the 1994 election. For the first time ever, Republicans controlled a majority of House seats in the South.

At the same time, moderate Northeastern Republicans, once a sizeable portion of the G.O.P. coalition, were experiencing a similar transformation. Their seats were largely being won by Democrats, thereby whittling away at the more moderate wing of the Republican Party in both chambers of Congress. In fact, the election of 2008 saw the last remaining Republican-held New England House seat fall to the Democrats. By some accounts, the ideological divide between the two major parties in Congress at the end of the first decade of the twenty-first century is as wide as it has been in over a century.

Along with the partisan and ideological shift in Congress came changes in the body's demographics. One consequence of the social movements of the 1960s was an expansion in the number of minorities and women in Congress. From just a handful of African Americans and women in the late 1960s, by the first decade of the twenty-first century almost 10 percent of the House was African American and over 15 percent of both chambers was made up of female lawmakers. When the Democrats gained control of Congress after the 2006 election, they elected the first female Speaker of the House, Nancy Pelosi (D–CA).

Changes to Congressional Structure and Rules

Despite the introduction of a new set of reformist lawmakers in Congress in the late 1960s, existing rules and norms in Congress—tight control of committee activities by chairs, deference to more senior lawmakers—made it difficult for these independent-minded, activist lawmakers to pursue their policy goals. To effect change in public policy, rank-and-file members had first to alter both the rules of Congress and the rules of their own party. For the most part, this meant making changes within the Democratic Party, which had, with only brief interruptions, controlled both chambers of Congress since the 1930s.

Under way since the mid-1960s, the reform process had the overall effect of breaking what had long been an authoritarian control over issue jurisdictions by very senior, very electorally secure, and often very socially conservative committee chairs. The changes both redistributed influence down to the rank-and-file through expanded subcommittee rights to consider and report legislation, as well as greater delegation of authority over the global agenda to the party leadership. Almost immediately, the House experienced its first major cracks in the old seniority system of granting committee chairs to the member with the longest continuous service on the panel. In 1975, propelled by a large freshman class of House Democrats, the majority caucus turned out three long-serving committee chairs. This action put all committee chairs on notice that the old system of committee fiefdoms would no longer be tolerated. The results of the reform effort were new rules bringing about a more open process of selection of committee chairs, the mandated referral of bills to subcommittees, "sunshine rules" designed to allow greater public scrutiny of congressional operations, and a fairer system of assigning members to committees.

Perhaps the most prominent changes to congressional procedures in the 1980s came in reaction to the mounting federal deficit driven by massive tax cuts initiated by President Reagan. In response, Congress enacted what appeared to be significant constraints on federal spending through the Gramm-Rudman-Hollings Balanced Budget Act. The measure was meant to put a cap on federal spending and eventually lead to a balanced federal budget. However, without hard rules to compel lawmakers to limit spending, such restrictions turned out to be largely ineffective.

The takeover of control by Republicans in 1995 allowed Gingrich to use his large cadre of loyal G.O.P. backbenchers to solidify his position as Speaker of the House and rewrite several key chamber rules to further consolidate control of the legislative agenda in the party leadership. The changes allowed party leaders to subsume the power to appoint committee chairs (the likes of which had not been seen since the early twentieth century), institute committee chair term limits to prevent the creation of policy fiefdoms, and control the hierarchy and workings of the critical Appropriation Committee.

The most significant change to House rules after the Democrats regained control in 2007 was the elimination two years later of term-limits on committee chairs. Democrats claimed that chair term-limits contributed to an environment of excessive campaigning for plum chairmanships among majority caucus lawmakers. It was also the case that term-limits were opposed by Democratic leaders, particularly those most affected by the limitation to their powers—existing committee chairs.

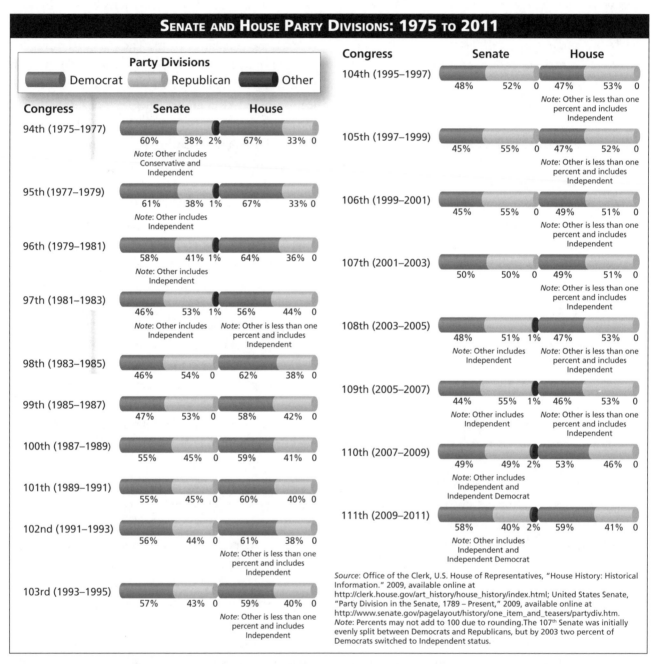

Although during the mid- to late 1970s Congress was controlled by the Democrats, the early 1980s saw split partisan control, with a Republican-dominated Senate and a Democratic-dominated House. The Democrats regained power by the late 1980s, but the mid-1990s found the Republicans ruling both chambers by a small margin for the majority of the period until the One Hundred Eleventh Congress ushered in Democratic control once again.

Unlike the House, the Senate had always operated with a fairly great degree of consensus. This had sometimes resulted in the death of important legislation due to the inability of bill proponents in the Senate to put together super-majority coalitions to overcome a filibuster. After years of attempting to make changes to the modern use of filibusters in the Senate, Democrats, in 1975, were able to change the number of votes required to invoke cloture (that is, to end debate or a filibuster) from two-thirds to three-fifths. This was significant at the time, inasmuch as Democrats held a 61-seat majority and even managed to expand their majority by one seat in the 1976 election. In 2009, the Democrats reached the 60-member mark again after the defection of Sen. Arlen Specter (PA) from the Republican Party and the end of litigation regarding the Minnesota Senate seat won by Al Franken.

Filibusters also underwent a transformation in the 1980s. The modern equivalent of the filibuster, the relatively anonymous "hold" that can be placed on legislation by an objecting lawmaker, became far more common as a dilatory and obstructionist tactic. No longer were senators compelled to engage in unending speeches on the Senate floor in order to block consideration of a bill. Once a filibuster was threatened, bill supporters would immediately seek the votes to invoke cloture. By the turn of the century, cloture votes would become the norm for getting controversial business done in the Senate and the number of cloture motions filed jumped dramatically.

Relations with the President and Policy Output

Throughout the history of the contemporary Congress there have been periods of ebb and flow in the relative strength of the president and Congress to control the policy agenda. Because much of this period is characterized by divided government—different parties controlling the presidency and one or both chambers of Congress—the struggle frequently comes down to the party of Congress attempting to resist the efforts of the presidential administration, with occasional instances of cooperation on particular issues or during times of crisis.

Many of the liberal Democratic lawmakers elected in the late 1960s and early 1970s were not elected on the coattails or beholden to the agenda of a same-party president. To the contrary, they were elected to fight against the political establishment both in terms of a conservative Republican president (Richard Nixon) and a similarly conservative Democratic Party power structure in Congress. The large cadre of "Young Turks" within the Democratic ranks, many of whom had their own thoughts about congressional priorities, resulted in President Carter's difficulties in winning congressional support for a number of his top-priority policy agendas, such as health care and welfare reform. On the other hand, when the Democratic Congress and president did come together to alter federal policy, many of their major efforts had the effect of shrinking rather than enlarging the role of government. These measures included deregulation of transportation industries and banking institutions, and relaxation of clean air and clean water measures. Alternatively, Congress and Carter also enacted a number of more liberal-leaning laws, such as a comprehensive energy package, expansion of food stamps, overhauls of Social Security and civil service, and toxic waste cleanup.

The unbroken chain of Democratic control of both chambers in Congress that had existed since 1955 and that had been a significant factor in the enactment of many important social and economic programs of the 1960s and 1970s ended in 1980. Reagan's election that year also brought with it a Republican majority in the Senate and a distinct conservative agenda to cut government programs and spending. Thus, the work of Congress in the early years of Reagan's administration was largely dominated by substantial tax cuts and a reprioritization of the federal budget away from government regulation and toward increased defense spending. Though the Democrats in the House resisted the severity of Reagan's initial tax cut proposals, enough concessions were made that a more than sufficient number of Democratic defectors in both chambers voted in favor of the Reagan budget and tax plans.

The disappearance of the centrist elements of both parties in the 1980s fostered more homogeneous party caucuses in Congress and stronger leadership on both sides of the partisan aisle. Speaker Tip O'Neill

(D–MA), working with a party that was composed of far fewer conservative Southern Democrats, was able to maintain tighter control over the agenda and to ensure that his party worked better as a unit than it had two decades earlier. As a result, by the mid-1980s, O'Neill was able to rally congressional Democrats to reassert their own agenda, first with a slowing of budget cuts and then measures that increased taxes, as well as a shoring-up of the Social Security system and an extension of the Voting Rights Act. Later, in Reagan's second term, as the administration was bogged down in the Iran-Contra scandal and wrangling over the deficit, Congress took advantage of the weakened president to cut large amounts of Reagan's proposed defense budget and the planned intercontinental MX missile, initiate tax reform and immigration reform, extend the Clean Water Act (even over President Reagan's veto), expand the superfund toxic waste cleanup program, and block much of Reagan's social agenda, such as efforts to permit prayer in public schools.

Perhaps more than any other factor influencing the legislative accomplishments of Congress during the one-term presidency of George H. W. Bush was the recession that took hold in the first few months of 1989. To bring government spending in line with revenues and reach agreement on a deficit reduction package with the Democrat-controlled Congress, Bush had to break his campaign pledge of no new taxes. With some significant exceptions—for instance, the rewriting of the Clean Air Act and the creation of the Americans with Disabilities Act of 1990—Congress had little interest in pursuing items on Bush's domestic agenda. Most of the political accomplishments during his presidency occurred in the realm of national security and foreign policy: the dissolution of the Soviet Union, a successful war to drive Iraqi forces out of Kuwait, and the democratizing of regimes in Central America and South Africa.

Though Bill Clinton entered office in 1992 with Democrats in control of both chambers of Congress, high expectations for policy accomplishments quickly evaporated and Republicans soon took control of both chambers. The first Clinton Congress did see several legislative successes, however, including the ratification of the North American Free Trade Agreement (NAFTA), a deficit reduction measure that included a tax increase, the Family and Medical Leave Act of 1993, and controls on handguns. However, the legislative record of Congress during the first two years of the Clinton administration is probably better known for what did *not* happen rather than for what did. The failure of the administration's health care initiative was partially grounded in the fragmented jurisdictions of Congress's committees and the desire of its many chairs to have a say in the legislation's future. Forces aligned against health care reform used the decentralized power structure to neutralize any momentum Clinton had to bring about meaningful changes to health policy.

This failure was an important part of the Republican strategy to wrest control of Congress from the Democrats in the 1994 midterm elections. Representative Newt Gingrich, the emerging leader of a more conservative and confrontational wing of the Republican Party, sought to define the Republican legislative agenda before the 1994 election with his manifesto, the "Contract with America." The document was a set of 10 policy goals intended to shrink and reform government, to which nearly all Republican House candidates had pledged their support. With Democratic legislative stumbles, a number of well-publicized scandals and embarrassments involving prominent Democratic lawmakers, and the Contract, Republicans were able to turn the national electoral tide against the majority party. The Democrats lost 54 seats in the House, 8 seats in the Senate, and majority control of both.

The new Republican-controlled Congress in 1995 entered with a political agenda defined through the Gingrich Contract and a perceived mandate to shift policy in a decidedly conservative direction. Within the first 100 days, the House had passed nearly all 10 of these agenda items that included provisions such as a statute to balance the federal budget and the curbing of unfunded mandates to states. However, progress on many of these proposals stalled in the more cautious Senate, where the "Contract with America" had fewer supporters. Only the least controversial measures—increased congressional accountability, reductions in federal bureaucracy, and limitations on unfunded mandates to state and local governments among them—were deemed acceptable to the Senate.

Gingrich's consolidation of a cohesive Republican leadership led to a number of policy successes and even some agreements with the Clinton administration, including welfare and telecommunications reform, a measure assisting workers in retaining insurance coverage, and an overhaul of the IRS. However, Republican unity and the strength of the Gingrich speakership began to crumble in the winter of 1995–1996, when a showdown with Clinton over budget bills led to two government shutdowns. Most polls showed that Americans blamed Gingrich and the Republicans in Congress for the gridlock, not Clinton. Gingrich's tenure as Speaker abruptly ended immediately following the 1998 election, as Republicans continued to hemorrhage seats in the House.

In an effort to provide stability and less controversy to the House Republican leadership, Dennis Hastert, an unassuming conservative lawmaker from Illinois, was tapped to become Speaker. Hastert maintained a low profile but presided over a House that was equally as partisan and contentious as that under his predecessor. As a rule, Hastert would refuse to bring forward any bill that did not have the support of a majority of Republicans.

The acrimony and confrontations between the Republican-controlled Congress and Clinton reached a crescendo in 1998 when the Republican leaders in Congress attempted to remove the president from office through impeachment over the circumstances surrounding his extramarital affair with a White House intern and the subsequent effort at cover up. Though Republicans were able to garner the necessary majority in the House to bring forward the articles of impeachment, a clear lack of public support for the effort prevented them from mustering even a simple majority in the Senate for conviction on the perjury charges. (A two-thirds majority is constitutionally required for conviction.) Despite these political confrontations, lawmakers were able to complete some major legislation in the last two years of the Clinton presidency, including financial services reforms and a relaxation of restrictions on trade with China.

Even in the aftermath of the contentious 2000 election, Congress was able to enact a number of important measures. And despite festering partisan tension, the majority Republicans were able to gain a significant number of Democratic votes to pass two of Pres. George W. Bush's legislative priorities—a major reform of elementary education and a tax cut. An opportunity for the Democrats to reassert their agenda emerged in June 2001 when then-Republican senator James Jeffords (VT) bolted from the party and began to caucus with the Democrats, thereby swinging control of the chamber in their direction. However, the terrorist attacks of 9/11 ended any effort by either party to control the political agenda and led to a period of security-oriented legislation largely characterized by bipartisanship. Such statutes included the anti-terrorism measure, the USA PATRIOT Act, as well as the creation of the Department of Homeland Security, and the resolution to use military force in Iraq. However, as the military efforts in Iraq wore on and the underlying partisan division reemerged, the number of policy areas where Democrats and Republicans in Congress were willing to work together diminished. Large Bush agenda items —Social Security and immigration reforms, and an overhaul of the alternative minimum tax—went nowhere in Congress. After the Democrats took control of Congress at the start of 2007, they did enact a number of important legislative changes, including an increase in the minimum wage and a reduction of the federal student loan rate. However, many of the major items in their program—such as an expansion of children's health insurance and a timetable for removal of troops from Iraq—would have to wait until after the 2008 presidential elections.

The election of Barack Obama presaged an opening of new opportunities for the Democrats to put their imprint on federal policy. Among the early actions by Congress were an expansion of children's health insurance, a monumental economic stimulus package to address the most severe economic downturn since the Depression, and the confirmation of the first Latina to the Supreme Court (Sonia Sotomayor). However, completion of the signature agenda item of the term and of the young Obama administration—health care reform—still looms on the horizon.

Ethics Issues

Lawmakers have long made headlines with their ethical lapses and personal scandals (for example, Adam Clayton Powell Jr. in late 1960s, and Abscam in the early 1980s), and these have often affected the public image of Congress. But by the 1980s, this phenomenon had undergone a notable shift with the ever-widening partisan divisions that developed in Congress and the opportunity to use personal scandal for political gain. As Gingrich and his group of conservative allies sought a wider array of strategies to gain a larger foothold in the House, they employed the tactic of hammering away on questions about the ethics of the Democratic leadership. Eventually, Speaker Jim Wright (D–TX) was forced to resign in 1989 over a number of questionable financial dealings—the only speaker to have been forced from office due to scandal. Almost simultaneously, Democratic Majority Whip Tony Coelho (D–CA) resigned under a cloud of suspicion regarding controversial personal investments. Hot on the heels of these scandals were revelations that hundreds of lawmakers would routinely overdraw their House bank accounts, and even the House post office was embroiled in its own scandal over money laundering and drug dealing. The relatively short span in which these scandals unfolded eventually served as fodder for Republicans eager to impugn the long-standing and complacent Democratic majority in Congress and assisted in Republican gains in the 1992 and 1994 elections.

Eventually, the politics of public scandal came back to haunt Speaker Gingrich, whom the House voted overwhelmingly to reprimand for ethics violations in 1997. It was the first time in the history of the chamber that a Speaker had been disciplined for ethical wrongdoing. Gingrich's ethical lapses were a significant contributing factor to his diminished leadership abilities, and the Republican losses in the 1998 election were the final straw—Gingrich resigned from both the speaker-ship and his congressional seat soon after the election. G.O.P. leadership fared no better in the immediate aftermath of the Gingrich downfall as the heir-apparent, Rep. Robert Livingston (R–LA), the conservative chair of the House Appropriations Committee, was also forced to resign over revelations of an extramarital affair. Livingston attempted to use his own resignation as an inducement for President Clinton to do the same over his affair with Monica Lewinsky, but to no avail. Attacks on the personal ethics of congressional leaders as a political strategy have continued into the twenty-first century, ensnaring powerful leaders such as House majority leader Rep. Tom Delay (R–TX), who was forced to step down in 2005.

The contemporary U.S. Congress is a somewhat different legislative body than it was 40 years ago. Though structurally the legislature is largely the same, the locus of power and the process of legislative production have shifted. No longer is it the case that committees command the lion's share of authority to determine the legislative agenda and hammer out the details of policy output. Parties and their leadership play a much more significant role in congressional operations and wide divisions in ideology and policy priorities have come to define both congressional proceedings and executive-legislative relations.

Bibliography and Further Reading

Binder, Sarah. *Stalemate: Causes and Consequences of Legislative Gridlock*. Washington, D.C.: Brookings Institution Press, 2003.

Hibbing, John, and Elizabeth Theiss-Morse. *Congress as Public Enemy: Public Attitudes toward American Political Institutions*. New York: Cambridge University Press, 1995.

Mayhew, David. *Divided We Govern: Party Control, Lawmaking, and Investigations 1946–2002*. New Haven, CT: Yale University Press, 2005.

Poole, Keith T., and Howard Rosenthal. *Ideology and Congress*. Piscataway, NJ: Transaction Publishers, 2007.

Quirk, Paul J., and Sarah A. Binder, eds. *Institutions of American Democracy: The Legislative Branch*. New York: Oxford University Press, 2006.

Rohde, David. *Parties and Leaders in the Postreform House*. Chicago: University of Chicago Press, 1991.

Sinclair, Barbara. *Unorthodox Lawmaking: New Legislative Processes in the U.S. Congress*, 3rd edition. Washington, D.C.: Congressional Quarterly Press, 2007.

Theriault, Sean M. *Party Polarization in Congress.* New York: Cambridge University Press, 2008.

Zelizer, Julian E. *On Capitol Hill: The Struggle to Reform Congress and Its Consequences, 1948–2000.* New York: Cambridge University Press, 2006.

E. Scott Adler

CONSERVATISM

Conservatism in contemporary American politics and society is an ideology grounded in support of both limited government involvement in the economy and vigorous use of state power to promote, uphold, and when necessary enforce proper codes of personal morality and behavior. The American conservative of the late twentieth and early twenty-first century possesses a strong faith in the ability of the market to appropriately direct economic affairs and an equally strong belief that government must use its coercive power to foster and induce proper personal behavior on the part of individuals. The contemporary American conservative also has good reason to be quite pleased: since 1980, conservatism has enormously influenced national, state, and local politics.

The Origins of Contemporary Conservatism

In some ways, conservatism has a long history in the United States. Certainly one can find conservative elements in the thought of many of the Founding Fathers—John Adams, Alexander Hamilton, and James Madison, to name but a few—and a reverence for tradition and the nation's past have long been part of America's national psyche. And if one wanted to point to the most politically conservative period in American history, one would be hard pressed to make a more appropriate choice than the years between 1921 and 1933 when three consecutive Republican presidents (Warren Harding, Calvin Coolidge, and Herbert Hoover) presided over a 12-year period of extremely limited government activity. But contemporary American conservatism is somewhat different than what came before it. To fully understand the conservatism of

today, we must turn to a period that many would consider the ideology's nadir in the United States—the end of World War II through the early 1960s.

To many observers, the immediate post–World War II era appeared to be the ultimate (and perhaps final) triumph of liberalism. Franklin Roosevelt and his fellow Democrats had dramatically expanded the size and scope of the federal government with the New Deal, and heavy federal government involvement in the economic realm was now viewed by many Americans as normal and beneficial. American involvement in and the outcome of World War II established the United States as perhaps the central figure in world affairs, a development that was also accepted, if not embraced, by a good deal of American society. Even the Republican Party— the party on the losing end during the New Deal era and the instrument of conservatism in the 1920s— appeared to be accepting of these changes. Thus the two central pillars of 1920s American conservatism—a laissez-faire approach to the domestic economy and rabid isolationism—appeared to have been widely discredited in less than twenty-five years. It is almost impossible to overstate the dramatic nature of these changes. Liberalism appeared to reign supreme.

Yet appearances can be deceiving, and even as liberals were convinced of their ideological victory a somewhat altered version of conservatism was slowly mounting a comeback. This revitalization of conservatism was fueled in part by economic arguments, in particular by economists who criticized the heavy government involvement of Keynesian economics and argued instead for a return to a reliance on free markets. The Austrian scholar Friedrich Hayek's *The Road to Serfdom* (1944) and the American economist Milton Friedman's *Capitalism and Freedom* (1962) are two of the most well known examples of works that argued that high levels of government involvement in the economy would ultimately result in the loss of freedom. Both books were widely read, and still today are part of the conservative canon in the United States.

The resurgence of conservatism had a political element as well. As early as 1937, a number of Southern Democrats in Congress banded together with some Republican members to create what came to be known as the Conservative Coalition, a bloc of legislators who were increasingly opposed to and also increasingly successful at blocking some of the more liberal proposals of the Roosevelt administration. Despite being thoroughly trounced by FDR in 1932, former Pres. Herbert Hoover did not withdraw from public life. Indeed, Hoover outlived Roosevelt by almost twenty years, and throughout the entirety of those years Hoover was a frequent and harsh public critic of New Deal liberalism. The think tank he started even before his presidency—the Hoover Institution, housed at Stanford University—would become an important resource in resuscitating conservatism in America. The American Enterprise Institute, founded in 1943 but rising to prominence in the 1950s, was another conservative think tank that was crucial in the dissemination of conservative ideas and that also served to bring together a critical mass of conservative intellectuals to contribute to the movement. Finally, the *National Review*, established by the conservative icon William F. Buckley in 1955, provided a national outlet for the presentation of conservative views and a space for conservative dialogue. All of these political elements of the new conservatism were in agreement that the federal government had grown much too large, and that liberty was at risk as a result.

Reliance on free markets and support for limited government were, of course, not new to American conservatism. Both ideas had long histories in the conservative tradition in the United States. But the resurgent conservatism of the postwar era did add one new component to the mix: virulent anticommunism and a willingness to be actively involved in international affairs in order to combat the "red menace." As noted above, American conservatism before World War II was staunchly isolationist and wanted to severely limit the nation's involvement in events beyond its borders. Conservatives of the postwar era went to the opposite extreme. They believed that it was the responsibility of the United States to confront communism anywhere and everywhere it appeared across the globe. Communism was a grave threat to American liberty, and thus must be thwarted by any means necessary, including the use of America's military might. The United States as a muscular, aggressive superpower was a crucial element of the conservative rebirth after World War II.

Barry Goldwater: Father of Contemporary Conservatism

As the 1950s drew to a close, American conservatism was defined by a fervent faith in free markets, a strong desire for limited government (especially at the federal level), and rabid anticommunism. Though still a minority viewpoint in the United States, it was also clear that conservatism was on an upswing. One man brought together all of these elements of conservatism and presented them to society for public consumption and discussion, and in the course of doing so likely did more than any other single individual to advance the cause of conservatism in late twentieth and early twenty-first century America. That man was Arizona senator Barry Goldwater.

Goldwater was a cocky military pilot, a new breed of politician from the still-untamed and rapidly expanding American West. He was defiant in his conservatism, and made no apologies for his views regarding destroying the Soviet Union (perhaps with nuclear weapons) or gutting the New Deal. Goldwater was a brusque, aggressive, no-nonsense politician adamant about the necessity of reducing the size of the federal government and eliminating the global communist threat. Goldwater's statement of conservative principles, *The Conscience of a Conservative* (1960), in many ways served as the manifesto of the new conservatism. This work has remained central to American conservatism to the present day.

Goldwater appealed to conservatives across the United States. But he scared many others, including many of the moderates and liberals who controlled the Republican Party. These individuals were appalled when Goldwater won the Republican nomination for president in 1964, and many hoped that the conservative takeover of the G.O.P. that Goldwater's candidacy represented would be a temporary development. Those holding such a hope would in the end be disappointed. Barry Goldwater lost badly in the 1964 presidential election, suffering one of the worst defeats in American history. But in so doing Goldwater pointed the way for future conservative growth and success. In 1964, conservatives took control of the Republican Party. They have yet to relinquish it.

Conservatism after Goldwater: Success Achieved

Richard Nixon was certainly paying attention to the growth of the conservative movement within both the Republican Party and American society as a whole. He noted Goldwater's (and also George Wallace's) popularity in the South and the West. Republican success in these areas—especially the South—represented a shift in the party's center of gravity, a shift that was due in large part to the growing importance of conservatism. Certainly, some of this newfound success had to do with Goldwater's opposition to federal government involvement in civil rights for African Americans, but conservatism's appeal was based on more than race. Desires for lower taxes and reduced government involvement in individuals' affairs were also crucial, as were a renewed emphasis on law-and-order and support for an aggressive foreign policy to defeat communism. Nixon clearly incorporated conservative views and themes into his presidential campaigns in 1968 and 1972, and though he might not have always governed as a conservative, it was clear that he realized that he needed the support of conservatives. Conservatives, however, were never completely comfortable with Nixon, and longed to get one of their own, a certified true believer, into the White House. The presidential election of 1980 would grant them this wish.

Ronald Reagan was an early convert to the postwar conservative resurgence. He was a regular speaker at conservative events throughout the 1950s and early 1960s, and it was a 1964 speech in support of Goldwater that launched Reagan to national prominence as a politician rather than as an actor. When Reagan won the presidency in 1980, American conservatism claimed control of the executive branch. As the noted conservative columnist George Will remarked after Reagan's win, Barry Goldwater had finally won the presidency, just 16 years after he had first run for the office.

Although there is clearly some truth to Will's observation, he was not entirely correct, either. Reagan's conservatism did embody the same belief in free markets, desire to shrink government, and militant anticommunism that marked the conservatism of Goldwater. But Reagan also represented one important addition to the ideology, the final piece that would result in the American conservatism of the current period. That piece is often labeled social or cultural conservatism and is composed of strong support for the use of state power to enforce proper codes of moral conduct. This final element is firmly rooted in religious, mostly Christian, conservative groups in the United States, and it is impossible to fully comprehend the substance of or the success of conservatism in the contemporary American context without taking into account this religious element.

Implications of the Rise of Conservatism

Though the election of Ronald Reagan as president in 1980 did in many ways represent the ultimate breakthrough of the conservatism of the period, by no means did conservatism's rise cease or even peak with Reagan. Since 1980, conservatives have only tightened their grip on the Republican Party. Republican Party activists are now overwhelmingly conservative. Republicans in Congress are more conservative now than perhaps ever before, and the ideological division between conservative Republicans and liberal Democrats has become the dominant division in both the House and the Senate. All Republican presidential candidates since Reagan have taken great pains to present themselves as true conservatives, and even the one successful Democratic presidential candidate from 1980–2004, Bill Clinton, went to great lengths to assure voters that he was not an old school liberal, declaring that "the era of big government is over" and promising to "end welfare as we know it."

Many conservatives initially viewed George W. Bush's victory in the 2000 presidential election as a prime opportunity to finally implement the full range of their policy goals, and during the early part of Bush's first term such views seemed warranted. Bush was able to enact large tax cuts, achieve substantial deregulation of financial markets, and rollback many environmental regulations that conservatives believed were onerous to business and representative of unjustified governmental meddling. His unambiguous public support for policies such as a constitutional

RELATED ENTRIES

THIS VOLUME
Neoconservatives; Republican Party

amendment banning abortion (with the possibility of some limited exceptions) and a constitutional amendment banning same-sex marriage led many social conservatives to believe that they were extremely close to achieving some of their most important goals. Bush's foreign policy in the post–9/11 world also pleased conservatives, especially the so-called neoconservatives, who were particularly supportive of strong American military involvement—unilaterally, if necessary—around the globe. Some events later in the Bush administration—in particular the establishment of the Medicare Part D prescription drug benefit and mounting federal deficits—disheartened conservatives, and the victory of the Democrat Barack Obama in the 2008 presidential election caused some conservatives to openly worry about the future of their movement. But even with such setbacks, the years of the late twentieth and early twenty-first centuries were good ones for American conservatives.

These conservative successes served to dramatically increase the relevance of ideology in contemporary American politics. Ideology became important in individuals' party identification and vote choice, with conservatives siding with the Republicans and liberals supporting the Democratic Party. Ideology also permeated almost all areas of partisan conflict in contemporary American politics, something that had never happened before. It was central to American politics, and in the clash of ideologies one can easily make the case that by the opening years of the twenty-first century conservatism had come out on top. In fact, conservatism—defined by a reliance on free markets, a belief in limited government in many areas, an aggressive foreign policy, and a willingness to use the power of the state to enforce proper moral behavior—was arguably more powerful in late twentieth and early twenty-first century America than it ever had been before in American history.

Bibliography and Further Reading

Abramowitz, Alan, and Kyle Saunders. "Ideological Realignment in the U.S. Electorate." *Journal of Politics* 60, no. 3 (August 1998): 634–652.

Berlet, Chip, and Matthew N. Lyons. *Right-Wing Populism in America: Too Close for Comfort.* New York: Guilford Press, 2000.

Brewer, Mark D. "The Rise of Partisanship and the Expansion of Partisan Conflict within the American Electorate." *Political Research Quarterly* 58, no. 2 (June 2005): 219–229.

Layman, Geoffrey C. *The Great Divide: Religious and Cultural Conflicts in American Party Politics.* New York: Columbia University Press, 2001.

Layman, Geoffrey C., and Thomas M. Carsey. "Party Polarization and Party Structuring of Policy Attitudes: A Comparison of Three NES Panel Studies." *Political Behavior* 24, no. 3 (September 2002): 199–236.

———. "Party Polarization and Conflict Extension in the American Electorate." *American Journal of Political Science* 46, no. 4 (October 2002): 786–802.

Micklethwait, John, and Adrian Wooldridge. *The Right Nation: Conservative Power in America.* New York: Penguin Press, 2004.

Patterson, James T. *Congressional Conservatism and the New Deal: The Growth of the Conservative Coalition in Congress, 1933–1939.* Lexington: University Press of Kentucky, 1967.

Phillips, Kevin P. *The Emerging Republican Majority.* New Rochelle, NY: Arlington House, 1969.

Stonecash, Jeffrey M., Mark D. Brewer, and Mack D. Mariani. *Diverging Parties: Social Change, Realignment, and Party Polarization.* Boulder, CO: Westview Press, 2003.

Mark D. Brewer

DEMOCRATIC PARTY

The experience of the Democrats since 1976 is a story of a party grappling with collapse and failure on the heels of great electoral and policy triumphs. Democrats confronted the need to revise their liberal ideology to meet changing circumstances and a more conservative public mood, but without becoming just a kinder and gentler version of conservative Republicans. Perhaps even more important, the Democrats sought to rebuild their political coalition, which had shattered along the lines of race, ethnicity, gender, and ideology.

Background

Few American political parties have fallen as far and as fast as the Democrats did between 1964 and 1972. At the beginning of this era, the Democrats were electorally and legislatively triumphant. Lyndon Johnson had crushed Barry Goldwater in the 1964 election and Democrats were in the midst of enacting the boldest legislative program since the New Deal. Many observers began to talk about the permanent liberal consensus in American politics. But by 1972 this sense of triumph had given way to defeat and division. The Democrats' presidential candidate, George McGovern, suffered a humiliating 49-state landslide defeat, and the party seemed more like an assemblage of feuding factions and insular interest groups than a serious national governing coalition. Perhaps worst of all, the party's liberal ideology seemed both outdated and out of the mainstream of American politics.

Division and Decline

The 1976 election was the second since the Democrats reformed their nominating system in 1972, effectively ending the power of party bosses to select their presidential nominee. As in 1972, the party picked a nominee—former Georgia governor Jimmy Carter—who would have had little chance under the old rules. Carter was barely known at the start of the campaign, but he did possess important political qualities that made him acceptable to various factions within the party. First, as a white Southerner, he had strong appeal in that region, but his racial views were acceptable to party liberals. Second, his homespun character, religiosity, and lack of Washington experience appealed to New Politics reformers, many of whom had supported McGovern in 1972. Perhaps most important, Carter seemed such an improbable choice for the nomination that his opponents failed to take him seriously until it was too late. Carter won a narrow victory, 50 to 48 percent, against incumbent Gerald Ford. Despite the close outcome, Carter seemed to have rehabilitated the old New Deal coalition of the South and the industrial Northeast and Midwest.

The Democratic victory was short-lived, however, doomed by events, Carter's own stumbles, and internal divisions. By 1979, skyrocketing inflation and unemployment, long lines at filling stations, U.S. hostages in Iran, and the Soviet invasion of Afghanistan had convinced many Americans that Carter and the Democrats were incapable of governing. The Democrats were also divided internally after Sen. Ted Kennedy of Massachusetts chose to challenge Carter for the Democratic nomination. Though Kennedy failed to seriously threaten Carter's hold on the party, the contest exposed clear divisions between the party's liberal and conservative wings. Carter eventually lost to the staunch conservative Republican Ronald Reagan by a sizeable margin, 51 to 41 percent. The election was not just a personal rejection of Carter, however. Many political observers hypothesized that the election had ushered in a Republican realignment.

Internal divisions remained on display for two more election cycles, reflecting the party's ideological, racial, and generational divides. In 1984, the front-runner in the presidential primary was Walter Mondale, Carter's vice president. Mondale represented those who believed in both the essential strength and the moral imperative of traditional Democratic liberalism. His main opponent was Sen. Gary Hart of Colorado, who presented himself as the candidate of new ideas and criticized Mondale for his links to unions and other Democratic interest groups. In doing so, Hart symbolized those who believed that recent election results represented a rejection of the Democrats' New Deal and Great Society visions, and that the party needed to rethink its ideology for a postindustrial, high-tech economy. Finally, the nomination process also saw the candidacy of the civil rights activist Jesse Jackson. Jackson represented a new political assertiveness among African Americans, who for decades had been the Democrats' most loyal but most controversial constituency.

Indeed, race had become one of the Democratic Party's biggest burdens. Not only had much of the white South abandoned the party in the wake of the civil rights movement, but also many Northern whites were profoundly unsettled by the changes in race relations since the 1960s. Mondale eventually won the nomination, but the contest had weakened his candidacy and exposed the deep rifts within the Democratic coalition. Aware of the difficult situation he faced against the popular Reagan, Mondale sought to capitalize on the growing gender gap in voting behavior by selecting Rep. Geraldine Ferraro of New York as his running mate, but any benefits that the Democrats received from the Ferraro nomination were lost in the

ensuing Republican landslide. Reagan won 49 states, with Mondale victorious only in the District of Columbia and his home state of Minnesota.

Change

The 1984 election left Democrats defeated and dispirited, and thus open to change. Many Democrats complained that the party reforms of the 1970s had given control of the nomination process to organized interests and liberal activists. Democratic presidential hopefuls thus had to move too far to the left in the pursuit of the nomination. This weakened them, perhaps fatally, in the general election, or if they did manage to win, as Carter did in 1976, they couldn't govern effectively because they had few links to Democrats in Congress. These complaints had led Democrats to introduce "superdelegates" in the 1984 electoral cycle. These superdelegates were state and national party leaders, along with Democratic elected officials, and they would prevent a dark-horse candidate from seizing the presidential nomination to the detriment of the party's interest in appealing to the center.

After the 1984 election, the Democratic National Committee (DNC) sought to reduce the perceived influence of special interest groups. The DNC chairman, Paul Kirk, removed official recognition of special interest caucuses within the national party. In addition, he eliminated the party's midterm convention to save money as well as to remove a perceived venue for special interest haggling. Kirk also sought to refocus the DNC by focusing on fund-raising, party-building, and candidate service.

Many moderate and conservative Democrats sought to shift the party even more through the creation of the Democratic Leadership Council (DLC) in 1985. The DLC initially focused on giving greater weight to moderate and conservative Democrats by creating a Southern regional primary in 1988. The DLC also succeeded in creating "Super Tuesday" in 1988, allowing nine Southern states to hold primaries on the same day.

The Super Tuesday results failed to boost a moderate candidate, however, and the remaining contests settled down to a battle between Massachusetts governor Michael Dukakis and Jesse Jackson. Even more than in

1984, Jackson's candidacy met with enthusiastic support from African Americans and many liberal whites. On the other hand, the party's liberal stands on racial issues were controversial, and Jackson was deeply unpopular among many of the moderate-to-conservative whites that Dukakis would need to win in the general election. When Dukakis eventually selected Sen. Lloyd Bentsen of Texas as his running mate, it only served to highlight the racial divisions among Democrats. Despite holding a large lead after the Democratic nomination, Dukakis eventually lost the election to Vice Pres. George H. W. Bush by a margin of 53 to 46 percent.

A Third Way

Going into the 1992 elections, the Democrats looked likely to lose their fourth straight election. In the aftermath of the Persian Gulf War, Pres. George H. W. Bush achieved approval ratings close to 90 percent. As a result, several nationally known Democrats decided against running. The race eventually became a contest between Gov. Bill Clinton of Arkansas and the former Massachusetts senator Paul Tsongas. As the former head of the DLC, Clinton sought to craft a new message for the party, describing himself as a "New Democrat" who sought to find a "third way" between Reagan-style conservatism and traditional Democratic liberalism. Clinton sought to further the image that he was not a traditional Democrat by publicly criticizing Jesse Jackson and then eschewing traditional ticket-balancing by selecting Sen. Al Gore, another moderate Southerner affiliated with the DLC, as his running mate. Clinton and Gore stressed their "New Democrat" credentials by calling for "an end to welfare as we know it" and trumpeting their support for middle-class tax cuts and the North American Free Trade Agreement (NAFTA). These positions were intended to insulate them from charges by Republicans (and some Democrats) that the party was too liberal, too beholden to the interests of minorities and labor unions, and too wedded to "tax and spend" policies.

Once in office, Clinton faced near unanimous Republican opposition and divisions among Democrats. The perceived failures of Clinton and the Democratic Congress, combined with a weak economy and vigorous efforts by congressional Republicans to nationalize the election through its "Contract with America," led to disastrous results for Democrats in the 1994 midterm elections. The party lost both the Senate and the House, the latter after 40 years of uninterrupted Democratic control. While Democrats throughout the country and from all points on the ideological spectrum faced problems in 1994, the greatest losses occurred among moderate and conservative Democrats, particularly in the South. For many years, these elected officials had been able to win in otherwise Republican areas by stressing their differences with the national party, but many failed in that effort in 1994. Perhaps ironically, these losses left the Democratic Party more ideologically unified than before.

President Clinton acknowledged that the center of gravity in American politics had indeed shifted away from Democratic liberalism. In January 1996, he famously declared that the "era of big government is over." Perhaps the most concrete sign of this was the passage of a Republican-sponsored welfare reform bill in the summer of 1996. Not only did President Clinton sign it into law, but a majority of Democrats in the House and the Senate also ended up voting for the bill.

Clinton managed to win reelection in 1996, becoming the first Democrat to do so since Franklin D. Roosevelt, but once again he achieved only a plurality of the vote, defeating the Republican candidate, Bob Dole, by a margin of 49 to 41 percent. The Texas billionaire Ross Perot also ran again as an independent, but he managed just over 8 percent of the vote. The presidential race represented more of a personal victory for Clinton, since Democrats managed to gain back only eight seats in the House and actually lost a net two seats in the Senate.

In his second term in office, Clinton continued to seek accommodation with Republicans in Congress, especially on legislation signed in 1997 to balance the budget. The revelation that Clinton had had an affair with a White House intern and then lied about it under oath dominated the rest of his second term. As a result, Clinton became only the second president to face an impeachment trial in the Senate. (The first was Andrew Johnson, in 1868.) Republican efforts to capitalize on the scandal backfired, however, and the Senate eventually acquitted Clinton, but the controversy highlighted a growing divide between Democrats and Republicans on the issue of moral values. Over the previous decades, Democratic voters, especially white Democrats, had become increasingly educated, urban, and secular, while Republican voters had become more rural and religious.

Despite a strong economy and Clinton's high approval ratings, the 2000 election proved to be one of the closest in American history. Vice President Al Gore won the popular vote by over five hundred thousand votes, but the outcome in the Electoral College hung on the outcome in Florida, where Gore trailed his Republican opponent, Texas governor George W. Bush, by just a few hundred votes. The ensuing recounts and legal disputes finally ended on December 12, when the U.S. Supreme Court ordered an end to the recounts and effectively declared Bush to be the winner. The outcome embittered many Democrats, since Gore had lost despite winning the popular vote. In addition, many Democrats believed that the Florida results raised serious questions of disfranchisement, especially of minority voters. Finally, the Supreme Court's five-vote majority in *Bush v. Gore*, 531 U.S. 98 (2000) came from justices appointed by Republican presidents.

Despite Gore's loss, the Democrats picked up four Senate seats, achieving a 50-50 tie (the House remained in Republican hands). In May 2001, the Democrats actually won control of the Senate when Sen. Jim Jeffords of Vermont quit the Republican Party to become an independent and decided to caucus with the Democrats. The Jeffords switch highlighted the growing strength of the Democrats in the Northeast and the growing polarization of the parties, for his defection seemed to counterpoise the movement of conservative Southern Democrats into the G.O.P.

This polarization came to an abrupt—but ultimately temporary—end with the attacks on the World Trade Center and the Pentagon in September 2001. Democrats gave strong support to President Bush in the aftermath of the attacks, voting overwhelmingly to authorize the use of force in Afghanistan and for the USA PATRIOT Act, which strengthened the ability of law enforcement to investigate potential terrorists. Democrats were more divided when it came to authorizing the use of force in Iraq. In the House, Democrats voted against the resolution, but only by a margin of 126 to 82. In the Senate, a majority of Democrats actually voted for the resolution. Despite this bipartisanship, Republicans used the 2002 midterms to paint the Democrats as weak on foreign policy, an issue that had dogged the Democrats since the 1960s. These attacks, combined with President Bush's high approval ratings, helped the Republicans to regain the Senate.

Disputes over foreign policy dominated the Democrats' 2004 nomination campaign. President Bush's primary justification for the invasion of Iraq in March 2003 was to eliminate stockpiles of weapons of mass destruction (WMDs). When these stockpiles proved nonexistent and the invasion resulted in a prolonged insurgency against American forces, Democrats became much more critical of both the war and President Bush. The 2004 election campaign between Sen. John Kerry of Massachusetts and President Bush focused largely on questions of foreign policy. Bush won 51 to 48 percent in the popular vote, but the switch of a few thousand votes in Ohio would have given an Electoral College victory to Kerry.

Bush's victory renewed speculation about the emergence of an enduring Republican majority. Republicans won the White House again, and they added to their majorities in the House and the Senate. In particular, the 2000 and 2004 elections seemed to mark the death of the Democratic Party in the South. Even with Southerners at the top of the ticket in 2000 (Al Gore) and at the bottom in 2004 (Sen. John Edwards of North Carolina), Democrats failed to win any Southern states in those two elections. In 2004, the Democrats also lost five Senate seats in the South, while Republicans gained a net of five seats in the House—an outcome due solely to the loss of five Democratic seats in Texas resulting from an unprecedented redistricting, which would normally occur only in the wake of the decennial U.S. Census.

Rebound

Yet Democratic fortunes began to rebound soon after the election. President Bush began his second term by launching a public campaign to reform Social Security with the creation of private contribution accounts. Democrats were nearly unanimous in opposition to the proposal, believing that it would likely destroy what they considered the party's programmatic achievement, and Bush's plan went nowhere.

Growing dissatisfaction with the Iraq War, along with inept handling of Hurricane Katrina in August 2005, drove down President Bush's approval ratings over the next two years and created a strong political environment for the Democrats going into the 2006 elections. The party won back majorities in both houses, gaining 31 seats in the House and 5 in Senate. The victory gave the House Speakership to Rep. Nancy Pelosi of California, the first woman ever to hold that position. The election results reinforced the ongoing regional shifts in the party coalitions. Democrats won a majority of the vote in every region but the South, and the party tightened its grip on the Northeast, winning all but one House seat in New England. What few seats the Democrats held in the South were largely in majority-minority districts.

At the start of the 2008 presidential campaign, most observers considered Sen. Hillary Clinton of New York to be the odds-on favorite to win the Democratic nomination, but Sen. Barack Obama of Illinois soon began to mount a serious challenge. The Clinton-Obama contest proved historic, since Clinton was the first woman to seriously contest for a major party presidential nomination, while Obama was the first African American to do so. In this respect, the two candidates represented two crucial parts of the Democratic coalition—women and minorities. To some extent, support for Clinton and opposition to Obama reflected the racial divides that had torn the party since the 1960s. On the other hand, the two candidates had few if any serious ideological or policy disputes, suggesting that the party had managed at last to overcome such divisions.

Obama eventually won the nomination after a long and close contest, and he went on to win the general election, 53 to 46 percent, over Arizona senator John McCain. He thus became the nation's first African American president. Obama's victory was, of course, greatly helped by the deep unpopularity of President Bush, but his victory seemed to provide historic vindication for the Democratic Party's support for civil rights in the 1960s. It also

RELATED ENTRIES

THIS VOLUME
Bush, George W.; Carter, Jimmy; Clinton, Bill; Clinton, Hillary Rodham; Election of 1980; Election of 1992; Election of 2000; Election of 2004; Election of 2008; Obama, Barack
OTHER VOLUMES
Democratic Party (vols. 3–6)

suggests that the party may have finally managed to work past the legacy of the 1960s. Obama is the first Northern Democrat to win the presidency since John Kennedy in 1960, and he is the most liberal since at least Lyndon Johnson, indicating that liberalism is no longer a fault line within the party, and that it is no longer a clear indicator of electoral defeat. More importantly, Obama's victory depended mostly on the increased support and turnout of racial and ethnic minorities, particularly African Americans, young people, and the well educated. In the aftermath of the 1960s, the support of these groups was often seen as an electoral liability for the Democrats. Yet in 2008, Obama and the Democrats managed to turn them into assets. Though much depends on the successes or failures of the Obama administration, the likely growth of these demographic groups suggests that the Democrats may have finally entered a new and more hopeful era.

Bibliography and Further Reading

Baer, Kenneth S. *Reinventing Democrats: The Politics of Liberalism from Reagan to Clinton.* Lawrence: University Press of Kansas, 2000.

Brewer, Mark D., and Jeffrey M. Stonecash. *Dynamics of American Political Parties.* Cambridge, UK: Cambridge University Press, 2009.

Cohen, Marty, David Karol, Hans Noel, and John Zaller. *The Party Decides: Presidential Nominations before and after Reform.* Chicago: University of Chicago Press, 2008.

Galvin, Daniel J. *Presidential Party Building: Dwight D. Eisenhower to George W. Bush.* Princeton, NJ: Princeton University Press, 2010.

Green, Donald, Bradley Palmquist, and Eric Schickler. *Partisan Hearts and Minds: Political Parties and the*

Social Identities of Voters. New Haven, CT: Yale University Press, 2002.

Karol, David A. *Party Position Change in American Politics: Coalition Management.* Cambridge, UK: Cambridge University Press, 2009.

Klinkner, Philip A. *The Losing Parties: Out-Party National Committees, 1956–1993.* New Haven, CT: Yale University Press, 1994.

Levendusky, Matthew. *The Partisan Sort: How Liberals Became Democrats and Conservatives Became Republicans.* Chicago: University of Chicago Press, 2009.

Radosh, Ronald. *Divided They Fell: The Demise of the Democratic Party, 1964–1996.* New York: The Free Press, 1996.

Rae, Nicol C. "Be Careful What You Wish For: The Rise of Responsible Parties in American National Politics." *Annual Review of Political Science* 10 (June 2007): 169–191.

Philip A. Klinkner

DEREGULATION AND PRIVATIZATION

The term *deregulation* refers to the process of reducing the role of past rules and restrictions on the behavior of companies and individuals. *Privatization*, meanwhile, refers either to the outright transfer of business ownership from the government to the private sector or, more significantly in the United States, transferring the operation of services such as waste removal, fire protection, libraries, prisons, and retirement pensions from the government to the private sector. Until the financial crisis that began in 2007 started a shift toward renewing and strengthening financial regulations, deregulation and privatization had been aspects of economic management since the 1970s, as the trend toward increasing the role of government that existed for much of the twentieth century was reversed. Areas most affected by deregulation include transportation, communications, and finance, while privatization had an impact on a number of social services that had previously been part of the government sphere. Though support of deregulation is generally the strongest within the Republican

Party—both Ronald Reagan and George W. Bush were noted supporters—the deregulation process enjoyed substantial bipartisan support during this time period, and much of the federal deregulation occurred during Democratic presidencies.

Political Philosophy of Deregulation and Privatization

How a person answers three critical questions can help to explain that individual's political views related to deregulation and privatization. First, does the invisible hand of the free market allocate economic resources to their most productive uses and create the largest possible welfare for society, or do various market failures in a liberalized economy lead to inefficiencies and waste? Second, even supporters of the free market realize there is a tradeoff between economic efficiency and equity, as the outcomes of market processes are not necessarily fair and equitable. Therefore, should the government intervene to produce fairer outcomes? Third, can government intervention in the economy improve outcomes, or will the government only make matters worse?

The role of government in the economy grew dramatically for much of the twentieth century. Coming in waves during the Progressive Era, the Great Depression, and the 1960s, regulations were designed to protect workers and consumers, to prevent business monopolies and promote competition, and to protect the environment. Liberal politicians tend to support such regulation because they have less faith in the efficiency and fairness of free market outcomes and believe that government intervention can improve situations. On the other hand, conservative politicians generally believe that the free market can produce the most efficient outcomes, that equality of opportunity ensures a fair chance for everyone to compete in the economy, and that government bureaucrats do not have the necessary tools to improve on market outcomes and may even make matters worse with misguided policies or by developing close ties with the industries they are meant to regulate.

Deregulation in the Transportation Sector

Regulation of the transportation industry began in earnest with the creation of the Interstate Commerce

Commission in 1887. The first major push for deregulation came in the transportation sector during the 1970s, after Depression-era regulations reduced the number of competing companies, increased prices, and limited the available services. The administration of Pres. Jimmy Carter worked hard with the Democratic Congress to deregulate the transportation industry. Perhaps most significantly, the Airline Deregulation Act of 1978 eliminated the Civil Aeronautics Board, which had been created in 1938 as the Civil Aeronautics Authority to promote airline safety, ensure plane routes reached all major regions in the country, and prevent excessive competition that might drive airline companies out of business. After the deregulation, the number of airlines, passengers, and routes grew; prices fell; and the hub-and-spoke model for airlines developed. However, some small airports lost access to routes, and airlines such as Pan American and Eastern went bankrupt as a result of increased competition. In similar ways, the subsequent Motor Carrier Act of 1980 deregulated the trucking industry and the Staggers Rail Act of 1980 deregulated the railroad industry.

Deregulation in the Communications Sector

The Telecommunications Act of 1996 deregulated the media industry considerably. It modified the Communications Act of 1934, which viewed the airwaves as public property, such that communications companies had significant duties to promote the public interest. One important change of the Telecommunications Act was to remove restrictions on media ownership, allowing companies to purchase more radio and television stations in multiple markets. The act also allowed telecommunications companies to enter any lines of business they chose to, so that cable television companies could provide Internet services, for example.

Deregulation in the Financial Sector

The banking sector also experienced large-scale deregulation during this time period. By 1976, American banks were highly regulated. For instance, banks were not allowed to open branches across state lines and had to meet the requirements of each state regulatory agency. This resulted in a large number of small local banks, in contrast to the existence of several large banks dominating the industry, as occurred in many other countries. Banks also faced restrictions on their asset holdings, such as the prohibition against owning stocks, and were required to keep minimum levels of capital and reserves on hand. In addition, Regulation Q prevented banks from paying interest on checking account deposits.

The original intention of many of the soon-to-disappear regulations was to reduce competition in the banking industry and dissuade banks from taking excessive risks, thus preventing the types of bank failures that were endemic in the Great Depression. Because the government provided deposit insurance to protect banks after the creation of the Federal Deposit Insurance Corporation (FDIC) in 1933, these regulations were seen as necessary to make sure banks did not seek excessive risks for the chance of high returns, knowing that bank depositors with insurance on their deposits would be less vigilant about monitoring bank activities to protect their assets.

But the high inflation of the 1970s made it difficult for banks to compete for deposits with other financial institutions that could offer high interest rates. The Depository Institutions Deregulation and Monetary Control Act of 1980 removed restrictions that prohibited banks from paying interest on checking account deposits, and it also removed ceilings on interest rates banks could pay for other types of deposits. This helped banks to compete for funds with other unregulated actors in the high interest rate environment of the time. Nonetheless, the process of financial disintermediation had begun, as nonbank institutions had created money market mutual funds and other products to attract depositors with higher interest rates than could be offered by the regulated banks. The 1980 act also deregulated thrift institutions, allowing easier entry and greater leeway for investment activities, which many commentators believe helped lead to the Savings and Loan crisis in the late 1980s.

Later, the Riegle-Neal Interstate Banking and Branching Efficiency Act of 1994 eliminated interstate banking restrictions, leading to bank consolidation as the number of banks reduced and the proportion of assets owned by the largest banks grew. The Financial Services Modernization Act of 1999 (also called the Gramm-Leach-Bliley Act) repealed the separation between commercial banks and investment banks that was created by the Glass-Steagall Banking Act of 1933. Prior to this time, commercial banks accepted deposits but could not provide brokerage services or underwrite corporate securities. While commercial banks were restricted in their risk-taking activities, the justification was that they enjoyed deposit insurance and access to credit from the Federal Reserve in order to help prevent bank runs. Investment banks were not as closely regulated but did not accept deposits. After the change, commercial banks were able to extend into more fields and take more risks.

Another deregulation of sorts developed as well, as the existing regulations did not extend to what the Nobel Prize–winning economist Paul Krugman has called the "shadow banking system." Since the 1970s, the growth of private equity firms, hedge funds, financial derivatives, and nonbank financial actors has occurred outside the scope of government regulations. Because regulations are meant to limit the actions of financial institutions, these institutions have strong incentives to find loopholes or other ways to legally avoid regulations. Because of the antiregulatory environment, new regulations were not created for many of these financial innovations. The growth of securitization, the holding of assets off the bank's balance sheet, and the lack of a centralized location for trading financial derivatives all contributed to the financial crisis whose roots began with the collapse of the subprime mortgage securities market in 2007.

Privatization of Social Services

Though ultimately unsuccessful, Pres. George W. Bush began his second term with a push to privatize part of Social Security with the creation of personal retirement accounts (PRAs). With PRAs, workers would obtain control over some portion of their payroll tax, and then invest this money for their own use during retirement. This would move the country closer to the president's goal of creating an "ownership society." Although President Bush spent a great deal of political capital on this matter, his proposals never made it through congressional committees, because

some conservative politicians viewed such reform as a type of "socialism," with the government playing the role of stock-picker, while many Democrats opposed the idea of tying so much of a worker's retirement pension to fluctuations in the stock market.

Though the attempts at Social Security privatization were unsuccessful, many state and local governments have experimented with privatization by contracting out to private companies the operation of prisons, police and fire departments, schools, libraries, toll roads, and other services traditionally viewed as part of the public sector. Job training and welfare programs have also been increasingly privatized in recent years. In 1997, the Council of State Governments' Survey on Privatization in State Government found that more than half of the social service agencies in the 27 states with respondents had privatized at least 15 percent of their programs and service. Candidates for this privatization also included child care and drug and alcohol treatment. The winners of these privatization contracts have included both for-profit and nonprofit organizations.

Supporters of privatization believe that private companies will have more incentives to reduce costs and improve efficiency than the government, while opponents believe that the quality of services will decrease after privatization. The city government in Phoenix, Arizona, experimented with this issue by allowing private companies to bid for waste collection contracts after much dissatisfaction developed regarding Phoenix's public works department. At first, the private companies won the contracts, but eventually the public works department improved its methods and costs and was able win back the contracts. Research on this issue is inconclusive, however, and the debate continues.

Future Outlook for the Regulatory Debate

Politicians will continue to debate the role of regulation in American life. For environmental policy, tools such as taxes or cap-and-trade schemes may be used more often to limit pollution to desired levels in ways that are more efficient than sometimes-arbitrary regulations. Cost-benefit analysis, a tool that compares the entire duration of future costs and benefits from different regulations, is used to determine which regulations pay for themselves and which may be a waste of resources. However, liberal politicians tend to view market-based solutions and cost-benefit analysis with suspicion, thinking that they provide a justification to remove necessary regulations.

After the prolonged economic boom of the 1980s and 1990s, which helped galvanize supporters of deregulation and free-market thinking, the financial crisis that began in 2007 pushed momentum in the direction of greater financial regulation, especially under the administration of Pres. Barack Obama. The reform process will be complicated, however, because the finance industry is constantly developing new products and techniques to bypass regulations. The industry also spends a great deal of effort lobbying politicians for favorable treatment, making it difficult for regulators to maintain control. Suggestions for financial reform have included ensuring that all financial institutions are regulated, temporarily nationalizing banks in order to get them to increase lending and supply credit to the economy, simplifying the regulatory apparatus that currently extends to many agencies, more carefully designing the capital requirements of financial institutions (including requirements to hold more capital during economic boom periods), increasing transparency by requiring different financial securities to all be traded through clearinghouses, and requiring housing mortgage initiators to maintain a larger stake in the mortgages they create.

Bibliography and Further Reading

Blinder, Alan. *Hard Heads, Soft Hearts: Tough Minded Economics for a Just Society.* Cambridge, MA: Perseus, 1987.

Carr, Edward. "Greed—and Fear: A Special Report on the Future of Finance." *The Economist,* January 24, 2009.

Gordon, John Steele. *An Empire of Wealth: The Epic History of American Power.* New York: HarperCollins, 2004.

Heilbroner, Robert L., and Aaron Singer. *The Economic Transformation of America: 1600 to the Present,* 4th edition. New York: Wadsworth Publishing, 1998.

Hughes, Jonathan, and Louis P. Cain. *American Economic History,* 6th edition. Boston: Addison-Wesley, 2003.

Krugman, Paul. *The Return of Depression Economics and the Crisis of 2008.* New York: W. W. Norton, 2009.

RELATED ENTRIES

THIS VOLUME
Economic Policy; Federal Reserve Bank; Financial Crisis of 2008; Regulatory Agencies; Savings and Loan Crisis; State-Federal Relations

Mishkin, Frederic S. *The Economics of Money, Banking, and Financial Markets,* 8th edition. Boston: Pearson Addison-Wesley, 2007.

Walton, Gary M., and Hugh Rockoff. *History of the American Economy,* 9th edition. Fort Worth, TX: Harcourt College Publishers, 2001.

Wade Donald Pfau

DRUG POLICY

In the late twentieth century, and particularly during the 1980s, federal policies to control the use and distribution of illicit drugs expanded in both scope and intensity. Declared first by Richard Nixon and then escalated by presidents Ronald Reagan and George H. W. Bush, the "war on drugs" spanned Republican and Democratic administrations and drew bipartisan congressional support. Although its effectiveness in reducing levels of drug abuse and availability was contested, the policy was backed by continually increasing federal funds, and it had a profound impact on criminal justice and national security institutions, policies, and outcomes.

Background and History

Federal policy has sought to curb the use and abuse of illegal drugs through reducing both the supply and demand for drugs. Supply-reduction strategies target drug production, trafficking, and sales through law enforcement measures. These include eradicating drug crops, interdicting shipments, and arresting and prosecuting sellers. Demand-reduction strategies seek to prevent or treat drug use and abuse. U.S. policy encompasses both approaches but has historically favored strategies of supply reduction through law enforcement.

The origins of this policy can be traced to the early twentieth century. Although the use of psychoactive substances had periodically raised public concern, it was not until 1914 that policy makers began a policy of federal drug control. That year, Congress passed the Harrison Act, which prohibited the sale of heroin, cocaine, and their derivatives, except with medical prescriptions. By the late 1920s, federal narcotics agents had taken steps that transformed this system of medical control into one that made the sale or possession of such substances illegal and subject to enforcement. Additional measures followed: the Marijuana Tax Act of 1937 effectively added marijuana to the list of prohibited substances, and new laws in the 1950s (the Boggs Act of 1951 and the Narcotics Control Act of 1956) imposed increasingly rigorous penalties on those who possessed or sold marijuana, heroin, or cocaine. Despite the growing punitive trend, the funding, scope, and impact of drug enforcement remained limited until the arrival of the Nixon administration in 1969.

Richard Nixon had made "law and order" a prominent theme in the 1968 presidential campaign, and he saw the use and abuse of drugs (particularly heroin) as central to the nation's crime problem. Nixon took steps to consolidate and expand federal antidrug laws and agencies. In addition to enforcement, Nixon saw drug treatment as an instrument for fighting crime. He significantly boosted federal funding for treatment, particularly methadone maintenance programs to control heroin addiction. Nixon also permanently extended the parameters of federal drug control beyond U.S. borders, through a campaign to stop production and trafficking in nations such as Turkey and Mexico.

The Ford and Carter administrations did not make drug policy a priority. President Gerald Ford lowered the rhetoric of the Nixon drug war but did not seek fundamental reform. President Jimmy Carter took halting steps to reverse elements of the existing policy, most notably through a modest but unsuccessful attempt to reform marijuana laws. Arguing that penalties for marijuana possession had become, in some cases, more damaging than actual use of the drug, Carter endorsed proposals to decriminalize marijuana and to impose civil fines rather than criminal penalties for possession. These proposals died on Capitol Hill, however. Meanwhile, the rise of teenage marijuana use in the 1970s triggered a growing parents' antidrug movement.

Turning Point: The 1980s

The 1980s marked a watershed in drug policy. Policy makers in these years built both the institutional capacity and the political will to pursue a sustained national policy of drug enforcement backed by substantial funding. Under presidents Ronald Reagan and George H. W. Bush, the federal antidrug budget increased from $1.5 billion to $12.3 billion; it continued to rise, though more gradually, in subsequent years. Beginning in the 1980s, approximately two-thirds was devoted to enforcement, and one-third to treatment and prevention, according to the White House Office of National Drug Control Policy (ONDCP).

Reagan's drug policy was shaped by an electoral coalition that included a broad conservative constituency opposed to the perceived permissiveness of the 1960s and 1970s; the parents' movement mentioned previously was part of this environment. Drug policy in the 1980s was also influenced by increases in powdered cocaine use and the spread of a cheap new cocaine derivative called "crack," which was particularly common in low-income urban communities.

Reagan drew a wide range of federal agencies into drug enforcement, and he pressed Congress to make it easier to arrest, convict, and imprison drug users and dealers. He also secured the involvement of the U.S. military in the drug war through an amendment to the 1878 Posse Comitatus Act, which had banned the military from civilian law enforcement efforts for over a century. Under Bush, the role of the military in fighting drugs was transformed from an occasional support function into a significant national security mission. Drug interdiction efforts increased, as did source-country campaigns to stop production, particularly of cocaine in South America.

Throughout the 1980s, national and state legislatures bolstered efforts to expand the drug war. In Congress, many debates occurred at the height of campaign seasons, when opinion polls repeatedly placed drugs high on the list of public concerns. Lawmakers passed major antidrug bills in 1986 and 1988. Among other provisions, these laws imposed severe new mandatory minimum sentences for drug violations. Several states adopted similar sentencing laws. By curtailing judges' discretion, these laws increased both the number of drug offenders who faced incarceration and the length of the average drug sentence.

By the end of the decade, the rapid expansion of drug enforcement had redefined key military missions and reoriented domestic law enforcement priorities, policing practices, and sentencing trends. Drug enforcement efforts not only increased the overall numbers of drug offenders, they also exacerbated racial disparities in the criminal justice and corrections systems despite similar drug use rates among racial groups. Strategic decisions to focus law enforcement efforts on low-income urban communities, where street-level drug dealing was more visible, helped drive a 199 percent increase in drug arrest rates for African Americans between 1980 and 1992, more than four times the increase for whites. Sentencing laws contributed to more severe punishments for black offenders within the system. This was in part due to the disparity in federal cocaine sentencing, introduced initially by the 1986 Anti-Drug Abuse Act and echoed in several state laws. The act specified that possessing or selling 5 grams of crack would trigger the same five-year federal mandatory minimum prison term as selling 500 grams of powdered cocaine.

The 1990s and Early 2000s

The administrations of Bill Clinton and George W. Bush devoted less attention to federal drug control, but neither altered the fundamental direction of the policy. President Clinton brought a more measured tone to the drug war and called for increased emphasis on treatment, but he made no significant change in resource allocations. Abroad, he expanded source-country efforts through a new drug-eradication initiative in Colombia in 2000. President Bush continued the emphasis on supply-reduction strategies at home and abroad: spending on drug eradication, interdiction, and arrests of dealers and users rose 47 percent between 2002 and 2008, while the amount spent on drug treatment and prevention increased 1.4 percent (ONDCP).

Overall, drug arrest patterns revealed a shift in enforcement priorities, from cocaine and heroin in the 1980s to marijuana in the 1990s and 2000s. Some in Congress, meanwhile, urged greater attention to localized methamphetamine use.

By the early 2000s, there were scattered signs of moderation in select state and federal initiatives. Partly in response to overcrowded prisons and budget pressures, several state legislatures reevaluated their stiffest sentencing laws beginning in the late 1990s. Over a dozen states created or expanded options for sentencing drug offenders to treatment (through "drug courts" and similar programs) or other alternatives to incarceration between 2004 and 2006. The number of drug courts grew to over one thousand six hundred by 2007. In late 2007, meanwhile, the U.S. Sentencing Commission lowered its guidelines somewhat for judges sentencing crack-cocaine offenders, and it repeated its calls for Congress to address the disparity in cocaine sentencing through legislative reform.

Conclusion

Even as the drug war faded from the public spotlight, the policies and institutions established earlier remained in place, producing a substantial impact on agency priorities, resources, and outcomes. Abroad and at the borders, U.S. military, intelligence, law enforcement, and Homeland Security agencies continued to define and confront the international drug trade as a national security threat, in some cases linking the trade to terrorist or insurgency threats. In 2008, over $5 billion was invested in efforts to disrupt the drug supply through interdiction and international drug control efforts (ONDCP).

At home, record rates of drug arrests, convictions, and sentences demonstrated the impact on criminal justice priorities and practices. Drug arrests more than tripled between 1980 and 2005, to over 1.8 million. In 1980, drug offenses reflected 5.9 percent of all arrests; by 2008, they were 12.2 percent of all arrests. For those convicted, mandatory minimum sentences increased the likelihood of a prison sentence. The number of drug offenders behind bars jumped 1,100 percent, from 41,100 to 493,800, between 1980 and

2003. Demographic breakdowns showed continued racial disparities: although African Americans represented 14 percent of monthly drug users, they represented 37 percent of drug arrests and 56 percent of those in state prison for a drug offense in 2003.

Meanwhile, the core strategy of federal policy—to lower drug use and abuse by reducing the supply of drugs—achieved few sustained or significant results in this period, producing an ongoing debate over the policy. Although casual drug use has diminished since the late 1970s, driven largely by decreased marijuana use, drug control strategies have not substantially lowered the rates or consequences of abuse and addiction for drugs such as heroin and cocaine. Given the record of results, and the financial and social costs of the supply-reduction strategy of drug enforcement, critics of the policy have called for alternative approaches, with many arguing for greater investment in reducing demand through treatment and prevention. Some have called for adopting a public health rather than a law enforcement approach to drug control; others have called for decriminalizing the use of certain drugs or implementing "harm reduction" strategies to minimize the damaging effects of drug abuse. As of 2008, however, the trajectory of federal drug policy remained largely within the parameters set in the 1980s.

Bibliography and Further Reading

Bertram, Eva, Morris Blachman, Kenneth Sharpe, and Peter Andreas. *Drug War Politics: The Price of Denial.* Berkeley: University of California Press, 1996.

Boyum, David, and Peter Reuter. *An Analytic Assessment of U.S. Drug Policy.* Washington, D.C.: American Enterprise Institute, 2005.

Katel, Peter. "War on Drugs." *CQ Researcher* 16–21 (June 2006): 481–504.

King, Ryan S. "Disparity by Geography: The War on Drugs in America's Cities." Washington, D.C.: The Sentencing Project, 2008. http://www.sentencingproject.org/doc/publications/dp_drugarrestreport.pdf (accessed November 16, 2009).

Mares, David R. *Drug Wars and Coffeehouses: The Political Economy of the International Drug Trade.* Washington, D.C.: Congressional Quarterly Press, 2006.

Massing, Michael. *The Fix.* New York: Simon & Schuster, 1998.

Mauer, Marc, and Ryan S. King. "A 25-Year Quagmire: The War on Drugs and Its Impact on American Society." Washington, D.C.: The Sentencing Project, September 2007. http://www.sentencingproject.org/doc/publications/dp_25yearquagmire.pdf (accessed November 16, 2009).

Musto, David F. *The American Disease: Origins of Narcotic Control,* 3rd edition. New York: Oxford University Press, 1999.

United States Sentencing Commission. "U.S. Sentencing Commission Votes Unanimously to Apply Amendment Retroactively for Crack Cocaine Offenses." News Release. Washington, D.C.: United States Sentencing Commission, December 11, 2007. http://www.ussc.gov/PRESS/rel121107.htm (accessed January 8, 2010).

White House Office of National Drug Control Policy (ONDCP). http://www.whitehousedrugpolicy.gov (accessed November 16, 2009).

Eva C. Bertram

ECONOMIC POLICY

In the United States, federal, state, and local governments engage in business and financial regulation, the provision of social insurance, and the promotion of trade with other countries. In the late twentieth and early twenty-first centuries, federal economic policymakers sought—with variable success—to maintain a golden mix of low inflation, high employment, and steady economic growth, increasingly through monetary policy but sometimes with a variant of fiscal policy that relied on tax cuts. With the financial crisis and deep recession that began in 2007, the federal government was thrust into activist stances that have not been seen in the United States since the 1930s.

For the period beginning in 1976, several particular characteristics of economic policy emerged. First, the government played an active role in managing the national economy with its tools of fiscal policy (taxation and expenditures) and monetary policy. Second, this period has also been associated with a rightward shift in government policy with fewer economic regulations and greater reliance on the free market—often achieved, ironically, through new regulatory initiatives. Third, the period witnessed a massive growth in federal government debt, as the President's Budget for Fiscal Year 2009 reports that debt as a percentage of Gross Domestic Product (GDP) grew from 36.2 percent in 1976 to an estimated 67.5 percent in 2008. Finally, there was a return of what the Nobel Prize-winning economist Paul Krugman called "depression economics"—that is, deep uncertainty about what to do in the face of a serious economic downturn coupled with calls to take enormously stimulative spending measures.

Background

After a prolonged economic boom starting at the end of World War II, by the early 1970s, America's economic situation took a turn for the worse. Inflation was already working its way into the economy by the late 1960s as growing government spending for the Vietnam War and Pres. Lyndon B. Johnson's Great Society social welfare programs pushed prices upward. In 1971, Pres. Richard Nixon ended the system of fixing the value of dollars to gold because rising prices and a growing trade deficit were making it increasingly difficult to stop the value of the dollar from falling. Later, the economic situation became more severe after an increase in oil and food prices in the early 1970s shook the economy. By 1976, the United States experienced "stagflation," a coinage denoting the high inflation and high unemployment of the period.

A stark contrast existed among politicians and economists relating to how the government should best confront these economic problems. The "classical" approach of economics for responding to such a downturn, as pursued for example by Herbert Hoover at the start of the Great Depression, was to maintain a balanced budget and not interfere with the free enterprise system. The classical economic view was that an economic downturn would lay the seeds for the eventual turnaround as the surplus of savings would push down interest rates until businesses were once again encouraged to expand. But the election of Franklin D. Roosevelt in 1932 had ushered in an era with a much more expansive government policy. Roosevelt's economic policies are often associated with Keynesianism, an economic philosophy that encourages an activist role for government in macroeconomic management. In 1936, Keynes published *The General Theory of Employment, Interest, and Money*. This book argued that economic downturns could last indefinitely if business remained pessimistic about the future and took no action to expand. Keynes argued that government could and should actively manage aggregate demand. During recessions, the government should run budget deficits by increasing spending or decreasing taxes. This view had been particular popular during the 1950s and 1960s, but by the 1970s, Milton Friedman and others argued from a Monetarist position that an activist economic policy by the government would create more problems and would only trigger further inflation without providing any relief for the unemployed.

Managing the National Economy

In the 1976 presidential election, stagflation presented a stark tradeoff for the government, as economic theory suggests that it is difficult to simultaneously reduce both inflation and unemployment. The Republicans advocated a need to "Whip Inflation Now," as President Ford's WIN campaign slogan stated it, even at the expense of unemployment, while the Democrats argued that reducing unemployment was more important. Though there were exceptions, Republicans tended to be more receptive to Monetarist ideas, while Democrats tended to side more with Keynesians. Macroeconomic problems persisted throughout the rest of the decade, and the economic problems would not be fully reversed until the end of a deep recession in the early 1980s, as the Federal Reserve under Paul Volcker pursued a contractionary monetary policy to reduce inflation. The Federal Reserve adopted Monetarist ideas by focusing on slowing the growth of the money supply, which sent short-term

interest rates to over 20 percent in the early 1980s. This led to a severe recession and unemployment rates as high as 11 percent. Eventually, however, the Federal Reserve's contractionary policy resulted in much lower inflation rates, as inflation decreased from 13.5 percent in 1980 to 4.1 percent in 1983, and a period of economic growth began that would last through the remainder of the 1980s. Even a stock market crash in October 1987, which sent the Dow Jones Industrial Average down 22.8 percent in one day, proved to be a temporary aberration as the Federal Reserve took decisive action to prevent economic damage and new stock market highs were again achieved in 15 months.

The presidency of Ronald Reagan in the 1980s brought with it increasing calls for lessened government involvement in the regulation of the economy—calls that had begun during the Carter administration. A number of industries, including airlines, banks, telephones, and electric utilities were "deregulated," or allowed to be more responsive to the free market. Government spending was also decreased for a number of social welfare programs including Medicare, food stamps, and others. In the Economic Recovery Act of 1981, Congress, under the prodding of the Reagan administration, passed the largest tax cut in America's history. Reagan's "supply-side" economic prediction was that lower taxes would create incentives for people to work harder and invest more which, in turn, would lead to larger tax revenues than would be possible with the higher tax rates. As it turned out, the Reagan tax cuts were accompanied by increased military spending that dwarfed the decreases in spending on domestic programs.

Following a mild recession in 1991, the 1990s turned out to be a period of sustained economic boom with low inflation, low unemployment, and a rapidly growing stock market. To enhance international trade, President Clinton signed the North American Free Trade Agreement with Canada and Mexico. In 1998, the federal government produced its first budget surplus in over thirty years. By the turn of the new century, the American economy was booming, with information technology (IT) leading the way. People even began to speak of a "New Economy" in which innovations in information technology and improvements in worker productivity would allow for rapid economic growth without the usual worries about inflation. These hopes were ultimately dashed with the stock market crash beginning in early 2000 and a subsequent recession. That downturn proved relatively brief, however.

But overshadowing the entire post-1976 period was the extremely serious economic downturn that began in 2007. Beginning with losses in the market for subprime mortgage securities, banks and nonbank financial institutions experienced substantial losses, which reduced capital bases and forced substantial deleveraging of financial firms. As companies reduced their investment spending and consumers increased savings in response to economic uncertainties, in early 2009 Pres. Barack Obama pushed through Congress a substantial fiscal stimulus package designed to jump-start the economy.

Continuing Challenges for Economic Policy

Aside from the great financial crisis and recession, other challenges as well continue to confront the American economy and government policy makers. Despite their country's riches, many Americans still live in poverty. In 2007, the Census Bureau estimates that 37.3 million Americans lived below the poverty line. This represents 12.5 percent of the population. More shocking, 18 percent of children in America live in poverty. Additionally, 45.7 million Americans have no health insurance, which represents 15.3 percent of the population. The poverty statistics reflect the fact that the income distribution in the United States is far from equal. Wage growth has stagnated at the lower income levels while most of the increases in household income are due to the rising fortunes of the top 20 percent of households. Reasons for this include global competition in manufacturing jobs, tax policies that provide more advantages for rich households, and cuts in government spending on social programs. As for economic policy, in 1996 President Clinton signed legislation that builds a stronger link between work effort and welfare payments.

America also faces a demographic problem that will strain its pension and health care systems. Fertility rates have been falling and, in 2010, the post–World War II baby boom generation will reach retirement age. This generation is quite large and decreasing mortality rates mean that these people will enjoy more years of retirement, which will put increasing stress on the younger generation of workers. The Social Security program's trustees are legally required to regularly issue forecasts of when the program will become insolvent. Those forecasts have tended to portray an increasingly lower horizon for insolvency—and thus signal the need for adjustments to the program to raise the horizon. The Medicare program faces a much more severe problem since increasing health costs for elderly retirees mean that the Medicare program is projected to become insolvent in the short run. The Clinton administration had pushed to invest a portion of the Social Security Trust Fund in the stock market to increase returns, and the Bush administration pushed to create personal retirement accounts with a portion of Trust Fund contributions, but politicians generally try to avoid Social Security reform, as benefits will only be seen in the long-run while the sacrifices of fewer benefits or high payroll taxes would occur much sooner. One exception was the Greenspan Commission in 1983, which persuaded Congress to pass a package of slight benefit cuts and tax increases to deal with the immediate financing problems. The Greenspan Commission set an important precedent by demonstrating the political tractability of the "Social Security crisis."

The financial crisis will have important implications for economic policy. The huge size of the government bailout for the financial sector has greatly expanded the size and role of government economic policy. Already, the Federal Reserve has expanded its powers to buy new kinds of financial assets from banks. This broadening power is also accompanied by large fiscal stimulus programs to boost the demand for goods and services as recommended by Keynesian economic policy. Accompanying this growing government activism is a push by President Obama to expand government infrastructure development and to broaden the availability of health insurance to the entire population. These matters raise important questions about the role of the government in the economy, and President Obama will likely push for a more active government role and less reliance on free market outcomes, reversing the Reagan-era goal of limited government.

Bibliography and Further Reading

Blinder, Alan. *Hard Heads, Soft Hearts: Tough Minded Economics for a Just Society.* Cambridge, MA: Perseus Books, 1987.

Gordon, John Steele. *An Empire of Wealth: The Epic History of American Power.* New York: HarperCollins, 2004.

Heilbroner, Robert L., and Aaron Singer. *The Economic Transformation of America: 1600 to the Present,* 4th edition. New York: Wadsworth Publishing, 1998.

Hughes, Jonathan, and Louis P. Cain. *American Economic History,* 6th edition. New York: Addison Wesley, 2003.

Krugman, Paul. *The Return of Depression Economics and the Crisis of 2008.* New York: W. W. Norton, 2009.

U.S. Census Bureau. *Income, Poverty, and Health Insurance Coverage in the United States: 2007.* Washington, D.C.: U.S. Government Printing Office, 2008. http://www.census.gov/hhes/www/poverty.html (accessed December 15, 2008).

U.S. Office of Management and Budget. *Historical Tables, Budget of the United States Government, Fiscal Year 2009.* Washington, D.C.: U.S. Government Printing Office, 2008. http://www.whitehouse.gov/omb/budget/fy2009/pdf/hist.pdf (accessed December 15, 2008).

Walton, Gary M., and Hugh Rockoff. *History of the American Economy,* 9th edition. Toronto, Canada: South-Western, 2002.

Wade Donald Pfau

EDUCATION POLICY

Over the past 30 years, education has become an increasingly important issue on the national political agenda, and the federal government's role in schools has undergone a remarkable expansion and transfor-

mation. In 1976, voters did not even rank education as one of the country's top 20 concerns, but by 2000 many polls showed it to be a vital issue on the minds of millions of Americans. This political shift has accorded debates over school reform a prominent place in congressional and presidential elections in the contemporary era, as well as in broader partisan and ideological struggles over the proper size and scope of the national government. The increased salience of education for voters, and increasing concerns about the inability of states to improve school performance or reduce educational inequities, ultimately led to the passage of the No Child Left Behind law (NCLB) in 2001. NCLB inaugurated a new era of educational governance in the United States, one that features a substantially larger and different role for the federal government in regulating the nation's schools.

Education Moves onto the National Agenda

Until the latter half of the twentieth century, the United States' powerful traditions of states' rights and local control of schools prevented the issue of education from emerging on the national political agenda, and precluded a major role for the national government in education policy. The Supreme Court's *Brown v. Board of Education,* 347 U.S. 483 (1954) decision initiated an ambitious and controversial effort to bring about school integration through mandatory busing. With the passage of the Elementary and Secondary Education Act (ESEA) of 1965, the federal government began to provide financial assistance and supplemental programs to high poverty school districts. During the 1970s, Congress enacted a number of grant-in-aid conditions that required states to adhere to federal mandates concerning school access and inputs in order to receive federal education funds. In 1979, a cabinet-level U.S. Department of Education was created, a reflection of both the greater activism of educational interest groups in national politics and the need for expanded bureaucratic capacity to administer the myriad federal education programs. But neither the department nor ESEA sought at this point to influence core policies concerning school governance, curriculum, assessment, or accountability.

By the 1980s, however, the continuing existence of large racial and socio-economic achievement gaps and the release of the widely-publicized *A Nation at Risk* report—which warned that America's global economic competitiveness was threatened by under-performing schools—resulted in increased attention to education by citizens, the media, and national policymakers. Responding to the newfound sense of a national education crisis, Democrats called for additional federal spending and regulation, while Pres. Ronald Reagan and the Republican Party argued that federal programs and regulations had been ineffective and even counter-productive and called for private school vouchers and the elimination of the U.S. Department of Education. President George H. W. Bush took a different approach, one strongly supported by the business community, when he advocated national academic standards and a greater national focus on student achievement. Bush was unable to enact his America 2000 proposal, however, due to continuing G.O.P. opposition to federal influence in education and Democrats' focus on increasing and equalizing school funding.

President Bill Clinton pushed Democrats to embrace a more centrist position on education and gained passage of two major school reform bills in 1994—Goals 2000 (which pushed states to establish academic standards) and a reauthorization of ESEA entitled the Improving America's Schools Act (IASA). Many of the reform ideas that would later form the core of NCLB—such as standards, assessments, adequate yearly progress, school report cards, and corrective action—found their first expression in the IASA. Though the new laws did not include many mandates for states, they nonetheless signified a sea change in federal education policy and codified the shift from the historical focus on ensuring resource equity for disadvantaged students to a new commitment to improve the academic performance of all students. IASA ostensibly required states to adopt standards, assessment, and accountability policies but was weakly enforced, and by 2002 only 16 states had fully met its requirements.

Under the leadership of Speaker Newt Gingrich, Republicans in the mid-1990s once again tried to reduce federal involvement in education by cutting federal spending, by converting it into block grants or vouchers, and by eliminating the Department of Education entirely. These conservative positions on education, though popular with the party's base, proved extremely unpopular with the general public and particularly with moderate swing voters. The extent of public displeasure with the conservative agenda on education was revealed forcefully in the 1996 presidential election, when voters favored Bill Clinton over Republican candidate Robert Dole on the issue by more than a two-to-one margin. Between 1984 and 1996, polls showed that Democrats maintained a double-digit advantage over Republicans in the percentage of the public who felt the party better addressed education.

By the end of the 1990s, the partisan "education gap" had become increasingly costly for the G.O.P. The failure of most states to comply with the 1994 federal mandates or to make significant progress in closing achievement gaps despite greatly increased federal and state education spending put pressure on national policymakers to undertake more substantive education reform. The unpopularity of the earlier Republican focus on deregulation and privatization and the discrediting of the Democratic focus on resources and process regulation led to a new bipartisan consensus on standards, testing, and accountability. In the 2000 election, millions of voters ranked education as the single most important issue of the election, and presidential candidates George W. Bush and Al Gore proposed remarkably similar plans for an expanded federal role in schools that became the basis for NCLB.

NCLB and an Expanded Federal Role

The centerpiece of NCLB was the requirement that states, as a condition of accepting federal funds, should establish academic standards to guide their curricula and adopt a testing regime aligned with those standards. States were required to test all students in math and reading in grades 3–8 every year, as well as once in high school. States were free to develop and use their own standards and tests, but every school, school district, and state had to make student test results publicly available and disaggregated for certain groups of students, including major racial and ethnic groups, major income groups, students with a disability, students with limited English proficiency, and migrant students.

NCLB mandated that every state and school district issue report cards to detail student test scores and identify those schools that failed to meet proficiency targets and were in need of "program improvement." NCLB explicitly required that states use this information to track their efforts to close the achievement gaps in reading and math between different student groups. States were required to establish a timeline (with regular benchmarks) for making "adequate yearly progress" (AYP) toward eliminating these gaps and moving all students to state proficiency levels by 2014. The law's accountability provisions required states to take a number of escalating actions with Title I (high-poverty) schools that do not reach state performance objectives. These actions included providing technical assistance to schools, and public school choice and tutoring to students. Schools that continued to fail to make AYP were required to implement corrective actions such as replacing staff, adopting a new curriculum, or undergoing more radical "restructuring." In exchange for meeting these new federal demands, NCLB provided a significant increase (approximately 49 percent in its first year) in federal education spending and new flexibility in how states can spend it.

NCLB and the expanded federal presence in education proved to be highly controversial, as state officials struggled to meet the law's ambitious goals and timetables and bristled at the intervention of the national government into historically local matters. Opponents argued that the law was an unfunded and unworkable mandate that stymied the creativity and flexibility of local teachers and school administrators and reduced education to mere test prep. The periodic reauthorization of ESEA—expected to occur sometime in 2009–2010—ensures that the fight over NCLB and the federal role in schools will continue, but early indications are that the central focus on standards, testing, and accountability are likely to be preserved.

The past 30 years have witnessed a dramatic shift in national politics and policymaking in education.

The issue has moved from the periphery to the center of the public agenda and thus to the heart of contemporary congressional and presidential campaigns. The new federal focus on academic performance and the extension of federal policy to cover every student and every school in the country mark a major shift in the governance of elementary and secondary education in the United States.

Bibliography and Further Reading

Anderson, Lee. *Congress and the Classroom: From the Cold War to No Child Left Behind.* University Park: Pennsylvania State University Press, 2007.

Chrismer, Sara, Shannon Hodge, and Debby Saintil, eds. "Assessing NCLB: Perspectives and Prescriptions." Special Issue of *Harvard Educational Review* 76, no. 4 (winter 2006).

Debray, Elizabeth, Kathryn McDermott, and Priscilla Wohlstetter, eds. "Federalism Reconsidered: The Case of the No Child Left Behind Act." Special Issue of *Peabody Journal of Education* 80, no. 2 (2005).

Hess, Frederick, and Michael Petrilli. *No Child Left Behind: A Primer.* New York: Peter Lang Press, 2006.

Kaestle, Carl, and Alyssa Lodewick, eds. *To Educate a Nation: Federal and National Strategies of School Reform.* Lawrence: University Press of Kansas, 2007.

Manna, Paul. *School's In: Federalism and the National Education Agenda.* Washington, D.C.: Georgetown University Press, 2006.

McGuinn, Patrick. *No Child Left Behind and the Transformation of Federal Education Policy, 1965–2005.* Lawrence: University Press of Kansas, 2006.

Patrick J. McGuinn

ELECTION OF 1980

Ronald Reagan's triumph in the 1980 election ushered in a period of conservative dominance in U.S. domestic policy and marked the end of détente and the resumption of a more confrontational U.S. approach in the Cold War with the Soviet Union. The 1980 election was also remarkable in that it took place in the shadow of the continuing incarceration of American hostages from the U.S. Embassy in Teheran, Iran. The hostage drama would play a major role in the outcome of both the Democratic primary campaign and the general election.

Carter's Problems

In 1976, former Georgia governor Jimmy Carter had leapt from political obscurity to win the presidency for the Democrats in the wake of the Vietnam War and the Watergate scandal. His margin of victory had been narrow, however, and Carter faced the additional problem of being a moderate Southern Democrat in a party that was becoming increasingly non-Southern and ideologically liberal. The situation was exacerbated by the Georgian's disdain for the deal-making endemic to domestic politics in Washington, which alienated his own party's congressional leadership. In foreign policy, Carter had some genuine successes such as the Camp David Middle-East Peace Accords and the Panama Canal Treaty (both signed in 1978), but these were overshadowed by the downfall of the U.S. ally the Shah of Iran in early 1979 and a concomitant rise in world oil prices that sank the U.S. economy into recession.

Carter's decision to allow the exiled and ailing Shah to enter the U.S. for cancer treatment prompted the seizure of 66 U.S. embassy personnel as hostages by the new Islamic revolutionary government in Iran on November 4, 1979. The hostage drama helped Carter at crucial moments due to the natural tendency of the American public to rally around the presidency in a foreign policy crisis, but the focus on the hostages also emphasized Carter's apparent haplessness in the face of challenges from hostile regimes. The Soviet invasion of Afghanistan at Christmas 1979 undermined Carter's hitherto conciliatory approach to relations with the U.S.S.R. and added to the atmosphere of crisis in foreign policy.

By the summer of 1979, it was clear that Carter would face a strong reelection challenge for the 1980 Democratic nomination from Sen. Edward Kennedy (D–MA). Carter could not have asked for a more formidable opponent than the younger brother of the modern Democratic Party's two greatest political martyrs: Pres. John F. Kennedy and Sen. Robert F. Kennedy. California's idiosyncratic Democratic governor Edmund G. "Jerry" Brown also indicated that he was likely to challenge Carter.

The Nominating Campaigns

Despite Carter's evident weaknesses, the incumbent clearly benefited from the intense media focus on the Iranian hostage crisis. Edward Kennedy's liabilities as a candidate also became apparent. At a time when the public mood had clearly shifted in a conservative direction, the Massachusetts senator's main argument against the Carter administration was that it had been insufficiently liberal. Kennedy's presidential candidacy also revived media interest in the 1969 Chappaquiddick incident in which Kennedy had driven off a bridge in Martha's Vineyard and his young female passenger drowned. Chappaquiddick dominated Kennedy's major primetime interview with CBS's Roger Mudd (broadcast the same day that the Iranian hostages were seized), and Kennedy stumbled when given the opportunity to articulate the reasons for his candidacy.

The early caucuses and primaries—Iowa, New Hampshire, Florida, Illinois—were all decisive victories for Carter, but the incumbent proved unable to eliminate Kennedy (Jerry Brown's campaign went nowhere). Every time he appeared on the brink of quitting, the Massachusetts senator would win a critical "big state" primary—New York, Pennsylvania, and California—to keep his campaign alive and thereby undermine the standing of the all-but-certain nominee Carter. At the Democratic convention (which opened in New York on August 11), Kennedy delivered a stem-winding concession speech that underlined all the Democratic liberals' misgivings about Carter. The lasting images of the convention were of the Massachusetts liberal icon, not the renominated Carter-Mondale ticket.

Sensing Carter's vulnerability, the race for the G.O.P. nomination attracted a strong field of candidates. Ronald Reagan, the former governor of the nation's largest state, a polished television communicator, and leader of the party's rapidly growing grassroots conservative movement, was a strong frontrunner. Reagan's vulnerabilities were also evident: His age (68 at the time) would make him the oldest president ever to take office if elected, and his hard-line stance against Soviet communism might give rise to potential charges of "extremism." Conservatives seeking a younger, less polarizing alternative to Reagan had several options. The most apparently formidable was former Texas governor, Nixon Treasury secretary, and Democrat, John Connally. Senators Robert Dole (R–KS), the G.O.P. vice-presidential candidate in 1976, and Howard Baker (R–TN), the minority leader in the U.S. Senate, were major Republican figures on Capitol Hill. These challenges never really materialized, however. Connally's millions in campaign funds secured him only one convention delegate, Dole had been a poor 1976 vice presidential candidate, and Baker was unpopular with conservatives for having supported Carter's Panama Canal Treaty.

Reagan's strongest opponents in the primary campaign were former CIA director George H. W. Bush and Illinois congressman John B. Anderson. Bush had the advantage of being a fresh face in presidential politics, with good conservative credentials, and extensive experience in foreign policy. Anderson, a veteran House Republican, was a former conservative who had moved closer to the political center as his party had moved to the right. A compelling speaker, Anderson's maverick style attracted rave reviews from the national press covering the campaign and even earned him a place in the popular *Doonesbury* cartoon strip.

Bush gained the early momentum in the nominating campaign by upsetting Reagan in the January 21 Iowa caucuses. The New Hampshire primary on February 26 became decisive for the Californian, who sacked his campaign manager and came out swinging

Ronald Reagan and wife Nancy wave to the crowd after he receives the presidential nomination at the Republican National Convention on July 17, 1980. Reagan's triumph over incumbent Jimmy Carter in the November election opened a sharp cultural divide between supporters of the increasingly Southern/interior Western and religiously conservative Republican Party and the more urban, coastal, and secular Democratic Party. The election of 1980 ushered in a period of conservative dominance of Washington that would continue through the first decade of the twenty-first century. (Bettmann/Corbis)

at Bush in the televised debates. Reagan's comeback victory in the Granite State arrested Bush's momentum and the Texan's campaign never really recovered as Reagan rolled up a succession of big primary wins in the South and West. Bush was able to win some other primaries such as Pennsylvania (April 26) and Michigan (May 20), but his withdrawal from the race on May 26 ended the G.O.P. contest. By wrapping up the Republican nomination while Carter was still fending off Edward Kennedy, Reagan was able to unify his party prior to the convention and get an early start on his general election campaign.

The only suspense at the G.O.P. convention (held in Detroit from July 13–16) was a failed last-minute effort (initiated by former Sec. of State Henry Kissinger) to have former Pres. Gerald Ford nominated as Reagan's running mate. Reagan instead nominated his defeated primary rival George Bush, which both reassured the moderate wing of the party and bolstered the foreign policy credentials of the ticket. Though the 1976 G.O.P. platform had taken an ambivalent position on abortion and supported the Equal Rights Amendment (ERA), the 1980 platform repudiated the ERA and demanded a constitutional amendment banning abortion. Both shifts underscored the enhanced influence of religious Southern conservatives over the G.O.P.

The Fall Campaign

For most of the fall campaign, a close contest between Carter and Reagan was anticipated. A complicating factor was the Independent candidacy of John B. Anderson. Anderson's bid was prompted by the enthusiastic media response to his maverick candidacy during the G.O.P. primaries. In the latter, Anderson had demonstrated his appeal to Northern Republican moderates uncomfortable with Reagan's conservatism, while his increasingly liberal issue positions had potential appeal to Kennedy Democrats increasingly estranged from Carter. Anderson got on the ballot on all 50 states and was polling 20–25 percent in early summer. Like most independent and third-party presidential candidates, however, his support had dropped to single digits by the last week of the campaign due to the potency of the "wasted vote" argument.

The Iran hostage crisis remained at the forefront of public attention during the campaign. Carter realized that bringing the hostages home before polling day might be an election-winning coup, but he was unable to make a deal with the Iranians. The continuing impasse allowed the Republicans to highlight Carter's "weakness" in foreign policy, but the Reagan campaign also concentrated heavily on the deepening economic recession. Carter's campaign strove to raise doubts about Reagan's temperament and intellectual capacity for the presidency, but these attacks also gave rise to charges of "meanness" on the part of the president.

The anticipated televised debates between the candidates became a point of contention as Carter's camp refused to debate Anderson since the Illinoisan had clearly become a greater threat to the Democratic ticket. Reagan and Anderson debated on September 21, a polite encounter that reflected well on both candidates at the expense of the absent Carter. The only debate between the two major party candidates took place on October 28, just one week before Election Day. Carter was aggressive and sought to demonstrate his grasp of the major issues at the expense of the allegedly disengaged Reagan. The key moments belonged to the Californian, however. Reagan's response of "there you go again" to one of Carter's attacks made the incumbent appear peevish. Reagan also encapsulated the key economic issue by asking the nationwide viewing audience "Are you better off than you were four years ago?"

The Result

The election result was a comfortable victory for Ronald Reagan, who carried 44 states and won a landslide 489–49 margin in the Electoral College. Reagan defeated Carter 51–41 percent, with Anderson securing just under 7 percent. The G.O.P. ticket made major gains among white Southerners, evangelical voters, and ethnic Catholic voters in the Northern cities. Carter carried only his home state of Georgia, five other "core" Democratic states (Hawaii, Maryland, Minnesota, Rhode Island, and West Virginia), and D.C. Anderson's support derived mainly from liberal enclaves and college towns.

Even more surprisingly, the Republicans gained 12 Senate seats and secured control of the chamber for the first time since 1954. They also gained 33 seats in the House and made major gains in state legislatures. Reagan's apparently strong coattails certainly contributed to the legislative successes of the "Reagan Revolution" in 1981 and reinforced the widespread perception of a new alignment of political forces in the United States.

Implications of the Election

The 1980 election set a pattern of Republican victories in presidential elections based on G.O.P. strength in the Southern and Western states and the suburban areas of the Northeast and Midwest that would be repeated in 1984 and 1988. Yet the Republicans suffered House losses in 1982 and lost control of the Senate in 1986, reflecting the traditional swing of the electoral pendulum against the president's party. The 1980 election did, however, initiate a sharp cultural divide between supporters of the Republican and Democratic parties. The Republicans after 1980 became an increasingly southern and interior western party strongly influenced by religious conservatives, while the Democrats became an increasingly "coastal" party strongly supported by minorities, urban social liberals, and secular voters.

Perhaps the greatest effect of the 1980 election was a decisive change in the direction of public policy. After 1980, both Republicans and Democrats moved in the direction of a more limited government approach in economic and welfare policy that lasted through the Democratic presidency of Bill Clinton (who proclaimed the "era of big government is over" in his 1996 State of the Union address). For American conservatives, the 1980 election and what it represented became as important as the 1932 election had been to the liberals of the New Deal era.

Bibliography and Further Reading

Abramson, Paul R., John H. Aldrich, and David W. Rohde. *Change and Continuity in the 1980 Elections.* Washington, D.C.: CQ Press, 1982.

Busch, Andrew E. *Reagan's Victory: The Presidential Election of 1980 and the Rise of the Right.* Lawrence: University Press of Kansas, 2005.

Cannon, Lou. *Reagan.* New York: G. P. Putnam's Sons, 1982.

Drew, Elizabeth. *Portrait of an Election: The 1980 Presidential Campaign.* New York: Simon & Schuster, 1981.

White, Theodore H. *America in Search of Itself: The Making of the President, 1956–1980.* New York: Harper & Row, 1982.

Nicol C. Rae

ELECTION OF 1992

In 1992, William Jefferson Clinton, a self-described "New Democrat," defeated the incumbent president George H. W. Bush, ending the conservative Republican revolution of Pres. Ronald Reagan (1980–1988). The resounding foreign policy successes of President Bush were witnessed by the nation and world in the fall of the Berlin Wall, the collapse of the Soviet Union that effectively ended the Cold War, the reunification of Germany, and the military expeditions to the Persian Gulf and Panama. However, these collective foreign policy successes could not obscure serious domestic economic problems that dissipated the coherence of the Republican Party and led to the "centrist" Clinton becoming the first Democratic president since Franklin Delano Roosevelt to win two terms in the White House.

Republican Foreign Policy Successes and the Remaking of the Democratic Party

Reagan's conservative revolution solidified an image of the Republican Party that had been launched during the Eisenhower and Nixon presidencies, one that was strongly anti-communist, staunch on national security, and highly patriotic in contrast to the Democrats' weaker image on these issues. Meanwhile, Republicans painted the Democratic Party as "wrong" on character, cultural, and social issues. The "Reagan Revolution" allowed the Republicans to dominate electoral competition at the presidential level with their adroit ability to frame certain key issues at the expense of the Democrats. At the same time, their financial prowess and ability to out-raise and outspend their Democratic opponents channeled both the print and electronic media to a "framing process" that defined the Democratic Party in negative and unflattering ways. The Democratic Party was portrayed as being at odds with mainstream values and American principles. In effect, the conservative revolution saw the Republicans winning three presidential elections in a row (1980, 1984, and 1988). They were declared to have a lock on the Electoral College through the turn of the century. In 1988, the Bush election campaign continued with their winning formula of portraying the Democratic Party negatively. Republicans associated the Democrats so effectively with a negative definition of the "L" word—as in "liberal"—that the Democratic presidential candidate Michael Dukakis would not even say the word until the last days of the campaign.

In February 1985, all of the negative name-calling and innuendo began to unravel with the creation of the Democratic Leadership Council (DLC). The DLC sought to move the image of the Democratic Party more to the center and away from the liberal label deployed by Republicans. Governor Clinton was not only one of the founding DLC members but also became chairman of the organization in 1991. Thus his presidential campaign was set to remake the Democratic Party's image during his run for the presidency and thereafter.

Perhaps ironically, it was the foreign policy successes of the Bush administration—the collapse of the Soviet Union and the end of the Cold War—that largely obviated the Republican Party's tactic of characterizing the Democrats as weak on defense and national security. That is, presidential candidate and later nominee Clinton had only to redefine, refashion, and re-label his party from the standpoint of domestic policy, not both domestic and foreign policy. Even the Republicans' attempt to pin a "draft-dodging" tag on Clinton during the primaries and the general election campaign got little traction because their foreign policy successes had eroded its effectiveness.

Clinton re-imagined his party by calling himself and running mate Al Gore New Democrats and by announcing that their ideology was "centrist" and not liberal. To this the Bush campaign had no real retort.

Clinton also announced that he would focus on the middle class in America. He used the occasion of the Rainbow Coalition convention, headed by the two-time African American presidential candidate and civil rights leader Jesse Jackson, to distance both himself and the Democratic Party from Jackson, a sometimes controversial figure and prominent liberal icon. During the campaign, Clinton flew back to Arkansas to watch the execution of an intellectually disabled African American man to prove to the nation's electorate that neither he nor the Democratic Party was "soft-on-crime," another label penned on the party by the Republicans.

In July, as the nation's economy slipped into a recession, Clinton found another opportunity to remake the Democratic Party's image by blaming the incumbent Bush administration for its fiscally irresponsible policies. All of this re-imaging of the Democrats was possible in large part because of the foreign policy successes of the Bush administration and the Republicans' inability to respond to attacks on their domestic policies. Even when they saw this re-imaging taking place, they had no strategy to deal with it except to repeat over and over again all of their defining critiques of the Democratic Party. Finally, they turned to such character issues as Clinton's marital infidelity and lying and gave the Democrat a nickname, "Slick Willy." Like other Republican attempts to frame the Democrats, the attack never gained much traction.

The Presidential Primaries

The Republican foreign policy successes worked not only in allowing the Clinton-led Democrats to re-imagine themselves but they served also to determine the nature of the Democratic challengers. When in March 1991 the first Persian Gulf War ended swiftly and victoriously, President Bush's approval rating in the polls rocketed to 91 percent. Since the development of public opinion polls in 1936, no president had enjoyed such a high approval rating. As a result, most of the first-tier potential Democratic presidential candidates, including New Jersey senator Bill Bradley and New York governor Mario Cuomo, decided not to challenge Bush's re-election bid.

That being the case, Clinton found himself facing second-tier candidates in the primaries, including senators Paul Tsongas (D–MA), Tom Harkin (D–IA), and Bob Kerrey (D–NE), and Gov. L. Douglas Wilder of Virginia and former governor Jerry Brown of California. The news media dubbed the Democratic field the "seven dwarfs." Even in such a weak field, however, Clinton did not win in either the Iowa caucus, where everyone deferred to Iowa favorite-son Harkin, or in the New Hampshire primary, which went to Tsongas, who was from the neighboring state of Massachusetts. In the March 3 primaries, Tsongas won Maryland, Clinton won Georgia, and Brown won Colorado. Then came Super Tuesday on March 10 with its large number of Southern primaries. Tsongas won three states, including Rhode Island, Delaware, and his home state of Massachusetts, while Clinton took nine states, six of which were Southern states. On March 17, Clinton won Illinois and Michigan, while Brown a few days later won Connecticut.

Tsongas and Brown had hoped to win in the April 7 primaries in New York, Wisconsin, Kansas, and Minnesota, but Clinton seized the first three states and tied with Tsongas in Minnesota. Brown in a long-shot effort to win in New York had announced that if he won there, he would choose Jackson as his vice presidential running mate. His campaign collapsed, but he refused both to bow out and to endorse Clinton. However, all of the other candidates either dropped out or dropped out and endorsed the presumptive nominee.

President Bush won all of the Republican primaries. However, he did face one major challenger in Patrick J. Buchanan, a speechwriter in the Nixon and Reagan White Houses. Bush also received a minor challenge from the Klansman and neo-Nazi David Duke of Louisiana. In the New Hampshire primary, Buchanan surprised the president with a strong third-place finish, capturing 37 percent of the vote and holding Bush to only 52 percent, dangerously close to the 50 percent mark so prized by incumbent candidates. Buchanan stayed in the primaries, attacking the president for his failure to maintain fidelity to Reagan's conservative principles and for compromising on his "no new taxes" pledge and on the Civil Rights Restoration Bill. In the end, President Bush simply steamrolled these opponents, but not before Buchanan's attacks revealed cleavages and fractures in

the Republican Party's electoral base. President Bush entered 39 primaries and won them all, while Clinton won 30 of 36 Democratic primaries.

H. Ross Perot: The Rise of the Third-Party Candidate

Two days after the New Hampshire primary on February 18, Texas billionaire computer services entrepreneur H. Ross Perot announced that, if the American people wanted him to do so, he would run for president. Inasmuch as he already had a national reputation for helping Vietnam War veterans and rescuing prisoners of war (as well as his own company executives from Iran), people started to listen to his dire warnings about the state of the nation and its descent from its position as the world's number-one economic superpower. This attention resulted in Perot getting his name on the ballot in all 50 states. On May 18, the concerted efforts of Perot volunteers got him on the ballot in the Oregon state primary via a write-in campaign. He received 13 percent of the votes using this technique, while Clinton won the primary and Brown placed second. Just prior to this vote, a Time/CNN poll on May 13–14 showed Perot receiving 34 percent of the vote, with Clinton and Bush each receiving 30 percent.

By June 3, Perot had announced the hiring of Pres. Jimmy Carter's chief-of-staff, Hamilton Jordan, and President Reagan's campaign strategist, Ed Rollins, in an attempt to demonstrate broad appeal to both Democrats and Republicans. On June 11, Perot addressed the NAACP National Convention in Nashville, Tennessee, but his speech included language that those in attendance considered patronizing and demeaning. A huge protest ensued and there was such extensive media coverage that on June 15 Rollins quit, declaring that Perot would not take his advice. A month later, when Clinton was giving his acceptance speech at the National Democratic Convention, Perot, at a press conference, abruptly announced his withdrawal from the race and gave his nod, but not his endorsement, to Clinton. Actually, Perot did not quit the race but continued his efforts to obtain a place on the ballot of all 50 states.

Perot officially reentered the presidential race during the general election phase on October 1. This was the second stage of his campaign and in both the first and second stages, Perot bitterly attacked President Bush. Clinton's strategy was simply not to respond to Perot's critiques. Eventually, he let the Bush-Perot battles play themselves out without entering the fray on either side. Nevertheless, Perot's re-entry into the race turned the 1992 election into a three-way —instead of the usual two-way—contest.

The National Conventions

On July 13, the Democrats held their national convention in New York, and Clinton used the occasion to redefine and imprint the party's new image. After satisfying the prerequisites of endorsing Clinton and having his speech approved by the Clinton campaign, Jesse Jackson was allowed to address the convention. Brown and Tsongas were given little opportunity to express their concerns. In securing the party's nomination Clinton received 79 (78.6) percent of the delegate votes to Brown's 14 (13.9) percent and Tsongas' five (4.9) percent. The Democratic platform gave the military a strong role, lowered expectations for the labor unions, and did not mention race or civil rights even in muted tones. The platform was fashioned so that it reached out to middle-class Americans.

The final tactic in redefining the Democratic Party was Clinton's selection of Al Gore as his running mate and vice president. This choice broke the traditional pattern of balancing the ticket by selecting a running mate from a region of the country different from that of the presidential nominee. This time, there were two baby boomers from the South. Hidden was the fact that this was a direct strategy, reinforcing an appeal to win back the South that had been taken over by the Republicans. Therefore, the party platform and the vice presidential selection had been used to make the image of the New Democrats.

On August 17, Republicans followed with their convention in Houston, Texas. To secure his base, President Bush gave Buchanan a prime time speech slot that was used to deliver a scathing attack on the Democrats and Clinton. Bush kept Vice Pres. Dan Quayle as his running mate and adopted a party platform that was a model of Reagan conservatism. In his acceptance speech, Bush apologized for his compro-

mise on the tax pledge and promised to continue the Reagan Revolution in conservatism. Thus, it came as no surprise that President Bush received 98 percent of the delegate votes in securing the nomination. Clinton left the Democratic Convention with a 23 point lead in the polls over President Bush; however, by the time of the Republican Convention, President Bush was only 18 points behind. When it ended, the president had reduced the Democrat's lead even further, but after only three days Clinton's polling figures rose back to the pre-convention levels.

The Presidential Debates

President Bush was not able to receive a significant bounce in the polls from his Republican Convention. With three scheduled presidential debates, the president had another opportunity to try and catch or overtake Clinton. The debates were set for October 11, 15, and 19, with the single vice presidential debate set for October 13. According to the debate polls, Perot won the first debate, Clinton won the second, and Clinton and Perot tied in the third. The president lost all three and managed to beat Perot just once in the second debate. Clinton maintained the lead that he had held since July. The handwriting was clearly on the wall. American voters did not trust and were not about to choose the president or Perot to handle and change the economy. The economic recession was now the major issue and concern in the 1992 campaign; it had trumped both national security and foreign policy issues.

The Election Outcome

On November 3, the Clinton-Gore Democratic ticket won 32 states and the District of Columbia. The incumbent president won 18 states. However, this large state-level victory translated into only a plurality of the popular vote: 43.3 percent for the Democrats, as compared to 37.7 percent for the Republicans and 19 percent for Perot's third party. In terms of actual votes, Clinton received 45 million, Bush 39 million, and Perot 20 million. Other third-party candidates received about 1.4 percent of the vote. Clinton beat Bush by some six million votes.

In 1988, Dukakis had won only 10 states and the District of Columbia. In 1992, the New Democrats,

RELATED ENTRIES

THIS VOLUME
Bush, George H. W.; Clinton, Bill; Third Parties

Clinton and Gore, had grown the party by winning 22 additional states, four of them from the Republican-dominated South. The Democratic candidates won their home states of Arkansas and Tennessee, and also seized Georgia and Louisiana. Elsewhere, Clinton won states in every region of the nation. On the other hand, President Bush, who won 40 states in 1988, lost more than half of them (22 states) by 1992. Among those that he did win was his adopted state of Texas but not his birth state of Maine. However, Clinton's real achievement came with the electoral votes. He won two-thirds of the electoral votes or 370 (68.8 percent) to President Bush's 168 (31.2 percent). Perot, for all of his strong popular vote showing, did not win a single electoral vote from any of the 50 states. In Texas, however, he was able to win a few counties.

Overall, the Clinton-Gore presidential victory in 1992 enabled the Democratic Party to return to competitiveness in presidential elections. This election showed how the party was able to win the White House in the post–civil rights era against the Republican Party that had previously captured the Solid South. A significant portion of the region had been won again by Southern native sons: Pres. Lyndon Baines Johnson in 1964, President Carter in 1976, and the Clinton-Gore ticket in 1992 and in 1996. These electoral victories broke up the original Republican presidential coalition, at least temporarily.

Bibliography and Further Reading

Ceaser, James, and Andrew Busch. *Upside Down and Inside Out: The 1992 Elections and American Politics.* Lanham, MD: Littlefield Adams, 1992.

Deskins, Donald, Jr., Hanes Walton, Jr., and Sherman C. Puckett. *Presidential Elections 1789–2008: County, State and National Mapping of Election Data.* Ann Arbor: University of Michigan Press, 2010.

Lewis-Beck, Michael, and Tom Rice. "Localism in Presidential Elections: The Home State Advantage." *American Journal of Political Science* 27, no. 3 (1983): 548–556.

Pomper, Gerald, ed. *The Election of 1992.* Chatham, NJ: Chatham House, 1993.

Rapoport, Ronald, and Walter Stone. *Three's A Crowd: The Dynamic of Third Parties, Ross Perot, and Republican Resurgence.* Ann Arbor: University of Michigan Press, 2008.

Rosenstone, Steven J. *Forecasting Presidential Elections.* New Haven, CT: Yale University Press, 1983.

Walton, Hanes, Jr. "African Americans, H. Ross Perot, and Image Politics." In *African American Power and Politics: The Political Context Variable*, edited by Hanes Walton, Jr. New York: Columbia University Press, 1997: 282–293.

———. *Reelection: William Jefferson Clinton as a Native-Son Candidate.* New York: Columbia University Press, 2000.

Hanes Walton Jr., Josephine A. V. Allen,
Donald R. Deskins Jr., and Sherman C. Puckett

ELECTION OF 2000

Between Franklin D. Roosevelt's first election in 1932 and Harry S. Truman's election in 1948, the Democrats won five consecutive presidential elections. But between Republican Dwight D. Eisenhower's election in 1952 and Democrat Bill Clinton's reelection in 1996, the political fortunes of the two major parties fluctuated far more. From 1952 through Republican Richard Nixon's reelection in 1972, neither party was able to win more than two elections in a row. And in 1976 and 1980, two incumbent presidents in a row were defeated (Republican Gerald Ford in 1976 and Democrat Jimmy Carter in 1980), a pattern that had occurred only once before in American history (1888 and 1892). Republican George H. W. Bush's election in 1988 broke this pattern of volatility; the G.O.P. had now won three elections in a row. But volatility returned in 1992 with Clinton bringing the Democrats back to power. He was easily reelected in 1996.

The 2000 contest thus gave the Democrats the chance to win three consecutive elections. Their first task was to find a nominee, since like Eisenhower in 1960 and Ronald Reagan in 1988, Clinton could not run for reelection because of Amendment XXII. Al Gore, Clinton's vice president, faced only one serious opponent, former senator Bill Bradley of New Jersey. Gore won every primary and caucus, and by March 9 Bradley had withdrawn. For his part, Texas governor George W. Bush faced several serious opponents, the most formidable being Sen. John McCain of Arizona. McCain won seven primaries, including the New Hampshire contest, which had often served as a launching pad for successful nominations. But Bush, who was more heavily funded and who had the support of many Republican leaders, prevailed fairly easily. On March 9, McCain conceded.

In the general election campaign, Gore's main decision was whether to associate himself with Clinton and to try to capitalize on the perceived economic successes of the Clinton administration, or whether to emphasize his own policies. He chose to do the latter. Moreover, because of the threat of losing votes to Ralph Nader, the Green Party candidate, he made populist appeals, especially late in the campaign. Bush ran as a moderate, claiming to be a "compassionate conservative." He deemphasized social issues, stressing the need to improve education and arguing that his administrative experience would enable him to carry out educational reform. Both campaigns focused on a relatively small number of battleground states, with Florida receiving the most attention—a decision that had fateful consequences. And both campaigns made a major effort at boosting turnout among their supporters.

The Election Outcome

Bush won a minority of the popular vote, and his party lost seats in both the U.S. House and the U.S. Senate. But Bush prevailed with 271 electoral votes to Gore's 266, with one elector abstaining. Gore won more popular votes than Bush, 50,992,335 (48.4 percent) to 50,455,156 (47.9 percent). But Bush's margin over Gore in Florida, where the official vote count gave Bush a 537 vote lead out of nearly six million votes, gave Bush the 25 electoral votes needed to gain his majority. Overall, 105,396,627 people voted, only 51.2 percent of the voting-age population and 55.6 percent of the eligible population.

Bush's victory in Florida came, however, after protracted court battles in which Gore demanded a recount in four counties. The Florida supreme court ordered a manual recount for the entire state. But on December 12, by a five-to-four vote, the U.S. Supreme Court overturned the Florida decision, ruling that its method for recounting was unconstitutional as there was not enough time to establish statewide standards. (*Bush v. Gore*, 531 U.S. 98 [2000]) The following day, Gore conceded. In effect, the Supreme Court refereed the presidential election of 2000—a first in American political development.

In the period between the popular vote election (November 7) and the *Bush v. Gore* decision, the Republican-controlled Florida state legislature voted to appoint 25 electors to vote for Bush for president and Dick Cheney for vice president. Although Article II, Section 1 of the U.S. Constitution specifies that states shall appoint electors "in such Manner as the Legislature thereof may direct," no state legislature had appointed electors since South Carolina in 1860. Whether a state legislature could appoint presidential electors after a popular-vote election was problematic. Although the Electoral Count Act of 1887 was designed to resolve disputes, its applicability to the Florida contest was questionable. But most analysts argue that Bush would have prevailed if the Florida recount had proceeded.

Bush won 30 states; Gore won twenty states and the District of Columbia. Ralph Nader came in third in all 48 states (including the District) for which results were reported. Pat Buchanan was on the ballot in every state except Michigan. Nader argued that if he received 5.0 percent of the popular vote, the Green Party would be entitled to federal funding in the 2004 election. He received only 2.7 percent, but his candidacy altered the outcome nevertheless. In two states, Florida and New Hampshire, Bush's winning margin was less than the number of votes cast for Nader. If Nader had not been on the ballot, it seems likely that Gore would have won Florida, although Bush would have held New Hampshire, where his margin over Gore was larger.

Bush was the first presidential candidate since 1888 to be elected without winning the plurality of the popular vote. Except for Richard M. Nixon in 1968, all the other Republican winners since 1896 had won a majority of the popular vote. Bush's electoral-vote victory was the second closest contest since 1828, the first year when the vast majority of states chose their electors by popular vote. Only the disputed contest of 1876, in which the Republican Rutherford B. Hayes defeated the Democrat Samuel J. Tilden by a single vote, was closer. George W. Bush carried every state that his father had carried in 1988, as well as every state Republican Bob Dole had carried in 1996. Gore, on the other hand, carried 9 of the 10 states that Democrat Michael S. Dukakis carried in 1988, as well as the District of Columbia. The 2000 contest was closer than George H. W. Bush's 1988 victory because George W. Bush failed to win 11 of the 40 states his father carried, while winning only one state that his father had lost. In 2000, Bush carried all 11 of the Southern states, gaining 147

of his electoral votes from the Old Confederacy. This was the fourth election since World War II in which the Republicans had won all 11 Southern states (the others were 1972, 1984, and 1988). The transformation of the South from an overwhelmingly Democratic region to a predominantly Republican one is the most dramatic change in postwar American politics.

The Reasons Bush Won

Why was the election so close? After all, it was its closeness that created the context in which the Court effectively awarded the election to Bush.

The question can be answered in several ways. First, one can look at the views of the electorate about the incumbent, the problems facing the country, and the parties. The NES survey shows that two-thirds of the

President-elect George W. Bush prepares to be sworn in on January 20, 2001. He stands with outgoing president Bill Clinton and outgoing vice president Al Gore, who had lost his bid for the presidency to Bush five weeks previous when the U.S. Supreme Court overturned a Florida supreme court order for a manual recount for the entire state. It was the first time in American political history that the Supreme Court rendered the final decision in a presidential election. (Tim Clary/AFP/Getty Images)

public approved of the job Bill Clinton was doing as president, and other surveys also showed relatively high approval. Moreover, just under half the respondents thought the government was doing a bad job solving what they considered to be the most important problem facing the country. And somewhat more thought the Democratic Party would do a better job of solving that problem than thought the G.O.P. would. All these evaluations were similar to those four years earlier when Bill Clinton prevailed by an 8.5 percent popular vote margin over Bob Dole. Based upon these "retrospective" evaluations, Gore had a clear advantage. But Gore did not do as well among those with a favorable view of Clinton, the condition of the country, and the Democratic Party as Clinton had done four years earlier.

Secondly, Bush ran an effective campaign. He ran as a moderate. And on several important issues, especially defense spending, government job guarantees, and aid to African Americans, the electorate was clearly closer to where it saw Bush than to where it saw Gore. And, although the electorate was more likely to favor Gore's position on abortion rights, Bush did an excellent job of obfuscating his "pro-life" position.

Thirdly, Bush's victory can also be seen as part of the long-term decline of the New Deal coalition. Despite populist appeals by Gore, he won only a small majority among white union members, whereas Bush won a small majority among white Catholics. There was virtually no relationship between social class, as measured by occupation, and the way people voted. Among the traditional social groups that made up the New Deal coalition, only African Americans and Jews voted overwhelmingly Democratic.

Lastly, although more Americans identified as Democrats than as Republicans, the Republicans had narrowed this margin. In 1980, 65 percent of all party identifiers were Democrats; in 2000, 59 percent were. Given that Republicans are more likely to vote than Democrats, the Democratic edge is actually somewhat narrower.

The Electoral Vote Balance

The narrow Republican presidential victory, along with small Republican losses in the U.S. House and Senate, underscored the relatively close balance in

RELATED ENTRIES

THIS VOLUME
Bush, George W; Third Parties

partisan forces as America entered the twenty-first century. Between 1988 and 2000, the G.O.P. had won two of these contests, the Democrats the other two. Sixteen states (with 135 electoral votes as of 2004 and 2008) had voted Republican in all four elections. The Republicans had won five additional states (with 64 electoral votes) in three of these contests. For their part, the Democrats had won nine states and the District of Columbia (with 99 electoral votes) in all four elections. In 12 states (with 166 electoral votes), the Democrats had won in three of these contests. And there were eight states (with 74 electoral votes) that split evenly between the parties, in all cases with the Republicans winning in 1988 and 2000 and the Democrats winning in 1992 and 1996.

Conclusion

Bush's 2000 victory led to important policy consequences. Although he had run as a "compassionate conservative" and although he won by a very narrow margin, he governed—in a way that sharply surprised Democrats in Congress—as if he had a mandate for major policy change. Bush's fiscal policies lowered taxes for affluent Americans, which contributed to massive budget deficits. His social policies usually were conservative, even when the public disagreed with them, such as his restrictions on embryonic stem-cell research. Most importantly, his reactions to the terrorist attacks on September 11, 2001, led to Operation Enduring Freedom, the invasion of Afghanistan in October 2001, and to Operation Iraqi Freedom, the invasion of Iraq in March 2003.

Despite the policy consequences of Bush's election, from the long-term standpoint of affecting the balance of partisan forces, the election did relatively little. Bush may have had the opportunity to restore the Republican Party to the dominance that it enjoyed before the Great Depression, but to do this he would have to win reelection and to establish a basis for a successor to win the White House. He succeeded in fulfilling this first goal, but badly failed in the second.

Bibliography and Further Reading

Abramson, Paul R., John H. Aldrich, and David W. Rohde. *Change and Continuity in the 2000 and 2002 Elections.* Washington, D.C.: CQ Press, 2003.

Ceaser, James W., and Andrew E. Busch. *The Perfect Tie: The True Story of the 2000 Presidential Election.* Lanham, MD: Rowman and Littlefield, 2001.

CQ Press. *Presidential Elections, 1789–2000.* Washington, D.C.: CQ Press, 2002.

Lewis-Beck, Michael S., William G. Jacoby, Helmut Norpoth, and Herbert F. Weisberg. *The American Voter Revisited.* Ann Arbor: University of Michigan Press, 2008.

Manza, Jeff, and Christopher Uggen. *Locked Out: Felon Disenfranchisement and American Democracy.* New York: Oxford University Press, 2006.

McDonald, Michael P., and Samuel L. Popkin. "The Myth of the Vanishing Voter." *American Political Science Review* 95, no. 4 (December 2001): 963–974.

Shaw, Daron R. *The Race to 270: The Electoral College and the Campaign Strategies of 2000 and 2004.* Chicago: University of Chicago Press, 2006.

Weisberg, Herbert F., and Clyde Wilcox, eds. *Models of Voting in Presidential Elections: The 2000 U.S. Elections.* Stanford, CA: Stanford University Press, 2004.

Paul R. Abramson

ELECTION OF 2004

The 2004 election raised the question of whether the incumbent president—George W. Bush—could win reelection. In 1976 and 1980, two incumbent presidents in a row were defeated, something that had occurred only once before in American history (1888 and 1892). Moreover, Republican George H. W. Bush failed to win reelection in 1992. Going into the election, however, George W. Bush argued that it would be dangerous for the country to change its leadership at a time of war. It was a powerful argument that helped to explain why the Democratic Party nominated a decorated war hero, Sen. John Kerry.

Bush himself faced no challenge in his bid for the G.O.P. presidential nomination, but many Democrats sought to oppose him. Four Democratic senators, one ex-senator, one former governor, two members of the U.S. House, and one retired general ran for the Democratic presidential nomination. Because many states had moved their primaries and caucuses to early in the delegate selection period, the contest was heavily "front-loaded." Howard Dean, the former governor of Vermont, was an early favorite, and he skillfully used the Internet to fund his campaign. But his poor showing in the Iowa caucuses severely damaged his prospects, while Massachusetts senator John F. Kerry's win helped propel him to front-runner status, and this status was reinforced by his first-place showing in the New Hampshire primary. By March 3, Sen. John Edwards of North Carolina, who had emerged as Kerry's strongest opponent, withdrew from the contest, effectively ensuring that Kerry would be nominated. Kerry later chose his former opponent as his vice presidential running mate.

The Democrats held a successful convention. Kerry was portrayed as a war hero who had earned three Purple Hearts, a Bronze Star, and a Silver Star for his service as a swift boat commander in Vietnam. But an independent "527" group called "The Swift Boat Veterans for Truth" questioned his war record. Kerry was slow to respond, and the term "swift-boated" entered the political vocabulary. Although Kerry was helped by his performance in the three televised debates with Bush, as the election approached the polls suggested that either candidate could win. Both candidates focused on a handful of battleground states, with Ohio receiving the most attention. And both made a great effort to get their voters to the polls, although it is generally acknowledged that the Republicans were more successful. President Bush's political advisor, Karl Rove, legendary for his obsessive preoccupation with tactics, worked well with the Republican National Committee's highly professional operation.

The Election Outcome

Bush's reelection extended Republican rule. He won 286 electoral votes to Kerry's 251 (with one vote cast for John Edwards). Unlike 2000, when Bush won fewer popular votes than Al Gore, in 2004 he won a majority of the popular vote. He gained 62,040,610 (50.7 percent) of the vote to Kerry's 59,028,439 (48.3 percent). There was a surge in turnout. Some

122,295,345 Americans voted, 55.3 percent of the voting-age population and 60.3 percent of the population eligible to do so. The Republicans gained three seats in the U.S. House, and had now won control of the House for the sixth consecutive election. They also gained four Senate seats, regaining majority control of that chamber.

The Republicans had now won 9 of the 15 elections since World War II; the Democrats had won six. Moreover, the Republicans had won the majority of the popular vote seven times since the war ended (1952, 1956, 1972, 1980, 1984, 1988, and 2004), whereas the Democrats had won a popular vote majority only twice (1964 and 1976).

But the 2004 presidential election was very close. Bush's 2.4 percent margin of victory was the narrowest popular-vote win for an incumbent in American history, and his electoral-vote margin was the second narrowest. Even so, in the 26 elections in which an incumbent president has run, he has been defeated 10 times, so being reelected is a significant achievement.

The most striking feature of the 2004 election was its similarity to that of 2000. Only 3 of the 50 states switched sides. Iowa and New Mexico narrowly voted Democratic in 2000, but they voted narrowly Republican in 2004. New Hampshire voted narrowly Republican in 2000, but it voted narrowly Democratic four years later. Bush gained 15 electoral votes between 2000 and 2004, and eight came from the switches among these three states. The remaining seven-vote gain resulted from the net increase in House seats among the 29 states that he won in both elections, which followed the reapportionment after the 2000 Census.

As in 2000, Bush carried all 11 of the states of the Old Confederacy, the fifth time since World War II that the G.O.P. had swept these states (the earlier elections were 1972, 1984, and 1988). Between the end of Reconstruction (1877) and the end of World War II, the Democrats were so dominant in these states that the region was viewed as the "Solid South." But since the end of the war, the Democrats have never swept this region. The transformation of the South from an overwhelmingly Democratic region to a predominantly Republican region has

been an enormously consequential metamorphosis in American politics because it has created a secure regional base for any Republican presidential candidate. The presidential elections of 2000 and 2004 appeared to consolidate this change.

Bush's victory had major policy consequences. Granted, the "political capital" that he claimed to have earned could not be spent to carry out many of his proposed reforms. But his reelection did lead to the appointment of two conservative justices to the U.S. Supreme Court—John H. Roberts as chief justice of the United States and Samuel A. Alito Jr. as associate justice. And despite Democrats regaining control of the U.S. House and Senate in the 2006 midterm elections, Bush was able to pursue his policies in Iraq, increasing U.S. military involvement in spite of Democratic opposition.

The Reasons Bush Won

Why was Bush reelected? The most important factor was that America was at war. Voters are risk-averse and "switching horses in midstream" is seen as risky. All four previous wartime presidents who had sought reelection had also prevailed.

Of the two wars the United States was fighting in 2004, Operational Enduring Freedom (Afghanistan) and Operation Iraqi Freedom, the latter was much more controversial. Although the major rationale for the war was that Iraq was developing weapons of mass destruction, no such weapons were found. The secondary rationale, that the Iraqi government had links with Osama bin Laden's al Qaeda ("The Base") terrorist organization, was questionable. The major national exit poll conducted by Edison Media Research/Mitofsky International (called the Pool Poll because it was conducted for a consortium of news organizations) showed that 53 percent of voters thought things were not going well in Iraq, but by 51 percent to 45 percent they still believed the decision to go to war was correct.

Second, other retrospective evaluations narrowly favored the G.O.P. A small majority of Americans approved of Bush's performance as president. According to the National Election Study (NES) survey, 51 percent approved of Bush's performance as president, while 49 percent disapproved. The Pool

Poll showed that 53 percent of voters approved of the job he was doing as president, while 46 percent disapproved. Other polls also showed a narrow margin approving of Bush.

The NES survey showed that 15 percent thought the government was doing a "very bad" job handling what they believed to be the most important problems facing the United States, while 24 percent thought it was doing a "bad job." Moreover, the public had a decidedly mixed view about which party would do a better job of solving problems facing the country. But on the question of the war on terrorism the Republicans held a decisive advantage. Moreover, the Pool Poll showed that 58 percent of voters said they trusted Bush to handle terrorism, while only 40 percent trusted Kerry.

Thirdly, Kerry ran an ineffective campaign. Despite his combat service in Vietnam, which contrasted favorably with Bush's service as a pilot in the Texas Air National Guard, Kerry was vulnerable to criticism because of his prominence as an anti-war protestor. He was also characterized as a "flip-flopper" who changed his positions to accommodate the popular mood, and he did little to dispel this criticism.

Fourthly, Bush's victory may be seen as a continuation of the long-term decline of the New Deal coalition. Kerry did hold together some components of this coalition. He won overwhelming support among blacks, solid support among Jews, and a clear majority of votes in union households. Social class, as measured by occupation, was only weakly related to the vote. Most importantly, Kerry, a Catholic, failed to win a majority of the Catholic vote. Forty-four years earlier, when Democrat John F. Kennedy, also a Catholic, ran for election, four of five Catholics voted for him.

Finally, although more Americans identified as Democrats than as Republicans, the Democratic margin was small. In 1980, 65 percent of all party identifiers were Democrats; in 2004, only 53 percent were. Given that Republicans are more likely to vote than Democrats, for all intents and purposes there was an equal balance between the two parties.

The Electoral Vote Balance

Despite small Republican gains in the House and solid G.O.P. gains in the Senate, Bush's narrow reelection in 2004 underscored the close partisan balance. During the five elections between 1988 and 2004, the Republicans won sixteen states (with 135 electoral votes) in all five contests. They won five additional states (with 64 electoral votes) in four of the five. The Democrats won eight states, as well as the District of Columbia, in all five elections (92 electoral votes). And they won 11 states (163 electoral votes) in four of these five elections. Seven states (70 electoral votes) voted Republican in three of these contests. Finally, the Democrats won three small states (14 electoral votes) in three of these elections.

Conclusion

Above all, the 2004 election demonstrates the importance of unexpected events. In the absence of the September 11, 2001, terrorist attacks, it seems unlikely that the United States would have started wars against Afghanistan and Iraq. In November 2004, a majority of Americans still thought that attacking Iraq was the correct decision, although by November 2006 the war cost the Republicans control of both the House and Senate. Bush's major asset in 2004 was that a solid majority thought that he would do a better job than Kerry in fighting the war on terror.

Even though shortly after the 2004 election many pundits and scholars thought that long-term Republican dominance was at hand, the war in Iraq continued and became increasingly unpopular. The Republicans lost control of the House and Senate in 2006. In 2008, the war continued and economic conditions had deteriorated. The Republicans suffered further congressional losses—and lost the presidency as well.

Bibliography and Further Reading

Abramson, Paul R., John, H. Aldrich, Jill Rickershauser, and David W. Rohde. "Fear in Voting Booth: The 2004 Presidential Election." *Political Behavior* 29, no. 2 (June 2007): 197–220.

Abramson, Paul R., John H. Aldrich, and David W. Rohde. "The 2004 Presidential Election: The

Emergence of a Permanent Majority?" *Political Science Quarterly* 120, no. 1 (Spring 2005): 33–57.

Abramson, Paul R., John H. Aldrich, and David W. Rohde. *Change and Continuity in the 2004 and 2006 Elections.* Washington, D.C.: CQ Press, 2007.

Ceaser, James W., and Andrew E. Busch. *Red Over Blue: The 2004 Elections and American Politics.* Lanham, MD: Rowman and Littlefield, 2005.

CQ Press. *Presidential Elections, 1789–2004.* Washington, D.C.: CQ Press, 2005.

Lewis-Beck, Michael S., William G. Jacoby, Helmut Norpoth, and Herbert F. Weisberg. *The American Voter Revisited.* Ann Arbor: University of Michigan Press, 2008.

Shaw, Daron R. *The Race to 270: The Electoral College and the Campaign Strategies of 2000 and 2004.* Chicago, IL: University of Chicago Press, 2006.

Paul R. Abramson

ELECTION OF 2008

On November 4, 2008, Barack Obama, a freshman Democratic senator from Illinois, was elected president. The son of a white mother from Kansas and a black father from Kenya became the first African American to win the nation's presidency.

But in many respects, the election was conventional. It continued the duopoly of the Democratic and Republican parties, which between them have won all 40 presidential elections since 1852. Although this duopoly has been challenged from time to time, no third-party or independent candidate has come close to winning.

Moreover, Obama's victory continued the pattern of postwar volatility that began with Republican Dwight D. Eisenhower's 1952 victory. From 1952 through Republican Richard Nixon's reelection in 1972, neither party was able to win more than two elections in a row. And in 1976 and 1980, two incumbent presidents in a row were defeated (the Republican Gerald Ford in 1976 and the Democrat Jimmy Carter in 1980), a pattern that had occurred only once before in American history (1888 and 1892). Republican George H. W. Bush's election in 1988 broke this pattern by winning for the G.O.P. a third consecutive election. But volatili-

ty returned in 1992 with Bill Clinton bringing the Democrats back to power.

When Clinton was reelected in 1996, the 2000 contest provided the Democrats the opportunity to win three consecutive elections. Although their candidate, vice-president Al Gore, won a plurality of the popular vote, Texas governor George W. Bush won a disputed electoral-vote majority. With Bush's reelection in 2004, the Republicans seemed poised to win three consecutive elections. Indeed, despite the closeness of Bush's reelection, some saw the election as a watershed that was likely to establish the Republicans as the dominant party.

But this bright scenario for the Republicans began to fade as the war in Iraq dragged on and became increasingly unpopular. In the 2006 midterm elections, the Democrats gained 30 seats in the U.S. House of Representatives and six seats in the U.S. Senate, regaining control of both chambers. The Democrats now had strong prospects of retaining control of both chambers in 2008 and good prospects of winning the presidency.

The Nomination Contest

Like Eisenhower in 1960, Ronald Reagan in 1988, and Clinton in 2000, Bush could not run for reelection because of Amendment XXII. Unlike all these previous elections, the sitting vice president did not seek the presidency. In 1968, when Lyndon B. Johnson announced that he would not seek reelection, his vice president, Hubert H. Humphrey, secured the Democratic nomination. The 2008 election was the first contest since 1928 in which neither an incumbent president nor a sitting vice president sought his party's nomination.

A large number of candidates were expected to run, and many did (8 Democrats and 10 Republicans). All the same, Sen. John McCain of Arizona won the Republican contest fairly easily. McCain ignored the Iowa caucuses and focused instead on the New Hampshire primary, which he narrowly won against former Massachusetts' governor Mitt Romney. Former New York mayor Rudy Giuliani did not compete until the Florida primary, and his third-place showing ended his candidacy. Although McCain won only nine of the twenty-two Republican contests on Super Tuesday (February 5), he won the three largest states, driving out Romney, although former Arkansas governor Mike Huckabee continued to compete until McCain won enough delegates to formally secure the nomination. McCain had essentially locked up the Republican nomination in March.

The Democratic contest developed into a protracted struggle between Obama and Hillary Rodham Clinton, the former First Lady and senator from New York. Stunned by her third-place showing in the Iowa caucuses, where she finished behind both Obama and former North Carolina senator John Edwards, she rebounded with a narrow win over Obama in the New Hampshire primary. On Super Tuesday, Obama won 13 of the 22 Democratic contests, while Clinton won 9. As all of the Democratic contests allocated delegates according to proportional representation, the delegate count remained close. But as the primary season neared its end, it was clear that Obama would win a majority of the elected delegates. One key to his victory was his success in caucus contests, where his superior organization prevailed. Obama won more delegates than Clinton in all 14 states that used caucuses.

However, one out of five Democratic delegates was chosen neither in the primaries nor caucuses, for the party allows states to select Democrats who hold elected office and other party officials. These "superdelegates" are free to vote as they choose. At the outset of the nomination contest, many superdelegates had favored Clinton. Although these superdelegates could have delivered enough votes to nominate her, doing so would have been politically risky, and would have been especially damaging among blacks. Gradually, even superdelegates who had declared a preference for Clinton switched to Obama. Facing inevitable defeat at the convention, Clinton conceded in early June and supported Obama.

Obama's choice of Delaware Sen. Joseph R. Biden Jr. as his running mate was quite conventional. Biden had the foreign policy experience that Obama lacked. McCain's choice of Sarah Palin, the governor of Alaska, however, was risky. Although Palin had challenged Alaska's established political leadership and was a social conservative who could mobilize the Republican base, she had little national exposure and no foreign policy experience.

The General Election Campaign

Obama rejected public funding, allowing him to raise more money than McCain. He used the Internet more effectively than McCain to both raise funds and to organize his supporters. His campaign sponsored get-out-the-vote efforts, specifically aimed at registering the young and racial and ethnic minorities. His main theme was that electing McCain would continue Bush's policies, whereas he would bring "change you can believe in."

McCain also promised change, arguing that he had the experience to implement it. To promise change, however, he needed to distance himself from Bush, a difficult task for a Republican. Although McCain performed well during the three debates when foreign policy was discussed, in all three a majority of television viewers thought that Obama had won. Moreover, by the time of the first debate economic conditions had seriously weakened McCain's prospects. The economic meltdown began in mid-September. Between the end of the Republican nominating convention in early September and mid-September, several polls showed McCain leading Obama. From mid-September on, Obama led in every published poll.

By the end of the campaign Obama was targeting several "red states" that Bush had won in 2000 and 2004. The only "blue state" McCain targeted was Pennsylvania. Palin did a good job of energizing social conservatives, but her one-on-one interviews provided fodder for satire. However, she committed no major gaffes in her debate with Biden.

The Election Outcome

Obama won 365 electoral votes to McCain's 173. He won 69,498,516 popular votes (52.9 percent) to McCain's 59,948,323 (45.7 percent). Obama carried all 19 states that John F. Kerry carried in 2004, as well as D.C., and also won nine states that Bush had carried. In addition, he won an elector from Nebraska's Second Congressional district. Obama's success in the

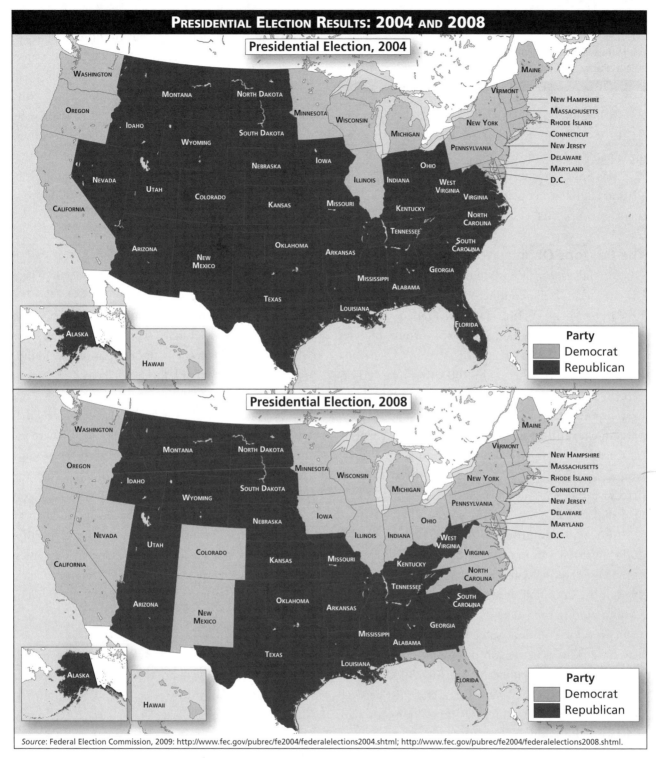

PRESIDENTIAL ELECTION RESULTS: 2004 AND 2008

Presidential Election, 2004

Presidential Election, 2008

Source: Federal Election Commission, 2009: http://www.fec.gov/pubrec/fe2004/federalelections2004.shtml; http://www.fec.gov/pubrec/fe2004/federalelections2008.shtml.

In the election of 2008, Barack Obama carried nine states that had been carried by the incumbent Republican president, George W. Bush, in 2004. These states included the typically conservative-dominated Southern states of North Carolina, Florida, and Virginia; Indiana, Iowa, and Ohio in the Midwest; and Colorado, Nevada, and New Mexico in the West.

South was particularly striking. He carried Florida, North Carolina, and Virginia, winning 55 of the South's 153 electoral votes. In addition to recaptur-ing the presidency, the Democrats gained 21 seats in the U.S. House of Representatives and eight seats in the Senate.

Although turnout was high by American standards, it did not reach the record levels that were anticipated. Turnout among the voting-age population was 56.8 percent, while turnout among the population eligible to vote was 61.7 percent, only a slight increase over 2004.

The Reasons Obama Won

Obama did especially well among blacks. According to the exit poll conducted by Edison Media Research/Mitofsky International (called the Pool Poll because it is conducted for a consortium of news organizations), 95 percent of African Americans voted for Obama, whereas in 2004 Kerry carried 88 percent of the black vote. Moreover, in 2008 blacks made up 13 percent of the voters, compared with 11 percent in 2004, suggesting that black turnout increased. Obama also did well among Hispanics, winning 67 percent of the vote, compared with 53 percent for Kerry, and Hispanics also may have made up a slightly larger share of the voters.

Although age-group differences were small in 2004, in 2008 Obama won two-thirds (66 percent) of the votes among voters between the ages of 18 and 29. But the Pool Poll shows no evidence of a surge in turnout among the young.

The Pool Poll does suggest that the Democrats may have done a better job of mobilizing their supporters than the Republicans did. In 2004, 37 percent of voters said they were Democrats, 26 percent said they were Independents, and 37 percent said they were Republicans. In 2008, 39 percent were Democrats, 29 percent were Independents, and 32 percent were Republicans. This shift probably also resulted from a movement in party loyalties away from the Republicans.

But Obama won mainly because most voters disapproved of President Bush. In 2004, 53 percent of voters approved of the job Bush was doing as president, whereas 46 percent disapproved. Bush won 90 percent of the vote of those who approved of his performance, but only 6 percent of those who disapproved. Four years later, only 27 percent of voters approved of Bush, while 71 percent disapproved. McCain did as well as Bush in holding voters who approved of Bush, winning 89 percent of their vote. And he did a better job among voters who disapproved of Bush, winning 31 percent. It appears that to some extent he was able to distance himself from an unpopular president, but not enough to prevail.

The Electoral Vote Balance

Between 2004 and 2008, there has been a clear shift in the electoral vote balance toward the Democrats. There are now only 13 states, with a total of 96 electoral votes, that have voted Republican in all five elections between 1992 and 2008. They have won six additional states (with 67 electoral votes) in four of the last five. And they have won eight states (with 86 electoral votes) in three of the last five elections. On the Democratic side, there are now 18 states and D.C. (with 248 electoral votes) that the Democrats have won in all five elections. There are three states (with 16 electoral votes) that the Democrats have won in four of the last five contests. And the Democrats have won two states (with 25 electoral votes) in three of the last five elections. The Democrats are now competitive in all major regions of the country, with a Republican advantage only in the South, Mountain West, and the Prairie states. But the Democrats have made inroads in both the South and the Mountain West.

Conclusions

In 1964, British Prime Minister Harold Wilson said, "A week is a long time in politics." Between November 2, 2004, when Bush was reelected and November 4, 2008, there were 208 weeks. In late 2004, many Republicans were euphoric, but in late 2008 they were engaging in postmortems and debating about how to rebuild their party.

On the other hand, the Democrats had no reason to be complacent. In late 2008, public opinion polls suggested that Obama had a reservoir of good will. But the problems he faces are far greater than those confronting Bush when he took office in 2001. At that time, America was at peace, although even then major terrorist attacks were being planned against New York and Washington. When Obama took office, America was engaged in two wars, and Obama had pledged to withdraw U.S. combat troops from Iraq by the summer of 2010. In 2001, the U.S. was in a period of relative prosperity. In early 2009, it faced the greatest economic crisis since the Great Depression.

Bibliography and Further Reading

Abramson, Paul R., John H. Aldrich, and David W. Rohde. *Change and Continuity in the 2008 Elections.* Washington, D.C.: CQ Press, 2010.

Ceaser, James W., Andrew E. Busch, and John J. Pitney, Jr. *Epic Journey: The 2008 Elections and American Politics.* Lanham, MD: Rowman and Littlefiled, 2009.

Cook, Rhodes, Alice V. McGillivray, and Richard M. Scammon. *America Votes 28: Election Returns by State, 2007-2008.* Washington, D.C.: CQ Press, 2009.

McDonald, Michael P. "2008 General Election Turnout Rates." http://elections.gmu.edu/ Turnout_2008G.html (accessed October 9, 2009).

Paul R. Abramson

ENVIRONMENTAL POLICY

Environmental policy in the United States consists of all governmental actions that impinge upon environmental conditions and processes at home and abroad. Though the term "environmental policy" was not coined until the 1960s, its roots in the United States are deep, and early laws governing land use, natural resource extraction, and wildlife management continue to shape environmental policy and politics today. The 1970s, however, represent the high point of environmental protection policies in the United States, when the public and policymakers were paying a great deal of attention to environmental problems and were optimistic about the government's capacity to solve them. Since then, many environmentalists, regulated industries, and policymakers have become somewhat disillusioned with the state of American environmental policy, albeit for different reasons. Many analysts believe that U.S. environmental policy stands at an important crossroads at the beginning of the twenty-first century; as a society, we must assess what environmental programs work, how to improve performance through policy redesign, and how we can effectively address emerging environmental problems like global climate change.

Historical Context

The earliest policies to shape the American landscape were tied up with questions of property rights and ownership. Land and other natural resources were seen as commodities, to be developed and extracted for individual gain and for colonial (and later national) economic growth and expansion. The nineteenth century was a critical period in U.S. environmental policy as the federal government embarked on a massive public land giveaway. Concern for the environment was largely absent as Southern farmers exhausted soils, loggers in the Midwest destroyed old growth forests, miners eroded mountains, and commercial hunters decimated some bird populations and other animal species. The West was soon settled, but at a significant cost to the environment.

Beginning in the late 1800s, the progressive conservation movement began questioning the mentality that fueled westward expansion and led to widespread environmental destruction. The conservation movement advocated for government retention of remaining public lands and the scientific management of natural resources. Though the conservation movement represented progress in terms of how the government managed natural resources, some urged an even more ecologically oriented perspective and policy. Preservationists like Sierra Club founder John Muir rejected conservationists' commodity-centered multiple-use philosophy and advocated an ethical, aesthetic view of nature that recognized the right of nature to exist free of human interference. The nascent environmental movement of the 1960s would build on Muir's legacy by voicing skepticism about the ability and willingness of natural resource agencies to manage for the public good, let alone ecological values.

In addition to the usual battles over public land use and natural resource management, the 1960s ushered in a relatively new set of concerns and conflicts over pollution and toxins in the environment. By this time, air and water pollution in urban areas was becoming an increasingly visible and serious problem, as symbolized by the fire that broke out on Ohio's polluted Cuyahoga River in 1969. Earlier in the decade, Rachel Carson raised alarm about the negative ecological and human health impacts of pesticides in her book *Silent Spring*. Carson urged caution regarding America's seemingly uncritical acceptance of new technologies and its belief in scientific expertise, suggesting that some technological innovations may cause more problems than they solve. Carson's message galvanized the public and transformed the environmental movement from one chiefly concerned about wildlife and wilderness protection to a broader movement that embraced a myriad of issues and demanded multiple policy changes.

Many of the changes advocated by the environmental movement were realized in the 1970s with help from supporters in Congress and the White House. Earth Day 1970 was a nationwide grassroots teach-in and protest designed to communicate to the nation's leaders widespread support for stronger environmental protection policies. It worked. Soon thereafter, Pres. Richard Nixon created the Environmental Protection Agency, and Congress passed landmark environmental legislation, including significant amendments to the Clean Air Act (1970), the Federal Water Pollution Control Act of 1972, and the 1973 Endangered Species Act (ESA). These new environmental laws consolidated federal power over environmental matters while preserving a role for the states in implementing and enforcing the laws. At the time, the laws were embraced by both Republicans and Democrats, as each party tried to capitalize on the high salience of environmental issues by showing their constituents that they were working for stronger regulation.

Waning Support and Growing Conflict

The bipartisan support for tough environmental standards waned as the 1970s came to a close. Implementation delays and high enforcement costs highlighted the challenges involved in meeting statutory goals. Industry increasingly resisted new regulation and tried to block implementation of existing laws, while environmentalists used the courts in an attempt to speed things up and enforce strict statutory

standards. The courts had opened their doors to environmental interests by relaxing rules of judicial standing, and environmentalists made good use of statutory rights to sue, now embedded in many environmental laws. This gave environmentalists an arena in which to fight attempts by hostile administrations to delay or weaken implementation, and later, the courts would become a means for bypassing a gridlocked Congress.

The Reagan administration represented one of the most direct challenges to the environmental movement. Reagan embraced a distinctly anti-regulatory approach to governing as part of his conservative ideology of small government and laissez-faire economics. He embarked on an executive strategy of defunding environmental programs and agencies and transferring regulatory authority to the states as a way of undercutting environmental protection programs. But his open hostility to the environmental agenda created a public backlash such that membership in environmental organizations increased dramatically during his two terms in office. Congress largely rebuffed his anti-regulatory efforts and strengthened the Resource Conservation and Recovery Act in 1984 by closing loopholes, such as one that allowed millions of metric tons of hazardous waste to be burned for energy recovery, while passing amendments to the nation's premier hazardous waste clean-up law, known as "Superfund," and enacting the Safe Drinking Water Act in 1986. On other issues, however, Congress remained gridlocked and failed to renew major environmental statutes such as the Clean Air Act and the Federal Insecticide, Fungicide, and Rodenticide Act.

Reagan's successor, George H. W. Bush, was not a particularly strong advocate for the environment, but he seemed to have learned an important lesson from the Reagan years and supported some key environmental policies, most notably the demanding Clean Air Act Amendments of 1990. This was a major legislative achievement for the president and a victory for environmentalists. However, other activities within the Bush White House, most notably the activities of Vice Pres. Dan Quayle's "Council on Competitiveness," signaled a return to Reagan-era attempts at environmental deregulation. In the international sphere, President Bush alienated much of the global environmental community by rejecting binding targets for greenhouse gas emissions and refusing to sign the Convention on Biological Diversity.

Environmentalists had high hopes when Bill Clinton was elected president in 1992, both because of the many environmental pledges he made on the campaign trail and because of his pick of Al Gore, who had a strong environmental record as a senator from Tennessee, as his vice president. The Clinton administration's record on the environment was mixed, however. It succeeded in reversing many of the anti-environmental executive actions of the Reagan and Bush administrations; one of its first actions was to disband the Council on Competitiveness. President Clinton also assembled a strong "green team" by appointing respected environmental leaders to key posts in the administration, such as Bruce Babbitt (once president of the League of Conservation Voters and former Arizona governor) as secretary of interior. Spending on environmental and renewable energy programs increased and new programs were introduced at the EPA to try to make environmental policies and processes more efficient and effective. And when his environmental agenda languished in Congress, Clinton at times used his executive powers to forward his goals, including strengthening the Environmental Protection Agency—an agency seriously weakened under Republican administrations.

Despite these gains, environmentalists criticized Clinton and members of his administration for backing down on other promised policy changes in the face of congressional opposition, including raising grazing fees on public lands and enacting a tax on the energy content of fuels in order to promote conservation. Many environmental groups faulted him for supporting the North American Free Trade Agreement (NAFTA) and the World Trade Organization (WTO), which they saw as potentially undermining domestic environmental laws when such laws were considered barriers to free trade. Perhaps the greatest disappointment came when Clinton failed to ask Congress to ratify either the Convention on Biological Diversity or the Kyoto Protocol to the Framework Convention on Climate Change, despite presidential support. By most accounts, President Clinton and Vice President Gore

feared that the Kyoto Protocol would be "dead on arrival" in Congress, and did not want to suffer such a public rejection of their policy proposals.

Environmental Policy in the Twenty-First Century

By the turn of the new millennium, environmental policy appeared to be at a crossroads. Though the public largely remained supportive of environmental policies, a targeted political backlash against environmentalism and a growing frustration with certain policies in particular suggested some real problems with past policies and approaches. Implementation of environmental regulations during the 1980s and 1990s had highlighted the costs of environmental protection, and hit a few industries and individuals especially hard. Property rights activists joined forces with the "Wise Use" movement to try to weaken land use and wildlife protection laws, while large industries argued that environmental regulations were overly burdensome and did not provide effective incentives for complying with the law. For example, critics suggested that the Endangered Species Act provided perverse incentives for landowners to destroy endangered species and their habitat so they would not be subject to the law, thereby undermining its intent. They suggested more collaborative and flexible regulatory approaches that would offer positive incentives for landowners to cooperate with government agencies and that would promise them a degree of regulatory certainty. Some of these changes in regulatory approaches were advanced by the Clinton administration and remain part of the Environmental Protection Agency's commitment to "reinvent" environmental regulation. Under the ESA, for example, landowners can sign "Habitat Conservation Plans" that allow an incidental "take" of threatened or endangered species as long as the landowner takes measures to minimize and mitigate the effects of their actions on the species. But new approaches to environmental regulation are often layered upon existing structures and institutions, creating a complex and unstable policy environment.

President George W. Bush entered office with promises to establish controls over carbon dioxide emissions and reduce mercury pollution from power plants. But environmentalists feared a Bush administration that they considered beholden to big industry like oil and gas companies. Indeed, environmentalists will remember the Bush presidency as a major setback. Not only did Bush use many of the same administrative tools as Reagan did to weaken U.S. environmental and energy policy but he also blocked progress on addressing looming environmental catastrophes like global warming. Included among the many perceived sins committed by the Bush administration are the relaxed rules on mountaintop removal coal mining, a new forest policy (eventually enacted by Congress) that could increase logging on federal lands, and adoption of a rule that undermined key provisions of the Clean Air Act. Many people outside (and some inside) the Bush administration accused the administration of suppressing the evidence and advice of career agency scientists. This was especially the case when it came to the issue of global warming; though Bush eventually acknowledged the human causes of global warming, his administration remained opposed to mandatory restrictions of U.S. greenhouse gas emissions.

The election of Pres. Barack Obama signaled yet another shift in environmental politics and policy. His appointments suggest a desire to strengthen environmental policy and move forward on the key problem of global warming. Even in the face of an economic crisis, President Obama appears committed to pursuing a new energy policy based on renewable technologies. He has argued that a strong economy *and* clean environment are both necessary and possible. The majority of the public seems to be on board with Obama's plans.

Public opinion polls suggest that American citizens support action on climate change and do not want to see environmental laws weakened (and for good reason—though U.S. environmental policies have not always achieved their goals in terms of improving environmental outcomes, there is no doubt that without them, the nation's environment would be worse off). However, further progress in environmental policy is threatened by the relatively low public salience of environmental problems compared to other policy issues. Even the issue of climate change, which started to attract a lot of attention in 2006 after the release of Al Gore's movie, *An Inconvenient Truth,* is not at the top of the public's agenda. Advocates for stronger environmental policy face other challenges. They must admit that it will be more costly, difficult, and controversial to gain additional environmental improvements, in part because the easier (and cheaper) problems have already been addressed. Newer and more complex problems, such as persistent toxins, non-point source pollution, and global climate change will require more fundamental changes to our economy and society. Politics must provide a means of spearheading and supporting such changes. It remains to be seen whether American political leaders will rise to this challenge.

Bibliography and Further Reading

Andrews, Richard N. L. *Managing the Environment, Managing Ourselves: A History of American Environmental Policy.* New Haven, CT: Yale University Press, 1999.

Fiorino, Daniel J. *Making Environmental Policy.* Berkeley: University of California Press, 1995.

Klyza, Christopher M., and David Sousa. *American Environmental Policy, 1990–2006.* Boston: MIT Press, 2008.

Rosenbaum, Walter A. *Environmental Politics and Policy,* 5th edition. Washington, D.C.: CQ Press, 2002.

Vig, Norman J., and Michael E. Kraft, eds. *Environmental Policy: New Directions for the Twenty-First Century.* Washington, D.C.: CQ Press, 2006.

Sarah B. Pralle

ETHICS

In the wake of the Watergate scandal that broke in the early 1970s, the American public experienced a growing concern with the erosion of ethical standards among government officials. Over the course of the later twentieth century, Congress reacted by setting new and stronger ethical standards for appointed officials and elected representatives. Ethics commissions, legislative regulations, and federal oversight marked a new chapter in ethics reform in American political history that entailed both behavioral guidance and direct enforcement.

Post-Watergate and the Establishment of the Office of Government Ethics

Watergate highlighted the corrupting influence of unethical conduct on the electoral process and the dangers of government secrecy in fostering illegal behavior of elected officials. In an effort to restore public confidence, Congress passed the Ethics in Government Act of 1978, which prohibited activities in conflicts of interest for public officials, forbid the use of nonpublic government information to further private interests, and disallowed the acceptance of gifts from persons or entities seeking official government action.

The act also created the administrative structure for the Office of Government Ethics (OGE), a separate agency within the executive branch responsible for ethics training, education, and oversight of executive branch officers and employees. Originally a small agency of fewer than 20 members, by 1990 the OGE had grown to more than 7,000 federal officials, many of whom were employed as Designated Agency Ethics Officers (DAEO). These special ethics officers were appointed within every executive department and agency to provide counseling, education, and guidance in ensuring compliance with a wide array of ethics regulations with a special focus on investigating financial disclosures and conflicts of interest cases involving elected officials and career civil servants. In addition, the act established the Office of Independent Counsel, which Congress or the attorney general could use to open special investigations of federal officials and which outlined the formal procedures needed to initiate independent investigations of high-level executive officials which encompassed the president, vice president, Cabinet members, top presidential aides, and other senior-level executive branch officials.

While OGE's jurisdiction extended to the employees of the executive branch, the Ethics in Government Act was influential in other areas of government. In response to the act, the legislative and judicial branches of government developed their own organizations that implement and enforce ethics guidelines. The House Committee on Standards of Official Conduct guides the U.S. House of Representatives, the Senate Select Committee on Ethics directs the U.S. Senate, and the Judicial Conference Committee on Codes of Conduct provides oversight for the judicial branch. Although the Ethics in Government Act provided the foundation for ethics guidance after Watergate, further amendments would be needed to expand the OGE's mandate as a result of government ethics violations in the mid-1980s.

The Persistence of Ethics Reform

Between 1981 and 1988, the Reagan administration found itself embroiled in what seemed like an endless series of controversies involving ethics violations. Over the course of Reagan's two presidential terms, more than a hundred federal officials, most of whom were political appointees, were indicted or charged with ethics offenses. These charges culminated in the resignation of Attorney Gen. Edwin Meese following OGE accusations that he had violated six of the general provisions of the federal standards of conduct. Such controversies served to intensify the debate over the need for renewed enforcement of ethics rules. Seeking to demonstrate a greater commitment to political ethics reform, Pres. George H. W. Bush made it his first executive order to create the President's Commission on Federal Ethics Reform in 1989. This commission was tasked with standardizing a single comprehensive set of ethics standards for the entire Executive Branch of the Government. The Ethics Reform Act of 1989 implemented several of the recommendations from the ethics commission pertaining to gifts, gratuities, conflicts of interests, and financial disclosures. It also enhanced the educational responsibility of the OGE by broadening the requirement of mandatory ethics training, coordinated by OGE's Office of Education and Training, for all employees and political appointees in the executive branch. Moreover, all presidential appointments were required to complete forms designating their former contacts with contracting and procurement officials prior to government service. Under the act, the OGE was also responsible for expanding the financial disclosure system and reviewing agency programs to guarantee compliance with the law. The act extended beyond the executive branch to include post-employment "revolving door" restrictions for the legislative branch, limitations on outside-earned-income for non-career employees in all branches of federal government, and additional conflicts of interest rules for legislative branch staff.

In carrying out a greater commitment to ethics reform, Pres. George H. W. Bush sought to ensure that all public officials act with "the utmost integrity" by instituting ethics standards that were "fair, objective, and consistent with common sense." Moreover, Bush endeavored to provide equitable ethical standards across all three branches of the federal government, making sure ethics guidelines were not so "unreasonable and restrictive" as to discourage citizens from entering public service. These basic principles provided the groundwork for future efforts to create a single model of standards of ethical conduct for all government officials.

In the 1990s, Pres. Bill Clinton came to office promising to restore trust in government by imposing even stricter ethical guidelines. Clinton pledged to continue ethics reform by replacing the "decade of greed" with innovative initiatives to reinvent government as he issued Executive Order 12834, which instituted the "five-year pledge." In hopes of stopping the assumption that the federal government was in the pocket of special interests, Clinton staff members pledged not to represent private parties in dealings with the government for five years after they left White House employment. Yet, despite a heightened commitment to government ethics reform, the 1990s saw further allegations and investigations regarding ethics violations.

Congress and Ethics

Infractions of ethic rules were not confined to the executive branch; between 1982 and 1990, the U.S. House of Representatives accumulated as many as 116 charges of corruption. In many cases, charges of abuses were related to Congressional prerogatives such as the franking privilege and overseas travel that resulted in serious violations of ethics rules. Congressional ethics violations reached a new level in 1991 when it was announced that during a period of 39 months, 20,000 checks were written against House members'

bank accounts for which there were insufficient funds. While House members attempted to explain the banking scandal to their constituents, the public witnessed the Senate Ethics Committee's publicized hearing of "the Keating Five." The 1992 Keating Five Affair featured five prominent U.S. Senators—Alan Cranston (D–CA), Dennis DeConcini (D–AZ), John Glenn (D–OH), John McCain (R–AZ), and Donald Riegle (D–MI)—and Charles Keating Jr. chairman of the Lincoln Savings and Loan Association. The senators were charged with improperly intervening on behalf of Keating, who was the target of a banking regulatory investigation, in return for the chairman's $1.3 million contributions to the senators' reelection campaigns. After an extensive investigation by the Senate Ethics Committee, three of the senators, Cranston, Riegle and DeConcini, were formally reprimanded; Glenn and McCain were cleared of acting improperly but criticized for exercising poor judgment.

The investigation brought to the forefront disturbing ethical questions regarding lobbyists' growing influence on political elections, which Congress addressed in the 1990s and 2000s by passing new laws that sought to regulate lobbying. In 1995, Congress passed the Lobbying Disclosure Act (LDA), which required persons directly lobbying members of Congress and officials of the executive branch to register and file electronic reports detailing government officials contacted, issues discussed, and income received by lobbyists. In 2007, Congress enacted the Honest Leadership and Open Government Act, which amended parts of the Lobbying Disclosure Act by strengthening public disclosure requirements concerning lobbying activities and funding sources, placing additional restrictions on gifts for members of Congress and their staff, and providing for mandatory disclosure of earmarks in expenditure bills. The following year, the House passed legislation that created an outside review panel to investigate possible ethics violations among House members. To ensure the bipartisan nature of the board appointments, the new Independent Office of Congressional Ethics is composed of a panel of non-lawmakers named jointly by the speaker and minority leader. From 2001 to 2008, new congressional ethics provisions were passed, including a legislative code of conduct as well as requirements for more extensive disclosure of personal finances. New federal campaign finance laws were also introduced that capped donations from union and corporate political action committees.

Over the past 25 years, state governments have mirrored the national discussion over political ethics by enacting a variety of ethics laws to regulate behavior of legislators at the local level. The provisions of these laws include restrictions on conflicts of interests, gift and honoraria limits, mandatory financial disclosure, and restrictions on post-government service employment. In addition, some states have established independent ethics commissions to enforce restrictions on legislative conduct.

The Role of the Media and the Politicalization of Ethics Probes

In the 1970s, when the *Washington Post* reporters Robert Woodward and Carl Bernstein exposed the Watergate political cover-up, the media acquired a prominent role in reporting political wrongdoing. Thus, during the Clinton administration, the political reporting surrounding the Lewinsky scandal, which emerged from a sexual relationship between Clinton and a White House intern named Monica Lewinsky, heralded an era of "new media" fueled by call-in talk show hosts, the 24/7 cycle of cable news, and tabloid cyberjournalists. Since Watergate, new technologies, the Internet, and real-time bloggers have created a digital feast for the public as the press has taken the role of political intermediaries in reporting ethics violations.

Like Watergate, the Lewinsky scandal and Clinton's impeachment and Senate trial represented a benchmark in terms of political ethics. In the past, agencies like the OGE stipulated that personal improprieties impinged on professional ethics when an official violated the law. However, with the media coverage of the Lewinsky scandal, the boundaries between personal and public ethical misconduct became less clear. The modern conception of political ethics blurred the line between individual behavior and professional responsibilities. With the Lewinsky scandal, the public debated the boundaries of what constituted ethics violations and questioned whether every breach of private morality by an elected

official was a public issue. The Lewinsky affair revealed that the public drew a sharp distinction between the two, while even congressional Republicans tried to blur the distinction. As revelations about Clinton emerged, his popularity—measured in opinion polls—rose.

The 1990s and 2000s marked a new chapter in political ethics as professional ethics standards were used in partisan attacks and breaches in personal ethics became political weapons. Between 1997 and 2008, the public witnessed prolonged periods in which one party leveled allegations of ethics violations against another party. In 1997, Rep. Newt Gingrich (R–GA), charged with violating 84 ethics rules, found himself at the center of a political maelstrom that made him the first sitting Speaker of the House to be reprimanded by his peers over ethics violations.

Media reports exposing evidence of corruption and ethics violations increased during the administration of Pres. George W. Bush. Over the course of eight years, Bush's Department of Education answered allegations of breaking "conflict of interest" rules regarding 4.8 million dollars worth of questionable discretionary contracts for their Reading First Program. The Department of Interior's inspector general described the Bush administration as "a culture of ethical failure" in a report outlining Interior officials' financial self-dealings, abuse of government expense accounts, and acceptance of gifts from energy companies that exceeded limits set by ethics rules. The Department of Homeland Security had to respond to charges of fraud after audits from the Government Accountability Office revealed widespread misuse of government credit cards tallying over $2 billion.

The ethical issues surrounding the Bush administration brought to light the central dilemma in drafting ethics codes for elected officials. If ethics provisions are written broadly to cover a wide range of potential activities, the ethics rules run the risk of being too ambiguous to provide clear behavioral guidance and may be subject to arbitrary interpretation. By contrast, the use of explicit rule-driven ethics codes often causes many officials to reason that they are free to engage in any type of conduct not clearly prohibited by the current list of ethics rules or regulations. In light of OGE's struggle to mandate a unified ethics code with clear rules and regulations, citizen groups and public advocacy organizations have served as important political intermediaries informing the public of specific ethics violations while placing added pressure on political officials for further ethics reform.

The Rise of Public Advocacy Groups and the Open Government Movement

Despite growing cynicism over repeated violations of the public's trust, the American people have come to expect and demand higher ethical standards of elected officials. Since the 1970s, the rise of ethics violations by elected officials has paralleled the emergence of a grassroots movement calling for open government, a political philosophy that maintains that the business of government and state administrations should be open at all levels to encourage direct public scrutiny and oversight. Public advocacy groups such as the Common Cause have called for regulations that focus on political and government transparency by encouraging openness of government decision-making processes, demanding open access to government meetings, transcripts, and financial disclosure information as well as petitioning for budgetary review, and audits as well as freedom of information legislation.

Since the 1970s, the Freedom of Information Act (FOIA) has provided the basic authority and procedure for the public to petition the executive branch for unreleased government records. Amendments to the act in the late 1970s, 1980s, and 1990s have expanded FOIA, making it the main vehicle for empowering individuals to hold government accountable to codes of ethical conduct. By filing lawsuits and launching successful public information campaigns, public advocacy groups called for elected officials to slow the revolving door as they moved from government service to lobbying positions, insisted on competitive bidding for all government contracts, and required lobbyists to register on an online federal database.

Public advocacy groups gained additional momentum by using information technology to shine a light on political ethics violations. The call for open government has become increasingly successful with the rise of the Internet, which has given the public free, open, and easy access to government information. With the rise of technology, new efforts have been made to improve government transparency online by centralizing informational databases of lobbying reports, ethics records, and campaign-finance reports. Heralding a new era of grassroots activism, groups such as Public Citizens Network, Taxpayers for Common Sense, Citizens Against Government Waste, Center for Responsive Politics, and the Institute on Money in State Politics have used an array of social networking tools to mobilize and educate millions of Americans on government fraud and ethical misconduct. As a result of public interests groups, ethical norms are continually evolving in response to changing circumstances and revisions of what constitutes acceptable individual and organizational interactions with government officials.

The post-Watergate code of political ethics was developed to heal internal divisions and restore public trust. As a result, the late twentieth and early twenty-first centuries have witnessed renewed efforts to combat political corruption by setting higher ethical standards for members of Congress, executive branch officials, government officers, and employees of the government. Serving as an important chapter in late twentieth century political history, the evolving nature of ethics standards and reform have provided the necessary counterbalance to the growing influence of special interest groups while ensuring the integrity of the political system and safeguarding the democratic process of American government.

Bibliography and Further Reading

Apostolidis, Paul, and Juliet William, eds. *Public Affairs: Politics in the Age of Sex Scandals.* Durham, NC: Duke University Press, 2004.

MacKenzie, G. Calvin, and Michael Hafken. *Scandal Proof: Do Ethics Laws Make Government Ethical.* Washington, D.C.: Brooking Institute Press, 2002.

Roberts, Robert N. *White House Ethics: The History of Politics of Conflict of Interests Regulations.* New York: Greenwood Press, 1988.

Rosenson, Beth A. *The Shadowlands of Conduct: Ethics and State Politics.* Washington, D.C.: Georgetown University Press, 2005.

Thompson, Dennis F. *Ethics in Congress: From Individual to Institutional Corruption.* Washington, D.C.: Brooking Institutions Press, 1995.

Angela Fritz

EXECUTIVE BRANCH

The last quarter of the twentieth century was a period of great structural dissonance for the federal executive branch. Presidents and other political actors strived to reconcile widespread disenchantment with the executive branch's phenomenal growth in the decades following World War II with the necessity of competent governmental administration in an ever-modernizing and globalizing world. The results included intermittent and often stymied efforts at reforming and streamlining the executive branch, interspersed with the creation of additional departments and agencies as new circumstances necessitated them, a trend that carried over into the first decade of the twenty-first century.

The Backlash Against Executive Branch Expansion

As the political scientists Karen M. Hult and Charles E. Walcott describe, the mid-1970s marked a "tipping point" in the development of the executive branch. Throughout the post–World War II era, the executive branch was transformed into an increasingly complex network of bureaucratic departments, agencies, and offices that became the centerpiece of the modern American political system. Federal agency budgets and personnel ranks swelled, new agencies were added and old ones reorganized to accommodate new exigent circumstances, and presidents developed a vast "counter-bureaucracy" under the aegis of the Executive Office of the President (EOP) as a means for advancing their agenda more effectively. These developments came to a head during the Nixon presidency (1969–1974), which was also the point at which popular disgruntlement with bureaucratic government reached its apex and the revelation of the Watergate scandal finally confirmed the fears of many critical observers that the postwar growth and increasing executive-centeredness of the federal government had spiraled out of control.

Against this backdrop, the Carter administration took pains to distance itself from these developments. During the 1976 election season, Carter campaigned as a Washington outsider who would bring more diversity to the federal bureaucracy, rely more heavily than previous presidents on the Cabinet, and, above all, initiate fundamental bureaucratic reorganization. In fact, Carter took steps to begin this process even before he was elected. Once he was assured of the Democratic Party nomination, he chose Jack Watson, who had overseen Georgia's state government reorganization when Carter was governor, to lead his transition team. Under Watson's direction, executive branch reform became one of the transition team's six major priorities and Harrison Wellford, a former congressional staffer, was tapped to oversee White House staffing and head up a task force on government reorganization.

Once in office, Carter dramatically reduced the size of the White House staff. He also did away with several advisory councils that had been established within the EOP by the Johnson and Nixon administrations, including the Economic Opportunity Council, the Federal Property Council, the Council on International Economic Policy, and the Energy Resources Council. Even more notably, he acted upon his campaign promise to reform the bureaucracy by establishing the Federal Personnel Management Project (FPMP) to devise a comprehensive reorganization plan. The end product of the FPMP's efforts was the Civil Service Reform Act (CSRA) of 1978, the first comprehensive reform of the federal civil service since its establishment by the Civil Service Act of 1883. As an omnibus piece of legislation, the CSRA included numerous provisions, including the creation of new merit pay and performance appraisal programs, the establishment of the Federal Labor Relations Authority to oversee labor practices and adjudicate labor disputes within the federal bureaucracy, and the abolition of the unwieldy

Civil Service Commission and the distribution of its responsibilities across three separate agencies: the Equal Opportunity Employment Commission, the Office of Personnel Management, and the Merit Systems Protection Board.

Although the Carter administration oversaw a net reduction in the size of the executive branch, it nevertheless carried on the by-then entrenched tradition of creating new executive offices and departments to deal with emergent policy concerns. For example, in 1977 Carter signed the Department of Energy Organization Act, which authorized the creation of a Cabinet-level Department of Energy with responsibility for energy policy and nuclear safety, two issues of mounting importance during the 1970s. Two years later, he signed the Department of Education Organization Act, which provided for the division of the existing Department of Health, Education, and Welfare into two separate Cabinet-level entities: the Department of Health and Human Services and the Department of Education. In addition, three new EOP units were established during his tenure: the Office of Administration and the Domestic Policy Staff in 1977, and the Office of the United States Trade Representative in 1979.

The trends set in motion during the late 1970s carried on well beyond the Carter presidency. As the Republican Party candidate for the presidency in 1980, Ronald Reagan denounced Carter as "the head of a government which has utterly refused to live within its means" and resolved to do away with deficit spending and initiate an "immediate and thorough hiring freeze on federal hiring." (Reagan) He also pledged to eliminate both the Department of Education, which he argued needlessly enabled the federal government to meddle in state and local affairs, and the Department of Energy, which he viewed as the quintessence of inefficient and inept government interference. As president, Reagan cut many federal agency budgets—more, in fact than any other modern president. Nevertheless, several departments, including the departments of Defense, State, and Justice, saw considerable increases in their spending during the 1980s. Moreover, Reagan did not fulfill his campaign promise to abolish the two

cabinet departments Carter had established; in fact, by the end of his presidency both the Education and Energy departments were still quite solvent, and Reagan's successor, George H. W. Bush, increased their budgets by 22.2 and 29.6 percent, respectively.

Effects of Deregulation, Privatization, and Devolution

The impetus for deregulation, or the reduction of government restrictions on economic activity, stemmed in part from the same concerns about federal government aggrandizement that prompted presidents Carter and Reagan to directly reduce executive branch unit staff sizes and budgets. During Carter's presidency, several deregulatory steps were taken, including the passage of the Airline Deregulation Act of 1978, which provided for the gradual phasing out of the Civil Aeronautics Board's powers to regulate aviation industry fares and routing. Carter also took steps to deregulate various other industries, including trucking, oil, and railroad. During the 1980s, the Reagan administration built upon these first steps taken by Carter to further deregulate the economy. As a candidate for the presidency, Reagan had pledged to eliminate "overregulation" by the federal government. Within his first month in office, he had established a Presidential Task Force on Regulatory Relief to review existing regulations and determine their net social benefits, froze all pending regulations, and issued an executive order (EO 12291) mandating that the societal benefits of any future regulations must demonstrably outweigh the costs. Furthermore, over the duration of his presidency, Reagan oversaw the continued deregulation of the aviation industry and a variety of other industries.

The flipside of deregulation, privatization, also picked up speed during this period. In 1982, Reagan appointed a Private Sector Survey on Cost Control (also known as the Grace Commission for its chairmanship by the businessman J. Peter Grace) to investigate the extent and sources of government inefficiency and make recommendations for reform. Then, in 1987, Reagan established a new, 13-member Commission on Privatization to further review the division of labor between the federal government and the private sector. Congress declined to act directly upon the Grace Commission's recommendations, and the Commission on Privatization issued its report with less than a year left for the Reagan administration to implement its proposals; however, federal spending as a share of the gross domestic product did decline slightly during Reagan's two terms in office and the contracting out of various government services rose substantially between 1981 and 1989.

Finally, in addition to deregulating industries and transferring business ownership and control from the public to the private sector, the last quarter of the twentieth century marked the "devolution revolution," or the movement to reassign many policy responsibilities from the federal government to the states. Like deregulation, this decentralizing trend began during the 1970s, with President Nixon's "New Federalism" initiatives and the passage of General Revenue Sharing legislation, which provided unrestricted federal funding to state and local governments. It came to full fruition during the 1980s, when President Reagan made the decentralization of policymaking and implementation a priority of his administration. During this "decade of devolution," there was a major push to transfer spending discretion to the states through the consolidation of categorical grants into block grants and, in 1987, Reagan issued Executive Order 12612, which restricted federal agencies' capacity to preempt state laws.

The obvious effect of all three processes—deregulation, privatization, and federal devolution—during the 1970s and 1980s was to curb the influence of the federal executive branch. Though the immediate postwar decades had empowered the federal government as a whole to shoulder new policy responsibilities and the executive branch in particular to take the lead in such initiatives, the new era brought with it an understanding that private-sector corporations and sub-national governmental units would work in partnership with the federal executive branch to produce policies and provide services to the American populace. In some ways, though, deregulation, privatization, and devolution also enhanced the executive branch's involvement. In particular, the Office of Management and Budget (OMB) attained new authority to administer contracts and grants and oversee deregulatory proceedings.

Reinventing the Executive Branch in the Post–Cold War Era

Though many factors had come together to promote the executive branch's accretion in the wake of World War II, the Cold War had always been a major force driving the postwar development of the executive branch. Above all, it created an aura of heightened exigency that empowered the federal government to develop a vast national security apparatus, including the Cabinet-level Department of Defense and numerous other administrative units such as the National Security Council and the Central Intelligence Agency. The end of the Cold War, then, augured the possibility of finally taming the bureaucracy by at least reducing the size and budgets of the national security units. At the same time, moreover, the United States was swept up in the worldwide New Public Management (NPM) movement that was cresting during the 1990s. According to NPM philosophy, governments should adapt to the modern, globalized world by streamlining their bureaucracies' organizational contours and procedures; or, as President Clinton once put it, "it's time our government adjusted to the real world, tightened its belt, managed its affairs in the context of an economy that is information-based, rapidly changing, and puts a premium on speed and function and service, not rules and regulations." (Quoted in Aberbach and Rockman 136)

The Clinton administration's efforts to "reinvent" American government during the 1990s exemplified NPM ideals. Six weeks into his presidency, Clinton placed Vice Pres. Al Gore in charge of the National Performance Review (NPR), which was to be a rigorous investigation into opportunities for improving management practices in the agencies of the federal government. Under Gore's leadership, more than three hundred "reinvention laboratories" were established within the various agencies to test-run new practices, and a series of town-hall-style meetings were held in a number of agencies to tease out reform proposals directly from employees. A Reinventing Government Summit held in Philadelphia's Constitution Hall that summer brought together public and private sector leaders to discuss business-style ideas for reforming government. The product of these activities was a Phase-I report that proffered 384 recommendations for improving government operations and promised over $100 billion in savings. Two subsequent phases, launched in 1995 and 1998, respectively, extended and refined the Phase-I initiatives.

As described in the Brookings Institution's "Fifth-Year Report Card" on the initiative's first five years, the NPR made some important inroads in its efforts to reinvent government. For example, it was quite successful at achieving procurement reform and improving customer service. However, it also produced more mixed results in some respects, such as its inconsistency in developing effective leadership at all management levels and improving popular trust in government, and fell very notably short in others, including the NPR's failure to identify governmental objectives and cultivate legislative support for the initiative. As such, despite its "A+" for effort, on balance the NPR earned only "a genuinely mixed review . . . great progress in some areas, little traction in others, some administrative disasters averted, others not prevented, strong academic complaint, government downsized, but only modest public awareness and little voter appreciation of the result." (Kettl 59)

The Executive Branch in the Age of Terrorism

The post–Cold War peacetime interlude, and its attendant opportunity for the diminution of the federal executive branch, came to an abrupt halt on September 11, 2001. The 9/11 terrorist attacks on the United States brought the post–Watergate ambivalence about the extent of the executive branch to new heights, as the federal government confronted both heightened demand for strong counterterrorist action and widespread disillusionment with its capacity to effectively coordinate the activities of the numerous administrative units that share responsibility for averting and responding to national disasters.

On the one hand, the 9/11 attacks heralded the most extensive executive branch reorganization since the creation of the Department of Defense conse-

quent to the National Security Act of 1947. Within a month of the attacks, President Bush established a new Office of Homeland Security that would lead the effort to coordinate the federal government's counterterrorist initiatives. In March 2002, Assistant to the President for Homeland Security Tom Ridge unveiled a new Homeland Security Advisory System, which employed color-coded terrorism threat levels to direct federal, state, and local government agencies as well as transportation facilities to implement coordinated preventive measures. Finally, on November 25, 2002, Congress passed the Homeland Security Act, which provided for the creation of the Department of Homeland Security (DHS), a new cabinet department charged with protecting the domestic territory of the United States from attack. The DHS subsumed 22 federal agencies and ranked among the largest federal departments, with nearly two hundred thousand employees and an annual budget of more than 30 billion dollars. Moreover, since the establishment of the DHS, additional initiatives were advanced to further streamline public and private sector disaster preparedness, including the development of the National Response Plan in 2004 and its 2008 update, the National Response Framework.

Even as these new opportunities for re-growing the executive branch were emergent, though, other political actors reacted in ways that served to curtail the Bush administration's War on Terrorism initiatives. Though Congress did sign on to most of the administration's counterterrorist initiatives, it also tussled repeatedly with the president over the power to exert control over the new Department of Homeland Security and its various bureaucratic units. Public opinion was similarly of two minds: although Americans by and large expressed strong support for governmental initiatives to prevent future terrorist attacks, many remained skeptical of the executive branch's capacity to do so effectively. For example, nearly three-quarters of Americans surveyed by the Gallup Organization in June 2002 approved of President Bush's plan to create the Department of Homeland Security, but only 20 percent believed that the new department would be very effective at combating terrorism.

Concerns about the executive branch's capacity to coordinate effective response to crisis situations were revitalized in September 2005, when Hurricane Katrina made landfall in New Orleans, Louisiana. Hurricane Katrina was the United States' costliest ever natural disaster in terms of monetary damage and was responsible for more than a thousand deaths in the Gulf Coast region. The recovery and relief effort was notoriously poorly run, as intergovernmental communication broke down and federal government resources arrived only belatedly and even then were allocated inefficiently. Critical attention focused especially on the shortcomings of the Federal Emergency Management Agency (FEMA), an agency that had earned accolades for its effective administration during the 1990s and one of the 22 agencies that had been incorporated into the Department of Homeland Security when it was established a few years earlier. As the political scientist Patrick S. Roberts explains, FEMA had performed admirably in both the aftermath of 9/11 and the relief effort following severe hurricanes that struck Florida a few years later. By the time Katrina struck, however, the agency's reorganization for incorporation into the DHS and its new counterterrorism mandate had eroded its capacity to respond as effectively as it once had to weather catastrophes. In the end, FEMA's ill-conceived response to the Katrina disaster not only brought about FEMA director Michael Brown's resignation and the agency's newfound status as the symbol of government malfeasance and inefficiency but it also revived public skepticism about the executive branch's capacity to deal with crisis situations more generally.

After 2005, several steps were taken to restore the image of both FEMA and the federal bureaucracy as a whole and improve the executive branch's capacity to respond more effectively in future crisis situations. On October 4, 2006, President Bush signed the Post–Katrina Emergency Management Reform Act, which reorganized FEMA, equipped it with greater autonomy within the DHS, and revamped the agency's preparedness mission. The DHS also stepped up its "Ready" campaign's public relations efforts to facilitate disaster preparedness among private individuals, businesses, and emergency relief and recovery organizations such as the Red Cross. Much work

RELATED ENTRIES

THIS VOLUME
Deregulation and Privatization; Ethics; Federal Emergency Management Agency; Homeland Security
OTHER VOLUMES
Executive Branch (vols. 2–6)

still remained to be done by the end of 2008; however, noticeable progress had been made to implement many of the Post–Katrina Act's numerous provisions, substantially more Americans reported having taken disaster preparedness actions in their homes and workplaces than had been the case three years earlier, and FEMA displayed improved capability in its response to that year's high-category hurricanes, Gustav and Ike.

In his 1996 State of the Union Address, Pres. Bill Clinton famously declared that "the era of big government is over," aptly capturing the overriding sense since the mid-1970s that the executive branch of the federal government had grown dangerously unwieldy as a result of its unbridled expansion in the postwar era. Reform efforts to roll back the recently expanded executive branch and rationalize its bureaucratic procedures were thus a prominent feature of the national political landscape since the mid-1970s. And yet various countervailing forces largely prevented reformers from fully realizing their goals. As a result, more than a quarter-century after Jimmy Carter unveiled the first presidential effort to streamline executive branch organization and procedures, the United States continues to grapple with the problem of ascertaining the optimal size and scope of its federal executive branch.

Bibliography and Further Reading

Aberbach, Joel D., and Mark A. Peterson, eds. *The Executive Branch.* Oxford, UK: Oxford University Press, 2005.

Aberbach, Joel D., and Bert A. Rockman. *In the Web of Politics: Three Decades of the U.S. Federal Executive.* Washington, D.C.: Brookings Institution Press, 2000.

Haynes, Wendy. "Seeing around Corners: Crafting the New Department of Homeland Security." *Review of Policy Research* 21 (2004): 369–395.

Hess, Stephen. *Organizing the Presidency*, 3rd edition. Washington, D.C.: Brookings Institution Press, 2002.

Hult, Karen M., and Charles E. Walcott. *Empowering the White House: Governance under Nixon, Ford, and Carter*. Lawrence: University Press of Kansas, 2004.

Kettl, Donald F. *Reinventing Government: A Fifth-Year Report Card*. Washington, D.C.: Brookings Institution, 1998.

Ingraham, Patricia W., and Carolyn Ban, eds. *Legislating Bureaucratic Change: The Civil Service Reform Act of 1978*. Albany, NY: SUNY Press, 1984.

Patterson, Bradley H., Jr. *The White House Staff: Inside the West Wing and Beyond*. Washington, D.C.: Brookings Institution Press, 2000.

Reagan, Ronald. "Time to Recapture Our Destiny," speech to the Republican National Convention, Detroit, MI, July 17, 1980.

Roberts, Patrick S. "FEMA and the Prospects for Reputation-Based Autonomy." *Studies in American Political Development* 20, no. 1 (2006): 57–87.

Shamira M. Gelbman

FEDERAL BUREAU OF INVESTIGATION

The decades since the mid-1970s have been a period of change and controversy for the Federal Bureau of Investigation (FBI). The 1975 congressional investigations exposed institutional excesses and violations of civil liberties committed in the name of domestic security; such disclosures prompted the FBI to return to a focus on law enforcement. However, FBI surveillance in the 1980s of opponents of the Reagan administration's policies in Central America renewed criticism that the Bureau and its political masters had failed to differentiate dissent from subversion. In the early 1990s, with the end of the Cold War, the Bureau began to put less emphasis on counterintelligence activities: but reversed itself mid-decade with the exposure of major spy cases within the Central Intelligence Agency. In 2001, the FBI discovered that one of its own had been spying for Moscow for 20 years. Later that year, the Bureau drew intense criticism for not having done more to prevent the terrorist attacks of September 11. As of late 2009, a political and bureaucratic effort to reposition the FBI as a law enforcement agency with a counterterrorism focus is ongoing.

Background

Established in 1908 to give the Department of Justice its own investigators for a small number of federal crimes, the FBI has seen its responsibilities expanded by presidents and Congress to include hundreds of crimes and such domestic security concerns as counterintelligence and countersubversion. The Bureau began domestic security activities in response to a German sabotage campaign prior to World War I. During the postwar Red Scare, the FBI was active in harassing and deporting noncitizens suspected of having revolutionary beliefs and tendencies. The involvement of Bureau personnel in the scandals of the Harding administration led to the elevation of a young Justice Department attorney, J. Edgar Hoover, to the directorship in 1924. He led the FBI for the next 48 years, becoming both an iconic and feared figure. Under Hoover, the FBI became an efficient and headline-grabbing law enforcement agency in the fight against crime in the 1920s and 1930s.

After World War II, the FBI seemed preoccupied with chasing communists. The Bureau's counterintelligence program (COINTELPRO) used illegal techniques such as wiretaps, bedroom bugs, and break-ins. It initially targeted American communists, but in the 1960s and 1970s was expanded to white hate groups, radical black groups, civil rights organizations, and the antiwar movement. COINTELPRO was ended in 1971 after its activities were brought to public attention; the later revelation that Martin Luther King Jr. had been the target of the Bureau's "dirty tricks" tarnished the FBI's image for years. The FBI has also been criticized for its slow response to the rise of organized crime. After the exposure in 1957 of a gathering of big-city crime bosses from around the country, the Bureau finally began collecting information on the Mafia. In the early 1960s, Attorney Gen. Robert F. Kennedy initiated an expansion of enforcement activities directed against organized crime. Later in the 1960s, Congress provided new tools for the FBI to pursue a coordinated campaign against organized crime—the Omnibus Crime Control and Safe Streets Act of 1968 and the Racketeer Influenced and Corrupt Organization Act of 1970.

A New Era Begins

J. Edgar Hoover's death in May 1972 signaled a new beginning in the FBI's organizational life. The next several years were difficult for the Bureau and its directors. Investigative journalists broke stories in late 1974 and early 1975 that detailed illegal domestic spying activities by the Central Intelligence Agency (CIA) and the FBI. Numerous questionable and illegal activities, including the full extent of the COINTELPRO operations and the maintenance of internal files on prominent politicians and civic leaders, were publicly exposed in hearings in 1975 in the House and Senate (the Pike and Church committees, respectively).

In 1977, the newly elected president, Jimmy Carter, appointed Edward Levi as his attorney general. Levi quickly established new and more restrictive internal guidelines for FBI counterintelligence investigations. Congress added further restrictions in 1978 when the Foreign Intelligence Surveillance Act, which requires approval by the Foreign Intelligence Surveillance Court for electronic surveillance in espionage cases, went into effect. That same year, William H. Webster, a former federal judge, was named FBI director; he served until 1987. Webster sought to return the FBI to its law enforcement roots, focusing efforts on investigating white-collar crime and political corruption. Convictions were obtained against members of the Mafia's ruling body, including major figures in New York City's crime families. A sting operation (code-named ABSCAM) targeted political corruption in New Jersey and Washington, D.C. Seven members of Congress, including a senator, were convicted of taking bribes. A similar operation (GREYLORD) in Cook County, Illinois, implicated numerous judges, clerks, lawyers, and police officers in the fixing of court cases.

Old habits die hard, though. Domestic opponents of Pres. Ronald Reagan's policies in Central America came under FBI scrutiny in the 1980s. Surveillance and break-ins targeting a wide range of organizations—from radical activists to student groups to religious orders—were undertaken in an effort to ascertain whether foreign terrorist groups were involved with or controlled these domestic actors. In the case of the Committee in Solidarity with the People of El Salvador (CISPES), FBI agents from 1981 to 1985 attended political rallies, infiltrated the group's meetings, took notes on political discussions, and opened files on thousands of individuals. No connection between CISPES and foreign or terrorist groups was ever found. In 1989, the Senate Select Committee on Intelligence concluded that the investigation of CISPES and affiliated groups, while certainly improper, was an "aberration" and that decisions about the investigation had not come from the director's office. A national civil liberties controversy had also erupted in 1987 over the revelations about an FBI operation called the Library Awareness Program, in which the FBI sought to recruit librarians to report on foreign-appearing patrons who expressed an interest in scientific or technology-related books.

Judge Webster headed the FBI during what is popularly known as "the year of the spy," when the nation was reminded that the Bureau was the primary federal agency in domestic security matters. During 1985, 17 individuals were charged with espionage-related crimes. Some cases involved relatively low-level efforts, but other instances were more serious. Although the breakthroughs in most of these cases came from information provided by defectors, the FBI proved adept at building the evidentiary base for U.S. prosecutors to obtain convictions. Significant espionage cases included the John A. Walker spy ring (broken through information from his former wife), which had targeted the navy's coded communications; Edward Lee Howard, a former CIA officer who was able to slip past FBI surveillance and defect to the Soviet Union; Ronald William Pelton, a former employee of the National Security Agency who was identified through hints from a Soviet defector; Jonathan Jay Pollard, a naval intelligence analyst who was spying for Israel; and Larry Wu-tai Chin, a retired

CIA employee who spied for the People's Republic of China for more than thirty years.

The Cold War Ends

The FBI transitioned out of the Cold War under William S. Sessions, director from 1987 to 1993. In the early 1990s, counterintelligence was deemphasized; and hundreds of counterintelligence agents were moved to criminal investigations. The deadly shooting incident at Ruby Ridge, Idaho, in 1992 and the disastrous end to the siege of the Branch Davidian compound near Waco, Texas, in 1993 brought stinging criticism from the media and Congress about the Bureau's ability to manage crises. Although public opinion was initially on the FBI's side in assigning blame for the deaths in these incidents, the criticism negatively affected internal morale and gave critics more examples for their accusations of the FBI's overuse of force with domestic extremists. In July 1993, Sessions, who had come under a cloud in the previous administration for improperly using his position for personal benefit, became the first FBI director to be fired. President Bill Clinton then appointed Louis J. Freeh to the directorship. Freeh's management style, which included personal involvement in major cases and a tendency to discount countervailing opinions, alienated many at the Bureau. Even worse, the relationship between president and director ultimately became rocky and even hostile.

The arrest in February 1994 of CIA officer Aldrich H. Ames brought the FBI's focus back onto counterintelligence and gave the Bureau a coup in its rivalry with the CIA. Lack of cooperation between the FBI and CIA was faulted for allowing Ames to spy for the Soviets and then the Russians for at least nine years. The result was an increase in FBI control over counterintelligence investigations. Freeh used the Bureau's jurisdiction over transnational crimes and the CIA's diminished stature in counterintelligence matters to begin an expansion of the FBI's overseas activities. Dozens of new legal attaché offices were opened around the world over the ensuing years. Domestically, FBI investigators performed with great professionalism in the case of the 1995 Oklahoma City bombing by arresting Timothy McVeigh and Terry Nichols within days and then amassing the evidence that convicted them.

The Ames case had barely disappeared from the headlines when another Russian spy in the CIA, Harold James Nicholson, was uncovered in 1996. This time, the two agencies stressed that their cooperation had worked to limit Nicholson's spying to two and half years. A month after Nicholson's arrest, one of the Bureau's own, Edwin Earl Pitts, was arrested for spying for Russia from 1987 to 1992. A worse shock was yet to come. In February 2001, veteran FBI special agent Robert Philip Hanssen was arrested and charged with spying for the Soviet Union and Russia for 20 of the 25 years he had worked at the Bureau. Hanssen, who had worked predominantly in counterintelligence, was said to have compromised American spies in the Soviet Union (at least three of whom were executed), important technical operations, investigative techniques, and thousands of pages of classified documents. The FBI inspector general's review of the Hanssen case pointedly criticized the Bureau's counterintelligence program and its lack of attention to internal security procedures. In the aftermath of the Hanssen case, the FBI took a number of steps to improve its internal security, including expanded use of the polygraph and greater attention to the financial situation of its employees.

The Impact of 9/11

Just as it was beginning to assess the counterintelligence, psychological, and other implications of Hanssen's betrayal, the FBI was hit with strong criticism for its role in the failure to prevent the terrorist attacks of September 11, 2001. In addition, a new director, Robert S. Mueller III, had taken over just before the attacks. Even more change was demanded of the Bureau. The recommendations of the National Commission on Terrorist Attacks Upon the United States (the 9/11 Commission) and the subsequently enacted Intelligence Reform and Terrorism Prevention Act of 2004 pushed the FBI to change its focus from the meticulous collection of the kinds of evidence required for a grand jury in a criminal case to the expeditious gathering, analyzing, and acting on intelligence to prevent future terrorist attacks. Organizationally, the Bureau's intelligence, counterintelligence, and counterterrorism components were placed under a single manager, who reports to both the FBI director and the newly established position of Director of National Intelligence. These and other changes were aimed at short-circuiting more radical proposals that would have stripped the FBI of its domestic security and counterintelligence responsibilities in favor of a new domestic intelligence agency, similar to the British Security Service (MI5). Such a move would have limited the Bureau to its federal law enforcement activities.

The FBI's effort to remake itself into an organization capable of fulfilling its law enforcement, counterintelligence, and counterterrorism responsibilities is ongoing. However, some serious problems have been encountered along the way. Efforts to replace the FBI's cumbersome and obsolete case filing system with secure and efficient information technology have failed at the cost of millions of dollars. A significant shortage of translators in the languages associated with the counterterrorism effort means that, at a time of relaxed surveillance guidelines, the FBI cannot process all the material from approved wiretaps. The language gap will take years or even decades to close. The FBI also faces a substantial cultural challenge—its institutional culture is predominantly a law enforcement or police culture that rewards the special agent in the field for identifying, locating, and arresting people who have broken the law. This essentially reactive nature of law enforcement—a catch-the-criminals mentality—is not the same as the proactive approach necessary for the counterintelligence and counterterrorism breakthroughs that can uncover spies or prevent future terrorist attacks. In addition, the kind of sit-at-the-desk analytical work necessary for unraveling conspiracies is not rewarded as well as that of the special agents.

A Delicate Balance

In addition to organizational and cultural difficulties, the FBI will continue to confront the conflict between providing security and protecting civil liberties. In 2000, Congress and civil liberties and privacy groups strongly questioned the Bureau's use of its Carnivore surveillance tool—software designed to intercept and analyze email, Internet chats, and Web browsing. In the wake of the 9/11 terrorist attacks, the use of wiretaps and searches without court approval, as well as intelligence-gathering operations against Islamic, environmental, and animal rights groups, have raised further concerns. The FBI's effort to apply law enforcement and intelligence methodologies in seeking to find and neutralize terrorists will continue to challenge the Bureau to maintain a balance between national security and personal liberties.

Bibliography and Further Reading

Clark, J. Ransom. *Intelligence and National Security: A Reference Handbook.* Westport, CT: Praeger Security International Reference, 2007.

Jeffreys-Jones, Rhodri. *The FBI: A History.* New Haven, CT, and London: Yale University Press, 2007.

Kessler, Ronald. *The Bureau: The Secret History of the FBI.* With epilogue. New York: St. Martin's, 2003.

National Commission on Terrorist Attacks Upon the United States. *Final Report of the National Commission on Terrorist Attacks Upon the United States.* New York: Norton, 2004.

Posner, Richard A. *Uncertain Shield: The U.S. Intelligence System in the Throes of Reform.* Lanham, MD: Rowman & Littlefield, 2006.

Theoharis, Athan G., ed. *The FBI: A Comprehensive Reference Guide—From J. Edgar Hoover to the X-Files.* With Tony G. Poveda, Richard Gid Powers, and Susan Rosenfeld. New York: Oryx, 2000.

Wise, David. *Spy: The Inside Story of How the FBI's Robert Hanssen Betrayed America.* New York: Random House, 2002.

J. Ransom Clark

FEDERAL EMERGENCY MANAGEMENT AGENCY

The Federal Emergency Management Agency (FEMA) has had a checkered history since its creation as an independent agency in 1979. The product of a reorganization intended to consolidate a bewildering collection of emergency authorities and programs, FEMA has suffered under unwise political appointments, inadequate agency capacity, insufficient political clout, and problematic intergovernmental relations to name but a few challenges. For most of its history, FEMA has been viewed with ambivalence at best. All the same, the success or failure of FEMA is of immense political importance when a major disaster is unfolding in the glare of the media spotlight. Despite FEMA's foibles and occasional folly, expectations surrounding the role the agency should play in times of disaster and the assistance it should mobilize and coordinate continues to grow.

Before FEMA: Laying the Groundwork

Emergency management policy in the United States is of relatively recent origin. Influenced by two sub-policy areas of civil defense (for nuclear attack) and disaster assistance, policy reflected the uncertainty and complexity that surrounded approaches to managing catastrophes. Development of this policy area tended to be characterized by fragmentation, incrementalism, and changing federal priorities and was primarily a response to specific events. Interest in civil defense corresponded to the threat of or declarations of war, while interest in disaster policy typically followed significant disasters. Beginning in 1950, Congress established in statute a permanent role for the federal government in both civil defense (Federal Civil Defense Act of 1950) and disaster relief (Federal Disaster Relief Act of 1950).

Emergency management was viewed as a shared-governance arrangement, although details of the intergovernmental "partnership" and the responsibilities of each party were not specified by law. Such lack of specification permitted the politicization of the process.

Dissatisfaction with the intergovernmental arrangements for emergency management led the National Governors Association (NGA) in 1977 to initiate a project to investigate the system. Their overall assessment pointed to a "lack of a comprehensive national emergency policy, as well as the dispersion of federal responsibilities among numerous federal agencies, which has hampered states' abilities to manage disaster situations." (National Governors Association ii)

Following this report, consensus grew surrounding the need to reorganize the federal emergency management function using a lead agency concept.

FEMA—The Early Years: 1979 to 1987

President Jimmy Carter created FEMA in 1979 to be the lead agency for emergency management. Numerous functions were transferred from existing agencies to FEMA: civil defense, certain elements of national preparedness, fire prevention and assistance, disaster relief, flood insurance, emergency broadcast and warning, earthquake hazards reduction, and dam safety.

Carter recruited his then-head of the Office of Personnel Management, John Macy, to serve as the first FEMA director. Macy's task was to unify an agency that was both philosophically and physically separated, with various parts of the agency located in five separate office buildings around Washington, D.C. Emphasizing the similarities between natural hazards preparedness and civil defense, Macy embraced the comprehensive emergency management concept advocated by the NGA and attempted to implement the lead-agency role. Consolidation of programs proved difficult, however, with a distinct separation of national preparedness functions and staff from state and local support programs and their personnel. National preparedness activities remained secret, required security clearances, and were the agency's priority until the Clinton administration. The integration of functions within one agency appeared to be cosmetic, with little attention paid to the few major disasters that occurred during this period.

Gradually, local civil defense programs became less viable and more controversial because of the lessening of Cold War anxiety. Intergovernmental tensions increased, however, with the election of Ronald Reagan to the presidency in 1980 and the appointment of Louis Giuffrida as director of FEMA in 1982. Guiffrida placed top priority on government preparedness for nuclear attack and realigned agency resources to elevate the agency's national security responsibilities, angering the state directors who had lobbied for the creation of FEMA. In February 1987, President Reagan issued a national security decision directive redefining U.S. civil defense policy. Among other provisions, the directive gave priority to the development of survivable state and local crisis management capabilities.

Growing Pains for FEMA: 1988 to 1993

The Robert T. Stafford Disaster Relief and Emergency Assistance Act passed in 1988 ushered in a significant expansion in the provision of federal disaster assistance as natural disasters increasingly became nationalized and politicized, fueled by media coverage and public expectations. These five or six years also witnessed rising costs caused in part by an increase in the number of federal disaster declarations, the occurrence of several unusually large disasters, and the extension of federal disaster assistance. Concurrently, intense media coverage and public scrutiny of disaster response often focused negative attention on FEMA. Such criticism prompted FEMA to streamline many of its disaster assistance processes, with improvements noted in the time it took the federal government to declare a disaster (and thus start the flow of assistance) and with such innovations as the national teleregistration process.

Nevertheless, FEMA came under increasing criticism and lost credibility with many of its constituents. The failed response to Hurricane Andrew in south Florida in 1992 prompted Congress to ask the National Academy of Public Administration (NAPA) to conduct a comprehensive study of government capacity to respond to major natural disasters. This report, issued in 1993, highlighted the numerous problems at all levels of government. A major focus of the study was inadequacies within FEMA and needed reforms. The report contended that FEMA was an "institution not yet built" and likened the agency to a patient in triage, suggesting that Congress and the president needed to decide whether to treat it or to let it die. Recommendations to strengthen FEMA included elevation of its placement within the federal bureaucracy, reduction of the number of political appointees, reorganization of functions, and the development of a new statutory charter.

Soon after Pres. Bill Clinton appointed former Arkansas state director of emergency management James Lee Witt to head FEMA in 1993, the agency was reorganized and former civil preparedness programs dismantled or renamed to emphasize natural and technological disasters. Witt's appointment ushered in a new approach to emergency management, with an emphasis on hazard mitigation.

The Witt Years: 1994 to 2000

The Witt years witnessed systems improvements for providing assistance and in the administration of FEMA. Considered a success story for the Clinton administration, FEMA embraced the Government Performance and Results Act of 1993 and its emphasis on broad policy goals that could only be achieved in partnership with state and local agencies and with private and nonprofit sector organizations. An emphasis on hazard mitigation and new ideas of sustainability and disaster-resistant communities took hold. For example, FEMA launched a popular national intiative called Project Impact with the goal of incorporating hazards risk management decisions into the community's everyday decision-making processes. Such disaster-resistant communities were expected to promote sustainable economic development, protect its natural resources, and promote a better quality of life for their residents.

The growing burden of federal disaster relief costs prompted Congress to reexamine federal disaster assistance policy. A 1994 House Bipartisan Task Force on Natural Disasters report voiced concern that state and local governments no longer viewed disaster assistance as a shared government arrangement but as solely a federal responsibility. "This not only raises the costs of disasters to federal taxpayers, but also to our society as a whole as people are encouraged to take repeated risks they think they will not have to pay for." (U.S. Congress, House 1) Nevertheless, Congress had little incentive to change how it conducted disaster assistance because it was "almost perfect political currency: serving mostly humanitarian (and rarely questioned) purposes, and largely funded out of supplemental appropriations (which does not officially add to the budget deficit)." (U.S. Congress, House 66)

Significant organizational changes within FEMA occurred during this time. FEMA was viewed as more open, flexible, and collaborative than it had been in the past. The importance of emergency management was validated when President Clinton elevated Director Witt to be a member of his Cabinet in 1996.

Mega Disasters: 2001 to 2005

The election of George W. Bush to the presidency ushered in many changes for FEMA. Bush appointed his former campaign manager and close personal friend, Joe Allbaugh, to head the agency, despite Allbaugh's lack of emergency management qualifications or experience. The friendship was viewed as a positive for the agency, and Allbaugh's lack of experience did not come up during his confirmation hearings.

The 9/11 terrorist attacks dramatically changed the landscape for emergency management. The focus rapidly shifted to terrorism, with natural hazards receding to the background. Bush quickly established the

White House Office of Homeland Security and the Homeland Security Council in October of 2001. A national strategy for homeland security was issued the following July; it called for greater integration of federal response plans and functions and the creation of a national incident management system. In response, the president and Congress instituted one of the most ambitious reorganizations in American history with the creation of the Department of Homeland Security (DHS) in November 2002. In 2003, FEMA was subsumed into the newly created DHS as the lead agency for emergency preparedness and response. Losing its independent agency status weakened FEMA's ability to coordinate and broker resources within the federal bureaucracy. FEMA became a very small entity within the massive bureaucracy of DHS. Director Allbaugh

Michael D. Brown (right), director of the Federal Emergency Management Agency, is briefed about Hurricane Katrina by members of FEMA at the Office of Emergency Management in Baton Rouge, Louisiana, on August 29, 2005, the day the storm made landfall. Although FEMA had experienced much criticism in its history for its handling of disasters, its history of political appointments such as Brown, and its bureaucratic infighting, it was Hurricane Katrina and its aftermath that highlighted the agency's shortcomings most starkly. (Jocelyn Augustino/CNP/Corbis)

decided to leave government service and was replaced by his deputy and close friend, Michael Brown, who also had no background in emergency management.

Ironically, soon after this reorganization, one of the most demanding years for disasters in the United States occurred in 2004–2005. The 2004 hurricane season, for example, saw five major storms hit the coast of Florida in just 48 days. The 2005 hurricane season was so active that the National Hurricane Center exhausted its list of alphabetical names and began using the Greek alphabet to name storms. Although the 2004 federal response was coordinated completely within FEMA using the former Federal Response Plan framework first promulgated in 1992, a new National Response Plan was signed in December 2004 based on the National Incident Management System (NIMS). The National Response Plan was established to help solve the problem of vertical fragmentation—the failure of various levels of government to effectively coordinate their emergency management responsibilities. NIMS provided a management structure and concept of operations to help responders at all jurisdictional levels and across all disciplines work together more effectively. The response to Hurricane Katrina would be the first real test of the new system now under the responsibility and direction of DHS.

Hurricane Katrina, which struck Alabama, Louisiana, and Mississippi on August 29, 2005, was one of the worst hurricanes ever to make landfall in the United States. As the disaster unfolded on television screens across America and around the world, disbelief and anger at the suffering and seemingly needless loss of life characterized the coverage for weeks. The response to this disaster by all levels of government was so problematic that it launched the most wide-ranging investigation of the U.S. emergency management system in history.

Brown was relieved of his operational duties on September 9, 2005, and soon resigned his position amid growing criticism of his failed attempts to coordinate the federal response. He was replaced as agency head by R. David Paulison, who came to his new post from the U.S. Fire Administration. Unlike Brown, Paulison brought an emergency response background and experience to the job.

FEMA: In or Out? 2006 to present

In the aftermath of Hurricane Katrina, calls came to restore FEMA's independent agency and Cabinet-level status. DHS secretary Michael Chertoff also announced a number of initiatives to strengthen FEMA's core functions, emphasizing logistics, customer service, communication, and coordination. FEMA went to work increasing its operational readiness by predesignating federal coordinating officers, increasing its cache of relief supplies, and upgrading systems.

In 2007, Congress passed the Post–Katrina Emergency Reform Act of 2006 that, although keeping the agency in the DHS, increased its organizational autonomy. DHS initiated a wide-ranging review of the National Response Plan in 2007 and also began a comprehensive catastrophic disaster preparedness project.

Barack Obama's election as the forty-fourth president of the United States generated renewed discussion about the placement of FEMA within the federal government. For example, at its annual meeting in November 2008, the U.S. Council of the International Association of Emergency Managers (IAEM-USA) called for FEMA to be restored to its former status as an independent agency reporting directly to the president. IAEM-USA also urged that the FEMA director be designated as a member of the president's Cabinet.

When reviewing the history of FEMA, what becomes clear is that FEMA operates in an environment that is, on the one hand, mostly inattentive because of the relatively low salience of disasters, but, on the other hand, unforgiving when a disaster does occur. FEMA has walked a political tightrope of competing national interests with respect to civil defense, natural disaster, and homeland security as well as struggling to establish effective working relationships with myriad partners in public, private, and nonprofit settings. Although many factors contribute to this challenging environment, the FEMA of the future will need strong executive support and sufficient resources to meet performance expectations. FEMA personnel must be highly qualified, especially FEMA leaders. Attention to the enduring challenges of emergency management in a federal system, particularly with respect to catastrophic disaster preparedness, requires frank, open, and ongoing dialogue.

Bibliography and Further Reading

Bea, Keith, et al. *Federal Emergency Management Policy Changes after Hurricane Katrina: A Summary of Statutory Provisions.* Washington, D.C.: Library of Congress, 2006.

Drabek, Thomas E, and Gerard J. Hoetmer, eds. *Emergency Management: Principles and Practice for Local Government.* Washington, D.C.: International City Management Association, 1991.

Dymon, Ute J., and Rutherford H. Platt. "U.S. Federal Disaster Declarations: A Geographical Analysis." In *Disasters and Democracy*, edited by Rutherford J. Platt, 47–68. Washington, D.C.: Island Press, 1999.

National Academy of Public Administration. *Coping with Catastrophe: Building an Emergency Management System to Meet People's Needs in Natural and Manmade Disasters.* Washington, D.C.: National Academy of Public Administration, 1993.

National Governors Association. *Emergency Preparedness Project: Final Report.* Washington, D.C.: National Governors Association, 1978.

Rubin, Claire B., ed. *Emergency Management: The American Experience 1900–2005.* Fairfax, VA: Public Entity Risk Institute, 2007.

U.S. Congress. House. *Report of the Bipartisan Task Force on Disasters.* 103rd Cong., 2nd sess., 1994.

U.S. General Accounting Office. *Disaster Assistance: Federal, State, and Local Responses to Natural Disasters Need Improvement.*Washington, D.C.: Government Printing Office, 1991.

Waugh, William L., Jr. *Living with Hazards Dealing with Disasters: An Introduction to Emergency Management.* Armonk, NY: M. E. Sharpe, 2000.

Jane A. Kushma

FEDERAL RESERVE SYSTEM

The Federal Reserve System (the Fed) has been a source of political controversy since its founding. Endowed with great powers to affect and stabilize the nation's economy, the Fed's role in shaping the country's economic welfare has evolved over the modern period. The 1970s was a time of relative political constraint for the Federal Reserve, numerous economic obstacles gave way to significant growth in its prestige and independence in the 1980s and 1990s. During the first decade of the twenty-first century, the asset bubbles that threatened to cripple the economy served to test the policy tools of the Fed and determine the limits of its economic capabilities within a dynamic political atmosphere.

Background

At its inception in 1913, the Federal Reserve System, often referred to as the nation's "central bank," was primarily designed to provide and guarantee a stable national currency. Over the course of the century, the policy tools of the Federal Reserve System were broadened—as was its mandate. By the late twentieth century, the Fed's most important job was determining monetary policy through the setting of the federal funds interest rate, the discount rate, and bank reserve requirements. Today, the Fed accomplishes most of its goals by conducting open market sales and purchases of government securities. The Fed was also charged with implementing foreign exchange policy as determined by the Treasury, acting as a lender of last resort, and, along with other agencies, supervising and regulating commercial banks and bank holding companies. Professional observers and citizens alike regularly think of it as among the most powerful and influential institutions in the world.

Because of the far-reaching mandate of the Federal Reserve and its pervasive role in the U.S. and global economy, its actions and motivations have been the object of public scrutiny and debate virtually from its beginnings. This was certainly the case in the mid-1970s, a period during which the Federal Reserve's credibility was being questioned by many in the financial world. In the eyes of some, the Fed had for many years served the financial interests of a deficit-burdened government and possibly the electoral concerns of Pres. Richard Nixon instead of managing the national economy. In light of the long period of stagflation—a combination of inflation and recession—during this time, many scholars have contended that Arthur Burns, chairman of the Federal Reserve from 1970 to 1978, was wrong to have kept the money supply high and growing. By maintaining very low interest rates, the primary policy instrument at the time, Burns's monetary policy set the stage for a decade of weak economic performance and for renewed attention to the importance of price stability.

The Beginning of the Great Inflation

The Federal Reserve had never before been confronted with anything like the painful supply shocks, mostly in the form of high oil prices, that fueled the deep recession and inflation of 1973–1975, and it was unsure as to how to address them. When Burns's term as chairman expired in 1978, President Carter chose to replace Burns with G. William Miller. Miller, like Burns, did not believe that inflation was solely a monetary phenomenon. In many ways, Miller's handling of the national economy while at the Fed was not much of a departure from that of Burns.

Miller's inability to break the back of inflation stemmed from both political constraints and bureaucratic inertia. With passage of the Humphrey-Hawkins Full Employment Act of 1978, Congress set out three possibly incompatible economic goals that it expected the Federal Reserve to meet: full employment, stable prices, and steady long-term growth. The act was most notable in its stress on combating both unemployment and inflation and its revision of the exclusive focus on employment embodied in the Employment Act of 1946. The Humphrey-Hawkins Act also reemphasized the Fed's ultimate responsibility to the legislature, requiring that the chairman specify goals for the growth in the money supply that would be reported to Congress once a quarter.

Volcker Forges the Way for an Independent Central Bank

The massive inflation of the decade of the 1970s was fully under way by the time Miller left the Federal Reserve for the Treasury—with few steps having been taken to address the economy-wide increases in prices. Although the Federal Reserve did begin to announce money supply targets in line with congressional goals embedded in the Humphrey-Hawkins Act, only with the advent of Paul Volcker as Fed

chairman (appointed by President Carter in 1979) did the Fed finally abandon its use of the federal funds rate as a primary policy tool. As president of the New York Fed, Volcker had been an inflation hawk and had developed a reputation for favoring tight money. A self-declared believer in "practical monetarism," a more moderate version of the idea that central banks should focus only on the growth of the money supply, Volcker lived up to his anti-inflation image and took actions meant to cut growth in the money supply, thus inducing the recession that so many monetarists had been willing to risk.

Presidents are often held responsible for the state of the economy, and as unemployment climbed ever higher, Carter's approval rating spiraled downward. After the first wave of monetary contraction from October 1979 to March 1980 forced interest rates to their highest levels in the postwar period, Carter invoked the 1969 Credit Control Act, which allowed the board of governors to impose special measures of credit restraint on the banks in a more unorthodox attempt to control prices. Subsequently, Volcker eased the tightening of the money supply and Carter dropped the request for the credit controls in May 1980. Four months later, however, the Federal Reserve again began restricting the money supply, seemingly certain in its political independence and resolute about tackling the nation's inflationary condition and psychology.

The public outrage at the Federal Reserve and Volcker was unprecedented. In 1982, the economy bottomed out at an unemployment rate averaging nearly 10 percent following a rise in the nominal federal funds rate to 20 percent in 1981. Indebted farmers, many driven to bankruptcy by the high and volatile interest rates, circled the White House with their tractors in protest. So great was the political invective against Volcker that he was given Secret Service protection. Nonetheless, Volcker did not waver in his commitment to bringing down the inflation rate, and he was able cut the double-digit inflation (as measured by the change in the Consumer Price Index) of the late 1970s and early 1980s to a mere 3.8 percent in 1982.

During this period, debates about appropriate monetary policy measures were renewed. Although the rampant inflation seemed to have been tamed, unemployment remained high and interest rates remained somewhat volatile. The velocity of—or demand for—money was becoming more variable, and the relationship between inflation and the traditionally defined money supply more tenuous. Furthermore, the Depository Institutions Deregulation Monetary Control Act of 1980, which changed the regulations affecting bank deposits and the law allowing interest to be paid on certain accounts, contributed greatly to political and economic confusion surrounding the appropriate definition of money. Economists debated what types of bank accounts and asset classes should be included in the measure. Also during this period, discussion about whether monetary policy should be guided by rules or discretion—a debate begun by the economist Milton Friedman—became relevant to the conduct of monetary policy. Those who favored hard-and-fast rules with respect to the growth of the money supply encouraged Congress to pass legislation stripping the Fed of almost all discretion, an action that would have forced the central bank to enlarge the money supply at a stable, constant rate. This extreme outcome did not come to pass, as many also recognized the importance of an independent Fed able to respond to crises in flexible and novel ways. For all of these reasons, however, the Federal Reserve chose to return to a policy of targeting interest rates rather than monetary aggregates in 1983—three years after the recession helped cost Carter his bid for reelection.

Supply-Siders vs. Monetarists

President Reagan's election brought a revolution in economic policy making to the country, and his appointments to the Federal Reserve Board reflected this shift. The governors chosen by Reagan over the course of his administration subscribed to supply-side economics, which revolved around the idea that tax cuts were the key to increasing productivity and improving the economy. Reagan's appointees wanted to lower interest rates and cut taxes to reduce unemployment and tame inflation. This ideology was at odds with Volcker's brand of monetarism, and Volcker had no qualms about expressing his displeasure with the president's large and increasing budget deficits.

Although Volcker maintained majority standing on the Federal Open Market Committee (FOMC), he had lost it on the smaller board of governors, which was more susceptible to presidential influence. Despite this constraint and the growing dissatisfaction of Congress and the public, Volcker managed to maintain the high federal funds and discount rates that he wanted. The rash of bank failures in the 1980s and early 1990s that followed in the wake of a continued tight monetary policy only strengthened the political appeal of the supply-siders' views, however.

The Reagan presidency found both the political and economic environment welcoming to financial deregulation. As high, volatile interest rates threatened to edge many financial institutions into bankruptcy, the effort to remove legal restrictions from the industry in order to foster expansion and competition appeared to be an innovative solution. Legislation like the 1982 Garn-St. Germain Depository Institutions Act, which allowed savings and loan institutions to diversify, was passed during this period (though ultimately it did little to save the thrifts from the specter of insolvency.)

When the Continental Illinois National Bank and Trust Company failed in 1984, the Federal Reserve took steps to prevent the country's financial system from grinding to a halt. This was one of the earliest implementations of the "too big to fail" doctrine, and, some scholars have argued, the beginning of a period of financial moral hazard. If banks believed that the government would bail out insolvent institutions, banks might be willing to take on more risk than rational decisions would otherwise dictate. Although the burden of these bailouts fell on the taxpayer, it was clear that if these institutions had been allowed to fail, the economy would have suffered above and beyond the cost of saving the institutions. Whether the actions taken by the Federal Reserve and the federal government did, in fact, induce excessive risk taking has become a matter of controversy.

After Volcker had been nearly outvoted by the board of governors in 1986 in a discount rate dispute, Reagan offered the chairman a third term at the helm of the Fed in 1987. The opposition to Volcker's policies from many parts of the political spectrum and Volcker's own distaste for Reagan's budget deficits led him to turn down the offer. The Fed's policies during his time as chairman pushed many in Congress to question whether the central bank was independent of Wall Street influence and whether it should be made more accountable to the public—either through political appointments or congressional oversight. Upon Volcker's departure, however, many of these questions faded from public discourse.

Greenspan's Low Interest Rates and Hands-Off Approach

When Reagan appointed Alan Greenspan as chairman of the Federal Reserve in 1987, the savings and loan crisis was already fully under way. Eventually, more than seven hundred thrift institutions would fail. This, in combination with the great stock market crash on October 19, 1987, quickly tested Greenspan's ability to lead. Greenspan's rapid response to the meltdown consisted mostly of pumping liquidity into the banking sector and lowering interest rates.

Although Greenspan was faced with a large number of various crises, from the World Trade Center attacks of 1993 and 2001 to the failure of the large, interconnected hedge fund Long-Term Capital Management, the age of Greenspan is often considered to be a golden age of economic prosperity. The 1990s saw an unprecedented period of economic expansion, low unemployment, and minimal inflation. Greenspan was able to harness the popularity and respect he commanded to speak publicly about a number of issues outside the Fed's policy sphere, including globalization, budget deficits, and deregulation. Many came to see the chairman as a far more public figure than his predecessors. Greenspan's tenure was also marked by the creation of a more open Federal Reserve. Prior to 1994, communication between the FOMC and the public was virtually nonexistent. As a result of Greenspan's push for transparency, the FOMC began issuing press releases after

each meeting and, in a move that ended the guessing-games of professional "fed-watchers," clearly and simply stated the near-term federal funds target.

Greenspan's association with the longest period of economic expansion in the postwar period, however, was not without its difficulties. The asset bubbles formed during Greenspan's tenure, most significantly the dot-com bubble of the late 1990s and the housing bubble of the latter half of the first decade of the twenty-first century, proved economically disastrous once they burst. Though many complex forces contributed to these price misalignments, critics have pointed to two important factors that could have been controlled by the Federal Reserve. The first is the deviation, in the first years of the twenty-first century, from the Federal Reserve's implicit Taylor rule (the "rule" that indicates how much to raise or lower the federal funds rate in reaction to shortfalls in output and gaps in inflation). A lower-than-optimal interest rate (as suggested by the rule) may contribute to too much liquidity in an economy and engender the belief that asset prices will continue to rise. The second factor identified by critics as contributing to the development of the bubbles, particularly the subprime mortgage debacle, was the growing financial deregulation that Greenspan and others had advocated and implemented. Financial "modernization" legislation such as the Gramm-Leach-Bliley Act of 1999 also encouraged a more laissez-faire approach to supervision.

The Return of Macroeconomic Uncertainty

The credit crisis of 2008–2009 brought new and difficult challenges to the leadership of the Fed. The housing bubble was near to bursting when Ben S. Bernanke was appointed chairman of the Federal Reserve in 2006; he faced mortgage and housing markets that were now firmly intertwined by debt securitization with the rest of the financial world. In the summer of 2007, Bear Stearns, a global investment bank and securities trading concern, began to suffer the consequences of the bubble and its overexposure to the mortgage market—eventually failing in the face of severe solvency problems. Not until the fall of 2008, however, did the macroeconomic situation begin to deteriorate rapidly with the failure of

Lehman Brothers and the impending bankruptcy of American International Group. Within days, two of the major remaining investment banks, Morgan Stanley and Goldman Sachs, actively chose to convert into bank holding companies, thus bringing themselves under the regulatory purview of the Fed, while a third investment bank, Merrill Lynch, was purchased by Bank of America.

In efforts to contain the financial meltdown, the Federal Reserve adopted several exceptional policy measures. In addition to extending financial assistance to several major banking institutions, the Federal Reserve chose to maintain a federal funds rate target between 0 and 25 basis points (the lowest in history), to pay interest on banks' excess reserves kept at the Fed, and to pursue credit easing by expanding the Fed's balance sheet through the purchase of mortgage-backed securities and long-term Treasury securities for the first time since the 1960s. These policy decisions have no precedent in the history of the Federal Reserve and may raise far-reaching institutional and political questions in the future. The Treasury and the Fed issued a joint press release stating that "The Federal Reserve's independence with regard to monetary policy is critical for ensuring that monetary policy decisions are made with regard only to the long-term economic welfare of the nation." (Board of Governors of the Federal Reserve System).

Bibliography and Further Reading

Axilrod, Stephen H. *Inside the Fed; Monetary Policy and Its Management, Martin through Greenspan to Bernanke.* Cambridge, MA: The MIT Press, 2009.

Board of Governors of the Federal Reserve System. "The Role of the Federal Reserve in Preserving Financial and Monetary Stability—Joint Statement by the Department of the Treasury and the Federal Reserve." Press release, March 23, 2009. http://www.federalreserve.gov/newsevents/press/monetary/20090323b.htm.

Duy, Tim. Tim Duy's Fed Watch. http://economistsview.typepad.com/timduy (accessed October 11, 2009).

Hetzel, Robert L. *The Monetary Policy of the Federal Reserve: A History.* Cambridge, UK: Cambridge University Press, 2008.

Overtveldt, Johan Van. *Bernanke's Test: Ben Bernanke, Alan Greenspan, and the Drama of the Central Banker.* Chicago: Agate, 2009.

Shull, Bernard. *The Fourth Branch: the Federal Reserve's Unlikely Rise to Power and Influence.* Westport, CT: Praeger, 2005.

Wells, Donald R. *The Federal Reserve System: A History.* Jefferson, NC: McFarland, 2004.

Carolyn Abott

FINANCIAL CRISIS OF 2008

The Financial Crisis of 2008 thrust the federal government into a more active role in economic policy making. Beginning with losses in the market for subprime mortgage securities, banks and nonbank financial institutions experienced substantial losses, which reduced their capital available to lend and forced the financial firms to reduce their debt. Ultimately, economies worldwide contracted. As companies reduced investment spending and consumers increased savings in response to economic uncertainties, the Nobel prize–winning economist Paul Krugman noted that this situation required the government to provide substantial fiscal stimulus if the economy was to recover. Responses to the crisis—including government spending, corporate bailouts, and interventions in the financial markets—created a deep political divide, however. Critics of the growing government role worried that the United States might be on the road to socialism and that such expansion of the government would reward the irresponsible behavior of wealthy financial professionals and greedy mortgage borrowers.

Events of the Financial Crisis

The financial crisis began in August 2007, when concerns about losses in subprime mortgage securities led to fears of counterparty risk (the risk that the other party to a financial arrangement will be unable to meet its obligations) and the freezing of financial markets around the world. The Dow Jones Industrial Index weathered that shock and peaked in October 2007—and then lost about 54 percent of its value by March 2009. In March 2008, the Bear Stearns investment bank collapsed, and the government helped arrange for it to be bought at a fraction of its previous value by JP Morgan Chase. In September 2008, the Lehman Brothers investment bank declared bankruptcy; the government engineered a takeover of "Fannie Mae" (Federal National Mortgage Association) and "Freddie Mac" (Federal Home Mortgage Corporation), the nation's two largest mortgage finance lenders; the Federal Reserve provided a bailout of the American International Group; Merrill Lynch was sold to Bank of America; and Morgan Stanley and Goldman Sachs both transformed themselves into traditional bank holding companies, thus making them more subject to federal regulation but also giving them access to federal support. This transformation ended the era of independent investment banks in the United States. In December 2008, stock broker and financial advisor Bernie Madoff was implicated in the world's largest Ponzi scheme scandal to date. Throughout this period, climbing unemployment as well as troubles in the automotive industry and other companies outside of the financial system ensured that the financial crisis affected almost every aspect of the wider economy.

Politics and Causes of the Financial Crisis

Many factors have been cited as a cause of the 2008 financial crisis, including the growth of complex and opaque financial derivatives, a glut of savings from developing countries that reduced the returns from taking risks and thus led financial actors to seek greater risk to achieve desired returns, and the low interest rate policy of the Federal Reserve while Alan Greenspan was chairman (1987–2006). One factor in particular, though, is closely related to American politics—the role of regulation. An important political divide exists over if the crisis was caused by too little or too much regulation. The argument of those who blamed deregulation was that it allowed banks and other nonbank financial entities to take excessive risks because bank officials believed that the government would come to the rescue if things went wrong. Financial analysts spoke of the "Greenspan put"—the idea that the Federal Reserve would act quickly to prevent economic downturns—and also of "too big to fail"—the idea that the government would not let large financial companies fail, as the costs to the over-

all economy would be too high. Since the 1970s, deregulation in the banking sector had included allowing banks to merge into larger units with more total assets, to pay interest on checking deposits, to remove the ceilings on interest rates that could be paid on other types of deposits, and, in 1999, even eliminated the separation between commercial banks and investment banks.

Deregulation expanded as new financial innovations and products grew outside the scope of existing regulations. Paul Krugman characterized this as the "shadow banking system." Since the 1970s, the growth of private equity firms, hedge funds, financial derivatives, and nonbank financial actors had occurred outside the scope of existing regulations. In the words of author and former banker Charles Morris, "The relentless deregulation drive that started during the Reagan administration steadily shifted lending activities to the purview of nonregulated entities, until by 2006, only about a quarter of all lending occurred in regulated sectors, down from about 80 percent twenty years before." (54) Because regulations are meant to limit the actions of financial institutions, these companies had and have strong incentives to find loopholes or other ways to legally avoid regulations. Because of the antiregulatory environment of the past three decades, many of these financial innovations were left unregulated. The growth of securitization, the holding of assets off a bank's balance sheet, and the lack of a centralized location for trading financial derivatives all contributed to the financial crisis.

The antigovernment side of the political spectrum, however, laid the blame for the financial crisis more squarely on government regulations such as the Community Reinvestment Act of 1977. While the intentions of the act were noble—it required banks to avoid discriminating against low-income members of the community when deciding about loans—critics charged that this requirement forced banks to lend money to those who were poor credit risks. Specifically, with the goal of increasing home ownership and reducing discrimination, the Clinton administration was blamed for strengthening the act by requiring Fannie Mae and Freddie Mac to purchase and securitize housing loans made to poor individuals with low credit ratings. By taking such action, these government-sponsored enterprises allowed the subprime mortgage market to grow more than it would have otherwise, though the specific degree of blame to be placed is a source of controversy as Pres. George W. Bush also supported similar policies. In addition, many subprime mortgage lenders operated outside of this system as a part of the shadow banking system, and these institutions were less concerned about credit quality because they sold the loans—packaged as securities—to other financial actors.

The Role of Politics in Formulating the Government's Policy Response

Regardless of the causes, clearly a strong policy-making response was needed to end the crisis and to avoid a prolonged economic downturn. These responses include providing fiscal stimulus through increased government spending or through tax reductions, using government funds to buy the troubled assets of financial institutions or to otherwise inject further capital into financial institutions, bailing out companies viewed as "too big to fail," and providing a coordinated international response to avoid both beggar-thy-neighbor policies and countries falling into protectionism.

As for fiscal stimulus, President Bush signed a $150 billion economic stimulus plan in January 2008; it provided $100 billion worth of tax rebates for businesses and individuals; President Barack Obama signed the much larger $787 billion American Recovery and Reinvestment Act of 2009 in February 2009. This bill included tax relief, greater unemployment benefits, and more government spending on infrastructure, education, and health care.

Using government funds to assist failing financial companies has more generally been the task of the Department of Treasury, the Federal Reserve, and the Federal Deposit Insurance Corporation. The Federal Reserve, in particular, dramatically expanded its role by printing money to inject into financial markets in various ways; as a result, the assets on its balance sheet grew from less than $1 trillion to more than $2 trillion in 2008. The Troubled Asset Relief Program (TARP), passed by Congress in October 2008, allowed the

Treasury and Federal Reserve to spend $700 billion to help some financial institutions stay solvent.

Politics, however, often constrains the necessary actions. Although most economists argued that ending the crisis required the government to aid in restoring the health of banks' balance sheets so that they could resume extending credit to the wider economy, the American public tended to view such actions with suspicion—either because they see this as rewarding irresponsible bankers or because they believe government action is the first step on the road to socialism. For example, in March 2009, the public and politicians were outraged by the revelations that officials at the American International Group (AIG) received $165 million in bonuses despite receiving a bailout of $173 billion of taxpayer monies. Politicians discussed creating special provisions for a 100 percent tax on such bonuses; AIG's actions also further threatened plans to provide financial assistance to similar firms. Economists were also concerned about and outraged by such cavalier actions; economists also maintained that this type of government intervention was the only way to normalize conditions in the financial sector and resume the growth of credit and lending in the economy. Treasury official turned academic Phillip Swagel has argued that political constraints have severely limited the role of government actors; for example, the Federal Reserve and Treasury desired a TARP-style program in March 2008 but knew such request to Congress was politically unfeasible. They had to wait until the financial crisis further escalated in September of 2008.

Economics and politics collided in the arena of protectionism. In their desire to take action and to garner votes, some politicians urged protectionist measures popular with the public but that will do long-term damage to the country after inevitable retaliation from other countries reduces global trade and further damages the American export industry. For example, in the debate over the Obama administration's stimulus package, much time was spent discussing "Buy American" provisions that would require stimulus funds only be used to purchase American-made products. Politicians also discussed whether banks receiving TARP funds only be allowed to make loans in the United States or to hire only American workers.

The Financial Crisis and Long-term Reforms

As a long-term response to the crisis, many reforms have been considered. For instance, rating agencies experienced conflicts of interest—they were paid by the organizations for which they were providing ratings and some consideration had been given to put regulations in place to prevent this behavior. In addition, financial actors initiating mortgage loans could be required to keep a stake in the mortgages they create so that they will pay more heed to credit risk. Complex financial derivatives might be regulated and sold through exchanges rather than in over-the-counter markets; such arrangement would help reduce counterparty risk and make the industry more transparent. Regulation in the future may also be designed to keep pace with new financial instruments and innovations and ensure that all financial actors are adequately regulated—admittedly a difficult task as the finance industry constantly develops new products and techniques to bypass regulations and also lobbies extensively for favorable treatment. The United States may, in the future, consolidate its many regulatory bodies and expand regulation to any financial entity that behaves like a bank or is "too big to fail." Economists have also discussed developing counter-cyclical capital requirements that force institutions behaving like banks to develop a larger capital cushion during boom times.

The financial crisis and very deep recession that began in 2007 thrust the federal government into an activist role unseen in the United States since the 1930s. In the coming years, the experience of the financial crisis of 2008 will certainly have important implications for economic policy. The enormous bailout provided to the financial sector greatly expanded the size and role of government in economic policy. This growing government activism raises important questions about the role of the government in the economy; President Obama can be expected to push for a more active government role and less reliance on free market outcomes, reversing the Reagan-era goal of limiting government.

Bibliography and Further Reading

Barbera, Robert J. *The Cost of Capitalism: Understanding Market Mayhem and Stabilizing Our Economic Future.* New York: McGraw-Hill, 2009.

Carr, Edward. "Greed—and Fear: A Special Report on the Future of Finance." *Economist*, January 24, 2009, 1–24.

Foster, John B., and Fred Magdoff. *The Great Financial Crisis: Causes and Consequences.* New York: Monthly Review Press, 2009.

Krugman, Paul. *The Return of Depression Economics and the Crisis of 2008.* New York: W. W. Norton, 2009.

Mishkin, Frederic S. *The Economics of Money, Banking, and Financial Markets*, 8th edition. Boston: Pearson Addison-Wesley, 2007.

Morris, Charles R. *The Trillion Dollar Meltdown.* New York: Public Affairs, 2008.

Swagel, Phillip. "The Financial Crisis: An Inside View." Brookings Papers on Economic Activity Spring 2009 Conference, April 2009. http://www.brookings.edu/economics/bpea/~/media/Files/Programs/ES/BPEA/2009_spring_bpea_papers/2009_spring_bpea_swagel.pdf (accessed May 28, 2009).

Wallison, Peter J. "The True Origins of This Financial Crisis." *The American Spectator*, February 2009. http://spectator.org/archives/2009/02/06/the-true-origins-of-this-finan (accessed May 13, 2009).

Wade Donald Pfau

FISCAL AND BUDGETARY POLICY

Contemporary American fiscal and budgetary policy is largely influenced by the ideological framework of the "Reagan Revolution." The Reagan presidency marked a critical juncture in American fiscal policy, one that produced remarkably persistent political discourse, policy choices, and the evolution of fiscal and budgetary rules. President George W. Bush invoked Reagan's 1981 tax cuts to legitimize the 2001 and 2003 tax cuts, while also echoing Reagan's claim that deficits were not responsible for creating high interest rates. The Democrats' response to Reagan was tepid; they failed both to defend their own neo-Keynesian macroeconomic models and to develop a coherent and alternative set of fiscal and budgetary policies. Both parties, in the face of political gridlock, turned to macrobudgetary rules to control spending and balance the federal budget, only to see these goals slip away in a new wave of massive deficit spending during the Bush administration.

The Reagan Revolution

Ronald Reagan's fiscal and social agenda decisively shaped the policy decisions of his era and influenced or constrained those of every president who followed. Not only did Reagan's policies clearly challenge those of the Democratic Party, they also signified a break from the fiscal assumptions and policies of previous Republican administrations. Prior to Reagan, Republican presidents called for balanced budgets and attempted to limit the growth of federal expenditures. They recognized, however, that the citizenry would never again tolerate government passivity in the presence of great economic dislocation such as the Great Depression or even a deep recession; they were also still influenced by Keynesian economics and believed in the efficacy of countercyclical deficit spending. President Dwight D. Eisenhower announced that he would engage in deficit spending under circumstances similar to what Roosevelt faced; President Richard M. Nixon declared that "We are all Keynesians"; President Gerald Ford continued to employ the language of neo-Keynesian full-employment economics in his budgets.

Reagan's administration differed from his Republican predecessors in that it undertook a full-scale assault on neo-Keynesian economics. Reagan's efforts were greatly aided by the breakdown in the neo-Keynesian hegemony among economists and the rise of stagflation in the late 1970s—both undermined the logic of the Phillips curve trade-off between inflation and unemployment. Although Reagan's economic advisors included traditional budget-balancing conservatives who disliked Keynesian deficits and monetarists who believed in the superiority of monetary policy, Reagan's presidency is noteworthy for offering supply-side economics as the theoretical rationale for his fiscal policy proposals.

Supply-side economists argued that major reductions in corporate and personal income taxes would spur investment, productivity, and an entrepreneurial spirit that would restore the nation's economic health. Inspired by their ability to keep more of their income, entrepreneurs would invest in new factories, hire more workers, and increase the production of goods to meet demand, thus lowering prices and combating inflation. All this would boost the economy, stimulate new federal revenues, and help balance the budget. Did supply-side proponents actually promise that their tax cuts would produce sufficient revenues to balance the budget? The answer is unclear, though the 1982 fiscal forecast of the Reagan administration predicted that such measures would result in a balanced budget within four years. Nevertheless, supply-siders tolerated budget deficits, clearly valuing tax cuts more than balanced budgets. Prominent supply-siders like Jack Kemp opposed a constitutional amendment requiring a balanced federal budget for fear the amendment might constrain the size of tax cuts.

Reagan's tax cuts came in the form of the Economic Recovery Tax Act of 1981 (ERTA), which cut federal taxes by an estimated $1.764 trillion between 1982 and 1990 and lowered the top marginal tax rate from 70 to 50 percent. ERTA proved to be the most important and lasting victory of the Reagan Revolution, with its symbolic importance to American conservatism far outweighing its immediate effects and policy implications. Conservatives continue to employ ERTA as their standard for evaluating fiscal policy, and woe to any Republican who fails to follow Reagan's lead. The reality, however, is that Reagan proved to be one of the great raisers of taxes in American history. After 1981, Reagan signed 13 major bills that either directly increased taxes, such as the Tax Equity and Fiscal Responsibility Act of 1982, the Social Security Amendments of 1983, and the Deficit Reduction Act of 1984, or were intended to be revenue neutral, most notably the Tax Reform Act of 1986, which lowered the top marginal rate to 28 percent. These laws collectively increased taxes by an estimated $693 billion during the same period. To the chagrin of supply-siders, Reagan approved tax increases that offset ERTA by more than one-third. Nonetheless, ERTA crystallized the conservative position on fiscal policy, drawing the line that for the foreseeable future separates "good" conservatives from questionable ones. The irony is that Reagan crossed this line repeatedly.

The Retreat of Democratic Fiscal Policy

Confronted by the intellectual and ideological challenge of the Reagan Revolution, the Democrats failed to defend the Keynesian and neo-Keynesian theories that had served them well since the days of Franklin D. Roosevelt and John F. Kennedy. Keynes's theories provided the intellectual framework and justification for the Democrats' activist fiscal policies and deficit spending during the Great Depression. Neo-Keynesianism's full-employment budget models distinguished an economically good deficit from a harmful one even when the economy was not in a recession. During a weak economy, a nominal budget deficit might actually be calculated as a balanced full-employment budget—based on estimated revenues and expenditures had the economy been at full-employment level. Having seemingly jettisoned the ideas of Keynes and without a publicly convincing, coherent alternative, the Democrats lacked an agreed-upon set of guidelines to frame and present their fiscal policies.

Rather than defend Keynesianism, the Democrats turned to more conventional understandings of fiscal policy. Georgia governor Jimmy Carter ran against Pres. Gerald Ford on a platform that promised to balance the budget despite the recession. Congressional Democrats during Carter's administration then ignored the policy prescription of running balanced full-employment budgets in favor of extra spending. During the 1980 election, Carter failed to note that the full-employment budget was actually balanced. Throughout the presidencies of Reagan and George H. W. Bush, the party of the New Deal and full-employment economics called for balanced budgets during the worst months of that period's recessions. During the 1992 election and then as president, Bill Clinton called for deficit reduction to lower interest rates, even as the economy attempted to climb out of a recession. As a consequence, throughout his administration, Clinton's legislative and spending initiatives, such as his health care plan, were inevitably subjected to the criticism that they added to the very

deficits that he claimed delayed economic recovery. By making nominally balanced budgets and deficits the measures of the nation's fiscal well-being, the Democrats undermined their basic logic of governance and constrained their vision of fiscal policy.

The Rise of Macrobudgetary Rules

The Reagan administration ushered in years of triple-digit budget deficits that dwarfed anything previously experienced in peacetime America; it also introduced new forms of macrobudgetary laws designed to address these massive fiscal imbalances. Although the federal deficit grew significantly during the 1970s, the Reagan deficits and those extending into the 1990s regularly reached previously unknown heights. From a low point of $78.9 billion for 1981, the last Carter budget, Reagan's deficits ranged as high as $221 billion, those of George H. W. Bush to $290 billion, and $255 billion under Clinton. At the same time, the ideologically polarized and deeply divided executive and legislative branches could achieve only budgetary gridlock. Rather than face and resolve this political conflict, politicians revised the budgetary process with macrobudgetary rules.

These macrobudgetary rules tried to impose centralized, top-down, front-loaded budgetary outcomes on elected officials in an attempt to achieve fiscal solutions by guiding and constraining the scope of their decisions. The Balanced Budget and Emergency Deficit Control Act of 1985, better known as Gramm-Rudman-Hollings, called for a balanced budget in 1990. The law established annual maximum deficit amounts and threatened automatic budget cuts or sequesters to the extent necessary to reach these amounts if they were exceeded. The law contained numerous loopholes. First, the politicians exempted some 70 percent of the budget, principally entitlements, from sequestration. Second, the gap between the maximum deficit amounts and actual deficits became so large that it would have created huge, politically unacceptable sequesters of 20 to 30 percent for nonexempted programs. Politicians then engaged in widespread budgetary gimmickry to avoid sequestration. These gimmicks included exaggerating economic assumptions, overestimating revenues and underestimating expenditures, shifting outlays to future fiscal years, and moving favored programs from the nonexempt to the exempt category. The law failed to set forth an institutional framework that could overcome the deep political divisions of the day. Politicians, however, recognized that despite their enacted spending cuts and tax increases, changes in the macroeconomy ultimately determined the size of the deficit.

The next set of macrobudgetary laws benefited from the lessons learned from the failings of Gramm-Rudman-Hollings. The Budget Enforcement Act of 1990 (BEA), passed by a Democratic Congress and signed by President Bush, avoided the mistake of making a balanced budget the law's goal. The Congress, instead, focused on laws that addressed the level of government spending, something the politicians could, indeed, control. BEA divided spending into three categories: defense, international, and domestic discretionary spending. The law created "firewalls" between the categories to avoid one category of spending being raided to fund another category. BEA retained sequestration, but it would be applied only to the spending category that exceeded its spending cap. Finally, the law created PAYGO (pay-as-you-go) rules to address the problem of growing entitlements. These rules required that any newly proposed increase in mandatory spending or the loss of revenues from tax cuts that increased the deficit must be "paid-as-you-go" with offsets of either equal levels of spending cuts or revenue increases. A Republican Congress and Pres. Bill Clinton incorporated BEA's rules into the Balanced Budget Act of 1997 (BBA).

Balanced Budgets

Faced with a deficit spiraling out of control, Pres. George H. W. Bush in 1990 signed both the BEA and a tax hike that caused him to renounce his "read my lips" pledge to avoid tax increases. To the outrage of conservatives, top marginal rates grew from 28 percent to 31 percent. President Clinton and congressional Democrats further raised the top rate to 39.6 percent in the Omnibus Budget and Reconciliation Act of 1993. The BEA and BBA, supported by congressional Republicans with their "Contract with America," proved to be reasonably effective in controlling federal spending. Aided by significant new revenues stemming

RELATED ENTRIES

THIS VOLUME
Economic Policy; Monetary Policy

OTHER VOLUMES
Fiscal and Budgetary Policy (vols. 5 & 6)

from the dramatic growth of the dot-com economy, the government balanced its budget for the first time since 1969 and ran surpluses from 1998 through 2001.

The Bush Administration and the Return of Deficit Spending

Within a stunningly short period, the government's surpluses turned into a long-term projection of large-scale deficits. The shift in the nation's fiscal fortunes began with Pres. George W. Bush's Economic Growth and Tax Relief Reconciliation Act of 2001. This legislation was the first of five tax cuts that collectively reduced government revenues by $1.988 trillion and that lowered the top marginal tax rate to 33 percent—a fiscal policy justified in the name of Ronald Reagan and his 1981 supply-side tax cut. In March 2001, the economy formally entered into an eight-month recession following the bursting of the dot-com bubble, which in turn was followed by a relatively flat, jobless recovery. The attacks of September 11, 2001, and then the invasions and occupations of Afghanistan and Iraq resulted in a major buildup of defense and homeland security operations and a consequent rise in expenses. Finally, the Republican-controlled Congress abandoned and then let expire the government's macrobudgetary rules, particularly its PAYGO requirements, even as it increased overall spending and enacted new entitlement programs. All of this new spending and the passage of significant tax cuts, mixed with at-best moderate long-term growth, produced renewed and ongoing deficit spending beginning in 2002; the national debt nearly doubled from $5.6 trillion in 2000 to $9.6 trillion in 2008. By the end of the George W. Bush presidency, large-scale deficit spending once again characterized American fiscal and budget policy.

Bibliography and Further Reading

Eisner, Robert. *How Real Is the Federal Deficit?* New York: The Free Press, 1986.

Ippolito, Dennis S. *Why Budgets Matter: Budget Policy and American Politics*. College Park: Pennsylvania State University Press, 2004.

Palazzolo, Daniel J. *Done Deal?: The Politics of the 1997 Budget Agreement*. Chatham, NJ: Chatham House Publishers, 1999.

Roberts, Paul Craig. *The Supply-Side Revolution*. Cambridge, MA: Harvard University Press, 1985.

Rubin, Irene S. *Balancing the Federal Budget*. Washington, D.C.: Congressional Quarterly Press, 2002.

Savage, James D. *Balanced Budgets and American Politics*. Ithaca, NY: Cornell University Press, 1988.

Schick, Allen. *The Federal Budget: Politics, Policy, Process*. Washington, D.C.: Brookings Institution Press, 2007.

White, Joseph, and Aaron Wildavsky. *The Deficit and the Public Interest*. Berkeley: University of California Press, 1989.

James D. Savage

FORD, GERALD R.

1913–2006
Thirty-eighth President of the United States

The thirty-eighth president of the United States, Gerald R. Ford, restored faith in American political institutions and in constitutional government in the aftermath of Watergate—a moment of grave constitutional crisis in American history. He was the first man to have become president without having been elected as president or vice president. After the resignation of Richard Nixon's vice president, Spiro T. Agnew, Ford was appointed to that office under the provisions of Amendment XXV of the Constitution.

Early Life

Gerald R. Ford was born in Omaha, Nebraska, on July 14, 1913, to Leslie Lynch King and the former Dorothy Gardner. His parents divorced when he was an infant. In 1916, Ford's mother married Gerald R. Ford, Sr., owner of a local paint store. The elder Ford adopted his wife's son and gave the boy his name. "Jerry"—as Ford was known to family and

friends—was a good athlete, an adequate student, and an Eagle Scout. Ford graduated from the University of Michigan in 1935. A star football player in college, he was offered a professional contract, but he sought a more stable occupation and set his sights on becoming a lawyer. He graduated from Yale Law School in 1941 and returned to Grand Rapids, Michigan, to practice law.

Although he initially embraced the isolationist sentiments of his native Middle West, Ford changed his mind after hearing 1940 Republican presidential hopeful Wendell Willkie make the case for providing American assistance to help Great Britain fend off Nazi conquest. After the Japanese attack on Pearl Harbor in December of 1941, Ford joined the navy and rose to the rank of lieutenant.

Congressional Career

In 1948, Ford, backed by local reformers and with an assist from Sen. Arthur Vandenberg (R–MI), successfully ran for the U.S. House of Representatives. While in the House, Ford championed balanced budgets, a strong national defense, internationalism, and civil rights. Ford endeared himself to colleagues with his clean-cut image, his earnestness, and the deference he showed to elders. In 1961, the American Political Science Association, in presenting Ford its Distinguished Service Award, described him as a "Congressman's Congressman." This appellation implied that Ford tended to the needs of his fellow members of the House as diligently as he did to those of constituents.

In his first term in the House, Ford landed a highly coveted seat on the Committee on Appropriations, the entity that funds government agencies and programs. From there, he began his slow ascent through the Republican ranks. In 1963, a group of self-proclaimed "Young Turks," led by Ford protégé Donald Rumsfeld catapulted Ford into the chairmanship of the House Republican Conference, the third highest party post in the House. That same year, Pres. Lyndon B. Johnson named Ford to the Warren Commission—the group charged with investigating the assassination of Pres. John F. Kennedy.

In 1965, after the Republicans lost 37 House seats, casualties of Johnson's landslide reelection victory,

Ford, again the choice of younger House members, ousted Charles Halleck as Republican minority leader. While supportive of civil and voting rights, Ford opposed most of Johnson's domestic agenda. More of a hawk than a dove on Vietnam, Ford accused Johnson of mismanaging the war. He also took issue with what he characterized as the president's "unhealthy passion for secrecy." In response, LBJ leveled two insults at Ford that political opponents and stand-up comics repeated for decades: (1) that Ford had played football too long without a helmet; and (2) that Ford could not walk and chew gum at the same time.

With the election of Richard Nixon, with whom he had served in the House, as president in 1968, Ford changed roles from administration critic to presidential foot soldier, according to historian Douglas Brinkley. Nixon had considered taking Ford as his running mate in both 1960 and in 1968. Out of loyalty to Nixon, Ford, in an action he later regretted, led congressional efforts to impeach Supreme Court justice William O. Douglas. Angered over Douglas's liberal opinions, congressional Republications cited Douglas's authorship of an article for a magazine that ran nude photographs as evidence of conduct unbefitting a jurist. Ford's statement that "an impeachable offense is whatever the majority of the House . . . considers to be at a given moment in history" would later be cited in subsequent efforts to impeach presidents Nixon and Clinton.

An Abbreviated Vice Presidency

After winning reelection to his 12th term in 1972, Ford resolved to retire from the House. When the G.O.P. failed to capture control of the House in that year (Nixon was reelected in a landslide), Ford concluded that he might not attain his lifetime ambition of becoming speaker of the House. After Vice Pres. Spiro T. Agnew resigned on October 10, 1973, as part of a plea bargain at the end of an extensive probe of Agnew's alleged tax evasion, money laundering, and bribery, Nixon nominated Ford to replace Agnew. Ford took the oath of office on December 6.

With both the House and the Senate conducting investigations into the Watergate break-in and with Nixon battling in the courts to deny Congress and

special prosecutors access to taped conversations between Nixon and his aides, commentators looked upon Ford's appointment as part of Nixon's strategy to repair relations with Congress. The appointment and confirmation came too late, however, to help Nixon. Ford continued to defend the president but stopped when he learned that a tape Nixon had surrendered on orders from the Supreme Court contained evidence that Nixon had participated in a cover-up of the burglary and bugging of the Democratic National Committee in the Watergate Hotel. On August 8, 1974, Nixon announced his resignation. Ford became president when the resignation took effect the next day.

Ford's 896-Day Presidency

"Our long national nightmare is over," Ford declared in his first remarks as president. His next sentence, "Our Constitution works; our great Republic is a government of laws and not of men," struck the tone the nation was hoping for as it sought to bring down the curtain on the prolonged Watergate scandal. A month later, Ford, without warning, issued Nixon a "full, free and absolute pardon" for "all offenses" he may have "committed or taken part in" while in office. A Gallup poll found a drop in the new president's ratings from 71 to 49 percent.

Conspiracy theorists charged that Ford had, prior to becoming president, made a secret deal in which Nixon agreed to resign in exchange for a pardon. Ford, waiving executive privilege, appeared before the House Judiciary Committee to refute such charges under oath. He defended the pardon as the only means by which he could put the Watergate matter behind the nation. In response to critics who asserted that Nixon should not have been pardoned prior to either a trial or an admission of guilt, Ford took to citing a 1915 Supreme Court decision that stated that acceptance of a pardon constituted an admission of guilt.

Ford's political situation deteriorated considerably after the 1974 congressional elections. Democrats, aided by the Nixon pardon, a downturn in the economy, and rising inflation, added greatly to their congressional majorities, picking up 49 seats in the House and 5 in the Senate. With the executive and legislative branches pulling in opposite directions, Ford made extensive use of the veto. Of the 66 vetoes he handed down, Congress overrode only 12. Most of the bills Ford vetoed were spending initiatives that Democrats maintained would spur the economy. Ford preferred spending cuts as a means of controlling inflation, which was being fueled by high oil prices, food shortages, and a growing money supply. During Ford's presidency, inflation reached 12 percent.

The most famous of Ford's vetoes was a financial bailout of New York City. A *Daily News* headline, "Ford to City: Drop Dead," severely and adversely affected Ford's popularity—even after he had reversed his position. (Ford changed course after New York submitted a proposal more to his liking.) Ford failed in his attempt to persuade Americans to combat inflation through voluntary constraints on spending and on demands for higher wages and prices. The press and the political opposition ridiculed his campaign to have citizens sport "WIN" (Whip Inflation Now) buttons. In 1975, Ford persuaded Congress to enact modest tax cuts as an antirecessionary move. The recession that year constituted the first characterized by both high unemployment and high inflation.

Foreign Policy

In March 1975, North Vietnam, in violation of the Paris Peace Accords Nixon had signed, launched a sustained assault on South Vietnam. (All American combat forces had been withdrawn more than a year before Ford took office.) Ford went before a joint session of Congress to request $722 million in military and economic aid for South Vietnam, but Congress refused. In a speech at Tulane University on April 23, Ford declared the war in Vietnam "finished" as far as America was concerned.

By April 30, North Vietnam's occupation of Saigon, the capital of South Vietnam, was complete. In anticipation, the United States had undertaken a mas-

sive helicopter evacuation of U.S. personnel and those Vietnamese who had sided with the United States in the war. While extensive, the effort proved unable to transport all who wished to leave. The sight of thousands of Vietnamese rushing to the rooftop of the American Embassy in the hope of finding room on the last departing helicopters became indelibly fixed in the American consciousness. Ford then threw his weight behind efforts to aid Vietnamese who took to the seas to escape. The media dubbed them "the boat people." Facing down opposition, much of it in Congress, Ford oversaw efforts to incorporate more than one hundred thirty thousand Vietnamese, approximately 1 per cent of the population of South Vietnam, into American society. "To do less would have added moral shame to humiliation," he said. A month after the fall of Saigon, Ford ordered American marines to rescue the crew of the merchant ship *Mayaguez* after the Cambodian government seized it. The successful effort to rescue the crew of 40 took the lives of an equal number of American military personnel.

Ford continued Nixon's policies of détente toward the Soviet Union and engagement with the People's Republic of China. In July 1975, Ford, Soviet premier Leonid Brezhnev, and the heads of 33 other nations signed the Helsinki Accords, which recognized as permanent Eastern European boundaries that had been in place since the end of World War II. American conservatives derided them as a strategic defeat for the West. Yet the Helsinki Accords' provisions that bound signatories to respect the human rights of all inhabitants became the vehicle through which dissidents within the Soviet bloc were able to attract the attention of the rest of the world.

The Election of 1976

Ford faced a stiff challenge for the Republican nomination in 1976. Former California governor Ronald Reagan, his would-be replacement, charged that détente, as Nixon and Ford practiced it, constituted nothing less than appeasement. Reagan's campaign gained momentum, particularly in the Southern states, when he attacked Ford's proposal to relinquish control of the Panama Canal to Panama. Ford prevailed over Reagan at the convention by a mere 117 votes.

Ford went into the general election trailing his Democratic opponent, Jimmy Carter, by 33 percent in the polls. Seeking to capitalize on not only Watergate, but also on congressional scandals, Carter cast himself in the role of an outsider, a reformer, and a representative of the new (nonsegregationist) South. Seeking to distance himself from Nixon, Ford stressed his integrity. As the election neared, Ford steadily eroded Carter's lead. He lost the popular vote to Carter by 2 percentage points.(In the Electoral College, Carter defeated Ford 297 to 240.)

Carter began his inaugural address with a unique and unprecedented tribute to the man he had defeated. "For myself and for our nation," Carter proclaimed, "I want to thank my predecessor for all he has done to heal our land." Restoring integrity to and faith in the American government after Watergate remains Ford's greatest legacy. His brand of Midwestern Republicanism, with its preference for balanced budgets, détente, and downplaying hot-button social issues gave way to a more assertive conservatism in both domestic and foreign policy heralded by Ronald Reagan, Newt Gingrich, and George W. Bush.

Bibliography and Further Reading

Brinkley, Douglas. *Gerald R. Ford*. New York: Times Books, 2007.

Cannon, James. *Time and Chance: Gerald Ford's Appointment with History, 1913–1974*. New York: HarperCollins, 1994.

DeFrank, Thomas. *Write It When I'm Gone*. New York: Putnam 2008.

Felzenberg, Alvin S. *The Leaders We Deserved (and a Few We Didn't): Rethinking the Presidential Rating Game*. New York: Basic Books, 2008.

Ford, Gerald R. *A Time to Heal: The Autobiography of Gerald R. Ford*. New York: Random House, 1979.

Greene, John R. *The Presidency of Gerald R. Ford*. Lawrence: University Press of Kansas, 1995.

Hartmann, Robert T. *Palace Politics: An Inside Account of the Ford Years*. New York: McGraw Hill, 1980.

Mieczkowski, Yanek. "Gerald Ford." In *The American Presidency*, edited by Alan Brinkley and Davis Dyer, 443–454. Boston: Houghton Mifflin, 2000.

Pham, Quang X. "Ford's Finest Legacy." *Washington Post*, December 30, 2006.

Porter, Roger B. "A President With a Purpose: Leadership Lessons from Gerald R Ford." *Harvard Magazine*, March–April 2007.

Alvin S. Felzenberg

FREE TRADE AGREEMENTS, RISE OF

One of the defining features of the world trading system, especially since the 1990s, has been the meteoric rise of bilateral and regional trade agreements. Until the 2000s, the United States had only a handful of free trade agreements, including the North American Free Trade Agreement (NAFTA) with Mexico and Canada, and a free trade agreement with Israel. Yet, as Lael Brainard of the Brookings Institution reported, between July 1999 and November 2007, Congress ratified 11 more free trade agreements. At the end of 2008, agreements with South Korea, Panama, and Colombia were awaiting congressional approval, and negotiations with Thailand, the United Arab Emirates, Malaysia, and the Southern African Customs Union were under way. Furthermore, plans for a Free Trade Area of the Americas remained on the table despite disagreements among participating countries. U.S. bilateral and regional trade agreements both respond to challenges posed by the multilateral trading system and, in turn, shape the multilateral system. These agreements remain politically sensitive both because of growing disenchantment with globalization and the perception that the agreements will have ill consequences.

Definitions

Bilateral agreements generally denote trade (and investment) agreements between two countries. The term *regional trade agreement* commonly refers to an agreement that forms a region out of several countries, for example, NAFTA. Regional trade agreements can also be agreements between two regional entities, for example, the ongoing negotiations between the European Union (EU) and Mercosur, which comprises Brazil, Argentina, Uruguay, and Paraguay. All of the above agreements are generally referred to as free trade agreements (FTAs) since they aim for elimination of trade barriers between participating countries—even though, in reality, they tend to achieve only a reduction of barriers. In addition to FTAs, the United States has also negotiated bilateral investment frameworks and trade and investment framework agreements; these aim to enhance trade and investment flows between the United States and other countries. Because FTAs, like customs unions, establish preferential reductions of barriers to trade and investment between parties to the agreement, they are often referred to as preferential trade agreements (PTAs). (Note, however, that members of a customs union apply a single external tariff, whereas parties to a free trade agreement retain external tariffs.)

The Debate

To understand the role PTAs play in U.S. policy making and the contentious relationship among them, the multilateral trading regime of the World Trade Organization (WTO) must be clarified. Article XXIV of the General Agreement on Tariffs and Trade and Article V of the General Agreement on Trade in Services allow for the formation of free trade areas and customs unions as long as "substantially all trade" between signatories to a PTA is liberalized. Furthermore, through the enabling clause, PTAs between developing countries are permitted by the WTO, and PTAs between developed and developing countries can be allowed under a waiver. Although the WTO should be notified of these agreements, the WTO estimates that currently about four hundred PTAs are in force—only some of which have been formally made known to the WTO. The current generation of PTAs increasingly links developed and developing economies and increasingly involves countries that are not geographically proximate—the U.S.-Morocco FTA is an example. Furthermore, PTAs encompass aspects of trade, including investment, that the WTO negotiations have not addressed comprehensively.

The proliferation of PTAs has intensified the debate about the compatibility of these agreements with the multilateral trading system. Inspired by the seminal work of Jacob Viner, a substantial part of the literature generated in the debate examines PTAs'

impact on welfare by examining trade creation versus diversion. For instance, trade diversion might occur if a regional agreement expands the production of less efficient members and reduces the production of more efficient outsiders. No blueprint exists delineating the welfare implications of these agreements and thus case-by-case analyses of PTAs may be more appropriate. Scholars have focused their debates on whether these agreements constitute stepping stones leading to multilateral free trade or whether they hamper the multilateral efforts of the WTO. For instance, the literature investigates, without reaching a consensus, PTAs' effects on members' external trade policies in an attempt to understand such agreements' implications for multilateral trade liberalization. Other scholars emphasize that these agreements may be undermining the multilateral trading system in a number of ways. PTAs lead to a "spaghetti bowl" of "criss-crossing preferences," including complicated rules of origin (which determine the origin of products). (Bhagwati 13) Also, negotiations for PTAs can strain the resources of countries large and small.

The PTAs of the United States

A brief overview of the PTAs of the United States reveals that these agreements have served to advance the U.S. trade agenda when the multilateral forum has become too cumbersome, while simultaneously affecting the multilateral level. In the 1960s, the United States initiated the Kennedy Round of multilateral trade negotiations in order to "counter the discrimination inherent in the creation of the European Common Market." (Bergsten) Similarly, during the 1970s, the United States encouraged the Tokyo Round in order to "counter additional discrimination from the [European] Community's expansion to include the United Kingdom." (Bergsten) Again, when the multilateral round of negotiations faltered in the 1980s, NAFTA was formed. Since all these multilateral negotiations eventually resumed, these few examples may suggest that regional formations can induce multilateral cooperation.

Nevertheless, PTAs have, over time, created an alternative path to economic interdependence. The allure of this alternative continues, as the WTO—with more than one hundred fifty members and reliance on consensus decision making—cannot negotiate rapidly. The competitive liberalization policy of the administration of George W. Bush became increasingly frustrated with this cumbersome multilateral decision-making. The term *competitive liberalization* initially denoted the rush by different countries worldwide to liberalization in the then-nascent global economy but grew to encompass the policy of seeking bold liberalization through bilateral and regional trade agreements in addition to multilateral agreements. Practically, the result has been that the United States pursues liberalization on any level—bilateral, regional, or multilateral. The rise in the number of PTAs of the United States, particularly since 1999, can thus be seen partly as a consequence of this policy.

In addition to competitively liberalizing, the United States has also been responding to a trend sparked by the EU and others. Former U.S. trade representative (USTR) Robert Zoellick remarked in 2001 that "other countries are moving forward with trade agreements while the [USA] has stalled." In 2007, the Business Roundtable, an association of chief executive officers of major U.S. companies, urged the Bush administration to forge ahead with free trade agreements, putting forward PTAs by China and the EU as reasons. Accordingly, U.S. PTAs can be seen as a response to the rising influence of other key economic actors.

PTAs also provide testing grounds for issues that either go beyond current WTO commitments or expand upon existing ones. As a USTR document explains, FTAs can serve as "laboratories for liberalization and models for global negotiations by establishing innovative new disciplines . . . such as e-commerce, intellectual property . . . labor and environmental cooperation and expanding services trade." ("Background Information on the U.S.-SACU FTA") Hence, U.S. agreements with developing countries seek provisions on intellectual property rights that are often considered "WTO-plus."

Finally, the increased use of PTAs as tools of foreign policy during the Bush administration contributed to the rise in U.S. PTAs. For instance, U.S. PTAs in North Africa and the Middle East, including agreements with Morocco, Oman, and Bahrain, fit with the broader strategic concerns of the United States in that region. Similarly, trade and investment framework agreements with Pakistan and Afghanistan were negotiated. The likely political—rather than economic—importance of these agreements is perhaps highlighted by the fact that U.S. exports to these PTA members represent a small portion of total U.S. exports.

The Unpopularity of PTAs

Although PTAs give American businesses favorable terms for access to foreign markets, they remain domestically unpopular. For instance, in the House of Representatives, Democratic Party support for the United States–Dominican Republic–Central America Free Trade Agreement was 7 percent (July 2005) and support for the U.S.-Morocco agreement was 59 percent (July 2004). Republican support for these two agreements was, respectively, 87 and 89 percent. The background of NAFTA provides a suitable example to examine domestic turmoil over PTAs. A variety of groups opposed NAFTA, including traditional protection-seeking industries that compete with imports (such as textiles), organized labor, environmentalists, and consumer groups. Only after Pres. George H. W. Bush agreed to negotiate labor and environmental standards separately did his administration win "fast-track authority," which allows negotiation of trade agreements with only an up-or-down vote in Congress. When Pres. Bill Clinton took office, he negotiated or renegotiated three side agreements—on import surges, environmental standards, and labor standards—to NAFTA to placate those who opposed the agreement in Congress. Even though NAFTA eliminated tariffs after a transitional period, it did not usher in unfettered free trade. As Hufbauer and Schoot emphasize, it included restrictive rules of origin in sensitive sectors, particularly textiles and automotive, and delayed liberalization in the agricultural market for import-sensitive products for 15 years. Concerns about NAFTA continue to focus on environmental and labor standards as well as the conviction that NAFTA caused loss of manufacturing jobs in the United States and put pressure on wages of unskilled workers. The reality remains complex: some studies confirm these contentions, while other studies demonstrate NAFTA's minuscule effect. Certainly, NAFTA's unpopularity among certain groups is part of a larger debate about the benefits of globalization and further economic interdependence. Globalization is blamed for job insecurity and wage inequality within the United States, although most studies demonstrate that technology favoring higher-skilled workers plays a larger role in bringing about this inequality. At the same time, those concerned with the economic development of the weaker trading partners of the United States worry that PTAs allow the United States to pursue its own goals—often at the expense of these partners. The diverse set of concerns about U.S. PTAs, as exemplified by the NAFTA debate, reveals the domestic bias against PTAs despite the multiplicity of purposes these agreements have served in responding to and shaping the multilateral trade agenda.

Bibliography and Further Reading

Bergsten, Fred C. "The Global Trading System and Developing Countries in 2000." IIE Working Papers 99-6, 1999. http://www.iie.com/publications/wp/wp.cfm?ResearchID=171 (accessed November 17, 2009)

Bhagwati, Jagdish. "America's Bipartisan Battle against Free Trade." *Financial Times*, April 9, 2007.

Bhagwati, Jagdish et al., eds. *TradingBlocs: Alternative Approaches to Analyzing Preferential Trade Agreements*. Cambridge, MA: MIT Press, 1999.

Blustein, Paul. "From Lima to Doha: Assessing the U.S. Trade Agenda." The Brookings Institution. http://www.brookings.edu/opinions/2007/1112_trade_blustein.aspx (accessed November 11, 2009).

Brainard, Lael. "Tracking Trade Votes." The Brookings Institution, http://www.brookings.edu/search.aspx?doQuery=1&q=Tracking%20Trade%20Votes (accessed November 11, 2009).

Business Roundtable. "We Cannot Stand Still: The Race for International Competitiveness." March 2007. http://74.125.93.132/search?q=cache:cD3OmfLdf98J:trade.businessroundtable.org/cant_stand_still.pdf+We+Cannot+Stand+Still:+The+Race+for+International+Competitiveness&cd=1&hl=en&ct=clnk&gl=us (accessed November 17, 2009)

Destler, I. M. *American Trade Politics*, 3rd edition. Washington D.C.: IIE, 1995.

Galal, Ahmed, and Robert Z. Lawrence. *Anchoring Reform with a US-Egypt Free Trade Agreement*. Policy Analyses in International Economics 74. Washington, D.C.: IIE, 2005.

Hufbauer, Gary C., and Jeffrey Schott. *NAFTA Revisited: Achievements and Challenges*. Washington, D.C.: IIE, 2005.

Kahler, Miles. *Regional Futures and Transatlantic Economic Relations*. New York: Council on Foreign Relations Press, 1996.

Kono, Daniel. "When Do Trade Blocs Block Trade?" *International Studies Quarterly* 51, no. 1 (2007): 165–181.

Lawrence, Robert. *Regionalism, Multilateralism, and Deeper Integration*. Washington, D.C.: Brookings Institution Press, 1995.

Mansfield, Edward D., and Helen V. Milner. "The New Wave of Regionalism." *International Organization* 53, no. 3 (1999): 589–627.

Milner, Helen V. *Interests, Institutions, and Information*. Princeton, NJ: Princeton University Press, 1997.

Office of the United States Trade Representative. "Background Information on the U.S.-SACU FTA." http://ustraderep.gov/Trade_Agreements/Bilateral/Southern_Africa_FTA/Background_Information_on_the_US-SACU_FTA.html (accessed November 11, 2009).

Schott, Jeffrey, ed. *Free Trade Agreements: US Strategies and Priorities*. Washington D.C.: IIE, 2004.

Stiglitz, Joseph. *Making Globalization Work*. New York: W. W. Norton, 2006.

Viner, Jacob. *The Customs Union Issue*. Carnegie Endowment for International Peace, New York, 1950.

Zoellick, Robert. "Free Trade and the Hemispheric Hope." Prepared Remarks of Robert B. Zoellick, U.S. Trade Representative, Council of the Americas, Washington, D.C., May 7, 2001. http://ctrc.sice.oas.org/geograph/westernh/zoellick_3.pdf (accessed November 17, 2009)

———. "Unleashing Trade Winds." *The Economist*, December 7, 2002.

Ayse Kaya Orloff

GAY AND LESBIAN RIGHTS MOVEMENT

The gay and lesbian rights movement in the U.S. began to experience rising expectations in the mid-1970s, only to face an enormous social, cultural, and medical crisis in the AIDS epidemic, coupled with federal governmental indifference, in the following decades. Activists became more radical in response to this crisis, challenging both U.S. laws and dominant cultural norms and constructions of sexuality. In the first decade of the twenty-first century, the movement came to be dominated by an emphasis on achieving marriage equality for same-sex couples.

Beginnings

Prior to the mid-1970s, lesbians and gay men faced an openly hostile political climate. Sodomy statutes prohibited not only anal intercourse, but they were often interpreted also to prohibit any oral-genital contact, whether among same- or different-sex couples, married or not. Police routinely raided gay bars and targeted gay male cruising places in order to arrest lesbians and gay men for solicitation and loitering with the intent to commit the illegal act of sodomy. During this politically repressive time, lesbian and gay activism was marked by assimilation and quiescence. The predominant lesbian and gay organizations, the Mattachine Society and the Daughters of Bilitis, focused primarily on self-help issues. Homophile activists tried to persuade psychological and religious authorities (and themselves) that

homosexuality was neither a sickness nor a sin, in the hopes that these professionals would then advocate for tolerance on behalf of homosexuals.

Grassroots organizations then began to proliferate as lesbians and gay men were emboldened by the sexual revolution of the 1960s and other political movements of the day to engage in more visible and daring tactics, including public protests. Although leaders differed in the extent to which they emphasized cultural over political change, they were clear that to gain either, they needed to generate publicity by creating a political movement. Some activists demanded entrance into mainstream institutions, while gay "liberationists" opposed those same institutions—a tension that continues to this day.

Departing from the homophile tradition, the emerging view that gays, not psychiatrists or religious authorities, were the experts on homosexuality laid the groundwork for mobilization efforts. The movement now employed both litigation and protest tactics in seeking to end government employment discrimination based on sexual orientation. By 1975, new U.S. Civil Service Commission regulations omitted the term "immoral [i.e., homosexual] conduct" from its employment guidelines.

In the context of political and cultural changes in the U.S. brought on by the student and nascent anti-war movements of the 1960s, gaining access to government jobs and gaining security clearances seemed quite mainstream. Young activists, influenced by the radical movements of the 1960s, joined older homophile organizations, and new organizations such as the Gay Activists Alliance emerged. Often glaring incidents of police abuse and inequality triggered the growth of new organizations and the use of more radical tactics. Activists pressed for an end to entrapment, police harassment, and employment discrimination. The Stonewall riots of 1969, which were a response to a police raid on a gay after-hours club in New York City, were but one in a series of uprisings by lesbians and gay men.

Drawing on the psychoanalytic theory of the German philosopher and sociologist Herbert Marcuse, gay liberationists held that humans were innately bisexual and that the movement should therefore try to pursue change by freeing the bisexual within, thus challenging gender roles and sexual norms. Liberationists also sought alliances with other oppressed peoples. Soon, however, due to infighting, gay liberation gave way to the gay and lesbian rights movement. Lesbian and gay liberation groups and lesbian and gay psychiatrists challenged the American Psychiatric Association (APA) view that homosexuality was a mental disorder. In 1973, protest-movement pressure and new empirical data led the APA to remove homosexuality from its list of mental disorders.

Culture, Politics, and the Meaning of Identity: 1987–2006

In 1986, the U.S. Supreme Court ruled in *Bowers v. Hardwick*, 478 U.S. 186, that there was no right to privacy for homosexual sodomy to be found in the U.S. Constitution. The defeat symbolized the intransigence of homophobia. In response to *Hardwick*, national lesbian and gay organizations organized a march on Washington in 1987 that sparked a resurgence in grassroots activism. Even the generally more timid national organizations began to focus again on the cultural meanings and challenges to the mainstream presented by lesbians and gay men. Activists sought to repeal sodomy laws, pass antidiscrimination and hate crimes legislation, fight anti-lesbian/gay rights initiatives, end the military's ban on lesbian and gay personnel, and obtain the right to marry.

Fury over government inactivity surrounding AIDS, anger at what had come to be seen as the timidity of the AIDS service organizations, anguish over the mounting number of AIDS cases, and the *Hardwick* decision led New York City activists to form the radical direct action group ACT UP in 1987. ACT UP had multiple targets, ranging from city, state, and federal elected officials, who were seen as ignoring the epidemic, to the Centers for Disease Control and Prevention (CDC) and the Federal Drug Administration (FDA). AIDS communities mobilized to attain access to drugs, money for research and treatment, and protection from discrimination based on the involuntary disclosure of HIV status.

By 1992, ACT UP's radicalism had waned. Groups working cooperatively with health care providers and government research agencies, such as the Treatment Action Group, gained prominence. Despite continued overlap in organizations and personnel, by 1990 the AIDS movement had become distinct from the lesbian and gay movement.

ACT UP's ideals were taken up by Queer Nation, formed in 1990. Like ACT UP, Queer Nation reframed the discourse around sexual orientation, employing new tactics and challenging the very categories of identity that had previously motivated activism. Self-proclaimed queer activists sought alliances with people of color, bisexuals, transgendered people, and anyone else defined by dominant discourse as somehow transgressing dominant cultural norms. Queer nationals also reappropriated the term "queer" to include lesbians, gay men, bisexuals, and transgendered (LGBT) people, as well as anyone else who challenged the dominant sex/gender system. "Queer" did not demarcate a person's sexual orientation, it was a statement against the normal.

During the late 1980s and 1990s, the Religious Right placed initiatives on the ballots of dozens of cities and states. If passed, such laws would have made it illegal for lesbians and gay men to organize politically, remove protection based on sexual orientation from existing antidiscrimination legislation, and essentially legalize anti-lesbian/gay discrimination. In response, groups such as the Lambda Legal Defense and Education Fund (Lambda Legal) and the National Gay and Lesbian Task Force (NGLTF) began to take on a greater leadership role, and litigation became ever more important to the movement. In 1992, Colorado

Members from the activist group Queer Nation hold up protest signs outside of a meeting attended by the Reverend Jerry Falwell in Houston, Texas, on August 19, 1992. Falwell, a member of the Religious Right who had often spoken out against homosexuality, was in Houston to discuss "family values," a topic that inspired many of the responses visible on the demonstrators' placards. (Najlah Feanny/CORBIS SABA)

passed Amendment 2, a statewide anti-lesbian/gay referendum. Lambda Legal and local Colorado lawyers immediately challenged the amendment, which was overturned by the U.S. Supreme Court in 1996.

In other arenas, activists demanded domestic partnership benefits from corporations, unions, and cities. Despite the still foundering federal anti-gay discrimination bill and a decade of Republican influence, lesbians and gay men helped pass the Hate Crimes Statistics Act in 1990. The act mandated the collection and publication of data on bias-related violence based on religion, race, ethnicity, and sexual orientation. This was the first time that Congress had ever passed any positive legislation that included the term "sexual orientation."

Bill Clinton's election as president in 1992 marked the end of 12 years of Republican presidential rule. During his election campaign, candidate Clinton had promised to end the military's ban on lesbian and gay personnel, pushing the issue to the forefront of lesbian and gay politics. The disappointing "Don't Ask, Don't Tell" policy that eventually emerged helped reify a mind-set in the armed forces that holds that statements about being gay or lesbian are evidence of a propensity to engage in "homosexual acts" and grounds for dismissal. The emphasis on the military was a major source of conflict within the lesbian and gay movement, as many activists decried militarism and saw the fight for inclusion as regressive. But when pushed, even those lesbians and gays opposed to the military as an institution agreed that sexual orientation should not be grounds for exclusion.

In the 1990s, as it looked likely that a Hawaii court might legalize same-sex marriage, the right to marry became the most important and controversial political issue for lesbian and gay activists. Many activists felt that rather than ape the patriarchal institution of marriage, the movement should create new ways of gaining legal protection for intimate relationships. Still others argued that gaining access to marriage was the first step toward reforming it. In 1996, the federal government passed the Defense of Marriage Act (DOMA) to permit states and the federal government to deny legal recognition of same-sex marriages lawfully performed in other states. As of November 2009, at least 73 statutory and constitutional DOMAs are in effect, and five states (Massachusetts, Connecticut, Vermont, Iowa, and New Hampshire) allow same-sex couples to marry. In 2003, the U.S. Supreme Court overturned the remaining sodomy statutes in *Lawrence v. Texas*, 539 U.S. 558, marking an important legal victory.

Summary

Denied basic rights of association, faced with laws against sodomy that defined them as criminal, subject to police harassment and medical "treatment," homosexuals and the fledgling homophile movement struggled for survival between 1940 and 1964. By educating straight professionals, activists hoped those professionals would, in turn, help increase tolerance of homosexuals and ease the legal sanctions against them.

Lacking access to political institutions and absent dense social networks from which to mobilize, lesbian and gay activists began to demonstrate publicly as lesbians and gay men in order to mobilize a mass movement. Activists challenged cultural understandings of homosexuality and achieved political gains. By contrast, Liberationists championed a universal bisexuality in order to challenge dominant gender and sexual norms.

As organized opposition and political access increased in the late 1970s, activists began to work with state agencies and focus on obtaining political and legal change.

By 1986, the government's lack of response to the AIDS epidemic and the *Bowers v. Hardwick* defeat sparked a reevaluation of the cultural and political meaning of sexual orientation. Denied meaningful political access, groups like ACT UP and Queer Nation stressed strategies designed to criticize dominant cultural practices. By contrast, others sought access to the nation's most conservative institutions: marriage and the military. The cultural and political meaning of sexual orientation remains contested, but it is clear that the shifting emphasis on political and cultural change are responses to changes in the political climate, and that the cultural and political impact of these diverse constructions (or deconstructions) varies over time and place.

Bibliography and Further Reading

Armstrong, Elizabeth A. *Forging Gay Identities: Organizing Sexuality in San Francisco, 1950–1994.* Chicago: University of Chicago Press, 2002.

Barclay, Scott, Mary Bernstein, and Anna-Maria Marshall, eds. *Queer Mobilizations: LGBT Activists Confront the Law.* New York: New York University Press, 2009.

Bernstein, Mary. "Celebration and Suppression: The Strategic Uses of Identity by the Lesbian and Gay Movement." *American Journal of Sociology* 103, no. 3 (1997): 531–565.

———. "Identities and Politics: Toward a Historical Understanding of the Lesbian and Gay Movement." *Social Science History* 26, no. 3 (2002): 531–581.

Bernstein, Mary, and Renate Reimann, eds. *Queer Families, Queer Politics: Challenging Culture and the State.* New York: Columbia University Press, 2001.

D'Emilio, John. *Sexual Politics, Sexual Communities: The Making of a Homosexual Minority in the United States 1940–1970.* Chicago: University of Chicago Press, 1983.

Epstein, Steven. *Impure Science: AIDS, Activism, and the Politics of Knowledge.* Berkeley: University of California Press, 1996.

Fetner, Tina. *How the Religious Right Shaped Lesbian and Gay Activism.* Minneapolis: University of Minnesota Press, 2008.

Vaid, Urvashi. *Virtual Equality: The Mainstreaming of Gay and Lesbian Liberation*. New York: Anchor Books, 1995.

Mary Bernstein

GINGRICH, NEWT

born 1943
Fifty-eighth Speaker of the U.S. House of Representatives

Newt Gingrich, the nation's 58th Speaker of the House, devised and implemented the strategy that produced the first Republican majority in the House of Representatives in 40 years. He remains a significant commentator, conservative political strategist, and author.

Formative Experiences

Newton ("Newt") Leroy Gingrich was born in Harrisburg, Pennsylvania, on June 17, 1943. His teenage parents, Newton Searles McPherson and the former Kathleen Daugherty, divorced when he was a year old. Two years later, his mother married Robert Gingrich, an army lieutenant, who adopted the three-year-old Newt. His immediate family would eventually include three half-sisters.

When he was ten, Gingrich lobbied state and local officials to establish a local zoo. His unsuccessful efforts made the local newspapers. Zoology and paleontology, along with politics, would rank high among his lifelong pursuits. When he was 15, Gingrich toured Verdun, the site of one of the bloodiest battles of World War I. He later attributed his decision to study history and enter politics to his realization that the horror that took place there might happen again.

After his family relocated to Columbus, Georgia, Gingrich declared his intention to build an effective statewide Republican Party in the then one-party (Democratic) state. Gingrich received his B.A. degree from Emory University in 1965, his M.A. in history from Tulane in 1968, and his Ph.D. in history from Tulane in 1971. He wrote his doctoral dissertation on Belgian educational policies in the Congo. While at Tulane, Gingrich worked on behalf of Gov. Nelson A. Rockefeller's campaign to win the 1968 Republican presidential nomination. Gingrich cited Rockefeller's strong commitment to civil rights as his reason for supporting the New York governor over former vice president Richard Nixon, an early hero of his, and the California governor and future Republican icon, Ronald Reagan.

His studies completed, Gingrich taught history at the University of West Georgia in Carrollton. He broadened his academic interests to include environmental studies and displayed a fondness for the works of futurist writers such as Alvin Toffler (*The Third Wave)* and John Naisbitt (*Megatrends*), as well as the management consultants Peter Drucker and W. Edwards Deming.

Electoral politics were his true calling, however, and Gingrich set his sights on the Sixth Congressional District. Running against an entrenched Democratic incumbent, John J. Flynt, Gingrich cast himself in the role of an outsider and reformer who would take on vested and corrupt interests. He also tore into Flynt's segregationist voting record. Running in years that proved favorable to Democrats in Georgia (1974, in the aftermath of Watergate, and 1976, with former governor Jimmy Carter heading the Democratic ticket), Gingrich nearly upended Flynt in two successive elections. After Flynt retired in 1980, Gingrich opposed the more liberal Democratic hopeful, the state senator Virginia Shapard. Campaigning as a social and fiscal conservative, Gingrich defeated Shapard by 9 percentage points, and he would win reelection to the House six times.

The Path to Power

Once in the House of Representatives, Gingrich eschewed the traditional freshman's role of tending to his district, performing journeyman-type roles on subcommittees, and biding his time as he acquired seniority. He set out to fulfill a higher ambition: winning Republican control of an institution that had been in Democratic hands since 1954. Toward that end, he used his well-honed capacity to attract press attention and his organizational skills to draw public attention to examples of Democratic corruption and abuses of power.

Gingrich used the House's custom of allowing members to deliver short speeches at the close of business as an opportunity for him and his colleagues to deliver coordinated party messages. With a new cable network, C-SPAN, broadcasting House proceedings, this tactic helped Gingrich build grassroots support and attract donors to his cause. The Democratic House Speaker, Tip O'Neill, ordered television cameras turned away from the speakers so that audiences would see that the Republican renegades were addressing a near empty chamber. But O'Neill's persistent and increasingly personal attacks against his youthful tormentor helped cement Gingrich's standing among his fellow conservatives as their leader.

Through the Conservative Opportunity Society he founded in 1983; the National Republican Congressional Campaign Committee, which he continually advised; and GOPAC, a group dedicated to getting Republicans elected, and which he chaired after 1986, Gingrich played a central role in recruiting candidates, devising campaign strategy, and fund-raising. Gingrich's motivational tapes, candidate training schools, and manuals remained staples of Republican party-building efforts for more than a decade.

At the same time, his continued focus on Democratic misdeeds began to yield dividends. Together with 77 other members, Gingrich filed ethics complaints against Jim Wright, O'Neill's successor as House Speaker. In 1989, the investigation the Republicans helped launch resulted in Wright's resignation. With the backing of the "newer breed" of Republicans he had helped elect to Congress, Gingrich prevailed in a closely contested race for Republican Minority Whip in 1989. Once in that post, he showed himself as willing to criticize Republican leaders as readily as he had Democrats.

Gingrich torpedoed the first budget agreement Pres. George H. W. Bush, a Republican, hammered out with congressional Democrats. Next, he put House Republican Leader Bob Michel on notice that, unless the long-standing G.O.P. stalwart took a more combative approach to Democrats, Gingrich would challenge Michel for the post of G.O.P. House leader. Michel then announced that he would retire after the 1994 election.

As he emerged as a national conservative spokesman, Gingrich remained true to two of his early signature issues: civil rights and environmentalism. He supported designating Martin Luther King Jr.'s birthday a national holiday, sanctions against the apartheid South African government, and the 1980 Alaska Lands Act (the largest wilderness protection measure up to that time).

Speaker Gingrich

With the Clinton administration floundering after its failed effort to steer its health care initiative through a Democratic Congress, and with the Democratic House majority beset with mounting scandals, Gingrich set out to "nationalize" the 1994 congressional election. Weeks before the election, he invited all the G.O.P. congressional candidates to sign a "Contract with America" on the Capitol steps. The document consisted of ten procedural changes the party promised to bring to a vote if it obtained majority status. "If we break this contract, throw us out," they proclaimed in an advertisement in *TV Guide*. (Garrett 2005, 306) With a pickup of 54 seats, the Republicans won control of the House, 230 to 204. (They also exercised control of the Senate, 52 to 48.)

Attention soon focused on the new Speaker of the House, whose name his followers attached to a movement they likened to a "revolution." Before he had even assumed his new office, Gingrich's critics had gone on the offensive. Weeks before the long-awaited G.O.P. takeover of Congress, *Newsweek* ran a cover story entitled "How the Gingrich Stole Christmas!"

However, Gingrich hampered his own public relations when he accepted a $4.5 million advance on a book that a media conglomerate that had business before the House agreed to publish. (He brought the controversy to an end by agreeing to accept a $1.00 advance and subsequent royalties instead.) Political adversaries, angered at Gingrich's past criticisms of Wright and other Democrats for ethics violations, filed a series of complaints against Gingrich throughout his tenure as Speaker. In his third year in the post, Gingrich agreed to pay a $300,000 penalty after he admitted that he had provided the House Ethics

Speaker of the House Newt Gingrich, surrounded by about 160 House Republicans with Republican National Chairman Haley Barbour, holds up a copy of the "Contract with America" on April 7, 1995. He and his colleagues were marking the first 100 days of the first Republican Congress elected in 40 years and the passage of several procedural changes they had promised to implement during the 1994 congressional elections. In an effort to "nationalize" those elections, Republicans advanced the "Contract" as a means of distinguishing them from the Democratic majority they sought to replace. Supporters and critics of their agenda referred to the transfer of power on Capitol Hill as the "Gingrich Revolution." (Richard Ellis/AFP/Getty Images)

Committee with inaccurate information about his fund-raising for partisan and nonpartisan activities.

Gingrich, in his early days as Speaker, received considerable praise for the speed with which he redeemed promises he had made in the previous campaign. Consistent with his vow, he brought each of the items in the Contract with America to a vote within the first hundred days of the new Congress. Most made it through the House.

Gingrich versus Clinton

Egged on by conservative activists, both inside and outside of Congress, Gingrich chose to confront rather than cooperate with the Democratic president. That strategy, at first, appeared a promising means of attaining results. In his first press conference after his party had lost control of both houses of Congress, Clinton, beset with hostile questions, protested that he was still "relevant."

As they forged ahead, Gingrich and his cohorts ignored warnings that, given the narrow size of the Republican House and Senate majorities, Clinton retained both a presidential veto and the capacity to make it stick. They also underestimated the skill with which the administration's economic team might, over the short term, finance the national debt in the absence of congressional authorization, thereby reducing pressures on the Democratic president to yield to Republican demands.

With the Republicans pressing for a balanced budget within seven years, tax cuts, and spending reductions, and with Clinton resisting cutbacks on projected spending increases for Medicare, Medicaid, the environment, and education, the two branches reached a standoff. After Clinton vetoed appropriations bills that Congress had passed and Congress refused to pass a continuing resolution to keep the government functioning, the government twice suspended all nonessential services (from November 14 to 19, 1995, and again from December 16, 1995, to January 6, 1996).

In the controversy over the budget, Gingrich undermined his bargaining position early on when he complained that Clinton had snubbed him and Senate majority leader Bob Dole on their return trip from the funeral of the assassinated Israeli prime minister Yitzhak Rabin. His adversaries charged that the Speaker had shut down the government in retribution. The *New York Daily News* ran on its cover a cartoon of the speaker, depicted as an infant throwing a tantrum under the headline, "Cry Baby."

Clinton, with reelection foremost on his mind, resolved that the way to forestall a challenge to his renomination was by shoring up his liberal base. That precluded his accepting spending reductions on favored Democratic programs the Republicans had been pressing for. His short-term objective attained, Clinton, having won the public relations battle against Congress, saw it in his best interests to compile a record on which he might make his case to the public for a second term. That entailed making good on promises he had made to balance the budget and reform welfare, two issues the Republicans had been pushing.

At the outset of 1996, Gingrich and his lieutenants achieved their stated goal of reversing the direction of national policy. Clinton signaled that change was at hand when, in his State of the Union address that year, he declared that the "the era of big

government" was "over." Together, Clinton and Gingrich balanced future budgets, turned deficits into surpluses, reformed welfare (along lines the G.O.P. had proposed), and cut taxes on capital gains.

Gingrich Departs the House

After the voters returned both the Democratic president and the Republican Congress to office, Gingrich became the second Republican Speaker reelected by his peers in 60 years. Within the Republican caucus, however, signs of dissatisfaction with Gingrich's leadership became increasingly visible. Nine Republicans, concerned over ethical controversies involving the Speaker, declined to vote for Gingrich's continuation in the parliamentary post. In the summer of 1997, Gingrich's peers within the House leadership, resentful of his attempts to centralize power within the House and angry over the slow pace at which the conservative agenda was being implemented, attempted, but failed, to oust him.

Ultimately, Gingrich's misjudgment of the national mood concerning Clinton's possible impeachment hastened his departure from both the Speakership and the House. After Independent Counsel Kenneth Starr presented Congress and the public with a report documenting that Clinton had twice committed perjury before a grand jury over alleged sexual misconduct with a White House intern, Gingrich allowed the House to vote out articles of impeachment before Congress adjourned for the 1998 congressional elections.

He predicted that, partly as a result of public disapproval of Clinton's alleged behavior with a White House intern, the Republicans would add at least 20 seats to their House majority. After the Republicans lost five seats, Gingrich, alert to continued disaffection with his leadership and renewed plans to replace him as Speaker, announced his resignation from Congress. He remains active in public affairs as a senior fellow at the American Enterprise Foundation, head of the Center for Health Transformation, chair of American Solutions for Winning the Future, and commentator for Fox News, and he is considered a leading contender for the 2012 Republican presidential nomination.

Bibliography and Further Reading

Drew, Elizabeth. *Showdown: The Struggle between the Gingrich Congress and the Clinton White House*. New York: Simon & Schuster, 1996.

Garrett, Major. *The Enduring Revolution: How the Contract with America Continues to Shape the Nation*. New York: Crown Forum, 2005.

———. *The Enduring Revolution: The Inside Story of the Republican Ascendancy and Why It Will Continue*. New York: Three Rivers Press, 2006.

Gillon, Steven M. *The Pact: Bill Clinton, Newt Gingrich, and the Rivalry that Defined a Generation*. New York: Oxford University Press, 2008.

Maraniss, David, and Weisskopf, Michael. *Tell Newt to Shut Up!: Prizewinning Washington Post Journalists Reveal How Reality Gagged the Gingrich Revolution*. New York: Simon & Schuster, 1996.

Steely, Mel. *The Gentleman from Georgia: The Biography of Newt Gingrich*. Macon, GA: Mercer University Press, 2000.

Williams, Dick. *Newt: Leader of the Second American Revolution*. Marietta, GA: Longstreet Press, 1995.

Alvin S. Felzenberg

GLOBALIZATION

Globalization is generally understood as the increasing interdependence of different parts of the world, particularly through the cross-border movement of goods, services, and capital, as well as the proliferation of multiple sources of authority alongside the state, including international organizations and nongovernmental organizations, that govern this interdependence. Although revolutionary advances in communications and transportation technology have played an important role in connecting distant parts of the world, U.S. leadership at the end of World War II in setting up an interdependent world—guided by open, liberal economic relations and mediated through multilateral institutions—has also been crucial in propelling globalization. In the 1980s, economic globalization accelerated thanks to the Reagan administration and its counterpart in the United Kingdom, led by Prime Minister Margaret Thatcher, championing economic liberalism (often referred to as "neoliberalism") with an emphasis on deregulation, privatization, and free markets. The collapse of communism in Eastern Europe at the end of the 1980s gave further impetus to globalization, as liberal democracy appeared to emerge triumphant. Despite the key U.S. role in facilitating both political and economic globalization, public support for globalization began to erode at the end of the twentieth century, and the official consensus of support began to be more tentative as well.

The key to the revival of a globalized world at the end of World War II was the Bretton Woods Conference of 1944. At the conference, under U.S. leadership and with key support from the United Kingdom, the World Bank (originally the International Bank for Reconstruction and Development) and the International Monetary Fund (IMF) were created. The International Trade Organization (ITO) was also envisioned at the conference, but instead of that institution, a less robust institution called the General Agreement on Tariffs and Trade (GATT) was created in 1947 to reduce barriers to international trade. GATT became the World Trade Organization (WTO) in 1995. These multilateral institutions were created not only to help reconstruct the war-wrecked countries but also to ensure that exchange rates were stable and international trade was resuscitated. The underlying normative impetus in the creation of an interdependent world was to ensure that the "beggar-thy-neighbor" policies and competitive economic blocs of the 1930s would not be repeated again.

Until about the early 1970s, the United States had affected the development of these institutions, and the regimes they embody, more than the institutions affected U.S. political development. For instance, the Bretton Woods Conference created a system of fixed but adjustable exchange rates, where currencies had fixed exchange rates to the U.S. dollar, and the dollar was fixed to gold. When Pres. Richard Nixon ended the free gold convertibility of the dollar in 1971, he also effectively ended this system of fixed exchange rates. Many commentators also point to the predominant position of the United States at key multilateral institutions in emphasizing how the political-economic architecture of globalization is affected more by the United States than vice versa. The United States holds the greatest voting power at both the IMF and the World Bank, and its market size confers on it considerable informal power in the WTO, where each member is formally entitled to one vote. In fact, the economic liberalization of the 1980s is seen partially as a result of U.S. influence over the IMF and the World Bank through the Washington Consensus, a term that refers to the application of a set of neoliberal principles, primarily through IMF conditionality and World Bank structural adjustment loans, in the developing world. This "consensus" denotes the convergence between the two multilateral institutions and the U.S. Treasury on these policy prescriptions for economic development. In short, viewed from outside the United States, globalization has, at the very least, served U.S. interests handsomely. Some commentators go further, contending that globalization can be understood as "Americanization."

Skepticism about Globalization in the United States

Although the United States played a crucial role in facilitating an interdependent world, public skepticism in the United States concerning this enhanced interdependence has been becoming widespread. For instance, the Pew Research Center found that 78 percent of the Americans it surveyed in 2002 thought global trade was "good" for their country, but this level of support dropped to 59 percent in 2007. In understanding the growing unpopularity of globalization within the United States, it is crucial to refer back to the spirit in which the multilateral order was created at the end of World War II. As the political scientist John G. Ruggie explains, the multilateralism of the post–World War II order was contingent upon domestic interventionism. Industrial nations agreed to an open multilateral world so long as they could intervene domestically to provide for their citizens' social and economic security. Ruggie calls this the "embedded liberalism compromise." The compromise can be understood not just as a bargain struck between the industrial countries at Bretton Woods, but also as an implicit or explicit deal struck between governments, including the United States, and their citizens. Leaving aside the question of the extent to

which the embedded liberalism compromise continues to be relevant, the concept captures nicely the notion that citizens expect their governments to shield them from destabilizing influences of globalization. As the perception that globalization disadvantages certain groups within the United States grows, so will the discontent against globalization, if the government cannot keep its side of the bargain in the embedded liberalism compromise.

Public Skepticism: The Case of International Trade

The case of international trade, which is one of the most prominent issues under the rubric of globalization, provides a good example to illustrate this growing discontent. Although some benefits of increased international trade are easily observable to consumers in the form of greater product variety and reduced prices, the view that globalization has been bad for the U.S. labor force has gained increasing acceptance in light of recent statistics. For instance, studies demonstrate average real-wage growth in the United States has been static, if not in decline, since the 1970s, while the premium earned by high-skilled workers, relative to less-skilled workers, has risen during the same period. Yet studies show that this phenomenon can only be partially attributed to globalization. Some commentators point out that trade with low-wage countries has put pressure on the wages of low-skilled workers in the United States and has also contributed to job insecurity. Still, the relatively more important factor in bringing about the mentioned inequality has been technological change favoring skilled workers. Transformations in labor market institutions, particularly the weakening of trade unions, as well as changes in the organizations of firms have also contributed to this wage inequality. Furthermore, offshore outsourcing, or the "purchas[ing] of services abroad," has been blamed for job losses. (Bhagwati et al. 93) While some scholars argue that offshoring has made a minor impact, others worry that it will likely become more disruptive for the United States. Overall, regardless of nuances in the debate, the public perception that globalization plays the leading role in generating the discussed economic ills has been increasing. Still, international trade continues to constitute a relatively small, albeit increasing, portion of the U.S. gross domestic product (GDP), and the U.S. market has always been relatively self-sufficient. While imports constituted roughly 4 percent of GDP in 1960, 5 percent in 1970, and 11 percent in both 1980 and 1990, they constituted 16 percent in 2005, according to the World Development Indicators. (Exports for these years constituted roughly 5 percent of GDP in 1960, 6 percent in 1970, 10 percent in 1980 and 1990, and 11 percent in 2005.)

Elite Skepticism: The Case of International Trade

Growing skepticism against globalization among U.S. political leaders parallels the public's discontent. The issue of international trade can be used to illuminate this point as well. As international trade scholar Judith Goldstein points out, given that the electoral units are relatively small, it is generally difficult for members of Congress, especially members of the House of Representatives, to ignore import-competing interests within their constituencies that press for protectionist policies. There may also be a larger problem. Starting in the 1970s, the number of groups demanding protection from trade increased to include industries that commonly do well internationally. Groups demanding protection have both diversified and increased in number. At the same time, the notion that countries in competition with the United States, such as Japan and China, have promoted their industries by putting the United States at an unfair disadvantage has gained traction. In turn, the notion that the U.S. government can intervene to protect industries, and that the United States should actively seek "fair" trade for U.S. importers and exporters has gained ground.

In general, the stronger the perception that other strong economies are not just partners but also rivals to the United States, as discussions regarding China in the 2000s and Japan in the 1980s demonstrate, the stronger the temptation to institute governmental protection against foreign trade. As international trade analyst Ian Destler demonstrates, over the last few decades, the shifting electoral bases of the Democratic and Republican parties have established

Democrats, despite intraparty differences, as the relatively more protectionist party, with labor as one of their core constituencies. At the same time, major labor unions have shifted their stance from selective protectionism to a more general protectionist attitude. Although the executive branch is generally considered to be relatively pro-liberalization, and hence pro-globalization, it is delimited by congressional oversight and delegation of authority. For instance, congressional delegation of "fast-track authority" to the executive branch for the negotiation of international trade agreements, with only an up or down vote in Congress, has not always been forthcoming. Overall, while it is premature to contend that the United States is moving in an anti-liberal—and hence anti-globalization—direction, pressures for policies not conducive to globalization have increased.

Multilateralism versus Unilateralism in U.S. Foreign Policy

Finally, the United States' engagement with other actors in a globalized world has been affected by political tensions within the country regarding what best serves the U.S. national interest: continued engagement with others through multilateral organizations, or unilateral stances on what political leaders consider to serve the country's interests. For instance, the United States has not ratified the Kyoto Protocol on global climate change, it is not a party to the International Criminal Court, and it launched the war against Iraq in 2003 without the full support of the international community. Although the motivations in refraining from such multilateral engagements remain diverse, U.S. recalcitrance for multilateral global efforts stems from fears that U.S. sovereignty will be undermined and national interests will suffer.

While some commentators, such as Charles Krauthammer, have regarded the struggle to have the multilateral stamp of approval as a pretense that the country can afford to forgo, others have emphasized that "global interests can be incorporated into a broad and farsighted concept of the national interest." (Nye 138) Still others suggest that the globalized world has compelled the pursuit of novel mechanisms for the pursuit of national interests, as well as for the definition

RELATED ENTRIES

THIS VOLUME
Environmental Policy; Free Trade Agreements, Rise of; Trade Policy

of "national interests." For instance, transgovernmental networks, formed between officials with similar responsibilities and expertise from different national governments, have become an increasingly important tool for pursuing national interests, and at times for clarifying what those interests are.

The United States has played the crucial leadership role in reviving a globalized world economy, and in creating the multilateral institutions to govern that economy. Further, it has generally remained committed to this interdependent world. Today, however, growing public and elite discontent with globalization have strained the U.S. commitment to globalization.

Bibliography and Further Reading

Acemoglu, Daron. "Technical Change, Inequality, and the Labor Market." *Journal of Economic Literature* 40, no. 1 (March 2002): 7–72.

Bhagwati, Jagdish. "America's Bipartisan Battle against Free Trade." *Financial Times*, April 8, 2007.

Bhagwati, Jagdish, Arvind Panagariya, and T. N. Srinivasan. "The Muddles over Outsourcing." *Journal of Economic Perspectives* 18, no. 4 (2004): 93–114.

Blinder, Alan. "Offshoring: Big Deal, or Business as Usual?" CEPS Working Paper No.149. Princeton, NJ: Center for Economic Policy Studies, June 2007. http://www.princeton.edu/~blinder/papers/07juneCEPSwp149.pdf.

Destler, Ian M. *American Trade Politics*, 3rd edition. Washington, D.C.: Institute for International Economics, 1995.

Goldstein, Judith. "International Forces and Domestic Politics: Trade Policy and Institution Building in the United States." In *Shaped by War and Trade: International Influences on American Political Development*, edited by Ira Katznelson and Martin Shefter, 211–236. Princeton, NJ: Princeton University Press, 2002.

Krauthammer, Charles. "The Unipolar Moment." *Foreign Affairs*, Winter 1990/1991.

Nye, Joseph S., Jr. *The Paradox of American Power: Why the World's Only Superpower Can't Go It Alone*. Oxford: Oxford University Press, 2002.

Pew Global Attitudes Project. *47-Nation Pew Global Attitudes Survey*. Washington, D.C.: Pew Research Center, 2007. http://pewglobal.org.

Ruggie, John G. "International Regimes, Transactions, and Change: Embedded Liberalism in the Postwar Economic Order." *International Organization* 36, no. 2 (1982): 379–415.

Scheve, Kenneth, and Matthew J. Slaughter. *Globalization and the Perceptions of American Workers*. Washington, D.C.: Institute for International Economics, 2001.

Slaughter, Anne-Marie. *A New World Order*. Princeton, NJ: Princeton University Press, 2005.

Stiglitz, Joseph. *Globalization and Its Discontents*. New York: W. W. Norton, 2002.

———. *Making Globalization Work*. New York: W. W. Norton, 2006.

Ayse Kaya Orloff

HEALTH CARE

Conflict and change have characterized the political context of medical care in the United States from the 1970s to the first decade of the twenty-first century. In addition, the perception grew during this period that the vast cost of health care did not measure up to the value provided.

The title of Sen. Edward Kennedy's (D–MA) 1972 book, *In Critical Condition: The Crisis in America's Health Care*, clearly expressed the sense of crisis pervading the public health-care discourse in the early 1970s. The hallmarks of this crisis—ongoing inflationary pressure in health care costs, fragmentation in the organization of heath care, and the uninsured or underinsured status of millions of Americans—forced politicians of all political persuasions to propose competing remedies. In 1974, for instance, the now-forgotten Kennedy-Mills proposal received extended consideration in the finance committees of Congress, as did the Nixon CHIP plan and the catastrophic health insurance bill of Sen. Russell Long (D–LA) and Sen. Abraham Ribicoff (D-CT).

In the 1980s, the picture was very different: very few figures of political significance confidently promoted government-financed universal health insurance for the nation or for a particular state. The deficits of the Reagan and Bush years continued to dominate political discourse and set severe limits on what seemed sensible and realistic to discuss. Intellectually, the 1980s inherited the debris of the reform mentality of the 1970s—a mentality that turned first to bureaucratic realignments as a means to rationalize the provision of medical care and financing through policies like diagnostic-related group payments to hospitals. After those approaches yielded little, the ideology of markets, which urged competition and privatization as a way to handle spiraling inflation, ascended. Indeed, inflation was a major factor in the health care crisis. Health care expenditures in the United States totaled about 7 percent of national income in 1970, about 9 percent by 1980, more than 11 percent by 1990, and nearly 16 percent in 2008.

The 1980s, in short, subordinated the possibility of national health insurance to a wide variety of other initiatives. At the state level, earnest, but unsuccessful, efforts were made to promote insurance expansion. Many business firms made noteworthy attempts to expand the scope of employment-related health insurance. A number of initiatives—some now forgotten—were undertaken, ranging from financing second opinions to wellness programs, from embracing pre-paid group practice plans as an option for employees to exercise facilities at the workplace. But fundamental reform of the rules of the American way of offering and providing medical care was expunged from the political agenda. What major changes were attempted came primarily from private initiatives. These included the expansion of health maintenance organizations (HMOs), a misleadingly named, largely Republican-backed variant of what had been the ideal of the pre-paid group practice model championed by American liberals. Private employers assumed an increasingly aggressive stance toward medical providers; one after another experiment was tried in attempts to address the persistent complaints about the costliness, fragmentation, and sheer complexity of American medical care.

Regulatory Promises and Failures: The Experience of the 1970s and Beyond

The governmental policies chosen to "rationalize" medical care in the 1970s and after were each alone certain to disappoint. Collectively, however, they were regarded as incremental steps toward more sensible public intervention in the regulation of medical care. The regulations that did emerge were dispersed bureaucratically, disconnected from the major public programs that financed care, and celebrated with visions of eventual success that no reasonable analyst should have accepted. Health planning, for instance, emerged in 1974—205 little agencies all over the country, equipped with the authority to say no to major capital expansion but lacking the financial carrots to induce anyone to move in a different direction. Professional Standards Review Organizations—established by the federal government to monitor quality of care—were relegated in 1972 to a different set of agencies, dominated by physicians and disconnected in practice from the payment systems of Medicare, Medicaid, or private health insurance plans. Medicare and Medicaid, once separate organizationally, were technically joined in an agency known as the Health Care Financing Administration. This new organization, however, failed to unify the administration of Medicare and Medicaid, much less have an impact on health planning. In all of these cases, the political struggles were intense, dominated by groups with financial and professional interests in the policies, and reported in the trade press and professional medical journals, but all fell short of attracting the national attention crucial to debates about national health insurance.

Throughout the 1970s, commentators complained about the uneven distribution of care and the relatively high rates of inflation in medicine, but little fundamental change was achieved. The Nixon administration tried wage-and-price controls and gave them up. The Carter administration supported legislation to contain hospital costs but was defeated in both 1978 and 1979 by a combination of hospital opposition and more general skepticism about whether the federal government could accomplish what it promised. Inflation continued unabated amid naïve rhetoric about a "voluntary effort" to control costs by the health industry.

Competition as an Answer

Attracted by the volume of funds flowing through a system of retrospective, cost-based reimbursement, many in the private sector came to see opportunity where the politicians had found causes for complaint. In the hospital world, small chains of for-profit hospitals—the Humana and Hospital Corporations of America, concentrated in the South, are the most prominent examples—grew into large companies throughout the disappointing regulatory decade of the 1970s. The growth of HMOs—at first slower than promised by the enthusiasts of the 1973 legislation—came to include for-profit firms as well and, in that legal form, grew substantially in the 1980s and 1990s. Major players in the health care industry, such as Baxter Travenol and American Hospital Supply, increased their competitive edge through vertical and horizontal integration. On the other hand, doctors lost some of their competitive power as a glut of physicians saturated the market.

A growing antiregulatory and anti-Washington rhetoric characterized the political context of these changes in U.S. health care. Policy analysis—influenced mostly by economists—played up the economic cost of decisions made by regulatory agencies, thereby questioning the quality of new policies. Both Democrats and Republicans listened to these criticisms and were influenced by them. What's more, these antiregulatory attitudes and directives reached across the entire U.S. economy. The deregulation of the Civil Aeronautics Board and the airlines industry became a symbol of the negative effects of government regulation. Additionally, medicine, conventionally considered more than simply an economic pursuit, became demythologized, as the convention of considering any set of related economic activities as an "industry" began to take hold. This environment—even before President Reagan took office—made increased government regulation of health care politically and ideologically distasteful.

There is great irony, therefore, in the fact that the most significant health initiative during the Reagan years—Medicare's prospective payment system by diagnosis-related groups—was highly regulatory: it was in effect a sophisticated system of administered pricing. What was more, the federal deficit made unthinkable a direct attack on the problem of the 30 to 40 million Americans lacking anything resembling decent health insurance. After over twenty years of grappling with the crisis in the U.S. health care system, little had been done to address it. The problems of access worsened throughout the 1980s and 1990s, as the number of uninsured and underinsured grew. The relative rate of medical inflation continued its relentless rise—except for a brief period in the mid-1990s—and showed no signs of slowing; truly extraordinary changes in the rules of professional medicine took place as American capitalism flexed its muscle. Medicine and medical practice, which once had been considered a higher calling, had become an "industry," accounting, by 1990, for over one-tenth of the economy.

Competition versus Regulation: The Nature of the Continuing Political Debate

At one extreme in the debate over increasing health expenditures is the idea of complete government control over and administration of medical care. According to the beliefs of some Americans, including policy makers and medical professionals, as well as ordinary citizens, successfully dealing with U.S. health care issues can only be accomplished through national programs such as those in Canada or Great Britain. However, many observers—citing rationing of care and long waits for all but the most essential treatments—view the British National Health Service with a good deal of distrust. The British system is also colored by the taint of "socialized" medicine, which invokes loss of choice and freedom on the part of both the practitioner and the patient. The Canadian system, however, holds more sway in some policy circles and versions of national health insurance based on the Canadian plan do have some support.

At the other extreme in American health policy debates from the early 1980s to the present are a set of ideas known as the "competitive health strategy." Although not monolithic in their ideas, advocates of this approach generally believe that the most critical element in a program to contain health care inflation is to restructure financial incentives. The central mechanism for remaking the incentive system, these advocates argue, is the introduction of greater price competition in the delivery of health care; widespread health insurance, therefore, would create a broad-based market that would encourage greater competition in insurance premiums. They also claim that substantially increased patient cost sharing would help. The striking feature of this perspective is the gap between the rhetoric of competition and the reality of constraints on room to maneuver. An important impediment to the enactment of pro-competitive legislation is the indirect connection between effective competitive markets and reductions in expenditures for medical care. A competitive strategy, even if implemented, does not produce visible gains in the short run. Even its most optimistic supporters concede that 10 to 15 years would be needed for a competitive market to develop.

The outcome of implementing any comprehensive competitive health care strategy remains cloudy. The reality of health politics in the 1980s and 1990s was one of incremental steps in both regulation and competition, which might be termed *agitated incrementalism*. During this time, there was little coherent public concern expressed about increasing health care costs, even though polls revealed growing anxiety about medical care. People appeared to be worried about the cost of health care to themselves (in increases in premiums or cost sharing), to employers (in rising insurance premiums), and to governments (in escalating program budgets—for Medicare at the federal level and Medicaid at both the state and federal level). The concern about relative inflation—the fact that aggregate spending on health care is higher than the value of benefits received—was relegated to the world of academia.

The United States may well be a country in which we receive insufficient "value for money," as Brian Abel-Smith noted some years back. Nevertheless, this lack of relative value is not at the top of the public's list of concerns: rather, concerns focus more on access, financial protection, and quality.

As a result, cost containment, when seriously attempted, comes from actions to control the rising costs of medical care to particular payers, most visibly the federal government and, hardly less so, specific states and corporations. However, this approach, as executed, has been flawed: policies that save government or corporate money do not necessarily translate into anti-inflationary measures. Indeed, actions at the federal level have simply shifted expense to other payers and have little—and in some cases, no—effect on spending aggregates.

This portrait is as accurate a description of decades of cost control politics as is available. The delivery of American medical care, as health policy scholar Kenneth R. Wing has said, "can be simultaneously described as a system on the brink of crisis and as a strong and growing industry, with seeming equal accuracy." (Quoted in Marmor 1994, 26) In attempting to explain this state of affairs, what must first be emphasized is the enormous influence of providers in the imbalanced political marketplace of many of the health policy struggles. Contributing to and worsening that imbalance is the lack of sustained public opinion marshaled around any one of the various suggestions to address the problems of cost, access, and quality of American medicine. Much of the explanation for the health care circumstances in the United States can be found in the pluralism of American politics and the dispersion of power in both the political and economic marketplaces. Our federalism has spread the authority for regulating medical care between the national government and the 50 states, while our financing splits private and public payers—with considerable discrepancies among these in each sector.

Two factors that account for inflationary pressures in U.S. medicine have become critical in this debate. One, medical care is regarded as a good, insured through work and a part of the private–public welfare state we have created in the United States. Two, the fragmentation of finance has resulted in payers separately addressing their own costs, rather than concentrating on the costs of American medicine in the aggregate. Pluralistic finance—coupled with broad-based third-party coverage—creates an inflation-friendly environment. Only countries whose systems concentrate the stakes of medical players—Great Britain, Canada, and Germany, for instance—have greater capacity to control health care inflation. Such countervailing power is only one necessary condition for restraint; political will is also essential. In some cases, as in Sweden, the stakeholders with concentrated authority have chosen to spend more on medical care. But they have made such choices through balancing the gains and losses of expenditures. In the United States, we have discovered our inflating health outlays, not chosen them.

2008: Moving beyond the Clinton Failure of 1993–1994

Striking surges of enthusiasm have nonetheless been evident. Over the course of the presidential election campaign of 2008, the candidates felt compelled to offer plans for universal health insurance. Such pressure was also present in the buildup to the election of 1992; what followed was the birth and death of the Clinton reform plan. Now, as then, huge majorities of Americans claim they want reform—universal insurance coverage—and disagree about what that would be. Then, as now, interest groups mobilize for battle, trading sound bites and horror stories, attacking and defending particular reforms. And, just as important, other fronts exist in the politics of health care: the moral disputes over abortion, euthanasia, and stem cell research; the distributive, intense local politics of hospital closures and clinic openings; the Washington and state capital fights in hearing rooms over the rules governing the practices of nurses, chiropractors, and physicians; the armies of lobbyists struggling to start or stop health insurance reforms in the states. In short, over the course of the past generation, health care politics became deeply woven into all the interstices and institutions of American politics.

Bibliography and Further Reading

Abel-Smith, Brian. *Value for Money in Health Services.* London: Heinemann Education Books, 1976.

Brown, Lawrence D. *Politics and Health Care Organizations: HMOs as Federal Policy.* Washington, D.C.: Brookings Institution Press, 1984.

Kennedy, Edward M. *In Critical Condition: The Crisis in America's Health Care.* New York: Simon & Schuster, 1972.

Marmor, Theodore R. *Political Analysis and American Medical Care: Essays.* New York: Cambridge University Press, 1983.

———. *The Politics of Medicare.* New Brunswick, NJ: Transaction Books, 2000.

———. *Understanding Health Care Reform.* New Haven, CT: Yale University Press, 1994.

———. "Universal Health Insurance 2007—Can We Learn from the Past?" *Dissent.* http://www.dissentmagazine.org/article/?article=863 (accessed November 23, 2009).

Marmor, Theodore R., and Jon B. Christianson. *Health Care Policy: A Political Economy Approach.* Los Angeles: Sage Publications, 1982.

Rushefsky, Mark E., and Kant Patel. *Politics, Power, and Policy Making: The Case of Health Care Reform in the 1990s.* Armonk, NY: M. E. Sharpe, 1998.

Starr, Paul. *The Social Transformation of American Medicine.* New York: Basic Books, 1984.

Theodore R. Marmor

HISPANIC AMERICANS

From the baseball stars David Ortiz and Albert Pujols to the performers Jennifer Lopez and Andy Garcia, the 2008 presidential candidate and New Mexico governor Bill Richardson, and the U.S. Supreme Court justice Sonia Sotomayor, Hispanics were at the center of American culture and politics in the opening years of the twenty-first century. By 2009, Latinos had become the nation's largest ethnic minority and accounted for more than half of U.S. population growth. (In this article, the terms *Latino* and *Hispanic* are used interchangeably.) As a result, they captured the attention of advertisers, media companies, and political strategists, and they were at the center of debates over national identity and security in post-9/11 America. Seen by many as the latest chapter of a proud immigrant history, Hispanics have been regarded by others, notably the distinguished political scientist Samuel Huntington, as a grave challenge to American culture and sovereignty.

Yet Latinos were barely visible only a few decades ago. In 1970, they accounted for less than 5 percent of the U.S. population, compared to 15 percent in 2009. Not until the 1976 presidential election were national exit poll data available on how they voted. At that time, Hispanics had barely come together under a single banner. In fact, the group now known as "Hispanics" was far less visible to other Americans than its constituent national-origin subgroups. People would think of Puerto Ricans and associate them with the New York gang portrayed in the musical *West Side Story.* Cubans would bring to mind exiles from Fidel Castro's communist revolution living in Miami, or perhaps Desi Arnaz, the husband and co-star of Lucille Ball in the 1950s sitcom *I Love Lucy.* Only Mexican Americans would have been identified with a political leader: César Chávez, whose United Farmworkers Union attained national visibility in 1968, when Chávez ended a 25-day fast with an outdoor mass attended by four thousand farm workers and Sen. Robert Kennedy.

E Pluribus Latino

How did these disparate groups come to be identified as "Latinos"? The reasons include sheer growth in numbers; intermarriage among the different subgroups; dispersion across the United States, particularly of Mexican immigrants to places like North Carolina and Georgia in the 1990s; and the growth of Spanish-language media, especially radio and television.

Another reason is prejudice and simple lack of discernment on the part of Americans who over time and with the growth in the number of new arrivals unthinkingly came to relegate all Spanish-speaking individuals (as well as many who may not speak Spanish) into a single group. As had happened before in American history, those who were categorized in this way responded by making that category their own.

More benign were appeals from leaders of the major political parties that had the effect of fostering a self-conscious Hispanic identity. In 1968, Congress authorized National Hispanic Heritage Week, which was extended to National Hispanic Heritage Month during the administration of Ronald Reagan. In 1969, Congress created the Cabinet Committee on Opportunities for Spanish-Speaking People, which the Nixon administration used to reach out to Mexican- and Cuban-origin voters. Nixon appointed more Hispanics to federal positions than any previous president, and it was he who ordered the U.S. Census Bureau to insert a separate Hispanic-origin question on its 1970 questionnaire. In 1975, the Voting Rights Act was amended to apply not only to blacks but also to Hispanics. Then, in 1976 Congress passed legislation requiring federal statistical agencies to produce separate counts of "Americans who identify themselves as being of Spanish-speaking background." Sponsored by the Los Angeles Democrat Edward Roybal, the first Hispanic from California to sit in Congress in the twentieth century (from 1963 to 1993), this is the only law in U.S. history to mandate the collection of data for a specific ethnic group.

Despite such policies, Hispanics today do not invariably identify as such. In a 2002 poll sponsored by the Pew Hispanic Center, 54 percent of Hispanics identified primarily with their family's country of origin (as Cubans, Mexicans, etc.); 21 percent identified themselves as "American"; and only 24 percent self-identified as "Hispanic" or "Latino." Eighty-five percent said that Hispanics from different countries "have separate and distinct cultures," and only 43 percent believed Hispanics were "working together to achieve common political goals."

Each national-origin subgroup has its own distinct history and socioeconomic profile. Puerto Ricans are born U.S. citizens, and they are therefore the only Hispanics who arrive here with that status. Not surprisingly, they are also the most likely to identify as "Americans." Comprising about 9 percent of all Hispanics, Puerto Ricans are the second-largest subgroup, with slightly more residents on the main-

land than the island (4.1 versus 3.9 million). Among the former, most live in the Northeast, but Puerto Ricans are increasingly concentrated in Florida. (The demographic data in this section are from the 2007 American Community Survey, as tabulated by the Pew Hispanic Center.)

Puerto Ricans are also the least Spanish-monolingual, and the most bilingual, of all these subgroups, which may explain why they have a high rate of high-school completion compared to other Hispanics. Yet Puerto Ricans also have one of the lowest marriage rates of all Hispanics and the highest percentage of births to unmarried mothers. Their poverty rate is also among the highest.

Because of the Cold War and the Communist regime of Fidel Castro, U.S. policy has long regarded Cubans more like refugees than immigrants. Since 1966, under the Cuban Adjustment Act, Cubans fleeing Castro have been afforded special status. Even under the stricter "wet-foot, dry-foot" policy inaugurated by the Clinton administration in the mid-1990s, Cubans who reach U.S. soil are put on an expedited path to permanent legal residency and eventual citizenship. This would explain why Cubans report to Pew pollsters that they "trust the government in Washington to do what is right" more than any other subgroup. After Puerto Ricans, Cubans have the highest citizenship rate, about 74 percent. Representing less than 4 percent of all Hispanics, they are nonetheless the third-largest subgroup. About two-thirds live in Florida, with smaller concentrations in New York and New Jersey.

Cubans are diverse, reflecting differences across successive waves of migrants. They are also older on average than other Latinos, as well as more educated and affluent. Cubans have by far the highest home-ownership rate among Hispanics, and they have the lowest rates of poverty and of births to unmarried mothers of all the subgroups.

The fourth- and fifth-largest subgroups are Salvadorans and Dominicans, the former accounting for a bit more than 3 percent of Hispanics, and the latter for somewhat less than 3 percent. Salvadorans are the largest contingent of Central Americans, who began arriving in the United States during the 1980s in flight from the region's civil wars and natural disasters.

Unlike Cubans, Salvadorans have arrived not as refugees but mostly as illegal immigrants. Many remain illegal, but many others have been granted Temporary Protective Status and eventually permanent residency and citizenship, for example under the 1997 Nicaraguan Adjustment and Central American Relief Act. With large concentrations in California and Texas, Salvadorans have a rate of births to unmarried mothers of around 37 percent, just about the average among Latinos generally. They have the highest annual household income, but also the lowest high-school completion rate, of all the subgroups. The latter statistic may well be due to the dislocations Salvadorans have endured, which also likely explain why the notorious MS-13 gangs have taken root in Salvadoran communities, both in the United States and in El Salvador.

Dominicans are highly concentrated geographically, with more than 80 percent in the Northeast and over 50 percent in metropolitan New York. Approximately three-fifths are foreign-born, which is a much higher percentage than Mexicans (about 40 percent) but lower than Salvadorans (about 66 percent). In any event, Dominicans in the United States maintain relatively close ties to their homeland, which has been reflected in their attentiveness to elections back home. Their poverty rate is the highest of all the subgroups, and their rate of births to unmarried mothers, at 50 percent, is second only to Puerto Ricans.

Finally, Mexicans are by far the largest subgroup, comprising about two-thirds of all Hispanics. Mexicans are also the most typical "immigrants," having come to the United States primarily for economic reasons. Yet because Mexicans as a group have been here so long, they actually have fewer foreign-born in their ranks than any other subgroup (except for Puerto Ricans). Mexicans have one of the lowest high-school completion rates (ahead of Salvadorans) among these subgroups, but they are otherwise typical of Hispanics, who struggle with higher poverty and lower income than white non-Hispanics. Finally, more than half of Mexican immigrants in the United States are undocumented.

"Hispanic" is therefore a category that papers over salient differences, not only across these subgroups but also between foreign- and native-born individuals.

This category is also racially ambiguous. As defined by the Census Bureau, "Hispanics can be of any race." And in 2000, 47.8 percent identified as white, 1.8 percent as black, 42.6 percent as "some other race," and 6.4 percent as multiracial (with the remaining few identifying as Asian, Native Hawaiian/Pacific Islander, or American Indian/Alaskan Native).

Such ambiguity is unlikely to be resolved, however, for the simple reason that "Hispanic" is a convenient political category for both outsiders and insiders. For outsiders, especially in the media and national politics, the term facilitates discourse. For members of the group, it can be used to present themselves either as an immigrant ethnic group or an aggrieved racial minority, or both. This encompassing category also increases each subgroup's overall numbers, visibility, and clout.

Hispanic Politics in Texas and California

It does, therefore, make sense to speak of "Hispanic politics." From 1976 to 2009, the dynamic center of Hispanic politics clearly shifted from Texas to California—with striking implications for national politics and policy. For much of the twentieth century, Texas was the incubator for Hispanic politics. Two pioneering organizations were founded in Corpus Christi: the League of United Latin American Citizens (LULAC) in 1929, and the American G.I. Forum in 1948.

In 1968 the Mexican American Legal Defense and Education Fund was established in San Antonio by the Ford Foundation. MALDEF was soon the nation's preeminent lobbyist and litigator for Mexican Americans and, over time, for Latinos generally. Its role in the passage of the 1975 Voting Rights amendments was critical. But its biggest victory came in the case of *Plyler v. Doe*, 457 U.S. 202 (1982), in which the U.S. Supreme Court ruled that public schools were required to educate illegal immigrant children. For another decade or so, MALDEF played a prominent if controversial role in the debate over immigration policy.

In 1974, San Antonio native, William C. (Willie) Velásquez, founded the Southwest Voter Registration Education Project. Like MALDEF, "Southwest Voters" relied on foundation support, but in this case to register Mexican-American voters throughout the

William ("Willie") Velásquez, founder of the Southwest Voter Registration Education Project, registers a Mexican-American voter in 1978. "Southwest Voters," as the organization was known among Hispanic leaders, played a critical role in the increase of Latino voters and officeholders in Texas and the Southwest in the 1970s and 1980s. Velásquez, who died in 1988, was an activist who transformed himself and his organization into a critical source of information on Hispanic voting trends at a time when few others were available. (Steve Northup/Time Life Pictures/Getty Images)

region. Around the same time, Ernesto (Ernie) Cortes founded a different kind of organization in San Antonio. Inspired by the success of community organizer Saul Alinsky and backed by the local Catholic bishop, Communities Organized for Public Service (COPS) took root in predominantly Mexican-American parishes and soon became a force in local and state politics, spawning sister organizations throughout Texas and the Southwest.

From this ferment emerged Henry Cisneros, who was elected mayor of San Antonio in 1981, at the age of 34. The first Hispanic to head a major American city, Cisneros was catapulted to national prominence in 1984 when Walter Mondale inter-

viewed him as a potential running mate on the Democratic presidential ticket. From 1993 to 1997 Cisneros served as secretary of housing and urban development under Pres. Bill Clinton.

Even prominent Hispanic politicians who began to emerge elsewhere came originally from Texas: Mario Obledo, the secretary of health and welfare under California governor Jerry Brown, and subsequently a Presidential Medal of Freedom recipient; and Federico Peña, the two-term mayor of Denver (1983–1991) who later became secretary of transportation and then secretary of energy in the Clinton administration.

Texas retained this edge through the 1980s. California's Latino population was booming, but mostly as a result of illegal immigration from Mexico. But even after many illegals obtained amnesty under the Immigration Reform and Control Act (IRCA) of 1986 and eventually became citizens, Latinos in California struggled to develop political muscle. While California was more open and tolerant than Texas, it lacked the Lone Star State's political traditions and institutions, which were less dominated by media and money and therefore easier for Latinos with strong community bases to crack. Notably, both Willie Velásquez and Ernie Cortes were not very successful when they attempted to replicate their Texas successes in California.

But Latinos in California began to make sustained political gains in the late 1980s, when labor unions there turned seriously to organizing immigrant workers. In 1988, the Service Employees International Union (SEIU) launched its confrontational Justice for Janitors campaign in Los Angeles. In 1990, SEIU called a strike that resulted in a dramatic contract settlement for Mexican and Central American workers. That victory led to other successful efforts among Latino drywallers, hotel workers, and home healthcare providers.

Latino labor leaders soon entered electoral politics. In 1994, the organizer Antonio Villaraigosa was elected to the California State Assembly from Los Angeles. Two years later, the Los Angeles County Federation of Labor helped Democrats regain control of the Assembly, and in 1999 Villaraigosa became Assembly Speaker. In 2005 he was elected mayor of Los Angeles. In the meantime, another Latino labor leader, Fabian Nuñez, moved up the Sacramento ladder and became Assembly Speaker in 2002.

This Latino-labor alliance has been evident elsewhere as well. In New York, Dennis Rivera, a Puerto Rican, forged black, Latino, and other immigrant hospital workers into 1199SEIU, one of the state's most powerful unions. And in Nevada, unions representing Hispanic tourist industry workers had a noticeable impact on the 2008 elections.

Yet California has clearly been in the lead. In February 2009 Hilda Solis, the daughter of immigrant union activists (father from Mexico, mother from Nicaragua), became the Obama administration's sec-

retary of labor. Her rise from a Los Angeles community-college board to Congress reflected labor backing. Eliseo Medina started out as an organizer with the United Farm Workers, and in the 1980s worked in Los Angeles with SEIU; as of 2009 he was the international executive vice president. In the late 1990s, Medina played a key role in persuading the AFL-CIO to change its position on immigration and actively pursue immigrant workers, including illegals, as potential union members.

This shift has been more than geographical. It also represents a change from public interest law firms like MALDEF and the Puerto Rican Defense and Education Fund, on whose board Justice Sonia Sotomayor sat from 1980 to 1992. With few or no actual members, such organizations have relied on financial support from foundations and other non-Latino national elites. Such sponsorship has allowed them to pursue goals such as voting rights and school finance reform that require technical expertise, hefty budgets, and patience. But these same factors suggest why such issues do not easily resonate with economically pressed, politically unsophisticated newcomers. In contrast, the Latino-labor alliance harks back to membership organizations such as COPS, rooted in local communities. Focusing on the bread-and-butter concerns around which working people can be more readily mobilized, such organizations also tend to get drawn directly into electoral politics.

Hispanics and National Politics

Hispanics may be increasingly visible, but their voting strength is diluted by many factors. While they make up about 15 percent of the U.S. population, Hispanics were only 7.4 percent of the electorate in the 2008 presidential election. By comparison, non-Hispanic whites were 66 percent of the population but made up 76.3 percent of the electorate, while blacks were 12 percent of the population and 12 percent of the electorate.

One factor here may be cultural. When asked by pollsters working with the Pew Hispanic Center if they agreed that "it doesn't do any good to plan for the future because you don't have control over it," 42 percent of Latinos said yes, as opposed to 15 percent of non-Hispanic whites. More immediately relevant to such low voting rates, though, are two demographic factors: about a third of Hispanics are below voting age; and about a third are not citizens, including many illegals.

Yet many Hispanics who are in the United States legally do not naturalize; and those who become citizens do not necessarily register and vote. In 2008, for example, barely 50 percent of Hispanic citizens 18 years of age or older actually voted, compared to more than 66 percent of non-Hispanic whites. Barriers of language, social class, and discrimination undoubtedly help to explain such outcomes. But an overlooked factor is how the Voting Rights Act has fostered the creation of single-member, majority-minority districts that ensure the election of Latinos. Given the large proportion of nonvoters in such districts, including illegals and other noncitizens, these become safe seats for Latino office-holders, who then experience reduced pressure either to respond to constituents or to mobilize new voters.

Nevertheless, the Hispanic electorate is growing, albeit gradually. The growth is in part due to competition between Democrats and Republicans, especially after 2000, when the results in Florida and New Mexico were decided by a few hundred votes and George W. Bush won 35 percent of the Hispanic vote nationally. Determined to increase that number, President Bush addressed gatherings such as the first National Hispanic Prayer Breakfast in 2002 and appointed Latinos such as Cuban-born Mel Martinez (as secretary of housing and urban development) and the Mexican American Alberto Gonzales (as attorney general) to his cabinet. Bush also established the White House Office of Faith-Based and Community Initiatives to fund programs run by, among others, Hispanic evangelicals.

Such efforts paid off in 2004, when Bush captured at least 40 percent of the Latino vote, a Republican record. Yet there are evident limits to Republican inroads here. While evangelical Hispanics are less likely to vote Democratic than their Catholic counterparts, they are hardly lock-step Republicans. Nor are Cubans as monolithically Republican as they are often depicted. About one-quarter of Latino voters consistently identify themselves as Republicans, but at least twice that figure have long identified as Democrats. And while there are a handful of prominent Hispanic Republicans, including the former Reagan White House aide and commentator Linda Chavez, there are ten times as many Democratic as Republican Latino elected officials.

In 2008, the Latino vote for the Republican presidential candidate John McCain dipped to 31 percent, compared to 67 percent for Barack Obama, the Democratic candidate. McCain's highly visible efforts in 2006 and 2007 with Sen. Ted Kennedy, a Democrat, to pass comprehensive immigration reform legislation responsive to Latino advocates apparently counted for naught. With many Americans anxious to restrict immigration, Republicans began a divisive internal debate about the wisdom of appeals to Hispanics based on liberal immigration policies.

Immigration clearly has the potential to stir Latino passions as well. This was evident back in 1994, when Californians passed Proposition 187, which would have denied most public services to illegal immigrants. The proposition was gutted by the federal courts, but the long-term effect was to mobilize more Latinos to vote, and to vote against Republicans, who had embraced the measure. Then, in the spring of 2006, hundreds of thousands of Latino protestors, including many undocumented immigrants, marched in the streets of countless American cities to protest legislation passed by the Republican-controlled House that would have made illegal presence here, as well as aiding illegal immigrants, felonies.

Yet while immigration clearly matters to Latinos, they consistently rank it lower in importance than family and pocketbook issues such as education, jobs, and health care. Nor, given their very divergent histories and experiences, are Hispanics of one view on this issue. As Americans enter the second decade of the new century, immigration is one of many aspects of Hispanic politics that are not as straightforward as they at first appear.

Bibliography and Further Reading

Frey, William H. "Race, Immigration, and America's Changing Electorate." In *Red, Blue, and Purple America: The Future of Election Demographics*, edited by Ruy Teixeira. Washington, D.C.: Brookings Institution Press, 2008. http://www.brookings.edu/reports/2008/0227_demographics_frey.aspx.

Gimpel, James G. *Latino Voting in the 2008 Electorate: Part of a Broader Electoral Movement*. Washington, D.C.: Center for Immigration Studies, January 2009. http://www.cis.org/latinovoting.

Graham, Hugh Davis. *Collision Course: The Strange Convergence of Affirmative Action and Immigration Policy in America*. New York: Oxford University Press, 2002.

Huntington, Samuel P. *Who Are We? The Challenges to America's National Identity*. New York: Simon & Schuster, 2004.

Kaplowitz, Craig A. *LULAC, Mexican Americans, and National Policy*. College Station: Texas A & M University Press, 2005.

Leal, David L. "Latinos and Religion." In *A Matter of Faith: Religion in the 2004 Presidential Election*, edited by David E. Campbell. Washington, D.C.: Brookings Institution Press, 2007.

Milkman, Ruth. *L.A. Story: Immigrant Workers and the Future of the U.S. Labor Movement*. New York: Russell Sage Foundation, 2006.

Pew Hispanic Center. "Country of Origin Profiles of U.S. Hispanics." Washington, D.C.: Pew Hispanic Center, September 2009. http://pewhispanic.org/data/origins.

Pew Hispanic Center, and the Kaiser Family Foundation. *2002 National Survey of Latinos*. Washington, D.C.: Pew Hispanic Center, December 2002. http://pewhispanic.org/reports/report.php?ReportID=15.

Skerry, Peter. *Counting on the Census?: Race, Group Identity, and the Evasion of Politics*. Washington, D.C.: Brookings Institution Press, 2000.

———. *Mexican Americans: The Ambivalent Minority*. New York: The Free Press, 1993.

Skrentny, John D. *The Minority Rights Revolution*. Cambridge, MA: The Belknap Press of Harvard University Press, 2002.

Peter Skerry and Devin Fernandes

HIV/AIDS

In the last decades of the twentieth century, HIV/AIDS was the most controversial public health problem in the United States, but it was much more than just a medical concern. Because HIV is most commonly spread through sexual contact or illegal drug use (via needles), it produced "morality politics" with strong divisions between cultural conservatives and liberals over homosexuality, "guilty" and "innocent" victims, and personal responsibility. AIDS also activated new political challenges to the medical establishment and the federal government over research and treatment, as well as producing new institutions, interest groups, and programs.

The acquired immune deficiency syndrome (AIDS) first emerged in 1981 when five sexually active homosexuals in southern California were diagnosed with a rare and deadly form of pneumonia. The subsequent spread of AIDS, and the human immunodeficiency virus (HIV) that causes AIDS, was both dramatic and traumatic. Between 1981 and 1985, the estimated number of individuals newly infected with HIV soared to a peak of about 160,000 annually. Deaths from AIDS also climbed alarmingly, finally cresting at over 50,000 in 1995. Although the infection and death rates have declined substantially since then, HIV/AIDS has been a heavy burden: by the end of 2005, over 550,000 residents of the United States had died of AIDS, and over 1 million were living with HIV.

Political Characteristics

AIDS is a nasty disease, with nasty political characteristics. Three features of the disease, as well as how it is spread and those it inflicts, are especially relevant. First, AIDS has proven resistant to medical cures or prevention. Though it can now be treated as a chronic disease, the treatments are expensive and last a lifetime, creating financial stresses for health insurers, especially Medicaid. Second, the vast majority of infections are caused by sexual contact or the sharing of needles used for (illegal) drug injections. These behaviors are difficult to change through public policies and cannot be "fixed" permanently. They also involve behaviors that are heavily moralized in the

Patsy Clarke (right) and Eloise Vaughn, both of whose gay sons died of AIDS, are pictured on September 28, 1996, with promotional materials for the political action committee they co-founded, Mothers Against Jesse in Congress (MAJIC), to remove North Carolina senator Jesse Helms from the U.S. Senate. In 1987, Senator Helms was staunchly opposed to any HIV/AIDS prevention, or "risk reduction," policies that seemed to "promote or encourage, directly or indirectly, homosexual sexual activities," and he successfully amended the AIDS funding bill to prevent the CDC from pursuing prevention activities that specifically targeted homosexuality. (Will Mcintyre/Time Life Pictures/Getty Images)

United States, to the effect that HIV/AIDS has never been treated as just a medical matter in the way that, say, cardiovascular illness is. Third, HIV/AIDS has always been heavily concentrated in marginalized or stigmatized groups: homosexuals, injection-drug users, and African Americans. This has made it more difficult for the groups most affected by the disease to obtain policy change on their own behalf.

The Politics of Prevention

Estimates from 2006 indicate that the discounted lifetime medical treatment costs for a person with HIV is over $385,000. This implies that, even if we spent nearly that amount to prevent a single case of AIDS, society would be better off. Yet prevention is chronically under-funded, typically accounting for less than 20 percent of federal spending on HIV/AIDS. Our health care system could save billions of dollars if more were spent on prevention.

Prevention is good policy but weak politics. The three political characteristics of AIDS have made political support for prevention feeble, at best. Precisely because HIV/AIDS is so expensive to treat, governmental budgets are stressed; consequently, more dollars are allocated to those with strong interests, organizations, and claims. Many institutions (pharmaceutical companies, hospitals, etc.) as well as individuals benefit from greater treatment spending, and have mobilized for it more effectively than have treatment advocates. Treatment is also morally uncontroversial. Although many Americans (especially politicians) are wary of promoting policies that engage with homosexuals and drug users, few Americans would advocate withholding medical care for the ill. Finally, the groups that could benefit most from prevention programs are ill-equipped to mobilize for it.

During the early years of the AIDS crisis, when effective treatments were not available and prevention especially important, the federal government did almost nothing to prevent the spread of HIV. Cultural conservatives (such as Sen. Jesse Helms, R–NC, and Rep. William E. Dannemeyer, R–CA) within Congress, as well as the administrations of President Reagan and Pres. George H. W. Bush, were fundamentally opposed to any "risk reduction" policies that featured or involved sexually explicit wording, medical conditions, or contraceptive devices, or that seemed to condone illegal drug use (e.g., that would make sterile needles available to drug addicts) or homosexuality. President Reagan, for his part, did not even publicly mention AIDS until 1987, by which time nearly sixty thousand Americans had died of the disease. That same year Senator Helms successfully amended the AIDS funding bill to prohibit the Centers for Disease Control (CDC) from funding any activities that "promote or encourage, directly or indirectly, homosexual sexual activities" and also obtained language barring any prevention activities that targeted homosexual behavior. Helms and his allies skillfully used AIDS prevention activities to paint homosexuals in a light that made some heterosexuals uneasy, making it difficult for health-minded members of Congress to support prevention. This strategy was bad for public health, but it was politically effective: it helped neutralize those who might have advocated for prevention, while at the same time mobilizing conservatives—including those in the Christian Right, led by preachers such as Jerry Falwell and Pat Robertson—who often portrayed AIDS as God's scourge upon homosexuals.

Although the Gay Men's Health Crisis (the oldest and most well-established gay organization focused on AIDS) successfully sued the government to strike down the Helms amendment, homosexuals gave relatively little organized attention to prevention. On the one hand, those already infected understandably focused their efforts on treatment. On the other, those not infected lacked the knowledge, incentives, or capacity to seek policy change (especially given the unfavorable political environment). As a result, the main political advocates of prevention have not been gays, but rather public health officials who have professional reasons for such advocacy.

Only two prevention activities have been politically easy. Early in the epidemic, many "innocent" (as they were labeled) individuals were infected through blood transfusions. This was politically a simple problem to fix: there was a technological preventative—better blood screening—that did not involve changing sexual behavior or anything to do with illegal drug use; and both individuals and institutions (such as the

Red Cross) had strong incentives to see that it was implemented. Beginning in 1985, all donated blood was screened, and since that time only a handful of HIV cases have resulted from tainted blood.

HIV can also be passed in vitro from infected pregnant women to their fetuses. Until the 1990s, there was no effective way to prevent such transmission. But after better HIV treatments became available in the mid-1990s, CDC recommendations for the routine screening, counseling, and treatment of pregnant women have reduced prenatal transmission by 95 percent. Again, a morally uncontroversial technological fix made policy change unproblematic.

The Politics of Treatment

Although less controversial than prevention, the politics of HIV/AIDS treatment has had its own checkered history. Two issues have dominated the political debate: how much would be spent, and how treatment research should be conducted.

Again, the federal government was slow to react. In 1985—the peak year for new infections—only about $200 million was devoted to all HIV/AIDS programs. Not until 1989 did federal funding exceed $1 billion; in 2006, over $21 billion was spent. The most significant single program to provide care to the poor and uninsured suffering from AIDS is the Ryan White Program, enacted in 1990 and reauthorized three times. Ryan was one of the "innocent" victims of AIDS—a white, middle-class youth who was infected through a blood transfusion. Because he was not in a stigmatized group, nor infected through sexual behavior or drug use, he was the ideal rallying-point for those advocating more funding for treatment. After Medicaid and Medicare, the Ryan White Program has been the largest source of funding for AIDS treatment.

The most significant political aspect of treatment research is the democratizing impact of gay activists. These activists transformed the procedures by which drugs are tested, the ways in which test results are interpreted, and the processes by which those interpretations are used in the licensing of drugs. The activists did so, in part, by becoming well versed in the language of treatment research; once they were fluent in this language, it was increasingly difficult for medical researchers to ignore their arguments.

HIV/AIDS imposed terrible burdens on those infected and those who love them. It has also imposed substantial costs on the American public through prevention and treatment programs, as well in the lost productivity of those infected. It again exposed—and heightened—the divisions between cultural conservatives and liberals. Because of these divisions, the political system responded with too little, too late, so that far too many lives were lost. By the beginning of the twenty-first century, however, the institutions, interest groups, and programs concerned with HIV/AIDS had become an established part of American political life.

Bibliography and Further Reading

Bailey, William A. "Politics, Drug Use, and Sex: The HIV Primary Prevention Picture in the United States." Paper presented at the 8th International AIDS Conference, 1992. Amsterdam, Netherlands.

Epstein, Steven. *Impure Science: AIDS, Activism, and the Politics of Knowledge*. Berkeley: University of California Press, 1996.

Rom, Mark Carl. "Gays and AIDS: Democratizing Disease." In *The Politics of Gay Rights*, edited by Clyde Wilcox, Ken Wald, and Craig Rimmerman. Chicago: University of Chicago Press, 2000.

Mark Carl Rom

HOMELAND SECURITY

The U.S. Department of Homeland Security (DHS) has faced a number of significant political, organizational, and intergovernmental challenges during its brief existence. As one of the more visible responses to the 9/11 terrorist attacks, the creation of this new department was the product of much political debate within Congress and the Bush administration. While many recognized that the federal government had extraordinary capabilities, it was also apparent that these capabilities were highly fragmented and com-

partmentalized. Ultimately, the new department was viewed as a way to assimilate the many disparate intelligence, law enforcement, and emergency management initiatives with respect to combating terrorism, and to promote their coordination. However, numerous implementation issues plagued DHS as it undertook the largest reorganization in the federal government since President Truman established the Department of Defense in 1947. In addition, an important goal for this new department was to create a national response system that would be able to integrate local, state, and federal civilian and military assets. This system was tested in 2005 following Hurricane Katrina and found to be seriously deficient. Many of the same federal response problems that occurred with September 11 were repeated for the hurricane. Events like the terrorist attacks and Hurricane Katrina have profoundly changed the American political landscape, and DHS has been at center stage in the nation's attempts to learn the lessons from such events and adapt to twenty-first century threats and challenges. While progress has been made, challenges continue to loom on the horizon.

The Political Origins of DHS

The devastating terrorist attacks of September 11, 2001, on the World Trade Center and the Pentagon rocked the nation and the world. One month after the attacks, Pres. George W. Bush established the White House Office of Homeland Security via executive order, and he brought in Pennsylvania governor Tom Ridge to head it. Early on, Bush was pressured by some members of Congress to create a new Cabinet-level department for homeland security, but Bush resisted, arguing instead for a more limited initiative, given his campaign promise to restrain the growth of government. With Ridge remaining a presidential appointee without congressional confirmation, however, his formal authority over federal departments and agencies with homeland security missions was limited because he did not have any influence over agency budgets or their personnel.

The Office of Homeland Security issued its national strategy for homeland security in July 2002. Since homeland security was a relatively new term, the document provided the following definition: "Homeland security is a concerted national effort to prevent terrorist attacks within the United States, reduce America's vulnerability to terrorism, and minimize the damage and recover from attacks that do occur." (Office of Homeland Security 2002)

The national strategy document also defined several key mission areas. The *intelligence and warning* mission involved the recognition or detection of possible terrorist attacks before they would occur, permitting the implementation of protective measures if such targets could be identified. Another important mission was *border and transportation security*, involving the prevention of infiltration of terrorists and the protection of land, water, and air transportation systems. The *domestic counterterrorism* mission focused on interdicting terrorist activity and prosecuting those who would fund or engage in terrorism in order to thwart terrorism plans, and to apprehend those involved in attacks. The mission to *protect critical infrastructure and key assets* was a strategy to defend critical buildings, transportation, technology, and other strategic resources, and to prevent attacks against likely targets (such as monuments or national symbols). *Defending against catastrophic threat* was a mission to prevent the proliferation of dangerous weapons and quickly detect and deal with the damage of major attacks. Finally, the *emergency preparedness and response* mission involved planning, training, and equipping emergency responders to react successfully to terrorist incidents.

The release of the strategy document coincided with a proposal that President Bush put before Congress to establish a new federal Department of Homeland Security, an attempt to preempt congressional efforts to define the new Cabinet-level department. In particular, the timing was influenced by the explosive testimony of Minnesota FBI agent Coleen Rowley before the Senate Judiciary Committee about how her superiors shelved her urgent requests (shortly before September 11) for a warrant to search the computer of Zacarias Moussaoui, whom she suspected of training to fly a hijacked plane. With even more evidence of the government failure to "connect the dots" with respect to intelligence prior to 9/11, Bush's proposal for the new department was welcomed by both houses of Congress and both political parties, but it fell far short of a comprehensive reorganization of the agencies that had responsibilities for national security. Ironically, President Bush's proposal did not address directly what many Americans believed to be the most important revelation from the September 11 attacks: the failure of the nation's intelligence agencies, particularly the FBI and the CIA, to share information. Bush's proposed department did not include the intelligence agencies. Instead, they would be "integrated" into homeland security through specific initiatives such as the Terrorist Threat Integration Center and the Office of the Director of National Intelligence. Administration officials argued that their frontline work was too important to be slowed by the reorganization demands.

The Homeland Security Act of 2002 creating DHS was passed in November, and the department became operational in January 2003. Tom Ridge was named DHS secretary. The threefold mission of the Department was to protect the United States from further terrorist attacks, reduce the nation's vulnerability to terrorism, and minimize the damage from potential terrorist attacks and natural disasters. The legislation was not restricted to the newly created department but transformed several other federal agencies as well, signaling that the U.S. government was crossing the threshold to a new era of governance.

The DHS Organization and Implementation Challenges

Merging some 22 agencies (or parts of agencies) and approximately one hundred eighty thousand employees, the new department was charged with bringing together related elements of the homeland security mission under one umbrella. The affected agencies included the U.S. Coast Guard, the Secret Service, the Federal Emergency Management Agency (FEMA), and the Immigration and Naturalization Service (INS). It was recognized, however, that putting these agencies under one umbrella would not automatically alleviate challenges associated with bureaucratic autonomy and boundaries, conflicting and competing missions, and vastly different organizational cultures. As the new department was starting up, the General Accounting Office (GAO, now called the Government Accountability Office) noted that DHS faced enormous challenges and designated the prospect "high risk" for three reasons: (1) the size and complexity of the effort, (2) the preexisting challenges the new component agencies brought with them, and (3) the potentially serious consequences for national security that "failure" would bring.

According to the reorganization plan submitted by President Bush (and required by the legislation), Secretary Ridge had one year to develop a comprehensive organizational structure for the department and name leadership for the new directorates. March 1, 2003, was the date established for most of the federal agencies designated in the legislation to begin their move into the new department, either physically or symbolically. Although a few of the agencies remained intact after the move, most were fully incorporated within one of the four new directorates: Border and Transportation Security, Information Analysis and Infrastructure Protection, Science and Technology, and Emergency Preparedness and Response. A fifth management directorate incorporated parts of the existing administrative and support offices within the merged agencies.

As the political scientist Donald Kettl notes, coordination is the central element of all bureaucracies, with problems of coordination being their most persistent pathology. The sheer number and diversity of agencies involved in homeland security, both inside and outside DHS, underline the difficulties that immediately arose. As might be expected, DHS agencies struggled to define their new homeland security mission vis-à-vis existing agency missions, with tensions surfacing for many. DHS agencies had other important missions for which they were responsible, but they were being asked to refocus their priorities. FEMA in particular struggled with how much attention to pay to its more traditional programmatic focus on natural disasters, resulting in a weakened agency when Hurricane Katrina struck. Similarly, the Coast Guard shifted many of its assets to homeland security, spending much less time on drug interdiction, in which it played a major role.

Another important organizational challenge for DHS was to mesh the quite different organizational cultures that the various agencies brought to the department. While some agencies focused on intelligence concerns and prevention, others addressed preparedness and response. Some were accustomed to information sharing and collaboration, while others tended to hold information close and protect their autonomy. Furthermore, according to the GAO, many DHS agencies brought with them at least one major management problem, such as issues associated with human capital, information technology, or financial management.

While it appeared that the basic organizational structure for DHS had been solidified by the end of Secretary Ridge's term of service in February 2005, incoming DHS Secretary Michael Chertoff pointed to several fundamental changes needed in the department's structure as a result of findings from his extensive Second Stage Review (2SR) released in July 2005. Chertoff announced a six-point agenda, based upon the 2SR findings:

- Increase preparedness with a focus on catastrophic events.
- Strengthen border security and interior enforcement and reform immigration processes.
- Harden transportation security without sacrificing mobility.
- Enhance information sharing with the U.S. government and private sector partners.
- Improve DHS financial, human resource, procurement and information technology management.
- Realign the DHS organization to maximize mission performance.

Unfortunately, six weeks after Chertoff announced the reorganization plans, Hurricane Katrina struck the Gulf Coast. The department was again reorganized after the 2005 hurricane season as a result of requirements specified in the Post-Katrina Emergency Management Reform Act of 2006.

Finally, a hallmark of post–9/11 investigations was a recurring reference to the phenomenon of "stovepipes," or "the tendency for organizations and agencies to closely guard information, carry out their own specialized activities in isolation from one another, and resist efforts to encourage cross-agency collaboration." (Tierney 411) While DHS was created to overcome these problems, some scholars have argued that some homeland security initiatives may actually have created new stovepipes or reinforced existing ones. For example, although law enforcement agencies at all levels of government may be more cooperative with each other in combating terrorism, there is little incentive for these agencies to collaborate beyond that particular function. Similarly, DHS has spawned many "special purpose" entities, including Joint Terrorism Task Forces, Metropolitan Medical Response Systems, Urban Area Security Initiatives, and the like, further complicating efforts to coordinate activities. Finally, other DHS initiatives, funded through special legislative "earmarks," have interfered with efforts to develop more comprehensive and integrated approaches to managing extreme events.

Intergovernmental Challenges

One of the foremost challenges for the Department of Homeland Security has been to tie together in a national system, under one homeland security umbrella, the many functions needed to deal with terrorism and other threats. The U.S. system of federalism has multiple levels of government with overlapping missions. Kettl has argued that homeland security places significant demands on this intergovernmental system by seeking to impose a highly integrated and coordinated administrative structure on what is a diffuse and loosely integrated system. He concludes:

> Homeland security is inevitably an intergovernmental function, with the national government using intelligence to identify security risks and state and local governments fielding the forces that provide security and manage the consequences of any attacks. Homeland security therefore challenges governmental leaders to balance the political attributes of federalism with the imperative of forging state and local governments into a reliable system that, in fact, makes the homeland safer. (Kettl 2003, 271)

State and local governments have repeatedly criticized how DHS has distributed grant money to prepare and train first responders. The initial formula distributed money based not only on population but also on a guarantee that every state would get at least 0.75 percent of the total. As a result, states with low populations got more money per capita than the most populous states, which are generally considered more likely terrorist targets. Funding has since moved to a more risk-based approach, but distributional conflicts remain a problem.

Another initiative intended to improve intergovernmental coordination was the development of a new National Response Plan (NRP) in 2004, which replaced the earlier Federal Response Plan (FRP) promulgated in 1992. While the FRP was developed through extensive planning between FEMA, other federal agencies, and others over a five-year period, the NRP was developed primarily by DHS in less than a year. Deficiencies in the more than 400-page plan would contribute to response problems during its first major test during the 2005 hurricane season. (The National Response Plan was amended in 2008 to a much-abbreviated National Response Framework, which emphasized guiding principles and more easily understood roles and structures.)

When Hurricane Katrina struck the Gulf Coast it caused unprecedented devastation, including levee failures in New Orleans. Numerous response failures at all levels of government were documented in investigative reports commissioned by the White House, Senate, and House of Representatives. The 2006 House report was particularly damning:

> Our system of federalism wisely relies on those closest to the people to meet immediate needs. But faith in federalism alone cannot sanctify a dysfunctional system in which DHS and FEMA simply wait for requests for aid that state and local officials may be unable or unwilling to convey. In this instance, blinding lack of situational awareness and disjointed decision making needlessly compounded and prolonged Katrina's horror. (A Failure of Initiative x)

Whereas the failure to prevent the September 11 attacks was dubbed a "failure of imagination" by the 9/11 Commission, the response to Hurricane Katrina was called a "failure of initiative" by the House committee investigating the disaster.

A vivid example of intergovernmental breakdown in Katrina was the New Orleans levee system failure.

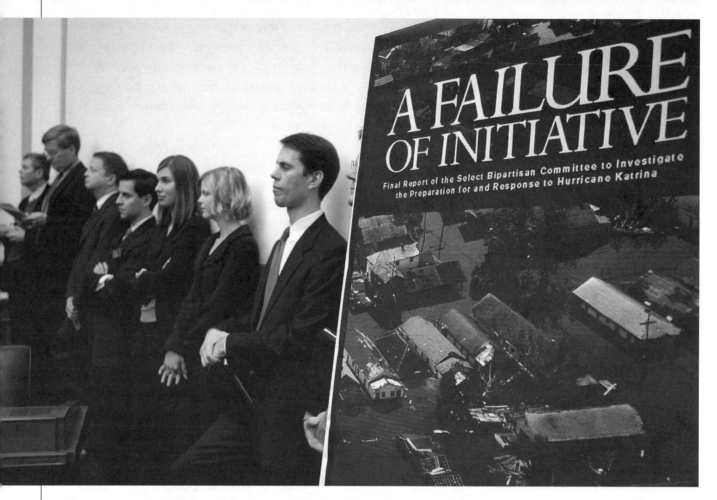

Congressional aides stand next to a poster showing the cover of the House Select Hurricane Katrina Committee's report on the federal response to the disaster during the committee's presentation on February 15, 2006, in Washington, D.C. The report detailed, in part, the failure of local, state, and national government to respond in the wake of the disaster and highlighted a problem that has plagued the Department of Homeland Security since its inception, namely the extreme difficulty of coordinating actions across a giant federal bureaucracy. (Joshua Roberts/Getty Images)

The U.S. Army Corps of Engineers, the Louisiana Department of Transportation, and five local levee boards shared responsibility for the region's flood control system. Because there was no plan to deal with levee failure, it took days for the different agencies to sort out how to accomplish needed repairs before the city could be pumped out.

There are no easy answers to the challenges federalism poses to homeland security. The essential problem with intergovernmental arrangements for homeland security is that often the attempt to promote joint action can lead to inaction. Although plans are important, they are useless if there is insufficient capacity or inadequate mechanisms to exe-

cute them. Participation in coordinated planning and preparedness must be a requirement of the partnership, not an option. Therefore, a significant challenge for DHS is the need to balance its numerous federal initiatives to protect the homeland with an improved understanding of the intergovernmental aspects of homeland security and the importance of working relationships. The Post-Katrina Emergency Management Reform Act of 2006 established several new leadership positions within DHS, moved additional functions into FEMA, created and reallocated functions to other components within DHS, and amended the Homeland Security Act. Whether these structural changes will lead to improvement in the area of intergovernmental relations for homeland security remains to be seen.

Prior to taking office, President Obama designated Janet Napolitano, then governor of Arizona, to run DHS. Secretary Napolitano was confirmed by the Senate and sworn in one day after Obama's inauguration. She brought a homeland security background to her appointment at DHS, having served as a U.S. attorney and Arizona's attorney general and governor. Early in her tenure, she noted several priority areas that she planned to emphasize, including improving state and local partnerships, signaling a recognition that problems of intergovernmental coordination remain an ongoing concern.

Homeland Security: A Work in Progress

The creation of the Department of Homeland Security was the largest, most complex federal reorganization in U.S. history. The demands for coordination and integration of the homeland security functions of intelligence, law enforcement, and emergency management have been daunting. Coordinating action among the 22 entities that have come to reside within the department seems inconsequential when considering the gargantuan task of coordinating actions across the federal bureaucracy, with subgovernments and numerous other stakeholders having a role in securing the homeland. Given the difficult challenges inherent in accomplishing the work of homeland security, including identifying threats and preventing attacks, as well as responding effectively when they do occur, the road has not been an easy one.

Now that DHS has transitioned from one presidential administration to the next, many questions have surfaced with respect to how the current political system will define the homeland security "problem." DHS will have to continue to tackle its organizational problems while remaining vigilant to environmental changes and responsive to its various constituencies. An important tenet of disaster response is to maintain "situational awareness," or the appropriate monitoring and processing of information, events and their implications, to aid in decision making. It would seem that DHS would do well to apply this approach.

Bibliography and Further Reading

Bullock, Jane A., George D. Haddow, Damon P. Coppola, and SarpYeletaysi. *Introduction to Homeland Security: Principles of All-Hazards Response,* 3rd edition. Boston: Elsevier, 2009.

Department of Homeland Security. "Department Subcomponents and Agencies." http://www.dhs.gov/xabout/structure/

Homeland Security Council. *National Strategy for Homeland Security.* Washington, D.C.: Homeland Security Council, 2007. http://www.dhs.gov/xlibrary/assets/nat_strat_homelandsecurity_2007.pdf.

House Select Bipartisan Committee to Investigate the Preparation for and Response to Hurricane Katrina. *A Failure of Initiative: The Final Report of the Select Bipartisan Committee to Investigate the Preparation for and Response to Hurricane Katrina.* 109th Cong., 1st session. Washington, D.C.: U.S. House of Representatives, 2006. http://katrina.house.gov.

Kettl, Donald F. "Contingent Coordination: Practical and Theoretical Puzzles in Homeland Security." *American Review of Public Administration* 33, no. 3 (2003): 253–277.

———. *System under Stress: Homeland Security and American Politics,* 2nd edition. Washington, D.C.: CQ Press, 2007.

Napolitano, Janet. "Testimony of Secretary Janet Napolitano before the House Committee on Homeland Security on DHS, The Path Forward." Washington, D.C.: U.S. Department of Homeland Security, February 2009. http://www.dhs.gov/ynews/testimony/testimony_1235577134817.shtm.

Office of Homeland Security. *National Strategy for Homeland Security.* Washington, D.C.: Office of Homeland Security, 2002. http://www.dhs.gov/xlibrary/assets/nat_strat_hls.pdf.

Relyea, Harold C., and Henry B. Hogue. "Department of Homeland Security Reorganization: The 2SR Initiative." Washington, D.C.: Congressional Research Service, 2005. http://www.law.umaryland.edu/marshall/crsreportscrsdocuments/RL33042_08192005.pdf.

Sylves, Richard. *Disaster Policy and Politics: Emergency Management and Homeland Security.* Washington, D.C.: CQ Press, 2008.

Tierney, Kathleen J. "Recent Developments in U.S. Homeland Security Policies and Their Implications for the Management of Extreme Events." In *Handbook of Disaster Research*, edited by Havidan Rodriguez, Enrico L. Quarantelli, and Russell R. Dynes, 405–412. New York: Springer, 2006.

U.S. General Accounting Office. *Major Management Challenges and Program Risks: Department of Homeland Security*. Washington, D.C.: Government Printing Office, January 7, 2003.
http://www.gao.gov/pas/2003/d03102.pdf.

U.S. Government Accountability Office. *Overview of Department of Homeland Security Management Challenges*. Washington, D.C.: Government Printing Office, April 20, 2005.
http://www.gao.gov/new.items/d05573t.pdf.

Jane A. Kushma

HOUSE OF REPRESENTATIVES

See Congress

HUMAN RIGHTS

A nation's human rights record is reflected in its domestic policy, its foreign policy, and its adherence to international treaties and conventions. In all these areas, the United States' commitment to human rights has always been more pragmatic than principled. As a result, its human rights record is mixed and does not present a coherent picture. The influence of human rights on American politics has increased steadily since 1976, in part because of the growth of international human rights law generally, and in part because the end of segregation and other changes in American life made the country more receptive to the idea of human rights.

Democratic administrations have tended to give more attention to human rights, as evidenced by personnel choices, public policy, and the signing of treaties. The Carter administration (1977–1981) was the first to emphasize human rights in its agenda, and the Obama administration is poised to follow suit. The Republican Party's emphasis on sovereignty has undercut official U.S. adherence to international human rights norms.

Domestic Policy

Americans do not usually discuss domestic policy in terms of human rights, because the United States protects civil rights and civil liberties and considers those statutes and constitutional guarantees enough to satisfy human rights requirements in international law. Nonetheless, persistent domestic problems such as poverty; disparities in access to health care, food, and shelter; racial inequality; and defects in the treatment of suspects and inmates may also deprive people of their human rights.

In 1976, the United States' domestic record on human rights was improving, as seen primarily in the abandonment of both de jure and de facto racial discrimination. However, in the 1980s, the dramatic rise in homelessness raised new concerns about protections for the human rights of Americans. In 2005, the government's response to Hurricane Katrina led to accusations that it did not do enough to protect the lives, homes, and dignity of those who lived on the Gulf Coast, although again this was rarely discussed in terms of human rights.

The most significant contemporary domestic issue to raise human rights concerns is the death penalty, which the United States has maintained since its founding in both state and federal jurisdictions. Between 1972 and 1976, the Supreme Court held that the death penalty, as administered, violated the Amendment VIII prohibition on "cruel and unusual punishment," but it was reinstated after the Court's decision in *Gregg v. Georgia*, 428 U.S. 153 (1976). Since then, more than one thousand individuals have been executed, nearly half of them in Texas. Although most states and the federal government have reinstated the death penalty since 1976, the Supreme Court in recent years has limited its application by prohibiting its implementation where the defendant was mentally retarded or under age, or, as in *Kennedy v. Louisiana* (2008), where the crime did not result in death (except for crimes against the state, such as treason).

Most discussions of human rights in America relate to the second Bush administration's response to the attacks of September 11, 2001, and the ensuing "war on terror." Domestically, the USA PATRIOT Act has been the principal target of criticisms about human rights, because it enhanced the federal government's ability to gather information from noncitizens and citizens alike, sometimes without a warrant, and because it expanded the government's authority to surveil, detain, and deport immigrants.

The war on terror also produced human rights abuses of detainees in Guantanamo Bay, Cuba, where hundreds of men have been held since 2002 without being charged and without recourse to the normal legal system. Moreover, there was evidence that the second Bush administration permitted the torture of detainees at Guantanamo, as well as in "black sites" at CIA facilities in foreign countries and through the practice of extraordinary rendition (in which prisoners are taken to foreign countries where torture is likely to take place but that are outside of U.S. jurisdiction). Extraordinary rendition predated the Bush administration, but it was used increasingly as a matter of policy in the "war on terror." It is now estimated that hundreds of people were subject to extraordinary rendition during this period. The most severe claims of torture during the Bush administration concern the Abu Ghraib prison in Iraq, where photographic evidence of sadistic abuse and humiliation was circulated throughout the world in 2004. Although some of those involved have been prosecuted, there has not been any full-scale investigation into torture by American forces.

Although torture was not a prominent issue in the 2008 presidential election, it did become a political issue during the 2007 nomination of Michael Mukasey to become the U.S. attorney general. Mukasey was eventually confirmed by the Senate, but his refusal to affirm that the practice of waterboarding was illegal led several senators to withhold their support for him. President Obama's attorney general, Eric Holder, emphatically repudiated his predecessor's stance on torture.

On his second day in office, President Obama signaled his commitment to human rights by issuing executive orders that required an immediate review of the status of all detainees at Guantanamo Bay, the closure of that detention facility, as well as of all CIA prison facilities throughout the world, an end to the practice of extraordinary rendition, and the humane treatment of all detainees, in conformity with international law.

Foreign Policy

America's foreign policy since 1976 (and even before) has featured paradoxical combinations of sensitivity and blindness to human rights while pursuing foreign policy interests. The policy of containment of communism virtually defined the nation's foreign policy agenda throughout the Cold War period. Containment was itself a human rights policy, given the authoritarianism of the Soviet Union, Maoist China, and their many client states. Thus, in 1980, the United States opened its borders to 125,000 refugees from Cuba during the Mariel boatlift. On the other hand, the United States had friendly relations with governments that opposed communism regardless of their human rights record. Under this principle, for example, the Reagan administration turned a blind eye toward human rights abuses in El Salvador, Chile, and Argentina, even as it vigorously supported the Solidarity movement in Poland.

Exceptions to this general rule include President Carter's support for the Sandinistas in Nicaragua, during the revolt against the Nicaraguan dictator Anastasio Somoza, and his criticism of the Paraguayan president Alfredo Stroessner and the Chilean president Augusto Pinochet, mainly on human rights grounds. The Carter administration also made efforts to normalize relations with China by lowering its diplomatic engagement with Taiwan. All presidents since then have chosen a policy of "constructive engagement" with China in an effort to encourage that nation to respect human rights. In the early 1980s, the Reagan administration tried to use constructive engagement to encourage South Africa to dismantle its policy of apartheid. However, the policy drew fire, as South Africa's intransigence grew. Eventually, national and international calls for action compelled the United States to abandon this soft diplomacy and enact a sweeping regime of sanctions against South Africa. Many people, including perhaps most forcefully Archbishop Desmond Tutu, viewed the policy of constructive engagement as antithetical to the anti-apartheid struggle and, insofar as it provided succor to the white minority government of South Africa, it may have delayed the end of apartheid.

In addition to the long struggle against communism, U.S. foreign policy has been largely defined by two major considerations: the need to protect oil supplies and, since 2001, the war on terror. U.S. foreign policy has consistently privileged these two interests over respect for human rights. Thus, when war and genocide have broken out in parts of Africa that have few natural resources that interest the United States (such as Rwanda in 1994, the Congo in the 1990s and 2008, and Darfur in 2004), or when a government visits rampant human rights abuses upon its citizens, as in Zimbabwe since 2000, the U.S. government has not intervened. The principal exception to this was the Clinton administration's support for NATO's humanitarian intervention in Bosnia and Kosovo in 1994.

The need to protect oil supplies (at reasonable prices) made the U.S. officially neutral in the Iran-Iraq war of the 1980s, but it prompted military intervention when Iraq invaded Kuwait in 1990. This priority also explains the friendly relations the United States has with such countries as Saudi Arabia and Uzbekistan, which have problematic human rights records.

Since 2001, U.S. foreign policy has also been defined by the Bush administration's "war on terror," as evidenced by increasingly close relations with countries such as Pakistan, notwithstanding its poor human rights record. On occasion, human rights has been the pretext for U.S. military action, as in the 1989 invasion of Panama and the 2003 invasion of Iraq. The 2001 invasion of Afghanistan, in response to the Taliban's sheltering of al Qaeda, was heralded as a human rights victory when the Taliban was ousted and replaced by a secular, pro-American government.

In many of these situations, America's position on human rights was shaped not by congressional mandates but by the executive's weighing of competing interests in an increasingly complex world. Consequently, flexibility, adaptability, and political considerations tend to define human rights policy more than legislative assertions of human rights law. One example was the 2008 decision by the Bush administration to disengage from the United Nations Human Rights Council, countered by the Obama administration's successful effort in 2009 to gain a seat on the Council.

The Ratification of Treaties

The United States adheres to fewer human rights treaties than any other Western democracy, although it has signed and ratified several important ones since 1976. During the Carter administration, both the International Covenant on Economic, Social and Cultural Rights and the International Covenant on Civil and Political Rights (ICCPR) were signed, but the former has never been ratified, and the latter was not ratified until 1992. The International Convention on the Elimination of All Forms of Racial Discrimination (CERD) was signed in 1966 but was not ratified until 1994, and the U.N. Convention against Torture and Other Cruel, Inhuman or Degrading Treatment or Punishment was signed in 1988 and ratified six years later. In general, the United States is far more comfortable with treaties that protect the kinds of civil and political rights that are guaranteed in the U.S. Constitution than with the types of social, economic, and cultural rights that would be nominally or actually protected under governments that have not copied the institutional forms of the Anglo-American democracies.

Other conventions—such as the Convention on the Elimination of All Forms of Discrimination against Women (CEDAW), the Convention on the Rights of the Child, and the Convention Relating to the Status of Refugees—have been signed but remain unratified as of 2008. All except the Convention against Torture were signed during Democratic administrations. Still others have never been signed by the United States, including many treaties and conventions relating to labor and employment, to education, and to statelessness and the rights of aliens. The Rome Statute, which created the International Criminal Court (ICC), was signed by President Clinton, but in an unprecedented move it was "unsigned" by President Bush. Indeed, the American Service-Members' Protection Act of 2002 protects American military personnel from international prosecution for human rights abuses. In its first few months, the Obama administration signaled a change in attitude toward the ICC.

Moreover, certain principles and practices under international and domestic law have limited the effect of international agreements in the United States. First, the United States has taken full advantage of a nation's right under international law to mitigate the impact of international treaties through understandings, exceptions, and reservations. For instance, upon signature of CERD, the treaty prohibiting racial discrimination, the United States made reservations with respect to free speech because the U.S. Constitution does not permit punishment for hate speech. Its ratification of ICCPR was limited by reservations with respect to freedom of expression and the death penalty. Likewise, the United States has stated that it will only adhere to the Convention against Torture and the Geneva Conventions to the extent that the practices covered by these treaties are already prohibited by the U.S. Constitution. In this way, the United States avoids any legal obligation beyond what would be required by the Constitution. Second, if a treaty is not self-executing (and most treaties are not under U.S. constitutional law), then a federal law is necessary to implement it before it can become enforceable in American courts, as explained by the Supreme Court in *Medellín v. Texas* (2008). For example, as of late 2009, there is no legislation implementing CERD or ICCPR, so obligations under these treaties cannot be enforced in American courts.

The United States has always held itself out as a beacon of human rights, and since 1976 the protection of human rights has become an increasingly important part of American political dialogue. And yet the United States' practice since 1976 reveals that other policy objectives have usually competed with its strong commitment to human rights, in both domestic and foreign arenas. The United States often appears to promote human rights only when it is pragmatic to do so, and rarely does it shine the international human rights spotlight on its own domestic policies.

Bibliography and Further Reading

Amnesty International. " 'Rendition' and Secret Detention: A Global System of Human Rights Violations; Questions and Answers." http://www.amnesty.org/en/library/asset/POL30/003/2006/en/dom-POL30003 2006en.html (accessed December 12, 2008).

Bayefsky, A. F. "The United Nations Human Rights Treaties." http://www.bayefsky.com (accessed October 26, 2009).

Donnelly, Jack. *International Human Rights*, 3rd edition. Boulder, CO: Westview Press, 2006.

Henkin, Louis, ed. *Human Rights*. Eagan, MN: Foundation Press 1999 (Supp. 2003).

House Select Bipartisan Committee to Investigate the Preparation for and Responses to Hurricane Katrina. *A Failure of Initiative: Final Report of the Select Bipartisan Committee to Investigate the Preparation for and Responses to Hurricane Katrina*. Washington, D.C.: U.S. House of Representatives, 2006. http://katrina.house.gov (accessed December 12, 2008).

Human Rights Library. "Ratification of International Human Rights Treaties—USA." http://www1.umn.edu/humanrts/research/ratification-USA.html (accessed December 12, 2008).

Lauren, Paul Gordon. *The Evolution of International Human Rights: Visions Seen*, 2nd edition. Philadelphia: University of Pennsylvania Press, 2003.

Mayer, Jane. "The C.I.A.'s Travel Agent." *The New Yorker*, October 30, 2006. http://www.newyorker.com/archive/2006/10/30/06 1030ta_talk_mayer (accessed December 12, 2008).

Powell, Catherine. *Human Rights at Home: A Domestic Policy Blueprint for the New Administration* Atlanta, GA: U.S. Human Rights Network, October 2008. http://www.acslaw.org/files/C%20Powell%20 Blueprint.pdf (accessed November 3, 2009).

Erin Daly

RELATED ENTRIES

THIS VOLUME
Civil Liberties; Civil Rights; War on Terror

IMMIGRATION POLICY

U.S. immigration policy has been one of the most controversial political and social issues facing the nation since the late 1970s. The immigration policy debate consists of three distinct components—legal immigration, refugee policy, and illegal immigration—each of which presents its own challenges and has generated its own attention and legislation. By far, concern over illegal immigration, and efforts to control the entry of undocumented aliens into the United States, has been the most contentious aspect of the U.S. immigration debate. Over the course of the past 30 years, efforts to combat illegal immigration have expanded from a regional issue confined to California and the southwestern border-states to a major national political issue affecting federal, state, and local levels of government in every region of the country.

Legal Immigration and U.S. Policy

U.S. immigration policy pertaining to the entry of legal immigrants has remained relatively unchanged since the passage of the Immigration Act of 1965, which abolished the use of national quotas in determining immigrant admissions. Since 1965, the number of immigrants permitted annually to enter the United States has increased, although the cornerstones of immigration policy have, essentially, remained consistent. The two primary bases for legal migration to the United States are entry for the purposes of employment and reunification with family members who already reside in the country.

In late November 1990, Pres. George H. W. Bush signed into law the most significant legislation regarding legal immigration in 35 years. The Immigration Act of 1990 raised the level of legal immigration to the United States to 675,000 persons annually beginning in 1995. The new law reserved most of the immigration slots for purposes of family reunification, although it also increased employment immigration. The 1990 act established annual limits of 140,000 permits for permanent immigrants and one hundred thirty-one thousand permits for temporary immigrants with skills, abilities, and experience in demand by U.S. employers. Furthermore, the law implemented a new immigration "lottery" system whereby 40,000 immigration permits would by awarded annually to persons from nations that historically had sent low numbers of immigrants to the United States.

Changes in U.S. Refugee Policy

The Refugee Act of 1980 represented the largest and most significant piece of legislation regulating U.S. refugee policy in the post-Watergate era. Signed into law by Pres. Jimmy Carter on March 17, 1980, the act revised the guidelines for the admission of refugees into the United States by expanding the definition of a refugee to refer to a person who faces a well-founded risk of persecution in his or her homeland on the grounds of race or ethnicity, religion, or political ideology. Before 1980, U.S. recognition of refugee status focused primarily on persons attempting to flee communist nations. The 1980 act allocated federal funding for the resettlement of refugees within the United States, and the law's passage coincided with the entry of large numbers of Indochinese refugees escaping war and violence in Cambodia, Vietnam, and Laos. Shortly after signing the legislation, however, President Carter came under sharp criticism during the so-called Mariel Boat Lift, a bargain struck between Cuban Americans and the Castro regime that ultimately relocated some 125,000 refugees from Cuba to the United States during the spring and summer of 1980. The influx of such a large number of refugees—most of whom settled in southern Florida—in such a short time alarmed many Americans, and concerns over the refugees grew amid media reports that a significant portion of *marielitos* possessed criminal records. The Carter administration soon made a deal with Havana to stop the influx of Cuban refugees.

The Immigration Act of 1990 established the immigration category of "Temporary Protected Status." The act authorized the attorney general of the United States to temporarily suspend the deportation of certain undocumented immigrants and allow them to reside within the United States, on the basis of dangerous political or social conditions in their home countries incurred through civil war or natural disasters. Temporary Protected Status was not the equivalent of political asylum or official refugee status, but the new category did provide a temporary postponement of deportation and granted temporary residency to certain migrant groups, including Nicaraguans and Hondurans fleeing Hurricane Mitch and Somali and Sudanese refugees escaping political violence.

Growing Concern Over Illegal Immigration

Unquestionably, the most contentious and acrimonious aspects of U.S. immigration policy since the 1970s has been the growing concern over illegal immigration, which occurs when foreign nationals enter the United States and take up residence without proper authorization from the U.S. government. It should be noted that illegal immigration did not exist prior to the implementation of the Chinese Exclusion Act in 1882, which barred the entry of Chinese immigrants, and the Immigration Acts of 1921 and 1924, which enacted

national quotas to strictly limit the influx of immigrants from Southern and Eastern Europe. Also in 1924, the federal government established the U.S. Border Patrol to restrict the entry of foreigners from Canada into the United States. Prior to the enactment of these legislative acts, the United States maintained a relatively open and unrestricted immigration policy.

In November 1986, Pres. Ronald Reagan signed the Immigration Reform and Control Act (IRCA) into law following several years of intense congressional debate. As the most extensive revision of U.S. immigration policy since the Hart-Cellar Act of 1965, IRCA contained two major provisions. The first offered amnesty and the chance to obtain legal permanent residency to those who could prove that they had resided in the United States since 1982 or earlier. The second major provision imposed criminal penalties on employers who knowingly hired illegal immigrants. Consequently, IRCA required employers to verify the eligibility of employees to work in the United States by requesting applicants to present documentation of citizenship or legal residency, usually in the form of a Social Security or alien registration card.

IRCA proved—and remained—controversial. Those strongly opposed to illegal immigration criticized it for rewarding "lawbreakers" with amnesty. For their part, some civil rights organizations have expressed concern that the employer sanctions provision may result in discrimination against Latinos and other prospective employees who appear to be foreign. Critics have also questioned IRCA's effectiveness in combating illegal immigration. Although illegal crossings and arrests along the U.S.-Mexico border declined during the first three years after IRCA went into effect, illegal immigration began to increase again during the early 1990s and has continued through the first decade of the twenty-first century. Also, employer sanctions have proven to be largely ineffective. To date, relatively few sanctions have been issued to employers who hire undocumented aliens, and the penalties that are issued usually consist of small, inconsequential fines.

California

During the mid-1990s, public furor over illegal immigration reached new heights in California and quickly became one of the state's hottest political issues. California Republican governor Pete Wilson emerged as a national spokesman against illegal immigration, publishing an editorial in national newspapers that criticized Pres. Bill Clinton for failing to enforce the nation's immigration laws. The Clinton administration ultimately responded by hiring an additional 600 Border Patrol agents, but a political backlash against illegal immigration had been born. During 1993, Wilson proposed several anti-illegal immigrant bills to the California state legislature, including the denial of health care, education, and driver's licenses to undocumented immigrants. Wilson's most controversial proposal called for the denial of U.S. citizenship to children born in the United States to undocumented mothers.

One of the most controversial and high-profile immigration bills in U.S. history emerged in California the following year. Proposition 187, also known as the "Save Our State" initiative, appeared on the 1994 California ballot as a referendum. Proposition 187 sought to bar illegal immigrants from receiving public education, non-emergency medical care, and publicly funded social services. The referendum also increased penalties for the production, sale, and use of fraudulent identification documents and called for public employees, such as police officers, teachers, and medical professionals, to report persons they suspected of being in the country illegally to what was then the Immigration and Naturalization Service (INS).

Proposition 187's reverberations were felt nationwide, and several high-profile political figures took stances on the ballot initiative. Wilson immediately backed the ballot initiative and made his support for it a centerpiece of his 1994 re-election campaign. President Clinton and Vice Pres. Al Gore opposed it, particularly its denial of public education to undocumented children, as did conservative Republicans former secretary of education William Bennett and former secretary of housing and urban development Jack Kemp. Texas governor (and future U.S. president) George W. Bush also opposed the measure.

California voters passed Proposition 187 by a margin of 49–41. Opponents immediately filed suit to block the implementation of the measure's provisions, and Proposition 187 would, ultimately, never

go into effect. Despite the proposition's political fate, the 1994 ballot referendum foreshadowed the rise of grassroots level opposition to illegal immigration and the emergence of illegal immigration as a major concern of national politics a decade later.

Some political experts point to Proposition 187 as a cornerstone in the transition of California from a once reliably Republican state to a solidly Democratic one. The measure is believed to have alienated many Latino voters, particularly younger ones who saw Proposition 187 and Governor Wilson's strong opposition against illegal immigration as pandering to anti-Mexican and anti-Latino sentiments. Approximately three-fourths of Latinos voted against Proposition 187. Since 1994, the majority of new Latino voters in California—one of the fastest-growing segments of the state's electorate—have registered as members of the Democratic Party.

National Action

After the Republican Party gained control of the Senate and the House of Representatives in the 1994 midterm elections, new proposals aimed at curbing illegal immigration emerged during the One Hundred Fourth Congress. In 1995, Speaker of the House Newt Gingrich assembled a House task force on illegal immigration, which included Brian Bilbray (R–CA) and Elton Gallegly (R–CA). Congressman Gallegly introduced a bill in January 1995 that called for the termination of birthright citizenship to children mothered by undocumented immigrants. Gallegly sponsored an additional bill, known popularly as the Gallegly Amendment, which granted permission for states to bar undocumented children from attending public schools. The House of Representatives approved the Gallegly Amendment in March 1996, although the Senate failed to pass a similar measure. In March 1995, Representative Bilbray introduced H.R. 1363, a proposed Citizenship Reform Act that sought to deny birthright citizenship to children born to undocumented parents. It did not pass.

Illegal immigration emerged as a prominent issue during the 1996 presidential campaign, with both political parties vying for control of the issue. Republican candidates came out strong against illegal immigration in the primary campaign. Governor

Wilson declared himself an early candidate for the Republican nomination, and he sought to capitalize on the nationwide recognition he had garnered in the debates over illegal immigration and Proposition 187. However, Wilson's presidential campaign was short-lived. Another outspoken critic of immigration policy who sought the G.O.P. nomination was the conservative commentator Patrick J. Buchanan, a veteran of the Nixon and Reagan administrations who criticized legal and illegal immigration for changing the racial and ethnic composition of America. Kansas senator Robert Dole, the eventual Republican presidential nominee, supported the Gallegly Amendment and expressed support for English to be declared the nation's official language. The 1996 Republican Party platform called for a constitutional amendment denying U.S. citizenship to children born in the United States to parents who were in the country illegally and also called for the declaration of English as the official language of the United States.

The presidential election looming, President Clinton sought $1 billion from Congress to bolster immigration enforcement during 1996. The Democratic Party's 1996 platform also aimed to crack down on illegal immigration by seeking to increase criminal and civil penalties against employers who hire undocumented workers. The Democrats also boasted that the Clinton administration had increased the size of the Border Patrol by 40 percent and had arrested and deported thousands of undocumented workers in 1995.

On September 30, 1996, President Clinton signed into law the Illegal Immigration Reform and Immigrant Responsibility Act of 1996 (IIRIRA). This law contained provisions aimed at reforming both legal and illegal immigration. The IIRIRA provided an additional five thousand Border Patrol agents over a five-year period, effectively doubling the size of the Border Patrol. The new law also imposed three- and ten-year bans on the legal entry of undocumented immigrants who had previously been apprehended and deported.

Recent Developments: Illegal Immigration in the Twenty-First Century

Illegal immigration reemerged as a major political issue in the middle of the first decade of the 2000s, by

which time an estimated 12 million illegal immigrants resided in the United States. Conservative Republican representative Tom Tancredo of Colorado quickly rose to prominence as the nation's most vocal critic of illegal immigration and the country's failure to control its borders. In addition to denouncing the costs undocumented immigrants pose to taxpaying citizens through their usage of education, medical care, and other social services, Tancredo explicitly declared that mass legal and illegal immigration posed a major threat to America's national and cultural identity.

On December 16, 2005, the Republican-controlled U.S. House of Representatives passed H.R. 4437 on a largely partisan vote. Sponsored by Republican congressman James F. Sensenbrenner of Wisconsin, the bill increased the presence of an undocumented person in the United States from a civil infraction to a criminal offense, authorized the construction of 700 miles of new fencing to be constructed along the U.S.-Mexico border, increased fines against employers who hired illegal immigrants, called for the abolition of the diversity lottery program which had been created under the Immigration Act of 1990, and penalized persons who knowingly aid and abet or provide assistance to undocumented migrants. Massive protests against H.R. 4437 occurred nationwide during the spring of 2006, carried out largely by undocumented immigrants, their supporters, and Latino civil rights and immigrants rights organizations. These rallies, which at times featured Spanish chants and displays of flags from Latin American nations, sparked counter protests and outrage on conservative talk radio and cable news networks from private citizens and political pundits opposed to illegal immigration. With illegal immigration deeply dividing the nation, Pres. George W. Bush announced in a televised speech in May 2006 that he would authorize six thousand National Guardsmen to assist the U.S. Border Patrol.

In contrast to the enforcement-only approach of H.R. 4437, the U.S. Senate opted to pursue a multifaceted approach to deal with illegal immigration. Senator John McCain of Arizona and Democratic senator Edward M. Kennedy of Massachusetts led the efforts to bring about comprehensive immigration reform, which consisted of increasing border patrol enforcement and enhancing criminal sanctions against the employers of illegal immigrants, while also providing a pathway towards legalization for undocumented aliens who passed a criminal background check, paid a fine, learned English, and met other eligibility requirements. Ultimately, however, the Republican-controlled Congress in 2006 and the Democratic-controlled Congress in 2007 failed to pass any significant legislation dealing with illegal immigration.

By the early twenty-first century, concern over uncontrolled immigration had become an issue that attracted politicians looking for an issue that would carry them into office. Relatedly, many cities and states in the U.S. have become notably more multicultural. Iowa and Georgia, for example, have become major destinations for immigrants. However, large immigrant enclaves exist throughout the nation. Minnesota and Maine, for example, have relatively large Somali immigrant populations in their major cities. Native-born American citizens have had contradictory reactions to the demographic shifts which have altered American society. Nevertheless, the bottom line, in terms of public policy, is acceptance of legal immigration—punctuated by highly symbolic but relatively inconsequential efforts at restriction of immigration and deportation of undocumented aliens. For the foreseeable future the United States will, paradoxically, continue to accept large numbers of seemingly unwanted immigrants.

Bibliography and Further Reading

Buchanan, Patrick J. *State of Emergency: The Third World Invasion and Conquest of America.* New York: St. Martin's Griffin, 2007.

Chavez, Leo R. *Shadowed Lives: Undocumented Immigrants in American Society.* Orlando, FL: Harcourt Brace, 1998.

Chavez, Leo R. *The Latino Threat: Constructing Immigrants, Citizens, and the Nation.* Palo Alto, CA: Stanford University Press, 2008.

Daniels, Roger. *Coming to America: A History of Immigration and Ethnicity in American Life.* New York: Harper Perennial, 2002.

Daniels, Roger. *Guarding the Golden Door: American Immigration Policy and Immigrants Since 1882.* New York: Hill & Wang, 2004.

RELATED ENTRIES

THIS VOLUME
Asian Americans; Hispanic Americans

OTHER VOLUMES
Immigration (vols. 2–4 & 6); Immigration Policy (vol. 5); Immigration Restriction (vol. 4)

Perea, Juan, ed. *Immigrants Out! The New Nativism and the Anti-Immigrant Impulse in the United States.* New York: NYU Press, 1996.

Justin D. García

IMPEACHMENT OF BILL CLINTON

President William Jefferson Clinton's impeachment and trial demonstrated the enormousness of the political divide and personal antipathy that had developed between Clinton and the Republican Congress. When Clinton entered office in January 1992, he became the focus of repeated efforts by Republicans to find new means to thwart Democratic policy initiatives. Clinton's impeachment was the culmination of these efforts, but by the time the unsuccessful impeachment effort had come to an end in February 1999, it had helped to undo the House leadership, destroyed Clinton's efforts to accomplish anything positive in his last two years in office, weakened the president's legacy, and tainted nearly everyone closely involved with the process.

Impeachment Before Clinton

Prior to Clinton's impeachment, only two other presidents had seriously faced the prospects of impeachment and removal from office. The first was Andrew Johnson, whom Radical Republicans in Congress wanted to remove because of his strident opposition to Reconstruction. In 1868, the House of Representatives impeached Johnson for unilaterally dismissing his secretary of war, Edwin Stanton, without first gaining the approval of the Senate in accordance with the Tenure in Office Act. The Senate effort unexpectedly fell one vote short of convicting and removing the president.

The next president to face serious impeachment troubles was Richard Nixon. Although Nixon was reelected in 1972 in a landslide, his popularity among the American people had never been strong and it suffered in the course of congressional inquiries into his possible involvement in a burglary of the Democratic national headquarters. Following a dramatic revelation in 1974 by a White House aide that Nixon had secretly taped all conversations in the Oval Office, Nixon refused to comply with a judicial subpoena to deliver the tapes to the special prosecutor investigating the burglary. After the Supreme Court unanimously ordered Nixon to turn the tapes over to the special prosecutor, Nixon begrudgingly complied with the order. The House Judiciary Committee approved three articles of impeachment against him—for obstructing justice, ordering the FBI and IRS to harass his political enemies, and refusing to comply with a legislative subpoena. When the contents of the tape became public, Nixon's popularity sank to its lowest level. In early August 1974, he resigned after Republican leaders in Congress told him that impeachment by the House and conviction by the Senate was a certainty.

The Impeachment and Trial of President Clinton

Rumors of widespread marital infidelity hounded Clinton both as a candidate for president and after he had won the election in 1992. He entered office with many conservatives and Republicans in Congress believing that he lacked both a mandate—he had won only a plurality of the popular vote—and the moral fitness to be president. Within his first few months in office, a former Arkansas state employee, Paula Jones, filed a civil lawsuit against him for sexually harassing her while he was governor. As lawyers in the suit were litigating the question of whether a sitting president could be sued for pre-presidential conduct, public complaints about Clinton's supposed moral depravity—and efforts to use the legal process to constrain his ability to be an effective president—intensified after Republicans took control of both the House and the Senate in the 1994 midterm elections. By the time Clinton was re-elected in 1996, Republican representative Bob Barr (R–GA), among others, had introduced impeachment resolutions against Clinton for abusing his powers to fire White House

employees and thwart investigations, but none had been approved. Many Republicans believed that Clinton's legislative successes stemmed in part from his efforts to steal, or at least to take the credit for, their initiatives. With each success Clinton seemed to be mocking Republicans, who believed that they had regained the majorities in both the House and the Senate based on their efforts to preserve traditional American values against Clinton's (and the Democrats') assault.

Nevertheless, in the course of discovery in the *Jones* case, which the Supreme Court had unanimously allowed to proceed while Clinton was president, Clinton lied under oath about having sexual relations with a former White House intern, Monica Lewinsky. Although a district judge agreed to dismiss Jones' lawsuit, citing a failure to produce evidence of a claim for which she could receive legal damages, the lie became the basis for an independent counsel investigation into whether Clinton had committed perjury in the *Jones* case or obstructed justice. The investigation was led by Kenneth Starr, who was already operating as an independent counsel investigating other charges against Clinton and the first lady, Hillary Rodham Clinton. On August 6, Lewinsky testified before a grand jury, followed by Clinton's testifying before the same body on August 17. Even though Jones's case was settled on August 13, Starr submitted a report to Congress on September 9, 1998, charging that Clinton, in the *Jones* case and before the grand jury as well as in private meetings in the White House, had committed as many as 11 impeachable offenses. The House leadership greeted the report with some enthusiasm; it believed that impeaching Clinton—or at least seriously mounting an effort to oust him—would be popular with many of their constituents, if not most Americans, and help them to increase their control of the Congress and regain the White House. Thus, two days after its release, the House voted 363–63 to publicize the Starr report. After reviewing the report, the Democratic leadership implored Clinton to tell the truth about his relationship with Lewinsky, and more than a hundred major newspapers urged Clinton to resign. Clinton's popularity was reaching its lowest point since he assumed the presidency.

The Clintons and their Democratic allies gradually developed two strategies in response. First, they demonized Starr as a partisan Republican. They reminded the public that Starr had not only served in past Republican administrations but had also advised Jones's lawyers and even been seen in public lunching with one of the judges who sat on the special three-judge tribunal that shortly thereafter appointed him to investigate Clinton's misconduct. Second, Democrats developed a strategy to "win by losing." With the House Judiciary Committee composed of 21 Republicans and 16 Democrats, Democrats understood that Republicans could dominate committee decision-making as long as the Republicans remained unified, and Democrats believed that if they held together it would appear as if they were constantly losing votes because of the Republican committee members' strident partisanship.

The mid-term elections of 1998 provided the first political test of the Democrats' strategy and Republicans' mounting effort to impeach Clinton. Although the House leadership expected to gain at least 25 seats, the impeachment effort proved to be unpopular and Republicans actually lost seats in the House. This loss of seats, coupled with concerns about House Speaker Newt Gingrich's strong-arm tactics in consolidating power, his slow pace in enacting the party's conservative agenda, and possible sexual indiscretions of his own, cost Gingrich the speakership. Nevertheless, the chair of the House Judiciary Committee, Henry Hyde, and Republican committee members were not deterred. They perceived their base—and their duty—as demanding an intensifying of their efforts to impeach Clinton. On December 11, the Judiciary Committee approved three articles of impeachment against the president, voting 21–16 on allegations of perjury before the grand jury and obstruction of justice and 20–17 on perjury in a civil deposition. The next day, December 12, the committee approved a fourth article of impeachment charging Clinton with abuse of power by making perjurious, false, and misleading statements to Congress. All the articles were modeled on the articles previously approved against Nixon. Later the same day, the committee rejected an alternative censure resolution proposed by the Democrats. Before the full House's consideration of the articles, on December 13, Clinton ordered missile strikes against Iraq in retaliation against

its thwarting of United Nations weapons inspections. On December 17, Speaker-Elect Robert Livingston refused to postpone the impeachment debate as Clinton authorized a second wave of attacks against Iraq. Later the same day, Livingston confessed his own sexual indiscretions. The House began its debate on the impeachment articles on December 18. The next day, Livingston announced that he was resigning because of his indiscretions and expressed the hope that Clinton would follow his example. The House then approved two impeachment articles against Clinton. First, with five members of each party breaking ranks, the House voted 228–206 to approve the impeachment article charging Clinton with perjury in his grand jury testimony. Second, the House voted 221–212 to approve an impeachment article charging Clinton with obstruction of justice. (The other two articles did not come close to passing.) In a show of solidarity later in the day, House Democrats rallied to Clinton's side, along with his wife and Vice Pres. Al Gore, on the south lawn of the White House.

Though Clinton's fate rested with the Senate, the outcome was never in doubt. None of the 45 Democrats were disposed to convict him, so he was never close to the requisite two-thirds for conviction and removal. Because every public aspect of the trial was broadcast nationally on cable and public television, the Republican leaders organized the trial so that it would be done as quickly as possible and with as little embarrassment to the Republicans as possible. Even so, Clinton's popularity, already high at the beginning of the trial, intensified throughout the proceedings. On February 12, the Senate acquitted Clinton on both impeachment articles. Ten Republicans joined all 45 Democrats to acquit the president, 55–45, on the perjury article, while five Republicans broke ranks to join all of the Democrats, to split 50–50 on the obstruction of justice article.

Final Assessment

Clinton's impeachment took its toll. Rather than taking on new legislative initiatives in his last two years in office, Clinton instead had to devote most of his efforts—and use most of his remaining political coinage in his party—to staying in office. Consequently, he had no significant legislative achievements in the remainder of his term. On April 12, 1999, the district judge in the *Jones* case found Clinton in contempt of court for violating her discovery orders, ordered him to pay $90,000 to Jones's lawyers, and referred his misconduct to the Arkansas Supreme Court, whose May 2000 order disbarring Clinton was obviated by a deal reached between Clinton and the independent counsel on his last day in office. In exchange for not being prosecuted criminally, Clinton acknowledged his misconduct, paid $25,000 in legal expenses, and agreed to a five-year suspension of his law license.

In the immediate aftermath of Clinton's impeachment, whatever gains his presidency might have given Democrats in the 2000 elections largely evaporated. The impeachment put Democratic candidate Vice Pres. Albert Gore in an awkward position. Not wishing to be associated with Clinton's ethical problems, Gore avoided taking full advantage of the president's remaining popularity and thus found himself in a much closer election than he might otherwise have been, an election so close that it came down to a virtual tie that the U.S. Supreme Court helped to resolve in favor of Gore's opponent, George W. Bush. Republicans also maintained firm control of the House, and held a bare majority in the Senate. Thus, as a political strategy designed to achieve Republican control over all three branches of government, impeachment seemed to have paid off, at least in the short run.

Bibliography and Further Reading

Baker, Peter. *The Breach: Inside the Impeachment and Trial of William Jefferson Clinton.* Scribner, New York, 2000.

Gerhardt, Michael J. *The Federal Impeachment Process: A Constitutional and Historical Analysis.* Chicago: University of Chicago Press, 2000.

Kyvig, David E. *The Age of Impeachment: American Constitutional Culture since 1960.* Lawrence: University Press of Kansas, 2008.

Posner, Richard A. *An Affair of State: The Investigation, Impeachment, and Trial of President Clinton.* Cambridge, MA: Harvard University Press, 2000.

Toobin, Jeffrey. *A Vast Conspiracy: The Real Story of the Sex Scandal that Nearly Brought Down the President.* New York: Simon & Schuster, 2000.

Michael Gerhardt

INCOME INEQUALITY

Income inequality looks at income distribution among families. Incomes have never been distributed equally in the United States, and the gap between rich and poor varies over extended periods. For example, from the 1940s through the early 1970s, income inequality fell when measured by the percentage of total income of those in the top income tiers. Income inequality has grown steadily from the mid-1970s through the early twenty-first century, with the top 10 percent of families holding 43 percent of all the income in 2004.

Income inequality matters because it shapes patterns of consumption, savings, and investment. Income distribution and equity are related to issues of economic mobility and opportunity and the role of the government in the redistribution of income. These concerns translate into the political arena through various economic and social policies; in times of extreme inequality, political unrest can result from such great disparities.

Family income consists primarily of family members' earnings but also includes income from ownership (such as rent, dividends, capital gains, and interest), government transfers (such as Social Security, unemployment insurance, and welfare cash assistance), and deferred income from pensions and other retirement vehicles. Changes in labor markets, family structure, and government income policies can all affect income distribution; since the 1970s, all three have experienced dramatic changes that have likely contributed to increased inequality. Greater globalization and trade have been credited with the steady reduction in the developed world of well-paying jobs and the median wages of males—while the rise of single-parent families has resulted in a larger number of lower-income families. Women's increased participation in the labor force has increased the number of families with two earners. Finally, since the late 1970s, the

United States has seen its tax law and social safety net policies change fairly radically: the wealthy had their tax burden reduced considerably while cuts were made to programs that primarily aided the poor.

The economic causes of and the possible political cures for income inequality are hotly debated. Economists concentrate on the relationship between equity and economic growth. One approach claims that a "rising tide lifts all boats"—that is, that economic growth brings more income equality. Another common argument claims a trade-off between equality and growth—smooth-running market production creates inequality. Reducing inequality, some argue, makes markets less efficient and reduces growth. A more recent view, however, is that too much inequality impedes growth. Despite economists' claims, historical data find no consistent empirical relationship between measures of economic growth and income inequality.

Similarly, no particular correlation appears to exist between increases in income inequality and the extension of democratic rights or political mobilization. Income inequality can bring increased power to elites in the form of political and economic influence over legislative processes. Growing income inequality can also serve to mobilize the populace to seek a range of remedies—including legislative ones—to combat becoming a nation of haves and have nots.

The historical relationship between economic arguments about income inequality and political parties in the post–World War II era is hazy. Prior to the 1970s, liberal politicians (primarily but not exclusively in the Democratic Party) successfully used income inequality—especially along the racial divide—in the midst of economic growth to affect significant political and economic change, including the recognition of civil rights and the expansion of the social safety net to reach people previously locked out of government programs. Since the 1980s, however, conservative Republican as well as moderate Democratic politicians have implemented inequality-creating policies with the rationale that the slow economic growth and increases in poverty that began in the late 1970s were the result of government policies that reduced income inequality. Promoting savings and investment among the rich as the way to spur economic growth, Pres. Ronald Reagan

RELATED ENTRIES

THIS VOLUME
Economic Policy; Globalization; Tax Policy

championed policies that cut taxes for high-income households and reduced spending on low-income households. Union membership also declined precipitously during his administration. In the 1990s, Pres. Bill Clinton to some degree continued these policies by successfully promoting unfettered markets (such as free trade agreements) and ushering in dramatic changes to cash assistance programs for low-income families (although his administration expanded tax credit programs and health insurance to low-income families and slightly increased tax rates on high-income households). During the administration of Pres. George W. Bush, economic growth slowed, with large segments of the U.S. population experiencing declines in their standard of living. As a consequence, debate over the economic costs and benefits of unequal income distribution was renewed in the 2008 presidential campaign.

Bibliography and Further Reading

Campano, Fred, and Dominick Salvatore. *Income Distribution*. Oxford, UK: Oxford University Press, 2006.

Kuznets, Simon. "Economic Growth and Income Inequality." *American Economic Review* 45, no. 1 (1955): 1–28.

Okun, Arthur. *Equality and Efficiency: The Big Tradeoff*. Washington, D.C.: The Brookings Institution, 1975.

Piketty, Thomas, and Emmanuel Saez. "Income Inequality in the United States, 1913–1998." *The Quarterly Journal of Economics* 118, no. 1 (February 2003): 1–39. Data updated to 2004 are available at http://elsa.berkeley.edu/~saez/TabFig2004prel.xls (accessed October 6, 2009).

Ryscavage, Paul. *Income Inequality in America*. Armonk, NY: M. E. Sharpe, 1999.

Tilly, Chris, and Randy Albelda. "Not Markets Alone: Enriching the Discussion of Income Distribution." In *Political Economy for the 21st Century*, edited by Charles Whalen, 195–212. Armonk, NY: M. E. Sharpe, 1996.

Randy Albelda

INTEREST GROUP SYSTEM

The interest group system consists of all non-governmental organizations that attempt to influence public policy at any level of government. Although interest groups have been a part of American politics since the founding of the country, the size of the interest group system has grown and the influence of its groups has evolved over time. Changes since the 1970s—including technological innovations that boosted the growth of mass-membership groups, the creation of political action committees (PACs), and the aftermath of the civil rights movement—have served to change who is represented in the system, caused shifts in contribution patterns in federal campaigns, and altered the norms of what it means for citizens to participate politically. Interest groups in the post-1970s era have mobilized segments of the voting population around new issues, pushed those issues onto the political agenda, and, in some cases, contributed to their passage.

The Interest Group Explosion

The late 1960s and early 1970s in particular were marked by an increase in the number of organizations representing citizens and dealing with social issues. Scholars attribute this "interest group explosion" to a series of factors. Social movements for civil rights, women's rights, consumers' rights, and environmental protection led to the creation of affiliated interest groups. The expansion of government programs, particularly in the realm of social policy, encouraged citizens to organize to protect the benefits they had just gained. Campaign finance reform in 1973 and 1974 made possible the creation of political action committees, through which interest groups could contribute to federal election campaigns, and the number of such organizations grew quickly. Technological innovations such as direct mail also helped citizen organizations more easily gather resources, while a more general societal shift from industrialization to post-industrialization encouraged the rise of values-based objectives rather than only needs-based goals. This focus on rights-based initiatives—from civil rights, to women's rights, to rights of the disabled—brought a wider range of participants into the political system and contributed significantly to the increase in the number of interest groups.

The 1970s also were characterized by the birth of a new type of group that continues to characterize public lobbies to date: mass-membership lobbies, funded by newspaper advertising and direct-mail solicitations. Under the leadership of John Gardner, a former cabinet secretary in Pres. Lyndon Johnson's administration, the citizen group Common Cause pioneered the use of mailed advertising to attract members, sending out 6.5 million pieces of mail in 1970 alone and gaining more than one hundred thousand members in its first six months. The technique was widely copied, making it possible for non-occupational organizations whose potential members were widely dispersed to form more easily than ever before. The political scientist Andrew McFarland argued that Common Cause departed from previous "good government" groups by strategically engaging in politics at the national level, emphasizing *process* over *ideology*, and sustaining itself on the individual donations of its members, solicited by mail. The legacy of the organization includes pioneering the disclosure of public officials' personal finances, and the now widely employed use of "sunset clauses" to force mandatory review (rather than automatic reauthorization) of governmental programs. More generally, Common Cause represented a model for future public interest groups to emulate.

Also, beginning in the late 1970s, and particularly during the Reagan administration, the federal government began increasingly to delegate responsibility for social service programs to the states. Both federal and state governments relied increasingly on nonprofit organizations to provide social services for children, the needy, the disabled, and other dependent populations. Although many of these organizations were not technically interest groups, inasmuch they were not explicitly involved in attempts to influence public policy, most of them did act as advocates for the disadvantaged.

Finally, the aftermath of the civil rights movement resulted in continued mobilization efforts waged by those seeking equality, including women who fought for a constitutional amendment ensuring equal rights; gays and lesbians, who sought legal remedies to affirm their right to privacy; and the disabled, who advocated for public accommodations in the workplace and beyond. The mobilization of the disadvantaged resulted in counter-mobilization efforts by groups who favored the status quo or viewed changing conditions as violating other principles. For example, as the movement now known as the Religious Right gained momentum, the fundamentalist minister Jerry Falwell formed the Moral Majority in 1979, drawing a following of primarily white, Southern, evangelical Christians into political activism.

Assessing the Growth of the System

As a result of these political and societal changes, the number of groups interested in public affairs and social welfare more than doubled between 1970 and 1980, and by 1995 the number of such groups had quadrupled. But despite this rapid growth, business organizations still outnumbered social welfare groups. In 1995, the Encyclopedia of Associations listed 3,973 business associations, compared with 2,178 public affairs organizations and 1,938 social welfare organizations. A study in 2001 by the political scientists Frank Baumgartner and Beth Leech indicated that more than 60 percent of the lobbyists in Washington were businesses or associations of business, and nearly 80 percent of the expenditures on lobbying activities came from businesses and business associations. Nonetheless, research indicates that citizen groups tend to be more prominent in policy debates than simple numbers would predict.

In an effort to document the number of lobbyists and the amounts being spent on lobbying, Congress in 1995 passed the Lobbying Disclosure Act. Anyone whose "primary purpose" was lobbying had long been required to register under the Federal Regulation of Lobbying Act of 1946, but the law had many loopholes and only about a quarter of the lobbyists active in Washington actually registered. The 1995 act requires registration with the House and Senate by any organization that spends more than $20,000 on lobbying in a six-month period, or any professional lobbying firm that is paid more than $5,000 by a client. The registration forms lists the total amount spent on lobbying (including salaries for lobbyists), names of the lobbyists working for the organizations, and the issues on which it lobbied, including the specific bills and regulations on which it lobbied. Records indicate that there were

more than ten thousand organizations registered in 2005, spending a total of $2.41 billion on lobbying efforts. Though the disclosure law is clearly more effective than its predecessor, it still is criticized for lack of enforcement, the omission of any information about grassroots lobbying, and varying degrees of specificity provided by the organizations that fill out the forms.

Interest Group Influence

An organization is just an organization unless it decides to advocate politically. It is this advocacy— this political activity—that makes an organization an interest group. Interest groups seek to exert influence on the political process in direct ways, with outcome-oriented goals, such as winning a legislative victory on the floor of Congress, or through indirect means, such as public relations campaigns that seek to affect the political agenda by influencing public opinion. Groups also advocate at varying stages of the policy-making process, ranging from agenda setting up through providing oversight of regulatory measures already in place. The political scientist Jeffrey Berry defines the lobbying behavior of groups as "just about any legal means used to try to influence government." (1997, 6) The democratic principles of federalism and separation of powers provide interest groups with multiple points of entry into the system.

Mass membership groups, especially those that are part of larger social movements, influenced the policy process during this period through elections as well. The proliferation of groups during this time period contributed to the creation of important electoral cleavages that were still felt in the twenty-first century. For example, feminist women organized under the National Organization for Women (NOW) and the National Women's Political Caucus (NWPC) fought to pass the Equal Rights Amendment (ERA) during the 1970s and early 1980s. Though the Ninety Second Congress passed the ERA, too few states ratified the Constitutional amendment by the 1982 deadline. Nevertheless, their nationalized campaign created a viable electoral constituency of women voters mobilized by women's issues. The resulting "gender gap" has meant that women voters have been more likely than men to vote

Democratic in every presidential election since Ronald Reagan was first elected in 1980.

In addition, the short-term victory of the ERA in the Ninety Second Congress facilitated the emergence of the Women's Lobby (1972), which brought various organized women's interest groups together in D.C. and achieved important policy gains for women. The women's lobby is credited with the inclusion of a minimum wage for domestic workers to the Fair Labor Standards Amendments; the passage of bills providing educational equity for women and granting women equal access to credit; gaining women admittance to American military academies; the establishment of a National Commission on the Observance of International Women's Year; and finally, the defeat of congressional attempts to weaken Title IX of the 1972 Education Amendments Act, which prohibits most forms of sex discrimination in federally funded educational programs.

Women were not the only organized interest to see their policy objectives borne out or to facilitate the emergence of an electoral constituency. In every presidential election since 1980, the Christian Right—which includes interest groups like the Christian Coalition—has focused on electing an executive Republican candidate to office because of the support this "bully pulpit" can lend to their moral campaign. A sympathetic president also can appoint like-minded individuals to policy-making positions. For example, President Reagan appointed Moral Majority leader Bob Billings to the Department of Education, and a known anti-abortionist to the surgeon general's post. Other policy victories include the implementation of a gag rule forbidding federally funded family planning agencies from discussing abortion with its patients. During the 1990s and the early twenty-first century, the Christian Coalition, Focus on the Family, and Concerned Women for America have become increasingly involved in lobbying Congress directly. Some of their successes included the 1996 Defense of Marriage Act (DOMA), which prevents the federal government from recognizing same-sex marriages; a 1997 ban on Internet pornography that passed Congress, but was ultimately overturned by the Supreme Court, and the 2003 ban on a late-term abortion procedure known to its critics as partial-birth abortion. Finally, the Christian Right is credited among Republican Party activists as being a central component to the election of Pres. George W. Bush.

Although interest groups and their lobbyists often claim the credit for such shifts in policy, it is far from clear how much of the credit should go to the interest groups and how much is simply a reflection of broader shifts in the electorate and in the ideologies of elected officials. Such credit claiming raises the question: How much influence do interest groups have? Despite occasional scandals over the years that have documented specific instances of improper influence, political scientists have had limited success in systematically demonstrating the effects of campaign donations or lobbying. One reason for these findings of minimal impact is that efforts by opposing interest groups often cancel each other out. In addition, however, a tendency to study well-known issues and to focus attention on the end stages of policy making (such as a final vote on a bill) means that the places where interest groups are likely to have the most influence are overlooked. Some studies have suggested that interest groups are likely to be more influential at early stages of the policy process, when the political agenda is being set, and are also more likely to be influential in technical "issue niches" where few other interest groups operate and to which the public, most government officials, and the media pay little attention. Most scholars agree that interest groups also have a good deal of indirect influence by providing information to government officials. This might be technical information regarding how a new environmental regulation would affect manufacturing or how lessening the regulation would affect water quality, or it might include political information about the feelings of interest group members who are also constituents of the government officials in question.

Membership in Groups

Since 1970, technological advances like direct mail, email, and Internet Web sites have helped boost the numbers of membership groups of all types. These innovations make seeking new members cheaper than ever for the interest groups themselves, and make joining easier than ever for the potential members. Most of these large public interest groups keep membership costs low and provide incentives to members for joining, such as magazines, tote bags, or calendars. The senior citizen organization AARP grew into the largest citizen group in the United States by following this pattern. For a membership fee of $12.50 (spouses included free), members receive a magazine (*Modern Maturity*) and a wide selection of other benefits, including senior discount cards and access to group insurance plans. In 2005 the group had more than 36 million members, and lobbied to affect legislation related to Medicare, prescription drugs, and retirement benefits, among other topics. The selective benefits and low membership costs mean that like many large membership groups, AARP gets only a small proportion of its operating expenses from dues. In 2005, it spent $925 million, but only $229 million of that came from dues. Membership organizations must make up such shortfalls using a combination of large gifts from individual donors, interest on endowments, private and/or government grants, and income from other types of fund-raising programs. The biggest portion of AARP's budget, for example, comes from advertising in its magazine and royalties on products, such as insurance policies, sold under AARP's name.

Though part of the growth in the interest group system can be attributed to advances in technology, the number of interest groups also has grown because there are greater opportunities for influence. The House Democratic Caucus in 1975 adopted rules, dubbed "The Subcommittee Bill of Rights," that increased power for subcommittees while decreasing the power of committee chairman. This decentralization of power meant more potential access points for interest group lobbyists. With so many policy-making locations, simply monitoring what was going on in Washington in any policy area became of central concern for many interest groups. More interest groups set up offices, and those that were already in Washington spent more time on advocacy related activities. The decentralization of power also made grassroots approaches to lobbying more attractive. Though grassroots lobbying has also been around as long as the nation itself, the approach grew and adopt-

ed new techniques such as the transmission of large numbers of faxes (fax blasts), seeking out sympathetic constituents by phone and then directly connecting them to the appropriate congressional offices to voice their opinion ("astroturf" lobbying), and connecting with and alerting existing interest group members about new letter-writing campaigns via email alerts.

New regulatory agencies—such as the Occupational Safety and Health Administration, created by Congress in 1970, and the Consumer Product Safety Commission, created by Congress in 1972—also brought with them new incentives to lobby. Consumer groups like the Consumer Federation of America became active advocates before the new commission, while businesses and trade associations mobilized to advocate more actively regarding regulations that might greatly effect their profits. The Clean Water Act of 1972 not only provided these same sorts of incentives for lobbying but also opened a window into the world of litigation as advocacy. The act gave legal standing to private individuals and organized interests, allowing them to file citizen suits against polluters.

The exact extent of individual membership within the group system is a topic of some dispute. Depending on how membership is measured and what is counted as membership, the percentage of the general population who are involved in at least one group ranges between 40 percent and 90 percent. The lower estimates exclude church membership, while the higher estimates include what is known as "checkbook advocacy," or supporters of a group who do no more than provide a donation to the organization. Participation by individuals in the group system tends to be by the same people who participate in other forms of political activity, and the more politically active individuals tend to be members of more groups. The interest group system is therefore often viewed as exacerbating differences in political representation that already exist in the political system more broadly.

The Group System and American Democracy

Interest groups have been an integral part of the American political system since the founding. They have been influential since 1976 (as well as previously) in large part because of the ways in which they work hand-in-hand with government officials on policies that are of mutual interest. Interest groups have been the leaders in this process—bringing new issues to the table, as we can see from the growth of rights-based groups. Interest groups have also been the followers in this process —as we can see from the reactions of business to the new regulatory order that began in the 1970s. Throughout, interest group advocacy has been an important voice in the policy process.

Bibliography and Further Reading

Ainsworth, Scott H. *Analyzing Interest Groups: Group Influence on People and Policies.* New York: Norton, 2002.

Baumgartner, Frank R., and Beth L. Leech. *Basic Interests: The Importance of Groups in Politics and in Political Science.* Princeton, NJ: Princeton University Press, 1998.

Baumgartner, Frank R., and Beth L. Leech. "Issue Niches and Policy Bandwagons: Patterns of Interest Group Involvement in National Politics." *The Journal of Politics* 63, no. 4 (November 2001): 1191–1213.

Berry, Jeffrey M. *The Interest Group Society.* Reading, MA: Longman Publishing, 1997.

Berry, Jeffrey M. *The New Liberalism: The Rising Power of Citizen Groups.* Washington, D.C.: Brookings, 1999.

Carroll, Susan J., and Richard Fox. *Gender and Elections: Shaping the Future of American Politics.* New York: Cambridge University Press, 2006.

Center for Responsive Politics. http://www.opensecrets.org (accessed October 20, 2009).

Costain, Anne. "Representing Women: The Transition from Social Movement to Interest Group." *The Western Political Quarterly* 34, no. 1 (March 1981): 100–13.

McFarland, Andrew M. *Common Cause: Lobbying in the Public Interest.* Chatham, NJ: Chatham House, 1984.

Smith, Steven, and Michael Lipsky. *Nonprofits for Hire: The Welfare State in the Age of Contracting.* Cambridge, MA: Harvard University Press, 1993.

Walker, Jack. *Mobilizing Interest Groups in America: Patrons, Professions, and Social Movements.* Ann Arbor: University of Michigan Press, 1991.

Johanna Dobrich and Beth L. Leech

INTERNET

Since the 1990s, the Internet has had a major effect on political activity in the United States. Now pervasive, it has shaped the way in which communication takes place within politics, changed the way in which citizens gather information and make decisions about the candidates, and, some suggest, influenced the outcome of political campaigns and elections. Politicians and campaigns are under more scrutiny, and, it can be argued, held more accountable for their actions. At the same time, Americans feel more involved in the political process than they have in recent decades.

President Bill Clinton and his vice president, Al Gore, were the first in the White House to use the Internet as a political tool, posting the texts of speeches, executive orders, proclamations, press briefings, and their biographies online. It was during the Clinton presidency that the White House Web site debuted on October 21, 1994, and other political movements and groups increased their use of the Internet in a visible way. By 1996, most major political nominees, parties, and organizations hosted Web sites of their own.

Campaigns

The Internet became a major campaign tool during the late 1990s. In 1998, the former pro-wrestler Jesse Venture was elected governor in Minnesota with many crediting his use of the Internet for his success. Facing bias because of his wrestling career, Ventura posted political papers online, and also used the Internet to raise money. In 1999, the growing role of the Internet in politics continued when the entrepreneur Steve Forbes formally declared his candidacy for the G.O.P. nomination online. Also in 1999, the Federal Election Commission allowed online donations to presidential campaigns to qualify for matching federal campaign funds, making it easier for candidates with little startup money to solicit donations.

Supporters of Democratic presidential candidate Howard Dean gather for a "Dean Meetup" in a Lower East Side bar on August 6, 2003, in New York City. The monthly meetups were organized nationwide over the Internet during the Democratic presidential primary leading up to the election of 2004. Dean emerged as a front-runner for the nomination thanks in large part to his harnessing of the Internet as a tool for fundraising, networking, and mobilizing support. Four years later, the Internet-savvy Obama campaign would have even greater success in using Web 2.0 applications as a mobilizing force during the campaign of 2008. (Mario Tama/Getty Images)

Many of these developments set the stage for former Vermont governor Howard Dean's 2004 campaign for the Democratic presidential nomination, which marked a pivotal change in the way in which politicians used the Internet to gain support. Regarded by most as the first Internet-based presidential candidate, Dean achieved early success due to his online fundraising. Early in his campaign, he allowed supporters to donate money online and was able to raise a large amount of money in the form of small donations, rather than relying on few large donors. In this way, some argue, the Internet began to level the playing field, making it possible for relative unknowns to compete against established, well-funded candidates. Besides online fundraising, Dean used Meetup, a Web site for identifying and organizing face-to-face social networking, to mobilize support for his platform, organize volunteers to canvas neighborhoods, write letters, and participate in other grassroots activities. Dean's use of the Internet enabled him to go from being virtually unknown to becoming a major contender for the Democratic presidential nomination.

The Internet also has influenced the way in which political movements operate. Advocacy, protest, and watchdog groups use the Internet to mobilize efforts, advertise, and operate. Notable groups include Moveon.org and the Center for Responsive Politics (CRP). MoveOn is a non-profit, liberal, political advocacy group that has raised millions of dollars for its political causes. Created in 1998 as a grassroots movement to bring "real Americans" back into the political process, MoveOn.org has since become a major political organization. The Center for Responsive Politics is a nonpartisan, nonprofit organization. Through its Web site OpenSecrets.org, it reports on spending in politics and tracks how money affects public policy. Though the information had been previously published in paper format, the 1996 launch of OpenSecrets.org made the information free and more widely available.

Web 2.0

The Internet has increased the opportunities for writers to report events and opinions to a wide audience at a low cost. Political commentary and investigative reporting are no longer limited to members of the traditional press; anyone with a little technological savvy can start a Web site or Weblog (a "blog") and share opinions and articles with a worldwide audience. For example, in 1998, Matt Drudge (of The Drudge Report) brought attention to the relationship between White House intern Monica Lewinski and Pres. Bill Clinton by posting an article on his Web site before the mainstream press reported on it.

The role of blogs as a media source for political news expanded with a September 2007 decision by the U.S. Federal Election Commission recognizing blogs as "media" for the purposes of U.S. electoral law. In practice, this meant that bloggers had become recognized members of the press, receiving invitations to national conventions with press credentials, and allowing them to attend briefings along with newspaper and television reporters. Though most blogs have few readers, a few have become important media vehicles, such as the liberal Daily Kos (http://www.dailykos.com) and Andrew Sullivan's conservative The Daily Dish (http://andrewsullivan.theatlantic.com), for political coverage. Unlike traditional media, political blogs tend to lean far to one side or the other, and are not known for unbiased coverage of any political scene.

Social networking Web sites like Facebook and MySpace allow users with common political interests to connect to each other online, form groups, share ideas, and post information. People use social networking sites to discover friends' political interests, obtain information about candidates and campaigns, "friend" (that is, receive messages and updates from) candidates, and join or start political groups. Becoming a "fan" of a political candidate in a social network can be compared to using a bumper sticker; it shows support to other users in the network, but its political influence is debatable. Nonetheless, this type of social networking creates a greater awareness of group activity and a stronger feeling of belonging to a group of like-minded people. According to the Web strategist Joshua Levy, social networking sites have become "integral parts of the political dialog young voters have begun." (Beyond 16)

The term "Web 2.0" describes the change in the Internet experience from reading static Webpages to engaging with dynamic web content by contributing, manipulating, sharing, and syndicating information. Blogs, RSS, and social networking Web sites are examples of web 2.0 technology. A number of popular Web 2.0 tools made their way into politics during the 2008 presidential campaign. Both the Democratic candidate, Barack Obama, and the Republican, John McCain, made use of YouTube, an online site on which users can post videos, for advertising, as well as for mounting political speeches and campaign trail videos. Campaign-related speeches and interviews posted on YouTube were widely viewed and circulated. Notable videos that replayed on YouTube during the campaign were the interview by Katie Couric (of CBS News) with the Republican vice presidential candidate Sarah Palin, and Obama's speech repudiating incendiary comments made by his former pastor, Jeremiah Wright. The Palin interview was generally acknowledged to be an embarrassment to the G.O.P. campaign, bringing attention to its candidate's lack of experience and policy knowledge. Obama's speech regarding his former pastor was played over 3 million times on YouTube, demonstrating the wide reach of the medium.

Reporters and supporters also used Twitter, a Web 2.0 tool that displays real time "tweets," thoughts described in 140 characters or fewer and sent via text messaging. Twitter allowed up-to-date information on political opinions to be posted during political speeches and events during the 2008 election, and a Twitter Web site called www.politweets.com posted all political tweets in one place. Many credit the Obama campaign's skillful use of Internet tools for his victory—a victory captured on yet another Web 2.0 tool, Flickr, where Obama's campaign posted candid picture of the candidate and his family on election night as they watched the results.

The Internet has enabled people to feel more involved in politics, and in fact it has allowed users to voice opinions on blogs, communicate through social networking sites, arrange face to face meetings, and communicate with the politicians. Computer-mediated communication has shaped communication norms and will continue to do so, and by necessity, political communication by voters, politicians, and the media, will continue to adjust to the latest norms.

Bibliography and Further Reading

"Beyond Boxers or Briefs?: New Media Brings Youth to Politics Like Never Before." *Phi Kappa Phi Forum* (accessed December 11, 2008, from Academic Search Complete database).

Owen, Diana, and Richard Davis. "Presidential Communication in the Internet Era." *Presidential Studies Quarterly* 38, no. 4 (December 2008): 658–673.

Smith, Aaron, and Lee Rainie. *The Internet and the 2008 Election. Pew Internet & American Life Project.* http://www.pewinternet.org/pdfs/ PIP_2008_election.pdf (access December 16, 2008).

Wolf, Gary. "How the Internet Invented Howard Dean." *Wired* 12(01), January 2004. http://www.wired.com/ wired/archive/12.01/dean.html (accessed December 16, 2008).

Sigrid Kelsey

IRAN-CONTRA AFFAIR

The Iran-Contra affair centered around two covert operations during the presidency of Ronald Reagan— one to provide prohibited military support to anti-communist rebels in Nicaragua; the other to sell weapons to Iran as part of a deal to free American hostages. When both of these secret policies were exposed in late 1986, the revelations generated the most significant political crisis of Reagan's tenure and placed some of his most cherished policies in jeopardy.

The Contra War

When Reagan took over the White House in January 1981, senior U.S. officials frequently spoke bluntly about the need to roll back communist gains in the developing world, especially Central America. Anti-communism had long been a hallmark of Reagan's worldview, and restoring U.S. global preeminence at the expense of the Soviet Union and its allies was a major plank in the Republican Party platform.

Although tiny El Salvador was the initial focus, the administration's priority soon turned to Nicaragua, where long-time ally Anastasio Somoza had been overthrown in July 1979 by a popular uprising spearheaded by the Sandinista National Liberation Front (FSLN). Since then, U.S.-Nicaragua relations had quickly deteriorated as the Sandinistas, whom Reagan officials dismissed as Marxist-Leninists, assumed leadership of the new government.

In March 1981, Central Intelligence Agency (CIA) Director William Casey proposed a covert action program designed to counter the perceived threat from Central American leftist forces. In addition to being relatively low cost compared to overt military action, clandestine operations had the advantage of flying below the public radar, an important consideration given the political unpopularity of a regional conflict for most Americans and the president's desire to focus congressional attention on his ambitious tax cut and defense spending packages. Initially targeting arms flows from Cuba and Nicaragua to guerillas in El Salvador, the scope of the program gradually expanded to include the ouster of the Sandinistas. However, in its legally mandated reporting to Congress, the administration claimed falsely that its objectives were much more limited.

By late 1982, national media reports openly described a "secret war" against Nicaragua, leading Congress to take steps to circumscribe the program. However, suspicions about the administration's true intentions continued to grow. After it was revealed in April 1984 that U.S. government operatives had helped to mine Nicaraguan harbors, technically an act of war, Congress adopted far-reaching legislation to discontinue all aid to the Contras by the CIA or any other U.S. agency involved in intelligence activities. The bill became known as the "Boland Amendment" after its chief sponsor, Rep. Edward P. Boland (D–MA).

Instead of complying with congressional demands, and despite the political risks, the administration chose to take the program further underground. Senior aides, including National Security Advisor Robert McFarlane and Casey, assigned responsibility for keeping the Contras together "body and soul," as the president had put it, to Lt. Col. Oliver L. North of the National Security Council (NSC) staff. Congress was kept completely in the dark about the ploy. Although administration officials later contended in public that the NSC was not subject to the Boland Amendment, documentary evidence reveals that key officials at the time privately held the opposite view.

From late 1984 to late 1986, North labored to keep the Contras alive as a fighting force. To compensate for the cut-off of U.S. aid, he worked with private fund-raisers to tap wealthy Americans for financial support, including arranging meetings for donors with the president and other top officials. Some of the funds raised went to purchase weapons for the rebels, contrary to U.S. law. Arms procurement and delivery became the purview of a loose network of private operatives dubbed the Enterprise. Organized by retired Air Force general and covert operations specialist Richard Secord, the Enterprise came to include a small air force, a cargo ship, front companies, and a series of Swiss bank accounts through which unofficial funds flowed.

Later investigations revealed that these funds came from many sources, and that top U.S. officials helped to obtain them. In addition to American donors, more than 20 foreign governments were solicited for support of various kinds. Saudi Arabia donated $32 million during the period. The Sultan of Brunei gave $10 million. Others approached for weapons, equipment, or money included China, Israel, South Africa, South Korea, and Singapore. President Reagan personally interceded with Central American heads of state in *quid pro quo* deals that offered expedited U.S. aid in return for help with the Contras. Some of these efforts raised troubling legal questions at the time. Secretary of State George P. Shultz warned the president and his senior aides in June 1984 that third-country solicitations could constitute an "impeachable offense."

For two years, officials who knew about the various Contra support activities hoped they would remain secret until Congress re-entered the funding picture. However, on October 5, 1986, an aging Enterprise C-123 cargo plane was shot down by the Sandinistas over Nicaragua, and the lone surviving crew member linked the supply program to the U.S. government. North closed down the operation immediately as the administration prepared for major congressional and legal investigations.

Iran

Iran became a hot-button political issue for the United States in early 1979 when the Shah was overthrown after 36 years as a U.S. ally and replaced by a virulently anti-American Islamic regime. Relations plunged to even lower depths in November when fundamentalists stormed the American embassy in Tehran and took U.S. diplomats and staff hostage for 444 days.

The Reagan administration took office on the day the hostages gained their release. In the early days of the new presidency, Sec. of State Alexander Haig declared that terrorism would be the top foreign policy priority. The president regularly spoke out on the issue, proclaiming his refusal to negotiate with terrorists. Furthermore, the State Department labeled Iran as a state sponsor of terrorism, in part because of its ties to Hezbollah, a group that had engaged in a spree of hostage seizures of American citizens in Lebanon starting in 1984.

It therefore came as a shock to the American public in November 1986 when it was revealed that Reagan had approved of secret deals with Iran to gain the release of those hostages. As part of the deals, the United States had sold American weapons and even sent former National Security Advisor McFarlane on a secret negotiating mission to Tehran.

The arms-for-hostages deals can be traced to nearly simultaneous initiatives within the U.S. and Israeli governments. In June 1985, McFarlane and other American officials prepared a draft presidential directive which included a proposal to allow Western allies to provide limited amounts of weapons to Iran. At the time, Iran was fighting a brutal war with Iraq and lacked steady access to military supplies thanks to an embargo the United States had put in place. Viewed from the traditional Cold War perspective, this eventually led some to fear that the Islamic Republic might reach out to the Soviet Union for support, which in turn would grant Moscow leverage with Tehran. Secretary of Defense Caspar W. Weinberger and Secretary of State Shultz immediately rejected the notion, but this did not diminish the underlying concerns of certain other U.S. officials.

In July, a senior Israeli official approached McFarlane on behalf of Israel Prime Minister Shimon Perez. He described the existence of a "moderate" faction in the Iranian government that was believed to be interested in closer relations with the United States, and he proposed extending a sign of interest to this group in the form of a token shipment of arms which they could use to raise their standing within the regime. For their part, the "moderates" would return the gesture by freeing the hostages in Lebanon.

McFarlane immediately took the proposal to the president. Reagan's primary interest in it was not its purported strategic value but the possibility it presented for gaining the captives' release. His views were encouraged by meetings with the families of American hostages as well as memories of the political problems caused by the Tehran hostage crisis. It was this motivation that drove the Iran initiative forward.

With the president's approval, a series of deliveries took place from August 1985 through October 1986 comprising a total of 2,004 TOW (Tube-launched, Optically-tracked, Wire-guided) anti-tank missiles, 18 HAWK anti-aircraft missiles, and related spare parts. Israel took the lead with the first several

deliveries, using weapons from its stocks which the United States replaced with more advanced versions. But after problems arose with the HAWK delivery in November 1985, the U.S. side decided to take control of the operation. On January 17, 1986, Reagan signed a presidential finding authorizing the direct sale of weapons to Iran. During the course of the operation, the United States also provided intelligence on Iraq's order of battle.

The arms deals resulted in three Americans gaining their freedom. However, during the same period another three were taken captive. Thus the president's main goal for the operation was not achieved. The Israeli-inspired notion of building a relationship with Iranian moderates was equally unrealistic.

Domestically, the operation created significant political and legal problems for the administration, undermining various official U.S. policies, ignoring presidential pledges regarding negotiations with terrorists, and disregarding legal restrictions. On the latter point, Weinberger's notes from a December 1985 White House meeting are illuminating: "President sd. he could answer charges of illegality but he couldn't answer charge that 'big strong President Reagan passed up a chance to free hostages.'" Later, public denials of wrongdoing and false statements about the nature and scope of the deals compounded these problems.

Aftermath

On November 25, 1986, the president and the attorney general announced at a press conference that there had been an illicit "diversion" of profits from the Iran arms sales to the Nicaraguan rebels. This revelation of a further illicit act tying together two already explosive programs had major ramifications. Numerous official investigations followed. Because these typically focused on the narrow issue of the diversion, knowledge of which Reagan could safely deny, he escaped serious legal scrutiny for the actions he did take which were similar to those for which several of his aides eventually faced criminal charges. (Impeachment was initially a genuine concern, according to declassified records.) Reagan did not, however, escape sharp public judgment about his role and his mismanagement of the NSC process.

The administration's policy goals suffered as well. The distractions following the scandal's exposure undoubtedly hampered the government's ability to pursue important priorities such as arms control negotiations with Moscow. The arms deals with Iran produced resentment and suspicion particularly among key Arab states, and the blatant contradiction of self-proclaimed principles undermined America's credibility overseas.

Finally, the scandal had repercussions for the U.S. political and policy processes. The NSC staff was swiftly returned to its policy coordinating role. Congress enacted new laws in an attempt to hold the executive branch more accountable for intelligence operations. And, although the Independent Counsel statute came under a storm of criticism from Republicans during Iran-Contra, it survived to become an even more potent tool in the investigation of Pres. Bill Clinton a decade later.

Bibliography and Further Reading

Byrne, Malcolm, and Peter Kornbluh, eds. *The Iran-Contra Affair: The Making of a Scandal*. Alexandria, VA: Chadwyck-Healey, Inc., 1989.

Cohen, William S., and George J. Mitchell. *Men of Zeal: A Candid Inside Story of the Iran-Contra Hearings*. New York: Viking, 1988.

Draper, Theodore. *A Very Thin Line: The Iran-Contra Affairs*. New York: Hill & Wang, 1991.

Kornbluh, Peter, and Malcolm Byrne. *The Iran-Contra Scandal: The Declassified History*. New York: The New Press, 1993.

Mayer, Jane, and Doyle McManus. *Landslide: The Unmaking of the President, 1984–1988*. Boston: Houghton Mifflin Company, 1988.

Tower, John G., Edmund S. Muskie, and Brent Scowcroft. *Report of the President's Special Review Board*. Washington, D.C.: U.S. Government Printing Office, 1987.

U.S. Congress. Senate Select Committee on Secret Military Assistance to Iran and the Nicaraguan Opposition. *Report of the congressional Committees Investigating the Iran-Contra Affair with Supplemental,*

Minority, and Additional Views, November 1987. 100th Congress, 1st Session, 1987.

Walsh, Lawrence E. *Final Report of the Independent Counsel for Iran/Contra Matters*, Vols I–III. Washington, D.C.: U.S. Government Printing Office, 1993.

———. *Firewall: The Iran-Contra Conspiracy and Cover-Up*. New York: W. W. Norton & Co., 1997.

Malcolm Byrne

IRAN HOSTAGE CRISIS
November 4, 1979–January 20, 1981

The Iran Hostage Crisis consisted of the attack upon, and subsequent occupation of, the U.S. embassy in Teheran, Iran. For 444 days, 52 members of the embassy staff (Foreign Service, Marine guards, and clerical staff) were held captive by radical students and hardliners who demanded, among other terms, the return of the recently deposed Shah (Emperor) Mohammad Reza Pahlavi to custody of the new revolutionary regime in order to stand trial for alleged crimes committed during his reign. This watershed event in U.S. history would prove a critical factor both in the defeat of Pres. Jimmy Carter by Ronald Reagan in the 1980 presidential election and in the rise of conservatism as a major political force. This episode also foreshadowed the advent of several new, ominous issues that would bedevil American foreign policy for decades afterward: the rise of Islamic fundamentalism and state-supported terrorism.

Background

In 1953, a Central Intelligence Agency (CIA)-assisted coup restored the Shah of Iran, Mohammad Reza Pahlavi, to power. As one of the few pro-Western leaders in an increasingly important part of the world, the Shah had enjoyed considerable favor with successive U.S. administrations. Pahlavi, however, was paranoid that the same nationalist elements that had earlier removed him from power might, if unchecked, attempt to do so again. As a result, his regime ruled with an iron-fist and sought to crush all opposition.

In the late 1970s, pent-up discontent with the Shah's regime exploded and eventually led to his departure in 1979. With the return of Ayatollah Ruhollah Khomeini, the spiritual leader of the revolutionary movement, from exile in France in February 1979, a new Islamic state began to organize.

On February 14, 1979, the U.S. embassy in Teheran was attacked by an angry mob. The occupation, however, only lasted a few hours before the demonstrators were driven off by Revolutionary Guard militia. In the subsequent months, a sense of normalcy returned to U.S.-Iranian relations. The tranquility, however, would come to an abrupt end in the fall of 1979.

Seizure of the Embassy

Fleeing Iran, the Shah went into exile first in Egypt and later in Mexico. In the fall of 1979, however, he was diagnosed with cancer. At the request of former Sec. of State Henry Kissinger and the banker and personal friend David Rockefeller, on October 22, 1979, the Shah was admitted into the United States to seek potentially lifesaving medical treatment. Although apprehensive about the potential reaction of both public and official opinion in Iran, the Carter administration decided on humanitarian grounds to allow the Shah into the United States. Washington had received assurances from Iranian Foreign Minister Ibrahim Yazdi that, if the visit was for medical treatment only, the government would take measures to protect the U.S. embassy, but he made no guarantees about the security of the compound or its personnel.

On November 4, 1979, Islamic militants from local universities operating under the banner *Muslim Students Following the Line of the Imam*, stormed the U.S. embassy in Teheran, seizing the compound and taking all present personnel hostage. The students' initial condition for release of the hostages was the return of the Shah to Iran to face trial for alleged crimes against the Iranian people. Over the course of the crisis, the Iranian government would add additional demands: an official apology from the U.S. government for its support of the Shah, a pledge of non-interference in Iranian affairs, and the return of wealth that the Shah had deposited in the United States.

Although not originally sanctioned by the government, the students soon received word of Khomeini's blessing for the takeover of the embassy. Indeed, hard liners on the Revolutionary Council saw the incident as an opportunity to simultaneously sweep away moderate elements (particularly Prime Minister Mehdi Bazargan), renew the revolutionary zeal of the general population, and consolidate the control of fundamentalist clerics and their radical allies over Iran's government. When he was unable to secure the hostages' release, Bazargan resigned. He was replaced by Abolhassan Bani-Sadr, a moderate elected in January 1980 whose loyalty to Khomeini was beyond question.

The reaction to the embassy seizure in the United States was shock and outrage, generating a powerful anti-Iran backlash among the American public. President Carter denounced the takeover as a grave violation of international law and demanded the immediate and unconditional return of both the hostages and the compound. The president, whose popularity had been sagging due to his handling of the economy, benefited from a "rally around the flag" effect. Gallup reported that Carter's approval numbers jumped from 32 percent in October 1979 to 61 percent in December.

Despite public anger over the incident, Carter made it clear from the start that the safe return of all hostages was his top priority, and therefore decided to pursue diplomatic and economic measures to secure their release. In an effort to utilize American economic leverage to pressure Iran, in November 1979, Carter placed an embargo on the purchase of Iranian oil and froze the Islamic regime's assets in the United States. In December 1979, the United Nations Security Council approved a resolution condemning the embassy seizure, but, due to threat of a Soviet veto, failed to take steps to punish Iran. The United States strengthened its position in the eyes of global public opinion when the International Court of Justice ruled that Iran's actions were violations of international law.

Bani-Sadr was able to secure the release of two small groups of hostages, composed mainly of women and African Americans, in November 1979. Negotiations to secure the release of the others proved fruitless, however, as moderate leaders such as Bani-Sadr and Foreign Minister Sadegh Ghotbzadeh saw their efforts undermined by hard liners on the Revolutionary Council led by Ayatollah Mohammed Beheshti.

President Carter became single-mindedly focused on securing the safe return of the hostages, to the virtual exclusion of all other issues of national importance. Carter declined to appear at public events and cancelled foreign trips in an effort to project an image of strong leadership and determination in a crisis. Although initially supported by the American public, by the spring of 1980, this so-called, "Rose Garden Strategy" began to make Carter appear weak and impotent. Public impatience was fueled by news coverage, which featured a daily count of the number of days the crisis had heretofore worn on. Especially noteworthy was ABC's *Iran Crisis: America Held Hostage*, a nightly summary of the day's events broadcast after the late local news. Hosted by Ted Koppel, this program proved so popular that in March 1980 its name was changed to *Nightline*, and it became a permanent part of the broadcast lineup.

The "Canadian Caper"

When the hostages were initially seized, several members of the embassy's staff had been either outside the main building or away from the compound. Some, including Charge d'Affaires Bruce Laingen, found themselves holed-up at the Iranian Foreign Ministry. The more fortunate of these personnel, however, found their way to the embassies of friendly countries, eventually ending up at the Canadian embassy.

In January 1980, the Canadian government authorized the issuing of passports to the six Americans that had sought refuge at its embassy. The CIA supplied counterfeit Iranian visa stamps showing that these "Canadians" had been admitted to Iran *after* the embassy seizure, thus lending greater credibility to their assumed identities. On January 27, 1980, the six managed to board a flight to Zurich, Switzerland. Canada closed its embassy immediately after the escape of the Americans and evacuated its personnel before the Iranians could discover the ruse.

Domestic Situation: Spring 1980

By the spring of 1980, popular support for President Carter was eroding. The public was growing increasingly impatient with the lack of progress in getting the hostages freed. Indeed, Carter's Rose Garden Strategy was beginning to backfire as the president himself, rarely seen outside of the White House since the beginning of the crisis, increasingly appeared to become an additional, albeit voluntary, "hostage" of the Iranians. With the presidential elections looming later in the year, Republicans charged that Carter's conduct of foreign policy, especially his management of the hostage crisis, had left the United States appearing as a pitiful giant, possessing tremendous military might but unable to use it. Carter also faced an increasingly serious challenge from the liberal wing of his own party when Sen. Edward Kennedy (D–MA) became a formidable threat to the president's chances to win the Democratic nomination for reelection.

By April 1980, Carter had come to the realization that the Khomeini regime was manipulating the crisis for its own purposes, both international and domestic. As a consequence, Carter formally broke relations with the Islamic regime on April 7, 1980, and increased pressure on Teheran by imposing mandatory economic sanctions.

Rescue Mission: Operation Eagle Claw

In the spring of 1980, Carter began to seriously contemplate the use of a military option to free the hostages. Pentagon planners had been working on devising a workable plan for months. Informed by intelligence assets within Iran that the hostages were still being held at the embassy, Carter decided to authorize a special operation to rescue them.

Operation Eagle Claw took place on April 24, 1980. The plan called for a small American force of about 90 Delta Force commandos to be landed at a remote airstrip in the southeastern Iranian desert. After the establishment of a base camp ("Desert One"), the commandos would be flown by helicopter into Teheran, infiltrate the embassy compound and rescue the hostages. The helicopters were to then fly back to Desert One, where the rescue team and the hostages would be loaded onto waiting C-130s and flown to safety.

Although its success would rely on flawless execution of the plan, the mission was plagued with troubles from the outset. Of the eight helicopters utilized, various circumstances rendered three unavailable for the mission. With fewer mission-ready helicopters than the plan called for, the field commander informed President Carter of the situation and the mission was scrubbed. The mission turned tragic when, during the subsequent evacuation of Desert One, one of the helicopters collided with one of the C-130s, killing eight U.S. servicemen.

On the morning of April 25, President Carter broke the news of the failed rescue mission to the American public in a televised address. Although the nation initially rallied to Carter, the support evaporated rapidly. Conservative critics pointed to the mission's failure as a damning indictment of what they perceived as Carter's neglect of the military. Reports of jubilant Iranians celebrating what they interpreted as Allah's divine providence served only to accelerate Carter's loss of public support.

After the rescue attempt, the Iranians scattered the hostages in an effort to preempt any future efforts to free them. Carter ordered the military to develop plans for another mission, but never pursued the option.

Political Developments

From April through September 1980, no serious negotiations took place. One of the hostages, Richard Queen, having developed what was diagnosed as multiple sclerosis, was released on humanitarian grounds, reducing the number of American held for the remainder of the crisis to 52.

Originally given sanctuary in Panama, the Shah ended his odyssey in Egypt, where he was welcomed by his friend, Pres. Anwar Sadat. The Shah finally passed away on July 27, 1980. In Washington, there was hope that with his passing the key Iranian demand was rendered moot and a major stumbling block to a negotiated settlement had been removed.

During the late spring and summer of 1980, Carter's political fortunes suffered major reversals. Senator Kennedy, taking advantage of Carter's decision not to campaign while the hostages remained in captivity, was able to win a series of primary victories over the president. Carter belatedly abandoned his Rose Garden Strategy and began to campaign. Although he eventually won the Democratic nomina-

tion, his fixation on the hostage crisis, the bruising primary battle, and his all-but-complete inattention to other items on his agenda left Carter in a weakened position for the general election.

Ronald Reagan, perhaps the most conservative presidential candidate since Barry Goldwater, won the Republican Party nomination. Campaigning against what he characterized as the president's inept handling of both the economy and U.S. foreign policy, Reagan began to erase Carter's lead in the polls as the campaign headed into the fall.

By early fall, foreign events offered a glimmer of hope that the hostage crisis might be brought to an end before the November elections. On September 22, 1980, Iran was invaded by Iraq. The Iranians, although possessing an impressive arsenal of weapons supplied by the United States during the Shah's reign, lacked critical spare parts and ammunition needed to use them due to the American embargo.

A Negotiated Resolution

Having concluded that all political advantage had by then been wrung from the hostage situation and needing, because of the war, to reverse its diplomatic isolation by the world community, by the fall of 1980 the Iranian regime showed increasing signs of readiness to seriously negotiate to resolve the standoff. For their part, the students and hardliners holding the hostages showed signs of weariness with their venture and were anxious to join the fighting against the Iraqi invaders.

Utilizing intermediaries, the Iranians sent word to Washington that they were finally willing to bring the episode to a conclusion. With Algeria acting as a mediator, the Iranians presented Washington with terms considerably scaled back from those demanded earlier, eventually settling on an unfreezing and return of Iranian assets and a U.S. pledge of non-interference in Iranian affairs. The negotiations would wear on for several months as both sides haggled for more favorable terms.

President Carter's hopes of concluding the hostage crisis in time for the presidential elections, however, went unfulfilled. On November 4, 1980, Ronald Reagan defeated Carter in a 51 percent–41 percent landslide. In addition, the Republicans were able to recapture the Senate for the first time since Eisenhower's presidency as several prominent long-serving Senate liberals, including Frank Church (D–ID), Birch Bayh (D–IN), and George McGovern (D–SD) were defeated by conservative Republican challengers.

After weeks of haggling over the specific terms, in January 1981 the United States and Iran finally arrived at a mutually agreeable settlement. In accordance with the terms of the Algiers Agreement, in return for Teheran's release of the hostages the Iranians would receive $2.88 billion in formerly frozen funds; an additional $3.7 billion would be used to settle outstanding U.S. debts, while $1.4 billion would be placed in escrow to pay any possible American claims disputed with Iran. Four billion dollars of Iran's assets in the United States would remain frozen and inaccessible by the Khomeini regime.

On Carter's last day as president, January 20, 1981, the Iranians turned over the hostages to Algerian officials at the Teheran airport, where they were loaded onto a waiting 727. The plane finally took off for Algiers at 12:25 EST. Approximately two hours into the flight, the plane entered Turkish airspace; the Iran Hostage Crisis was officially over.

The Iran Hostage Crisis proved to be greater than the sum of its parts. The seizure of the embassy and the consequent holding of 52 Americans hostage for 444 days had profound implications for U.S. political history. Domestically, this event was clearly a critical factor in Jimmy Carter's loss to Ronald Reagan in the 1980 presidential election. Conservatives were able to make convincing arguments that Carter's inability to secure the release of the hostages projected an image of American weakness to potential adversaries. The failure of the April 1980 military rescue mission, in particular, underscored a popular perception of U.S. military weakness that, conservatives argued, virtually invited future attacks on American interests abroad. Due in large measure to the fallout of this episode, the political mood of the country became considerably more hawkish for the following decade. With the

swing of the political pendulum to the right, the Republicans were able to win three consecutive presidential elections (1980, 1984, 1988), take control of the Senate for six years (1981–1987), and forge a conservative coalition of Republicans and conservative Southern Democrats in the House of Representatives.

Iran has remained a focus of U.S foreign policy; in 2001, Pres. George W. Bush went so far as to group it with North Korea and Saddam Hussein's Iraq as part of an "Axis of Evil." Teheran's ongoing involvement in state-sponsored terrorism would remain a major impediment to improvement of U.S.-Iranian relations.

In the collective mind of a broad sector of the American public, the Iran Hostage Crisis may single-handedly have shaped an image of Islam as a religion of violent fanatics willing to use any means to accomplish their ends. This view would be reinforced by the terrorist attacks on New York and Washington on September 11, 2001. Over the intervening years, a number of writers and scholars have suggested that this episode represented the first battle in a "long war" with Islamic fundamentalism.

Bibliography and Further Reading

Abernathy, Glenn et al. *The Carter Years: The President and Policy Making.* New York: St. Martin's Press, 1984.

Bowden, Mark. *Guests of the Ayatollah: The First Battle in America's War With Militant Islam.* New York: Atlantic Monthly Press, 2006.

Brinkley, Douglas. *The Unfinished Presidency: Jimmy Carter's Journey Beyond the White House.* New York: Viking/Penguin Putnam, Inc., 1998.

Farber, David. *Taken Hostage: The Iran Hostage Crisis and America's First Encounter With Radical Islam.* Princeton, NJ: Princeton University Press, 2005.

Haas, Garland. *Jimmy Carter and the Politics of Frustration.* Jefferson, NC: McFarland and Company, Inc., 1992.

Harris, David. *The Crisis: The President, the Prophet, and the Shah: 1979 and the Coming of Militant Islam.* New York: Little, Brown, 2004.

Kaufman, Burton I., and Scott Kaufman. *The Presidency of James Earl Carter.* Lawrence: University Press of Kansas, 2006.

McManus, Doyle. *Free at Last*. New York: New American Library; Los Angeles: Los Angeles Times, 1981.

Glenn J. Antizzo

IRAQ WAR

2003–

The March 2003 invasion of Iraq launched by Pres. George W. Bush and the subsequent Iraq War, though controversial internationally, were initially supported by a majority of Americans. By the end of the Bush presidency in 2008, American troops were still fighting in Iraq and had suffered over 4,200 killed and 44,000 wounded since the war began. Revelations that faulty evidence was used to justify the invasion and the subsequent mismanagement of the war resulted in a shift in public opinion against the war and against the Bush administration and Republican Party, allowing a Democratic sweep of Congress in the 2006 midterm elections, and aiding the victory of Barack Obama in the 2008 presidential election. The Iraq War served to undo the major political gains the Republican Party had achieved since the presidency of Bill Clinton.

U.S.-Iraq Relations before 2003

The United States previously went to war with Iraq in 1991, when Pres. George H. W. Bush launched Operation Desert Storm to remove invading Iraqi forces from Kuwait. Bush, Sec. of Defense Dick Cheney, and Chairman of the Joint Chiefs of Staff Colin Powell opted not to depose Saddam Hussein after liberating Kuwait, believing an invasion would cost too many American lives and would require a commitment larger than could be justified to American voters. Instead, American forces withdrew but ensured the protection of persecuted ethnic minorities in Iraq by establishing and patrolling "No-Fly Zones" in the northern and southern regions of the country. The international community implemented economic sanctions against Iraq and deployed a team of weapons experts to assess and monitor Iraq's weapons programs. It was discovered in the aftermath of the 1991 Persian Gulf War that Saddam Hussein's attempts to develop a nuclear weapon were considerably more advanced than had been expected before the war.

Throughout the 1990s, American and British airplanes continued to patrol Iraqi airspace, at times bombing Iraqi radar and weapons installations. In October 1998, Pres. Bill Clinton signed the Iraq Liberation Act into law, making it official U.S. policy to support regime change in Iraq. In support of this goal, U.S. and British air forces undertook an intensive four-day bombing campaign of Iraq in December 1998, resulting in the destruction of some weapons facilities but also Saddam's refusal to allow re-entry of international weapons inspectors. A number of neoconservative journalists and academics, frustrated by the U.S. decision not to remove Saddam Hussein in 1991, had pushed for and supported the Iraq Liberation Act. The membership of the most prominent collection of neoconservatives concerned with Iraq, the Washington, D.C., think-tank Project for a New American Century (PNAC), included a number of former government officials and neoconservative thinkers who continued to press for regime change in Iraq. Significantly, over half of PNAC's membership was later appointed to positions in the administration of Pres. George W. Bush, including Donald Rumsfeld and Paul Wolfowitz, the secretary and deputy secretary of defense, respectively.

During the 2000 presidential campaign, candidate George W. Bush signalled his primary concern in international relations was with major states such as Russia and China. The Bush campaign indicated the removal of Saddam Hussein was desirable, but would be achieved by supporting Iraqi dissenters. Bush made clear he did not believe U.S. military forces should be employed in nation-building operations and presented this as a defining difference in foreign affairs policy between Republican and Democratic candidates. This distaste for post-conflict reconstruction programs, such as Pres. Bill Clinton had undertaken in Bosnia, significantly influenced planning for post-war Iraq.

The Decision for War

Following the terrorist attacks of September 11, 2001, the Bush administration sought a strategy for destroying the terrorist networks responsible and limiting the likelihood of a repeat attack. A number of administration officials who had previously been concerned by Saddam Hussein's continued presence in the Middle East, including Wolfowitz and Richard Perle, chairman of the Defense Policy Board, focussed on Iraq as a potential target. They were concerned that Saddam Hussein had been involved in the attacks due to his well-publicized hatred for the United States. Others, including Rumsfeld, believed that even if Saddam had not been involved in the attacks, he nonetheless would participate in a future attack and provide chemical, biological, or even nuclear weapons to terrorists. Paul Wolfowitz, deputy secretary of defense, later explained how officials in the Bush administration had several different concerns motivating an invasion of Iraq, but the one on which all could agree was Iraqi possession of weapons of mass destruction.

The Bush administration launched a major public relations campaign to convince the American public, Congress, and the international community that the invasion of Iraq was legal and necessary. In late 2002 and early 2003, the president, Vice Pres. Dick Cheney, and various other White House and congressional figures made public speeches and appeared on Sunday morning political talk shows to warn of the danger posed by Saddam Hussein's alleged stockpile of weapons of mass destruction. The Bush administration was extraordinarily successful in convincing the American public of the need for war, aided by public fear of another terrorist attack. Although some experts and politicians doubted the cause for war, Republican control of the relevant Senate committees prevented a thorough examination in Congress of the need for war. Similarly, American news outlets were later accused of presenting the administration's case for war without a critical evaluation of the consequences of an invasion.

In September 2002, senior House and Senate leaders were invited to the White House and shown intelligence intended to demonstrate the need to invade Iraq. The right to pre-emptively attack threatening states had been asserted in the president's new National Security Strategy released that month. Bush, then an extremely popular wartime president, won the support of most of the Republican congressional leadership, while the Democratic leadership was deeply divided. These divisions carried on into the October 10, 2002, vote granting the president power to use military force against Iraq. The vote passed easily in both the House and the Senate due to a Republican majority, but the Democratic caucus was divided over the necessity of the war. Some Democrats voted for the resolution concerned that a vote against invasion would cause them to look soft on terrorism and contrary to the popular president with congressional midterms less than a month away. With the authority for war granted, the looming invasion of Iraq played little part in the 2002 midterms.

In September 2002, Bush announced that the United States would work through the United Nations to solve its concern over Iraq's alleged weapons stockpiles. In November 2002, the United Nations Security Council passed an ambiguous resolution calling on Iraq to prove a standard of disarmament. By January 2003, the U.S. government was arguing that Iraq had not complied with the resolution, and military intervention had been authorized by the November 2002 resolution. British Prime Minister Tony Blair, a key ally of the Bush administration, had promised the British people that he would gain a second resolution explicitly allowing for the use of military force. In an attempt to achieve a second resolution, Sec. of State Colin Powell detailed the American case for war to the Security Council of February 5, 2003. Powell presented sound recordings of Iraqi soldiers allegedly discussing the disposal of weapons of mass destruction, photographs of delivery vehicles and mobile weapons laboratories, and a vial of imitation anthrax to make his case. It was later revealed that much of the intelligence used in Powell's report was provided by a source the Bush administration had been warned was unreliable. Powell's presentation failed to build enough support for a second resolution, and the U.N. Security Council never granted its explicit authorization for war.

Several traditional U.S. allies chose not to support the war. France in particular was the target of significant public backlash in the United States. Americans publicly dumped bottles of French wine in the street, American veterans who had fought to liberate France in World War II returned medals awarded by the

French government, and Congress voted to have all Capitol Hill menus rename French Fries as "Freedom Fries." But antiwar sentiment was also high around the world, with millions of demonstrators taking to the streets of major international capitols to protest the impending war.

Preparations for War and Post-War

Secretary of Defense Donald Rumsfeld's goal of transforming the military into a leaner, modern fighting force with heavy dependence on technological superiority manifested itself in the planning for the Iraq War. Rumsfeld altered the shape and reduced the size of the invasion force against the recommendations of senior military commanders. In February 2003, Army Chief of Staff Gen. Eric Shinseki testified before the Senate Armed Service Committee that a successful war in Iraq would require several hundred thousands of troops, while Rumsfeld and his deputies believed a force closer to one hundred thousand troops would suffice. Civilian officials from the Office of the Secretary of Defense publicly rebuked Shinseki for his statement, and he was subsequently forced to retire from the military. Shinseki's humiliation demonstrated the difficult relations between the uniformed military and the civilian defense leadership prior to the war. The result of all of this was that the U.S. force that invaded Iraq was strong enough to defeat the country's armed forces but not large enough to secure the country after the invasion.

Disagreements between the Department of Defense and State Department led to difficulties in planning for post-war Iraq. Department of Defense officials and neoconservative pundits in favor of the invasion predicted U.S. forces would be greeted as liberators, and Iraqis would take peaceful control of their country, allowing an early withdrawal of troops. Some officials in the Central Intelligence Agency and the State Department disputed this notion. Condoleezza Rice, a relatively weak national security advisor, poorly managed the National Security Council where these issues could be raised and debated. As a result, Powell and Rumsfeld took their concerns directly to the president, eliminating any chance for effective interagency cooperation and exchange.

The Department of Defense was given responsibility for reconstruction operations, but U.S. forces would enter Iraq without an effective plan to secure and police Iraq after Saddam Hussein's army had been destroyed, and without sufficient personnel or resources to rebuild Iraq's governance structure. Bitter interagency infighting, and a distaste for reconstruction efforts prevented appropriate funding and staffing to allow effective reconstruction of Iraq.

The Invasion of Iraq

The invasion of Iraq was remarkably successful in terms of speed and the limited loss of life suffered by U.S. forces. American troops avoided the expected high levels of urban warfare by skirting Iraqi cities and charging directly to Baghdad. The initial success seemed to confirm administration claims that Iraqis would greet the American troops as liberators.

In agreement with the military, various television and press reporters were embedded with various U.S. combat units in the lead-up to and invasion of Iraq. The embedded reporters provided the American public with an unusual level of access to the battlefield. In a number of cases the embedded reporters, who often lived and shared hardships with their assigned military units, provided a lopsided image of the war with little critical evaluation of the cause and consequence of the invasion. This enhanced the strong public support for the war, and strengthened the American public's connection with U.S. forces. The Bush administration would use this connection to great effect in later speeches and campaigns, implying criticism of the decision to invade Iraq showed an unpatriotic lack of support for American fighting men and women.

The Occupation and Insurgency

On May 1, 2003, in a carefully stage-managed event that saw the president land on the USS *Abraham Lincoln* in a warplane and dressed in a flight suit, Bush announced major combat operations in Iraq were over. Three weeks later, on May 23, 2003, the U.S. civilian administration in Iraq disbanded the Iraqi army, accidentally encouraging a large pool of unemployed young men to join the small insurgency operating against American troops. By midsummer

2003, a guerilla war was underway, fought both by nationalist Iraqis and foreign jihadists. Although claims that Saddam Hussein had supported al Qaeda before September 11 were disproved, the invasion resulted in the infiltration of al Qaeda fighters into

President George W. Bush stands aboard the nuclear aircraft carrier USS *Abraham Lincoln* in front of a banner reading "Mission Accomplished" to announce that major combat operations in Iraq are over and that the United States and its allies "have prevailed." This event on May 1, 2003, would come back to haunt the president throughout the rest of his time in office, as critics would point to it as an encapsulation of the Bush administration's flawed approach to and execution of the war. (Stephen Jaffe/AFP/Getty Images)

Iraq. Spectacular bombing attacks in August and September, including one that destroyed the United Nations headquarters in Iraq, indicated success in Iraq was not as close at hand as administration speeches implied. Violence worsened in 2004, and the fighting in Iraq took on an increasingly sectarian character between Sunni and Shi'a Iraqis.

In April 2004, a television news program reported that U.S. reservists had sexually assaulted and tortured Iraqi prisoners. Later, it was learned that in one case a man was beaten to death. Photos of the events, which occurred at Abu Ghraib prison, were leaked publicly and resulted in scandal for the Bush administration and particularly Sec. of Defense Donald Rumsfeld. As a result of the beatings, a small number of enlisted reservists were court-martialled, but the Bush administration appeared largely unaccountable for incidents that had caused significant international and domestic outrage. Despite calls from major media outlets for Rumsfeld's resignation, Republican majorities in the House and Senate ensured little support for a congressional investigation.

The Bush administration suffered another significant political setback in 2004, when the Iraq Survey Group determined that Saddam had not rebuilt his weapons programs as the president had claimed, and international inspectors and sanctions, combined with American and British bombing, had eliminated Saddam Hussein's capacity to create weapons of mass destruction. The Iraq Survey Group's report confirmed growing speculation that the U.S.'s primary reason for invading Iraq was false.

Despite indications the war had been launched on false pretenses and was not progressing as expected, Bush made Iraq, terrorism, and national security a significant element of his campaign platform in the 2004 presidential election. Bush argued that America was succeeding in Iraq, having handed over sovereignty to an interim Iraqi government in June. In an unusual role for a national security advisor, Condoleezza Rice also contributed to the campaign with political speeches. Exit polls showed that Americans who approved of the war voted overwhelmingly for Bush; those who opposed the war voted overwhelmingly for his Democratic rival, Sen. John Kerry (D–MA). At the time of the election, more

Americans approved of the war than disapproved. In his 2005 inaugural speech, Bush focussed on the promotion of democracy abroad as a goal of the United States. Increasingly in administration speeches, the promotion of democracy in Iraq replaced weapons of mass destruction as the primary goal of the Iraq War.

In early 2005, intelligence reports suggested Iraq was on the verge of civil war. Sectarian violence continued to escalate and death tolls climbed dramatically. Previously mixed neighborhoods in Baghdad were increasingly polarized by population shifts meant to avoid ethnic violence. Despite the sectarian violence and increasing American casualties, President Bush continued to claim progress was being made in Iraq and no new strategy was needed.

In late 2005, the House Democrats strengthened their calls for the administration to define its strategy in Iraq. Significant bureaucratic infighting in 2006 made a coherent internal policy review impossible. Concern that an attempt to redefine strategy, if leaked, would be a political burden on the Republican Party in the 2006 congressional elections prevented the White House from undertaking a formal strategy review. In March 2006, Congress appointed a bi-partisan panel, the Iraq Study Group, to make recommendations as to how the United States should proceed in Iraq, but its final report was not released until after the 2006 midterms.

In summer 2006, Democrats in Congress increased their public criticism of the war. In September 2006, with the midterm election less than two months away, polls found more than half of Americans believed the invasion of Iraq was a mistake. In November, the Democrats soundly defeated the Republicans, gaining a majority in both the House and Senate. Democrats largely attributed their victory to public dissatisfaction with the war in Iraq. The new Speaker of the House, Nancy Pelosi, expected the Democratic majority could force a drawdown of troops in Iraq by controlling funding for the American war effort and the Iraqi government.

The Surge

The calls from Democrats for a withdrawal from Iraq coincided with the primary recommendation of the Iraq Study Group. Despite the public and political expectation of a troop drawdown, President Bush chose to pursue another strategy of increasing the number of American troops in Iraq known as the "troop surge." After an election widely interpreted as a rebuke of the Bush administration's handling of the war, and with Democrats and some high-profile Republicans against an increase of troops in Iraq, Bush's decision was a major political risk. The White House actively sought the support of Sen. John McCain (R–AZ), who backed the surge and helped to argue for a troop increase. Bush's speeches shifted tone and indicated a spirit of bipartisanship. Bush also accepted the resignation of Sec. of Defense Donald Rumsfeld, who had been the target of intense criticism in the election campaign and had promised to resign if the Republicans lost control of either the House or the Senate. To replace Rumsfeld, Bush appointed former Director of Central Intelligence Robert Gates in December 2006. Gates was a far more conciliatory figure who focussed on building a better relationship with Congress and gaining bipartisan support for a continued U.S. presence in Iraq.

Despite continued criticism of a surge in Congress, notably from Speaker Pelosi and Sen. Barack Obama (D–IL), an increasing number of troops were deployed to Iraq from January through March 2007. Although the surge was designed to quell violence, the increase of troops and their expanding operations in Iraq resulted in an increase of violence. In another controversial move, made necessary by the heightened need for American troops, all units in Iraq had their tours extended from 12 to 15 months. This policy was extremely unpopular with military families in the United States. The extended tours, combined with the increase in violence, suggested the surge had caused the situation in Iraq to deteriorate further. The Republican caucus in Congress was breaking with the president and public support for the war reached its lowest point. In April 2007, both the House and Senate passed a bill that tied funding for the war to a requirement to begin withdrawing troops in October. Bush employed his presidential veto to reject the bill, and Congress eventually passed a bill providing the funds without a requirement for withdrawal. Bush's veto demonstrated he would continue with the surge despite congressional objections. In May 2007, Congress took the unusual step of passing a law requiring the U.S. commander in Iraq, Gen. David Petraeus, to return to Capitol Hill in September 2007 and testify regarding U.S. strategy in Iraq. Frustrated with their inability to control the president's strategy, this was an alternate way for Congress to attempt to influence the course of the war.

Petraeus returned to Washington, D.C., and testified before Congress. His testimony was mildly optimistic about the prospects for Iraq, buoyed by data showing attacks in Iraq had declined 50 percent from their pre-surge level. The troop surge, combined with a new American policy of targeting and killing individual insurgent leaders and the decision by a number of militant Sunni Iraqis to turn against al Qaeda terrorists in Anbar province and Baghdad contributed to the reduction of violence. The appointment of Petraeus and his frank testimony, combined with the declining violence in Iraq, succeeded in lessening criticism of the surge and taking some political pressure off Bush.

2008 Presidential Election

Iraq policies played a large role in defining candidates in the Republic and Democratic 2008 primaries. Republican candidates generally argued it was unwise to withdraw American troops from Iraq until violence had lessened further. Democratic candidates largely expected dissatisfaction with the war would propel a Democrat to the presidency, and most candidates promised to start withdrawing American troops. The last remaining Democratic contenders, senators Hillary Clinton and Barack Obama, promised to withdraw American troops from Iraq but to leave some troops to counter terrorist threats. During the presidential election campaign, Obama promised to withdraw U.S. combat troops within 16 months of his inauguration and to focus on Afghanistan. The Republican candi-

date, Sen. John McCain, expected American forces would withdraw by 2013 but refused to set a timetable for withdrawal. In November 2008, dissatisfaction with the Iraq War proved too much for McCain to overcome and contributed to Obama's victory.

In a surprising move in light of the Republican mismanagement of the Iraq War, Pres.-elect Barack Obama announced that Robert Gates would remain secretary of defense in his administration. Although some Obama supporters were critical of this decision, it demonstrated the general success of the 2007 Bush policy to increase troops in Iraq in order to quell violence, and Gates's success in gaining bipartisan support for a continued American presence in Iraq. In November 2008, the Iraqi Parliament ratified a status of forces agreement with the United States, requiring American troops to leave Iraqi cities by June 30, 2009, and to leave Iraq by the end of 2011.

The Iraq War serves as the defining event of the presidency of George W. Bush. The scandals of the war, including the faulty intelligence used to justify the invasion and the torture of Abu Ghraib, marked his administration as manipulative and unaccountable, while the sluggish rate with which the administration adapted policy to meet events in Iraq indicated a poorly managed bureaucracy. The lack of preparation and unexpected violence in Iraq thoroughly discredited the neoconservative proposition of improving the world by force of American military might. The number of casualties and the high cost of years of military operations were higher than expected, and resulted in the American public turning against a war they had supported when previously assured of its necessity and short duration. Voter dissatisfaction, fuelled by the Iraq War, reduced the Republican Party from controlling the House, Senate, and presidency in 2002 to controlling only the presidency by 2006. In 2008, the Democratic Party took control of the presidency in addition to the House and Senate.

Bibliography and Further Reading

Drogin, Bob. *Curveball: Spies, Lies, and the Con Man Who Caused a War.* New York: Random House, 2007.

Isikoff, Michael, and David Corn. *Hubris: The Inside Story of Spin, Scandal, and the Selling of the Iraq War.* New York: Crown Publishers, 2006.

Mann, Jim. *Rise of the Vulcans: The History of Bush's War Cabinet*. New York: Viking, 2004.

Packer, George. *The Assassins' Gate: America in Iraq*. New York: Farrar, Straus & Giroux, 2006.

Pillar, Paul R. "Intelligence, Policy, and the War in Iraq." *Foreign Affairs*, March/April 2006.

Ricks, Thomas E. *Fiasco: The American Military Adventure in Iraq*. New York: Penguin Press, 2006.

Woodward, Bob. *Plan of Attack*. New York: Simon & Schuster, 2004.

———. *State of Denial*. New York: Simon & Schuster, 2006.

———. *The War Within: A Secret White House History, 2006–2008*. New York: Simon & Schuster, 2008.

Timothy Andrews Sayle

LABOR

The American labor movement's purpose is to use the power of numbers—workers united in action—to democratize decision making at work and in government to achieve social justice. The American Federation of Labor-Congress of Industrial Organizations (AFL-CIO) has been a premier electioneering organization in American national politics for liberal Democrats, regularly turning out union members at higher rates than the general public and thereby accounting for a disproportionately high percentage of actual voters. Substantially reducing labor's political influence, however, is its badly faltering efforts to organize employees at their places of work in the last generation. In 2005, the AFL-CIO split apart when seven unions left to form the Change to Win (CTW) coalition, with CTW moving more aggressively to organize workers. Nevertheless, the two labor federations have so far been unsuccessful in their organizing attempts. In 2008, about 16 million workers belonged to unions. The return of unified Democratic control of the national government in 2009 may presage a revival in liberal reform that might help union organizers.

Labor and Political Development

The rise and diminution of organized labor's size and influence in American politics should be considered in the context of historical developments in American politics and society. The major explanations for labor's role in political life can be grouped by their emphasis on economic and institutional forces, situational factors like opportunities to form coalitions and organizing efforts, and ideological visions about the place of labor in American society. Some of the forces that have shaped the labor movement's long-term slide continue to operate today, including the changing nature and location of jobs, while others have offered unions potential advantage—for example, improved race relations and immigrant mobilization. Perhaps most important for union survival is whether liberals from the professional and business classes will again support union goals for employment and income security that, in recent years, have seemed incompatible with a globalizing and innovating economy.

The changing place and influence of unions in American politics can be seen in the declining rate of union membership—from 27.3 percent of the workforce in 1970 to 23 percent in 1980, 16.8 percent in 1988, 13.5 percent in 2000, to about 11 percent in 2008. The rate in the private sector is about 7.5 percent. Changes in the economic structure of the United States partly account for this trend because such changes affect patterns of employment. Unions have suffered huge membership losses in manufacturing since the 1970s as millions of jobs have disappeared while the potential for union organizing in the growing service industries has only begun to be tapped. However, such changes are far from the whole explanation for the shifting place of unions in America. The ability to organize workers depends on the institutional rules of employer-employee relations and business strategies, which, in turn, depend on the broader organization of American electoral politics and the leadership projects that animate those politics.

The national profile of union membership illustrates the changing contours of American party politics. Well into the 1970s, union membership was very high in the U.S. manufacturing region—which stretched from the Northeast to the Northwest—but very low in agricultural areas and in all sectors of the South. The regionalism of union membership was an outcome of the coalitional quality of the Democratic Party— Southern Democrats successfully shaped the National Labor Relations Act of 1935 to omit union rights for agricultural workers, perpetuated racial discrimination in private sector employment until the 1964 Civil Rights Act, enabled Southern legislatures to block union organization through the 1947 Taft-Hartley amendments to the NLRA, and denied public sector collective bargaining rights in the 1970s. During the civil rights revolution of the 1960s, white Southern voters began to shift rapidly to the Republican column in presidential elections, a trend that eventually spread to congressional and state elections in the 1980s and 1990s. Therefore, even though equal employment opportunity was established and the economy of the South was industrialized, low union membership in the South was maintained in the context of expanding social and business services sectors. Distinct regional differences in union membership continue in the twenty-first century.

The decline of union membership in the North was partly a result of the same regional disparity in party politics and labor policy that preserved the South as a nonunion employment arena in which private employers dominated. The movement of Northern factories to the South to escape union organization was an issue throughout the era. Moreover, firms based in the South that grew as the region's economy expanded sought to do business nationwide on a nonunion basis. Southern firms led a determined antiunion movement among national employers, which contributed to the formation of the Business Roundtable, the lobbying organization of top chief executive officers. One outcome of the successful

employers' movement was to hobble the administration of the national labor law by the National Labor Relations Board and to encourage the shift in policy to deregulation and welfare retrenchment. The Business Roundtable was instrumental in blocking labor law reform in Congress in 1978 and electing Ronald Reagan to the presidency in 1980; President Reagan appointed an outspoken leader of the antiunion movement to chair the NLRB in 1981. The antiunion movement also was very effective in defeating union organizations in meatpacking, garment manufacturing, mining, and elsewhere in the 1980s and 1990s. Finally, when foreign-based manufacturing firms began to invest in the United States in the 1980s, they also located in the nonunion states of the South. For example, Japanese and German auto companies established extensive nonunion operations in the United States to supply the U.S. market, which reduced the number of union jobs in the auto industry. Loss of (or failure to establish) union density made it much harder for unions to enforce industry-wide employment standards; such inability exacerbated competitive labor market conditions and placed increasing pressure on the contract terms in the unionized segment. Since the 1980s, manufacturing unions have engaged in defensive concessions bargaining. In 2007, in collective bargaining with the American auto companies, the United Auto Workers union chose to protect pay and benefits for its senior members and to abandon newly hired workers to market-rate (i.e., much lower) pay. The federal rescue of GM and Chrysler in early 2009 stipulated nonunion labor relations benchmarks for the American companies.

The American government structure framed the partisan politics of postwar economic development and the role of organized labor in the economy. The nationalizing qualities of labor reform of the New Deal were blunted by sectoral and subnational forces, especially in Southern legislatures and local governments. The weakening of Northern-based unions since the 1960s and their failure to penetrate the South undermined voter support for liberal Democrats and turned a number of Northern states into competitive arenas for Republican presidential and gubernatorial candidates in the 1970s and 1980s. Republican Party leaders capitalized on union weaknesses and managerial strength by adopting neo-liberal policies to deregulate labor markets, protect managerial authority in labor-management relations, and to press for international commercial and financial integration, all of which furthered the unions' troubles with declining membership.

Labor's Responses to Political Change Since the 1970s

The political problems of organized labor in the late twentieth and early twenty-first centuries were threefold. First, the Republican Party and the antiunion employers out-organized unions. Second, the Democratic Party changed because of the mass social movements of the 1960s and 1970s. Supporters of African American civil rights, Chicano rights, women's rights, gay rights, anti-imperialism, and the environment—these and others all found a home in the Democratic Party, turning it into a collection of reform factions of which unions were simply one (even if an especially resourceful one). Many traditional labor leaders felt threatened by the new movements' demands and became estranged from the New Democratic officeholders. Although the Democrats adopted a more socially liberal platform, the labor movement found itself sidelined by the Democrats' shift to neo-liberal economic strategies. Third, the economy changed in ways that required unionists to rethink their vision of social justice. The primary challenge was and is to demonstrate how unions are still relevant when laws are in place to protect civil rights at work and national economic borders are open.

Some argue that the key to a stronger liberal Democratic Party and union movement is the coming together of the movements and organized labor to agree on a new agenda for international justice. About a dozen unions have worked together since the 1970s independently of the AFL-CIO Executive Council to reweave the tattered fabric of their alliances with nonlabor liberals in such coalitions as the Progressive Alliance, the Citizen Labor Energy Coalition, the Central America Working Group, Jobs with Justice, and immigrants' rights groups. In contrast, top union leaders' responses to their declining influence were remarkably nonchalant until the 1980s. The AFL-CIO had one president, George

Meany, from 1955 to 1979; he was committed to Cold War liberalism and excoriated critics of U.S. foreign policy, including other union leaders. The AFL-CIO's organizational structure favored continuity of leadership and close relations with congressional Democrats rather than internal debate and reassessments of political strategies. Reagan's election motivated Meany's successor, Lane Kirkland, to search for new methods to bolster union influence on economic policy. Among these were an Organizing Institute, a public relations office for the labor movement, and a study of the transformation of work.

Labor Regroups, Twice

Kirkland's initiatives gained little traction in the larger political arena. Unions were battered in the workplace and Democrats offered little support. Although the AFL-CIO and the Clinton administration Labor Department worked well together on international labor standards, the administration's initiative for labor law reform was stillborn; it promoted trade and social reform policies that were anathema to organized labor. When the Republican Party won control of both the Senate and House of Representatives in 1994 for the first time since 1954, the crisis became acute for labor unions. A committee of 11 union leaders of the AFL-CIO launched the first-ever open campaign for the federation's presidency. The insurgents called themselves the New Voice campaign and elected John Sweeney in 1995. Sweeney's coalition then took over most of the top leadership positions, brought more people of color and women into the leadership, including former New Left unionists, and launched fresh initiatives to raise labor's profile in national political debates and in American government.

A significant theme in Sweeney's leadership was to recommit organized labor to a broad social reform mission, which led to new alliances with many nonlabor liberal groups, plus new links with gay and lesbian activists and support for immigration and immigrants' rights. The AFL-CIO achieved a few legislative victories in the late 1990s—including an increase in the minimum wage and defeat of fast-track trade authority and the Republican's TEAM Act (which would have allowed companies to form labor-management groups outside the collective-bargaining process). The AFL demonstrated that it could regain its footing as an electoral organization, contributing to Democratic gains in the congressional elections of 1998, 2000, and 2006, plus the presidential victory of Bill Clinton in 1996 and the popular vote majority for Al Gore in 2000. However, the AFL-CIO was not able to raise the rate of union membership, although some unions achieved success in that area. The collapse of effective union organizing was partly an outcome of weak enforcement by the NLRB of employee rights to unionize. In response, the AFL-CIO moved to gain union representation without the NLRB, first by launching pressure campaigns to convince employers to allow union recognition by the card-check method rather than an NLRB election and, second, by lobbying Congress to pass the Employee Free Choice Act (EFCA), which would require employers to recognize unions established by the card-check method. The failure of Sweeney to make much progress led to a new split in the labor movement— four unions formed the New Unity Partnership as a separate union organizing alliance. In 2005, these unions—eventually seven in all—quit the AFL-CIO to form the Change to Win coalition (CTW). CTW is an alliance of union leaders—a small executive committee with centralized decision-making authority— who are devoted to a strategy to increase union density in specific industries in order to increase workers' influence on wages and working conditions. The CTW industries are sectors whose products are largely not tradable (i.e., not much affected by international trade competition), such as home health care and hospitals, hotel and hospitality, trucking, construction, and farm labor and food processing. CTW is led by Andy Stern of the Service Employees International Union (SEIU), Sweeney's old union. While CTW leaders emphasize rank-and-file organizing campaigns, Stern has sought to make deals with employers in organizing campaigns and social reform. CTW tactics have created intense debates within the

SEIU and the broader labor movement. As the 2008 presidential election approached, the CTW abandoned its aversion to electoral action and rallied its members to support Barack Obama's candidacy.

Unions initially supported a variety of candidates in the presidential primaries, but the AFL-CIO and the CTW waged vigorous campaigns to elect Barack Obama; in November 2008, 65 percent of union members voted for the Democrat. The Steelworkers Union was especially energetic in urging its white male members to vote for Obama in Pennsylvania and Ohio. Both Obama and his vice president, Joseph Biden, were Senate sponsors of the Employee Free Choice Act; even before Obama's victory, the U.S. Chamber of Commerce and antiunion employers launched a public campaign against EFCA. With Obama in the White House, leaders of both the AFL-CIO and CTW are seeking to reunify the movement.

The Challenge of Labor for American Politics in the Twenty-First Century

Unions have often demonstrated their electoral skills and their capacity for innovative coalition building and lobbying. What remains is to convince liberal coalition partners in the Democratic Party that unions are critical to their agenda in the early twenty-first century. Many nonlabor middle-class voters have prospered in an economy that is deregulated, flexible, and dependent on high-end professional skills. The middle classes have benefited from cheap imports and low-wage services. Nonunion workers have benefited from the rights revolution. What alternative vision of a successful and just economy can union leaders offer to political allies to convince them that working-class organization is in their interests? Without a reformed institutional framework for labor relations, organized labor seems unlikely to regain the status and power that it once had in American society.

Bibliography and Further Reading

Battista, Andrew. *The Revival of Labor Liberalism*. Urbana: University of Illinois Press, 2008.

Dark, Taylor. *The Unions and the Democrats: An Enduring Alliance*. Ithaca, NY: Cornell University Press, 1999.

Fletcher, Bill, and Fernando Gapasin. *Solidarity Divided: The Crisis in Organized Labor and a New Path toward Social Justice.* Berkeley: University of California Press, 2008.

Milkman, Ruth. *L.A. Story: Immigrant Workers and the Future of the U.S. Labor Movement.* New York: Russell Sage Foundation, 2006.

Mishel, Lawrence, and Paula B. Voos, eds. *Unions and Economic Competitiveness.* Armonk, NY: Sharpe/Economic Policy Institute, 1992.

Moberg, David. "Dissent in the Ranks: SEIU Is the Nation's Fastest Growing Union—But at What Cost?" *In These Times,* April 10, 2008.

Schlozman, Kay Lehman, Sidney Verba, and Henry E. Brady. "Civic Participation and the Equality Problem." In *Civic Engagement in American Democracy*, edited by Theda Skocpol and Morris P. Fiorina, 427–460. Washington, D.C.: Brookings Institution/Russell Sage Foundation, 1999.

Teixeira, Ruy, and Joel Rogers. *Why the White Working Class Still Matters.* New York: Basic Books, 2000.

Weiler, Paul C. *Governing the Workplace.* Cambridge, MA: Harvard University Press, 1990.

Weir, Margaret. "States, Race, and the Decline of New Deal Liberalism." *Studies in American Political Development* 19, no. 2 (Fall 2005): 157–172.

Stephen Amberg

LIBERALISM

American liberalism after 1976 was a political ideology and political movement that advocated active government in order to promote liberty, equality, and security for all citizens. As a political ideology, liberalism favored active use of the legislative, fiscal, regulatory, diplomatic, military, and other powers of government for a variety of purposes: to regulate the economy; provide social welfare; ensure an inclusive and tolerant political community; protect the natural environment; and guarantee national security. Liberals advocated active government within the framework of individual rights and representative institutions inherited from the classical liberalism of the eighteenth century and expanded by the democratic liberalism of the nineteenth and twentieth centuries. As a political movement, liberalism competed for power through the Democratic Party and a variety of allied organizations, including interest groups and think tanks. While most liberals were Democrats, the Democratic Party was a large and diverse party in which liberals competed for influence with moderates (or centrists) and some conservatives. Among the most important liberal interest groups were labor unions, civil rights and civil liberties organizations, women's groups, and environmental groups. Influential liberal think tanks included the Economic Policy Institute, the Center on Budget and Policy Priorities, and the Center for American Progress.

During much of the twentieth century, liberalism was the ascendant or dominant public philosophy and political movement in the United States. It was born and rose to influence in the Progressive Era (ca. 1900–1917), became the dominant approach to government during the New Deal (1933–1941), and revived its energy and power in the Great Society period (1964–1968). Liberal ideas and movements varied considerably across the Progressive, New Deal, and Great Society eras, but in all three periods liberals pursued social reform, state building, and political inclusion. During these periods, and others like World War II (1941–1945), liberalism deeply shaped American society and politics by using the authority of democratic government to regulate economic activity, build a welfare state, promote a strong labor movement and industrial democracy, incorporate women and racial minorities into full citizenship, conserve resources and protect the environment, and create both a strong military and international institutions to ensure the security of the nation. Throughout these decades, liberals were sometimes divided, their power was always constrained, and their vision and accomplishments were often limited. For instance, both the civil rights movement and the pressures of ideological competition in the Cold War were needed to finally commit liberalism to the cause of racial equality. Nevertheless, over the first seven decades of the twentieth century, liberalism more often than not set the course of American political development. Then it fell from power. The last three decades of that century, and the early years of the twenty-first century, were largely dominated by the resurgent conservatism of the Republican Party and its allies. In these years, liberalism experienced decline, transformation, and, perhaps, revival.

The Decline of Liberalism

Liberalism's fall from power began in the late 1960s, when the Democratic Party's success in national elections waned. Between 1968 and 2004 inclusive, the Democratic Party won only 3 of 10 presidential elections—1976, 1992, and 1996. The Democrats maintained majority control of Congress through 1980, but lost control of the Senate between 1981 and 1987 and then lost majority status in both houses of Congress from 1995 until 2007. The decline of Democratic success in national elections after 1968 resulted in a decline of liberal influence over government and public policy.

Liberal influence also receded within the Democratic Party following the crushing defeat of the party's liberal presidential nominee, South Dakota senator George McGovern, in 1972. Thereafter, the increasingly conservative climate of national politics and the efforts of moderate and neoconservative Democrats to expand their influence in the party allowed centrists to dominate the presidential nominating process of the Democratic Party. The two Democrats elected to the White House between 1968 and 2004—James Earl (Jimmy) Carter in 1976 and William Jefferson (Bill) Clinton in 1992 and 1996—were moderates or centrists who combined generally progressive social views with fiscal conservatism and a readiness to curb the regulatory and welfare functions of government. Although Carter and Clinton could claim liberal initiatives and accomplishments in office, their willingness to accommodate conservative views and business interests often antagonized liberals.

The waning strength of Democrats in national elections and of liberals in the Democratic Party reflected their declining appeal to the public. The percentage of Americans who identified themselves as Democrats fell from 52 in 1974 to 47 in 1994; the percentage who identified themselves as liberals fell from 21 in 1974 to 14 in 1994, according to American National Election Studies data (note, however, that the percentages fluctuated from year to year in both

decades). But public opinion is as much an effect as a cause in politics, and the faltering public image of liberalism had many sources.

The decline of liberalism was, in part, a product of the upheavals of the 1960s. The passage of the Civil Rights Act of 1964 initiated a realignment of Southern whites from the Democratic to the Republican party that was central to the decline of Democratic presidential and congressional majorities and thus of liberal influence in government and public policy. The urban disorders, racial tensions (over school busing and affirmative action), and culture wars (over abortion, gay rights, and other issues) of the 1960s and later years also weakened the Democratic Party and liberalism among Northern white voters. The Vietnam War deeply divided and weakened both liberals and the larger Democratic Party for years; indeed, the divided liberals and Democrats paid a price in public support both for escalating the war and for trying to end it.

The social and political upheavals of the 1960s were not the end of liberalism's troubles. The recession of 1974–1975 marked the end of the long post–World War II era of stable economic growth, and the ravages of stagflation—the conjunction of high unemployment and inflation—during the Carter administration did much to undermine support for liberal economic, labor, and social welfare policies. The continued decline of unionism (which had begun in the mid-1950s) after that recession was also highly damaging to liberalism, as unions had for decades provided a significant share of the votes, money, activists, and lobbying skill that had sustained liberal electoral and legislative success.

Finally, liberals and Democrats declined in the last third of the twentieth century because conservatives and Republicans competed more effectively in elections, public debates, and legislative battles. Conservatives and Republicans developed and parlayed many advantages in political competition: superior financial resources; greater political unity; more effective campaign technologies; a more elaborate and coordinated infrastructure of think tanks, fundraising organizations, lobbying groups, and media outlets; more active social movements, especially among Christian conservatives; and more ideologically confident and assertive leaders. Such advantages enabled conservatives to define liberalism, for many voters, as racial favoritism, elitist social engineering, fiscal and regulatory excess, moral and cultural laxity, and military weakness. Liberalism became, as the Republican presidential candidate George H. W. Bush called it during the 1988 election campaign, the "L word." When Bush and other Republicans relentlessly attacked the Democratic presidential candidate in that campaign, the moderate Massachusetts governor Michael Dukakis, as a liberal and a "card-carrying member" of the American Civil Liberties Union, Dukakis refused to defend liberalism and asserted that the election was about competence—not ideology.

The decline of liberalism never amounted to total collapse or complete loss of influence, however. Moderate Democratic presidents at times advanced liberal goals, like Clinton's expansion of "earnings support" for low-wage workers through increases in the minimum wage and the Earned Income Tax Credit. Democrats maintained majority control of Congress for most of the years before 1995, developed more liberal voting records from the late 1970s on, and enacted liberal policies like family and medical leave for employees and expanded health insurance for children. Organized liberal groups like union members, minorities, women, and environmentalists retained sufficient clout to defeat some appointments, laws, regulations, and ballot propositions. Above all, liberals in and out of government retained substantial defensive power that allowed them to preserve many major liberal gains that conservatives had targeted, including Social Security. In addition, during the last quarter of the twentieth century, public attitudes continued to move in a liberal direction on many cultural issues—gay rights and gender equality among them. Still, liberalism's fall from power after the late 1960s was steep, long-lasting, and consequential.

The Transformation of Liberalism

Liberalism underwent transformation as well as decline in the late twentieth century. As a product of the New Deal and the Cold War, mid-century liberalism emphasized management of the economy, provision of social welfare, and containment of communist power abroad, and drew support from the working and lower middle classes, ethnic and religious minorities, urban and social reformers, and the unions, fraternal associations, civil liberties groups, and reform organizations that represented them. Then the new social movements of the 1960s—the civil rights, antiwar, women's, and environmental movements—enlarged and altered both the issue agenda and the support base of liberalism. Racial and gender equality, an end to the Vietnam War, protection of the natural environment, and a more participatory democracy became leading liberal issues and priorities. Their supporters among newly enfranchised Southern blacks, women, environmentalists, educated upper-middle-class reformers, and the many new civil rights, feminist, and public interest groups that they formed, became key liberal constituencies and organizations. The grafting of this New Politics liberalism, as it was called, onto the older New Deal–Cold War liberalism was full of tensions and conflicts, but liberalism proved capable of expanding its ideals of liberty, equality, and security to incorporate the varied concerns and demands of its broadened constituency.

This transformation entailed two further changes. First, as the New Politics movement of the 1960s gradually split apart, liberalism became a fragmented ideology and political movement, divided into four segments: New Deal liberalism, civil rights or multicultural liberalism, public interest liberalism, and neoliberalism. New Deal liberalism focused on the use of government authority to manage the economy and provide social welfare, and was chiefly supported by organized labor and less well off citizens. Civil rights or multicultural liberalism emphasized the use of government power to ensure equal civil and political rights, economic opportunities, and cultural recognition for groups that suffered discrimination and disadvantage; it drew support from racial and ethnic minorities, women, gay men and lesbians, the disabled, and their political organizations. Public interest liberalism stressed the use of government authority to promote broad public interests in a healthy natural environment, safe consumer products, and an open and accountable democracy; it was supported by environmental, consumer, and government reform groups and their well-educated and professional members. Finally, neoliberalism urged government to promote economic growth by curbing expensive social programs and burdensome regulations and supporting high technology firms and entrepreneurs, and found support among affluent suburbanites and some business sectors.

These variants of late-twentieth-century liberalism were not in a state of war, but they did have serious family squabbles. The fragmentation of liberalism weakened it in the face of ideological and political competition.

Second, as a result of its transformation, liberalism's once-strong connections to two great currents of American politics, populism and nationalism, were attenuated. Between the 1930s and 1950s, liberalism and the Democratic Party derived legitimacy and power from their public image as the ideology and the party that represented "the people" against powerful interests and elites and that promoted national interests, unity, and strength against parochial groups and external enemies. In the last few decades of the twentieth century, the changed issue agenda and social composition of liberalism and the Democratic Party eroded their populist and nationalist credentials and thus their legitimacy and power.

The Revival of Liberalism?

The decline of liberalism had consequences for the direction of public authority and policy in the last quarter of the twentieth century and the early years of the twenty-first. Chief among these consequences, however they are judged, were a sharp drop in union membership and power, the stagnation or decline of wages for many workers, the fraying of the social safety net, widening inequalities of income and wealth, the impairment of regulatory agencies and policies, and a less progressive tax code. The decline of liberalism also had consequences for the larger pattern of American political development in the twentieth cen-

tury. Liberalism had generated or guided three major features of that development: periodic economic and social reforms; growth of the roles and authority of national government; and inclusion of new or formerly excluded groups into the political community. Its decline meant that these political developments were either halted, stalled, or redirected—at least until liberalism could manage to revive itself.

In fact, efforts to resuscitate liberalism were already under way by the mid-1970s. Many liberals sought to diagnose the sources of liberal decline, to revive liberal ideas and policies, to strengthen liberalism's institutional infrastructure, and to devise more effective political strategies. From these efforts emerged new journals, Web sites, and magazines, like *The American Prospect*; new think tanks, such as the Economic Policy Institute; and new political organizations, like the Campaign for America's Future. Less well-known were the many organizations—the Progressive Alliance, Citizen Labor Energy Coalition, National Labor Committee, and Jobs with Justice—established by labor unions to rebuild and modernize the labor-liberal coalition and thereby fortify liberal politics. Labor leaders played a key, though little understood and appreciated, role in the many and varied efforts to revive liberalism. Even the shift of power at the nation's labor federation, the AFL-CIO, in 1995 was motivated by the desire of many unions and labor leaders to revive liberalism as well as unionism.

Perhaps these and other attempts to strengthen liberal ideas and politics had some effect. In the five presidential elections from 1992 through 2008, Democratic candidates (if relatively moderate ones) won the popular vote four times; only in 2004 did the Republican candidate win both the popular vote and the Electoral College vote. (Although Vice President Gore won the popular vote in 2000, he lost the Electoral College vote following a crucial Supreme Court decision.) The terrorist attacks on the United States on September 11, 2001, and the forceful response of Pres. George W. Bush allowed his conservative administration and party to retain power in 2004. But the increasingly unpopular war in Iraq, crises in the housing and financial markets, and a looming recession allowed Democrats to regain majority control of Congress in 2006 and to win the White House in 2008. These Democratic victories created the possibility, but not a guarantee, of a renewal of American liberalism.

Bibliography and Further Reading

American National Election Studies. "The ANES Guide to Public Opinion and Electoral Behavior." University of Michigan, Center for Political Studies. http://www.electionstudies.org/nesguide/nesguide.htm (accessed December 29, 2009).

Baer, Kenneth S. *Reinventing Democrats: The Politics of Liberalism from Reagan to Clinton.* Lawrence: University Press of Kansas, 2000.

Ball, Terrence, and Richard Dagger. *Political Ideologies and the Democratic Ideal.* New York: Pearson Longman, 2008.

Gerring, John. *Party Ideologies in America, 1828–1996.* Cambridge: Cambridge University Press, 1998.

Patterson, James T. *Restless Giant: The United States from Watergate to Bush v. Gore.* New York: Oxford University Press, 2005.

Shafer, Byron E. *Partisan Approaches to Postwar American Politics.* New York: Chatham House Publishers, 1998.

Starr, Paul. *Freedom's Power: The True Force of Liberalism.* New York: Basic Books, 2007.

Taylor, Andrew J. "The Ideological Development of the Parties in Washington, 1947–1994." *Polity* 29, no. 2 (winter 1996): 273–292.

Wilentz, Sean. *The Age of Reagan: A History, 1974–2008.* New York: HarperCollins, 2008.

Andrew Battista

MARSHALL, THURGOOD

1908–1993
Supreme Court Justice

Thurgood Marshall, the first African American to sit on the U.S. Supreme Court, spent much of his life at the center of important legal and political battles over racial issues and civil liberties. After graduating from Howard University School of Law in 1933 and joining the Legal Defense and Educational Fund of the National Association for the Advancement of Colored People, Marshall became among the most famous and important lawyers in the nation—winning numerous cases that struck down segregation and other forms of racial discrimination. His most significant triumph came in *Brown v. Board of Education of Topeka (I)*, 347 U.S. 483 (1954), in which the Supreme Court struck down legally segregated public schools.

Marshall's judicial career began when John F. Kennedy appointed him to the U.S. Court of Appeals for the Second Circuit in 1961. Lyndon B. Johnson named Marshall solicitor general of the United States in 1965 and two years later nominated him to the Supreme Court. A strong believer in racial integration and using law as an instrument for reform on behalf of the disadvantaged, Marshall found himself somewhat isolated as American politics, and the Supreme Court, moved in a more conservative direction during the late 1970s and 1980s.

Judicial Philosophy

Whereas conservatives upheld the deciding of cases based on the "original intent" of the Constitution, Marshall staunchly insisted that the Constitution could usefully address—and adapt to—changing circumstances. "I am constantly left, on balance, unable to determine exactly what was intended," he once said, referring to originalist ideas that the Founders' intent was the primary source of the Constitution's meaning. (Quoted in Tushnet 1997, 191) Marshall, indeed, thoroughly resisted original intent because he viewed the Constitution as an initially deeply flawed document that supported slavery when proposed and adopted. In a 1987 speech marking the bicentennial of the Constitution, Marshall called it "defective from the start, requiring several amendments, a civil war, and momentous social transformation to attain the system of constitutional government, and its respect for the individual freedoms and human rights, that we hold as fundamental today." (Quoted in Tushnet 2001, 282) Believing that "those who refused to acquiesce in outdated notions of 'liberty,' 'justice,' and 'equality,'" had advanced liberty more than had the Founding Fathers, Marshall contended "the true miracle was not the birth of the Constitution, but its life."

Marshall strongly maintained that the courts had an obligation to ensure equal treatment of all citizens. For too long, he suggested, justice had depended on race and class, with wealthy whites receiving treatment different from that meted out to nonwhites and the poor. During his many years as a lawyer, he once recalled, he had routinely seen "first hand evidence of a frightening attitude by those who make and administer the laws—that there are people in the United States that just don't matter." To Marshall, the accused often did not receive fair trials, people were arrested without charges (or on trumped-up charges), and too many in custody had been victims of police brutality or offered coerced confessions. Marshall became famous for using vivid anecdotes from his extensive encounters with racial or class discrimination to appeal to colleagues to base their ruling on the context of the case more than on legal precedent. These stories, Justice Sandra Day O'Connor later observed, led her and others "to respond not only to the persuasiveness of legal argument but also to the power of moral truth." (Quoted in Ball 204)

Civil Rights for African Americans

Marshall stood with a liberal majority during his early years on the Court, but from the mid-1970s through his retirement in 1991 the Court moved in a more conservative direction as a result of several appointments made by Republican presidents Richard Nixon, Ronald Reagan, and George H. W. Bush. Indeed, Marshall spent most of his tenure on the Court angrily firing off dissents from majority opinions on a host of issues, including civil rights for African Americans.

Marshall believed that the courts had played an integral and crucial role in advancing racial equality during the 1950s and 1960s, but the conservative turn left him disillusioned and fearful that some of the gains he had fought for were in danger of being rolled back. Marshall sometimes even questioned whether some of his fellow justices were racist. Certainly, Marshall felt that most of his colleagues were woefully ignorant of the conditions facing African Americans. "What do they know about Negroes?" he bluntly asked in 1990. Marshall also thought his colleagues mistakenly applied abstract notions of "color blind" equality and opportunity to a world where racism was still endemic. He regularly told the story of how he had once met an African American railroad worker who told him he "had never been in any city in the United States where he had to put his hand up

in front of his face to find out he was a Negro." (Quoted in Tushnet 1997, 116)

Marshall's belief in the persistence of racism shaped his thinking on affirmative action, one of the most controversial battles of the 1970s and 1980s. At the heart of the debate was the question of whether race could be taken into account in decisions about education, employment, or other areas. Citing Marshall's own work in the *Brown* case, the equal protection clause of Amendment XIV, and the Civil Rights Act of 1964, conservatives claimed that it could not. Marshall and other liberals saw no contradiction, however, and maintained such considerations were valid. To Marshall, affirmative action constituted a new means to achieve his longtime goal of equality. Although he, too, was troubled by race-conscious thinking in its most insistent forms, Marshall saw affirmative action as a temporary necessity that would help make up for generations of discriminatory policies by governments, schools, and employers. The government, he argued, had to permit more aggressive efforts to open up opportunities for African Americans and others—simply saying that discrimination was illegal was insufficient.

The Court first confronted affirmative action in *Regents of University of California v. Bakke*, 438 U.S. 265 (1978). A California medical school maintained separate admission standards and reserved 16 places in a class of 100 for "disadvantaged" students, most of whom were African Americans. Allan Bakke, a white student, claimed he had been discriminated against when the school denied him admission despite his having higher test scores than some African American applicants. The Court struck down the use of rigid quotas in admission decisions but allowed race to be considered as one factor in those decisions. Although he supported the latter policy, Marshall viewed *Bakke* as a setback.

Over the next 13 years the Court would confront affirmative action 10 more times. Much to the disappointment of conservatives, affirmative action did not disappear as the Court upheld some form of the policy in 7 of the 10 cases. Conservatives won a few battles, however, and Marshall became alarmed over the Court's narrowing of the circumstances in which

Thurgood Marshall sits with Pres. Lyndon Johnson on August 21, 1967, following Marshall's appointment to the Supreme Court. Marshall believed strongly that it was incumbent on the courts to ensure equal treatment of all citizens, and his support of affirmative action policies and his opposition to the death penalty were illustrative of this view. Although Marshall's early years on the Court were marked by liberal successes, by the time of his retirement, he had begun to despair of the rightward shift the Court had taken in the wake of appointments by Republican presidents from Richard Nixon to George H. W. Bush. (Keystone/Getty Images)

affirmative action could be applied. In *Wygant v. Jackson Board of Education*, 476 U.S. 267 (1986), the Court ruled that school districts could not take race into account to keep African American teachers while firing more senior white instructors. In *Wards Cove Packing Co. v. Atonio*, 490 U.S. 642 (1989), the Court ruled that a high number of one race or another in certain job classifications did not, by itself, constitute discrimination. In *Richmond v. J. A. Croson, Co.*, 488 U.S. 469 (1989), the Court declared that a program in Richmond, Virginia, to award 30 percent of the city's business contracts to minority-owned

firms over five years was illegal unless an individual contractor could prove that he or she had been discriminated against in the past. Awarding contracts to make up for a general history of discrimination, the Court announced, was unconstitutional. Marshall characterized the Court's rationale "exceedingly myopic" given that the city had excluded African American-owned firms in the past.

Civil Liberties

Marshall believed passionately in the need to protect individual civil liberties, especially those of the marginalized. He upheld the right to privacy, including a woman's right to choose an abortion, and viewed the 1976 Hyde Amendment, which forbade the use of federal Medicaid funds to pay for abortions for poor women, as profoundly unjust. Indigent women deserved (and had) the same rights as the wealthy, Marshall insisted. The only justice of his era to have defended someone accused of a capital crime, Marshall described the death penalty as "morally unacceptable." Noting that most of those sentenced to death were poor and/or nonwhite, he also denounced it as an arbitrary punishment. His conservative colleagues, however, disagreed, and the Court affirmed the death penalty in 1976 after it had struck it down four years earlier. During the next 15 years, Marshall was usually in the minority as the Court expanded police powers and restricted rights of the accused. Similarly, Marshall supported few limitations on speech and held to a strict separation between church and state. Here, too, Marshall grew dismayed at the conservative swing. "This Court has gone to pot," he declared near the end of his career. (Quoted in Ball 380)

Marshall's pessimism was overstated. By the early 1990s, the Court had moved away from the liberal thrust of the 1960s, but important victories from that era remained in place, albeit sometimes in weakened form. When Marshall died in 1993, liberals hailed him as a symbol of the ability of government to ameliorate social problems and as a defender of civil liberties. Conservatives, on the other hand, saw Marshall as embodying a judicial philosophy that they believed had contributed to the social and moral decay of the nation.

Bibliography and Further Reading

Ball, Howard. *A Defiant Life: Thurgood Marshall and the Persistence of Racism in America.* New York: Crown, 1998.

Davis, Michael D., and Hunter R. Clark. *Thurgood Marshall: Warrior at the Bar, Rebel on the Bench.* New York: Citadel Press, 1994.

Rowan, Carl T. *Dream Makers, Dream Breakers: The World of Justice Thurgood Marshall.* Boston: Little, Brown, 1993.

Tushnet. Mark V. *Making Constitutional Law: Thurgood Marshall and the Supreme Court, 1961–1991.* New York: Oxford University Press, 1997.

Tushnet. Mark V., ed. *Thurgood Marshall: His Speeches, Writings, Arguments Opinions, and Reminiscences.* Chicago: Lawrence Hill Books, 2001.

Williams, Juan. *Thurgood Marshall: American Revolutionary.* New York: Random House, 1998.

Timothy N. Thurber

NADER, RALPH

born 1934
Activist and Presidential Candidate

Ralph Nader, who came to symbolize the campaigns for consumer empowerment and participatory democracy that began in the 1960s, ran in each of the presidential races from 1996 to 2008. His political career illustrates the effectiveness of well-directed lobbying and the constraints facing independents and minor party candidates. He has been praised as a vigorous campaigner and denounced as a willful electoral "spoiler."

Advocacy

Born into an immigrant Lebanese American family in Winsted, a small town in Connecticut, Nader graduated from Princeton in 1955 and Harvard Law School in 1958. In 1964, Nader moved to Washington, D.C., to work as an aide for Assistant Sec. of Labor Daniel Patrick Moynihan in the Kennedy and Johnson administrations. Nader came to the public eye when he published *Unsafe at Any Speed*, an indictment of the American automobile industry, in 1965. Efforts by General Motors to find evidence that might discredit him prompted Nader to bring a lawsuit alleging "invasion of privacy." Against this background, he became widely known as an advocate for consumer empowerment and, at the same time, a critic of both government corruption and what he regarded as corporate greed. In

1971, Nader established Public Citizen, an advocacy group that brought together the various campaigning organizations that he and his supporters had created and built. Their focus included safety, health, environmental, and antitrust issues as well as the need for more open forms of government. Nader's campaigning is said to have prompted the recall of millions of defective motor vehicles and the passage of at least eight federal consumer protection laws. These include the National Traffic and Motor Vehicle Safety Act of 1966 and the Safe Drinking Water Act of 1974 as well as legislative reforms regulating conditions in coal mines, meatpacking and poultry production, and addressing the dangers posed by gas pipelines and the radiation emissions generated by televisions. He has also been credited with the creation or reform of federal government agencies such as the Occupational Safety and Health Administration, the Environmental Protection Agency, the Consumer Product Safety Commission, and the Federal Trade Commission. His calls for more open forms of government laid the groundwork for the Freedom of Information Act of 1974.

Political Thinking

Nader's political thinking and the strategies he used as both a consumer advocate and political campaigner have drawn, at least in part, upon populist themes rooted in his youthful experiences in New England town meetings as well as concepts of reinvigorated citizenship. Nader ties his commitment to popular participation in the policy process to a stress on the ways in which markets have failed to deliver optimum outcomes, an emphasis on the responsibilities of government, and a critique of the larger corporations. His thinking incorporates some of the ideas popularized by John Kenneth Galbraith—for instance, the ways in which advertising creates artificial wants. However, it has also drawn upon the progressive tradition, the concept of a managerial revolution, and the critiques of elite rule that were propounded by writers such as C. Wright Mills in *The Power Elite*. From Nader's perspective, those who manage and direct the large corporations and monopolies not only control the flow of income and the stock of wealth and neglect the public good but also hold disproportionate political power. The citizen is thereby denied representation.

Taken together, these strands have shaped and structured the character of Nader's activism from the 1960s onward. In his early campaigning for automobile safety, he maintained that whatever an individual driver's "fault" might be in losing control of a car, car companies should nevertheless bear much more responsibility because of their failure to construct "a crash-worthy car." During the 1970s, when he led Public Citizen, he brought calls for corporate responsibility and a commitment to consumer protection together with a broader agenda that included an emphasis on open government and freedom of information, sustainable energy development and usage, environmental protection, and health care reform. By 1992, Nader was offering a "Democracy Toolbox" that included calls for term limits, the extended public financing of election campaigns, referendums to recall public officials, measures that would offer the public greater access to information, reforms to give shareholders more control over the companies and pension funds in which they had invested or saved, and the opening up of the legal system to those without funds.

He and those who worked with him (dubbed "Nader's Raiders") were also tactically astute. Nader quickly grasped the publicity value of congressional hearings and the need for lobbying techniques that were structured around the realities of congressional life: "How do you get a key member of Congress who can lever other members of Congress to do the right thing on this issue? . . . you often beat them on weekends. You see, they stop working Friday at 5:00 P.M. And it's on weekends that you really make the difference." (Academy of Achievement)

In the foreign policy arena, Nader has spoken of "waging peace," attacked corporate globalization, criticized trade liberalization policies, and called for the reorientation of institutions such as the World Bank and the International Monetary Fund so as to combat "global infectious diseases." At times, he seems to be speaking in isolationist language; at other times, he talks of promoting democratic visions, defending the rights of indigenous peoples, and crusading for a more rational and egalitarian use of the world's resources.

Presidential Candidate, 1996 and 2000

Nader first ran as a presidential candidate in 1996—although earlier efforts had been made to draft him and he had allowed his name to go forward as a write-in candidate in some 1992 Democratic Party primaries. In 1996, he was nominated by various states' Green parties but ran only a limited campaign. He declined contributions and refused to advertise or build a campaign organization. He committed himself to spend only $5,000, a move that enabled him to avoid Federal Election Commission (FEC) reporting requirements

Nader's 2000 campaign had much greater substance. He was formally put into nomination at a nominating convention organized by the Association of State Green Parties in Denver. Some questioned his relationship with the Greens, arguing that he lost credibility by tying his fortunes to those of a minor party. For their part, some Green activists saw Nader as a representative of "old" class-based politics. They pointed to his seeming neglect of issues such as race, gender, and sexuality.

In his acceptance speech at Denver, Nader acknowledged the consequences of "environmental devastation" but also sought to reposition Green politics in terms of the broader populist goals that he championed. Much of the speech was directed against large corporations and inequalities of both wealth and power. He stressed the importance of maintaining "the commonwealth of assets that the people of the United States already own" and resisting what he depicted as the encroachments of big business. He invoked such overarching ideals as community and self-reliance.

Nader, who drew crowds of up ten thousand, ran a professional and well-organized campaign. In contrast to 1996, he established a formal campaign committee, employed paid organizers, and raised funds. Commentators suggested that Nader's principal goal was to secure 5 percent of the vote, thereby winning federal funding for the party and beginning the process of placing it on the political map. It was a realistic target—particularly given the factional fights and fragmentation of the Reform Party, which had in 1992 seemed capable of making an electoral breakthrough. Nader may also have had hopes of shifting the political agenda in the way that Reform candidate Ross Perot had done. Perot's 1992 run for the White House ensured that the major party candidates addressed issues such as the federal budget deficit.

Nader and his running mate, Winona LaDuke, a rights activist for indigenous peoples, secured a place on the ballot in 43 states and the District of Columbia. However, from September onward, Nader began to campaign with particular vigor in the battleground states where support for Republican candidate George Bush and Democratic candidate Al Gore was almost evenly divided. Nader may have been bidding for long-term influence, but such campaign decisions led to accusations that he was simply a "spoiler." Some concerned Democrats and Greens established "trading" arrangements whereby those in the battleground states could avert a Republican victory by voting for Al Gore while a Democratic voter in a state where the outcome was certain would, in return, support Nader.

Although Nader only secured 2.74 percent of the popular vote, far short of the 5 percent threshold for FEC funding, the 97,488 votes that he won in Florida were widely seen as pivotal. (The Nader vote was also greater than the electoral margin between Bush and Gore in seven other states.) Despite Nader's denials and claims by his supporters that the campaign had won the backing of nonvoters rather than registered Democrats, embittered Democrats believed that he handed the presidential election to George W. Bush.

Had Nader not run, it was said, many of those votes would have been cast for Al Gore and he would have been assigned Florida's 25 Electoral College votes, thereby giving the White House to the Democrats.

The 2004 Campaign

The close character of the 2000 contest led to fears that Nader's candidacy would again deny the Democrats victory in 2004. Commentators also suggested that although the 2000 campaign might have strengthened the Greens, it had cost Nader his credibility as a campaigner.

Nonetheless, despite pleas from former backers and some prominent Democrats, Nader submitted a program, Spirit of the Common Good, to the chairpersons of the Democratic and Republican parties at the end of October 2003 and sought a response to the issues addressed in it. Judging that their responses were inadequate, Nader announced that he would again stand for election. However, this time, Nader ran as an independent, calling for the "responsible withdrawal" of troops from Iraq over a six-month period, a system of health insurance modelled after that of Canada, and the provision of a guaranteed living wage for all workers.

The campaign and the results disappointed. Efforts to secure the Green Party's endorsement failed. Nader appeared on just 35 ballots, secured limited funding, and won only 0.4 percent of the vote— less than one-sixth of his 2000 total. At most, Nader had a marginal impact on the Democratic campaign.

Some commentators considered Nader's showing to be the death-knell for him and for hopes of building a progressive political movement His announcement that he would seek the presidency again in 2008 did little to change such judgments. Others, particularly those who emphasize his lobbying work, have offered a much more positive interpretation. According to Dennis Kucinich, the Ohio representative who sought the Democratic Party's presidential nomination in both 2004 and 2008, Nader's career has illustrated the extent to which the individual citizen can reshape the public policy process. Although Nader's detractors would not accept such interpretations, they would concede that his campaigns, particularly those conducted during his early political life, contributed to the growth of consumer rights, added to expectations of democratic government, and popularized a more complex understanding of citizenship. As his career progressed, he increasingly offered a vision that represented a structured ideological alternative in an era often defined by conservatism and faith in markets.

Bibliography and Further Reading

Academy of Achievement. "Ralph Nader: Consumer Crusader." http://www.achievement.org/ autodoc/page/nad0bio-1 (accessed May 3, 2008).

Berg, John. "Spoiler or Builder? The Effect of Ralph Nader's 2000 Campaign on the U.S. Greens." In *The State of the Parties: The Changing Role of Contemporary American Parties,* 4th edition, edited by John C. Green and Rick Farmer, 323–336. Lanham, MD: Rowman & Littlefield, 2003.

Burden, Barry C. "Ralph Nader's Campaign Strategy in the 2000 U.S. Presidential Election." *American Politics Research* 33, no. 5 (2005): 672–699.

Martin, Justin. *Nader: Crusader, Spoiler, Icon*. New York: Basic Books, 2003.

Nader, Ralph. "Acceptance Statement of Ralph Nader, for the Association of State Green Parties Nomination for President of the United States, Denver, Colorado, June 25, 2000." http://www.ratical.org/co-globalize/ RalphNader/062500.html (accessed October 24, 2009).

———. *Crashing the Party: How to Tell the Truth and Still Run for President*. New York: Thomas Dunne Books, 2002.

The Nader Page. "Ralph Nader: Biographical Information—The Essential Nader." http://www.nader.org/enbio.html (accessed October 23, 2009).

Shane, Scott. "The 2004 Election: The Independent; Nader Is Left with Fewer Votes, and Friends, after '04 Race. *New York Times*, November 6, 2004. http://select.nytimes.com/search/restricted/article?res =F20F16FF39580C758CDDA80994DC404482 (accessed April 3 2007).

Silverstein, Ken. "Candidate Nader." *Mother Jones,* July/August 2000. http://www.motherjones.com/ news/feature/2000/07/nader.html (accessed April 2, 2007).

Edward Ashbee

NATIONAL ENDOWMENT FOR THE ARTS

The establishment of the National Endowment for the Arts (NEA) grew out of a Cold War political ideology of contrasting visions. An effort to counterbalance the militarism of the Cold War era, the NEA was the result of Pres. John F. Kennedy's commitment to celebrating and reaffirming a democratic political philosophy that showcased American free will and promise of freedom through creative expression. Such support for free artistic expression would be in stark contrast to the repression of unapproved art by Communist regimes. In addition to disseminating the underlying democratic political ideals of American culture abroad, a federally funded arts program served an important domestic role, as public art projects exposed the citizenry to a variety of visions and improved the quality of life for everyday Americans.

Although Kennedy did not live to see the creation of a federal arts program, the NEA would be established by his successor, Pres. Lyndon B. Johnson, as part of the Great Society on September 29, 1965. The government had a history of supporting arts under the Works Progress Administration (WPA) during the Great Depression. Yet the New Deal art programs originated from the government's efforts to give employment to members of the art community. While the WPA of 1935 supported artists as part of a jobs program, the National Foundation on the Arts and Humanities Act created the country's first national funding agency to promote the arts. The agency was given a broad mandate that included advocating and recognizing the importance of the arts, ensuring financial and creative support for

National Endowment for the Arts Chairman Dana Gioia holds up material of the national theater initiative Shakespeare in American Communities as he testifies on March 10, 2005, during a hearing before a House Appropriations subcommittee focused on the organization's 2006 budget request. The NEA had experienced political turbulence in the 1970s and 1980s during a conservative backlash against some of the publicly funded art that proved to be controversial, but it weathered the political divisiveness of the 1980s and the reduced federal funding of the 1990s and emerged in the new century with an expanded and diversified base of support from corporations, foundations, and state and local public agencies. (Alex Wong/Getty Images)

artists, encouraging cultural diversity, and increasing access and appreciation of the arts for all citizens. During its first years, the NEA funded countless projects, ranging from artists' residencies to public art commissions to touring exhibits; arts projects were funded in museums, theaters, dance companies, and educational institutions.

Appreciation for the arts and funding of the NEA paralleled the economic boom of the 1960s and early 1970s. President Richard M. Nixon greatly expanded funding for the NEA—from $7 million in 1968 to $64 million in 1974. In the 1970s, however, the NEA

entered turbulent artistic waters as it began to receive and grant requests for support that focused on more politically radical forms of artistic expression, including feminist art, performance art, and populist art forms. By the 1980s, the NEA had become involved in a political debate about the limits of federal support for public art projects.

In the midst of inflation, high interest rates, and growing federal budget deficits, cultural and fiscal conservatives denounced taxpayers' financial support of what they viewed as "immoral" and "obscene" art. Conservatives voiced outrage as they pointed to examples of government-funded art that included the homoerotic photography of Robert Mapplethorpe and a crucifix suspended in urine by artist Andres Serrano. Some Republican leaders, including Jesse Helms (R–NC) and commentator Patrick Buchanan, called for the abolition of the NEA. In response to growing pressure from the Religious Right, Pres. Ronald Reagan slashed federally funded arts programs. The political divisiveness of the 1980s marked the beginning of a series of culture wars that heightened political tensions between conservatives and liberals over the limits of artists' right to free expression and ideological boundaries of public support for the arts; such disagreements tested the federal mandate of the NEA. The 1990s brought dramatic changes for the agency as Congress substantially reduced funding, eliminated direct grants to artists, and required 40 percent of the NEA's budget go to state-supported local arts programs.

To weather shifting political tides, federal arts projects were recast as cultural projects that fostered economic development and contributed to larger urban renewal campaigns. In 2000, the NEA gained cultural capital as it expanded its base of support to include foundations, corporations, and individuals as well as a network of state and local public agencies; such diversity allowed the NEA to frame nonprofit arts as important in contributing to local economic activity and growth. The agency sponsored a series of national initiatives, including Shakespeare in American Communities, Poetry Out Loud, and The Big Read. Offering myriad arts programs at the community level, the NEA has begun its latest chapter by including a vibrant public arts initiative that has become an important component of cultural public policy and that requires active collaboration of the NEA, Congress, the president, and a lobbying coalition of arts interest groups around the country.

Despite a series of challenges and controversies, the NEA has endured in the face of changing political and cultural agendas. Originating as a way to cele-brate the spirit of American democracy during the Cold War, the history of the NEA has tested the limits of democratic idealism, personal freedom, and creative expression as well as brought to light the complexities of free speech in government-funded cultural activities. In the context of American political history, the debate over the NEA has contributed to a national discussion about the boundaries of artists' freedom of expression as well as called into question the fundamental principles guiding an American democratic political philosophy grounded in rights guaranteed by the First Amendment.

Bibliography and Further Reading

Binkiewicz, Donna M. *Federalizing the Muse: United States Art Policy and the National Endowment for the Arts, 1965–1980*. Chapel Hill: University of North Carolina Press, 2004.

Brenson, Michael. *Visionaries and Outcasts: The National Endowment for the Arts, Congress, and the Place for Visual Arts in America*. New York: New Press, 2001.

Larson, Gary O. *The Reluctant Patron: The United States Government and the Arts, 1943–1965*. Philadelphia: University of Pennsylvania Press, 1983.

Marquis, Alice Goldfarb. *Art Lessons: Learning from the Rise and Fall of Public Arts Funding*. New York: Basic Books, 1995.

Smith, David A. *Money for Art: The Tangled Web of Art and Politics in American Democracy*. Chicago: Ivan R. Dee, 2008.

Angela Fritz

NATIONAL ENDOWMENT FOR THE HUMANITIES

The National Endowment for the Humanities (NEH) is a small, independent federal agency that was begun in 1965. Since its inception, controversy has surrounded the question of the extent to which the federal government should fund the humanities and whether the NEH should function principally as a grant-making organization for scholarly research or should undertake broader public initiatives to infuse more deeply American culture with the humanities. The agency has been attacked often by both liberal and conservative critics who allege politicization of its funding decisions and goals. The agency's rigorous internal procedures, however—for example, the refusal to use the same peer-reviewer more than once in an annual review cycle—have given it a strong reputation for objectivity.

Establishment

The NEH was established by Congress through the National Foundation on the Arts and the Humanities Act of 1965, which was signed into law by Pres. Lyndon B. Johnson. The initiative to create a federal agency for the humanities began during the Kennedy administration and culminated in the 1964 report of the National Commission on the Humanities, which argued that after a decade of growth in federal support for scientific research, the nation needed to address its limited support of the humanities. Although the bill moved very rapidly through both the House and Senate, its birth was not without controversy. President Johnson had publicly supported the creation of a humanities endowment, placing the value of the humanities alongside that of science and technology. Republican opposition was significant, with some Republican members of Congress expressing concern that federal influence would stifle or politicize creativity in the humanities, while others questioned whether such need for federal support had been demonstrated. The agency's early years were, nevertheless, characterized by a high level of bipartisan support. President Richard M. Nixon doubled the NEH budget to $29.7 million for 1972 and noted with admiration NEH's institution of the prestigious Jefferson Lecture in the Humanities, the greatest recognition the federal government confers for distinguished intellectual achievement in the humanities.

Evolution

Charges of politicization of NEH leadership began with Pres. Jimmy Carter's 1977 appointment of Joseph Duffey to head the agency. Duffey had played a key role in Carter's presidential campaign; criticism of its funding decisions soon followed. The debate about whether NEH should primarily support scholarship or programs of public interest intensified, reverberating in hearings held by Sen. Claiborne Pell (D–RI) and Rep. Sidney Yates (D–IL); new arguments arose over whether the NEH adequately embraced cultural diversity and appropriately supported small, underfunded institutions in its grant making. Much of the political history of the NEH at that time, and subsequently, revolved around the tension between a perceived national humanities agenda and a deep-seated aversion to developing a cultural ministry like those in Europe; this tension was found in both political parties.

The Republican chairmen appointed by presidents Ronald Reagan and George H. W. Bush, William Bennett and Lynne Cheney, vigorously articulated agendas that emphasized (though hardly exclusively) the value of traditional approaches to the humanities, including the exploration and teaching of Western civilization and the development of Great Books courses. Beginning with the tenure of William Bennett (1981–1985) and continuing through the service of Lynne Cheney (1986–1993), NEH chairmen took strong positions not only on the role of the humanities but also on general education policy, including elementary and secondary education. Cheney published a number of reports on the state of the humanities, addressing such issues as low standards in public schools, national curriculum and tests, the breakdown of academic freedom in universities, the promotion of theoretical approaches at the expense of traditional understanding of history and literature, and ignorance of significant ideas and contributions of Western civilization. In such areas as the humanities in K–12 education, these reports signaled new emphases within NEH grant making—in this case, the report was followed by the growth of seminars and institutes for schoolteachers.

As the presidency changed from 12 years of Republican administration to the two terms of Democratic control under Bill Clinton, the NEH embraced a broadly pluralistic and multicultural agenda—first in *A National Conversation on American Pluralism and Identity*, published by chairman Sheldon Hackney (1993–1997) and more strongly still under his successor, William Ferris (1997–2001), whose signature program was the Regional Humanities Centers, followed by the 1999 program, My History Is America's History.

In addition to the stated intention of the 1994 Congress to reduce the federal budget, controversy over NEH support of the National History Standards, deemed to be overly critical of American values and deficient in coverage of major political leaders, including the Founders, led to increased criticism. In 1995, at a House committee hearing, the two previous Republican chairs, Bennett and Cheney, joined in calls for abolishment of the agency on the grounds that it was inimical to American values. Funding for the agency was reduced from a 1994 level of $177.5 million to $110 million in 1996. The NEH budget remained flat through 1997, with only a $0.7 million increase for 1998 and 1999.

The NEH received significant bipartisan support under the direction of chairman Bruce Cole (2001–2009), largely as the result of his efforts to focus the agency's resources on deepening understanding of American history and institutions as a necessary part of the nation's ability to defend its democratic processes, an initiative that he argued was made more urgent by the September 11, 2001, terrorist attacks on the United States. The We the People initiative was announced by Pres. George W. Bush on September 17, 2002, and received more than $66 million of targeted funding from Congress between fiscal years 2004 and 2008. Thus NEH's overall budget grew at a time of limited federal discretionary spending to $144.7 million in 2008. The final initiative of the Cole chairmanship, Picturing America, placed more than seventy thousand poster sets with images of American visual arts in classrooms, libraries, and Head Start programs.

Bibliography and Further Reading

Cheney, Lynne V. *Telling the Truth*. Washington, D.C.: The National Endowment for the Humanities, 1992.

Commission on the Humanities. *The Humanities in American Life: Report of the Commission on the Humanities*. Berkeley: University of California Press, 1980. http://ark.cdlib.org/ark:/13030/ft8j49p1jc/ (accessed October 31, 2009).

———. *Report of the Commission on the Humanities*. New York: The American Council of Learned Societies 1964. http://www.acls.org/uploadedFiles/Publications/NEH/1964_Commission_on_the_Humanities.pdf (accessed October 31, 2009).

Hackney, Sheldon. *The Politics of Presidential Appointment: A Memoir of the Culture War*. Montgomery, AL, and Lousiville, KY: NewSouth Books, 2002.

Miller, Stephen. *Excellence and Equity: The National Endowment for the Humanities*. Lexington: University Press of Kentucky, 1984.

The National Endowment for the Humanities. *Informed Patriotism. We the People at Five Years*. Washington, D.C.: The National Endowment for the Humanities, 2008.

Michael Poliakoff

NEOCONSERVATIVES

Neocons, or new conservatives, were liberal intellectuals who grew disillusioned with the Democratic agenda, particularly the ballooning liberal welfare state and the Democrats' prosecution of the Cold War. The neocons emerged in the mid-1960s and contributed to the rise of the right in the 1970s and the revamping of conservatism during the years of the Reagan presidency. By the 1990s, they had brought the culture wars to the forefront of policy debate and advocated the controversial policy of building democracy in the Middle East. A backlash against the neocons, inspired by their advocacy of the 2002 U.S. invasion of Iraq, damaged both their position and legacy.

Background of the Neocons

The neocons were dominated by individuals of the Jewish and Roman Catholic faiths with urban, working-class roots. Children of immigrant parents and witness to the devastation of the Great Depression, they aligned with the New Deal coalition. World War II taught them the dangers of fascism and, for a time, some future neocons flirted with its opposite extreme—Marxism and its variants. In fact, author and editor Irving Kristol, widely acknowledged as the founding father of neoconservatism, and his wife, the historian Gertrude Himmelfarb, met at a Trotskyist gathering at City College in New York but would soon reject the philosophy. Other founders include the sociologists Daniel Bell, Nathan Glazer, and Seymour Martin Lipset as well as the political scientist Norman Podhoretz. Because of their experiences with leftist organizations and the emergence of the Cold War, the neocons considered communism to be the most dangerous threat in the world. On the domestic front, they advocated equality of opportunity, defended the general principles of capitalism, and preached the bourgeois values of hard work and delayed gratification, drawing especially on their religious convictions in their support of such beliefs.

The neocons continued to align with the Democrats during the postwar period. Not only had the party emerged, under Pres. Harry S. Truman's leadership, as staunchly anticommunist, it had also committed itself to economic growth policies that simultaneously boosted the economy and smoothed the rough edges of capitalism through such programs as a minimum wage and fair housing. Furthermore, the party defied its Southern wing in 1948 to adopt a strong civil rights plank. The Republican Party, in contrast, seemed old-fashioned at best and reactionary at worst. The G.O.P. was perceived as a tool of business interests and lacking sophistication in foreign policy. The latent effects of the party's unwillingness to prepare for World War II stood in sharp relief to its Red-baiting and embrace of nuclear weapons in the postwar period.

Intellectual Development in the 1960s and 1970s

The neocons began to question Democratic policies in the mid-1960s. Although they supported Pres. Lyndon Johnson—some had even worked in his administration—they grew uncomfortable with his Great Society programs as they grew more expansive. They soon identified with what they called the "unintended consequences" of Johnson's efforts. For example, Glazer originally had joined the Johnson administration as a domestic policy consultant but ultimately concluded that government programs actually weakened traditional ways, such as neighborhood associations or churches, that people had previously used to handle social and economic distress. The neocons considered these traditional organizations important because they provided a safety net without giving more responsibility and power to the state. While the neocons did not abhor all federal programs, they did question the initiatives that weakened mediating structures. Such endeavors seemed to create more problems than they had been originally designed to solve.

Even more than Democratic policies, the neocons began to have doubts about the liberal perspective itself. They criticized the bureaucratic structures established to administer federal programs, claiming that a "new class" of professionals had emerged, consisting of city planners, social workers, educators, and others who cared more about maintaining their jobs than actually solving problems. The neocons also grew skeptical of the liberal faith in the production and consumption of goods. The Keynesian focus on consumer demand essentially gave federal endorsement to the self-fulfilling aspects of consumer culture and undercut the bourgeois behavior—hard work, delayed gratification, thrift, and so on—that made capitalism triumphant and with which the neocons identified. Neocons also criticized the liberal focus on racial integration. They did not believe a "color-blind" society was possible and questioned the assumptions driving the civil rights movement as it traveled north and endorsed busing and affirmative action, policies the neocons believed promoted a double standard by focusing on equality of results instead of opportunity. Underlying these complaints was the dismay that neocons felt about the growing influence of the New Left and the counterculture on the liberal ethos, which led them to be more critical of liberalism. For example, *The Public Interest*, an influential journal edited by Kristol, focused almost exclusively on the "unintended consequences" of liberal programs. Likewise, as the editor of *Commentary*, Podhoretz led an aggressive campaign against the counterculture. Such editorial direction led sociologist Michael Harrington to derisively devise the term *neoconservative*.

Influence in 1970s and 1980s

The targets of Harrington's disdain at first bristled at the label, since they considered themselves loyal Democrats. They supported the Democratic candidate

Hubert Humphrey in the 1968 presidential election and rallied around Sen. Henry "Scoop" Jackson, a conservative Democrat from Washington state. However, the Democratic Party seemed to ignore the neocons' warnings and instead "caved" to the radicals by adopting affirmative action, embracing an expansive welfare policy, and softening the party's anticommunist agenda in the early 1970s. When the Democrats nominated the liberal dove George McGovern in 1972, Kristol, Himmelfarb, the historian Oscar Handlin, and the philosopher Sidney Hook all voted for Richard Nixon in his reelection bid for president. In the meantime, the Democrat Daniel Patrick Moynihan even worked

in the Nixon administration. Soon, neocons began embracing the "new conservative" label, because they saw the attention that nomenclature gave as a way to bring a new perspective to the conservative agenda, especially as the Republican Party foundered in the wake of the Watergate scandal. The time was ripe to "modernize" the G.O.P.

Neoconservatives during the 1970s augmented the conservative infrastructure and contributed to the overall rise of the right. They joined such conservative think tanks as the American Enterprise Institute, the John M. Olin Foundation, and the Heritage Foundation, published articles in conservative newspapers like the *Wall*

Former foreign policy advisor to Pres. Ronald Reagan and U.S. ambassador to the United Nations Jeane Kirkpatrick sits behind a desk during a UN session in New York in 1983. An important neoconservative thinker, Kirkpatrick was a committed anticommunist whose so-called Kirkpatrick Doctrine advocated U.S. support of anticommunist governments across the globe, including authoritarian dictatorships, who, she believed, could be led toward democracy through the United States' example. (Bernard Gotfryd/Getty Images)

Street Journal and the *Washington Times*, and filled the ranks of the fiercely anticommunist Committee on the Present Danger. With their policy proposals, the neocons avoided being associated with the laissez-faire economic policies and apocalyptic anticommunist scenarios that had characterized the Republican Party in the past. Regarding economic policy, Kristol gave important support to Arthur Laffer and Jude Wanniski for their theories on supply-side economics and helped sell their ideas on Capitol Hill. Not only did Kristol believe that supply-side economics would address the problem of stagflation that plagued the country for much of the 1970s but that the supply siders' emphasis on working, saving, and investing would revivify virtues he considered to be on the wane. Republican presidential candidate Ronald Reagan would advocate the supply-side approach on the campaign trail in 1980 and implement it in 1981. Furthermore, the neocons addressed some of the important societal questions Americans were asking in the 1970s, such as the causes for rising divorce, crime, drug use, and illegitimacy rates.

The neocons also brought attention to welfare reform. First through the work of Moynihan and then the political scientist Charles Murray, the neocons publicized how the welfare system seemed to reward fatherless households and advocated the negative income tax as a better way to help the working poor, a policy implemented in 1992. As foreign policy advisors to Reagan, the neocons also led the charge in a renewed anticommunism but eschewed the talk of "rolling back" communism by deploying nuclear weapons that had hurt the Republicans in previous decades. Jeane Kirkpatrick, the U.S. ambassador to the United Nations from 1981 to 1985, was one such influential voice.

These various efforts had an important impact, as they helped the G.O.P. construct a newly relevant conservatism that offered legitimacy to Reagan and allowed the Republicans to emerge as the majority party. However, disagreement has arisen about the neocons' role in Reagan's most celebrated achievement—ending the Cold War. While their champions emphasize Reagan's tough talk and massive nuclear buildup in bringing the Soviets down, their critics claim that Reagan's pursuit of détente and disarma-

ment with Soviet premier Mikhail Gorbachev, a policy the neocons denounced, was more important.

Culture Wars and Democracy Building

At the end of the Cold War, critics questioned the relevancy of neoconservatism without anticommunism. Furthermore, a number of individuals who were identified with the neocons, such as two-time secretary of defense Donald Rumsfeld, were not "new" as the label suggested but had always considered themselves conservatives. Neoconservatives, however, turned their attention to new matters, and in their policy prescriptions continued to distinguish themselves as a unique strain in the G.O.P. On the domestic front, Kristol led the charge in the culture wars—the belief that American society, influenced by the counterculture, had become unable to distinguish right from wrong. This vacillation, neocons charged, led to a tolerance and even celebration of behavior once considered abhorrent and resulted in intolerable government policy on such matters as abortion, school prayer, pornography, and the funding of the arts, among other issues. The politician William Bennett, Himmelfarb, the historian Lynne Cheney, and the legal scholar Robert Bork wrote prolifically on the culture wars and grew increasingly harsh during the Clinton years (1993–2001), as they considered the president to be representative of the worst of the baby boom generation. The "culture of corruption" and moral decay they believed Clinton represented became an important issue in the 2000 presidential election and boosted the candidacy of the victor, Republican George W. Bush.

On foreign policy matters, the neocons advocated a more proactive approach than either George H. W. Bush or Bill Clinton had embraced. In the post–Cold War environment, the neocons maintained that the United States should not be disengaged from international problems. Stressing the universality of democracy, they argued that the United States should promote freedom and democracy abroad through the support of pro-democracy movements, foreign aid, and even military intervention. Disgusted by George H. W. Bush's unwillingness to overthrow Iraqi dictator Saddam Hussein during the Persian Gulf War (1990–1991) and Clinton's reliance on the United Nations for foreign policy decisions, the neocons finally saw a shift toward their position with the promulgation in 1999 of the Clinton Doctrine, which argued that American intervention is justified where American values are at stake. After the September 11 terrorist attacks in 2001, the neocons' influence grew dramatically, first with the Bush Doctrine, which argued not only that preemptive military action is justified to protect the United States from the threat of terrorism or attack but also that America should look for opportunities to spread democracy. One result was the 2002 invasion of Iraq. Paul Wolfowitz, protégé of Scoop Jackson and long-time Defense Department official, was among the primary architects of these policies. As Bush's deputy secretary of defense, Wolfowitz argued that the United States needed to preemptively thwart terrorist attacks by pressuring countries that harbored or supported terrorists. That pressure could range from diplomacy to actual invasion, the approach Wolfowitz favored in Iraq. Those who agreed, including National Security Advisor Condoleezza Rice and Sec. of Defense Donald Rumsfeld, gained influence in the Bush administration, while those who did not, like Sec. of State Colin Powell, were marginalized.

As their influence grew, the neocons were criticized by both the left and traditional Republicans. The left decried the neocons' militarism and lack of concern for the United Nations, while traditional Republicans condemned what they considered the neocons' overly idealist commitment to nation building. Indeed, as the Iraq War continued and turned into what most observers agreed was a civil war, the neocon philosophy came under fire. The controversy surrounding the Iraq War began to erode the neocons' longtime influence on both domestic and foreign policy. Neocons simplistically became equated with hawks. The neocon label even entered popular culture. The well-known bands The Rolling Stones and Offspring both released songs, "Sweet Neo Con" and "Neocon," respectively, criticiz-

ing these thinkers. Whereas neocons had once enjoyed an enigmatic influence, the Iraq War both illuminated and damaged their status. Concurrently, the Bush administration suffered in the polls. Indeed, the neocons' reputation, as much as President Bush's, hinged on the Iraq War.

Bibliography and Further Reading

Blumenthal, Sidney. *The Rise of the Counter-Establishment: From Conservative Ideology to Political Power.* New York: Times Books, 1986.

Demuth, Christopher, and William Kristol, eds. *The Neoconservative Imagination: Essays in Honor of Irving Kristol.* Washington, D.C.: AEI Press, 1995.

Gerson, Mark. *The Neoconservative Vision: From the Cold War to the Culture Wars.* Lanham, MD, New York, and Oxford: Madison Books, 1997.

Glazer, Nathan. *The Limits of Social Policy.* London: Harvard University Press, 1988.

Kristol, Irving. *Neoconservatism: The Autobiography of an Idea.* New York: The Free Press, 1995.

Murray, Douglas. *Neoconservatism: Why We Need It.* New York: Encounter Books, 2006.

Podhoretz, Norman. *Breaking Ranks: A Political Memoir.* New York: Harper & Row, 1979.

Seltzer, Irwin, ed. *The Neocon Reader.* New York: Grove Press, 2004.

Emilie Raymond

NETWORK TELEVISION AND NEWSPAPERS

From 1976 to the present, American news media have gone through three distinct transformations, each with consequences for American politics. By 1976, television had become a fixture in American households. Political campaigns had changed as a result, with an increasing reliance on television commercials—including negative advertisements. The 1980s were a period of media expansion, with the growth of cable television providing more and more segments of the public with additional viewing options. The passage of the Telecommunications Act of 1996, the first major overhaul of U.S. telecommunications policy in 62 years, along with the emergence of the Internet, helped spur a period of media consolidation and convergence in which a few media giants began to acquire many different kinds of information and entertainment entities. News Corporation, for example, oversees various print media such as the *Wall Street Journal* as well as television and movie studios through Fox Broadcasting Company. Late in the first decade of the twenty-first century, such consolidation was followed by a period of media disruption in which changes to long-standing revenue streams and the availability of new modes of production forced several large conglomerates into bankruptcy. Throughout these decades, the trend has been toward greater choice for media consumers, which came at the cost of shared, common understandings of what constituted "news."

Media Expansion

In the mid-1970s, the United States was firmly entrenched in the broadcast era of television and newspaper coverage. More than 96 percent of households had at least one television set, and the large majority of those televisions received a small number of network television channels. American electoral politics had adapted to the ubiquity of televised content, with a shift from party-centered campaigning that focused on field mobilization of voters to candidate-centered campaigning focused on persuading undecided voters through television commercials and other appeals. Throughout the 1980s and into the early 1990s, American news media were primarily characterized by an expansion of the choice environment, as captive audiences became somewhat less captive. The percentage of households with access to cable channels grew from under 20 percent in 1976 to nearly 70 percent in 1996; as the audience for cable television grew, cable offerings expanded.

As news media expanded, the social benefits of the so-called spillover effects that result from a limited-choice environment declined. Very few American citizens actively chose to seek out political information through television or print journalism. During the broadcast era, many Americans were, nonetheless, exposed to political information in the course of watching the six o'clock news or reading the morning paper. When news is the only program available on television, Americans tend to watch news. As the choice environment expanded, many began to watch sports, drama, or comedy instead. The Cable News Network (CNN), founded in 1980, vaulted into the spotlight during the 1991 Persian Gulf War and became a 24-hour information source for those whose television preferences favored news content. The knowledge gap between those who chose to learn about politics and those who did not was relatively small during the broadcast era because political knowledge "spilled over" to less-interested segments of the public. Media expansion allowed many citizens to avoid political news, while also giving the politically interested more. Thus, an unintentional consequence of giving the viewing public greater choices is an increasing disparity between the politically knowledgeable and the politically unaware.

Media Consolidation and Convergence

The passage of the Telecommunications Act of 1996 marked the first major change in government media regulations since the Communications Act of 1934. The new regulatory framework relaxed restrictions on station ownership, allowing media conglomerates such as Viacom, Disney, News Corporation, and Time Warner to acquire large percentages of both television and print news markets, while conglomerates such as Clear Channel did likewise with radio stations. Two major trends and one unexpected effect emerged from this consolidation. The first trend was the development of competing niche markets among the conglomerates. Just as Disney owns the sports channel ESPN and News Corporation owns Fox Sports Net—leading the two similar networks to carve out different niches in an attempt to attract viewers—the 24-hour news stations MSNBC, CNN, and Fox News fall at different points on the ideological spectrum. Fox News generally features a more conservative set of commentators, while MSNBC offers airtime to more liberal hosts, and CNN attempts to occupy the political center. Among the segment of the populace that watches cable news, this fairly reliable delineation leads to further ideological polarization, as viewers self-select news content that reinforces their views on specific topics and frames issues in a manner that comports with their thinking. Critics of media consolidation have also noted that these major channels all share a strong pro-corporate bias, which, in turn, has given rise to various attempts to build alternative news venues.

The second trend has been toward the development of multi-platform media experiences. The growth of the Internet fueled the growth of traffic to the Web sites of CNN, *Time* magazine, and the *New York Times*. After some initial reluctance to move their reporting online, these sites and the media conglomerates that own them began experimenting with extensive multimedia ventures. An example of this trend is *American Idol*, which teaches a form of civic participation—voting, but not for public office—far removed from public life and also includes heavy cross-promotion between a media conglomerate's print, television, film, and gaming franchises. Likewise, such crossovers have involved journalists moving into the blogosphere and bloggers moving into journalism—blurring the distinction between citizens, journalists, and citizen-journalists as various media properties adapt to the new digital landscape.

One unexpected effect of all these media acquisitions was the precarious state they put the greater industry in. As media conglomerates bought additional properties, they assumed that each property would continue to grow and produce sufficient revenue to make the acquisition worthwhile—monies necessary to repay funds borrowed to purchase the outlet. Those media giants that went deeply into debt were thus put particularly at risk in the first decade of the twenty-first century as the entire sector entered a period of Internet-fueled disruptive innovation.

Media Disruption

The rise of the World Wide Web has led to a complex set of communications tools. Several of these have been actively embraced by major media corporations, but others have served to undercut them. Three such, in particular, have served to undermine traditional revenue streams—forcing many news organizations into bankruptcy and moving the industry as a whole into a state of frantic experimentation. The first of these is also the most unobtrusive, demonstrating the surpris-

ing nature of media disruption. Founded in 1995 and incorporated in 1999, the craigslist.org online community grew in the early 2000s to become the major hub in numerous cities and locales for the posting of local classified ads. Furniture, home rentals, dating profiles, jobs, and services can all be posted anonymously on the site. Throughout its early years, craigslist was ignored by media giants as an unsophisticated Web space unrelated to the business of journalism. But classified advertisements provide a major revenue stream for local newspapers, and as craigslist grew in popularity, it took advertising from newspapers. As of 2009, craigslist was one of the top 25 Web sites on the entire Internet, far exceeding either the *New York Times* or CNN sites in unique visitors per day. Without directly challenging or seeking to displace news production practices, craigslist became one of the major causes of turmoil in the print media.

The second more directly challenged news reporting: the rise of the political blogosphere. Although, as previously mentioned, major news organizations have hired bloggers or asked their journalists to blog, political bloggers have fashioned a variety of alternatives to traditional news outlets and production. Blog sites such as the left-leaning Huffington Post and Talking Points Memo, which won the prestigious Polk Award for Legal Reporting in 2007, provide alternate venues for investigative journalism while incurring far lower overhead costs than the media conglomerates. Although many such blogs reject the long-standing commitment to objective journalism that many media conglomerates gave at least lip service to, the bloggers are new entrants into the media system, further expanding the range of choices available to the public.

Third, as information migrates online, the prices that can be charged for it are reduced significantly. Much of the costs involved in producing a newspaper lie in the physical production and distribution of newsprint; such costs are passed along to the consumer. As more Americans get their news online, pricing structures have been disrupted by competitors who offer reporting and commentary for free. Although the large media sites attract millions of visitors and, therefore, generate revenue from online advertising, this cash stream is substantially less than what they had realized from offline advertising. In addition, most information on the Internet can be found with the help of the Google search engine and is available for free. Both television and print journalism face crisis-level challenges as their deeply in debt corporate parents adapt to new and reduced revenue streams and competition from Internet start-ups with much lower overhead costs. The closing of the *Rocky Mountain News* of Denver, Colorado, may be emblematic of the future of regional and local print media; since it shut down in February 2009, a number of other local papers have been forced into bankruptcy.

American media from 1976 to 2009 began with a small number of broadcast, print, and television outlets. The 1980s and early 1990s were characterized by media expansion, particularly with the growth of cable television. Beginning in 1996, this expansion gave way to a period of media consolidation and convergence, with a few conglomerates buying up diverse media platforms and developing multimedia entertainment and niche political content. The later years of the first decade of the twenty-first century saw a period of media disruption, with traditional revenue streams undercut by various Internet ventures.

Competition from new media organizations has led to a dizzying array of choices for American citizens about where to turn for news. This expansion of options has further broadened the gap between political knowledge seekers and those who, in the broadcast era, obtained a fair amount of political knowledge through spillover effects. How journalism will be financed and produced in the twenty-first century remains an open question, as do the political implications of an increasingly complex media environment.

Bibliography and Further Reading

Aufderheide, Patricia. *Communications Policy and the Public Interest: The Telecommunications Act of 1996.* New York: Guilford Press, 1999.

Baum, Matthew, and Samuel Kernell. "Has Cable Ended the Golden Age of Presidential Television?" *American Political Science Review* 93, no. 1 (1999): 99–114.

Jenkins, Henry. *Convergence Culture: Where Old and New Media Collide.* New York: NYU Press, 2006.

Prior, Markus. *Post-Broadcast Democracy: How Media Choice Increases Inequality in Political Involvement and Polarizes Elections.* Princeton, NJ: Princeton University Press, 2007.

Sunstein, Cass. *Republic.com.* Princeton, NJ: Princeton University Press, 2002.

David Karpf

9/11 COMMISSION

The 9/11 Commission was an independent, bipartisan investigatory body established by Congress in 2002. The commission was responsible for explaining the events of September 11, 2001—the airplane hijackings and the use of the airplanes as missiles to crash into buildings—that killed nearly three thousand people in New York, Pennsylvania, and Virginia. The commission's report, released in 2004, described the central role of the al Qaeda terrorist organization in the planning and execution of the September 11 attacks. It also proposed a series of government policy reforms designed to prevent the types of failures in intelligence and response that enabled al Qaeda to break through the nation's civil defenses. The commission's findings were an important part of the retooling of U.S. national security policy that occurred in the wake of the September 11 attacks.

Creation

The commission that was created by federal statute on November 27, 2002, was the result of months of compromise and negotiation. Shortly after the September 11 attacks, some officials began calling for the creation of an independent commission, similar to the Roberts Commission that was formed to investigate the 1941 bombing of Pearl Harbor. During an October 21, 2001, edition of NBC's *Meet the Press*, U.S. senators John McCain (R–AZ) and Joseph Lieberman (D–CT) both called for an independent commission to review the mistakes that permitted the attackers to breach U.S. defenses on September 11 and make recommendations for preventing future system failures.

In the following months, many congressional Democrats would rally behind the idea of an independent commission. President George W. Bush and many Republicans in Congress argued, instead, that the investigation should be carried out by the intelligence committees of the House and Senate. House majority whip Tom DeLay (R–TX) called the idea of an independent commission "ill-conceived," in part because it would publicize information about the government's security weaknesses.

At that time, the House and Senate intelligence committees did conduct their own joint inquiry into the September 11 attacks. The Joint Inquiry began work in February and filed its report in December 2002. Democrats and some Republicans, as well as many September 11 survivors and family members of victims, were not satisfied by the intelligence committees' inquiry. They continued to press for a comprehensive investigation that would look beyond just the problems of the intelligence community.

The Bush administration continued to oppose the commission throughout the summer of 2002, fearing that an independent commission might simply launch, as the *New York Times* put it, a "political witchhunt" of administration officials. After negotiating with members of Congress for several months, the Bush administration finally agreed to a compromise plan. A 10-person commission of 5 Republican and 5 Democratic citizens would be established. The president would be allowed to appoint the chair, and the Senate majority leader, Tom Daschle (D–SD), would appoint the vice chair. The House and Senate leadership of each party would each appoint two of the remaining members. Under the compromise, the commission would be allowed to subpoena witnesses, but any subpoena would require the bipartisan support of either the chair and vice chair or at least six commission members. Such provision prevented Democrats from voting as a bloc to subpoena Bush administration officials and was an important demand of the White House.

President Bush signed the compromise plan into law on November 27, 2002, stating that "an aggressive investigation into September the 11th, with a responsible concern for sensitive information . . . [would] allow [the United States] to win the war on terror [and] contribute to the security of [the] country."

Commission Membership

President Bush initially appointed former secretary of state Henry Kissinger to chair the commission, but Kissinger withdrew his name shortly afterward—citing a conflict of interest. Former New Jersey governor Thomas Kean was then appointed as his replacement. Former U.S. representative Lee Hamilton, a Democrat from Indiana, was appointed to serve as vice chair. The remaining Democratic commission members included: former Watergate prosecutor Richard Ben-Veniste, former Clinton deputy attorney general Jamie Gorelick, former Nebraska governor and U.S. senator Robert Kerrey, and former U.S. representative from Indiana Timothy Roemer. The remaining Republican commission members included: former Reagan White House counsel Fred Fielding, former U.S. senator from Washington Slade Gorton, former Reagan secretary of the navy John Lehman, and former Illinois governor James R. Thompson. The commission members' distinguished public service backgrounds promised to ensure that its investigation and findings would be taken seriously by the president, government agencies, and the American public.

Investigation

Over the course of 21 months, the 9/11 Commission conducted one of the most expansive investigations of security policy in U.S. history. Commissioners interviewed presidents and their closest advisors, questioned representatives from a range of government agencies, and evaluated the performance of state and local disaster response teams. The commission collected a large body of data on the al Qaeda organization and its tactics and took a close look at the pre-9/11 intelligence-gathering techniques used to monitor terrorist groups.

The most visible feature of the 9/11 Commission's work was the televised questioning of high-level public officials. While presidents Bill Clinton and George W. Bush and vice presidents Al Gore and Dick Cheney testified before the commission in private, many of their advisors spoke during high-profile public hearings. One key witness was former counterterrorism chief for the Bush White House, Richard Clarke. Testifying before the commission on March 24, 2004, Clarke argued that terrorism policy was an "important but not urgent" priority before September 11, 2001. According to Clarke, Bush and National Security Advisor Condoleezza Rice did not devote serious attention to the terrorist threat despite repeated warn-

ings from both Clarke and CIA Director George Tenet. Following his testimony, Clarke appeared on CNN's *Larry King Live*, alleging that Rice had not convened the frequent interagency meetings that were necessary to coordinate intelligence and build a clearer picture of the terrorists' plans for September 11.

After some initial resistance, the Bush administration allowed Rice to appear before the commission on April 8, 2004. Testifying in the wake of Clarke's strong accusations, she faced tough questioning about the level of attention the Bush administration had devoted to the al Qaeda threat prior to the

National Security Advisor Condoleezza Rice is sworn in on April 8, 2004, to testify before the independent commission investigating the Sept. 11, 2001, terrorist attacks. A member of George W. Bush's cabinet, Rice defended the White House's handling of the terrorist threat and maintained that "there was no silver bullet that could have prevented the 9/11 attacks." The 9/11 Commission's report, released on July 22, 2004, criticized the administrations of both Bill Clinton and George W. Bush for a "failure of imagination" with regard to the danger a terrorist group such as al Qaeda posed to the homeland. (Scott J. Ferrell/Congressional Quarterly/Getty Images)

September 11 attacks. Rice insisted that President Bush had made al Qaeda an important priority and had been pursuing new strategies to address terrorist threats. Rice did admit that an "inability to connect the dots" between the intelligence of foreign and domestic security agencies had been a serious problem. Rice pointed out that these problems had been corrected by merging intelligence agencies into a single Department of Homeland Security and by creating a single terrorism threat information center to coordinate bits of intelligence collected by the various security agencies.

Clarke and Rice were joined by a host of other prominent officials, including former Clinton secretary of state Madeleine Albright, Sec. of State Colin Powell, former Clinton secretary of defense William Cohen, Sec. of Defense Donald Rumsfeld, Director of Central Intelligence George Tenet, former Clinton assistant to the president for national security Samuel Berger, Deputy Sec. of State Richard Armitage, former Clinton attorney general Janet Reno, Attorney Gen. John Ashcroft, former New York mayor Rudolph Giuliani, and New York mayor Michael Bloomberg.

Various mid-level bureaucrats, first responders, and others with firsthand knowledge of the 9/11 response were also called to testify before the commission. According to chairmen Thomas Kean and Lee Hamilton, commissioners were even allowed to submit questions to al Qaeda operatives held in U.S. detention facilities. While commissioners were not allowed to meet with the detainees, some of their questions were asked by trained interrogators and answers were returned in transcript form.

The commission also examined intelligence on the al Qaeda threat that existed prior to September 11. The most publicized piece of intelligence was an August 6, 2001, President's Daily Brief (PDB) titled "Bin Laden Determined to Strike in US." News of the August 6 PDB first surfaced during the joint congressional inquiry in 2002, but, citing executive privilege, the administration had initially refused to make the document public. Following a series of tense negotiations with the White House, 9/11 commission chairmen Kean and Hamilton and several staff members were allowed to read the August 6 PDB and

some of the other pre-9/11 PDBs related to al Qaeda. The August 6 PDB proved to contain little new intelligence and was eventually declassified and included in the commission's report.

Main Findings and Policy Impact

On July 22, 2004, the commission issued a 585-page report on the September 11 attacks. The report called attention to the serious threat posed by radical Islamic terrorism, especially the al Qaeda terrorist organization, and documented that radical Islamic terrorists were extremely well funded and well organized. Estimates suggest that al Qaeda's operating budget prior to the September 11, 2001, attacks was a remarkable $30 million per year.

The report also highlighted some core problems of U.S. counter-terrorism policy. It suggested that while both the Clinton and George W. Bush administrations had seen al Qaeda as a threat prior to the 2001 attacks, both suffered a "failure of imagination" about the level of damage that the terrorists could inflict. Some intelligence officers had suggested the possibility of terrorists using airplanes as weapons, but the intelligence system as a whole had not been designed to detect the signs of an attack, for example, suspected terrorists enrolling in flight schools. As a result, the significance of critical warning signs had not been appreciated.

The commission report contained a number of recommendations designed to prevent future intelligence system failures. Some of these recommendations were adopted under the Intelligence Reform and Terrorism Prevention Act of 2004 (IRTPA). One of the recommendations established by the IRTPA was the creation of a new director of national intelligence (DNI) to oversee the workings of the intelligence community. The DNI is responsible for managing the Central Intelligence Agency, the Federal Bureau of Investigation, the National Security Agency, and 13 other member bodies of the U.S. intelligence community. The DNI has authority over the community's budget and can transfer staff among the various intelligence agencies.

Another commission recommendation adopted by the IRTPA was the creation of a National Counterterrorism Center (NCTC). The NCTC is designed to facilitate information sharing among various national security agencies. The failure of government departments to share information had been identified as a major weakness during the 9/11 Commission hearings. For instance, the Federal Bureau of Investigation had not been fully informed by the Central Intelligence Agency about the domestic threats posed by al Qaeda's operations overseas.

Commission members, however, did not believe that Congress and the Bush administration had gone far enough in enacting their recommendations. After the 9/11 Commission formally disbanded, its members formed the 9-11 Public Discourse Project to inform the public about the progress of the reform efforts. While commissioners praised the creation of the DNI and NCTC by Congress, they expressed concern that by 2005 progress was still very slow at the bureaucratic level. For instance, problems were still in evidence with information sharing across all agencies, and the NCTC was severely understaffed. Despite commission recommendations to improve FBI intelligence capabilities, that agency was still severely lacking in necessary personnel and expertise. Commissioners also criticized Congress for failing to act on recommendations to consolidate and strengthen congressional oversight of the intelligence community. The 9/11 Commission Report had suggested either a joint intelligence committee modeled after the former Joint Committee on Atomic Energy or a single intelligence committee in each chamber with both authorizing and appropriating authorities.

Public Reaction

The public response to the 9/11 Commission Report was mostly positive. Senators McCain and Lieberman, who had been among the greatest champions of the commission since the September 11 attacks, immediately began assembling a coalition to enact the commission's recommendations. The IRTPA was introduced in the Senate in September 2004, pushed through Congress at an unusually rapid pace, and signed by President Bush on December 17, 2004. At the signing ceremony, President Bush praised the 9/11 Commission and stressed the important role of the new director of

national intelligence, saying that the act would "ensure that the people in government responsible for defending America have the best possible information to make the best possible decisions."

Criticism of the 9/11 Commission erupted briefly in 2008 with the publication of a new book by *New York Times* reporter Philip Shenon. In *The Commission: The Uncensored History of the 9/11 Investigation*, Shenon alleged that 9/11 Commission Executive Director Philip Zelikow, a prominent historian from the University of Virginia, had close ties to Bush administration officials Karl Rove and Condoleezza Rice. Shenon claimed that Zelikow had consulted with Rove frequently during the commission's work and had worked to temper criticism of the Bush administration and of Rice during the investigation and in the final report. While Shenon's book may have given some ammunition to Bush administration critics, its accusations went largely unnoticed and did not cast serious doubt on the 9/11 Commission's report and policy recommendations.

Historical Significance

The 9/11 Commission conducted its work at a critical juncture in U.S. political history. At the commission's inception, what was clear was that significant changes in U.S. foreign and national security policies were necessary, but opinions varied about what changes would be most effective. The commission's investigation provided a forum for national debate about the causes and consequences of the 9/11 attacks and what might be done to prevent future attacks. It gave Americans an opportunity to learn about the new enemy that had emerged and how this enemy had managed to break through the nation's civil defenses. The commission also played a key role in the post–9/11 overhaul of U.S. national security policy—pinpointing key structural and organizational problems, gathering recommendations from many of the concerned agencies and officials, and suggesting ways to improve government's ability to respond to the threat of organized terrorism around the world.

Bibliography and Further Reading

Kean, Thomas, and Lee Hamilton. *Without Precedent: The Inside Story of the 9/11 Commission.* New York: Alfred A. Knopf, 2006.

National Commission on Terrorist Attacks upon the United States. *The 9/11 Commission Report: Final Report of the National Commission on Terrorist Attacks upon the United States.* New York: Barnes & Noble Books, 2004.

The 9/11 Public Discourse Project. *Report on the Status of 9/11 Commission Recommendations, Part II: Reforming the Institutions of Government.* October 20, 2005. http://www.9-11pdp.org/press/ (accessed October 20, 2008).

Shenon, Philip. *The Commission: The Uncensored History of the 9/11 Investigation.* New York: Twelve Publishing, 2008.

The White House. *Transcript: President Signs Intelligence Reform and Terrorism Prevention Act.* December 17, 2004. http://www.whitehouse.gov/news/releases/2004/12/20041217-1.html (accessed June 30, 2008).

Daniel Preston Parker

NUCLEAR WEAPONS AND PROLIFERATION

The United States maintained an arsenal of nuclear weapons during the Cold War in order to deter the Soviet Union from invading Western Europe or attacking North America; it also periodically engaged in negotiations with the U.S.S.R. to slow the nuclear arms race. As a major element of American foreign policy, nuclear weapons policy was a politically charged topic that was debated between and within the Republican and Democratic parties with long-lasting implications. Following the Cold War, nuclear proliferation gained political importance as a possible source of weapons for terrorists. The question of how best to limit nuclear proliferation and ensure that weapons were not obtained by terrorist organizations resulted in high-profile political

debate during several presidential administrations and elections.

Nuclear Weapons and the Cold War

The Ford Administration

In 1976, Pres. Gerald Ford hoped to build on the success of Richard M. Nixon's negotiations with the Soviet Union and entered into a second round of Strategic Arms Limitation Talks (SALT II). Ford came under increasing pressure from Republicans in Congress as well as Democrats led by Sen. Henry "Scoop" Jackson (D–WA) for being perceived as too conciliatory toward the U.S.S.R. Some of Ford's own Cabinet officials, including Sec. of Defense Donald Rumsfeld, were opposed to SALT II and the talks were considered too contentious to engage in in an election year.

During the 1976 presidential election, a number of lobbying groups argued that the United States had become too complacent about the Soviet Union's increasing nuclear capability and accused the Central Intelligence Agency of misjudging the U.S.S.R.'s intentions. The most notable of such groups was the Committee on the Present Danger, which continued to lobby throughout the Carter administration for an American nuclear buildup.

The Carter Administration

In his first months as president, Jimmy Carter hoped to enter new arms control talks, but his initial proposals were ultimately rejected by the Soviets. Carter was unable to advance proposals that might have been acceptable to the Soviet Union because of deep divisions within the Democratic Party and threats that a new SALT treaty would not be ratified in the Senate. In 1979, after SALT consultations were successfully reinitiated, Carter began a major public relations campaign to convince the American people of the importance of reducing American and Soviet nuclear weapons. The Committee on the Present Danger, neoconservative pundits, and Republicans continued to vocally oppose the negotiations, while the most stinging criticism came from within Carter's party when Scoop Jackson characterized the policy as "appeasement."

In a concession to his domestic opposition, Carter changed course in 1979 and agreed to authorize development of a new system of MX missiles (later known as the LGM-118 Peacekeeper). Despite this shift in policy, the 1979 Soviet invasion of Afghanistan cast doubt on Carter's wisdom in undertaking disarmament negotiations with the Soviet Union and contributed to the weakening of the Democratic Party and the loss of the presidency in the 1980 election.

The Reagan Administration and Beyond

In the 1980 election campaign, Reagan promised to take a harder line against the U.S.S.R. and warned the American public to prepare civil defenses in case of nuclear war. Following his election, Reagan filled many senior positions with members of the Committee on the Present Danger (including Sec. of State George Shultz, National Security Advisor Richard Allen, Director of Central Intelligence William Casey and Asst. Sec. of Defense Richard Perle), adding substance to his highly anti-Soviet rhetoric. In his first term as president, Reagan dramatically increased defense spending in a move to modernize the command and control systems of American nuclear weapons and to deploy the Peacekeeper missile system and submarines carrying Trident ballistic missiles. In 1983, Reagan announced a Strategic Defense Initiative (SDI) to develop a ballistic missile defense system to destroy Soviet missiles before they could detonate in the United States. SDI, or "Star Wars" as it was widely known, was unpopular with American allies who were concerned that it represented an obstacle to negotiations with the Soviet Union and presaged a new, more dangerous phase of the Cold War.

Reagan's first-term nuclear weapons policies fueled public outcry from American antinuclear groups, coalescing in the major protest marches and rallies of the Nuclear Freeze Movement. Reagan disagreed strongly with this movement, and his policies during his first term cast doubt on claims that the movement directly affected his administration's nuclear policies. Nonetheless, despite his frustrations with the Freeze Movement—and less than one year after the initiation of Star Wars research, Reagan announced a significant change in policy toward the Soviet Union that would have a deep impact on American nuclear weapons through arms reductions.

The shift in policies was not directly attributable to the public outcry against the Reagan administration but was linked to the president's personal experiences. In October 1983, Reagan prescreened the television movie *The Day After*, which depicted the impact of nuclear war on the United States. Not long after watching the movie, Reagan learned that the Soviet Union had misinterpreted the NATO exercise Able Archer 83 as an indication of a coming attack and readied its nuclear forces. The demonstration of how easily an accidental nuclear war could be triggered combined with the emotional impact of the film strengthened Reagan's resolve to end the possibility of a nuclear war.

Reagan's new interest in arms reductions, combined with changes in the Soviet Union, resulted in a 1986 agreement to remove intermediate-range nuclear missiles from Europe. Although disarmament agreements between the United States and the Soviet Union were complicated by the American decision to begin research on a ballistic missile shield, negotiations continued through the 1980s. Despite the obvious shift in Reagan's policy in 1984, neoconservatives, including Richard Allen, argued that Reagan's more belligerent first-term policies and increased expenditure on American nuclear weapons had achieved the defeat of the Soviet Union. Scholars have discounted this linkage.

After the collapse of the Soviet Union in 1991, presidents George H. W. Bush and Bill Clinton maintained American nuclear weapons to deter rogue states and to hedge against a resurgent Russia. In 2002, the administration of Pres. George W. Bush conducted a review of the U.S. nuclear posture that concluded nuclear weapons should be kept to provide a deterrent against a wide range of threats; concurrently, however, the administration agreed to a Strategic Offensive Reductions Treaty to reduce the size of its nuclear arsenal. In 2007, although announcing a further reduction in the stockpile of nuclear weapons, the United States restarted production of nuclear weapons for the first time since 1992.

Nuclear Proliferation in the Post–Cold War Era

The United States has sought to limit the proliferation of nuclear weapons in other countries by participating in the Nuclear Non-Proliferation Treaty and by carefully controlling exports of weapons-related technology. Following the end of the Cold War, several agencies of the United States worked to secure unguarded and unwanted nuclear weapons in the former Soviet Union, preventing them from being sold on the black market.

During the Clinton administration, it became clear North Korea was attempting to develop a nuclear capability. In a move to persuade the North Koreans to abandon their plans, the United States agreed to provide that country with alternative nuclear energy reactors that could not be used to produce weapons-grade material. The agreement was extremely unpopular with the Republican-controlled Congress elected just after the signing of the agreement in 1994. Senator John McCain (R–AZ) was one of many Republicans speaking out against the agreement, favoring instead the use of force to prevent nuclear proliferation. Other critics, such as Richard Perle of the Defense Policy Board, called the agreement an act of appeasement. In the 2000 presidential campaign, Condoleezza Rice attacked the Democrats' approach to North Korea as a failure and advocated a more aggressive stance.

The terrorist attacks of September 11, 2001, increased concern that a subsequent terrorist attack might include the use of nuclear weapons supplied by the three countries that George W. Bush characterized as the "Axis of Evil": Iraq, North Korea, and Iran. Saddam Hussein's alleged attempts to develop nuclear weapons and their possible distribution to terrorist groups were the primary justification used by the Bush administration to gain bipartisan political support for the 2003 invasion of Iraq.

Also in 2003, the agreement between the United States and North Korea collapsed completely. President Bush, who had a well-known dislike of the North Korean government, limited his public rhetoric against North Korea because his administration was focusing on the war with Iraq. As that war continued, Bush found no public or political support for strong action against North Korea and a diplomatic stalemate ensued.

During George W. Bush's second term, Vice Pres. Dick Cheney fueled speculation that the United States would undertake military action against Iran to attempt to destroy its fledgling nuclear program. Such action was unpopular with Democrats, the American public, and some military leaders, including Adm. William Fallon, Commander of U.S. Central Command, who disagreed publicly with those urging war against Iran.

Debates over the best way to curtail production of a nuclear capability in Iran affected the 2008 Democratic primaries, with a significant difference of thought and opinion between Sen. Hillary Clinton (D–NY) and Sen. Barack Obama (D–IL) about how best to approach the Iranian government. Obama's willingness to meet with the Iranian president with no preconditions was attacked by Clinton, and later Republican presidential candidate John McCain, as naïve. During the presidential election campaign, Obama continued to argue it was best not to ignore enemies but did not rule out military strikes. McCain, who had been an advocate of force against North Korea and who had made clear he would be willing to use force against Iran if necessary, found little public support for his position among the electorate.

Nuclear weapons played a significant role in American political development from 1976 through 1989 as a visible point of disagreement between Republicans and Democrats. Perhaps of more significance, disagreement over nuclear weapons policy resulted in the weakening of the Democratic Party in 1980 and the shift of many high-profile neoconservative thinkers to the Republican Party. Following September 11, 2001, nuclear weapons and the possibility of a terrorist nuclear attack increased public fears and provided impetus for the invasion of Iraq and a tougher stance toward Iran and North Korea. Toward the end of the Bush administration, the best means for preventing the proliferation of nuclear weapons were still a matter of debate, and the Obama administration entered office embroiled in diplomatic standoffs with both Iran and North Korea and with lingering concerns over terrorist access to nuclear weapons.

Bibliography and Further Reading

Chernoff, Fred. "Ending the Cold War: The Soviet Retreat and the US Military Buildup." *International Affairs* 67, no. 1 (1991): 111–126.

Ehrman, John. *The Rise of Neoconservatism: Intellectuals and Foreign Affairs, 1945–1994.* New Haven, CT: Yale University Press, 1995.

Fischer, Beth A. *The Reagan Reversal: Foreign Policy and the End of the Cold War.* Columbia: University of Missouri Press, 1997.

Garthoff, Raymond L. *Détente and Confrontation: American-Soviet Relations from Nixon to Reagan.* Rev. ed. Washington, D.C.: Brookings Institution, 1994.

Norris, Robert S., and Hans M. Kirstensen. "Nuclear Notebook—U.S. Nuclear Forces, 2008." *Bulletin of the Atomic Scientists* 64, no. 1 (2008): 50–53, 58.

Public Broadcasting Service. "Frontline: Kim's Nuclear Gamble." http://www.pbs.org/wgbh/pages/frontline/shows/kim/ (accessed Otober 31, 2009).

Rhodes, Richard. *Arsenals of Folly: The Making of the Nuclear Arms Race.* New York: Alfred A. Knopf, 2007.

Wittner, Lawrence S. *The Struggle against the Bomb.* 3 vols. Stanford Nuclear Age Series. Stanford, CA: Stanford University Press, 1993.

Woolf, Amy F. "Congressional Research Service Report for Congress: Nuclear Weapons in U.S. National Security Policy: Past, Present, and Prospects." October 29, 2007. http://italy.usembassy.gov/pdf/other/RL34226.pdf (accessed November 9, 2009).

Timothy Andrews Sayle

OBAMA, BARACK

born 1961
Forty-fourth President of the
United States

On January 20, 2009, Barack Hussein Obama became the forty-fourth president of the United States. Americans celebrated his inauguration as a redemptive moment during bleak economic times. America's first black president, Obama had been a charismatic 48-year-old senator and best-selling author whose eloquent campaign theme affirming "Yes We Can" moved millions. His defeat of Hillary Rodham Clinton in the Democratic primaries and repudiation of Pres. George W. Bush during the general election promised to bring a new, syncretizing, post-baby-boom sentiment to American politics.

Just as Ronald Reagan launched his political career with a nationally televised address during Barry Goldwater's losing 1964 campaign and William Jennings Bryan seized the 1896 Democratic nomination after his "Cross of Gold" speech, Obama's spellbinding 2004 Democratic National Convention debut catapulted him to public prominence. At the time, Obama was an obscure Illinois state senator running for the U.S. Senate. Rejecting the popular division pitting a provincial, rural, conservative "red" America against a cosmopolitan, urban, liberal "blue" America, Obama celebrated a red, white and blue, "*United* States of America."

Preaching a nationalist gospel for a multicultural America, and resurrecting a national sense of community amid the selfishness of the boom years, Obama proclaimed, "If there's a child on the south side of Chicago who can't read, that matters to me, even if it's not my child." Acknowledging the Reaganite critique of Lyndon Johnson's Great Society as addicted to big government programs, Obama sounded a moderate note, saying, "People don't expect government to solve all their problems. But they sense, deep in their bones, that with just a slight change in priorities, we can make sure that every child in America has a decent shot at life and that the doors of opportunity remain open to all." Perhaps most dramatically, he repudiated "the pundits" who "like to slice and dice our country into red states and blue States." In what became arguably his most famous riff, Obama declared "We worship an awesome God in the blue states, and we don't like federal agents poking around our libraries in the red states. We coach little league in the blue states and, yes, we've got some gay friends in the red states."

An Unlikely Journey

Barack Obama's admittedly "unlikely" journey to the presidency began on August 4, 1961, in Honolulu, Hawaii. Obama's father, Barack Obama, Sr., was a student from Kenya. His mother, Stanley Ann Dunham, was a Kansan—with some slaveholders reportedly among her ancestors. The marriage was short, and Obama only saw his father one more time, and then only briefly. Obama's mother then married Lolo Soetoro, an Indonesian student. In 1967, Barry, as the young Obama was called, moved with his mother and her new husband to Indonesia. When he returned to Hawaii in 1971, his mother remained abroad.

Obama's grandparents, Madelyn and Stanley Dunham, enrolled him in Honolulu's exclusive Punahou School. There, Obama began seeking his identity, torn by his proximity to Hawaii's elite and his feelings of rootlessness and inadequacy. By his own admission, Obama internalized some of the sev-

enties' African American anger, indulged in the era's excesses, and luxuriated in the anomie of young, reflective seekers. After graduating from high school in 1979, Obama attended Occidental College in Los Angeles. When he transferred to Columbia University for his junior year, he became more serious about his studies. Still, after graduating in 1983, he drifted. After four years in New York, he eventually became a community organizer in Chicago. There, he solidified his identity as a black man and a social activist committed to working within the system.

Barack Obama delivers the keynote speech during the second night of the Democratic National Convention in Boston on July 27, 2004, a speech that launched his national political career. At the time a candidate for the U.S. Senate from Chicago, Obama went on to win his election and become the third black senator since the nineteenth century. On February 10, 2007, he declared his candidacy for the presidency and, after a hard-fought primary, he prevailed against front-runner Hillary Rodham Clinton and won the Democratic nomination. His decisive victory over opponent John McCain in the general election was widely seen as a strong rebuke of George W. Bush and his administration's policies. (Rick Wilking/Reuters/Corbis)

In 1988, Obama enrolled in Harvard Law School. He rose to the presidency of the *Harvard Law Review*, displaying a remarkable ability to mediate between the most radical African Americans and the more skeptical whites. The fame he garnered through his election as the prestigious journal's first black president landed him a book contract. The result—after years of delays—was *Dreams from My Father: A Story of Race and Inheritance*. The book described Obama's journey to find himself by making peace with his father, traveling all the way to Africa to visit his paternal relatives. This memoir first received respectable attention in 1995, then became a blockbuster bestseller after Obama's 2004 Democratic National Convention Speech.

Upon graduation, Obama settled in Chicago, practicing civil rights law and teaching at the University of Chicago Law School. In 1996, he entered politics, winning a race to serve as state senator. Four years later, he failed to unseat the four-term congressman Bobby Rush, a former Black Panther. Some interpreted this defeat as a lion of the old, once-radical African American establishment defeating a younger, more moderate upstart. But the setback was temporary. Obama served as a state senator until January 2005, at which time he joined the U.S. Senate as the junior senator from Illinois.

A National Superstar

In the Senate, Obama was most distinguished as a national spokesman rather than as a legislative whiz. Obama's 2004 convention speech positioned him as one of the Democratic Party's superstars during the 2006 midterm campaign. His best-selling second book, *The Audacity of Hope: Thoughts on Reclaiming the American Dream*, kept him in the public eye and articulated what would be his vision for the presidential campaign. Obama proudly identified as a liberal, committed to social activism and social justice. But he tempered his faith in government by relying on culture, the family, and the church, a reflection of the post-1960s skepticism that government can solve all the country's problems. Having synthesized the New Deal with the Reagan Revolution, Obama asserted his post–baby boomer sensibility. He repudiated the bruising, highly charged politics of both Bill Clinton and George W. Bush, seeking consensus and a more temperate approach to politics.

Obama ran for president facing the formidable U.S. Senator from New York and former First Lady, Hillary Rodham Clinton, among other more experienced opponents. While linking Senator Clinton to the 1990s' destructive all-or-nothing rhetoric, Obama emphasized his early opposition to the Iraq War. His eloquence inspired millions, attracting many younger voters into politics. Obama also put his experience as a community organizer to good use. He and his campaign advisors—in particular, chief strategist David Axelrod and campaign manager David Plouffe—used the social networking tools of the Internet brilliantly. They organized millions of avid supporters, working particularly hard for every extra delegate in the often-overlooked states that used informal caucuses rather than primaries for selecting nominees. Obama's surprise win in the Iowa caucuses flummoxed Clinton. In the hard-fought nomination campaign that ensued, Obama came across as more disciplined than his rival, as well as the better manager, strategist, and speaker. Still, he only won the nomination narrowly, after a protracted battle throughout the spring of 2008. Moreover, Senator Clinton tried tagging Obama as an elitist, while embarrassing videotapes of Obama's fiery pastor, the Rev. Jeremiah Wright, engaging in harsh, unpatriotic accusations against America forced Obama to break with a man who had played the role of spiritual father.

Obama's victory over his Republican opponent, Sen. John McCain of Arizona, in the general election was more decisive. The Democrat benefited from the great financial meltdown and the backlash against the unpopular Republican president George W. Bush's fiscal mistakes, Iraq War quagmire, and managerial incompetence, the latter demonstrated most starkly when Hurricane Katrina flooded New Orleans in August 2005. Americans were hungering for a change—and that is what Obama promised.

During the three presidential debates, Obama appeared unruffled, seeming more mature than his 72-year-old opponent. Thanks to his Internet fundraising, his impressive ground forces, and the traditional array of Democratic big donors, Obama raised over $600 million. Moreover, he suffered minimal political damage for rejecting public campaign financing. Like many political upstarts, including Bill Clinton, George W. Bush, and Jimmy Carter, Obama carefully shrouded his political ideology in ambiguity. Leftists embraced him as one of their own, wooed by his historic candidacy, his antiwar stance, and his eloquent calls for social justice. At the same time, moderates became quite comfortable with him, too, swayed by his preternatural calm, his eloquent calls for civility, and his post-1960s understanding about the importance of the flag, faith, and family.

Obama won an impressive victory, with 53 percent of the popular vote and 365 electoral votes. His electoral coalition included African Americans and Latinos, Jews and Catholics, and young voters and women. Still, if in 1980 Ronald Reagan won an "ABC" victory—meaning Anybody But Carter—in 2008 Barack Obama won thanks to the broad backlash against George W. Bush's presidency.

On election night, following the announcement of Obama's victory, McCain conceded graciously. Crowds cheered across the world. Even many Republicans acknowledged how special the moment was, considering America's history of racism. In his victory speech, Obama spoke lyrically, reaching out to Republicans and urging all Americans to work together.

Forty-five years earlier, Martin Luther King Jr. had dared to dream of equality and dignity for his children. Obama's remarkable ascent reflected the civil rights movement's great success. Obama's youth and relative inexperience demonstrated that celebrity, eloquence, and hope could trump experience in a meritocratic and media-besotted America. Facing a sobering global economic crisis, wars in Afghanistan and Iraq, the possibility of a nuclear Iran, and the still potent threat of international terrorism, Obama entered office with a crowded agenda, a Democratic majority in both Houses of Congress, and an anxious nation yearning for leadership.

Bibliography and Further Reading

Balz, Dan, and Haynes Johnson. *The Battle for America: The Story of an Extraordinary Election*. New York: Viking, 2009.

Obama, Barack. *The Audacity of Hope: Thoughts on Reclaiming the American Dream*. New York: Crown Publishing, 2006.

———. *Dreams from My Father: A Story of Race and Inheritance*. New York: Crown Publishing, 1995, 2007.

Plouffe, David. *The Audacity to Win: The Inside Story and Lessons of Barack Obama's Historic Victory*. New York: Viking, 2009.

Wolffe, Richard. *Renegade: The Making of a President*. New York: Crown Publishing, 2009.

Gil Troy

O'CONNOR, SANDRA DAY

born 1930
Supreme Court Justice

Sandra Day O'Connor was the first woman to sit on the U.S. Supreme Court. As with many influential justices, her stances were influenced by the composition and tenor of the Court on which she served. Although O'Connor's tendencies were toward compromise and judicial moderation, she nevertheless frequently found herself in dissent during the early 1980s, when a moderate-liberal majority was in control. As the Court shifted rightward in the late 1980s and early 1990s, O'Connor found herself at the center of the Court without having changed the substance of many of her views. And, in situations in which her ideological commitment outweighed her compromising instincts, she found herself unable to shape legal developments. Despite this, the temperament of Justice O'Connor is often cited as one of the primary reasons that the expected counter-revolution to the liberal Warren Court did not occur, and why, to the contrary, rights expanded in the conservative Burger and Rehnquist Court eras.

Early Years

O'Connor was born on March 26, 1930, in El Paso, Texas, and attended Stanford University, where she received an AB in 1950 and a law degree in 1952. Her future colleague on the Supreme Court, Chief Justice William Rehnquist, was valedictorian of O'Connor's

President Ronald Reagan, who had pledged during the presidential campaign that he would appoint the first female justice to the highest court, sits with newly announced Supreme Court nominee Sandra Day O'Connor in the rose garden of the White House on July 1, 1981. Although O'Connor would more often vote with the conservative wing of the Court, her jurisprudence was marked by a pragmatic centrism, particularly with regard to controversial areas such as abortion choice, separation of church and state and the free exercise of religion, affirmative action, and the balance of power between state and national government. (Keystone/CNP/Getty Images)

law school class, and the two dated briefly. She graduated high in her law class and was selected as an editor of the *Stanford Law Review*.

Despite her outstanding academic achievements, O'Connor was unable to find legal work with a major law firm. When she applied for a position in the firm in which future Attorney Gen. William French Smith was a partner, O'Connor was instead offered a position as a secretary. The difficulty that she faced as a woman trying to secure a position with a law firm was a defining point in her life, and would influence her Supreme Court decisions. After serving briefly as deputy county

attorney for San Mateo County, California, she worked as a civilian attorney for the army while her husband served his tour of duty. In 1965, she served as assistant attorney general in Arizona and in 1970 was elected to the Arizona senate, eventually rising to the post of majority leader. In 1975, she was elected to a local judgeship on the Maricopa County Superior Court and in 1979 was appointed to the Arizona Court of Appeals. In 1981, Pres. Ronald Reagan selected O'Connor to fill the seat of retiring U.S. Supreme Court justice Potter Stewart, fulfilling a campaign pledge to appoint the first female justice to the nation's highest court. The Senate voted 99–0 in favor of her appointment to the Supreme Court.

Swing Voter

At the core of O'Connor's jurisprudence was the view that the Court should balance competing interests and rights rather than make bright-line rules that could retard such attempts at balance in future cases. However, her evolution to pragmatic centrist on the Court took some years. O'Connor frequently agreed with conservative colleagues Rehnquist and Chief Justice Warren Burger during the first part of her tenure on the Supreme Court, when she wrote or joined dissents from some of the more liberal, rights-expansive decisions in the early 1980s. While feminist scholars initially attempted to explain her jurisprudence as somehow qualitatively different than that of her male colleagues, they foundered upon the emergence of her cautious conservatism whose "feminine" features were difficult to identify at first.

With the solidification of the conservative voting bloc in the 1990s, following the appointments of justices Antonin Scalia (1986) and Clarence Thomas (1991), O'Connor emerged as an influential "swing vote" on the Rehnquist Court on a wide range of cases, including privacy rights (specifically abortion rights), affirmative action, and church-state separation. Even on federalism and criminal procedure cases where she joined conservative majorities, O'Connor demonstrated a preference for a balancing approach to constitutional law and a case-by-case particularism, a stance that created many heated conflicts with Justice Scalia, who modeled himself as an originalist, though perhaps a less doctrinaire one than Justice Thomas.

Abortion and Gay Rights

O'Connor supported the fundamental right of abortion choice; however, she did not approve of what she considered the formalism of *Roe v. Wade*, 410 U.S. 113 (1973), in which pregnancy was segmented into three trimesters, with the state interest only supported in the third trimester, except where the health and life of the mother was at risk. This is evident in her dissent in *Akron v. Akron Center for Reproductive Health*, 462 U.S. 416 (1983), in which the court struck down an

Ohio law setting procedural restrictions on second- and third-trimester abortions. O'Connor argued that an undue burden test be applied to the regulations without reference to the stage of pregnancy. This test would have permitted states to restrict abortion unless regulations placed an undue burden on the fundamental right of a woman to choose. She issued a similarly forceful dissent in *Thornburgh v. American College of Obstetricians and Gynecologists*, 476 U.S. 747 (1986), in which the Court invalidated several Pennsylvania laws designed to regulate abortion. O'Connor disputed "not only the wisdom but also the legitimacy of the Court's attempt to . . . pre-empt state abortion regulation" and reiterated the undue burden standard. These decisions gave O'Connor a reputation of holding anti-abortion views similar to those of Rehnquist and Justice Byron White (the two *Roe* dissenters), who had joined her in her *Akron* dissents.

In *Webster v. Reproductive Health Services*, 492 U.S. 490 (1989), however, when the state of Pennsylvania (and her anti-abortion colleagues) called on her and the Court to overrule *Roe*, she declined the invitation. In *Planned Parenthood v. Casey*, 505 U.S. 833 (1992), she broke ranks with conservative colleagues to uphold the "core holding" of *Roe*. *Casey* reaffirmed the fundamental right of abortion choice but adopted O'Connor's "undue burden" standard, which allows state actions to discourage abortions by suggesting alternatives, if such alternatives do not impose an undue burden on the fundamental right of abortion choice. Following *Casey*, O'Connor continued to chart a middle course on abortion rights. Her most significant role in later abortion cases was her tie-breaking vote in *Stenberg v. Carhart*, 530 U.S. 913 (2000), a case in which the Supreme Court struck down a ban on intact dilation and extraction abortions (so-called partial-birth abortions) that made no exception for the health of the mother.

On gay rights issues, O'Connor joined the majority in *Bowers v. Hardwick*, 478 U.S. 186 (1986), which refused to recognize a "fundamental right of homosexual sodomy," but concurred in *Lawrence v. Texas*, 539 U.S. 558 (2003), which struck down a Texas anti-sodomy statute as violating due process. O'Connor favored an Equal Protection rationale, as she did in

Romer v. Evans, 517 U.S. 620 (1996), based on the view that states could not pass laws based on the moral disapproval of gay men and lesbians.

Church and State

In separation of church and state and free exercise of religion cases, O'Connor again took a pragmatic stance between Court colleagues who wanted a strict separation of church and state and those who sought a jurisprudential regime that required more government accommodation of religion than had been present in the past. O'Connor's concurrence in *Lynch v. Donnelly*, 465 U.S. 668 (1984) was important to Establishment Clause law, which was lapsing into incoherence in the early 1980s as criticism of the *Lemon* test mounted both on the Court and in the federal circuits. In *Lemon v. Kurtzman*, 403 U.S. 602 (1971), the Supreme Court had established a tripartite test for determining whether government actions violate the constitutional separation of church and state. For a statute or government action to be constitutional under the *Lemon* test (1) it must have a secular legislative purpose, (2) its primary effect must be one that neither advances nor inhibits religion, and (3) it must not foster an excessive government entanglement with religion. Instead of applying the *Lemon* test, which many contended made the state an adversary to religion, O'Connor argued that the Court should limit its inquiry to whether a government program and law resulted in excessive entanglement with religion, and whether the government was endorsing or disapproving of religion by its actions. This "endorsement or disapproval" test became the de facto standard for determining where government relationships with religion cross the constitutional line when the *Lemon* test is applied. She refined the endorsement test in *Wallace v. Jaffree*, 472 U.S. 38 (1985), a case in which the Court found unconstitutional Alabama's statute that allowed a "moment of silence" in its schools. In doing so, O'Connor emphasized that the Court must determine whether a moment of silence law endorsed religion by looking at the history and administration of such a statute in each state.

O'Connor was concerned about the message that any government endorsement of religion might send to nonbelievers. In *Allegheny County v. ACLU*, 492 U.S. 573 (1989), she and Justice Harry Blackmun engineered a Solomonic compromise whereby a holiday menorah display passed Establishment Clause muster, but a nativity scene did not. The approach, which O'Connor pioneered, was context-bound and fact-centered, and since the 1980s it has become characteristic of church-state law relating to public displays of religious iconography. Finally, as the pragmatic centrist, O'Connor provided the necessary fifth vote to uphold public vouchers for religious schools in *Zelman v. Simmons-Harris*, 536 U.S. 639 (2002).

Affirmative Action

A similar pattern of pragmatic but principled centrism determined O'Connor's support for affirmative action programs under certain conditions. O'Connor authored an important majority opinion in *Richmond v. J. A. Croson*, 488 U.S. 469 (1989) barring the use of racial preferences in local government contracting assignments where no history of de jure racial discrimination in that area of business had been shown. *Croson* reaffirmed Justice Lewis Powell's approach in *Regents of the University of California v. Bakke*, 438 U.S. 265 (1978) and deployed strict scrutiny against so-called "benign" racial preference regimes. Yet *Croson* allowed for racial diversity, which the state could pursue as a government interest as long as there were no strict quotas and each applicant's admission file had been individually analyzed. O'Connor's most celebrated role in the development of the Court's affirmative action jurisprudence was her majority opinion in *Grutter v. Bollinger*, 539 U.S. 306 (2003), upholding the University of Michigan Law School's admissions policy, which assigned extra points based on applicants' minority status. O'Connor endorsed the achievement of diversity in higher education as a compelling state interest, essentially reaffirming the middle course that Justice Powell charted in *Bakke*, and the same course that the military, business, and educational institutions had argued for in their amici briefs to the Court.

Federalism

In contrast to her usual pragmatic approach, O'Connor was ideologically committed to a conservative vision of federal-state relations, favoring sharp reductions in Congress's power to regulate purely local activities. She authored the majority opinion in *New York v. United States*, 505 U.S. 144 (1992), endorsing an "anti-commandeering" doctrine that forbade the federal government from utilizing state officers to achieve its policy goals with regard to the disposal of radioactive waste. She joined the conservative bloc in several Amendment XI decisions, extending state sovereign immunity to preclude federal suits against states by their own citizens—a notable example is *Seminole Tribe v. Florida*, 517 U.S. 44 (1996). She also joined the majority in *United States v. Lopez*, 514 U.S. 549 (1995) and *United States v. Morrison*, 529 U.S. 598 (2000), landmark decisions that imposed limits on Congress's authority to pass laws under the Commerce Clause, especially when the Court determined that the regulation resulted in federal government intervention in traditional state functions.

Criminal Procedure

O'Connor usually sided with the Rehnquist Court when it followed its predecessor, the Burger Court, in limiting access to federal courts for state criminal defendants and declining to expand procedural rights articulated during the Warren Court years. Some think that O'Connor's *habeas* jurisprudence owed something to her respect for state institutions, including state courts; she generally opposed giving defendants another chance to hear their case by allowing them to go to federal courts with (for O'Connor) the negative implications such decisions cast on the competence of state judicial systems.

However, as a believer in *stare decisis* (the rule of precedent), O'Connor joined the majority in *Dickerson v. United States*, 530 U.S. 428 (2000), declining to overrule the venerable *Miranda v. Arizona*, 384 U.S. 436 (1966) on the right for defendants to remain silent when arrested by police. She authored the plurality opinion in *Hamdi v. Rumsfeld*, 542 U.S. 507 (2004), a compromise position that allowed the national government to afford accused citizen "enemy combatants" less legal process than ordinary defendants are entitled to, but that rejected the extreme position that executive decisions regarding detention and interrogation of terrorist suspects were not subject to judicial review.

Explaining O'Connor's Jurisprudence

Scholars differ as to the reasons for O'Connor's fairly distinctive approach to judging. Some cite the influence of her time as a state legislator to account for her tendency to moderate the effect of potentially far-reaching decisions and her willingness to seek compromise with colleagues of widely divergent ideological orientations. Others criticize her for lacking a coherent judicial philosophy. Critics allege that her fact-bound opinions had the effect and possibly the intent of preserving her influence on the Court and giving her the ability to both set the law essentially single-handedly on some important constitutional issues as well as to depart from prior positions in cases where it suited her. Although O'Connor is accurately described as at the center of the Rehnquist Court, she was actually a solidly conservative justice by recent historical standards, and she voted with the conservative wing (Thomas, Scalia, Rehnquist, and Anthony Kennedy) considerably more often than with the moderate-liberal wing (Stephen Breyer, David Souter, Ruth Ginsburg, and John Paul Stevens).

Defying the expectations of some legal commentators, Sandra Day O'Connor did not develop a jurisprudence that was distinctively feminine, perhaps reflecting the lack of a clear concept of what such a jurisprudence would look like. Ultimately she argued for a pragmatic centrism, which would sustain basic rights in such areas as abortion choice, separation of church and state and the free exercise of religion, and affirmative action, and, most importantly, which would maintain the power of states in an era of expanding national government power. By grounding basic rights in pragmatism, in a Court clearly divided into conservative and liberal wings, O'Connor was a major force in determining what the Constitution meant in the last decade of her service on the Supreme Court (she retired from the Court on January 31, 2006) and for later decades.

Undoubtedly O'Connor's most notable opinion was issued in *Casey* (somewhat ironically, given that she did not write most of that opinion herself). The decision in *Casey* had implications far beyond the abortion context. Most importantly, in *Casey* the joint opinion makes a strong case for a certain approach to judicial decision-making that can be called "non-originalist"—that is, that the explicit statements of the Founders and the bare structure of the constitutional text are by no means the governing considerations in arriving at Court decisions. This stance has indeed become a major point of disagreement between conservative and liberal justices on the high court throughout the 1990s and into the twenty-first century, as evidenced in the landmark gay rights case *Lawrence v. Texas* (2003). In the end, O'Connor was remarkable for having cast the deciding vote in more important cases than any other justice of the post–World War II decades.

Bibliography and Further Reading

Biskupic, Joan. *Sandra Day O'Connor: How the First Woman on the Supreme Court Became Its Most Influential Justice*. New York: HarperCollins, 2005.

Cook, Beverly. "Justice Sandra Day O'Connor: Transition to a Republican Court Agenda." In *The Burger Court, Political and Judicial Profiles*, edited by Charles Lamb and Stephen Halpern. Urbana and Chicago: University of Illinois Press, 1991: 238–276.

Greco, Joan. "Sandra Day O'Connor." In *The Supreme Court Justices: A Biographical Dictionary. The Supreme Court Justices: A Biographical Dictionary*, edited by Melvin I. Urofsky. New York: Garland Publishers, 1994: 339–345.

Greenburg, Jan Crawford. *Supreme Conflict*. New York: Penguin Press, 2007.

Kahn, Ronald. "Social Constructions, Supreme Court Reversals, and American Political Development: *Lochner, Plessy, Bowers,* But Not *Roe*." In *The Supreme Court and American Political Development*, edited by Ronald Kahn and Ken I. Kersch. Lawrence: University Press of Kansas, 2006: 67–113.

Maveety, Nancy. *Justice Sandra Day O'Connor: Strategist on the Supreme Court*. Lanham, MD: Rowman and Littlefield, 1996.

O'Connor, Sandra Day. *The Majesty of the Law: Reflections of a Supreme Court Justice*. New York: Random House, 2003.

Ronald Kahn

RELATED ENTRIES

THIS VOLUME
Abortion; Affirmative Action; Civil Liberties; Rehnquist, William; Supreme Court and the Judiciary

PATRIOT ACT

See USA PATRIOT Act

PERSIAN GULF WAR

1990–1991

The Persian Gulf War was a watershed in U.S. and international politics. The first significant international conflict of the post–Cold War era, it laid the groundwork not only for other conflicts but also for how the United States would deal with subsequent international security challenges, including the conflicts in Afghanistan and Iraq. The war created two post–Cold War illusions that would haunt international politics and U.S. foreign policy for nearly two decades: first, that there existed an international consensus as to whether and how to deal with troublesome "rogue" regimes; second, that the style of war-fighting developed by the United States to cope with the threat posed by Iraq's invasion of Kuwait was not only effective in that operational theater but could also be readily transferred to other conflicts and other locales. Success led the military to believe that future wars would be conventional wars and could be easily won, thereby removing any incentive military planners might have had to adapt their doctrine and organization to meet the challenges of unconventional warfare and counterinsurgency. Success also exposed the foreign policy making establishment to the perils of unipolarity: in the absence of serious constraints on

U.S. power, all manner of foreign adventures seemed feasible.

Origins

The war had its origins in the end of two others: the Iran-Iraq War (1980–1988) and the Cold War between the United States and the Soviet Union. Begun over a border dispute over the Shatt al-Arab waterway, the Iran-Iraq War was, and remains, the largest and deadliest inter-state war since World War II. Both countries exited the war exhausted. Iraqi president Saddam Hussein had borrowed heavily from his Arab neighbors and faced domestic unrest over his deteriorating economy. To solve both problems simultaneously, he decided in the summer of 1990 to annex the neighboring emirate of Kuwait. The rich Kuwaiti oil fields would be a solution to his debt problem, and another foreign war could serve as a temporary distraction for a restive public. Coincidentally, the end of the Cold War in 1989 meant that the United States could for the first time in decades contemplate international action without Soviet opposition.

When Iraqi forces crossed into Kuwait on August 2, 1990, the first response was regional: the Arab League demanded immediate withdrawal. But the Arab states refused to take any meaningful action, and the crisis thus went global. Citing the audacity of the Iraqi aggression, the United States invoked the full force of international law to manage the situation. Over four months, the presidential administration of George H. W. Bush secured United Nations approval for a sequence of Security Council resolutions beginning with condemnation and the demand for immediate withdrawal on August 2 (Resolution 660). Further resolutions established sanctions, air and sea embargoes, and humanitarian assistance. Finally, on November 29, Resolution 678 gave the Iraqis until January 15, 1991, to withdraw or else face an international community poised to use "all necessary means" to roll back the annexation. Of the permanent members of the Security Council, only China voted other than yes (an abstention), with the rotating members Cuba and Yemen voting against. It was only the second time—and first since the Korean War—that the United Nations had authorized the use of force. At the time of that earlier conflict, the Soviets had been boycotting the council. Now, by contrast, the Soviets, including Pres. Mikhail Gorbachev and Foreign Minister Eduard Shevardnadze, were involved from the beginning, conferring with Bush on everything from how to conduct ship inspections, to the drafting of resolutions, to the decision to use force. During the Cold War, this degree of collaboration would have been unthinkable. The end of that conflict made the international legal response to the Iraqi invasion possible.

Indeed, a consideration of the end of the Cold War and its repercussions can help add perspective to our understanding of the first Gulf War. In June of 1991, the United States did not have a fully formed understanding of its changed national security interests in the Middle East, and, early in the crisis, the signals it sent to Iraq contributed to Hussein's decision to invade Kuwait. Iraq had been important to the U.S.'s Middle East strategy in the 1980s as a bulwark against the revolutionary Islamic republic in Iran. The United States had sided with Hussein in the Iran-Iraq War, and relations between the two governments were cordial, if arms-length. And there was a semblance of legitimacy to Hussein's postwar grievances against the Kuwaiti regime. Iran was a serious threat to conservative Sunni regimes, so in waging war against Iran, Hussein thought that he was doing his Arab neighbors a favor. When Hussein threatened Kuwait in June, he did so with the (incorrect) understanding that other states in the region, and the United States, accepted his campaign to extract remuneration from those who

had benefitted from the Iran-Iraq War. The U.S.'s first response to Iraqi pressure on Kuwait was ambivalence. In a now-famous July 25 meeting between U.S. Ambassador to Iraq April Glaspie and Hussein, Glaspie declared the issue was for the Arabs to resolve, and that the United States did not have an "opinion on inter-Arab disputes such as your border dispute with Kuwait… and Secretary of State Baker had directed our official spokesman to reiterate this stand." (Quoted in Freedman & Karsh 53) Yet eight days later, when Iraqi troops moved across the Kuwaiti border, the Bush administration decided that it did indeed want to roll back Iraqi aggression. International factors and domestic political concerns explain this shift and dictate why and how the United States chose to take on the challenge.

President Bush and his advisors worried about the effects of the crisis on world oil supplies. But they were also internationalists and worried that the end of the Cold War would bring a return of isolationist sentiment in U.S. public opinion. They saw Hussein's surprise invasion of Kuwait as the perfect opportunity to show the American public the value of continuing international engagement and at the same time define a post–Cold War role for the United States as the defender of a legitimate international order. This explains the moral and legalistic tone of Bush's rhetoric—condemning Iraq's "naked aggression" that "will not stand" and branding the U.S. response evidence of a "New World Order." (Mueller 18) Polling in the immediate wake of the Iraqi invasion showed only soft support for a war to defend Kuwaiti sovereignty (in late August, 49 percent of those polled thought the situation merited war). Support remained steady until the January 15 deadline, when it peaked above 70 percent.

The administration had an additional concern: the armed services were still under the pall of the so-called Vietnam Syndrome. General Colin Powell, then Chairman of the Joint Chiefs of Staff, opposed military intervention because the occupation of Kuwait was not a clear and immediate threat to American national security and because he feared the conflict could not be won quickly with few casualties. Its experience in Vietnam had served to render the military leery of engagements without clear objectives

General Norman Schwarzkopf, commander of the U.S.-led Operation Desert Storm, speaks to troops in Saudi Arabia. As the first significant international conflict of the post–Cold War era, the Persian Gulf War was meant to telegraph to the world what Pres. George H. W. Bush called the "New World Order" following the end of the United States's decades-long superpower conflict with the Soviet Union. The quick success of the campaign would also lead the American military to wrongly assume that future wars would be conventional in nature, an assumption that would be roundly discredited a decade later during the wars in Iraq and Afghanistan. (David Turnley/Corbis)

and battlefield environments that promised to turn into quagmires. The solution for the administration was to use the crisis to prove that the United States could win wars in the developing world quickly and cleanly. This impulse, combined with the American people's supposed aversion to casualties, decisively shaped the decision whether to confront Iraq and how to wage war against it. Where Powell saw only a quagmire, Bush and his advisors saw a weak target. The application of massive military might, beginning with an immense air campaign, would solve the problems of the past and lay down an American gauntlet

on a new era. But even on the verge of war, domestic support was precarious. The House voted 250–183 to defeat an anti-war bill, and the Senate authorized war by a narrow 52–47. Thus, from a political perspective, it was imperative that the conduct of the war dispel any lingering skepticism.

The Campaign

The campaign succeeded spectacularly. For Operation Desert Shield, the administration placed over two hundred fifty thousand allied troops in Saudi Arabia to defend against an Iraqi invasion of the Kingdom from

Kuwait. As Desert Shield gave way to Desert Storm in January of 1991, allied forces conducted a five-week bombing campaign to weaken Iraqi defenses, then swept around the massed Iraqi forces in a massive left hook, moving across the Saudi-Iraqi border, outflanking the Iraqis, and ending ground combat in just four days. Iraqi air defenses were devastated and allied forces freely attacked retreating Iraqi soldiers along the "Highway of Death" leading back into Iraq.

The war was also a success at home. The Pentagon imposed extraordinary controls on the press—embedding reporters with army and marine units (with a media officer), or keeping them in briefing rooms in Kuwait City. (The Vietnam experience had convinced the military that unattended reporters in the war zone impeded military operations and were bad for civilian morale). Strategy and media converged on the new 24-hour satellite news channels. The air war was compelling television and gave the conflict an immediacy that even TV coverage of Vietnam had lacked. Footage of plane after plane taking off and landing from airstrips and aircraft carriers, shots of bombs spilling through aircraft bomb-bays, cameras mounted on the tips of cruise missiles, Baghdad lit up at night—all seemed to back up the military's claims that the new precision weaponry made for a clean, surgical, low-casualty war. It worked. Media coverage was enthusiastic. Television reporters routinely used the first-person plural "we" and "us" when describing U.S. military action, and public support for the war soared. Though scholars think the military's claims were oversold, the technology of battle and mass communications combined to convince the government and the American people that military power could serve the ends of policy, even in the Middle East. The coalition had suffered only 379 casualties, nearly half of which were lost to friendly fire, while the Air Force estimated Iraqi casualties at around 20,000 (other estimates place the figure half as high). The battle was won; the Vietnam Syndrome was dead.

Impact

To avoid additional casualties, the administration decided not to pursue a policy of regime change in Baghdad. The Hussein regime was instead constrained by an elaborate set of international legal restrictions: so-called no-fly zones in the north and south prevented the Iraqi air force from using all its sovereign airspace, arms inspectors inside the country thwarted the regime's nuclear ambitions, and a sanctions regime restricted trade.

The war, however, made it easy for U.S. foreign policy-making elites to succumb to the temptations of the lone superpower. Victory in the Cold War had led to victory in the Gulf War, which surely meant that victory could be achieved anywhere the lone superpower chose to direct its attention. No international problem was too complicated or too difficult. In short order, the United States intervened in Somalia, Haiti, Bosnia, Kosovo, Afghanistan, and Iraq. Some of these were humanitarian missions. Others mixed concerns for national security with the U.S.'s reputation and the prestige of America's international order. All proved much harder than they looked, and all suggested an overconfidence in the efficacy of American military power. The military learned that the cure to the Vietnam Syndrome was to not fight unconventional wars and to rely on precision weaponry for a clean, telegenic, low-casualty style of war. Thus it spent the 1990s grudgingly doing humanitarian missions, or turning them into repeats of the Gulf War, as was the case in Kosovo.

When finally thrust into Afghanistan and Iraq, two wars that required counter-insurgency tactics and strategy, the U.S. armed forces were ill-prepared. It took four hard years of ineffectual fighting before the army rewrote its counter-insurgency manual and Gen. David Petraeus was given the authority to shift tactics. Meanwhile, the American public learned to embrace armed interventions of all sorts. They would at times sour on particular missions (Somalia), but force was the solution they appear to understand best. The attitudes of these three actors in the drama of U.S. foreign policy-making—civilian elites, military, and public—thus combined to create a heavily militarized foreign policy that dwarfs, and most often supplants, the diplomatic efforts of the State Department. The Gulf War established the tone and content of post–Cold War U.S. foreign policy and even now, nearly 20 years on, its influence has scarcely faded.

Bibliography and Further Reading

Baum, Matthew A. *Soft News Goes to War: Public Opinion and American Foreign Policy in the New Media Age.* Princeton, NJ: Princeton University Press, 2003.

Biddle, Stephen. *Military Power: Explaining Victory and Defeat in Modern Battle.* Princeton, NJ: Princeton University Press, 2004.

Bush, George H. W., and Brent Scowcroft. *A World Transformed.* New York: Alfred A. Knopf, 1998.

Freedman, Lawrence, and Efraim Karsh. *The Gulf Conflict, 1990–1991: Diplomacy and War in the New World Order.* Princeton, NJ: Princeton University Press, 1993.

Keaney, Thomas, and Eliot A. Cohen. *Gulf War Air Power Survey.* Washington, D.C.: United States Department of the Air Force, 1993.

Mueller, John E. *Policy and Opinion in the Gulf War.* Chicago: University of Chicago Press, 1994.

Press, Daryl G. "The Myth of Air Power in the Persian Gulf War and the Future of Warfare." *International Security* 26, no. 2 (fall 2001): 5–44.

Priest, Dana. *Mission: America's Military in the Twenty-First Century.* New York: Norton, 2003.

Rozell, Mark J. "Media Coverage of the Persian Gulf War." In *The Presidency and the Persian Gulf War,* edited by Marcia Lynn Whicker, James P. Pfiffner, and Raymond A. Moore. Westport, CT: Prager, 1993.

Geoffrey L. Herrera

POLITICAL POLARIZATION

Political polarization in the United States is the sorting of liberals and conservatives into the Democratic and Republican parties. It rests on a greater alignment between a party's leaders and its base; a more diverse and active interest group landscape; and an increasing divisiveness in the domestic and foreign policy stands adopted by the two major parties. In recent decades, cultural issues—for example, abortion, gay marriage, the death penalty, and prayer in schools—have emerged alongside the preexisting gulf between the parties over the size of government and the degree of government intervention in society and markets.

Party and congressional reform also have played a part in increasing polarization. Party reform, instigated at the 1968 Democratic Convention and effective for the 1972 Democratic Convention, affected both parties to varying degrees. More and more, Republican and Democratic positions on issues like abortion, affirmative action, civil rights, and other cultural issues became the arenas for intra-party battles. Further, congressional reforms in both parties allowed committee chairs and ranking members to be removed by an internal party vote if they failed to represent party agendas. For the Democrats, this process took place in the 1970s, and for the Republicans it occurred in the 1980s and 1990s. These changes helped parties to become more cohesive, allowing new members to develop programmatic policies as campaign and party-leadership vehicles.

The Debate over Polarization

Polarization has sparked considerable controversy. The culture of Congress in particular has changed. Policy stances are decided along party lines rather than through long-term committee friendships and committee-based policy agreements across party lines. Not only are there fewer bipartisan friendships, but it is also estimated that as many as a hundred members within each party caucus do not even talk with opposing party members, many of whom have come to view the other party as the enemy. Further, procedural battles and parliamentary tactics are increasingly deployed as means to defeat legislation. Rather than a win or loss based on a show of forces, political strategy based on personal attacks and ethics charges have produced a "fight club politics" in which efforts to undermine the opposing party's leadership have become another tool within the party arsenals. (Eilperin 2006) These efforts to attack leaders have ranged from the 1998 impeachment of Pres. Bill Clinton, to the earlier 1988 ethics charges lodged against then-Democratic speaker Jim Wright (who resigned his seat) by then-G.O.P. whip Newt Gingrich. Gingrich, who became speaker in 1995 with the new Republican majority, faced 84 ethics charges lodged against him, primarily by House Democratic whip David Bonior. (Gingrich was sanctioned by the House Ethics Committee in 1997 and later resigned his speakership and his seat after Republican candidates went down to defeat in the 1998 elections.) Other examples of polarization include refusals (in the Senate) to confirm judges, giving rise for some months in the early 2000s to the threat by the G.O.P. leadership (their party then in the majority) of abolishing the filibuster altogether. These internal battles have created hard feelings that persist even after the immediate political issue has faded.

Though some focus on the problems of polarized politics, polarization started with grassroots protests in the 1960s and reflects a greater democratization of American politics that has transformed the political landscape from one in which many groups were shut out of politics to a more inclusive politics. Partisanship used to stop at the borders, but polarization is now found in all areas of American politics, including foreign policy. The result is a more conflictual but also a more open political system. Though cultural issues do matter, they have not replaced economic issues. And even though parties sometimes focus too much on strategy to manipulate the agenda of policy debate to the extent of creating areas of false disagreement, the politics of setting the policy agenda has permanently moved toward party organizations, just as the responsible party approach would prescribe, supplanting older, less transparent bargaining processes between the president and Congress.

Bibliography and Further Reading

Baer, Denise L., and David A. Bositis. *Elite Cadres and Party Coalitions: Representing the Public in Party Politics.* New York: Greenwood Press, 1988.

Eilperin, Juliet. *Fight Club Politics: How Partisanship Is Poisoning the House of Representatives.* Lanham, MD: Rowman and Littlefield, 2006.

Fiorina, Morris P., Samuel J. Abrams, and Jeremy C. Pope. *Culture War? The Myth of a Polarized America.* New York: Longman Publishing Group, 2005.

Poole. Keith T. "The Decline and Rise of Party Polarization in Congress During the Twentieth Century," *Extensions,* Fall 2005.

Poole, Keith T., and Howard Rosenthal. "The Polarization of American Politics," *Journal of Politics,* 1984, 1061–1079.

Rhode, David W. *Parties and Leaders in the Postreform House.* Chicago: University of Chicago Press, 1991.

Stimson, James A. *Tides of Consent: How Public Opinion Shapes American Politics.* New York: Cambridge University Press, 2004.

Denise L. Baer

POLITICAL ACTION COMMITTEES

Political Action Committees (PACs) became more vigorous elements of the national election cycle following the campaign finance reforms of the 1970s. Indeed, it is now difficult to imagine how any national political figure could accumulate the necessary funds for a campaign without some assistance from PACs.

Although much has been written regarding the influence that PACs have on members of Congress and public policy, most voters still do not fully understand the rise and role of PACs in the last several decades. An examination of the early onset of what would become known as PACs deserves discussion. Moreover, the effect of Richard Nixon's 1972 campaign on the regulation of money is of vast significance in the growth of PACs. The explosion of PACs also includes lesser known "offshoots" that are imporant players in the electoral process. Perhaps of most concern is the influence of PACs on the political discourse and on members of Congress. One prevalent criticism of PACs includes the allegation that candidates and elected officials are beholden to them to the extent that they have abandoned the interests of the common citizen. PACs have evolved into an institutional element of the U.S. political process, and their influence merits attention.

Defining PACs

PAC is the common term for organizations that raise and spend campaign funds to assist or defeat candidates. Most PACs are connected to an interest group of some kind. The technical term for PACs is "separate segregated funds," because the money they collect must be kept in a separate bank account from the general funds for a corporation or a union.

Early Group Influence

Money influenced politics even before the advent of PACs and before they became a prevalent element of the U.S. political process. Businesses and corporations heavily subsidized William McKinley's 1896 presidential bid. Later, Theodore Roosevelt helped to bring about the Tillman Act of 1907, which prohibited direct corporate contributions to federal campaigns. Following this was the passage of the Federal Corruption Practices Act of 1925, which established the first public disclosure rules at the federal level, placed spending limits on parties in Congressional races, and banned corporate contributions of all kinds. The 1925 act would be the last effort at campaign reform until the 1970s.

The History of PACs

The notion of a PAC actually began with labor. The Congress of Industrial Organizations (CIO-PAC) raised money in 1944 for the re-election of Pres. Franklin Roosevelt. In reaction to the labor PACs, various business PACs were formed. In 1963, the Business-Industry Political Action Committee (BIPAC) was established by the National Association of Manufacturers. Even prior to the PAC movement, many corporations had already developed some type of pre-PAC political contribution method, some of them as simple as cash contributions in envelopes.

A Brief Background on the 1974 Reform Efforts

The rise of PACs cannot be understood without a discussion of the campaign reform of the 1970s. There were two major efforts at campaign reform in the 1970s. The 1971 Federal Election Campaign Act (FECA) dealt with the regulation of broadcasting, and the 1974 amendment addressed the regulation of money in elections. One unintended consequence of the 1974 reform was the tremendous growth of PACs. The legislation followed on the heels of the

Senate's Watergate investigation. By 1975, 19 corporations had been convicted of making illegal campaign contributions to the Nixon reelection effort. This event, along with other allegations, empowered the Democrats to amend the 1971 Federal Election Campaign Act. The 1974 law ushered in systematic contribution limits, thereby making it more difficult for candidates to raise the money necessary to mount serious campaigns. Since PACs are more likely to donate to incumbents than to challengers, the 1974 restrictions gave an advantage to the former and to the status quo.

It appears that the intent of the 1974 law was to make certain that wealthy individuals and economic institutions did not simply overwhelm the efforts of small, individual donors. Also included in the 1974 reform law was the provision, pushed by union lobbyists, for PACs to be legalized to raise money for election activities. At the time, speculation had it that this would give unions an enduring fundraising advantage over business.

Modern Era of PACs

What is considered to be the modern era of PACs began as a result of the 1974 reforms. The campaign reforms of the 1970s included a provision that granted the right to corporations and labor unions to form, administer, and raise funds for their PACs and to cover all organizational expenses from corporate and union treasuries. Outside of this provision, the changes of the 1970s did not affect PACs directly, but their indirect effect did limit other sources of campaign money, creating greater reliance among candidates on PAC funding.

Because the 1974 reforms created public funding for presidential elections but not for congressional races, PACs also began to focus more exclusively on the former.

The Growth of PACs in Elections

PACs grew tremendously in the years following the campaign reform measures of the 1970s. In 1972, there were 113 PACs; 608 in 1975; 2,551 in 1980; and 3,525 by 1983. PAC spending in elections jumped by 900 percent in one decade, rising from

$19.1 million in 1972 to $190.2 million in 1982. Even when adjusting for inflation, this amounted to a 350 percent increase. However, it is important to note that all campaign donations increased in this decade. By the early 1980s, PAC donations consisted of almost one-third of campaign funds for a House candidate and almost one-fifth of the funds for the standard Senate candidate.

By 2009, approximately 40 percent of donations for U.S. House candidates was derived from PACs. The influence of PACs in the Senate is less because the Senate races are much more expensive and rely more on individual donors. There were 399 House members running for reelection in 2008. Over $577 million was raised by all House members; of that, over $258 million was donated by PACs, and more than $290 million donated by individuals. Thirty members of the Senate sought reelection in 2008. Over $221 million was raised by these candidates. Over $59 million was donated by PACs and over $134 million was donated by individuals. In contrast to individual donors and PACs, political parties donated a much smaller amount to House and Senate candidates.

PACs Formed by Candidates

A lesser-known element of PACs includes the formation of PACs by elected officials. Many members of Congress have their own PACs to solicit funds aggressively on their own behalf. If they are not threatened by a serious challenger, they may donate part of their funds to the reelection effort of colleagues. These PACs have more leeway when it comes to spending. Elected officials who are able to disperse funds from their leadership PAC do so not only to hold or increase their party's numbers in Congress but also to elevate their clout within the party. House Minority Leader John Boehner (R–OH) and House Majority Leader Steny Hoyer (D–MD) each raised and spent millions from their leadership PACs on congressional races in the 2008 cycle.

Stealth PACs

In addition to PACs which are officially registered with the Federal Election Commission, there also exists an entity known as "stealth PACs." These hold tax-exempt status but may participate in political activities. Many are advocacy groups which are trying to influence federal elections with voter mobilization. In the 2008 election cycle, stealth PACs reported receipts totaling over $240 million and expenses of over $258 million. Some of the more notable of these PACs include EMILY's List, which was founded to fund female Democratic candidates supportive of abortion rights. In the 2008 election cycle, EMILY's List reported receipts totaling over $13 million and expenditures amounting to over $12 million.

Other notable examples of these "527" groups (so-named because of their IRS tax status) include the conservative Swift Vets and POWs for Truth, which gained notoriety in the 2004 election cycle for its ads questioning whether Democratic presidential nominee and Vietnam veteran John Kerry had actually deserved some of his service medals. The Swift Boat Veterans raised over $17 million and spent almost $22 million in an effort to profile Kerry's military record, though the credibility of this group has been called into question due to misleading or inconsistent statements.

Do PACs Buy the Votes of Members of Congress?

A great deal of the controversy surrounding PACs centers around the suspicion that PAC donations "buy" the votes of members of Congress. For instance, a House member who accepted regular contributions from the tobacco lobby then might be more inclined to vote in favor of the interests of tobacco producers. A number of studies conducted on this point have resulted in some interesting findings. PACs argue that contributions to candidates buys them *access*, not votes. Admittedly, it is difficult to get the ear of a member of Congress amidst the many demands and obligations associated with his or her various legislative positions. A donation by a PAC helps ensure that the member will at least listen to a PAC's proposal or position on a topic.

Studies find some correlation between PAC contributions and voting patterns on *some* issues but this

Senator Hillary Clinton greets people as she attends a luncheon of the EMILY's List PAC at the Hilton Washington Hotel on January 18, 2009, in Washington, D.C. Referred to as a "stealth PAC" because of its tax-exempt status, EMILY's List was founded in 1985 by Ellen Malcolm to raise money for pro-choice female candidates. As part of its mobilization efforts, the group provides members with information about candidates and encourages them to donate to their campaigns directly. (Alex Wong/Getty Images)

will not influence voting every time, and the correlations vary according to the visibility of the issue and the degree of specialization of the issue. The bottom line, quite counter-intuitively, of the great majority of the analyses is that the vote of a member of Congress is not affected by PAC contributions when the member's party, ideology, and constituent needs and wishes are taken into account.

The Public's View of PACs

Public opinion of PACs is generally not positive. Those who have an opinion regarding PACs tend to believe that PACs "own" the candidates and that elected officials are more responsive to the wishes of

the special interest groups than to the needs and desires of their constituents. In fact, the implication that a candidate is owned by a PAC can be a serious threat to his or her election hopes. Ironically, because it is so difficult to raise the funds to launch a legitimate, strong campaign, a candidate who refuses to accept PAC money might find it difficult to be taken seriously as a candidate.

PACs are given some "cover" from scrutiny due to the fact that so much of the American public does not even know what a PAC is. When voters do express opinions about PACs, their responses tend to depend on the wording of the question and on which PAC they are asked about.

The Influence of PACs on the Political Process

There is disagreement as to the ramifications of PACs for the U.S. electoral and legislative process. Some argue that PACs are a healthy element of public participation. Others maintain that the rules regulating PACs have made the process more open and transparent than the days of quietly collecting money from groups and employees and delivering it to candidates in plain envelopes. Still others point out that individual contributors, and not PACs, remain the most important element of campaign donations and that PACs are unfairly singled out by the media and some elected officials, even those who accept money from them.

Critics have developed a lengthy and detailed list of the negatives associated with the rise of PACs. It is accurate to suggest that PACs are incumbent-biased and therefore help to maintain the status quo, inhibiting the possibility of change or the injection of fresh ideas into the system. To the extent that PACs are the "children" of special interest groups, it can be argued that organizations of which only a tiny minority of Americans belong are effectively influencing public policies that effect everyone. Further, PACs are yet another indicator of the decline of political parties in the United States. The party mechanism to motivate voters and the grassroots approach have been lost to the world of direct mail, pollsters, advertisers, television, and accountants.

PACs, however, remain entrenched as a key element of the U.S. political system. They are the result of Congress attempting to limit the influence of a small, wealthy group of people. The subject of PACs cannot be addressed without a discussion of campaign finance reform. However, as history has shown, when one leak is plugged in the campaign finance process, yet another appears as participants scurry to find legal venues around the restrictions. True campaign reform is not likely to occur given the dynamics of Congress. In addressing campaign finance reform, Congress will always act to maintain the status quo, regardless of which party controls the body. Some have suggested that the solution to the issue of PACs would be the public financing of congressional elections. This was proposed decades ago, but Congress rejected it for the simple fact that it would mean that challengers would be eligible for public funding as well. Unless pressed by the voters, there is little chance that Congress will move in the direction of public financing of their elections.

Additionally, the proliferation of PACs is not only present at the national level. There has been rapid growth of PACs in states and local governments, as well. Indeed, many of the national PACs have offshoots at the state and local level and they function in similar fashion to the national PACs. Even if successful steps are taken to curb the influence of PACs in elections and the legislative process, no doubt PACs will find ways around the rules in order to achieve their goals. PACs are a systematic part of the U.S. political process.

It is proposed by some that PACs represent an exercise of the electorate's First Amendment rights. In contrast to this argument, it has been suggested that the Founding Fathers never envisioned or intended for the U.S. structure of government to be influenced in this manner. Regardless of who is correct, PACs are an entrenched part of the system and show no signs of weakening.

Bibliography and Further Reading

Cigler, Allan J., and Burdett A. Loomis. *Interest Group Politics.* Washington, D.C.: CQ Press, 2002.

Fiorina, Morris P., Paul Peterson, Bertram Johnson, and William G. Mayer. *America's New Democracy.* New York: Penguin Academics, 2009.

Sabato, Larry J. *PAC Power: Inside the World of Political Action Committees.* New York: W. W. Norton, 1984.

Samples, John. *The Fallacy of Campaign Finance Reform.* Chicago: The University of Chicago Press, 2006.

Sorauf, Frank J. *What Price PACS?* Report of the Twentieth Century Fund Task Force on Political Action Committees. Background paper. New York, 1992.

Witko, Christopher. "PACs, Issue Context, and Congressional Decisionmaking." *Political Research Quarterly* 59, no. 2 (2006): 283–295.

Lori J. Owens

PRESIDENCY

The development of the modern presidency has been the result of changing sources of presidential power that have relied on the president's legislative skills, managerial experience, public persona, and leadership-building abilities. Post-Watergate presidents, more so than earlier officeholders, have been expected to initiate and seek support for their legislative actions and policies through media outreach and congressional coalition building. During those instances in which bipartisan coalition building seems an unlikely possibility, modern presidents have resorted to unilateral policy making through executive directives, government initiatives, and other actions not ratified by Congress. In order for the president to accomplish his domestic and foreign policy goals, a greater emphasis has been placed on the president's ability to rally other actors to his side through the art of political persuasion. In addition, the president's public image has become much more important. The late twentieth-century's dynamic political environment and communication revolution has influenced the rhetorical and media strategies used by presidents to garner support from the general public.

Formal Presidential Powers and Congressional Coalition Building

The president's formal powers range from commander-in-chief of the armed forces to chief administrator of the executive branch of government. Although the president's formal powers are wide reaching, much of his authority over foreign and domestic affairs is shared with Congress. Fearing that the concentration of power in the hands of one person would result in executive tyranny, the framers of the Constitution created a system of "checks and balances" within the three branches of government. The Founders intended that presidential power be kept in check by Congress and the judicial branch, as well as by other regulations built into the political system, to ensure that governmental decision making did not become too centralized in the executive branch. However, the precise patterns of shared authority and balance of power were kept deliberately ambiguous.

Despite the power of congressional oversight, presidential administrations in the post–World War II period have been associated with strong centralized power and executive authority. After 1945, the Cold War gave rise to fears of nuclear proliferation and a foreign policy doctrine of containment that ushered in an era of "imperial presidents" whose focus on national security eclipsed Congress in the shaping of both domestic and international policies. However, with the administration of Richard M. Nixon (1968–1974), public and congressional satisfaction with a strong presidency dissolved due to the growing dissent over the Vietnam War and the exposure of political corruption in the Watergate scandal. In the late 1970s, the public witnessed a series of Watergate-era reforms in which Congress and the courts sought to limit some of the president's formal powers.

After Watergate, the legislative branch attempted to assert greater independence through strong congressional leadership and by reasserting its executive oversight role. In the post-Watergate political climate, Congress reaffirmed its constitutional power through an array of bills meant to make the president more accountable to Congress. This included curbing the executive branch's tendency toward secrecy and its ability to withhold information from the public by passing the Freedom of Information Act of 1976 and the Privacy Act of 1974. Congress had already attempted to restrict the president's unilateral war-making powers with the passage of the War Powers Act of 1973. Congressional oversight has become increasingly important in the late twentieth century. Modern-day congressional authority has taken on the role of watchdog, deploying a variety of oversight tools including select committee investigations, specialized subcommittee hearings, informal meetings, and House impeachment proceedings.

The late 1970s brought dramatic changes in how the president asserted influence, as presidential administrations focused more on congressional coalition building to pass carefully crafted legislative agendas. Modern presidents have relied on extra-constitutional powers, especially in terms of influence and bargaining, in order to effectively govern. Some presidential administrations have built bipartisan coalitions of organized interest groups as a means to forward their legislative agendas. For example, the Carter administration (1977–1981) focused on structured bipartisan coalitions by using White House staff in a liaison role that included direct communication with members of Congress. Carter's presidency adopted an approach to legislative coalition building that attempted to balance social reform with fiscal restraint. This new approach was designed to merge presidential and congressional policy-making initiatives, yet transformed the goals and resources of like-minded interest groups into political assets for the White House.

Although Carter faced many challenges in furthering his legislative agenda, he devised a White House legislative liaison system which required substantial legislative leadership and coalition-building skills. Indeed, one of the most pronounced characteristics of the post-Watergate presidency has been a more formalized White House liaison system, its goal to shape the legislature's agenda through coalition building, often across party lines.

The success of this process often depends on the extent to which the president's coalition constitutes a working majority in both houses of Congress. As a rule, presidential power increases when one political party controls the presidency and both houses of the legislature. For example, after the election of Pres. Bill Clinton in 1992, Democrats gained full control of Congress. Clinton passed the Family and Medical Leave Act of 1993, the North American Free Trade Agreement (NAFTA), and the Brady Handgun Violence Prevention Act of 1993 before losing control of Congress in the mid-term elections in 1994. Throughout much of the later twentieth century, the visibility of the president as party leader offered multiple opportunities for the passage of legislation with primary control vested in the executive office. Although coalition building has been a key component in the implementation of the president's domestic and international agenda since the late 1970s, a presidential administration often runs the risk of being temporarily drawn into a myriad of conflicting political party and special-interest demands.

Unilateral Action and Presidential Directives

In times of divided government, presidents have relied less on congressional alliances and instead have resorted to the use of unilateral action in the form of presidential directives, such as proclamations, executive agreements, and executive orders, to expand presidential power. In this case, the president needs neither congressional nor judicial approval for his policies to be put in place. Unilateral policies are most likely to be used when Congress is ready to enact sweeping legislation that the president opposes. Acting independently, the president can preempt Congress by blocking legislation with a veto and issuing a series of presidential directives.

Historically, the president has employed a variety of tools to, in effect, govern without the consent of Congress. Most widely used of these is the executive order, a directive issued by the president, usually to a U.S. executive officer or member of the executive branch, to direct operational procedures. Traditionally, presidents have issued executive orders to implement the constitutional powers of the office and, as a result, the tactic has a long historical precedent. For example, Pres. Franklin D. Roosevelt drew on executive orders more than any other tool to guide the country through the Great Depression and World War II. In more recent history, a greater number of executive orders have been issued in times of divided government due to the fact that executive orders dissuade congressional oversight. President William J. Clinton exercised his power to write executive orders after the Republicans gained congressional control in 1994. Clinton passed executive orders on affirmative action, labor law, and wilderness conservation. He also used an executive order to authorize military intervention in Kosovo in 1999.

Although some directives have been given to the president through specific legislation—such as the authority to create an executive budget—other powers, which presidential historians have referred to as "discretionary powers," have been assumed by the president in times of national or international crisis. These directives have, historically, often proved the most controversial in twentieth-century presidential history. For example, seeking to expand executive authority, Pres. Ronald Reagan took advantage of loopholes in the War Powers Act (1973) as license to engage in limited military action, to determine arms-control policy, and to end treaties, all of which constituted presidential prerogatives without congressional oversight.

Another Reagan-era initiative calculated to enhance the power of the presidency was the instigation of the so-called signing statement. The signing statement provides the president with the means to detail his own interpretation of a given statute. Whether the president issues a signing statement or a series of executive orders, exerting executive privilege through presidential directives remains controversial because some have argued that the use of these tools exceeds the office's constitutional boundaries.

The Public Presidency and Image Building

Public opinion, the media, and interest groups can either enhance or limit the president's use of unilateral powers. Through the explosion of communication technology, the late-twentieth-century conception of the presidency has entailed far greater media visibility than what the Founders experienced. Subsequently, modern presidents have additional ways of expanding executive power through media outlets. Modern presidents have used the media as an extension of presidential power, allowing for more timely communication of political messages to a larger audience than has been possible during any other time in American history. This so-called "public presidency" encompasses the use of media images, rhetorical strategies, powerful symbols, and the ceremonial duties of the office to appeal directly to the public. Through the use of these tools and well-planned communication strategies, presidents have sought to garner public support in hopes of rallying public opinion and forcing powerful political actors to comply with the president's policy agenda.

The twentieth century communication revolution and the rise of cable television has contributed to an elevation in the symbolism and power of the office of the president, while significantly reducing the strength and function of political parties to act as a conduit between the president and the voters. Television, in particular, offers a means by which presidents can present themselves and their agendas directly to voters, and can serve as a medium by which presidents can expand their popularity, develop a coherent communication strategy, and concentrate attention on specific social, economic, and political issues. For example, Ronald Reagan was known as the "Great Communicator" because he used televised speeches and State of the Union addresses to garner public support for his domestic and foreign policy initiatives. Bill Clinton conducted televised "town hall meetings" in order to engage the public in "two-way conversations" on his domestic policy agenda.

There is, of course, a downside to this arrangement, for even as television has enhanced the president's position as the nation's supreme political symbol, it has also established the office as the focal point of economic downturns, political scandals, and public dissent and protest. It also has tended to highlight the president's personal foibles and physical miscues. For example, Pres. Gerald Ford found it difficult to project a powerful public image. During his presidency, the public was treated to images of the president slipping down the steps of Air Force One and taking a spill during a skiing trip. With the help of late-night comedians and television show parodies, Ford's physical mishaps became part of a larger media image of presidential ineptness.

In addition, media sources can provide an important check on misuse of executive power and, as a result, make the president more responsive to public opinion. Any new president becomes open for criticism through media sources if he does not quickly produce visible results, usually in his first 100 days. The expansion of political media outlets has placed a greater importance on presidential style, leadership, and personality, as well as the president's organizational skills and managerial experience.

The Managerial Presidency and the Expansion of the Executive Branch

As post-Watergate presidents have added executive departments, they have also actively defined the scope of democratic representation as well as expanded informal avenues of presidential power. The president's influence has grown alongside the domestic responsibilities of the federal government. By providing for the public's welfare, health care, and safety, new executive departments significantly add to the federal bureaucracy and contribute to the overall power of the office.

The "institutional" presidency, which is characterized by a large, functionally specialized, and White House-centered presidential staff system, has had the effect of channeling, structuring, and making routine much of presidential behavior and activity during the late twentieth century. Though the "institutionalization" of the presidency has led to the expanded bureaucratization of the federal government, it has also increased presidential resources to influence administrative and policy-making processes. Modern presidents have had to shape and use the existing bureaucracy and consolidate power within the White House complex, thereby significantly strengthening the political power within the office of the president.

The Reagan administration (1981–1989) marked a turning point in the management of the executive departments by centralizing policy making, personnel decisions, and the budget process within the White House. During the 1980s, both conservatives and moderate liberals criticized the expansion and mismanagement of government social service policies, pointing to government fraud, bureaucratic waste, the scarcity of low-income housing, and the marginalization of the working class. In the 1980s, Reagan took office promising to end the "era of big government." With supply-side economics declared as the new political panacea, executive departments lost their prestige and political influence. Many executive agencies were forced to defend themselves against a presidential administration that sought to restrict each agency's effectiveness, power, and influence through a massive reorganization that targeted the entire executive branch of government.

The Clinton administration (1993–2001) continued this trend in the 1990s. President Clinton's "New Democrat" policies steered away from the expansion of government services of the New Deal and the Great Society. During his first six months in office, Clinton announced plans for a major overhaul of the federal government. Promising to reinvent government by promoting efficiency and cutting red tape, Clinton's reorganization plan was presented in a 1993 report entitled *Creating a Government That Works Better and Costs Less*. With the rise of the federal bureaucracy, recent presidents have struggled to balance administrative efficiency and government accountability with the politicization of public policy and the rising influence of special interests. In order to exert greater managerial control over the behemoth federal bureaucracy, presidential power and decisions have been centralized and concentrated in the White House.

In addition to legislative coalition building, presidential directives, and communication plans, presidential administrations of the late twentieth century have focused on developing a comprehensive organizational strategy for White House staff which has become crucial in orchestrating a president's political message and policy objectives, and has also aided the president's management of the growing federal bureaucracy. These organizational plans begin with a president's approach to decision making characterized, first and foremost, by the degree of control a president asserts over the policy-making process within the White House.

If the president wants to make a final decision with ultimate authority, staff organization will resemble a hierarchical system with the president at the top of the formal chain of command. Information gathering and decision making, as well as the responsibility to define and propose solutions to newly emerging problems, tend to occur at lower levels and rise up the chain of command to the president. For example, the Reagan administration's staff structure was characterized by a hierarchical decision tree made up of a group of high-level senior staff members.

If, on the other hand, the president rules by consensus or concurrence, he is less likely to rely on the use of a formal hierarchical pattern of authority. Instead, the president will institute an informal pattern of decision making, one that is more inclusive and is constructed and reconstructed as particular issues arise. The president will be at the top of the chain of command but he will purposely choose to involve others directly in decision making, welcoming varying opinions on policy initiatives and relying on more informal channels of authority and information gathering. For example, President Clinton relied on a team-building approach to decision making, seeking a wide range of opinions and perspectives from diverse policy groups who provided feedback on possible options to advance his domestic and foreign policy agendas.

Presidential transition teams have been confronted by the difficult and complex task of staffing the White House with those who can effectively convey organizational strategies and successfully use managerial tools. This may explain the growing importance of the chief of staff who oversees White House operations, relaying the president's managerial philosophy as well as setting the tone for the work-style and organizational culture of the administration. In addition, the president's organization of White House personnel has become increasingly significant in managing information and conflict resolution, a crucial component in preventing embarrassing "leaks" to the media. In the late twentieth century, presidential historians have argued that individual presidential management strategies and organizational styles have been critical to the success or failure of presidential administrations. During the post-Watergate period, chiefs of staff such as Andrew Card (under George W. Bush), John Podesta (under Bill Clinton), and Donald Regan (under Ronald Reagan), have been powerful political actors helping to centralize control, manage crises, and contain communication leaks within the White House.

The Imperial Presidency Revisited

In the aftermath of the terrorist attacks on September 11, 2001, Pres. George W. Bush presided over a his-

torically unprecedented consolidation of presidential power. Bush's augmentation of presidential power was aligned with efforts by many previous administrations to expand the presidency and diminish executive oversight of Congress by exerting executive privilege, conducting national security initiatives without congressional interference, increasing unilateral policy making, and centralizing government control and decision making within the White House.

Emerging from the September 11 terrorist attacks, the Bush administration tasked the White House Office of Homeland Security with developing government policies to secure the country's borders, synthesize intelligence information, and protect the nation's infrastructure. Citing the "dangers of a new era," Bush signed the Homeland Security Act, giving the Department of Homeland Security Cabinet-level status on November 25, 2002. The legislation, which called for the largest reorganization of the executive branch since the post–World War II period, mandated the consolidation of 22 federal agencies responsible for counterterrorism, thereby centralizing control in the White House.

A wave of executive assertions after September 11 has strengthened the Office of the President in unprecedented ways, marked by a reassertion and expansion of presidential power and unilateral decision making. President Bush redefined national security to include the defense of the country's economic infrastructure, creating a new kind of executive order, the Homeland Security Directive. Through a series of anti-terror laws, which included the USA PATRIOT Act, the Financial Anti-Terrorism Act, and the Aviation and Transportation Security Act, Congress granted the president additional authority to provide intelligence and law enforcement agencies with an array of new powers while creating a growing unease among the public regarding threats to civil liberties. One of the president's most important claims was the unilateral power to declare individuals, including U.S. citizens, "enemy combatants" who could be detained by federal authorities under adverse legal conditions.

The informal and formal powers of the post-Watergate presidency have been characterized by a delicate balance between congressional coalition building, the use of bold unilateral action to further domestic and foreign policy agendas, effective management of a growing bureaucracy, and the reliance on communication skills to craft a powerful public image. This complex array of presidential activities serves to augment the influence and political capital of the executive branch in light of the ever changing political landscape of the late twentieth and early twenty-first centuries.

Bibliography and Further Reading

Cronin, Thomas E., and Michael A. Genovese. *The Paradoxes of the American Presidency.* New York: Oxford Press, 1998.

George, Alexander L., and Juliette L. George. *Presidential Personality and Performance.* Boulder, CO: Westview Press, 1998.

Gould, Lewis L. *The Modern American Presidency.* Lawrence: University Press of Kansas, 2003.

Greenstein, F. I. *Leadership in the Modern Presidency.* Cambridge, MA: Harvard University Press, 1988.

Howell, William G. *Power Without Persuasion: The Politics of Direct Presidential Action.* Princeton, NJ: Princeton University Press, 2003.

Nichols, D. K. *The Myth of the Modern Presidency.* University Park: Pennsylvania State University Press, 1994.

Pfiffner, J. P. *The Modern Presidency.* New York: St. Martin's Press, 1994.

Rudalevige, Andrew. *The New Imperial Presidency: Renewing Presidential Power after Watergate.* Ann Arbor: University of Michigan Press, 2005.

Shogan, Colleen J. *The Moral Rhetoric of American Presidents.* College Station: Texas A&M University Press, 2006.

Stuckey, Mary E. *Defining Americans: The Presidency and National Identity.* Lawrence: University Press of Kansas, 2004.

Angela Fritz

PUBLIC OPINION POLLING

By the mid-1970s, public opinion polls were widely visible in American political and social life. The mass media routinely described the public's political attitudes, behavior, and personal attributes based on poll results. With improved computer technology, responses to questions could be counted, statistically analyzed, and interpreted with increasing speed. More and more polls were conducted by survey researchers or pollsters (the terms are synonymous today): the widely known Gallup and Harris polls and those of other commercial pollsters; academic surveys conducted by university-based research centers; and the newest players—the news media themselves, which began sponsoring and conducting their own polls on an unprecedented scale. Polls were also conducted for non-profit organizations and interest groups, and, most important, increasingly by political parties and election campaigns that treated their polling information as proprietary and used it for strategic purposes. By century's end, the number of polls had expanded enormously, and, just as important, their expansion had itself become highly politicized, prompting new debates about public opinion research.

Debates about Public Opinion and Polling

Academics and commentators continued to debate the positive impact on American democracy that George Gallup felt public opinion polling could have. Many critics doubted that the public was sufficiently knowledgeable, attentive to politics, skilled in interpretation and analysis, and wise enough to deserve attention in governing beyond casting its vote in elections. Rather, the public had to defer to political leaders and experts. Conversely, defenders of the "rationality" of public opinion argued that the public—as individuals and especially as a collective—was sufficiently capable of taking cues or learning from political leaders and other sources. Indeed, the public had defensible reasons for its opinions to warrant ongoing attention in the political process. One innovative survey method, called the "deliberative poll," attempted to improve the quality of such data by influencing the dynamics and quality of public opinion itself. This poll draws a random sample of the public through a probability sampling method, surveys respondents in person, and then brings the sample together to meet and learn about issues and through briefing materials, meetings with experts and political leaders, and small-group discussions, to see how public opinion is transformed through information and debate.

Both sides of the "rational public" debate were concerned with the operational problems of survey-based opinion research and with pollsters' persistent efforts to remedy them. Polls continued to vary in their type, scope, and quality, as both innovations and new problems emerged. As survey researchers tried to get good estimates of the opinions and behavior, the problems often cited in the early days of polling remained: sampling coverage—identifying and representing a population and obtaining a sufficiently high response rate; statistical sampling error, assuming acceptable sampling coverage; the effects of questions' wording; the use of fixed choice versus open-ended questions; the treatment of "don't know," "no opinion," and "undecided" responses; effects of question order ("context effects"); the fuzziness of research questions being studied and the assumptions made about respondents' familiarity with a particular issue or topic; whether reported behavior validly represents actual behavior (in the past, present, or future); interviewer effects on responses; and the effects of the type of survey method used ("mode effects").

Further Developments in Polling

Most polls through the early 1970s relied on face-to-face interviewing. Some research may have included longer intensive interviews and the use of small group conversations, later widely known as "focus groups," which were often used in commercial research and later in political campaigns. The use of "exit polls"—that is, sampling voters as they left polling precincts—expanded to include projecting, in addition to explaining, election results. The single most important development in polling was the expansion of telephone interviewing through the use of Random Digit Dialing (RDD) or related list-assisted methods. Telephone polling was less costly than in-person interviewing, inasmuch as it eliminated travel costs, and was easier than in-person interviews to monitor and validate. With the use of Computer Assisted Telephone Interviewing (CATI) systems, the speed and accuracy of data processing improved, and polling became highly efficient. What enabled pollsters to justify shifting to the telephone were, first, the fact that by the 1970s over 90 percent of households had telephones, and second, studies showing that the responses to questions fielded at the same time by separate telephone and in-person surveys yielded basically the same results. Telephone surveys did face a tradeoff, however: they excluded households without telephones and they potentially had higher rates of non-response due to households that are not reached (or even identified) by phone. Additionally, phone respondents were less likely to participate than those contacted in person, owing to the difficulty of establishing a rapport over the phone.

The use of CATI technology allowed polls to be done quickly and relatively cheaply, facilitating more polling and enabling news media outlets (often working in partnerships) to conduct their own polls. The same occurred for polling by political parties, candidates, and advocacy and interest groups. The impetus for the media to engage directly in their own polling was that they had more control of, and input into, public opinion research and were not forced to rely on the reports of commercial pollsters. The media could do state and local as well as national polling, and they could integrate poll results more closely with news writing. Perhaps most important, the media became less vulnerable to manipulation by reports of polls by political parties, candidates, and organized groups that might use such data for their own purposes. The news media could verify claims by others about the state of, or changes in, public opinion.

New Challenges and the Politics of Polling

The proliferation of polling created new challenges for pollsters and for the study of public opinion. Since the mid-1970s, there was an increase not only in public polling but also in market research, telemarketing, and telephone solicitations of all kinds that imposed on people's time. Such telephone calls became increasingly disruptive and annoying to households, who became less willing to participate and who gained the ability to screen calls through answering machines and caller-identification devices. Lower response rates increased the potential for "selection" or "non-response bias" in polls. In-person surveys still done for major academic studies, such as General Social Surveys and the American National Election Studies; and government surveys, including the U.S. Census, encountered similar problems. These maintained high response rates only through greater public relations and spending efforts. Compounding the problem of households without phones has been the increasing use of cellular phones not only to supplement regular "land-line" phones but also to replace such phones. The new challenges posed by cell-phone only households is likely to adversely affect survey response rates and costs.

These problems have led pollsters to turn to other methods using relatively new technology—the Internet. Because there is no available listing of electronic mail addresses, and because not everyone has computer and Internet access, one approach has been to use RDD or other sampling methods to draw representative samples of adults, giving respondents without Internet access such access, and forming "panels" who participate in multiple surveys, thereby reducing the costs of drawing repeated samples. A highly controversial variation of this method recruits thousands of volunteers to join panels through invitations on Internet sites; this approach assumes that any selection bias can be corrected through sophisticated methods of weighting.

Despite such methodological problems, polls have remained important on the political scene in the United States. In addition to survey results reported widely in the press—those that political actors and the public pay at least some attention to—polling by presidents has also increased. Presidents' pollsters have been acknowledged as important figures in the contemporary political landscape. Among them are Patrick Caddell (Jimmy Carter), Richard Wirthlin (Ronald Reagan), Robert Teeter (George H. W. Bush), Stanley Greenberg (Bill Clinton), and Dick Morris (Bill Clinton). Despite his

disparaging claims about political leaders using polls, George W. Bush appointed an academic public opinion and foreign policy expert, Peter D. Feaver, as a member of his national security team dealing with public support for the Iraq War. The relationship between polling and presidential administrations has been an extension of campaign politics, with private polls paid out of political party or campaign funds.

Though the common wisdom, beginning with George Gallup, held that polls enabled political leaders to learn about public opinion and to follow the public's wishes, the reality is that political leaders are not always under such immediate pressure; they have room to maneuver and to attempt to lead—or even manipulate—public opinion by using polling information to learn how best to "craft" their messages for this purpose. This has raised classic questions: To what extent do political leaders follow or lead public opinion? What are the implications for this for American democracy? Some critics have argued that the existence of polling gives the public the false sense that its voice is amply represented in the political process. Public opinion and polling research have remained major parts of campaigns—from the use of focus groups and other means of message testing, to initial benchmark polls that offer basic public opinion information to candidates, to periodic trend polls to compare to the benchmarks, to the even more frequent (weekly or even daily) tracking polls that have increasingly become the pulse of political campaigns. With the aid of polling and other data, political campaigns can "micro-target" both voters and vote-getting activities in increasingly precise ways.

Given such attention to public opinion, how the results of polls are reported has become an increasingly important academic and political issue. Journalists have been widely criticized for their shortcomings in reporting about polls, often accepting them uncritically without researching their quality and the questions asked in them. In particular, the accuracy and reporting of polls tend to matter to candidates most early in a political campaign when how well a given candidate performs in early polls can affect his or her ability to raise money from wary donors. Such problems have also occurred in the case of exit polls, once thought as setting the "gold standard" for polls and used substantially in election projections because they interviewed actual voters and could be done accurately with solid response rates. Television news networks and other press outlets initially conducted their own exit polls. To save costs and coordinate their activities, they eventually entered into a single exit poll consortium. The reputation of exit polling was tarnished in the 2000 presidential election controversy, and the 2004 exit polls showed a substantial Democratic candidate bias in many states, one that remained significant in the 2006 and 2008 elections (before the data were weighted by the actual vote to facilitate further analysis). This development overshadowed an earlier debate, which took full form after the 1980 election, concerning how the early reporting of exit poll results in some states led to the early projection of a winner in the presidential election and may have thereby affected voters in other states who had not yet cast their ballots. Thus, the opportunities for democracy first offered by polling still also pose challenges for the pollsters—and for American democracy.

Bibliography and Further Readings

Asher, Herbert. *Polling and the Public: What Every Citizen Should Know*. Washington, D.C.: CQ Press, 2007.

Eisinger, Robert M. *The Evolution of Presidential Polling*. New York: Cambridge University Press, 2003.

Erikson, Robert S., and Kent L. Tedin. American Public Opinion: Its Origins, Content, and Impact. New York: Pearson Longman, 2007.

Glynn, Carroll J., Susan Herbst, Garrett J. O'Keefe, Robert Y. Shapiro, and Mark Lindeman. *Public Opinion*, 2nd edition. Boulder, CO: Westview, 2004.

Gollin, Albert E., ed. "Polls and the News Media: A Symposium." *Public Opinion Quarterly* 44 (winter 1980).

Heith, Diane J. *Polling to Govern: Public Opinion and Presidential Leadership*. Stanford, CA: Stanford University Press, 2004.

Jacobs, Lawrence R., and Robert Y. Shapiro. *Politicians Don't Pander: Political Manipulation and the Loss of Democratic Responsiveness*. Chicago: University of Chicago Press, 2000.

Jacobs, Lawrence R., and Robert Y. Shapiro, eds. *Special Issue: Polling Politics, Media, and Election Campaigns*. *Public Opinion Quarterly* 69, no. 5 (2005).

Moore, David W. *The Superpollsters: How They Measure and Manipulate Public Opinion in America*. New York: Four Walls Eight Windows, 1992.

Robert Y. Shapiro

RACE

Forty-three years after Congress passed the Voting Rights Act, Americans elected their first African American president. Barack Obama won 53 percent of the vote in 2008, the largest winning margin by a Democratic candidate since Lyndon Johnson's 1964 landslide victory. Obama's election may or may not lead to a shift in the fortunes of the Democratic Party, but it does mark the end of a turbulent period in which racial conflict immeasurably changed the lives of many African Americans and profoundly altered American electoral politics.

In the wake of the civil rights movement and the passage of the 1965 Voting Rights Act (VRA), African Americans made impressive political gains. Black voter registration and turnout was up across the country, particularly in the 11 former states of the confederacy, where almost two-thirds of all eligible blacks were registered to vote by 1976. By comparison, only one-quarter of Southern blacks were registered in 1956. Black voter turnout in presidential elections has averaged 53 percent since the VRA passed, and in 2008 it surpassed the peak turnouts of the 1960s. African Americans have been elected to office in all regions of the country and at all levels of government. In 1970, there were 1,466 black elected officials, 38 percent of whom held office in the South. Thirty years later, at the turn of the century, there were 9,040 black elected officials, 70 percent of whom were elected to office in Southern states.

African American political incorporation was neither swift nor smooth, however. Questions of racial equality and inclusion have been at the core of electoral politics and policy debates since the 1970s. The mobilization of African American voters provoked a white backlash that set in motion a realignment of the political party system, as race supplanted the social class divisions that defined the party system of the New Deal era. Racially polarized voting—elections in which large majorities of whites refuse to vote for black candidates—characterized many state and local elections in Northern cities and the South. With the nationalization of America's racial divide by the mid-1970s, race dictated political party strategies, influenced the outcome of presidential elections, and left the country deeply divided over the question of what should be done to remedy racial inequalities. As a result, social welfare and criminal justice policies became entwined with race and defined one of the key differences between liberals and conservatives. In this political environment, blacks achieved significant electoral gains only by dint of hard-fought, contentious elections and enforcement of the Voting Rights Act. But the emergence of a powerful national Republican electoral majority limited the fruits of those gains.

Black Politics and Elections after the Civil Rights Movement

Initially, African Americans made important political gains in mayoral elections, largely in Northern cities and legislative districts. There were 278 black mayors by 1985, two-thirds of whom were elected in black-majority cities. Big cities outside the South were more likely to elect black mayors. In 1967 the first African Americans were elected mayor in a major city since Reconstruction: Carl Stokes won the mayoral election in Cleveland, Ohio, and Richard Hatcher took office the same day in Gary, Indiana. Their victories were followed by the election of black mayors in other major cities in the next 17 years, including Newark, Detroit, Atlanta, Los Angeles, Chicago, and Philadelphia. In these elections, African American candidates faced substantial opposition not just from Republicans but also from white Democrats. The presence of a black mayoral candidate motivated both black and white voters to turn out to vote, and although mayoral elections in many cities were more competitive as a consequence, they were also racially polarized. Rarely did black mayoral candidates pick up more than one-fifth to one-quarter of the white vote. This first generation of black mayors ascended to power by forging coalitions of energized black voters and white liberals, professionals, and, in some cases (such as in Atlanta), the white business establishment. Middle-class and blue-collar white Democrats rarely voted for black mayoral candidates.

Even though Southern blacks made impressive electoral gains in small towns and some cities after 1976, the enfranchisement and mobilization of African Americans did not translate readily into political representation and power in the South. Less than one-third of black-majority cities in the South had elected black mayors compared to almost three-quarters of Northern cities with sizeable black populations. Only three blacks were elected to the Ninety-Fourth Congress (1975–1976) from the South. By comparison, 14 blacks represented non-Southern congressional districts in that same Congress, a gain of 8 seats since 1965. There were almost twice as many black state legislators elected to office in non-Southern states in 1975 as in the 11 former states of the confederacy (182 black state legislators in non-Southern states, compared to 94 in the South).

Legislative Representation and Racial Gerrymandering

White opposition to black candidates was nowhere more apparent than in congressional and state legisla-

tive elections in the 1970s and 1980s. In the 30 years after the VRA was enacted, black candidates won seats in only 35 of the 6,667 elections in white-majority congressional districts. In the North, the concentration of large African American populations in cities paved the way for electoral gains and greater representation in legislative bodies. In the South, on the other hand, racial gerrymandering of legislative districts and city elections persisted for years after the VRA was enacted. Many Southern states and cities used multimember legislative districts (or at-large elections in cities) instead of single-member districts. Even if African Americans made up 40 percent of the eligible voters in a multimember district, it was almost impossible for an African American candidate to win a legislative seat. In fact, many Southern cities shifted from single-member districts to at-large elections in order to circumvent black voting power.

As a result of racial gerrymandering and racially polarized voting, no Southern white-majority congressional district had elected an African American to Congress as of 1985, and only 1 percent of Southern white-majority state legislative districts had elected blacks to Congress. By comparison, 77 percent of Southern black-majority districts had elected African Americans to state legislatures. By 1990, 25 years after the passage of the VRA, there were only five black members of Congress from the South, a region in which 20 percent of the population was African American, and few Southern blacks were elected from multimember state legislative districts or in at-large elections in cities. This is the main reason fewer blacks were elected mayor in black-majority cities in the South than in the North. Hispanics in states like California, where most cities used at-large elections, were similarly disadvantaged.

This situation changed when the U.S. Justice Department used its powers under the Voting Rights Act—specifically the requirement that states submit changes to electoral districts for approval—to mandate the creation of single-member districts in states and cities and new black-majority or black-Hispanic–majority congressional districts in the early 1990s. As a result, 14 additional African Americans were elected to Congress in 1992, bringing the total number in the One Hundred Third

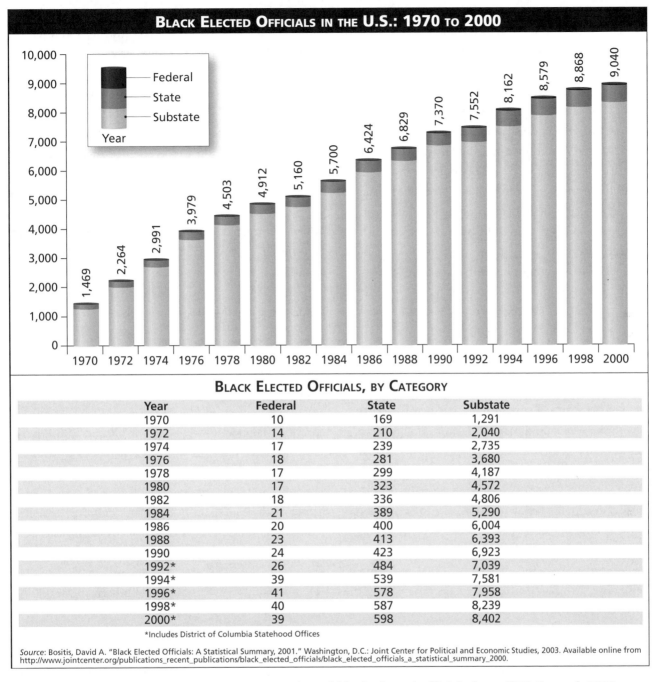

BLACK ELECTED OFFICIALS IN THE U.S.: 1970 TO 2000

BLACK ELECTED OFFICIALS, BY CATEGORY

Year	Federal	State	Substate
1970	10	169	1,291
1972	14	210	2,040
1974	17	239	2,735
1976	18	281	3,680
1978	17	299	4,187
1980	17	323	4,572
1982	18	336	4,806
1984	21	389	5,290
1986	20	400	6,004
1988	23	413	6,393
1990	24	423	6,923
1992*	26	484	7,039
1994*	39	539	7,581
1996*	41	578	7,958
1998*	40	587	8,239
2000*	39	598	8,402

*Includes District of Columbia Statehood Offices

Source: Bositis, David A. "Black Elected Officials: A Statistical Summary, 2001." Washington, D.C.: Joint Center for Political and Economic Studies, 2003. Available online from http://www.jointcenter.org/publications_recent_publications/black_elected_officials/black_elected_officials_a_statistical_summary_2000.

Though there was a steady increase in the number of black elected officials from 1970 through 2000, data show that the proportion of federal positions to the overall group remained fairly constant. The largest growth over the 30-year span is found in the substate category, which includes county, municipal, judicial and law enforcement, and education positions.

Congress to 39. Of the new members of the House of Representatives, 12 were elected from new black-majority districts created in the South. Moreover, by 2008, 303 (about 50 percent) of the 608 African Americans elected to state legislatures represented districts in Southern states, a dramatic change from the mid-1970s.

African Americans made up 8 percent of all state legislators in the United States in 2008, but they made up 17 percent in the South, which was almost proportional to the Southern black population (19.8 percent) in that year. The number of Hispanics elected to Congress and state legislatures increased during the 1990s as well.

Without the federal government's strong enforcement of the Voting Rights Act and the creation of majority-minority districts, it is likely there would have been far fewer African Americans and Hispanics elected to Congress and state legislatures. There is some evidence, however, that the level of racial polarization in state and local elections has diminished since the 1990s. Once African Americans are elected mayor or elected to a legislative seat in a white-majority city or district, they typically win reelection. Incumbency has its advantages. The seven black incumbents running in white majority congressional districts in 2008 were reelected with an average margin of 73 percent. The number of black state legislators winning in white-majority districts rose from 16 percent in 2001 to 30 percent in 2008. At the same time, a second generation of African American mayors governed 39 of the 100 largest cities by 2007, and Massachusetts elected its first African American governor, Deval Patrick, in 2006.

Race and Party Politics in National Elections

The emergence and consolidation of a powerful Republican electoral majority based on polarized racial voting blocs in presidential elections during the 1970s offset African American political gains in state and local government. Prior to 2008, Republicans won 7 of the 10 previous presidential elections and dominated political discourse. The Republican Party rose to power partly by cultivating white racial resentment, beginning with Barry Goldwater's decision during the 1964 election to troll for white votes in the South, and continuing with Richard Nixon's two presidential campaigns. The issue of race and racial equality was a key factor shaping voters' political attitudes and identity on both sides of the color line over the 1970s and 1980s, and it was vital to the rightward shift of national social welfare, crime, and tax policy agendas.

Intent on building a new majority coalition, Republican Party activists wielded a language of racial conservatism that appealed to whites' resentments and fears of racial equality by equating affirmative action and school busing with an assault on the freedoms of ordinary Americans. They eschewed the racist rhetoric so common to political campaigns before the civil rights revolution. Instead, Republican Party activists appealed to resentful whites with implicit racially coded language that invoked fear of crime and lawless blacks, anger at government handouts of jobs and welfare to undeserving blacks, and the idea that race-conscious policies were a form of "reverse racism," and thus unfair. The power of this racially coded political rhetoric in political campaigns depended on the avoidance of explicit racial appeals that ran afoul of a normative presumption of racial equality. During the 1988 presidential contest between Michael Dukakis and George H.W. Bush, the notorious Willie Horton ad, which linked black criminality with Dukakis, benefited the Republican candidate only so long as its racial message was implicit. Once the underlying racial message was exposed, it lost its appeal to voters.

Racial Voting Blocs

By the time of the 1984 election, voters and activists sharply distinguished between the Republican and Democratic Party positions on racial issues. In the 10 presidential elections between 1972 and 2008, overwhelming numbers of white voters defected from the Democratic Party, especially in the South, and voted Republican. Only an average of 40 percent of white voters cast their ballots for Democratic presidential candidates in these elections, while African Americans became the most loyal supporters of Democratic presidential candidates (87 percent of blacks voted Democratic, on average). Racial polarization, the difference between the proportion of African Americans and whites voting Democratic, averaged 48 percentage points in these 10 elections and peaked in the 2 elections that Richard Nixon won and Ronald Reagan's 1984 victory and the 1988 election. Indeed, 1972 and 1988 stand out as elections in which racially coded campaign statements were especially salient to Republican activists and white voters. (Racial polarization was also high in 2008 largely because of the surge in black turnout).

For both white and black voters racial issues overrode questions of social class and income, particularly during the 1980s, though this effect was more pronounced in the South than elsewhere. Nonetheless, in the three elections from 1972 to 1980, large majorities of white voters in all four regions of the country, swayed in part by the racially coded appeals of the Republican Party, displayed a similar hostility to the Democratic Party. Almost two-thirds (64 percent) of white voters voted for Ronald Reagan in 1980, and there was no difference between white voters in the Northeast, Midwest, and South.

Racial bloc voting is strongest in the South, which has been transformed from a Democratic Party stronghold into the Republican Party's core base of support. An overwhelmingly large number of Southern whites were reliable Democratic voters before the civil rights revolution. By the 1980s, however, only one-third of all Southern whites called themselves Democrats, and the proportion of reliably Democratic counties in the South had declined to 14 percent. The Republican takeover of Congress in 1994 consummated the Southern realignment, as Southern whites cast their ballots for Republicans in all offices, not just in presidential elections.

Since the early 1990s, racial bloc voting and racial resentment have declined everywhere but in the South. White voters in the South remain staunchly Republican; in the 2000, 2004, and 2008 presidential elections, only 30 percent of Southern whites voted for the Democratic candidate, compared to about 47 percent in the rest of the nation. In the Northeast in these three elections, white voters divided their votes evenly between Republican and Democratic presidential candidates. Regional differences in racial bloc voting have widened significantly. Fewer whites in the Deep South (the six states between the Mississippi Delta and the Atlantic coasts of Georgia and South Carolina), voted for Barack Obama in 2008 than voted for John Kerry in 2004. Yet in 2008, a majority of whites in the New England states, the Mid-Atlantic States, and four key Midwestern industrial states voted for Barack Obama.

The Ironies of African American Political Inclusion

Since the 1970s, African Americans have succeeded in gaining political representation and inclusion. Even though racial polarization is diminishing—Barack Obama's election is a reflection of this change, not its

RELATED ENTRIES

THIS VOLUME
African Americans; Civil Liberties; Civil Rights; Hispanic Americans

cause—African American political inclusion was contingent on the creation of black-majority electoral districts, mainly in the South. The Voting Rights Act was instrumental to this development.

The irony is that Republican politicians forged a new national majority by capitalizing on white resentment toward black political mobilization. Their success in implementing conservative tax, budget, law and order, and social welfare policies undercut black political gains. In the context of racially polarized elections, party competition was geared in part to assuaging the anxieties of white voters on racial issues, leaving African Americans on the periphery of many policy debates. The racial politics of the 1980s through the first decade of the 2000s precipitated the abolition of one of the main welfare programs for the poor, Aid to Families with Dependent Children, and its replacement with limited aid and strict work requirements. It also contributed to a massive increase in incarceration rates and eroded policies predicated on reversing racial inequality. African Americans have been disproportionately affected by these policies. For example, poor African Americans are more likely to be subjected to harsh punitive welfare rules; black men are far more likely to be imprisoned or sentenced to death than white men; and labor market discrimination remains a reality for many African Americans. Thus, diminishing racial polarization does not mean we have entered a post-racial age. The legacies of this period ensure that race will continue to influence elections and policy debates.

Bibliography and Further Reading

Canon, David T. *Race, Redistricting, and Representation: The Unintended Consequences of Black Majority Districts.* Chicago: University of Chicago Press, 1999.

Carmines, Edward G., and James A. Stimson. *Issue Evolution: Race and the Transformation of American Politics.* Princeton, NJ: Princeton University Press, 1989.

Frymer, Paul. *Uneasy Alliances: Race and Party Competition in America*. Princeton, NJ: Princeton University Press, 1999.

Hajnal, Zoltan L. "White Residents, Black Incumbents, and a Declining Racial Divide." *American Political Science Review* 95, no. 3 (2001): 603–617.

Handley, Lisa, and Bernard Grofman. "The Impact of the Voting Rights Act on Minority Representation: Black Officeholding in Southern State Legislatures and Congressional Delegations." In *Quiet Revolution in the South: The Impact of the Voting Rights Act, 1965–1990*, edited by Chandler Davidson and Bernard Grofman. Princeton, NJ: Princeton University Press, 1994.

Kousser, J. Morgan. *Colorblind Injustice: Minority Voting Rights and the Undoing of the Second Reconstruction*. Chapel Hill: University of North Carolina Press, 1999.

Lublin, David Ian, and Katherine Tate. "Racial Group Competition in Urban Elections." In *Classifying by Race*, edited by Paul Peterson, 245–261. Princeton, NJ: Princeton University Press, 1995.

Mendelberg, Tali. *The Race Card: Campaign Strategy, Implicit Messages, and the Norm of Equality*. Princeton, NJ: Princeton University Press, 2001.

O'Hare, William. "City Size, Racial Composition, and Election of Black Mayors Inside and Outside the South." *Journal of Urban Affairs* 12, no. 3 (1990): 307–313.

Valentino, Nicholas A., and David O. Sears. "Old Times There Are Not Forgotten: Race and Partisan Realignment in the Contemporary South." *American Journal of Political Science* 49, no. 3 (2005): 672–688.

Michael K. Brown

REAGAN, RONALD

1911–2004
Fortieth President of the United States

Ronald Reagan, the fortieth president of the United States, restored the American people's confidence in their country after a period marked by assassinations, the Vietnam War, Watergate, double-digit inflation, the hostage crisis in Iran, and a series of failed presidencies. He changed long-held assumptions about the role the federal government should play in American life and in its economic affairs, reduced taxes and regulations, and slowed the growth of government spending and programs. (Some termed this approach "Reaganomics.") While Reagan's critics maintained that Americans did not equally share in the economic expansion that ensued during his presidency, under Reagan the nation experienced one of the longest periods of economic growth in its history. Reagan is also credited for ending the Cold War peacefully and on terms beneficial to the United States. Historians debate whether he "won" the Cold War, as his admirers claim, or simply accelerated a process that had been years in the making. Most agree, however, that he handled the Cold War's conclusion masterfully.

Formative Experiences and Early Career

Ronald Wilson Reagan was born on February 6, 1911, in Tampico, Illinois. Biographers credit Reagan's sunny disposition, optimism, love of reading, and dramatics to the influence of his mother, the former Nelle Wilson, a Protestant fundamentalist. They attribute Reagan's sense of humor, fondness for storytelling, interest in politics, and love of everything Irish to his Roman Catholic father, Jack Reagan. Ronnie was the second son born to the couple. He graduated from Eureka College in 1932 and briefly worked as a radio sports announcer.

In 1937, Reagan signed a contract with Warner Brothers, and over the next 15 years he appeared in more than 50 films. His most famous roles were the Notre Dame football star George Gipp in *Knute Rockne, All American* (1940) and Drake McHugh in *King's Row* (1942). While Reagan never attained the superstar status of the "leading men" of his era (such as Cary Grant, James Stewart, and Clark Gable), he always had steady work. During World War II, Reagan was a second lieutenant in the Officers Reserve Corps of the U.S. Cavalry. Declared unsuitable for combat because of poor eyesight, Reagan made recruitment, training, and propaganda films and participated in campaigns to sell war bonds. He was discharged in 1945 with the rank of captain.

Transition into Politics

Known for his affable nature and keenly interested in the workings of the entertainment industry, Reagan was elected to the board of the Screen Actors Guild in 1941. He served as the union's president from 1947 to 1952 and again from 1959 to 1960. In that position, Reagan perfected his negotiating skills as he worked to increase wages, broaden benefits, and provide better working conditions for union members. Reagan entered union politics at a time when Communist agents, loyal to Moscow, sought to infiltrate the motion picture industry. He resisted their attempts to pack meetings, shout down speakers, and intimidate union officials. In testimony before House Un-American Activities Committee (HUAC), Reagan maintained that Hollywood was better able than the government to keep its "own house" free of subversives.

With his movie career waning after World War II, Reagan made the transition into the then new medium of television as host of *General Electric Theater*. When not on camera, Reagan toured the country, promoting GE products and delivering pep talks to its employees. While on the lecture circuit, Reagan found his politics gradually shifting from liberal Democrat to conservative Republican. He recalled in his memoirs that after he had reached the peak of his earning capacity (in what was then the 94 percent income tax bracket), he found that it was no longer profitable for him to accept additional work because he could only keep six cents out of every additional dollar he earned. This realization completed his political conversion into the ranks of the nascent post–World War II conservative movement.

In 1960, Reagan served as national chairman of "Democrats for Nixon." He officially switched his party registration to Republican in 1962. On October 27, 1964, Reagan made his national political debut on television. In a 28-minute paid political broadcast, he laid out the case why Barry Goldwater should be elected president. Although Goldwater lost to Pres. Lyndon Johnson in one of the largest landslides in U.S. history up to that point, Reagan's address, "A Time for Choosing," won universal acclaim as the one bright spot in an otherwise bleak campaign.

Governor Reagan

In 1966, Reagan ran for governor of California, and he defeated the incumbent governor, Edmund G. ("Pat") Brown, by almost one million votes, carrying

58 percent of the vote. His two major promises—to "send the welfare bums back to work" and "clean up the mess at Berkeley" (referring to the contemporary student demonstrations)—gave voice to two widely held opinions of the electorate.

Once in office, Reagan made balancing the budget and welfare reform his highest priorities. He accomplished the first through a 10 percent across-the-board cut in state spending, a hiring freeze, and, to the consternation of some conservatives, an increase in state income taxes. Working with the Democratic legislative leadership, Reagan reduced welfare rolls by tightening eligibility requirements, while also increasing assistance to the truly needy. As governor, Reagan fought to establish the Redwood National Park, opposed a measure that would have banned homosexual teachers from classrooms, and signed a law liberalizing abortion, an action he later said he had come to regret. As anticipated, he also had repeated run-ins with campus protestors and college administrators.

Reagan made his first stab at the Republican presidential nomination in 1968. Announcing his availability on the eve of the convention, he mustered only 182 votes against former vice president Richard Nixon and New York governor Nelson Rockefeller. In order to blunt Reagan's appeal to conservatives, especially within Southern delegations, Nixon adopted a "Southern strategy." He pledged to "go slow" on civil rights and appoint conservative, "strict constructionist" judges.

Reagan was reelected governor in 1970, pulling in 53 percent of the vote against the Democratic candidate, Assembly Speaker Jesse Unruh. Still, Reagan often found himself in conflicting roles, serving as a conservative spokesman on the one hand and as a party loyalist on the other. During Nixon's first term, Reagan had opposed many of the president's liberal-leaning economic policies. After Nixon declared his intention to visit the People's Republic of China (PRC), reversing a decades-old policy of refusing official recognition to the PRC, he recruited a skeptical Reagan to reassure conservatives that he had not gone back on American promises to defend Taiwan. (Formal diplomatic relations between the United States and China commenced during the Carter administration.)

The Path to the White House

After stepping down as governor in 1975, Reagan devoted increased attention to his role as conservative spokesman. He commenced a syndicated newspaper column, delivered five-minute radio commentaries, and returned to the lecture circuit. Doing much of his own writing, especially for the radio commentaries, Reagan took as his major themes issues with which he would be identified for the rest of his career, especially tax cuts and anticommunism. Convinced that the Soviet Union had taken advantage of American preoccupations with Vietnam and Watergate, Reagan became increasingly critical of the détente policies of presidents Nixon and Ford. He also opposed relinquishing American control of the Panama Canal, which proved a winning issue in the 1976 presidential primaries when Reagan challenged President Ford, who had become president after Nixon resigned, for the nomination.

Nonetheless, Ford edged out Reagan for the nomination by 117 votes. Ford's narrow loss to his Democratic challenger, Jimmy Carter, and Ford's disinclination to seek the presidency again, made Reagan the instant frontrunner for his party's presidential nomination in 1980. After losing the Iowa caucuses to George H.W. Bush, Reagan sailed through the remaining primaries to an easy nomination.

In a hard-hitting campaign, Reagan kept his Republican base intact while attracting the votes of millions of voters who, like the candidate, had traditionally voted Democratic. He ran well among union and nonunion working households, Roman Catholics, Southern whites, and religious conservatives. This "Reagan coalition" would be a powerful force in American politics for more than a generation. With Bush as his running mate, Reagan handily defeated Pres. Jimmy Carter, winning 51 percent of the popular vote to Carter's 41 percent and third-party candidate John B. Anderson's 7 percent. In the Electoral College, Reagan trounced Carter, 489 to 49. Double-digit inflation, rising unemployment, high gasoline prices, energy shortages, and the prolonged hostage crisis in Iran all worked in Reagan's favor. He captured the mood of the country in his only debate with Carter, when he asked voters whether they were better off than they had been four years earlier. He said that as president his three major priorities would be to cut taxes, increase defense spending, and balance the budget.

In his inaugural address, Reagan outlined the direction he wished his administration to take. With 13 percent inflation and 7.5 percent unemployment (it would later peak at 10.8 percent), Reagan proclaimed that government was not the solution to the nation's ills, but rather the source of the problem. With the speech primarily focusing on domestic matters, commentators made less note of Reagan's bold assertion of his vision for the nation and its place in the world. "It is time for us to realize that we are too great a nation to limit ourselves to small dreams," he said, adding, "We have every right to dream heroic dreams," picking up on a theme he had articulated in his campaign. In accepting his party's nomination, Reagan had quoted Thomas Paine's assertion, "We have it in our power to begin the world all over again." During the next eight years the nation and the world learn that Reagan intended to do nothing less.

Domestic Policy

Once in office, Reagan proposed cutting marginal income tax rates by 30 percent over three years. He argued that lower marginal tax rates would spur business investment and quicken economic growth. This, he said, would reduce unemployment and bolster the real income of average households. His efforts to enact his program stalled briefly as he recovered from an assassination attempt that nearly took his life. Reagan's ability to joke at his own misfortune, entreating his attending physicians to tell him they were "all Republicans," reassured a jittery nation, and conveyed a sense of his stamina.

Working with Congress, where the Republicans controlled the Senate by 7 votes and the Democrats controlled the House by 57 votes, Reagan steered to passage a measure that cut individual tax rates by 25 percent over four years, reduced taxes on capital gains, expanded tax incentives for business investment and retirement savings, indexed tax brackets for inflation, and reduced the windfall profit tax on oil companies enacted under the Carter administration. In response to Reagan's holding all of the House's 191

Republicans behind the plan and persuading 61 Democrats to vote for it, Democratic Speaker "Tip" O'Neill proclaimed Reagan's lobbying efforts the "greatest selling job" he had ever seen.

To curb inflation, Reagan, unlike his predecessors, proved willing to allow the Federal Reserve to pursue a "tight money policy," even if it meant a prolonged recession. He showed equal fortitude when he went through with an ultimatum he had given striking air traffic controllers to return to work or be terminated. The August 1981–November 1982 recession and the rising unemployment that accompanied it cost the Republicans dearly in the 1982 congressional elections. Reagan's popularity dropped to 39 percent. Yet Reagan's "stay the course" approach worked. Inflation dropped to 4 percent in 1983 and remained low for the rest of his presidency and well into those of his successors. At the same time, unemployment fell to 5 percent. By the end of his eight years in office, the U.S. economy had grown approximately 3.4 percent on average each year, resulting in the creation of 20 million new jobs. "I wonder why they don't call it 'Reaganomics' anymore," the president joked.

Reagan was criticized for large federal budget deficits and the resulting increase in federal debt. Reagan boosted defense outlays in both inflation-adjusted dollars and as a percent of GDP (gross domestic product). Combined with congressional reluctance to reduce domestic outlays after 1981, the federal deficit increased to 6 percent of GDP in 1983 before falling to 3.1 percent of GDP in 1988 as the economic expansion boosted federal revenue. Publicly held federal debt grew from $712 billion (33 percent of GDP) in 1980 to $2.1 trillion (52 percent of GDP) in 1988. While Reagan expressed disappointment at his failure to balance the budget, he viewed higher defense outlays as a short-term necessity that could be safely reduced once they achieved his intended foreign policy and defense objectives.

Foreign Policy

Early in his presidency, Reagan sent U.S. marines to Lebanon as part of a peacekeeping force to curb an ongoing civil war. When a terrorist attack in Beirut on October 23, 1983, took the lives of 241 U.S. service personnel, Reagan changed course and ordered the remaining U.S. forces to be removed. Two days after the tragedy, he sent American forces to depose a Marxist-Leninist government that had seized power in Grenada. Reagan maintained that he acted at the behest of the Organization of Eastern Caribbean States and out of concern for the security of the rest of the region and the safety of hundreds of American medical students at St. George's University. Three years later, after a terrorist bomb exploded in a Berlin discotheque, killing two American servicemen and injuring 230, including 50 American servicemen, Reagan, citing "irrefutable proof" that Libya was culpable, ordered a series of air attacks against that country.

Reagan's overall strategy toward military engagement was simple. He was prepared to act with overwhelming force to protect American interests, but he was unwilling to commit American troops to prolonged and poorly defined missions.

Reelection

Buoyed by an expanding economy and a restored sense of national pride, and running on a theme of "Morning in America," Reagan won reelection by a wide margin in 1984. He and George H. W. Bush prevailed over the Democrats Walter F. Mondale and Geraldine Ferraro, winning 59 percent of the popular vote. In the Electoral College, Reagan prevailed by a margin of 525 to 13. Mondale carried only his native Minnesota and the District of Columbia.

Ending the Cold War

Reagan devoted the remainder of presidency to his major goal, pushing back the boundaries of Soviet influence without resorting to war. Buoyed by reports that the Soviet economy was in worse shape than was commonly believed, Reagan concluded that the Soviet Union could not sustain its then-current military outlays, let alone increase them to counter a U.S. build-up, with an emphasis on high-tech weaponry. Publicly, Reagan justified higher defense outlays on the grounds that the United States was dangerously close to losing its historic military superiority over the U.S.S.R. Privately, Reagan realized the Soviet Union would bankrupt its economy if it were to match this challenge. Reagan worked to weaken the Soviet economy on other fronts, such as when he pressed Saudi Arabia to increase its oil production, driving down the price of the U.S.S.R.'s primary export.

Powerful rhetoric remained an important weapon in the arsenal Reagan had assembled against ideological adversaries. In 1982, before the British Parliament, Reagan sentenced Marxism-Leninism to the "ash heap" of history. To the National Association of Evangelicals, Reagan declared the Soviet Union to be an "evil empire." He reassured skeptics that "the world would not end if an American president told the truth." Relations between the United States and the Soviet Union stayed frosty after the Soviet military downed Korean Air Lines Flight 007, killing hundreds, including Rep. Larry McDonald (D–GA).

After the Soviet Union deployed medium-range missiles directed at Western Europe, Reagan, over the protests of the growing nuclear freeze movement, placed Pershing II and cruise missiles in West Germany. He astounded his critics when he maintained that the way to reduce the nuclear threat was by increasing U.S. arms. Few believed him when he said that his ultimate goal was a world free of nuclear weapons.

In 1985, Reagan found in Soviet leader Mikhail Gorbachev someone who shared the president's view that the U.S.S.R. faced a choice between making accommodations to the West and economic ruin. While both agreed to reduce the number of intermediate-range nuclear weapons and allow inspections of nuclear sites ("trust, but verify"), Reagan refused to abandon the Strategic Defense Initiative he had proposed to act as an impenetrable shield against incoming missiles. In 1987, Reagan and Gorbachev signed the Intermediate-Range Nuclear Forces (INF) Treaty, which eliminated an entire class of nuclear weapons. A year later, Gorbachev unilaterally reduced Soviet conventional forces and promised to withdraw troops from Eastern Europe. As Reagan prepared to leave office, the Cold War was all but over. The British prime minister, Margaret Thatcher, declared that Reagan had won it "without firing a shot."

Iran-Contra

Reagan's presidency suffered a major jolt in November 1986 when the press reported that Reagan, in violation of a pledge not to negotiate with terrorists, had authorized the selling of arms to Iran in exchange for the release of Americans held hostage by Iranian-backed terrorists in Lebanon. Proceeds from these sales, in violation of the expressed wish of Congress, found their way to anticommunist forces fighting to overthrow the Marxist government in Nicaragua. Officials at the National Security Council who ordered these actions later admitted to having destroyed documents detailing these transactions.

A commission Reagan named to investigate what became known as the "Iran-Contra Affair" faulted the president for not exercising appropriate oversight of his subordinates and for an overall sloppy management style. Reagan responded by reorganizing his White House team. Waiving "executive privilege," he allowed congressional and other investigators to peruse White House records. In an address to the nation, he assumed full responsibility for the episode. He said that he still did not believe that he had traded "arms for hostages," but that the evidence had persuaded him that he had.

The "Great Communicator"

Although he insisted that his many successes as president resulted not from his abilities as a communicator, but to the communication of "great things," Reagan made the most of his ability to persuade the public of the rightness of his cause. Strong public support, both at home and abroad, greatly enhanced Reagan's ability to move his program through Congress and pull foreign leaders his way. Among his many gifts as a communicator was his capacity to give voice to the sentiments of others. After the Space Shuttle *Challenger* disaster, Reagan echoed the nation's grief, saying that the astronauts had "slipped the surly bonds of earth to touch the face of God." Standing before the "Boys of Pointe du Hoc" 40 years after the Normandy Invasion, Reagan spoke of common service and sacrifice: "We were with you then; we are with you now. Your hopes are our hopes, and your destiny is our destiny." In Berlin, Reagan's voice of defiance ("tear down this wall") was heard on both sides of the Iron Curtain.

In his last public communication, when he revealed that he suffered from Alzheimer's disease, Reagan bid a farewell filled with optimism and hope:

"In closing let me thank you, the American people, for giving me the great honor of allowing me to serve as your president. When the Lord calls me home, whenever that may be, I will leave with the greatest love for this country of ours and eternal optimism for its future. I now begin the journey that will lead me into the sunset of my life. I know that for America there will always be a bright dawn ahead."

Reagan's Impact

As Barack Obama, the nation's forty-fourth president, recognized, Ronald Reagan ranks among the major "transformational" presidents in American history. Like Jefferson, Jackson, Lincoln, and Franklin Roosevelt, he reordered the nation's priorities, realigned its politics, and inspired a movement that remained influential for more than a generation after he left office. Reagan's lasting influence is threefold: he redefined the role of the federal government within the American political system, he rekindled the sense that a strong and assertive United States could be a force for good in the world, and, like John F. Kennedy, he inspired countless others to enter public life with the goal of picking up where he left off.

Bibliography and Further Reading

Cannon, Lou. *President Reagan: The Role of a Lifetime.* 1991. Reprint, New York: Public Affairs, 2000.

Edwards, Anne. *Early Reagan: The Rise to Power.* New York: Morrow, 1987.

Evans, Thomas W. *The Education of Ronald Reagan: The General Electric Years and the Untold Story of His Conversion to Conservatism.* New York: Columbia University Press, 2006.

Hayward, Steven F. *The Age of Reagan: The Conservative Counterrevolution , 1980–1989.* New York: Crown Forum, 2009.

Hayward, Steven F. *The Age of Reagan: The Fall of the Old Liberal Order, 1964–1980.* New York: Forum Prima, 2001.

Kengor, Paul. *God and Ronald Reagan: A Spiritual Life.* New York: Regan Books, 2004.

Mann, James. *The Rebellion of Ronald Reagan: A History of the End of the Cold War.* New York: Viking, 2009.

Reagan, Ronald. *An American Life: The Autobiography.* New York: Simon & Schuster, 1990.

———. *The Reagan Diaries,* edited by Douglas Brinkley. New York: HarperCollins, 2007.

———. *Reagan in His Own Hand,* edited by Kiron K. Skinner, Annelise Anderson, and Martin Anderson. New York: The Free Press, 2001.

Tygiel, Jules. *Ronald Reagan and the Triumph of American Conservatism.* New York: Pearson Longman, 2006.

Alvin S. Felzenberg

REFORM PARTY

See Third Parties

REGULATORY AGENCIES

The history of regulation in the United States has been characterized by periods of stability punctuated by salient events and periods of rapid and substantial change. The decade of the 1970s was one of rapid change, initially driven by the mobilization of environmental, labor, and consumer advocates, and ultimately by the problem of stagflation. Whereas the initial mobilization resulted in the creation of new social regulatory agencies, stagflation created a window of opportunity for deregulation and regulatory review. Following this tumultuous period, regulation entered a prolonged period of stability, an equilibrium that was ultimately punctuated by the financial collapse of 2007–2008.

Stagflation and Deregulation

The decade of the 1970s began with the most ambitious and costly regulatory initiatives in the nation's history. President Richard M. Nixon created the Environmental Protection Agency (EPA) in 1970, and Congress passed new statutes to control air and water pollution. Congress also created the Occupations Safety

RELATED ENTRIES

THIS VOLUME
Bush, George H.W.; Carter, Jimmy; Cold War, End of; Conservatism; Economic Policy; Election of 1980; Fiscal and Budgetary Policy; Iran-Contra Affair; Nuclear Weapons and Proliferation; Political Polarization; Presidency; Republican Party; State-Federal Relations; Tax Policy

and Health Administration (OSHA), dramatically strengthening the nation's regulation of workplace injuries and diseases. EPA and OSHA were emblematic of the new social regulation. Older economic regulatory agencies controlled conditions of entry and exit, pricing, and competitive practices on an industry-specific basis. The new social regulatory agencies, in contrast, had economy-wide jurisdiction and were charged with reducing the negative externalities (such as costs stemming from industrial activity that are borne by society) of industrial production. Armed with ambitious and complicated mandates, agencies like EPA and OSHA imposed regulatory costs that were far greater than those imposed by older economic regulatory agencies.

The decade that began with the creation of new agencies and the introduction of ambitious regulatory mandates ended with deregulation and regulatory reform. Following the 1973 OPEC (Organization of the Petroleum Exporting Countries) oil embargo, stagflation became a core concern for policymakers. Economic regulatory agencies had recently come under heavy assault both by the consumer movement and Chicago school economists. Consumer advocates compiled case studies of regulatory failure at the Federal Trade Commission and the Interstate Commerce Commission (ICC) that reinforced earlier scholarly works on regulatory capture (regulated industries dictating the terms of regulation) and life cycles. At the same time, economists of the Chicago school were developing an economic theory of regulation, modeling regulation as a series of exchanges between profit-maximizing firms and vote-maximizing members of Congress, resulting in the *de facto* cartelization of industries. Despite the ideological differences, there was a consensus that many economic regulations protected regulated interests and forced the costs onto the public, thereby contributing to inflation. Stagflation created a window of opportunity for policy change.

Over the course of the 1970s, deregulatory initiatives were introduced in air and surface transportation, communications, energy, and commercial banking. In some cases, these initiatives had devastating consequences for well-established regulatory agencies. For example, the Civil Aeronautics Board (CAB) had been responsible for the regulation of commercial aviation since 1940. It controlled entry, assigned route authority, and regulated fares. There was clear evidence that CAB's prohibitions on price competition and regulatory barriers to entry elevated prices, thereby contributing to inflation. The Airline Deregulation Act of 1978 phased out existing regulations and eliminated the CAB, thereby opening the industry to fierce price competition. A similar set of events beset the Interstate Commerce Commission (ICC), which had regulated the railroads since its creation in 1887, and then interstate trucking as well, following the passage of the Motor Carrier Act of 1935. Like the CAB, the ICC had functioned as a classic economic regulator, controlling entry, exit, the terms of competition, and pricing. The Railroad Revitalization and Regulatory Reform Act of 1976 provided the ICC with greater discretionary authority to find that regulation was unnecessary for entire categories of traffic. Four years later, the Staggers Rail Act of 1980 allowed railroads to adjust rates and engage in price competition. Ultimately, the ICC was eliminated in 1995.

Deregulation was not simply an effort to reduce costs. In the case of finance, inflation placed significant stress on the regulatory system erected during the New Deal. The Glass-Steagall Banking Act of 1933 separated commercial and investment banking and empowered the Federal Reserve, through Regulation Q, to set interest rates for savings while prohibiting interest for demand deposits (i.e., checking). It also created deposit insurance, through the Federal Deposit Insurance Corporation (FDIC). By the end of the 1930s, regulations had created distinct financial subindustries (such as commercial banks, savings and loans, and credit unions), each defined by the products and services it offered, and each with its own set of regulators. Under inflationary conditions, banks that were constrained from offering attractive interests rates (or interest rates at all on demand deposits) had difficulties attracting funds. Nonbank banks (i.e., institutions that accepted deposits but did not make loans, and thus fell outside of the regulatory framework) began to offer higher rates of return, thereby making them preferable to their regulated counterparts. The resulting disintermediation—the flow of funds outside of regulated intermediaries—created a regulatory crisis, and forced deregulation to accommodate market innovations. Over the course of the next few decades, a series of statutes would eliminate controls on interest rates and financial products, and many of the regulatory distinctions established under the New Deal system.

During the 1980s, savings and loans, burdened with large portfolios of fixed rate mortgages, used the greater freedom afforded by deregulation to make speculative investments and better compete for funds at market rates of interest. The institutions were willing to incur high and imprudent levels of risk because they could rely on the Federal Savings and Loan Insurance Corporation (FSLIC) to insure deposits, a problem referred to as "moral hazard." By the end of the decade, more than 500 savings and loan failures led to the bankruptcy of the FSLIC, forcing Congress to create the Resolution Trust Corporation to restructure failing institutions. Yet despite the largest wave of financial failures since the Great Depression, deregulation continued. Ultimately, the Financial Services Modernization Act of 1999 permitted the consolidation of commercial banks, investment banks, securities firms, and insurance companies in financial holding companies, thereby eliminating the last vestiges of Glass-Steagall.

Regulatory Review

Deregulation was only one part of the reform agenda. Beginning in the early 1970s, presidents established ever more demanding systems of cost-benefit–based regulatory review for agencies seeking to introduce significant new regulations. With Executive Order 11821 (1974), Pres. Gerald R. Ford required agencies to prepare inflation impact statements to accompany significant new regulations (i.e., those with an annual impact greater than $100 million). The analyses were reviewed by the newly created Council on Wage and Price Stability, which was placed in the Executive Office of the President (EOP). The application of review based on cost-benefit analysis continued in the Carter presidency with Executive Order 12044 (1978), which required agencies to prepare regulatory analyses, which would be reviewed by the newly created Regulatory Analysis Review Group, once again placed in the EOP.

In 1981, Reagan's Executive Order 12291 marked a sea change in regulatory review. It required agencies to submit regulatory impact analyses grounded in cost-benefit analysis to the Office of Management and Budget's Office of Information and Regulatory Affairs (OIRA). If agencies failed to make the affirmative case that new regulations generated net benefits, OIRA was authorized to prohibit them from publishing a notice of rulemaking in the *Federal Register,* thereby stopping the regulatory process. Even if new social regulatory agencies eluded the deregulatory fervor of the period, they were deeply impacted by the new review requirements. Although subsequent presidential administrations would allow for the consideration of a broader range of factors in regulatory review, cost-benefit analysis and a centralization of oversight functions in the OIRA would become permanent features of the regulatory state.

Regulatory Reinvention

During the period 1980–2008, there would be few significant new regulatory statutes (the major exception being the Clean Air Act Amendments of 1990, creating a cap-and-trade system for controlling acid rain). Lacking new statutory authority, agencies increasingly formed partnerships with corporations, trade associations, advocacy groups, and research institutions to collaborate in addressing regulatory problems. These partnerships became the centerpiece of the Clinton administration's regulatory reinvention efforts. Consider the case of the EPA. For two decades, critics had indicted the EPA for its command-and-control regulations and its adversarial relationships with business. During the Clinton presidency, the EPA initiated a new set of partnerships premised on the belief that corporations, if given the correct incentives, could find efficient and innovative means of preventing pollution. Many of these partnerships were designed explicitly to create a means of coordinating corporate efforts and disseminating best practices. This reliance on partnerships and corporate voluntarism was embraced by other regulatory agencies and was continued by the Bush administration.

Stability and Change in Regulation

Many policy areas have enjoyed long periods of equilibrium, characterized by a broad consensus regarding policy goals and stable relationships between congressional committees, regulatory bureaucracies, and regulated interests. In the 1970s, this equilibrium was punctuated by stagflation. By the end of the 1980s, however, it appeared that the system had once again become relatively stable. The rapid and substantial deregulatory efforts and the battles over regulatory review that marked the 1970s and early 1980s had come to a close. With the exception of the savings and loan industry, deregulation appeared, in fact, to benefit consumers, increase competition, and lower prices. Deregulation continued to occur, albeit incrementally, and there appeared to be a bipartisan consensus on the efficacy of cost-benefit-analysis-based regulatory review centralized in the OIRA. Even if there were few new regulatory statutes, agency budgets grew at a steady pace. In 2008, the last year of the Bush presidency, the combined regulatory budget was $48 billion. To place this number in perspective, inflation-adjusted regulatory budgets had grown by 310 percent since 1980. During this same period, inflation-adjusted GDP (gross domestic product) grew by 227 percent. As one might expect, social regulatory agencies claimed some 85 percent of overall regulatory spending. However, even the budgets for economic regulation expanded faster than the economy.

The stable equilibrium surrounding regulatory agencies was punctuated once again in the last year of the Bush presidency, as real estate markets collapsed and unleashed a financial panic that devoured the largest investment banks and forced an unprecedented effort to rescue the financial system. During the previous decades, liquidity had been added to real estate markets through the securitization of mortgage debt and the issuance of credit-default swaps (insurance contracts on mortgage-based securities). In a deregulated environment, large institutional investors had become highly leveraged and acquired significant stakes in these securities. As the market collapsed and created effects that cascaded throughout the economy, regulators were forced to take unprecedented steps to prevent the recession from turning into a depression. These events increased the salience of regulation and raised profound concerns over the unintended consequences of deregulation. With the election of Pres. Barack Obama and Democratic control of both houses of Congress, there was strong support for regulatory change. The immediate focus was the financial services industry. But proposals for carbon regulations to combat climate change and significant changes in labor regulations were also elevated on the policy agenda. As of this writing, it is impossible to predict the form that regulatory change will assume. But the changes will likely be substantial and will mark a significant departure from the stable equilibrium that emerged around deregulation.

Bibliography and Further Reading

Baumgartner, Frank R., and Bryan D. Jones. *Agendas and Instability in American Politics.* Chicago: University of Chicago Press, 1993.

De Rugy, Veronique, and Melinda Warren. *Regulatory Agency Spending Reaches New Height: An Analysis of the U.S. Budget for Fiscal Years 2008 and 2009.* Fairfax, VA: Mercatus Center at George Mason University, 2008. http://www.mercatus.org/uploadedFiles/Mercatus/Publications/1-regulatoryagency20080807_wc-regulators_budget_09.pdf (accessed October 31, 2009).

Derthick, Martha, and Paul J. Quirk. *The Politics of Deregulation.* Washington, D.C.: Brookings Institution, 1985.

Eisner, Marc Allen. *Governing the Environment: The Transformation of Environmental Protection.* Boulder, CO: Lynne Rienner, 2007.

Eisner, Marc Allen, Jeff Worsham, and Evan J. Ringquist. *Contemporary Regulatory Policy*, 2nd edition. Boulder, CO: Lynne Rienner, 2006.

Harris, Richard A., and Sidney M. Milkis. *The Politics of Regulatory Change: A Tale of Two Agencies*, 2nd edition. New York: Oxford University Press, 1996.

McGarity, Thomas O. *Reinventing Rationality: The Role of Regulatory Analysis in the Federal Bureaucracy.* Cambridge, UK: Cambridge University Press, 1991.

Marc Allen Eisner

REHNQUIST, WILLIAM

1924–2005
Sixteenth Chief Justice of the
United States

William Rehnquist, who served on the U.S. Supreme Court for over 30 years as associate justice and then chief justice, was the first true judicial conservative appointed to the Court in the post–Warren Court era. It was he who provided many of the intellectual and precedential foundations for the Court's swing back to the right during the 1980s and 1990s. As an associate justice, he was praised by most for his intellectually rigorous conservatism, even though he sought to limit the Court's intervention to aid the disadvantaged constituencies that the Court had developed during its liberal heyday of the 1960s. As chief justice, he played a key role in what is sometimes called a "federalism revolution" during the 1990s, and consistently steered the Court in a more conservative direction on a variety of doctrinal issues.

Loyal Republican to Chief Justice

Upon receiving his LLB from Stanford Law School in 1952, William Rehnquist went to work as a clerk for Justice Robert H. Jackson during the 1952 and 1953 terms. While serving in this capacity, he authored a controversial memo regarding the Court's landmark determination in *Brown v. Board of Education*, 347 U.S. 484 (1954) that was to dog him for the rest of his career, but especially during his Supreme Court confirmation hearings. In that memo, Rehnquist expressed opposition to the judicially ordered desegregation of public schools and asserted that the rights of minorities will always be determined by electoral majorities, regardless of the Court's ameliorative efforts. Following his clerkship, Rehnquist set up a private practice in Arizona, and it was there that he became involved in state politics. His support for Barry Goldwater's 1964 presidential campaign helped him to forge connections with the national Republican Party, and when Richard Nixon became President in 1969, Rehnquist accepted a position as assistant attorney general for the Office of

Legal Counsel in the Justice Department under Attorney General John Mitchell.

Nixon turned to Rehnquist relatively late in the process of choosing a replacement for Justice John Marshall Harlan, who was generally considered to be a judicial moderate. Rehnquist's 1971 nomination hearings were contentious, with the aforementioned clerk memo emerging as a focus of opposition to the nomination from civil rights groups. It was also alleged that he had harassed black voters as a poll watcher in Arizona. Despite these concerns, Rehnquist managed to win confirmation on a 68–26 Senate vote, quite close by the standards of prior successful nominations. Rehnquist was Nixon's ideal "strict constructionist," articulating a vigorous vision of judicial conservatism even from the beginning of his time on the Court. During these early years, he was often relegated to dissent and laying the foundations for a later conservative legal resurgence. He earned the nickname "Lone Ranger" for the perceived frequency with which he was left writing solo dissents.

Upon Warren Burger's retirement in 1986, Pres. Ronald Reagan immediately tapped Rehnquist for the top spot on the Court, invoking the substantial reputation that his 15 years on the Court had earned him in conservative legal circles. His confirmation hearings for promotion to chief justice were, if anything, even more acrimonious than his original hearings. The liberal opposition resurrected their former arguments against his nomination and added 15 years' worth of staunchly conservative opinions to bolster their case that Rehnquist was too far outside the mainstream of American society to lead the nation's highest court. This time around, women's rights groups—citing Rehnquist's dissent in *Craig v. Boren*, 420 U.S. 190 (1976)—added their voices to the chorus of opposition. In his dissent, Rehnquist had objected to the Court's decision requiring courts to review gender classifications in laws to ensure that they are not based on invalid stereotypes of what are expected of men and women in the workplace and other venues. Despite opposition, Rehnquist's promotion was ratified by a 65–33 vote.

Federalism

By the time he became chief justice, several broad features of Rehnquist's jurisprudence were already apparent: an ideology of judicial restraint, favoring the Court's non-interference with policy choices by more democratically accountable political actors, even (or perhaps especially) where claims of individual constitutional rights were concerned; a textualist/originalist mode of interpretation which used the structure and wording of the constitutional text to ground answers to cases and controversies exclusively in the explicit and inferred views of the Founders; and a deep and abiding commitment to federalism, accompanied by a desire to restore judicial policing of the boundaries between national and state governments. It was this latter feature that most consistently characterized Rehnquist's jurisprudence throughout his lengthy tenure on the Court (both as associate and chief) and came to symbolize the conservative achievements of the Rehnquist Court of the 1990s.

One of Rehnquist's early federalism triumphs was *National League of Cities v. Usery* 426 U.S. 833 (1976), in which he articulated the concept of an irreducible core of state functions upon which Congress had no power to infringe. This analysis failed to produce a workable standard for distinguishing between permissible and impermissible impositions upon the state governments by the federal government, and *National League of Cities* was overruled less than a decade later by *Garcia v. San Antonio Metropolitan Transit Authority*, 469 U.S. 528 (1985). Rehnquist's dissenting prediction in *Garcia* that federalist principles would "in time again command the support of a majority of this Court" proved prescient.

Beyond Federalism

In other areas of constitutional law, Rehnquist was a doctrinaire conservative who held the intellectual line against the fairly liberal majority that had formed on social issues during the later Burger Court years. Rehnquist dissented from *Roe v. Wade*, 410 U.S. 113 (1973), the landmark privacy decision recognizing a woman's right to terminate her pregnancy. Rehnquist did not consider *Roe* to be legitimately derived from the constitutional text, and made a sustained but ultimately unsuccessful effort over two decades to achieve its substantial modification or outright overruling. He consistently dissented in cases in which a majority of the Court voted to invalidate government action based on the guarantees of Amendment I, particularly as regarded freedom of speech and establishment of religion cases. And he opposed heightened scrutiny for gender classifications under the Equal Protection Clause, holding fast to his stated view that Amendment XIV was intended only to protect against invidious (intentional) racial discrimination, narrowly defined. On criminal procedure, he was a strong critic of the *Miranda v. Arizona*, 384 U.S. 436 (1966) decision that the police must inform suspects of their rights before questioning and of federal *habeas* review for defendants convicted in state courts.

Notably, Rehnquist's strongly worded dissents in these diverse areas of law did not always lay the foundations for later doctrinal revolutions. As with many justices who follow precedents that do not violate deeply held personal views on constitutional rights and theories of how to interpret the Constitution, Rehnquist, as chief justice, grew to accommodate or tolerate doctrinal innovations that he had initially vigorously opposed as an associate justice.

Chief Justice on a More Conservative Supreme Court

By the early 1990s, the Rehnquist Court's conservative wing had been bolstered to the point of dominance, with the retirement of long-serving liberals William Brennan and Thurgood Marshall and the appointment of the moderate-conservative Anthony Kennedy and the conservative originalist Clarence Thomas. Conservatives expected that this newly ascendant conservative wing of the Court would finally put the long-stalled conservative counterrevolution into practice, and reverse what they saw as the overreaching of the Warren and Burger years.

In some regards, these legal scholars and politicians were vindicated. Most especially in the broad category of constitutional law known as federalism, the Rehnquist Court broke new and innovative ground. But a more thorough-going counterrevolution in the sense of severe trimming back or overruling of old "liberal activist" decisions never came to fruition under Rehnquist, although this was not primarily due to lack of effort on the chief's part. Although it is certainly true that moderates Sandra Day O'Connor and Anthony Kennedy acted to prevent rollbacks in constitutional law in diverse doctrinal areas, preserving the liberal gains made under previous Courts, it is also true that Rehnquist, especially toward the end of his time on the Court, either came to suffer from battle fatigue after three decades' worth of sparring over similar legal issues, or else became somewhat more willing to compromise on issues upon which he had little hope of winning outright.

Federalism

Undoubtedly, the Rehnquist Court is most known for and will probably best be remembered in the context of its pronouncements on federalism; the doctrinal changes achieved in this area were real and substantial, and are likely to shape developments for years to come. The more radical, but possibly less decisive, shift occurred in the Court's Commerce Clause jurisprudence. Rehnquist's majority opinions in *United States v. Lopez*, 514 U.S. 549 (1995) and *United States v. Morrison*, 529 U.S. 598 (2000), which found unconstitutional the Gun-Free School Zone Act of 1990 and the Violence Against Women Act of 1994, respectively. These laws were viewed as going beyond Congress's authority under the Commerce Clause; they also stood for the proposition that it was the Court's duty to police the boundary between matters of national and local concern. These cases marked the first time since 1937 that the Court had invalidated a federal law on Commerce Clause grounds.

Both of these decisions came under strong criticism from the Court's four moderate-liberal members. In *Gonzales v. Raich*, 545 U.S. 1 (2005), handed down three months before Rehnquist's death, the Court reversed course, with justices Kennedy and Antonin Scalia crossing ideological lines to vote against a California medical marijuana law and endorse a Commerce Clause jurisprudence that suggested the Court might return to the Court's doctrine prior to *Lopez*, which was to trust Congress to police the boundaries between matters which were of national and state concern under the Commerce Clause.

Less noted in the popular press, but potentially more lasting, was the new direction in which the Rehnquist Court took Amendment XI guarantee of state sovereign immunity from lawsuits. Two of the most notable cases in this area were *Seminole Tribe of Florida v. Florida*, 517 U.S. 44 (1996) and *Alden v. Maine*, 527 U.S. 706 (1999). Both cases held that Congress's powers under Article I did not provide for the abrogation of state sovereign immunity, and barred the suit of states or state officials in federal courts to produce compliance with federal statutory schemes. The sovereign immunity doctrine as expanded by the Rehnquist Court has considerable bite; it is no longer the case that Congress can take for granted its power to enforce policy choices by threatening recalcitrant states with lawsuits.

Equal Protection, Amendment I, and Defendant Rights

In areas other than federalism, Rehnquist was sometimes less determined to carry the principles enunciated during his "Lone Ranger" days to their logical conclusions, or even to go as far (as chief justice) as he had explicitly demanded that the Court go in the past. For example, he concurred in *United States v. Virginia*, 518 U.S. 515 (1996), a case mandating inclusion of women at the all-male Virginia Military Institute. In doing so, Rehnquist accepted as binding the intermediate scrutiny for gender classifications formula that he had harshly criticized during the 1970s.

With regard to criminal procedure and defendant rights, in *Dickerson v. United States*, 530 U.S. 428 (2000), he wrote the majority opinion accepting the much-maligned *Miranda* decision as part of the basic fabric of American society, and turning back a congressional attempt dated to the 1960s to overrule *Miranda* by statute.

Whether these instances of apparent retrenching were simply reflections of the practical realities that O'Connor and Kennedy were not willing to go as far as Justice Rehnquist had been in 1971, or whether considerations like institutional stability and *stare decisis* (that is, a concern for following precedent) played a role in bringing Rehnquist to accommodate some doctrinal innovations he initially resisted is somewhat unclear, because the chief justice generally declined to acknowledge that his later positions were inconsistent with his earlier ones, even when the contradictions were clear. It may also be the case that Rehnquist felt comfortable passing the reins of conservative iconoclasm to justices Scalia and Thomas, focusing his own energies on managing the Court as an institution.

As Leader of the Supreme Court

One notable area in which Rehnquist was not criticized was his leadership of the Court. Though his predecessor Burger was derided by colleagues and Court historians alike for underhanded opinion assignment tactics and generally poor leadership qualities, Rehnquist garnered the respect of his colleagues of all ideological stripes for his efforts to reduce the Court's docket from its bloated peak of around 120 cases per term during the Burger years to 80, a number closer to the average. Rehnquist's concern for the efficiency of the Court's operations apparently coincided with the interests of the other justices. The respect of the nation, and his respect for the Office of Chief Justice and the Court, is also evidenced by the politically neutral way in which he presided over the Senate's impeachment trial of Pres. Bill Clinton. However, Rehnquist was severely criticized for joining his conservative colleagues on the Supreme Court in *Bush v. Gore*, 531 U.S. 98 (2000), a 5–4 decision which had the effect of stopping vote recounting in Florida and determining who would be the next President of the United States.

If Rehnquist's leadership has not had as profound an influence on the landscape of American law as, say, Earl Warren, that deficit is due less to any personal shortcomings and more to the sometimes fractured and contentious group of justices that Rehnquist presided over during his tenure as chief. The Rehnquist Court did not reverse the Warren Court, but it did develop a distinctly post-Warren conservative constitutional jurisprudence. Rehnquist was a conservative chief justice for a conservative political

era, and he will probably be remembered as a near great chief for his many contributions to judicial conservatism and his steady leadership of the Court during a period of ideological transition.

Bibliography and Further Reading

Bradley, Craig, ed. *The Rehnquist Legacy*. New York: Cambridge University Press, 2006.

Davis, Derek. *Original Intent: Chief Justice Rehnquist and the Course of American Church/State Relations.* Amherst, NY: Prometheus Books, 1991.

Davis, Sue. *Justice Rehnquist and the Constitution*. Princeton, NJ: Princeton University Press, 1989.

Greenburg, Jan Crawford. *Supreme Conflict*. New York: Penguin Press, 2007.

Rehnquist, William. "The Notion of a Living Constitution." *Texas Law Review* 54 (1976): 693.

Savage, David. *Turning Right: The Making of the Rehnquist Supreme Court*. New York: Wiley, 1992.

Whittington, Keith. "William H. Rehnquist: Nixon's Strict Constructionist, Reagan's Chief Justice." In *Rehnquist Justice*, edited by Earl Maltz. Lawrence: University Press of Kansas, 2003.

Yarbrough, Tinsley E. *The Rehnquist Court and the Constitution*. New York: Oxford University Press, 2000.

Ronald Kahn

RELIGION

Scholars long ignored, or at least marginalized, religion as a factor in U.S. political development. Since the 1970s, however, with the rise of the evangelical right, many analysts have recognized religion as a key political variable. In the 1970s, in part as a reaction to the perception of cultural decline, and also to the Supreme Court decision in *Roe v. Wade*, 410 U.S. 113 (1973) that legalized abortion, conservative religious leaders began to mobilize evangelical and "born again" Christians into a powerful political movement. By the 1980s the movement known as the "Christian Right" or "Religious Right" had become a fixture on the national political scene, and it has remained an important force ever since. Nonetheless, with the elections of a Democratic Congress in 2006 and Barack Obama as president in 2008, there has been significant interest in the emergence of progressive religious politics.

It was Pres. Jimmy Carter, a socially progressive Democrat and a proud born-again Christian, who played the initial key role in mobilizing evangelical Christians, especially those in the South, into national politics. Yet many Southern evangelicals who had rallied to Carter's candidacy ultimately turned against him because of disappointment with his social policies, particularly after he announced that abortion should be legally protected. Partially because of Carter's electoral success, a group of secular conservative leaders saw an opportunity. Such noted "New Right" leaders as Howard Phillips, Richard Viguerie, and Paul Weyrich believed that if they could build a coalition of secular and religious conservative groups, they could make the Republicans the dominant party for years. They reached out to the prominent Virginia televangelist Rev. Jerry Falwell, who in 1979 formed a national political organization called the Moral Majority. They also convinced Republican presidential candidate Ronald Reagan to make direct appeals to conservative evangelicals, believing that, if successfully mobilized, this group could deliver millions of new votes to the G.O.P.

The Christian Right Era: Reagan to George W. Bush

The 1980 Republican landslide surprised most observers, and Falwell claimed that his Moral Majority had helped to mobilize nearly four million new evangelical voters for the G.O.P. Falwell became an instant major player in U.S. politics, and the rise of the Christian Right was the big story of the newly resurgent Republican Party. The traditionally solid Democratic South had begun to transition to a competitive two-party region, with primarily white conservative evangelicals leading the march toward the G.O.P. This Republican courting of evangelicals significantly changed the U.S. electoral map, with the South moving increasingly into Republican hands.

The key power of the Christian Right is within the Republican Party, where the movement has succeeded in helping to nominate socially conservative candidates for various offices, and also to lead various platform and rules committees. In the early period of Christian Right mobilization, there was a fierce battle for party control between social conservatives and party moderates. It is widely acknowledged that, over time, the social conservatives won. But the story is a little more complicated than one group ousting another. What actually happened was that the Christian Right had learned how to play the political game in a smarter way, and thus became a stronger force in the Republican Party and U.S. politics.

The first wave of the Christian Right, which lasted from the 1970s to the end of the 1980s, is widely seen as a failure. By the end of the 1980s, two terms of the Reagan presidency had delivered very little on social policy, the Moral Majority was bankrupt and disbanded, and most coverage of the evangelical movement focused on several high-profile televangelist scandals. Rev. Marion G. (Pat) Robertson of the *700 Club* had campaigned for the Republican nomination for president in 1988, only to be soundly defeated by the socially moderate George H. W. Bush. At that time, many scholars and journalists had started writing the obituary of the Christian Right. They agreed that the movement had failed due to a lack of political sophistication among the leaders, who tended to use extreme rhetoric and eschew the necessity of compromise.

Yet the movement endured. In 1989, Robertson formed a new organization, the Christian Coalition. For its political director he chose Ralph Reed, a young political operative who could give a fresh look to the Christian Right. Unlike Falwell and some of the other early leaders of the movement, Reed could speak the secular language of politics as well as he could communicate with fellow evangelicals. The Christian Coalition made a major effort to build state, county, and local organizations around the country. Reed recruited state and local leaders whose backgrounds were in business, interest group politics, or civic activity, marking a major shift from the Moral Majority strategy of recruiting local pastors. This shift in strategy enabled the Christian Coalition to build a broadly ecumenical organization that reached out to social conservatives from a variety of faith traditions, with a special effort to recruit pro-life Catholics.

Not all of these efforts were successful, but they did evidence recognition of the importance of coalition building at the grass roots. Thus, the second wave of the Christian Right, in the 1990s, was a politically maturing movement that had learned from the mistakes of the first wave. Studies of the Christian Right during this decade found the rhetorical appeals of leaders to sound more moderate and the issue appeals more broad-based. In addition, the movement's organizers had built more broadly ecumenical bases and stronger grassroots networks than the first wave of the movement.

Reflecting its new strategy, the Christian Right moved its argument against abortion from moralistic appeals to asserting that *Roe v. Wade* should be overturned because it was bad constitutional law. Reed himself argued that he merely wanted the issue of abortion remanded to the states, in keeping with the constitutional Framers' notion of federalism, rather than have the Supreme Court mandate a one-size-fits-all approach. Other major movement figures, such as Robertson and Phyllis Schlafly, made similar appeals.

Many leaders in the movement also recognized that abortion rights could be more effectively reduced by focusing on secondary restrictions, such as parental notification and consent laws, ending taxpayer funding, restricting or eliminating late-term abortions, imposing mandatory waiting periods and counseling for those seeking abortion, and restricting what health care professionals and educators can tell young women about abortion options. Many of these issue positions are popular with voters outside of the Christian Right. Thus, in areas where the Christian Right position dovetailed with broader public sentiment, the movement had some successes at the state level.

In the 2000s, the Christian Right consolidated its position within the G.O.P. with the election and reelection of George W. Bush as president. In the 2000 Republican nominating contest, it was strong support from religious conservative voters that gave the edge to Bush over his chief rival, Sen. John McCain. Evangelical voters overwhelmingly favored Bush over Democratic presidential nominees in 2000 and 2004, and many observers concluded that the religious "values voters" were the key constituency to Bush's 2004 reelection. Indeed, exit polls showed that Bush won 78 percent of the evangelical vote in

that election. The polls also showed a significant difference in voting between those who regularly attended religious services and those who did not. Regular attenders of religious services voted strongly Republican, whereas occasional attenders and non-attenders voted strongly Democratic. Although many attributed Bush's victory largely to his strength among evangelicals, he also won a majority of Catholic voters and significantly improved his outcome among Mainline Protestant and even Jewish voters.

The electoral successes of George W. Bush evidenced the wisdom of a strategy of political pragmatism by the Christian Right. When Bush first ran for the G.O.P. nomination in 2000, there were several much more socially conservative candidates in the race. Bush actually had positioned himself as a social moderate on many issues. Nonetheless, prominent leaders of the Christian Right backed Bush's candidacy over those of the more conservative candidates because of the belief that he could win the presidency and the more ideologically pure candidates could not. Key support from Pat Robertson and other leading figures played prominently in the G.O.P nominating contest. And once elected, unlike some past successful Republican candidates for various offices, Bush did not turn his back on his supporters in the Christian Right. Instead, he placed prominent figures of the movement in top positions in his administration, and he appointed social conservatives to federal judgeships, including on the Supreme Court. Bush issued an executive order prohibiting federal funding for international agencies that provide abortions and abortion counseling. And perhaps most important, he created the federal Office of Faith-Based and Community Initiatives to provide government funding of church-based programs for delivering social services.

Despite these and other gains, Christian Right leaders and activists often complained that Bush did not place sufficient emphasis on the social issues agenda. They were especially disappointed after Bush's reelection, when the president made social security reform the priority of his domestic agenda and did little to promote issues that had mobilized the "values voters" for his candidacy. Furthermore, as the Bush presidency was mired in a failing war in Iraq, social conservatives became impatient with the lack of social initiatives. In the 2006 midterm elections, U.S. voters delivered a strong rebuke to Bush and the Republican Party by electing the Democrats as the majority party in both houses of Congress. Exit polls showed that although the Republican Party did well with evangelical voters, that group had slightly shifted its voting toward the Democratic Party, leading some observers to suggest that the evangelical alliance with the Republican Party was beginning to splinter. The election of the Democrat Barack Obama as president in 2008, along with the overall strong showing of his party across much of the country, further emboldened progressive religious leaders to build a movement to counter the Christian Right.

The Religious Progressive Movement: The Obama Era and Beyond

To many Americans, the religious progressive movement seemed almost silent or politically insignificant for many years. That began to change in 2004, when a number of progressive leaders took up the task of competing with the Christian Right in the arena of "God talk." *Sojourners* magazine, a leading force of progressive evangelicals, formed a petition campaign called "God is Not a Republican or Democrat," and over one hundred thousand people signed on. A number of groups became active in spreading the message of what some have called the "Religious Left." These included the Christian Alliance for Progress, Faithful America, the Center for American Progress and its Faith and Progressive Policy Initiative, and the Interfaith Alliance, among others. Although the 2004 elections were a disappointment for these progressive groups, like the Christian Right movement, they did not give up due to short-term failure but instead dedicated themselves to long-term political involvement. The elections of 2006 and 2008 showcased the benefits of their persistence. The Democratic Party's big successes in those election cycles have emboldened religious progressive leaders to try to build a powerful and lasting force in U.S. politics.

The greatest challenge for the religious progressive movement in organizing politically has been its very diverse base. Whereas the Christian Right appeals mainly to conservative evangelicals and conservative Catholics, thus enabling a wide consensus on key issues within that movement, the religious progressive movement includes black Protestants, Latino Catholics, predominantly white Mainline Protestants, Jews, and a variety of Eastern faiths and New Age groups. It is highly complicated to mobilize such a diverse base into common political action. Progressive religious groups also lack the issue intensity or fervor of the Christian Right. Indeed, in accepting a religiously open and pluralistic philosophy, the progressive groups find it difficult even to find common ground on many policies. Black Protestants and Latino Catholics have not been highly receptive, for example, to progressive appeals on gay rights issues.

The 2008 election results evidenced some shifting in voting among different religious groups. The Pew Forum on Religion and Public Life notes that Barack Obama won the Catholic vote by 9 percentage points, though Bush had won this group handily in 2004. Obama improved the Democratic Party showing among evangelicals by 5 percentage points. The shift among Catholics, long a big target of the Christian Right, was the most politically significant. Yet the core constituency of the Christian Right, the evangelical vote, was still heavily Republican, even if slightly less than it had been in 2004, according to the Pew Forum. A key to the potential success of the religious progressive movement is whether it can break this stranglehold over evangelicals.

Several significant developments suggest the possibility of a future shift in political loyalties among evangelicals and the emergence of a potentially powerful religious progressive movement. First, after the 2004 elections, certain prominent evangelical leaders began to signal their intention to focus on environmental protection, poverty, Third World debt, and AIDS, among other issues. Most of the issues identified as a new focus for evangelicals are more commonly identified with the Democratic Party than the Republican Party. This effort to shift the agenda focus away from such core issues as abortion has caused a significant rift in the evangelical community and thus created an opportunity for Democratic politicians. Whereas the moral issues agenda in the 2004 campaign focused on gay marriage and abortion, by 2008 much of the discourse had shifted to the environment, poverty reduction, affordable health care, and standards of U.S. conduct regarding war, torture, and secret prisons.

Second, the Democratic Party itself has started to make a serious effort to reach out to many evangelical voters who have identified with the G.O.P. for years. Although a difficult task, Democrats are talking much more about religion and moral values in the hope of attracting at least some of those voters who for years only listened to Republicans. Much of this task has been made more credible by the electoral success of Barack Obama, whose eloquent speeches in the 2008 campaign often reminded people of an evangelical style of discourse. His comfort in discussing religion presented a significant contrast with past Democratic presidential nominees such as John Kerry (2004) and Al Gore (2000), and thus made Obama appear more "authentic" as an advocate of moral issues.

Third, there is some evidence of a generational divide among evangelicals, with the younger voters being more politically independent than their parents. Although the younger evangelicals express a broad interest in issues beyond the social agenda, they retain strongly prolife views and still tend to vote Republican, even though they are not as likely as their parents to identify themselves as members of the G.O.P. This trend suggests the possibility of a shift in political alliances among evangelicals over the long term, especially if the Republican Party continues to be seen by younger voters as lacking a credible agenda on such issues as poverty, AIDS, Third World debt, and the environment.

Significant challenges remain for religiously motivated political activists. For the Christian Right in the Obama era, and with increased evidence that the core issues of the movement have lost much of their salience, the future looks potentially difficult. Yet experts often have written obituaries of the movement only to see it reemerge as a strong political force. For the religious progressive movement, the lack of a clear issue focus or central message, along with the diverse pluralistic nature of its core, presents strong barriers to effective political mobilizing over the long term.

Bibliography and Further Reading

Green, John C., Mark J. Rozell, and Clyde Wilcox, eds. *The Values Campaign?: The Christian Right and the 2004 Elections.* Washington, D.C.: Georgetown University Press, 2006.

Kohut, Andrew, John C. Green, Scott Keeter, and Robert C. Toth. *The Diminishing Divide: Religion's Changing Role in American Politics.* Washington, D.C.: Brookings Institution Press, 2000.

Moen, Matthew. "The Changing Nature of Christian Right Activism." In *Sojourners in the Wilderness: The Christian Right in Comparative Perspective*, edited by Corwin Smidt and James Penning, 21–40. Lanham, MD: Rowman & Littlefield, 1997.

Pew Forum on Religion and Public Life. "Voting Religiously." http://pewresearch.org/pubs/1022/exit-poll-analysis-religion (accessed May 12, 2009).

Rozell, Mark J., and Clyde Wilcox. *Second Coming: The New Christian Right in Virginia Politics.* Baltimore, MD: Johns Hopkins University Press, 1996.

Reed, Ralph. "What Do Christian Conservatives Really Want?" Paper presented at the Colloquium on the Religious New Right and the 1992 Campaign, Ethics and Public Policy Center, Washington, D.C., 1993.

Wilcox, Clyde, and Carin Larson. *Onward Christian Soldiers: The Religious Right in American Politics*, 3rd edition. Boulder, CO: Westview Press, 2006.

Wilson, J. Matthew, ed. *From Pews to Polling Places: Faith and Politics in the American Religious Mosaic.* Washington, D.C.: Georgetown University Press, 2007.

Mark J. Rozell

RELIGIOUS RIGHT

The "Religious Right," also known as the "Christian Right," is an umbrella term for the social movement comprising primarily theologically conservative Christians that mobilized to participate in American politics beginning in the 1970s. Since the election of 1980, the Religious Right has been a core voting bloc of the Republican Party. Traditionally, Christian Right organizations and activists have advocated in support of the "traditional" family and against abortion and gay rights; many have also argued in favor of prayer in public schools. In the twenty-first century, the political agenda of some Religious Right organizations has begun to broaden to include international human rights and other issues.

Early History

After decades of disengagement from politics, evangelical and fundamentalist Christians regained an interest in political activity in the 1960s and 1970s. Through much of the 1970s, evangelicals were more likely to identify as Democrats than Republicans, reflecting support for New Deal programs and the high percentage of evangelicals in the heavily Democratic South.

Originally called the "New Christian Right," and later shortened to Christian Right or Religious Right, the movement mobilized around concerns about the erosion of traditional values in American society. Works such as Hal Lindsey's *The Late Great Planet Earth*, a best-selling book of the 1970s, popularized a particular reading of biblical prophecy that foretold inevitable moral decline leading to the end of the world. Activism began with grassroots advocacy against sex education in public schools, which gained momentum in the late

At a polling station in Miami Beach, Florida, Anita Bryant, carrying a sample ballot, looks around for her voting booth as her husband, Bob Green, waits to sign in on June 7, 1977. Bryant was successful in organizing and mobilizing Christian activists to vote against a Dade County ordinance that would have prohibited discrimination on the basis of sexual orientation. Although Bryant would ultimately prove a divisive cultural figure, her successful campaign was one example of the grassroots-level reengagement of the Christian electorate in politics and political activism during the 1970s. (Bettmann/Corbis)

1960s, and battles to protect the tax-exempt status of Christian schools. Theologically conservative Christians organized in Kanawha County, West Virginia, in a battle over school textbooks in 1974, and assistance from a newly formed conservative think tank, the Heritage Foundation, increased their national visibility. Anita Bryant, a former beauty queen and pop singer, organized Christian activists in Dade County, Florida, to defeat a gay rights ordinance in 1977. The movement to defeat the Equal Rights Amendment gained momentum in the early 1980s, due largely to Phyllis Schlafly, the conservative Catholic founder of "Stop ERA." Each of these campaigns raised the national profile of grassroots efforts by religious conservatives concerned about perceived threats to traditional family values and the culture's moral decline.

The 1976 presidential election was a catalyst that energized religious voters for a national campaign. In the wake of the Watergate scandal and President Nixon's resignation, Jimmy Carter's biographical campaign attracted support. Carter spoke openly of his Christian faith, describing himself as "born again." At a time when both parties had legitimate opportunities to compete for the conservative Christian vote, Carter captured much of their support. The perceived influence of religious voters in Carter's election raised the national profile of evangelical Christians, leading *Newsweek* magazine to devote a cover article to the "Year of the Evangelicals."

Abortion Emerges as a Defining Issue

Many evangelicals who had regained interest in politics with Carter's 1976 campaign became more politicized in their opposition to abortion during his presidency. Due in part to emphases on other political issues and an initial reluctance to partner with Catholics, conservative Protestants did not immediately join the right-to-life movement in the aftermath of *Roe v. Wade*, 410 U.S. 113 (1973), the Supreme Court case that declared abortion was constitutionally protected. The evangelical theologian Francis Schaeffer and the pediatric surgeon C. Everett Koop's book and film series *Whatever Happened to the Human Race?*—and their accompanying 1979 speaking tour—called attention to the growing acceptance

of abortion, infanticide, and euthanasia, and energized evangelical audiences to connect the abortion issue with the sanctity of human life. Carter's moderate stance on abortion now became a political liability. Carter upset feminist activists by his refusal to support the public funding of abortion, but he likewise alienated conservative Christians, who expected him to be more proactive in working against *Roe v. Wade*.

By the early stages of the 1980 presidential campaign, leaders in the Religious Right had lost confidence in Carter. Protestants and Catholic activists began to join forces in opposition to abortion, and the issue solidified as the centerpiece of the Religious Right. Republican Party activists seized the opportunity to expand their political base and built alliances with disaffected Christian conservatives, encouraging them to support Ronald Reagan. Beginning with the 1980 election, the Republican Party platform included planks appealing to the Religious Right, such as support for constitutional amendments permitting organized prayer in public schools and defining human life as beginning at conception.

Around the same time, prominent religious leaders were founding national organizations to raise awareness of culturally conservative political issues. Reverend Jerry Falwell, pastor of what was then the largest independent Baptist church in the United States, founded the Moral Majority in 1979. Contending that supporters of pro-family issues made up a "silent majority" of the American public, Falwell encouraged political participation and voter registration to build and organize support for socially conservative policies. Other Christian Right organizations founded around this time included Ed McAteer's Religious Roundtable (later shortened to the Roundtable), which was designed to organize like-minded pastors; the Christian Voice, originally founded in California to lobby against a gay rights law; and the National Christian Action Coalition, founded in 1978 in support of Christian schools.

The leaders of these emerging groups came together with other grassroots movements in support of Reagan's 1980 presidential bid. Although not a professing evangelical like the other two candidates, Jimmy Carter and John Anderson, Reagan supported the newly broadened conservative agenda, which included a set of policy positions that were beginning to be relabeled as "pro-family" issues. Evangelical Christians represented an important Republican voting bloc in the federal elections of 1980 and 1984, helping solidify the connection between Religious Right organizations and the Republican Party.

In the early 1980s, Christian Broadcasting Network founder Pat Robertson organized the Freedom Council, a national network of local groups designed to train political activists and educate voters (it ceased formal operations in 1986). When Robertson began exploring a possible bid for the presidency in 1988, he drew key support from the grassroots networks built by the Freedom Council and its successor groups. Although he did not win the Republican nomination, Robertson's strong showings in several early states, including a surprise second place finish in the Iowa Caucus, demonstrated the growing political strength of religious conservatives.

Changing Tactics in the 1990s

By the late 1980s, many of the early Religious Right organizations were declining. High-profile scandals plagued televangelists Jim Bakker and Jimmy Swaggart, and the image problems carried over to other well-known media evangelists. The most prominent of the early organizations, Jerry Falwell's Moral Majority, changed its name in 1986 to the Liberty Foundation, and it closed in 1989.

Meanwhile, other conservative Christian organizations were building strength. The most significant organization of the 1990s, the Christian Coalition, grew out of the network that supported Pat Roberston's presidential campaign. Founded by Robertson and directed by a young and ambitious political operative, Ralph Reed, the Christian Coalition helped lead the Christian Right in a new direction. With little fanfare, the coalition built a network of state and local affiliates to train and prepare individuals for political activism. Eschewing much overt Christian rhetoric, Reed advocated a more pragmatic and less religious approach, broadening the agenda to include a wider range of issues and building coalitions with nonreligious groups. The organization gained fame for utilizing a network of churches each election year to distribute millions of "nonpartisan" voter guides that compared candidates on a range of pro-family issues. By 1995, the Christian Coalition boasted 1.6 million members and 1,600 local chapters. Reed left after the 1996 election, and the organization's influence has waned since then.

Focus on the Family, the ministry founded in 1977 by the child psychologist Dr. James Dobson, began nationwide daily radio broadcasts in 1981. In 1987, the organization had an annual budget of over $30 million; ten years later it grew to well over $100 million. In 1983, Dobson founded the Family Research Council (FRC), a Washington-based policy organization. After a rocky first decade, FRC developed a greater advocacy focus under the direction of Gary Bauer. By 1999, it had a $14 million budget and a mailing list of five hundred thousand. Other advocacy groups, including Concerned Women for America, the Traditional Values Coalition, and the American Family Association, also grew in size and influence during the 1990s.

In May 1998, Republican congressional leaders sponsored a "Values Summit," bringing evangelical leaders to Washington for input on public policy. Momentum from the summit led to the formation of the Values Action Team (VAT), spearheaded by Rep. Joe Pitts (R–PA). VAT gathered representatives from Religious Right organizations to meet weekly on Capitol Hill, coordinating political strategy and exchanging information about pro-family legislation. As they developed more political savvy, Religious Right organizations adopted new strategies, moving away from bold demands for change in favor of more incremental (and politically feasible) legislation. This shift led to a series of victories for abortion opponents, including the defeat of a Republican-favored bankruptcy bill with an amendment unfriendly to abortion protestors and the passage of three largely symbolic pro-life bills: the 2002 Born-Alive Infants Protection Act, the 2003 ban on the so-called partial-birth abortion procedure, and the 2004 Unborn Victims of Violence Act.

New Century, New Opportunities, and New Challenges

The election of George W. Bush in 2000 energized religious right leaders and organizations. For the first time since the Religious Right reentered politics, the movement could claim a president who shared their central policy goals and was openly faithful. Although he never described himself as an evangelical, Bush's frequent references to his life-changing religious conversion and his open discussion of his faith aligned him firmly with theologically conservative Christians. Bush was a strong advocate for many issues of principal concern to the Religious Right, especially upholding the right to life and the appointment of conservative judges. In the 2004 campaign, Religious Right organizations aggressively rallied their supporters to reelect Bush, likely helping him secure his narrow victory. As the Iraq War intensified and foreign policy took center stage, Bush faced increasing criticism from James Dobson and other movement leaders for not giving enough attention to pro-family issues.

As Republicans regained control of national political institutions, Christian Right organizations changed tactics once again. The Arlington Group, "a secret society of the Religious Right's top power brokers," began meeting in June 2003 to discuss their political agenda and resolve disagreements away from public scrutiny. (Gilgoff 157) Comprised of leaders of approximately seventy organizations, the group convenes every six weeks to plan strategy and encourage a united front.

While many leaders of the traditional Religious Right worked together to spotlight their pro-family agenda, other groups made steps to broaden evangelicals' policy concerns beyond just abortion and gay rights. For example, the National Association of Evangelicals, an umbrella group representing over sixty denominations and related organizations, issued *For the Health of the Nations*, a document calling evangelicals to civic engagement and outlining a broad public policy agenda. This redefinition of evangelical politics was well received by many evangelicals, but it also angered some Religious Right leaders.

The publication of the 2005 bestseller *God's Politics* turned the media spotlight on Jim Wallis, the head of Sojourners/Call to Renewal, an antipoverty and social justice ministry, and his mobilization of the so-called Evangelical Left. Capitalizing on growing disaffection with the Iraq War and Republican leadership in Washington, Wallis and others offered a counterpoint to the Religious Right that emphasized social justice issues instead of the cultural issues often associated with religious conservatives. Although it is yet unclear if these efforts will gain significant momentum, this attempt to refocus the agenda of religious voters may pose a challenge to the Religious Right.

The rise of the Religious Right in the late 1970s ended decades of political disengagement and reestablished organized efforts to encourage political participation among religious conservatives, reclaiming the historical connection between American politics and religious beliefs and values. The 1980 election began an uneasy but significant alliance between this burgeoning social movement and the Republican Party. Given the importance of the Religious Right in helping secure Republican victories early into the twenty-first century, it is easy to forget that the evangelicals and other conservative religious adherents who mobilized in the late 1970s could have found a political home in the Democratic Party. Thus, the recent alignment between Republicans and the Religious Right, although strong, is not necessarily permanent. However long this alliance holds, the influence of the Religious Right on American politics will endure for decades in the careers and activism of an entire generation trained by Religious Right organizations and now serving in staff positions and elected office at all levels of government.

Bibliography and Further Reading

Flint, Andrew R., and Joy Porter. "Jimmy Carter: The Reemergence of Faith-Based Politics and the Abortion Rights Issue." *Presidential Studies Quarterly* 35, no. 1 (March 2005): 28–51.

Gilgoff, Dan. *The Jesus Machine: How James Dobson, Focus on the Family, and Evangelical America are Winning the Culture War.* New York: St. Martin's, 2007.

Green, John C., Mark J. Rozell, and Clyde Wilcox, eds. *The Values Campaign? The Christian Right and the 2004*

Elections. Washington, D.C.: Georgetown University Press, 2006.

Marsden, George M. *Fundamentalism and American Culture*, 2nd edition. New York: Oxford University Press, 2006.

Martin, William. *With God on Our Side: The Rise of the Religious Right in America.* New York: Broadway Books, 1996.

Wald, Kenneth D., and Allison Calhoun-Brown. *Religion and Politics in the United States*, 5th edition. Lanham, MD: Rowman & Littlefield, 2007.

Wilcox, Clyde, and Carin Larson. *Onward Christian Soldiers: The Religious Right in American Politics*, 3rd edition. Boulder, CO: Westview, 2006.

Amy E. Black

REPUBLICAN PARTY

Political parties compete with each other to control government, and thus to influence—to their adherents' advantages—the allocation of a nation's economic and moral values. For more than a century and a half, Democrats and Republicans have fought for their different values in American elections and public offices. Fragmented by geography, ideology, and class, and by the American political system itself, the parties are constantly vulnerable to internal and external forces that can lead to large election losses and irrelevance. The Republican Party (also known as the G.O.P., short for "Grand Old Party") moved through this entire cycle of irrelevance, dominance, and irrelevance again in the period from 1975 through 2008. Starting the era at such a low point that some foresaw its possible extinction, the G.O.P. recovered by combining social and economic conservatism, and by nominating Southerners and Westerners at the top of its ticket. For a time this Southern and conservative strategy was highly successful, but by 2008 it had, apparently, run its course. The G.O.P. seemed once again adrift ideologically and restricted geographically, reduced to clear minority status at the national level.

From Founding to Near Death

Until the late 1960s, much of the social support for the Republican Party came largely from the upper middle class and corporate and financial interests, as the party's leaders generally favored freer economic markets and limited federal government intervention. Geographically, the Northeast, Midwest, and Plains were historic G.O.P. strongholds, with the South and most of the nation's major cities being more Democratic. In addition, Republicans often disagreed with each other on foreign policy, with an internationalist Northeast at odds with a more isolationist Midwest and Plains.

In the 1960s, this began to change. National G.O.P. leaders began a "Southern Strategy," advancing a brand of pro-military and "law and order" patriotism designed to attract culturally conservative Southern Democrats. Americans had elected and reelected the Republican Richard Nixon as president in 1968 and 1972. As both a candidate and president, Nixon exploited Democratic divisions on civil rights and foreign policy. His first election was greatly aided by the third-party candidacy of George Wallace, who stripped away Southern votes from their Democratic moorings. Nixon's first term was marked by improved relations with China and the U.S.S.R., what appeared to be steps toward resolving the Vietnam War, and reasonable economic performance. In 1972, Nixon easily defeated the South Dakota senator and antiwar Democrat George McGovern, carrying every jurisdiction except Massachusetts and the District of Columbia.

Nixon's 1968 and 1972 successes were more personal than party-wide, but scandals involving him and Vice Pres. Spiro Agnew devastated his party. Agnew resigned in October 1973 in a political corruption scandal dating from his days as Maryland governor. Revelations of White House involvement in the 1972 Watergate affair led to Nixon's resignation in August 1974 and the ascension to the presidency of Agnew's replacement, the former House member Gerald Ford of Michigan. Ford tried to disassociate Republicans from the scandals, but substantial G.O.P. congressional losses in 1974 were unavoidable. Ford also faced serious policy problems throughout his truncated term, including high unemployment, rising inflation, high interest rates, huge budget deficits, and questions over how to

At the 1976 Republican National Convention in Kansas City, Missouri, Ronald Reagan addresses the crowd as his rival for the nomination, Pres. Gerald Ford, who would win a narrow victory over Reagan, looks on. That year, the party was at a demoralizing low point, but four years later it would successfully broaden its electoral support by embracing social and economic conservatism, a political ideology embodied by Reagan, who would win the presidency in a landslide in 1980. He and his successor, George H. W. Bush, changed the face of the Republican Party, and the successes of the Reagan era in particular would cast a long shadow over the party as they faced electoral defeat in 1992, misread the electorate in the mid-to-late 1990s, and failed to live up to the managerial competence the Republicans had displayed during their 1980s heyday. (Pictorial Parade/Getty Images)

wrap up the Vietnam War. Criticized by moderates for doing too little to address the economy, and by conservatives for being too weak in Vietnam and against the party's domestic opponents, Ford had to hold off a serious 1976 presidential primary challenge from the conservative Ronald Reagan of California. Ford did so, and in the general election strove mightily but ultimately unsuccessfully to close a wide gap with Georgia Democrat Jimmy Carter. After Carter's victory, the Republican Party was at its

modern low. The G.O.P. had only 12 governorships (compared to 36 for Democrats), controlled only 4 state legislatures (compared to 35 held entirely by Democrats), and held slightly less than one-third of the seats in the House of Representatives (143 of 435) and slightly more than one-third of the seats in the Senate (38 of 100). The Republican's public party identification gap was a huge 21 points, with 52 percent of voters identifying with Democrats and only 31 percent with Republicans.

1976–1980: Quick Recovery

Carter's presidency and the G.O.P.'s response to its own weaknesses created a remarkably quick recovery. On the latter point, the remaining G.O.P. leadership invested heavily in better fund-raising techniques and extensive party-building work at the local, state, and national levels, often working with economic and, later, social conservatives who saw an opportunity for greater party influence. Carter's peculiar combination of moralism and naiveté resulted in disastrous policy results and a disenchanted evangelical voting bloc, who thought they were electing one of their own in Carter. Disappointed by the Democratic president's failure to implement socially conservative ideas that many voters thought should follow from his faith, evangelicals, particularly in the South, were ripe for Republican recruitment.

Ronald Reagan and those around him seized the opportunity. In his primary challenge to Ford in 1976, Reagan had piloted his vision of America renewed by traditional values and muscular patriotism. By the late 1970s, Reagan had found a third leg of his campaign stool, the painless economics of "supply side" fiscal policy, which emphasized job- and wealth-generating tax breaks above painful spending cuts.

1980–1993: Presidential Parity

This combination of economic, social, and foreign policy ideas catapulted Reagan into the White House in 1980, and the rest of the G.O.P. benefited as well. The number of Republican governors jumped to 23, a near doubling since 1977. The G.O.P. surprisingly won a majority in the U.S. Senate, and its gains in the U.S. House were large enough to create, albeit briefly, a conservative coalition majority.

Together, the new president and Congress enacted in 1981 the essential parts of the Reagan program—very large hikes in defense spending, small growth in domestic spending, and major tax cuts. The policy revolution Reagan brought on was brief, however, particularly in the domestic arena. After significant changes in 1981, Reagan and Congress governed in a more reformist than radical vein in domestic policy during the president's last seven years. Social security was reformed in a bipartisan manner in 1983, and

the federal tax structure was simplified and streamlined in 1986, with similar bipartisan cooperation. On foreign policy, Reagan's decisions to more directly challenge the Soviet Union's military and international strategies generated more controversy. Legally and politically questionable activities in Central America and the Middle East are illustrated succinctly by the Iran-Contra controversy in which proceeds from U.S. sales of arms to Iranians to gain release of American hostages in late 1985 through most of 1986 were diverted to aid the Contras fighting the Communist-friendly Sandinista Nicaraguan government. Through it all, Reagan remained popular. The general thrust of his domestic and foreign policy was preserved, and conservatism came to be defined as Reagan presented it—free economic markets, traditional personal behavior, and proud patriotic nationalism.

Republican electoral results were still mixed, however. In 1984, Reagan routed Walter F. Mondale, taking 59 percent of the popular vote and 525 of 538 electoral votes. Party identification finally moved slightly toward Republicans, as election surveys gave the G.O.P. 39 percent affiliation compared to 48 percent for Democrats. In Congress, however, Republicans lost two Senate seats but retained control, while Democrats continued to control the House. This pattern continued in 1986 and 1988, as Democrats narrowly regained a Senate majority in 1986 and held it in 1988, when the Republican vice president, George H. W. Bush, succeeded Reagan to the presidency.

The first President Bush started well, and his impressive prosecution of the Persian Gulf War in 1990 and early 1991 led to approval ratings near 90 percent. However, a recession began in 1990, and the president's perceived indifference to it swiftly reversed his public standing. In 1992, the Democrat Bill Clinton, abetted by third-party candidate Ross Perot, captured the presidency and a more solid Democratic congressional majority.

The 12 years of Republican executive leadership under Reagan and Bush changed the face of the party. At the presidential level, the Southern Strategy put the G.O.P. at least at parity with, if not usually favored over, the Democrats. The more uniform conservatism seemed to be working well in the South, even in local elections, more than offsetting G.O.P. losses in the Northeast and slippage elsewhere. Ideologically, the G.O.P. remake was completed in 1992, as a majority of the party's leaders blamed Bush's loss on insufficient conservatism, ignoring the equally plausible notion that Bush failed to address middle-class concerns with economic ideas to complement cultural appeals. To most Republicans, the loss of the presidency was a "blip," though hopes for a Republican congressional majority still seemed impractical.

1994–1999: A Misinterpreted Earthquake

Because congressional Republicans saw the 1992 election as a rejection of Bush and not conservatism, they felt emboldened to challenge the new Democratic president. In 1994, having blocked most of Clinton's legislative agenda the previous two years, House Republicans mounted an aggressive midterm campaign, engineered by party leaders Newt Gingrich of Georgia and Dick Armey of Texas, to seize House control through a 10-issue "Contract With America." Conservative and poll-tested popular, the issues worked to gain a House Republican majority for the first time in 40 years. The 1994 elections also brought large change to other parts of political landscape. The U.S. Senate returned to Republican control, and state legislatures finally showed a G.O.P. advantage, as those under full Republican control soared from 8 to 19 (one more than the Democrats). There were also 30 Republican governors in the 50 states, and exit polls showed the narrowest Democratic advantage in party identification in modern times: it stood at 6 points, 47 to 41 percent.

In a numerical sense, the 1994 election was a political earthquake, the release of the tension built up over decades of Democratic seat-holding advantages that led to liberal policies and the centrist ideology of American voters. But Republican leaders also saw the election ideologically, as a public newly embracing consistent and clear conservatism. In response, congressional Republicans and President Clinton both moved to the right—but for the former it was a further move to the extreme, and for the latter it was another step to the center.

President Clinton's centrism was embodied in his 1996 agreement to Republican-driven welfare reform.

That decision riled his liberal co-partisans, but it took much of the wind out of the sails of that year's G.O.P. presidential candidate, elder statesman Robert Dole of Kansas, whose lackluster campaign never gelled. An emerging bifurcated public assessment of the presidency also benefitted the incumbent. President Clinton argued that the public could and should separate its view of his scandalous behavior—which they frowned upon—and his centrist policies—the effects of which they liked. Resisting this argument, congressional Republicans expected to profit in the 1998 midterm elections from months of bad publicity regarding Clinton's relationship with White House intern Monica Lewinsky and his misleading denials of it. Republicans were shocked that in the 1998 elections they failed to gain seats from this strategy. Undeterred, the Republican House carried through its impeachment proceedings later that year. In the Senate trial early the next year, however, Democrats even found a few Republicans to join them in a vote to acquit.

2000–2008: Missing the Chance to Govern

National Republican optimism returned for the election of 2000, and a notably upbeat G.O.P. convention formally nominated Texas governor George W. Bush, the son of the former president, as its candidate to challenge Clinton's vice president, Al Gore, for the presidency. The younger Bush campaigned in the primaries as a "compassionate conservative," whose evangelical Protestantism brought humility and concern for "the least of these," as well as a clear endorsement of limited national government and traditional social mores. It was, it seemed, a slight elaboration of the traditional strategy, in recognition of its regional and ideological limitations.

Whereas economic and policy indicators predicted a fairly easy Democratic victory in 2000, voters apparently took out on Gore their disapproval of Clinton's personal excesses. The presidential election was a virtual tie, with its fate ultimately decided by the U.S. Supreme Court ruling on Florida legislative and judicial maneuvering on ballot recounting. Elsewhere on the ballot, Republicans held their own or lost a bit. Public party identification and state-level partisan indicators changed little. The G.O.P. lost a handful of seats in both the House and Senate, retaining control of the latter body only through the tie-breaking vote of the new vice president, Dick Cheney. Whatever slight policy modifications were implied by Bush's compassionate conservatism, they were swamped by the extreme partisan polarization of the election's aftermath. The narrow Senate G.O.P. advantage changed soon when, in May 2001, Vermont Republican senator James Jeffords resigned his party to become an Independent and caucus with Senate Democrats. This threatened some legislation, but the 2001 terrorist attacks soon brought a whole new range of issues to the fore.

Politically, the attacks brought a short period of congressional bipartisanship and a longer period of presidential approval. In 2002, Republicans regained control of the Senate, and in other arenas Republican fortunes moved up a notch. The 2004 elections repeated the 2002 results, but at the presidential level as well, as Bush and Cheney defeated Democratic senators John Kerry and John Edwards, and Republicans added slightly to their majorities in both the Senate and the House. The G.O.P.'s strategy of energizing its base of religious and socially conservative voters was credited as decisive in victory, particularly in 2004. Many of the remaining few Southern Democratic seats in Congress finally flipped to the Republican side. While candidate Bush had rarely raised military policy in his 2000 campaign, his administration's reactions to the terrorist attacks, attributed to neoconservative influence inside and outside the government, followed very much in the strain of Reagan's proud patriotism.

The Republican's decline after 2004 was as swift as its rise 25 years before. Public discontent with a poorly executed Iraq War combined with a rash of congressional G.O.P. scandals led to large Republican losses in 2006. That year, the G.O.P. lost control of the House and the Senate, and party identification, the number of G.O.P. governors, and the number of G.O.P.-controlled state legislatures all fell markedly. Two years later, Republican losses were also widespread. In the aftermath, the party was weakened in numbers and narrower in its geographic base. Besides losing the presidency, G.O.P. governorships fell from 28 before the 2006 elections to 21 after the 2008 elections. The party also lost 14 of the 55 U.S. Senate seats and 50 of

the 232 U.S. House seats it held before the 2006 elections. The 2008 elections eliminated the few remaining congressional Republicans in the nation's Northeast, geographically illustrating both the success and limitations of the party's Southern Strategy.

The Southern Strategy helped Republican majority-building efforts for a time, but more recently its geographic and ideological limitations have become obvious. There is very little G.O.P. presence in the Northeast and shrinking representation in the Midwest, Plains, and West. It is difficult to be a national party when only Southern states are secure. The party has largely failed to govern responsibly when its conservative ideology has been given the chance. Although Reagan was able to combine conservative rhetoric with reasonably good management, the record of later Republican presidents and Congresses has been mixed at best.

The party apparently learned only one of the two lessons of Reagan, its reigning hero. Reagan painted an appealing picture of the renewed America that would result from the application of conservative ideas in economics, social policy, and international affairs. This picture was so appealing that conservatism itself was redefined. That was lesson one. Lesson two was to competently run the programs one inherited even as one tried to rework them. Reagan's one revolutionary year was followed by seven years of domestic reform. The younger Bush's two terms were particularly at variance with lesson two. On foreign affairs, Bush's attempt to build democracy in Iraq was far more ambitious and difficult than Reagan's pushback against the Soviets and their weapons and proxy wars. On domestic affairs, Reagan's tax cuts were balanced with a willingness to limit spending and share the responsibility of decisions with the other party. Bush's tax cutting fervor seemed, on the other hand, to be imprudently matched with domestic expansions like Medicare and expensive international conflicts in Afghanistan and Iraq, with little regard to good management or fiscal practice. Pragmatic American voters eventually want responsible government management, as most expect at some time to need at least temporary government aid. Republicans have not done a good job resolving the tension between cutting and managing government, and they have faced the negative electoral consequences of this failure more quickly because the swift pace of globalization makes the nation—and its citizens and policies—more vulnerable to global trends and events.

As an American political party, the Republican Party is necessarily a coalition of state and regional parties that have some common but malleable principles and interests. The Southern Strategy shifted the party's geographic base to the South and its ideological base to more consistent conservatism. The strategy helped the G.O.P. regain the presidency and make historical gains in Congress, state and local offices, and even party identification. But after the party's loss in the 2008 elections, the G.O.P. finds itself once again a regional, rather than a national, political party, and it is thus very limited in its ability to appeal to a majority of the nation's voters.

Bibliography and Further Reading

Black, Earl, and Merle Black. *The Rise of Southern Republicans.* Cambridge, MA: Harvard University Press, 2002.

Douthat, Ross, and Reihan Salam. *Grand New Party: How Republicans Can Win the Working Class and Save the American Dream.* New York: Doubleday, 2008.

Edsall, Thomas B., with Mary D. Edsall. *Chain Reaction: The Impact of Race, Rights, and Taxes on American Politics.* New York: W. W. Norton, 1991.

Edwards, Lee. *The Conservative Revolution: The Movement that Remade America.* New York: The Free Press, 1999.

Gould, Lewis L. *Grand Old Party: A History of the Republicans.* New York: Random House, 2003.

Nesmith, Bruce. *The New Republican Coalition: The Reagan Campaigns and White Evangelicals.* New York: Peter Lang, 1994.

Rae, Nicol C. *The Decline and Fall of the Liberal Republicans: From 1952 to the Present.* New York: Oxford, 1989.

Taylor, Andrew J. *Elephant's Edge: The Republicans as a Ruling Party.* Westport, CT: Praeger, 2005.

Douglas L. Koopman

ROBERTS, JOHN

born 1955
Seventeenth Chief Justice of the United States

In 2005, John Roberts was appointed by Pres. George W. Bush, and confirmed by the U.S. Senate, to be the 17th chief justice of the U.S. Supreme Court. The appointment was seen as an attempt to solidify a conservative-leaning Court, which had been the hope of Republican presidents from Richard Nixon to George W. Bush. Yet conservatives have been frustrated in this hope. Despite a number of Republican appointments to the Court, the Court has not overturned the liberalism of the Warren and Burger courts, though it has moved in a conservative direction on many issues and worked at developing a conservative approach to rights-based jurisprudence. As a result, the Supreme Court is more conservative today than it was in 1976. To be sure, the Court has declined to firmly side with the strong claims of executive prerogative that were propounded by President Bush. And with the election of Pres. Barack Obama, any further move to the right now seems unlikely. But as of the beginning of 2010 Roberts commands a 5–4 conservative majority, if he can lead it.

Political Background and Judicial Views

After graduating from Harvard Law School in 1979, Roberts clerked for Judge Henry J. Friendly, a well-respected judge on the Court of Appeals for the Second Circuit. Friendly was known for his careful legal analysis and insistence upon judicial modesty, the belief that judges should have a limited view of their power. Roberts went on to clerk for William Rehnquist, who was then an associate justice of the

Supreme Court. He joined the Reagan administration in 1981 as an aid to the attorney general, where he worked, among other things, on executive power. In the Reagan administration, Roberts fit neatly with a group of extraordinarily talented conservative lawyers who were engaged in rethinking the law against what they perceived as entrenched liberalism. This group included lawyers drawn from the Federalist Society, an organization created to push back against the liberal leanings of the legal academy and bench. While Roberts himself was not at the time a member of the Federalist Society (he later served on a steering committee), he certainly shared its skeptical view of the liberalism of the Warren and Burger courts.

Roberts worked in the administration of George H. W. Bush as principal deputy solicitor general, where he argued a number of cases before the Supreme Court. In one case, *Lee v. Weisman*, 505 U.S. 577 (1992), Roberts argued that a nondenominational prayer at a junior high school graduation, which was not compulsory to attend, did not violate the separation of church and state. Roberts left government in 1993 to enter private practice. As a private lawyer, he would go on to argue a number of cases before the Supreme Court, where he was widely acknowledged as a superb advocate. President George W. Bush appointed Roberts to the D.C. Circuit Court of Appeals in 2003 and, two years later, he appointed him to the Supreme Court.

While Roberts's champions included lawyers and associates from the Federalist Society, his dedication to the law was widely praised outside of conservative circles in much the manner that his mentor Judge Friendly was praised; that is, he was seen as a modest judge who was serious about legal craftsmanship. Laurence Tribe, a liberal constitutional scholar at Harvard Law School, and a teacher of Roberts, has described him as "conservative in manner and conservative in approach . . . but he is someone quite deeply immersed in the law, and he loves it. He believes in it as a discipline and pursues it in principle and not by way of politics." (Purdum, et al.) Roberts has described his own view of the law and the Court in a similar manner, insisting that he does not "have an all-encompassing approach to constitutional interpretation; the appropri-

ate approach depends to some degree on the specific provisions at issue." (Purdum, et al.)

The Court as an Institution

Roberts has suggested that his biggest challenge as chief justice will be getting the Court to speak with a more uniform voice and less like nine individual law firms—as the Court has at times been described. Roberts sees this as essential to create stability in the law and respect for the Court as an impartial institution. According to Roberts, the number of different opinions issued by the Court—with a majority opinion, concurring opinions, and dissenting opinions—tends to undermine the Court as an institution. To be sure, the modern Court, particularly in the late twentieth century and beyond, has spoken with a more fragmented voice than earlier courts. It would be an important political development if Roberts got the Court to move away from this tendency. Institutionally, this approach comports with Roberts's vision of a more modest role for the Court, insofar as bringing a divided Court together is likely to require compromise, which would require settling legal and constitutional issues on narrower ground. As part of restoring a more modest judicial role, Roberts has sought to narrow standing (what qualifies one to bring suit in court), so the Court is deciding cases based on a "tangible injury." For Roberts, the chief justice can aid both of these processes by cultivating the proper judicial temperament—a temperament willing to work with other justices, including compromising and moderating positions, for the institutional good of the Court.

Roberts notes that most chief justices have been failures in this regard. Roberts himself has been partly successful in this endeavor. In his first term, the Court handed down more consecutive unanimous opinions than any other Court in recent history, and in his first term, 49 percent of cases were decided without dissent, and the number of 5–4 opinions and separate opinions declined. While it is far too early to know whether this trend will endure, the second and third terms of the Roberts Court saw a more divided Court with fewer unanimous opinions and more 5–4 splits over the most divisive issues in constitutional law.

Political and Constitutional Development

Roberts wrote majority opinions for the Court in cases upholding abortion restrictions (*Gonzales v. Carhart*, 550 U.S. 124 [2007]), narrowing race-based classifications in schools (*Parents Involved in Community Schools v. Seattle School District No. 1*, 551 U.S. 701 [2007]), limiting student speech (*Morse v. Frederick*, 551 U.S. 393 [2007]), and narrowing the reach of the McCain-Feingold campaign finance spending limits (*Federal Election Commission v. Wisconsin Right to Life*, 551 U.S. 449 [2007]). This has led critics to argue that the Court has moved in a more conservative direction, and on a number of issues it has. Yet it has done so without overturning leading liberal precedents on these very issues and there have been liberal victories on the Court. Still, Roberts certainly represents a challenge to the New Deal/Great Society liberal order that conservatives have been challenging since Ronald Reagan was president.

More intriguing, from the perspective of American political development, are the claims of sweeping executive power made by the Bush administration. Such claims had not been made since Franklin Roosevelt's presidency. As a young lawyer in the Reagan administration, Roberts supported a view of executive power called "the unitary executive," and he may well prove to be strongly influenced by this theory. In simple terms, the "unitary executive" view argues that Article II of the Constitution vests all of the "executive" power in the president. This allows the president to remove and direct lower-level executive officials. Congress, accordingly, cannot create entities in the executive branch that it, rather than the executive, controls. This debate has often been confused—by both the Bush administration and its critics—with claims of inherent executive power. While there is occasional spillover in this debate, a leading defender of the "unitary executive" argues that "inherent, secretive powers, particularly in regard to foreign policy are not a necessary part of the unitary executive and may undermine its vision." (Calabresi 2008, 411) The reach of executive power may well come to define the Roberts Court. And Roberts may well represent the fruit of conservative efforts, as they argue, to recapture a proper understanding of executive power, which critics see as a distortion of executive power that threatens constitutional rights. Such an understanding has certainly been evident in Roberts's opinions.

Roberts has tended to support the claims of executive power, or to defer to the executive branch, in both domestic cases and foreign policy cases. In *Hamdan v. Rumsfeld*, 548 U.S. 557 (2006), which challenged President Bush's use of military tribunals to try enemy combatants, Roberts recused himself because he had found against Hamdan and for the government while on the D.C. Circuit. In the 2008 case of *Boumediene v. Bush*, 553 U.S. ___, Roberts sided with the Bush administration and wrote a dissenting opinion that was joined by three other justices. In this case, the Court decided that aliens detained as enemy combatants have a constitutional right to challenge their detention in an American court. In his dissenting opinion, Roberts accused the Court of overstepping its bounds in a manner that would not necessarily help alien enemy combatants who might be illegally detained. Indeed, Roberts argued that Congress and the president had put procedural protections in place for aliens detained as enemy combatants, with protection from the D.C. Circuit Court. Roberts then insisted that these procedures ought to be given a chance to work before being prematurely displaced by the Supreme Court: "It is grossly premature to pronounce on the detainees' right to habeas without first assessing whether the remedies the DTA [Detainee Treatment Act] system provides vindicate whatever rights petitioners may claim." This fit with Roberts's insistence that courts should defer to the executive and legislative branches and not reach out to settle unnecessary legal and constitutional questions—particularly as the Court did not provide a clear process of its own for dealing with enemy combatants or clarifying what process they were, in fact, due. Critics insist that Roberts is far too deferential to executive power in such cases.

Roberts has cast himself as a chief justice who would like to speak for the Court and, in doing so, recast the Court's institutional role in the political order. For Roberts, this means narrowing the Court's role against an entrenched liberalism. Time will tell how successful Roberts is in this endeavor.

Bibliography and Further Reading

Calabresi, Steven G., and Christopher Yoo. *The Unitary Executive: Presidential Power from Washington to Bush.* New Haven: Yale University Press, 2008.

Dworkin, Ronald. "Judge Roberts on Trial." *New York Review of Books* 52, no. 16 (October 20, 2005).

Greenberg, Jan Crawford. *Supreme Conflict: The Inside Story of the Struggle for Control of the United States Supreme Court.* New York: Penguin, 2007.

Kmiec, Douglas. "Overview of the Term: The Rule of Law & Roberts' Revolution of Restraint." *Pepperdine Law Review* 34 (2007): 495.

Purdum, Todd S., Jodi Wilgoren, and Pam Belluck. "Court Nominee's Life Is Rooted in Faith and Respect for Law." *New York Times*, July 21, 2005. http://www.nytimes.com/2005/07/21/politics/21nominee.html (accessed October 31, 2009).

Rosen, Jeffrey. "The Roberts Court and Executive Power." *Pepperdine Law Review* 35 (2007): 504.

———. "Roberts Rules." *Atlantic Monthly* January/February, 2007. http://www.theatlantic.com/doc/200701/john-roberts (accessed October 31, 2009).

George Thomas

RELATED ENTRIES

THIS VOLUME
Rehnquist, William; Supreme Court and the Judiciary

SAVINGS AND LOAN CRISIS

The Federal Home Loan Bank System (FHLBS) failed spectacularly during the 1980s. The savings and loan associations (S&Ls, or thrifts) that belonged to it went bankrupt in record numbers at extraordinary cost. More than twelve hundred thrifts collapsed between 1980 and 1990, while another six hundred were insolvent but remained open for business. More important for the taxpaying public, the Federal Savings and Loan Insurance Corporation (FSLIC), which insured savings deposits at S&Ls, went bankrupt, suffering what was at the time the largest deficit ever reported by a public or private corporation. FSLIC's failure cost the American taxpayers between $125 billion and $153 billion.

The FHLBS was, in many ways, a policy and political failure. Too much regulation and changing economic circumstances caused the industry's problems—too little regulation dramatically worsened them. The Federal Home Loan Bank Board (Bank Board), the regulatory agency of the FHLBS, proved to be mostly impotent, often inept, and generally overwhelmed. Congress, too, appeared to be asleep at the wheel, failing to enact legislation to forestall the crisis and, when it did act, approving policies that were often inadequate if not counterproductive.

The "thrift tragedy" had a number of political causes, some still being debated today. The conventional wisdom had it that "[t]he savings and loan bankruptcies give sordid evidence of immoral financial buccaneers, incompetent regulators, and compliant politicians." (Weinstein) This view is supported by most popular books on the topic as well as by "public choice" scholars. Public choice analysis has emphasized that the tragedy's principal political causes lay in the government's structure and, especially, in officials' attention to their own self-interest. From this perspective, electoral incentives were the essential component that led members of Congress to intervene to protect individual thrifts and to delay giving the FSLIC the resources it needed. Regulators deferred to the wishes of the thrift industry, thus greatly increasing FSLIC's losses.

This portrayal contains some truth, but hardly gives the entire picture. An alternative "public spirit" view contends that bank regulators and members of Congress mainly acted as conscientiously as they could in the face of an evolving and novel crisis. From this perspective, the debacle unfolded as bureaucrats and politicians generally sought to promote the public interest while remaining true to their conflicting goals and prior policy commitments and trying to act in the face of their uncertainty over policy consequences. The FSLIC failed despite the best intentions of policy makers, not because of their worst instincts.

Background

Originally, S&Ls were formed to bring together the personal savings of individuals and issue home mortgages to families. Since the Depression, government policy had deliberately encouraged such saving and lending. In 1932, Congress created the FHLBS and the Federal Home Loan Bank Board to charter, regulate, and supervise thrifts (states had similar systems) and to promote home ownership through various policies, most especially by inducing S&Ls to finance long-term mortgage loans with fixed interest rates. To encourage homeownership, thrifts were required to invest most of their assets in home mortgages. To prevent ruinous competition among thrifts and other financial institutions for savings deposits, interest ceilings were imposed. In addition, the FSLIC was encouraged to protect savings through deposit insurance.

Between the Depression and the 1960s, the thrift industry was prosperous and popular. Thrifts made money by granting mortgages at slightly higher interest rates than they paid on deposits. But that simple model was subject to risk. Whenever interest rates rose, thrifts faced a serious dilemma: if they did not offer higher interest rates on deposits, money would be withdrawn and placed elsewhere; if they did, the "spread" between what they paid on deposits and what they earned on mortgages shrank or, worse, vanished. Moreover, when interest rates rose, fewer mortgages were originated. As interest rates spiked repeatedly after the mid-1960s, the position of the industry became more and more tenuous.

By the 1970s, policy makers were grappling with the industry's difficulties. The President's Commission on Financial Structure and Regulation (better known as the Hunt Commission) in 1972 and the Financial Institutions and the Nation's Economy (FINE) study, commissioned by the House Banking Committee in 1975, both called for granting thrifts broader and more flexible asset and liability powers—in particular, the ability to issue adjustable-rate mortgages (revenues would thus increase if interest rates rose) and to diversify their assets. Throughout this decade, however, when fundamental reform probably would have prevented the future crisis, Congress declined to act except to make minor changes. Congress likely avoided major restructuring because the FHBLS had *generally* worked well (and, it was thought, would continue to work if interest rates only returned to the low and stable levels of previous decades) and because Congress believed that thrifts *should* concentrate their assets in

home mortgages, rather than in a more diversified portfolio, and that S&Ls *should* continue relying on savings deposits to fund them.

By the late 1970s, the elements of the meltdown were in place. The thrift business, relying on short-term savings deposits to finance long-term mortgages, had a dangerous maturity mismatch. Short-term interest rates skyrocketed between 1979 and 1981, peaking at more than 16 percent, triple the level of five years earlier. Net new deposits plummeted, as did profits. The number of thrift insolvencies handled by FSLIC exploded from 4 in 1978 to 39 in 1980, 81 in 1981, and 252 in 1982. For the first time since its inception, the FSLIC spent more money handling insolvencies than it earned from insurance premiums. The thrift business and its federal insurer were on the edge of disaster.

Political Response to the Crisis

Congress largely ignored the ominous warnings of the Hunt Commission and the FINE study, but it could not overlook the fact that the thrift industry was actually heading toward bankruptcy in 1979. Action was not easy, however, for two primary reasons. First, genuine disagreements arose about what should be done to remedy the S&L problems: all remedies had the potential to make the problems worse. Second, because the financial industry was highly segmented legally (that is, thrifts, banks, and brokerages were all regulated separately), changing the rules for any one sector would affect all the other sectors and each sector would move to protect its own interests and priorities. Congress, nonetheless, reacted to the widespread turmoil in the financial markets and, in 1980, passed and President Carter signed the Depository Institutions Deregulation and Monetary Control Act (DIDMCA), widely considered to be the most important financial legislation since the Depression. DIDMCA's most important provisions for the thrift industry included phasing out deposit interest ceilings (to allow S&Ls to compete more effectively for deposits), allowing them to offer checking accounts, and providing higher deposit insurance limits (so that depositors would feel safer).

Strengthening the ability of thrifts to obtain funds proved insufficient to rescue the thrift industry, however:

S&Ls also needed to be able to earn more income. Accordingly, in 1982, Congress enacted and President Reagan signed the Garn–St. Germain Depository Institutions Act, which substantially deregulated the industry's investment authority. Thrifts were no longer limited to making (primarily) home mortgage loans—now, they could make commercial and consumer loans as well as invest in nonresidential real estate and high-yield ("junk") bonds, among other powers. The act also injected capital into weak thrifts in an effort to tide them over. The Bank Board, for its part, used its limited powers to implement numerous regulatory initiatives in an attempt to forestall or at least contain the growing emergency.

These measures appeared to work. Deposits flooded into thrifts between 1982 and 1984, and interest rates declined precipitously. In 1982, the FSLIC's insurance reserves stopped shrinking and began once more to grow. These new laws, regulations, and some good economic luck appeared to have averted a disaster.

This was an illusion. Policy makers soon came to recognize that, despite falling interest rates, rapid deposit growth, and reported profits, the thrifts' problems were growing worse. By 1984, the Bank Board had become concerned that many thrifts were using their new powers to attract funds and make loans too aggressively. This aggressiveness, the Bank Board believed, would lead to further insolvencies and losses to the FSLIC. The Bank Board moved to curb the thrifts' rapid growth and reckless investment by limiting their new powers to borrow and lend. It doubled FSLIC's insurance premiums and also doubled its examination and supervisory staff between 1984 and 1986.

Despite these measures, the Bank Board could not handle the growing number of failing thrifts. Thrift profits plunged in 1986 and 1987 and the number of insolvencies grew apace. Consequently, in 1985, the Bank Board asked Congress to provide the FSLIC with $15 billion in additional capital. Congress waited almost two years to approve this request; then, with the Competitive Equality Bank Act of 1987, it awarded FSLIC only two-thirds the amount requested. The reasons for the delay and the reduced funding involved both policy and politics. The S&L industry strongly opposed FSLIC's refinancing because if the

RELATED ENTRIES

THIS VOLUME
Federal Reserve System

FSLIC had no money, it could not shut down insolvent thrifts—and insolvent thrifts continued to insist that they would recover if just given time. Moreover, healthy S&Ls contested the recapitalization because, ultimately, they would be forced to pay for it through higher insurance premiums, which would, in turn, weaken their own stability and competitiveness.

When FSLIC shut a bankrupt thrift, it had to pay off all insured depositors; Congress had not given the FSLIC nearly enough funding to do this. In an effort to shut insolvent thrifts before they lost still more money, the FSLIC used creative financing techniques to stretch its new capital as it disposed of 205 failed S&Ls in 1988. Its efforts, however, did not stabilize the S&L industry. Thrifts lost a record after-tax $15 billion in 1988, and more than six hundred S&Ls were still insolvent but open for business at the end of the year. Worse, bankrupt thrifts increasingly "doubled down" by making even riskier investments in an attempt to regain profitability and many engaged in fraudulent activities to conceal or remedy their condition.

Shortly after his inauguration, Pres. George H. W. Bush proposed a sweeping program to end the thrift crisis once and for all. This proposal called for an additional $50 billion to be spent to close bankrupt thrifts and imposed tighter regulations on S&Ls. Lacking friends either in Congress or in the thrift industry, the Bank Board and FSLIC were both abolished and their functions were transferred to other federal agencies. Congress approved the president's program in the Financial Institutions Reform, Recovery, and Enforcement Act (FIRREA) of 1989. Although additional funding to close bankrupt S&Ls would, in fact, be needed after FIRREA, as losses were even larger than estimated, the passage of this law effectively ended the thrift crisis of the 1980s.

At the time, the thrift crisis was the largest financial market disruption since the Depression and the biggest federal government bailout ever. These events served as a prelude to the subprime mortgage mess and subsequent credit market meltdown and federal rescue package of

2008–2009. In both cases, regulatory structures and policies that were historically suitable were not appropriate for changing economic conditions and technological circumstances; financial deregulation allowed and perhaps encouraged ill-advised risk taking; Congress did not react quickly enough, and when Congress did act, it alternated between being too little, too late and panicky overreaction.

Bibliography and Further Reading

Adams, James Ring. *The Big Fix: Inside the S&L Scandal.* New York: John Wiley & Sons, 1989.

Barth, James R. *The Great Savings and Loan Debacle.* Washington, D.C.: American Enterprise Institute, 1991.

Day, Kathleen. *S&L Hell: The People and the Politics Behind the $1 Trillion Savings and Loan Scandal.* New York: W. W. Norton, 1993.

Kane, Edward J. *The S&L Insurance Mess: How Did It Happen?* Washington, D.C.: The Urban Institute Press, 1989.

Mayer, Martin. *The Greatest Ever Bank Robbery: The Collapse of the Savings and Loan Industry.* New York: Charles Scribner's Sons, 1990.

Rom, Mark Carl. *Public Spirit in the Thrift Tragedy.* Pittsburgh, PA: University of Pittsburgh Press, 1996.

Romer, Thomas, and Barry R. Weingast. "Political Foundations of the Thrift Debacle." In *Politics and Economics in the Eighties*, edited by Alberto Alesina and Geoffrey Carliner, 175–209. Chicago: University of Chicago Press, 1991.

Weinstein, Michael M. "Is the Peace Dividend at Risk?" *New York Times.* April 15, 1990.

White, Lawrence R. *The S&L Debacle: Public Policy Lessons for Bank and Thrift Regulation.* New York: Oxford University Press, 1991.

Mark Carl Rom

SCIENCE AND TECHNOLOGY POLICY

In the last decades of the twentieth century and the opening years of the twenty-first, science and technology policy in the United States has revolved around a series of recurring issues, including the role of the federal government in the funding of basic versus applied science research, the role of scientists as advisors to the president, the role of science in mission-oriented agencies, the efficacy of "Big Science" projects, and the use of science in driving economic development. These issues have been debated in the larger context of the more fundamental question of government's role in science. The importance of these themes has fluctuated depending on the larger political currents in the nation. As presidents have changed, so have priorities in science and technology policy.

Background

Up until the late 1960s, World War II and the Cold War defined much of U.S. science policy. The federal government supported more than 70 percent of the nation's investment in research and development (R&D). Much of this funding went into applied science with specific application in the military. More than 90 percent of the government's support was through the Department of Defense (DoD), the Atomic Energy Commission (AEC) and the National Aeronautics and Space Administration (NASA). Support for basic research was largely funneled through the National Science Foundation (NSF) for physical sciences and the National Institutes of Health (NIH) for life sciences. Scientists came into the executive branch, including the White House, to serve as advisers or administrators of technical programs. The concept of Big Science—large interdisciplinary and collaborative projects costing millions, or sometimes billions, of dollars—became accepted as the United States competed with the Soviet Union in a range of technical areas, with the Apollo Moon landing concluding the 1960s in spectacular fashion.

The 1970s

Two important issues defined science policy in the decade of the 1970s. The first was a growing concern over the environment, first raised with the publication of Rachel Carson's *Silent Spring* in 1962, and embodied in the Environmental Protection Agency (EPA, established under President Nixon in 1970). The EPA initiated a new link among scientific research, advocacy, and regulation in support of environmental quality. Industrial pollution and its impact on health became prominent in regulatory affairs under the EPA. The agency represented a forceful attempt by the federal government to comprehensively regulate and protect the environment. There had been earlier efforts at "regulatory science" through agencies such as the Food and Drug Administration. However, environmental regulation and the science that legitimated it were especially contentious. Under the EPA, science played a direct role in assessing risks that led to the regulation of pollutants in the natural and man-made environment.

The second issue was the growing importance of energy in light of the crises spurred by the OPEC oil embargo in 1973 and the Iranian Revolution in 1979. In 1974, the Ford administration created the Energy Research and Development Administration (ERDA) as the federal government's R&D arm for energy, giving it a broad mandate to research alternative sources of energy, including solar, wind, and geothermal energy. ERDA was later dismantled and subsumed into the Department of Energy (DOE), which Pres. Jimmy Carter gave Cabinet status in 1977. The desire for independence from Middle East oil sources was reflected in sustained increases in federally supported energy R&D through much of the 1970s. Energy R&D in virtually all areas grew during the decade, culminating in 1980 with President Carter's Big Science initiative to develop synthetic fuels.

The 1970s also saw the continuation of the debate regarding the role of the federal government in supporting basic versus applied scientific research that had begun in the late 1960s during the Vietnam War. In 1966, the DoD had sponsored the Project Hindsight study to assess the source of technologies that had helped in the development of military capabilities. The study concluded that few ideas from basic research had led to the development of specific DoD weapons. This conclusion contributed to the concern in both Congress and the executive branch that the government should be funding more applied scientific research to maximize its returns from investments in science. In an effort to limit the DoD's role in university basic research, Sen. Mike Mansfield (D–MO) sponsored an amendment to the fiscal 1970 defense authorization bill requiring that no appropriations be used to fund projects unless they contributed to a specific military function. This amendment led to the transfer of several long-term research projects and facilities, such as the Materials Research Laboratories, to the NSF and other civilian agencies.

The transfer of these research projects to NSF contributed to a dispute over the role of the NSF in basic versus applied research. In 1968, Pres. Lyndon Johnson had signed the Daddario Amendment, which explicitly authorized the NSF to fund applied research and the social sciences, thereby broadening the NSF's charter. The NSF established the Research Applied to National Needs (RANN) program in 1971 to promote applied science in meeting civilian needs. The RANN projects were mainly focused on environment, energy, and urban problems. In 1975, the energy programs were transferred from the NSF to ERDA. RANN and, more generally, NSF's expanded charter were very controversial, as the National Science Board was concerned that the NSF lacked the administrative background and capacity to effectively pursue and manage applied research. Further, the board was worried that Congress's support for applied science at the NSF would come at the expense of basic science.

Despite efforts to limit the DoD's role in basic science, the Defense Advanced Research Projects Agency (DARPA), which had been established as ARPA by the DoD in 1958, continued to thrive through much of this period. DARPA's role was to exploit innovative ideas that were often on the "far side" of technology (i.e., as high-risk, cutting-edge research that would not attract private funding) and develop new core capabilities for DoD. As such, DARPA played a critical role in the federal government's R&D programs, particularly in defense aviation. However, there are two technologies currently used by the average consumer that owe their genesis to DARPA: the Internet was based on DARPA's ARPANET (Advanced Research Projects Agency Network), which was designed to revolutionize the way data were transmitted over networks; and the global positioning system (GPS), which was based on technology DARPA developed to launch satellites and guide the navigation of U.S. Navy ships. While the first permanent ARPANET link was made in 1969, much of the network's growth occurred during the 1970s, and it was not until 1983 that MILNET, the military portion of ARPANET, was spun off as a separate network.

The mechanisms for making science policy, downplayed during the Nixon administration, experienced a resurgence under President Ford in the mid-1970s. Nixon, angry that some of his science advisors openly disagreed with certain decisions, such as his support of a Supersonic Transport (SST) plane, had abolished the position of presidential science advisor and the accompanying advisory committee and staff. However, when President Nixon resigned, President Ford expressed concern with the broken link with the scientific community. He signed the National Science and Technology Policy, Organization, and Priorities Act of 1976 to reestablish the science advisory apparatus in the White House. This revival of interest in science policy in the Ford administration continued into the Carter administration. In addition to energy, President Carter pursued economic competitiveness as a mission for science.

The ascension of economic competitiveness on the national agenda in the late 1970s was partially due to the rise of Japan as an economic giant. The new emphasis on economic competitiveness continued into the 1980s, with Congress passing the Stevenson-Wydler and Bayh-Dole Acts in 1980. The Stevenson-Wydler Technology Innovation Act of 1980 required federal laboratories to take a more active role in cooperating with potential users of federally developed technology. The Bayh-Dole Act permitted universities and small businesses to maintain exclusive rights over intellectual property resulting from federally funded research, and to grant licenses for use to third parties. These acts aimed to encourage the transfer of federally funded research by national laboratories and universities to industry.

The 1980s and Early 1990s

The dominant themes of the Reagan years (1981–1989) were missions in defense R&D and space technology. The Reagan administration also approached government and science issues from a strong ideological bent. This approach was seen in issues of basic versus applied research and the government's role in energy R&D. As oil prices declined and the energy crisis that worried Carter seemed to disappear, Reagan cut back on federal support for energy R&D. Regarding civilian science and technology, Reagan and his appointees also believed that the government's role was limited to basic research. They saw Carter's aim for the development and demonstration of specific energy technologies (such as synthetic fuel and solar and wind power) as beyond the government's responsibilities. Reagan also deemphasized civilian economic competitiveness as a federal effort. Basic research was acceptable, and the NSF did establish research programs in selected fields related to economic competitiveness, but applied research and development were cut back or eliminated in favor of the "market" as a driver.

Reagan also deemphasized environmental regulation and the science that supported it. Instead, Reagan gave a huge push to defense-related science and technology. In 1983, he proclaimed the need for a space-based missile defense system, which media and critics dubbed "Star Wars." This Big Science program immediately became controversial, as many scientists questioned both its feasibility and desirability. Reagan persisted, however, convinced that he had a responsibility to defend the nation in case of an atomic attack. In 1984, he also gave the go-ahead to another Big Science effort: the building of a space station by NASA. After the Challenger disaster in 1986, he agreed to a replacement to keep the space shuttle fleet at four.

Missile defense continued after Reagan left office, but its most exotic, space-based elements were dampened by his successor, George H. W. Bush. President Bush also made civil space a priority, proclaiming in 1989 his desire that NASA return to the Moon and eventually go to Mars. This initiative drew little congressional or public support, and it died when Pres. Bill Clinton took office in 1993. President Bush also recognized the rise of global environmental problems on the national agenda, and he enhanced this research area greatly, authorizing NASA to launch a major new program of Earth-observing satellites and backing the multiagency U.S. Global Change Research Program in 1989. He resisted going beyond R&D on climate change, however, saying the science had to first determine the nature of the problem before government could institute emission controls.

The Mid- and Late 1990s

In line with his overall policy of economic revitalization, President Clinton wanted to establish a stronger link between science and economic development. He increased funding for basic research in emerging technologies with economic potential, including computer science, biotechnology, and nanotechnology. With the Cold War over, President Clinton also linked space with foreign policy to forge a new relationship with Russia. The Russians joined the U.S.-led space station program, now called the International Space Station (ISS). The development of the station has actually involved 16 nations, including the United States, Russia, Japan, Canada, and various European nations.

Another major project that received greater visibility and presidential attention under Clinton, although it began earlier, was the Genome Project, an effort to sequence the human genetic code. Along with the International Space Station, the Genome Project symbolized a new model of Big Science, in which there was a much greater international collaboration. England was the major partner of the United States in the Genome Project, and individual scientists from many other nations were involved. For Big Science, at least, international partnership seemed on its way to becoming a virtual requirement in the post–Cold War world. The inability of the DOE to forge such a partnership was one reason Congress killed the Superconducting Super Collider (SSC), America's largest particle physics accelerator project, in 1993.

The Clinton administration continued President Bush's major R&D program concerning climate change. However, prompted by Vice Pres. Al Gore, President Clinton argued that the science now justified regulatory action on emissions control. When the Republicans took control of Congress in 1995, however, they sought major funding cutbacks in climate research. The White House pushed back at Congress and largely prevented the most serious cuts. However, the whole issue of climate change escalated as a political issue, and scientists were drawn into the contest. The signing of the Kyoto Protocol in 1997 worsened relations between the two branches on climate policy. Congress had warned the Clinton administration not to agree to emissions limits unless the developing countries (such as China and India) did so also. Gore signed the treaty anyway on behalf of the United States. President Clinton did not try to get Senate ratification for the Kyoto Protocol, but the climate issue festered and made the science used to justify regulation increasingly subject to political debate.

The New Millennium

The two terms of Pres. George W. Bush were eventful and turbulent for science and technology policy. The terrorist attack of September 11, 2001, gave rise to the establishment of the Department of Homeland Security. As other mission agencies had done, this department initiated an R&D mission oriented to its role in anti-terrorism. At the same time, the National Institutes of Health initiated research on bioterrorism. Security concerns also caused greater attention to be paid to cybersecurity and the role of foreign graduate students in U.S. research.

The Bush administration engendered a heightened conflict between government and the scientific community, resulting in the perception within the scientific community that President Bush was "antiscience." Early on, Bush drew fire from scientists for his attempt to arrest embryonic stem cell research. In addition, he stoutly refused to accept the increasing evidence scientists provided about climate change. The longstanding question of the reality and seriousness of climate change, controversial under Clinton, gained far higher visibility with President Bush's rejection of the Kyoto Protocol and his "muzzling" of government scientists who warned of a clear and present danger. However, following the release in 2007 of a report by the UN's Intergovernmental Panel on Climate Change that conclusively accepted proof of the reality of manmade climate change, President Bush admitted that climate change was a problem, though he remained reluctant to act on the issue. To act meant serious regulatory controls on emissions affecting industry. The president pointed to his support of research into various technologies that could mitigate climate change, but critics called his support far too little in relation to the need. The Bush administration's energy R&D budget, for example, was less than that of President Carter.

Although Bush did not appear particularly interested in science, he made one decision on Big Science that was potentially historically significant. The Columbia shuttle disaster of 2003 killed seven astronauts. The subsequent inquiry called for a goal more worthy of risking human lives than the ISS. In response, in 2004, Bush directed NASA to return to the Moon by 2020, with an eventual journey to Mars. This was a mission his father had articulated but which had died in 1993. Although the mission survived throughout the Bush years, it did not evince large public enthusiasm, owing in part to more pressing events of the Bush years, such as the Iraq and Afghanistan wars, Hurricane Katrina in 2004, and the economic crisis in 2008.

Emerging Priorities

As the Bush presidency ended, there were several issues in science and technology policy rising on the national agenda. Economic competitiveness was one of the major issues, as many other nations rapidly developed and challenged the United States in a host of economically relevant fields. A report issued by the National Academies' Committee on Science, Engineering, and Public Policy, titled *Rising Above the Gathering Storm: Energizing and Employing America for a Brighter Economic Future*, pointed to these problems and called for rebuilding the nation's human capital in science and technology. The second issue concerned energy. The wars in the Middle East and the acceptance of climate change as a threat gave rise to growing concerns about the nation's energy dependence on fossil fuels.

President Barack Obama sought to rebuild bridges between government and science, and also put scientific and technological advice more effectively to work in areas of national priority. He spoke about the importance of science and the need to inspire the next generation to go into technical fields. He appointed a number of prominent scientists to important positions in his administration, notably, Steven Chu, a Nobel Prize-winning physicist, as secretary of energy. He indicated that the United States would take the lead among nations in climate change. There was no guarantee he could do all he said he wanted to do, but there was optimism that a robust government-science partnership would be restored and sustained.

Bibliography and Further Reading

Brooks, Harvey. "The Evolution of U.S. Science Policy." In *Technology, R&D, and the Economy*, edited by Bruce L. R. Smith and Claude E. Barfield. Washington, D.C.: Brookings Institution and American Enterprise Institute, 1996.

Guston, David H. *Between Politics and Science: Assuring the Integrity and Productivity of Research*. New York: Cambridge University Press, 2000.

Lambright, W. Henry. "Government and Science: A Troubled, Critical Relationship and What Can be Done About It." *Public Administration Review* 68, no. 1 (2008): 5–18.

———. *Powering Apollo: James E. Webb of NASA*. Baltimore, MD: Johns Hopkins University Press, 1995.

Mooney, Chris. *The Republican War on Science*. New York: Basic Books, 2005.

National Academies, Committee on Science, Engineering, and Public Policy. *Rising Above the Gathering Storm: Energizing and Employing America for a Brighter Economic Future*. Washington D.C.: National Academies Press, 2007.

Pielke, Roger, Jr. *The Honest Broker: Making Sense of Science in Policy and Politics*. New York: Cambridge University Press, 2007.

Sarewitz, Daniel. *Frontiers of Illusion: Science Technology, and the Politics of Progress*. Philadelphia: Temple University Press, 1996.

W. Henry Lambright and Tamara Hafner

SENATE

See Congress

SEPTEMBER 11, 2001, ATTACKS

On September 11, 2001, a date that became known as "9/11," Islamist terrorists affiliated with Osama bin Laden's al Qaeda organization carried out a series of attacks on the United States by crashing hijacked commercial airliners into U.S. commercial and government landmarks in New York City and near Washington, D.C. The terrorists flew two airliners into the World Trade Center in New York City, destroying it. Another airliner crashed into the Pentagon, damaging it, and a fourth crashed in rural Pennsylvania. The attacks, which killed more people than any other act of terrorism in history, marked a radical escalation of al Qaeda's campaign against the United States and its allies. In response, the United States invaded Afghanistan, used the attacks, in part, to justify its invasion of Iraq, and enacted the most sweeping security reforms since the aftermath of World War II.

The Origins of 9/11

The September 11 attacks were part of the campaign against the United States that al Qaeda began to wage in the 1990s. In the 1980s, bin Laden, the son of a wealthy Saudi construction magnate, helped to organize radical Islamists to fight against the Soviet occupiers of Afghanistan. Following the Soviet-Afghan War, bin Laden turned al Qaeda (which means "the base") into an organization that provided training and financial and logistical support to radical Islamists in both Muslim and non-Muslim countries. Suspected of involvement in attacks on U.S. troops in Somalia in 1992 and in Saudi Arabia in 1996, bin Laden issued a fatwa calling on Muslims to drive American soldiers from Saudi Arabia in August 1996. In February 1998, bin Laden and his associate Ayman al-Zawahiri, a fugitive Egyptian, published a fatwa in the name of a World Islamic Front; the fatwa called on all Muslims to murder any American anywhere in the world.

On August 7, 1998, suicide terrorists affiliated with al Qaeda drove truck bombs into the U.S. embassies in Nairobi, Kenya, and Dar es Salaam. In retaliation, on August 20, 1998, Pres. Bill Clinton ordered attacks on a Sudanese factory mistakenly identified as an al Qaeda facility and on al Qaeda training camps in Afghanistan. Bin Laden had lived in these training camps since 1996, when he was forced out of Sudan, his home since 1992, by pressure from the United States and Saudi Arabia (which had stripped bin Laden of his citizenship in 1994). On October 12, 2000, jihadists affiliated with al Qaeda carried out a suicide bombing attack against the U.S. Navy destroyer USS *Cole* in the port of Aden, Yemen.

During much of this time, planning for what became the 9/11 attacks was under way. On February 26, 1993, a truck bomb exploded beneath the twin towers of the World Trade Center in New York. While only six people died, one of the terrorists involved in the bombing, Kuwaiti national Ramzi Yousef, said that he had hoped to kill 250,000 people. Yousef's uncle, Khalid Sheikh Mohammed, was involved in both the 1993 attack on the World Trade Center and a plot to blow up commercial airliners leaving Manila (averted by Philippine police in January 1995), and became the central figure in the 9/11 conspiracy.

At a meeting in Tora Bora, Afghanistan, Khalid Sheikh Mohammed presented Osama bin Laden with options for terrorist attacks against the United States, including the idea of training pilots to crash airliners into U.S. buildings. In late 1998 or early 1999, according to the U.S. government, with bin Laden's approval, planning was begun for what was known within al Qaeda as the "planes operation." Having initially planned to use existing members of al Qaeda, the architects of the plan chose instead to use Egyptian-born Mohamed Atta and other members of a jihadist cell in Hamburg, Germany, who were fluent in English. Members of the Hamburg cell used tourist and student visas to become residents of the United States and pursued flight training in Florida and Arizona with the help of money wired to them by Khalid Sheikh Mohammed. During the summer and fall of 2000, al Qaeda selected "muscle hijackers" and trained them in Afghanistan before sending them to the United States, where most of them temporarily resided in Florida.

Coordinated by Mohamed Atta, the hijacking teams, now numbering a total of 19 individuals including the pilots, selected as their targets commercial jets on cross-country flights whose fuel tanks would be full shortly after takeoff. They moved to hotels near the airports. On the morning of September 11, all 19 passed through security and boarded their scheduled flights.

The Attacks

American Airlines Flight 11, which left Boston's Logan airport for Los Angeles with 81 passengers and a crew of 11, was the first plane to be hijacked. At around 8:14 a.m., the terrorists, led by Atta, took control of the plane, stabbing several people with box cutters or knives and spraying an irritant to force passengers to the rear of the plane. The plane swerved south and at 8:46 American 11 crashed into the north tower of the World Trade Center.

Around this time, United Airlines Flight 175, which had also taken off from Logan on a trip for Los Angeles, was seized by terrorists, who stabbed a flight attendant and killed both pilots. At 9:03 a.m., United Airlines Flight 175 crashed into the south tower of the World Trade Center, killing its crew of 9 and its 56 passengers, including the hijackers.

American Airlines Flight 77, with 58 passengers and a crew of 6, had taken off from Washington's Dulles International Airport at 8:20 a.m. for its scheduled flight to Los Angeles. Between 8:51 and 8:54, the hijackers seized control of the plane and turned it south. At 9:37, Flight 77 crashed into the Pentagon, demolishing a large section of the building.

The last plane to take off, United Airlines Flight 93, departed from Newark Liberty International Airport for San Francisco at 8:42 a.m. The hijackers, who may have intended to destroy the White House or the Capitol in Washington, D.C., took control of the plane around 9:30. Learning from cell phones and onboard phones about the earlier attacks on the World Trade Center, passengers attempted to retake the plane. Shouting "Allah is the greatest," the hijackers deliberately or inadvertently put the plane into a steep dive and it crashed into a field in Shanksville, Pennsylvania, shortly after 10:00 a.m.

The Initial Response

The impacts of the jets and the spilling of their fuel ignited both towers of the World Trade Center. After burning for nearly an hour, the south tower collapsed around 10 a.m. and the north tower fell at 10:28 a.m. Damaged by debris from the collapsing towers, a third building in the World Trade Center complex, 7 World Trade Center, collapsed at 5:20 p.m. Many emergency response personnel, including more than three hundred New York firefighters who had rushed to the scene, were killed during the collapse of the Twin Towers.

Following the crash of the second airliner, Flight 175, into the World Trade Center, the Federal Aviation Administration (FAA) shut down all New York City–area airports at 9:17 a.m. At 9:40 a.m., shortly before American Airlines Flight 77 crashed into the Pentagon, the FAA, for the first time in history, shut down all flight operations at U.S. airports, following the statement of President Bush, in Sarasota, Florida, that the United States had experienced an "apparent terrorist attack." While the president left Florida, the White House was evacuated beginning at 9:45 a.m. and many institutions in Washington, D.C., and New York, including the State and Justice departments and the United Nations, were evacuated. Worldwide, most governments and media organizations condemned the attacks and expressed sympathy for the United States.

Excluding the hijackers, the dead numbered 2,974—2,603 in New York City in and around the World Trade Center, 125 at the Pentagon, and 246 on the planes. In addition, 24 people were listed as missing.

Al Qaeda Admits Responsibility

Like other traumatic events in U.S. history, including the Japanese attack on Pearl Harbor and the assassination of Pres. John F. Kennedy, the 9/11 attacks quickly became the subject of conspiracy theories and mythology, with some claiming that the attacks were staged by the U.S. government in order to provide it with an excuse to enlarge its powers or wage wars for oil in Afghanistan and Iraq. Such speculations have no basis in fact.

Arrested on March 1, 2003, in Rawalpindi, Pakistan, Khalid Sheikh Mohammed admitted his role in the attacks. Initially, bin Laden denied responsibility for the attacks, in a statement broadcast on September 16, 2001, by the Al Jazeera Arabic network based in Qatar. However, in November 2001, the United States recovered a videotape from Afghanistan in which bin Laden spoke to an ally about his advance knowledge of the attacks. Bin Laden admitted directing the hijackers in a videotape broadcast by Al Jazeera on October 30, 2004. In a tape aired by Al Jazeera on May 23, 2006, bin Laden stated "I was responsible for enlisting the 19 brothers" and on September 7, 2006, Al Jazeera aired a videotape showing bin Laden planning the attacks with two of the hijackers, Wail al-Shehri and Hamza al-Ghamdi, and Ramzi Bin al-Shibh, who, after he failed to gain entry to the United States in order to be one of the pilots, served as a coordinator between Khalid Sheikh Mohammed and Mohammed Atta. Although all of the details are not known, no doubt remains about the role of Osama bin Laden and al Qaeda in authorizing, planning, and funding the attacks on the United States on September 11, 2001.

The Wars in Afghanistan and Iraq

On September 21, 2001, President Bush told Congress and the nation, "the evidence we have gathered all points to a collection of loosely affiliated terrorist organizations known as al Qaeda." The president then demanded that the Taliban government of Afghanistan arrest and turn over al Qaeda members and other terrorists within its borders and close down terrorist training camps on its soil while making them accessible to U.S. inspectors.

When the Taliban rejected these demands, the United States went to war to topple the regime. Following the attacks on 9/11, the government of Pakistan, which had been sympathetic to the Taliban, aligned itself (under pressure) with the United States and provided support during the war. Known as Operation Enduring Freedom, the war began on October 7, 2001, with the United States and Britain dropping bombs in support of operations by the Afghan Northern Alliance. U.S. and British troops began ground combat missions in early 2002. Following its surrender to the interim government of the last city it controlled, Kandahar,

RELATED ENTRIES

THIS VOLUME
9/11 Commission; Bush, George W.; USA PATRIOT Act; War on Terror

on December 7, 2002, the Taliban persisted as an insurgent group.

The Bush administration justified the U.S. invasion of Iraq, Operation Iraqi Freedom, which began on March 20, 2003, in part as a response to 9/11 and the overall War on Terror, even though the regime of Saddam Hussein had no significant links to al Qaeda. Following the fall of Saddam, Sunni extremists, many of them from other countries, entered Iraq to battle U.S. occupation forces. Native Sunni and Shia militias also fought U.S. troops and each other. A group called al Qaeda in Iraq was organized by Abu Musab al-Zarqawi, who was killed by U.S. forces in 2006.

Osama bin Laden, Ayman al Zawahiri, and other al Qaeda leaders had escaped being captured or killed during the U.S. invasion of Afghanistan. From hiding, they continued to deliver videotaped messages in the subsequent years. Al Qaeda's role changed from providing a logistical infrastructure for Islamist militants to one of providing inspiration for largely independent terrorists like those who carried out bombings or attempted bombings in Madrid (2004), London (2005), London and Glasgow (2007), and Mumbai (2008).

The Domestic Response

At home, the U.S. government responded to the attacks of 9/11 by engaging in the most radical restructuring of the executive branch since the creation of the Department of Defense and the CIA in the years following World War II. On March 25, 2002, the Homeland Security Act established the Department of Homeland Security, which brought together a number of previously unrelated agencies, including the Federal Emergency Management Agency (FEMA) and the former Bureau of Immigration and Customs Enforcement, in what immediately became the third largest federal agency. For several years following the 9/11 attacks, the Department of Homeland Security intermittently issued color-coded terrorist threat alerts, which critics accused of contributing to a climate of fear.

President George W. Bush, standing with New York City firefighters and New York governor George Pataki, speaks to rescue workers, firefighters, and police officers from the rubble of Ground Zero on September 14, 2001. In the wake of the attacks, the country largely rallied around the president: his approval rating jumped from 55 percent on September 6 to 86 percent seven days later. Bush would see another spike in approval in the run-up to and in the first months of the Iraq War, but as the war dragged on and the Bush administration's strategies in the War on Terror came under increased criticism, Bush's numbers began a steady decline that would continue to the end of his term. (Eric Draper/White House/Getty Images)

Earlier, on October 26, 2001, President Bush signed the USA PATRIOT Act, which expanded the powers available for law enforcement agencies to engage in surveillance of suspected terrorists. Many argued that the act went too far in weakening civil liberties. Equally controversial was the decision of the Bush administration to classify suspected terrorists as "enemy combatants" to whom the Geneva Conventions governing the treatment of prisoners of war did not apply; to detain them on the U.S. naval base in Guantanamo, Cuba, known as "Gitmo"; and to establish a system of military tribunals to try them outside of the civilian U.S. criminal justice system. The treatment of prisoners at Guantanamo was widely denounced abroad and the subject of repeated litigation in federal courts. Following his inauguration on January 20, 2009, one of the first acts of Pres. Barack Obama was to order that the prison for terrorists at Guantanamo be closed and that the military tribunal system established by the Bush administration be reviewed.

Although President Obama signed an executive order on July 23, 2009, that ordered that Guantanamo be closed by the end of the year, the closing subsequently was postponed as a result of congressional opposition, judicial challenges, and the challenges of housing prisoners elsewhere or releasing them. On November 13, 2009, Attorney Gen. Eric Holder announced the forthcoming trial in New York of Khalid Sheikh Mohammed and four other Guantanamo detainees, including Abd al-Rahim al-Nashiri, who was a suspect in the bombing of the USS *Cole*.

The Lasting Effects of 9/11

One lasting effect of 9/11 was a trend in the United States and other countries toward a greatly increased role for the state in domestic security—ranging from airport security to border fencing, to electronic surveillance and the proliferation of police video cameras in public. Like the adoption of metal detectors in airports following the wave of airplane hijackings in the 1960s and 1970s, these measures were likely to become permanent.

In domestic politics, the intense fear generated by the 9/11 attacks initially benefited the Republican Party. From the Vietnam War until the end of the Cold War, the Republicans had dominated the White House largely because of their image as the more hawkish of the two parties. President George W. Bush and many conservatives described the war in Iraq as part of a global "War on Terror" or "Long War."

While public anxiety about terrorism helped George W. Bush be reelected, in the absence of further jihadist attacks on American soil, a high level of public anxiety could not last. In only a few years, the new Department of Homeland Security's color-coded threat alerts became a subject of derision and the media ceased to acknowledge them. By 2006, a majority of American voters had turned against the Iraq War and returned the Democrats to a majority in both chambers of Congress. Nor did the issue of national security work for the Republicans in 2008, when John McCain, a Vietnam War hero and foreign policy hawk, was defeated by Barack Obama, who had opposed the Iraq War. The global economic crisis that began in September 2008 marked the end of an era in American politics defined by the terrorist threat and the beginning of a new period as

the threat of the greatest recession since the Depression became the focus of public attention and political debate.

Bibliography and Further Reading

Bergen, Peter. *Holy War, Inc.: Inside the Secret World of Osama bin Laden.* New York: The Free Press, 2001.

Coll, Steve. *Ghost Wars: The Secret History of the CIA, Afghanistan, and Bin Laden, from the Soviet Invasion to September 10, 2001.* New York: Penguin Press, 2004.

Miller, John J., and Michael Stone. *The Cell: Inside the 9/11 Plot, and Why the FBI and CIA Failed to Stop It,* edited by Chris Mitchell. New York: Hyperion, 2002.

The 9/11 Commission Report: Final Report of the National Commission on Terrorist Attacks Upon the United States New York: W. W. Norton, 2004.

Wright, Lawrence. *The Looming Tower: Al Qaeda and the Road to 9/11.* New York: Knopf, 2006.

Michael Lind

SOCIAL SECURITY REFORM

Since the mid-1970s, the debate over the future of Social Security has divided citizens, interest groups, and politicians. This debate has led to incremental changes, rather than radical reforms that could have altered the basic structure of Social Security—one of the most enduring legacies of the New Deal and a central aspect of contemporary American politics. Because advocating reform of Social Security has become risky for politicians, the program is known as "the third rail of American politics."

The 1977 Amendments

In the late 1960s and early 1970s, a number of ad hoc benefit increases, as well as the enactment of an automatic indexation system, produced a major expansion of Social Security. Only a few years after this expansion, however, a less favorable than expected economic situation triggered the emergence of an unexpected crisis in Social Security. What became clear in the mid-1970s was that the indexation system enacted in 1972 generated unexpectedly high benefit increases, thus creating major fiscal challenges that could endanger the program's survival.

Although federal policy makers quickly understood the need to restore fiscal balance to Social Security, reforming this popular program was politically challenging. As the shift from expansion to retrenchment began in the mid-1970s, Social Security became a difficult issue for politicians, who had to cut benefits or increase taxes. Yet, as the fiscal crisis intensified, inaction became politically riskier than reform. Because any reform would feature unpopular payroll tax increases, the Carter administration decided to accelerate the reform process in order to enact legislation as soon as possible to put as much distance between such reform and voters going to the polls in the 1978 midterm elections. In May 1977, President Carter put forward a legislative proposal aimed at improving Social Security's short- and long-term fiscal status. Congress took less than six months to debate, revise, and enact the administration's proposal, and President Carter signed the 1977 amendments to the Social Security Act on December 20. The 1977 amendments slightly increased the payroll tax and, more important, pushed the "wage base" up (i.e., the range of earnings subject to the payroll tax) from $22,900 in 1979 to $29,700 in 1981. The legislation also established a less generous indexation system. To avoid a political backlash from those already receiving Social Security benefits, the 1977 amendments specified that the less generous indexation system would only apply to individuals who reached age 62 in 1979 and after. As the 1978 midterm elections approached, however, a growing number of voices in Congress wanted to roll back the payroll tax hikes, but President Carter was successful in opposing such change.

The 1983 Amendments

Although President Carter claimed that these measures would ensure the short- and long-term solvency of Social Security, deteriorating economic conditions created a new crisis soon after Ronald Reagan's election to the presidency in 1980. Responding to the crisis, Reagan proposed reducing early retirement benefits (for those age 62) significantly and making disability benefits harder to qualify for—faced with strong opposition, however, the president rapidly withdrew his controversial proposal. Hoping for political cover, Reagan then formed the bipartisan National Commission on Social Security Reform, chaired by economist Alan Greenspan, whose one objective was to create a legislative compromise that could be supported by the president, the Republican-controlled Senate, and the House's Democratic majority. In this context, President Reagan, Senate Majority Leader Howard Baker, and House Speaker Tip O'Neill each nominated 5 of the 15 members of the commission. Nevertheless, by November 1982, the commission had not reached a consensus because Democrats pushed for payroll tax increases while Republicans preferred benefit cuts.

To forge an agreement, a few prominent Democratic and Republican members of the commission, including former Social Security commissioner Robert Ball, met secretly with a handful of top congressional and White House officials. These private meetings resulted in a bipartisan deal that the commission as a whole adopted in January 1983. Ultimately, the Greenspan Commission advocated a complex set of small-scale benefit cuts and tax increases that did not fundamentally alter the program's structure. Largely because quick action was necessary, Congress rapidly enacted the 1983 amendments to the Social Security Act. During the legislative debate, however, Rep. J. J. Pickle (D–TX), chairman of the House Subcommittee on Social Security, introduced a controversial measure to the legislation that gradually increased the Social Security retirement age from 65 to 67, scheduled to go into effect between 2000 and 2022. Despite the opposition of interest groups like the AARP, Congress adopted this provision. President Reagan signed the 1983 amendments to the Social Security Act on April 20. Stressing the bipartisan nature of the legislation, the president succeeded in his attempt to share with both Democrats and Republicans in Congress the responsibility for painful changes in Social Security.

Social Security Privatization?

From a strictly actuarial standpoint, the 1983 amendments were successful—no new short-term fiscal crisis in Social Security developed after their enactment. Yet, during the 1990s and early 2000s, the issue of Social Security reform moved to the forefront of the federal policy agenda on two occasions. First, during the second half of the 1990s, exceptional stock-market performance and the fear that the imminent retirement of the large baby boom generation would lead to a future fiscal crisis led a number of conservatives to campaign for privatizing the system in order to "save" it. Under privatization, workers would have been able to invest part of their Social Security contributions in equities like stocks, which, reformers argued, would give retirees larger benefits than the current program. They also argued that Social Security is a "bad deal" for younger Americans and that the creation of personal savings and investment accounts as part of the program would be a better option. Those defending the traditional program responded that personal savings accounts would reduce the economic security of elderly citizens, whose Social Security benefits would become increasingly vulnerable to financial cycles and bad investment choices, among other risks. They warned against replacing a defined benefit system with a defined contribution system whose yield would be determined by the financial markets. To attack this type of policy alternative, opponents of Social Security privatization also pointed to higher administrative costs and the greater economic vulnerability of women and minorities. Unfortunately for supporters of privatization, Pres. Bill Clinton, after a period of uncertainty, formally rejected this policy alternative in his 1999 State of the Union address. In the unusually contentious context of the impeachment debate, no room was left for a bipartisan compromise that could have favored the enactment of major Social Security reform.

Second, during the first half of 2005, Pres. George W. Bush toured the country to promote privatization. Democrats in Congress and key interest groups like the AFL-CIO and the AARP depicted the president's plan as a Wall Street–driven attack against economic security that would increase poverty among the elderly without solving the long-term fiscal unbalance in Social Security. Ultimately, the president and his allies failed to generate strong political support for privatization. As his popularity

RELATED ENTRIES

OTHER VOLUMES
Social Security (vol. 5)

declined in the aftermath of the Iraq War and the Hurricane Katrina disaster of late summer 2005, President Bush abandoned his active campaign for privatization of Social Security.

During the 2008 presidential campaign, Republican candidate John McCain did not try to revive the privatization debate—rather, he advocated for the adoption of new personal savings accounts *alongside* the existing federal program. As for Democratic candidate Barack Obama, he strongly opposed Social Security privatization. With his election, privatization is unlikely to move back to the center of the federal agenda during his presidency. Nevertheless, enduring long-term demographic and fiscal challenges should keep alive the debate on Social Security's future, which should remain prominent in the years and perhaps the decades to come.

Bibliography and Further Reading

Béland, Daniel. *Social Security: History and Politics from the New Deal to the Privatization Debate*. Lawrence: University Press of Kansas, 2005.

Berkowitz, Edward D. *Robert Ball and the Politics of Social Security*. Madison: University of Wisconsin Press, 2003.

Califano, Joseph A., Jr. *Governing America: An Insider's Report from the White House and Cabinet*. New York: Simon & Schuster, 1981.

Campbell, Andrea Louise. *How Policies Make Citizens: Senior Citizen Activism and the American Welfare State*. Princeton, NJ: Princeton University Press, 2003.

DeWitt, Larry W., Daniel Béland, and Edward D. Berkowitz. *Social Security: A Documentary History*. Washington, D.C.: Congressional Quarterly Press, 2007.

Light, Paul. *Still Artful Work: The Continuing Politics of Social Security Reform*. New York: McGraw-Hill, 1995.

Pierson, Paul. *Dismantling the Welfare State? Reagan, Thatcher, and the Politics of Retrenchment*. Cambridge: Cambridge University Press, 1994.

Daniel Béland

SPACE POLICY

With the *Apollo 11* landing on the moon in 1969, the United States won the race that had galvanized American political leaders and the public into supporting a massive commitment to space exploration. In the decades following, support for the space program declined because of growing concerns about costs and the end of the Cold War, which had been the impetus for the program. For the remainder of the twentieth century and into the twenty-first century, space policy was determined by budgetary constraints and changing international relations. The result was an emphasis on reusable space craft; cheaper, more quickly developed unmanned probes of space; and international cooperation.

Retrenchment

Following the success of the Apollo missions, the space program went into an almost decade-long retrenchment. In 1969, Pres. Richard M. Nixon established the Space Task Group to develop new policy goals. Led by Vice Pres. Spiro T. Agnew, the group issued a report recommending that future space projects include a space shuttle, a 12-person space station, a 100-person space base, a lunar space station, a lunar research laboratory, nuclear-powered launch vehicles, and a Mars mission. The report was not well-received. The Bureau of the Budget maintained that these projects had too long of a lead-time and were too expensive; the administration, focused on domestic unrest and the increasingly unpopular war in Vietnam, did little to support the recommendations. In 1972, Nixon finally approved a small portion of the program—building a reusable vehicle that would provide routine access to space (the space shuttle)—but only after the National Aeronautics and Space Administration (NASA) cut the estimated costs by half. To maintain a permanent presence in space, he approved the Skylab program, which used modified Apollo equipment to develop an orbital laboratory.

Reflecting his lack of interest in space, Nixon abolished the policy-making National Aeronautics and Space Council in 1973, but he did not abandon space entirely. He continued using it as an arm of foreign policy. As relations between the United States and the Soviet Union thawed, space became a setting for détente, highlighted by the 1975 U.S.-Soviet Apollo Soyuz Test Project, which involved an *Apollo* spacecraft rendezvousing and docking with a Soviet *Soyuz* capsule in orbit.

Funding for space projects remained limited throughout much of the 1970s; neither Gerald Ford nor Jimmy Carter offered any bold initiatives. With little support from the White House or Congress, NASA was forced to protect its existing programs and to try to limit the regular cuts to its budget. President Carter did support development of the space shuttle, however, because of his interest in arms control, especially the balancing of armaments between the United States and the Soviet Union. Carter believed that the space shuttle could be used to deploy reconnaissance satellites that could then monitor Russia's ballistic missiles and aircrafts.

On April 12, 1981, NASA successfully launched the first reusable spacecraft, space shuttle *Columbia*. Over the next 10 years, the agency constructed four additional vehicles: *Challenger*, *Discovery*, *Atlantis*, and *Endeavour*. By 2009, NASA had utilized these vehicles for more than one hundred missions that conducted scientific experiments, performed environmental studies, deployed and serviced unmanned satellites, and engaged in military reconnaissance operations. Yet, the program remained controversial. The shuttle was never cost-efficient nor did it provide routine access to space as originally intended. It was also plagued by disasters: in 1986, *Challenger* exploded on launch, killing all aboard; in 2003, the space shuttle *Columbia* disintegrated on reentry. As part of his 2004 Vision for Space Exploration policy initiative, Pres. George W. Bush announced that the shuttle would be retired in 2010.

Beginning in the 1970s, NASA pursued unmanned programs to explore nearby planets and deep space. These comparatively inexpensive robotic missions yielded significant scientific observations and discoveries and revolutionized scientific understanding of the sun, planets, asteroids, and comets. In the summer of 1977, for example, the space agency launched two Voyager spacecraft that, over the next 20 years, provided the scientific community with pictures of Jupiter, Saturn, Uranus, and Neptune.

A cloudy trail of engine exhaust, solid rocket booster plume, and expanding gas fill the sky after the explosion of the space shuttle *Challenger* above the Kennedy Space Center in Florida on January 28, 1986. The disaster claimed the lives of seven crew members, including that of Christa McAuliffe, the first participant of the Teacher in Space Project. The tragedy seriously damaged public enthusiasm for space exploration in general, and the shuttle program in particular. (Bettmann/Corbis)

But these missions, while generating considerable temporary attention, never commanded the sustained public interest necessary to reenergize the space program.

Another response to the budgetary constraints of the late 1970s was increased collaboration with other space agencies. Among NASA's most successful efforts was the development of the Hubble Space Telescope in conjunction with the European Space Agency (ESA). NASA had begun developing places for a space telescope in the 1960s, but across-the-board public spending cuts by the Ford administration ended funding in 1974. Astronomers then began a nationwide lobbying effort that resulted in Congress funding a portion of the project. Only when the ESA agreed to provide additional funds did the project go forward. Technical delays and the temporary shutdown of the space shuttle following the *Challenger* disaster delayed deployment until 1990. Immediately following deployment, astronomers discovered that the Hubble had a faulty mirror, resulting in increased criticism of NASA. (NASA repaired the flaw during a series of space walks in December 1993.)

Space Station *Freedom* and the International Space Station

Space policy received renewed attention under Pres. Ronald Reagan. Over the course of his two terms, he steadily increased funding for NASA; in January 1984, he directed the agency to build a new space station, which he christened Space Station *Freedom*. The proposed orbiting laboratory experienced problems from the beginning. Budgetary overrides and developmental constraints slowed progress so that construction went years beyond the decade Reagan had mandated. Nevertheless, in 2000, the space station, in the form of the International Space Station, was built in cooperation with other nations—including Russia—and became operational.

In keeping with his general philosophy of limiting the role of government, Reagan encouraged the commercialization of space activities and the privatization of parts of the space program. During his watch, NASA began providing launch services for the commercial sector and sourced out shuttle maintenance. Reagan also pushed responsibility for space programs beyond NASA and the Department of Defense to federal agencies such as the Department of Transportation—which was placed in charge of commercial space launch activities.

Space Exploration Initiative

Shortly after he assumed the presidency, Pres. George H. W. Bush attempted to recapture the bold vision that had characterized the space program's early days. He revived the National Space Council and, in July 1989, during a ceremony marking the twentieth anniversary of the *Apollo 11* lunar landing, he announced the Space Exploration Initiative, a three-step plan for human exploration of space. The initiative outlined a short-term goal of completing the space station, an intermediate goal of a permanent return to the moon, and a long-term goal of landing a crew on Mars in 30 years. The estimated cost was to be $400 billion and would require significant annual increases in NASA's budget. The vague proposal met with a largely negative reaction both from Congress and the public. Senator Al Gore (D–TN), for example, remarked that "President Bush offers the country not a challenge to inspire us, but a daydream." (Hogan 4) Negative reaction increased in the fall when NASA issued a detailed plan for the project, now estimated to cost $541 billion. NASA had developed the plan largely in secret, without policy guidance from the White House or consultation with supporters of space exploration in Congress. With no support, the initiative faded, a victim of poor planning, a growing federal deficit, and an economic downturn.

Faster, Better, Cheaper

The downfall of the initiative, well-publicized problems with the space shuttle and Hubble, and charges that NASA undertook programs that were too costly, took too long to develop, and occurred too infrequently, prompted a reorientation of the agency. In 1992, Pres. George H. W. Bush responded by appointing Daniel S. Goldin as the new NASA administrator. Goldin established a "faster, better, cheaper" vision for the American space agency with programs such as Discovery, a series of highly specialized missions costing under $425 million individually that were developed in no more than 36 months. His tenure proved controversial, however, with critics claiming that he failed to provide a long-term vision for the agency. Goldin was constrained by the political atmosphere of the period, with both Pres. Bill Clinton and Congress focused on reducing the federal deficit.

Vision for Space Exploration

In the aftermath of the *Columbia* disaster, Pres. George W. Bush outlined a new policy that was designed to reignite public enthusiasm for space exploration. On January 14, 2004, he announced the Vision for Space

Exploration, which authorized NASA to complete the International Space Station by 2010, retire the space shuttle fleet, implement a robotic program to investigate the solar system, and develop a new spacecraft that would allow astronauts to return to the moon and explore Mars. The president's plan reaffirmed the nation's commitment to manned space exploration, and it provided NASA with new goals and objectives for the twenty-first-century. With the president and a Republican Congress no longer concerned about deficits, the program received initial funding. However, in 2006, a Democratic-controlled Congress cut funding in order to finance social programs. When recession struck, NASA received additional funding under the American Recovery and Reinvestment Act of 2009 as part of President Obama's effort to revitalize the economy.

Bibliography and Further Reading

Dethloff, Henry C. *Suddenly, Tomorrow Came . . . A History of the Johnson Space Center*. Washington, D.C.: NASA History Series, 1993.

Heppenheimer, T. A. *Countdown: A History of Space Flight*. New York: John Wiley & Sons, 1997.

Hogan, Thor. "Lessons Learned from the Space Exploration Initiative." *NASA History News and Notes* 24, no. 4 (November 2007): 1–2, 4.

Jenkins, Dennis R. *Space Shuttle: The History of Developing the National Space Transportation System*. Marceline, MO: Walsworth Publishing, 1996.

McCurdy, Howard E. *The Space Station Decision: Incremental Politics and Technological Choice*. Baltimore, MD: John Hopkins University Press, 1990.

McDougall, Walter A. *The Heavens and the Earth: A Political History of the Space Age*. New York: Basic Books, 1985.

Sietzen, Frank, Jr., and Keith L. Cowing. *New Moon Rising: The Making of America's New Space Vision and the Remaking of NASA*. Burlington, Ontario: Apogee Books, 2004.

Kevin M. Brady

STATE-FEDERAL RELATIONS

From the 1930s to the 1960s, the functions and responsibilities of the national government increased substantially. Education, welfare, and health care, to name a few, once viewed as the sole prerogative of the states, gradually crept into the purview of the federal government. However, beginning in the 1970s, the process of nationalization, along with the political influence of New Deal Democrats, waned with the rise of the conservative wing of the Republican Party. From 1980 to 2000, these states' rights Republicans attempted to use the presidency, and eventually Congress and the federal courts, to decentralize federal programs and return greater control and responsibility to the states. The Republicans were able to implement some of their political objectives, but their successes were short-lived. From 2000 to 2008, decentralization slowed—even halted in some policy areas—as the federal government increased its authority and power over states and localities.

The Devolution Revolution: Federalism in the Late 1970s and 1980s

In the late 1970s, Democratic president Jimmy Carter both expanded and contracted the powers of the federal government. On the one hand, he increased the size of the federal government by convincing Congress to create the Department of Energy in 1977 and, two years later, the Department of Education and Department of Health and Human Services. On the other hand, Carter decreased the role of the federal government by deregulating the railroad, trucking, banking, and airline industries. Overall, the line separating federal and state powers in the late 1970s did not move substantially one way or the other to increase the powers of either level of government. But indications of a devolution revolution were evident—a returning of power and responsibility to states and local governments as Americans grew increasingly frustrated with the federal government's inability to ameliorate economic conditions despite its increased power in economic and social affairs.

In his first Inaugural Address, Pres. Ronald Reagan revealed his intention to reach economic stability and improve the welfare of the people by contending that "Government is not the solution to our problems; government is the problem." The Reagan administration—and like-minded Republicans—believed that moving the political system away from cooperative federalism (big government) and closer to the dual federalism (limited government) was in keeping with the constitutional design of the Framers, as well as a way to achieve administrative efficiency. To decentralize power at the national level, Reagan proposed tax cuts, budget reductions, and economic deregulation. Such policies not only would diminish federal involvement in social and economic affairs but also would promote individual responsibility and give Americans incentive to work hard, which, in turn, would increase productivity and help the economy flourish. Despite opponents accusing Reagan's policy proposals of being ideologically unsound and of favoring wealthy Americans and major corporations, Congress acquiesced and reduced the personal income tax by 25 percent for all income levels over the course of three years. It also dropped the top tax rate from 70 percent to 50 percent, as well as lowered the maximum capital gains tax from 28 percent to 20 percent.

Like Pres. Richard M. Nixon, Reagan tried to pull back the federal government's supervisory role over state budgets. He championed the policy of revenue sharing—the practice of the federal government sharing its revenue with state officials—who were free to spend as they wished. To the disappointment of state officials, this practice ended in 1986 because of soaring federal budget deficits, which resulted in the use of more block grants—appropriated federal funds transferred to states for a broad purpose with few supervisory strings attached.

States generally prefer block grants to categorical grants because of the increased discretionary authority over spending federal dollars. Categorical grants force state and local recipients of federal funds to adhere strictly to national preferences. Between 1960 and 1980, Congress had authorized only five block grants, ranging from community development to law enforcement to job-training programs. During that time, categorical grants were more popular because Congress could dictate to the states the specific purpose of the federal funds (such as building bridges, roads, or dams, or paying for school lunches). The level of authority the federal government possessed over states and localities through categorical grants was agreeable to liberal Democrats but not to Reagan and states' rights

Republicans, who wished to increase state sovereignty over local government projects and programs. Consequently, Reagan demanded that Congress consolidate some 85 categorical grants into various block grants to give more budgetary authority to state and local communities.

For the most part, Congress complied with Reagan's budget requests. Together, they passed the Omnibus Budget Reconciliation Act of 1981, which converted 77 programs into 9 block grants. In the area of social programs, education funding went from 50 to 30 programs. Reagan also persuaded Congress to slash $1.6 billion from the Food Stamp Program, reduced subsidizes for school lunches, and slashed workplace programs. Reagan also continued President Carter's policy of deregulating the airline industry and relaxed various environmental regulations.

Despite Reagan's devolution policies, the federal government continued to dominate state governments and even received support from an increasingly conservative Supreme Court. Passed in 1984, the National Minimum Drinking Age Act established a national drinking age of 21 and authorized the secretary of transportation to withhold 5 percent of highway funds from any state refusing to raise its minimum drinking age to the national standard. A year later, in *South Dakota v. Dole*, 483 U.S. 203 (1987), the Supreme Court upheld the act and asserted that as long as the federal government exercised its spending power for the "general welfare" of the nation, no intrusion was being made on the traditional police powers of state governments.

Congress also used federal mandates, both funded and unfunded, as mechanisms to ensure authority over state governments. Essentially, mandates command states to take some action or face federal repercussions. In the 1980s and early 1990s, more than thirty mandates were in effect that controlled—and regulated—decisions of state governments. For example, in 1982, Congress extended the Voting Rights Act of 1965 for another 25 years. That law required 22 states with histories of racial discrimination to submit any changes in voting standards and procedures to the Department of Justice for federal approval. To protect disabled young Americans and guarantee their education, Congress passed the Handicapped Children's Protection Act of 1986. And, in 1990, Pres. George H. W. Bush approved the Americans with Disabilities Act, which mandated that states—and private businesses—publicly accommodate disabled Americans with wheelchair ramps, elevators, and parking spaces, among other such adaptations. Unlike other grants, federal mandates do not give states a choice about participation; rather, they force states into compliance with, or without, federal funding.

Reviving Amendment X: Federalism in the 1990s

The Republican congressional victory in the midterm elections of 1994 swung the political pendulum even more toward support of states' rights. Sensing an electorate frustrated with big government, conservative Republicans, led by Rep. Newt Gingrich (R–GA), devised a series of policy proposals under the rubric, "Contract with America." Gingrich's plan contained 10 major legislative proposals, prefaced with the assertion of ending "government that is too big, too intrusive, and too easy with the public's money." On the agenda were a balanced budget amendment, Medicaid reform, unfunded mandate reform, and welfare reform. The opportunity for Republican legislative success seemed promising given that Pres. Bill Clinton seemed to go along with the central premise of this movement by proclaiming that the "era of big government is over."

The House Republicans who campaigned on the Contract moved quickly to translate their campaign promises into law. They offered a balanced budget amendment to check federal spending and "restore fiscal responsibility to an out-of-control Congress." In addition, a Medicaid bill proposed converting that entitlement program to a block grant, which, had it been passed, would have imposed caps on federal spending and given states the power to decide eligibility requirements for health care beneficiaries. Despite a more conservative Congress, both bills failed to pass. Opponents argued that legally restricting federal government spending was impractical and that turning the

Medicaid program into a discretionary block grant would harm many patients.

Other bills, however, did pass and, in effect, shrunk the federal government. For example, many state and local officials complained about the financial burdens imposed by unfunded mandates. In 1995, Congress provided states with some relief by passing the Unfunded Mandates Reform Act. The law requires the Congressional Budget Office and federal agencies to issue a report to Congress detailing the impact of any proposed unfunded mandate on states' budgets. If the cost of a mandate is too burdensome for state governments, then Congress can amend the legislation, choose not to pass it, or keep it as is and force compliance.

The foundation of the Republican policy proposals was welfare reform. On the operating table was the 61-year-old New Deal entitlement program Aid to Families with Dependent Children (AFDC). Passed under the Social Security Act of 1935, the AFDC provided financial assistance to low-income, unmarried mothers. As the number of single mothers increased, so did federal spending. Many conservative Republicans thought the program too costly and administratively inefficient. After two failed legislative attempts, Congress finally persuaded President Clinton to sign the Welfare Reform Act of 1996. The new law replaced the AFDC entitlement program with the block grant—Temporary Assistance for Needy Families— that gave states authority to determine eligibility requirements for welfare recipients and stipulated that such recipients would have two years to gain employment and five years to wean themselves entirely off federal financial assistance.

Throughout the 1990s, over the objections of liberal Democrats, conservative Republicans continued their campaign to devolve the power of the federal government. Entering the battle was an increasingly conservative Supreme Court, which ushered in a period of rebirth for Amendment X and states' rights in several high-profile cases: *United States v. Lopez*, 514 U.S. 549 (1995), *Printz v. United States*, 521 U.S. 898 (1997), and *United States v. Morrison*, 529 U.S. 598 (2000). Each case involved Congress's attempt to use its power to regulate interstate commerce to expand the federal government's regulatory control over traditional state functions.

In *Lopez*, the Supreme Court invalidated the Gun-Free School Zones Act of 1990 because the federal government provided insufficient evidence to show how guns in local school zones "substantially affect" interstate commerce. Two years after Congress's effort to regulate guns in school zones, the Court reviewed the constitutionality of another federal law. In *Printz*, the Court voided the Brady Handgun Violence Prevention Act, a law that had required state and local law enforcement agencies to implement and administer federal gun-control policies, such as a five-day waiting period for all gun purchases. The Court increased state sovereignty by ruling that the "Federal Government may neither issue directives requiring the States to address particular problems, nor command the States' officers, or those of their political subdivision, to administer or enforce a federal regulatory program." In the *Morrison* case, the Court struck down the 1994 Violence Against Women Act, a federal law that attempted to curtail gender-related violence by permitting the federal government to prosecute any individual who commits a crime motivated by the sex of the victim—rape, for example. The Court reasoned that if the law was upheld, "Congress might use the Commerce Clause to completely obliterate the Constitution's distinction between national and local authority" and later try to regulate other crimes, like murder and divorce, which fall under the regulatory powers of states. In all three cases—*Lopez*, *Printz*, and *Morrison*—the Court bolstered state sovereignty by forcing Congress to respect the traditional police powers of state governments in the process of passing national laws.

The New Millennium: Federalism in the 2000s

Nevertheless, from 2000 to 2008, the decentralization that had begun under President Reagan faded, as the federal government again expanded its powers over state governments. The governing philosophy of George W. Bush's administration strayed from that of the Reagan administration in the 1980s and from that of the congressional Republicans in the 1990s. The Supreme Court, which, during the 1990s, seemingly had shifted its thinking on federalism toward expanding states' rights and minimizing federal powers, made several decisions affecting federal-state relations.

The 2000 presidential race between George W. Bush and Al Gore was ultimately decided by the Supreme Court. Although Gore had won the popular vote by a narrow margin, the Electoral College results remained unclear. Because of voting irregularities in Florida, the state supreme court ruled that the results of a recount would determine the winner of Florida's 25 electoral votes and, thus, the presidential election. However, the Supreme Court, in *Bush v. Gore*, 531 U.S. 98 (2000), overturned the state court's ruling and stopped the recounts, giving as a reason that they violated the equal protection clause of Amendment XIV. Accordingly, Bush was considered to have won Florida and the presidency, leaving many public officials and constitutional law scholars questioning the authority and jurisprudence of the Supreme Court in regard to federal-state relations.

As president, Bush signed several bills into law that expanded federal power into policy areas traditionally managed by state and local governments—education, for example. In an attempt to overhaul the nation's education system, Congress passed the No Child Left Behind Act of 2001, which mandated that states devise and implement a system of standardized testing to assess academic performance in each grade from third through eighth, and once between grades 10 through 12. The legislation, which did offer some financial assistance to the states, had properties both of a block grant and a categorical grant. On the one hand, it was a block grant in the sense that states were free to use the federal dollars to develop plans for measurable improvements in education. On the other hand, it was categorical because if state schools failed, they would lose their federal financial aid. Thus, the categorical side to No Child Left Behind, setting strict federal guidelines for states to follow as a condition of aid, granted the federal government an expansive supervisory role over the education policies of state and local governments.

After the *Bush v. Gore* decision, the Supreme Court handed down other rulings that influenced federal-state relations. One case involved California's Compassionate Use Act, a 1996 referendum that legalized the use of marijuana for medical purposes. The California law conflicted with the Controlled Substance Act, a federal law that prohibited the possession of marijuana. In 2006, the Court ruled that the use of medicinal marijuana in California, despite it being a local activity, did have "aggregate impact on the national market," one that is "substantial" enough to fall within Congress's regulatory powers (see *Gonzales v. Raich*, 545 U.S. 1 [2005]). A year later, in *Kennedy v. Louisiana*, 554 U.S. ___ (2008), the Court held that a Louisiana law that imposed the death penalty for child rape violated Amendment VIII and, therefore, forced Louisiana, along with any other states with similar laws, to either revise or expunge such law from its books.

Throughout American political history, factions have grappled over where to draw the line separating federal and state functions and responsibilities. Liberal, or New Deal, Democrats expanded the federal government's powers over states to address problems that were overwhelming the nation—the Depression in the 1930s and the social crisis of the 1960s. The result was bigger government. But the rise to power of states' rights Republicans in the 1980s, along with their congressional victories in the 1990s, provided enough impetus to turn the focus of national policies in the direction of smaller government. From 2000 to 2008, however, national policies reverted to big government, as spending increased and as more power centralized at the national level. As for the future of federal-state relations, it is debatable. What is certain, though, is that the balance of power will be subject to the state of the union, to the philosophical principles underpinning political factions, and to the judgment of the American people about which level of government can meet their social and economic needs and achieve administrative efficiency.

Bibliography and Further Reading

Beer, Samuel H. *To Make a Nation: The Rediscovery of American Federalism*. Cambridge, MA: The Belknap Press of Harvard University Press, 1998.

Conlan, Timothy J. *From New Federalism to Devolution: Twenty-Five Years of Intergovernmental Reform*. Washington, D.C.: Brookings Institution Press, 1998.

Elazar, Daniel J. *American Federalism: A View from the States*, 3rd edition. New York: Harper & Row, 1984.

Gerston, Larry N. *American Federalism: A Concise Introduction*. Armonk, NY: M. E. Sharpe, 2007.

Grodzins, Morton. *The American System*. Chicago: Rand McNally, 1974.

Karmis, Dimitrios, and Norman Wayne, eds. *Theories of Federalism: A Reader*. New York: Palgrave MacMillan, 2005.

Walker, David B. *The Rebirth of Federalism: Slouching Toward Washington*, 2nd edition. Washington, D.C.: Congressional Quarterly Press, 1999.

Kyle T. Barbieri and Mitchel A. Sollenberger

SUBURBS

See Urbanization and Suburbanization

SUPREME COURT AND THE JUDICIARY

When the Republican Party came to power in the late 1960s, it aimed to remake the Supreme Court. Although this makeover did not happen immediately and was not consistent in all areas, it was largely successful. Just as the Court from the late 1930s through the 1960s operated as an extension of New Deal-Great Society liberalism, so, too, did the Court from the 1970s onward operate as an extension of New Right conservatism. Whether considering the Burger Court's occasional resistance to what it perceived as its predecessor's liberal excesses during the 1970s and 1980s, the Rehnquist Court's federalism offensive of the 1990s, or the Roberts Court's reconsideration of key liberal and moderate precedents in the early 2000s, the Supreme Court of the last quarter of the twentieth century and early part of the twenty-first century—composed largely of justices appointed by Republican presidents—ushered in a period of conservative ascendancy in American constitutional jurisprudence.

The Burger Court, 1969–1986

When Earl Warren announced his retirement as chief justice in the summer of 1968, the chance to replace the liberal legend initially fell to Pres. Lyndon B. Johnson, who had previously announced that he would not seek reelection that fall. Warren's indication that he would leave the Court once a suitable replacement was confirmed left the possibility that the Democratic president might choose the next chief justice. Once Johnson turned to old friend and advisor Justice Abe Fortas, however, Republicans and Dixiecrats in the Senate resisted. Questioning Fortas about his close relationship with the president and raising the specter of financial improprieties, senators filibustered Fortas's nomination and hastened the path to his resignation from the Court the following year. Less than a month from the 1968 presidential election, Johnson declined to make a second nomination, ultimately leaving the opportunity to replace Warren to Republican Richard Nixon. The result was federal appellate judge Warren Burger. a leading critic of Warren and a man who Nixon and the Republicans believed would reverse the trend of aggressive liberal policy making that had consumed the Court since the early 1950s. Burger's conservative politics and strict constructionist judicial philosophy certainly represented a change from the Warren Court; however, the jurisprudential outcomes of the late 1970s and early 1980s were a decidedly mixed bag. Nixon and his fellow Republicans envisioned the Burger Court as a conservative counterweight to the Warren Court, but quirks of membership and leadership charted a more hesitant path.

In the three years following his successful nomination of Burger as chief justice, Nixon would add three associate justices, appointing (after two failed attempts) Burger's longtime friend and federal appellate judge Harry Blackmun to replace Fortas in 1970, Virginia lawyer and former American Bar Association president Lewis Powell to replace New Dealer Hugo Black in 1972, and Asst. Attorney Gen. William Rehnquist to replace John Harlan in 1972.

After Nixon's resignation amidst the Watergate controversy in 1974, Gerald Ford added one more Republican to the Supreme Court—naming federal appellate judge John Paul Stevens as a replacement for the long-serving William O. Douglas in 1975. With Jimmy Carter having the unfortunate distinction of being the first president since Andrew Johnson not to appoint a single justice to the Court, the Burger Court experienced only one change in membership between 1976 and Burger's resignation in 1986: in 1981, Ronald Reagan fulfilled a 1980 campaign promise to add a woman to the Supreme Court by tapping Arizona judge Sandra Day O'Connor to replace Potter Stewart. While the sequence of appointments from Burger to O'Connor consisted of six consecutive Republican additions by presidents Nixon, Ford, and Reagan, the Court did not become the conservative anchor those Republican presidents had hoped it would be—at least not yet. In part because Blackmun and Stevens would each drift toward the liberal wing of the Court (anchored by Warren Court holdovers William Brennan and Thurgood Marshall), in part because Powell and O'Connor were each relatively moderate justices, and in part because Burger failed to exert the kind of strong leadership and direction of the Court that Warren had, the Burger Court foundered in finding its vision and its voice, rolling back liberal precedents in some areas, chastening further liberal progress in others, affirming or even extending liberal legal positions in yet others.

The Burger Court's clearest contribution to constitutional law came in articulating and upholding a strict interpretation of the Constitution's separation of powers between the three branches of the federal government. In *Nixon v. Fitzgerald*, 457 U.S. 731 (1982), the Court declared that the constitutional separation of powers granted the president absolute immunity from civil liability for his official acts. In *INS v. Chadha*, 462 U.S. 919 (1983), the Court held that the "legislative veto"—a statutorily-provided veto issued by one house of Congress against the action of an executive branch officer—was a violation of the separation of powers and lawmaking process provided by the Constitution. In *Bowsher v. Synar*,

478 U.S. 714 (1986), the Court struck down the Gramm-Rudman-Hollings Balanced Budget and Emergency Deficit Control Act of 1985, asserting that it violated the separation of powers because it delegated legislative power to an executive branch official. All three decisions pointed toward a formalist reading of the separation of powers as a structural foundation of American politics that was to be maintained assiduously, even if the result was a clunky or undesirable outcome. As Chief Justice Burger insisted in *Chadha*, "[c]onvenience and efficiency are not the primary objectives—or the hallmarks—of democratic government."

In virtually all other jurisprudential realms, the Court was seemingly adrift, searching for the values it wished to promote and the approach it wished to take. As a result, this period in the Court's history is characterized more by a series of significant (and often high-profile) stand-alone decisions or changes in course in a variety of areas than by a consistent defining thrust in a few. On affirmative action, the Court—in a deeply divided opinion that saw four justices agree with the swing-vote Justice Powell on one key question and the other four justices agree with Justice Powell on the other key question—supported the use of race as one factor in decisions about college and university admissions but struck down systems that mechanically used race as the sole or determining factor. This decision, *Regents of the University of California v. Bakke*, 438 U.S. 265 (1978), proved to be incredibly controversial, spawning not only a series of related examinations of racial preferences in employment by the Court during the 1980s and 1990s but also prompting a full-scale reappraisal (and, ultimately, reaffirmation) of affirmative action in higher education as late as 2003. On gay rights, the Court upheld a state law criminalizing sodomy between consenting adults in *Bowers v. Hardwick*, 478 U.S. 186 (1986). Although the law punished both heterosexual and homosexual sodomy, the majority opinion framed the issue as one of the "right to engage in homosexual sodomy," a right it found was not encompassed by the right to privacy. Coming at a time when the gay rights movement was still nascent, the decision delivered a blow to gay and lesbian

equality; as education and awareness of gay and lesbian issues increased, however, the decision was eventually overturned in 2003. In both instances, the Burger Court issued a landmark ruling on a controversial issue and then, effectively, left the issue alone; in both instances, however, the issue would return to the Court at a later date, with the Burger Court's core holding surviving in the case of affirmative action but discarded in the case of gay rights.

In three other controversial areas, the Court handed down important decisions only to retreat from them within a short time. On sex discrimination, the Court suggested that gender was a "suspect classification" deserving of "strict" scrutiny in the context of the equal protection clause of Amendment XIV in *Frontiero v. Richardson*, 411 U.S. 677 (1973) before creating a new "quasi-suspect" level of classification and "intermediate" scrutiny only three years later in *Craig v. Boren*, 429 U.S. 190 (1976). On capital punishment, the justices memorably declared the death penalty, a sentence applied somewhat arbitrarily and beset with racial disparities, to be a violation of Amendment VIII's ban on cruel and unusual punishment in *Furman v. Georgia*, 408 U.S. 238 (1972); it subsequently reconsidered the issue—and lifted what had been an effective moratorium on the death penalty in the states—by outlining more specific constitutional standards in *Gregg v. Georgia*, 428 U.S. 153 (1976). On federalism, a slim majority ruled in *National League of Cities v. Usery*, 426 U.S. 833 (1976) that Amendment X forbade Congress from regulating matters that were considered "traditional governmental functions" of the states before reversing course and calling that approach "unsound in principle and unworkable in practice" in *Garcia v. San Antonio Metropolitan Transit Authority*, 469 U.S. 528 (1985). In the first two instances, the Court's about-face resulted in a more conservative ruling that, though modified slightly, remained fundamentally intact. In the case of federalism, the Court settled on a more liberal—more favorable to national power, less solicitous of states' rights—position, but its decision would serve only as a precursor to the Rehnquist Court's more sustained and aggressive attempt to recalibrate the balance between federal and state power in the 1990s.

The Rehnquist Court, 1986–2005

Chief Justice Burger's retirement in 1986 (to serve as chairman of the Commission on the Bicentennial of the Constitution) presented Ronald Reagan with his second opportunity to shape the Court. Proposing to elevate Associate Justice William Rehnquist—who had delighted conservatives with his support of school prayer, his opposition to abortion, and his attempt in *National League of Cities* to devolve government power back to the states—to the chief justiceship, Reagan actually shaped it doubly. First, by placing Rehnquist in the Court's center chair, Reagan gave the experienced jurist additional resources (speaking first in conference, assigning opinions when he was in the majority) to continue the conservative transformation of the institution. Second, by filling Rehnquist's old seat with committed conservative federal appellate judge Antonin Scalia, who was projected to be a more aggressive and reliable conservative than Burger (the justice he was effectively replacing), Reagan shifted the ideology of the Court as a whole to the right.

With the retirement of the moderate Lewis Powell in 1987, the president attempted to cement that shift even further with a staunchly conservative appointment. His first nominee, federal appellate judge Robert Bork, sparked substantial controversy over both his past political behavior (as acting attorney general during Watergate, he executed Nixon's order to fire Special Prosecutor Archibald Cox) and his likely judicial rulings (Democratic senators and liberal advocacy groups alleged that Bork would vote to reverse key civil rights decisions as well as undercut the right to privacy). As a result, the Senate ultimately rejected the nomination in one of the more caustic confirmation battles in American history. Reagan's second choice, federal appellate judge Douglas Ginsburg, also found himself embroiled in controversy—this time over the revelation that he had smoked marijuana both as a student and a professor—before withdrawing his name from consideration. Ultimately, after the seat had remained vacant for more than seven months, Reagan turned to federal appellate judge Anthony Kennedy, a seemingly less conservative—but also less controversial—nominee whom the Senate confirmed without a dissenting vote.

If Reagan's failure to solidify the Court's conservative bona fides with a heavyweight like Bork angered Republicans, then George H. W. Bush's failure to capitalize on the 1990 retirement of the Court's leading liberal, William Brennan, surprised them. With Brennan extending Warren Court ideology throughout the 1970s and 1980s, the opportunity to replace him with a more conservative jurist presented a unique chance to push the Court substantially to the right with a single appointment. But with the Bork and Ginsburg debacles fresh in his mind, Bush reached for an easily confirmable nominee in federal appellate judge David Souter. Although Souter came highly recommended by New Hampshire senator Warren Rudman and White House chief of staff (and former New Hampshire governor) John Sununu, he was regarded as a "stealth" nominee—one who, while deemed a reliable conservative by his Granite State supporters, would not provide the kind of paper trail Democrats could use to undermine his confirmation. While Souter was confirmed easily, he did not prove to be conservative in the least, siding more often than not with the liberal wing of the Court.

The year following Brennan's replacement by Souter, the Court's other liberal—the legendary Thurgood Marshall—retired, offering Bush a second chance to name a justice to the bench. Of course, replacing the first and (to that point) only African American to serve on the Court—and one who, as a lawyer, had famously and successfully argued before the Court in *Brown v. Board of Education of Topeka (I)*, 347 U.S. 483 (1954)—was a delicate matter. Bush responded by nominating federal appellate judge and former chairman of the Equal Employment Opportunity Commission Clarence Thomas, an African American whose policy positions could not have been more different from those of his predecessor. Following a bruising, highly publicized, and highly contentious confirmation battle that saw one of his former employees accuse him of sexual harassment and senators pointedly question his policy positions, Thomas joined a Court of seven other Republican appointees (only Byron White, nominated by John F. Kennedy, had been appointed by a Democrat) at the age of 43, promising to bring his brand of originalist judicial philosophy and conservative political ideology to the Court for decades to come.

Although the Rehnquist Court era formally began with Rehnquist's elevation in 1986, the Rehnquist Court that will be remembered in history is the one that began in 1994 and lasted—without a single change in membership—a full 11 years until the death of Rehnquist in 2005. That Court, completed by Bill Clinton's largely uncontroversial appointments of federal appellate judges Ruth Bader Ginsburg and Stephen Breyer (both moderate Democrats) to replace Byron White and Harry Blackmun in 1993 and 1994, respectively, consisted of seven Republican appointees and two Democratic appointees, yet it routinely divided along 5–4 lines on controversial issues. Sorting out these issues over the course of a prolonged period of stable membership, the Court made its mark in the closing years of the twentieth century and the opening years of the twenty-first. Its legacy was substantively different from that left by the Warren Court, but it may ultimately be regarded as equally forceful and similarly transformative.

Unquestionably, the jewel in the Rehnquist Court's jurisprudential crown was federalism. From instituting (essentially for the first time since the New Deal) limits on congressional exercise of commerce clause authority in *United States v. Lopez*, 514 U.S. 549 (1995) and *United States v. Morrison*, 529 U.S. 598 (2000) to emphasizing the "dual sovereignty" component of the Constitution's federal structure in *Printz v. United States*, 521 U.S. 898 (1997) to infusing new life into Amendment XI idea of "state sovereign immunity" in *Alden v. Maine*, 527 U.S. 706 (1999), a bare majority of the Rehnquist Court justices—the so-called federalism five of Rehnquist, O'Connor, Scalia, Kennedy, and Thomas—set out to shrink the scope of federal government authority and return power to the states. When a physically weakened Rehnquist was unable to convince Justice Scalia and Justice Kennedy to join the rest of the federalism five in striking down a federal statute criminalizing the use of medical marijuana (a practice several states had condoned) in *Gonzales v. Raich*, 545 U.S. 1 (2005), it appeared that the federalism revolution—the heart of the Rehnquist Court's vision—was over. Whether the pre-*Raich* federalism decisions will lead to the type of enduring decentralization and localism

desired by spirited advocates of federalism or whether those decisions were effectively undermined by *Raich* is open to debate, but, at least in the 1990s, they displayed the Court's willingness to challenge both Congress and enduring liberal precedents as part of a sustained and thorough reconsideration of the vertical division of power in American politics.

The Rehnquist Court also displayed a willingness to reconsider previous decisions and intervene in a variety of political disputes in other jurisprudential areas as well. On separation of powers, the Court moved away from the formalist conception of the Burger Court to adopt a more flexible and pragmatic approach by upholding the constitutionality of an independent counsel to investigate executive branch wrongdoing in *Morrison v. Olson*, 487 U.S. 654 (1988), condoning the creation of the United States Sentencing Commission in *Mistretta v. United States*, 488 U.S. 361 (1989), and denying the president absolute immunity from a civil suit stemming from actions before he took office in *Clinton v. Jones*, 520 U.S. 681 (1997). On gay rights, the justices directly overturned *Bowers* by striking down a Texas ban on homosexual sodomy in *Lawrence v. Texas*, 539 U.S. 558 (2003). On gender discrimination, they struck down the all-male admissions policy at the Virginia Military Institute, subtly elevating the burden required to sustain a gender classification from a "substantial relationship to an important governmental objection" (as *Craig v. Boren* had required) to an "exceedingly persuasive justification" in *United States v. Virginia*, 518 U.S. 515 (1997). On affirmative action, the Court heard two cases—*Gratz v. Bollinger*, 539 U.S. 244 (2003) and *Grutter v. Bollinger*, 539 U.S. 306 (2003)—that forced a reevaluation of *Bakke* but ultimately decided them in such a way that was largely consistent with the Burger Court's previous ruling that race could be a consideration but not the single determinative factor in admissions. On private property, it broadened the previously narrow concept of a "taking," and thus strengthened the protections of Amendment V, with its decisions in *Nollan v. California Coastal Commission*, 483 U.S. 825 (1987), *Lucas v. South Carolina Coastal Council*, 505 U.S. 1003 (1992), and *Dolan v. City of Tigard*, 512 U.S.

374 (1994) before allowing a municipal government to use its power of eminent domain to transfer property from one private citizen to another for the purpose of economic redevelopment in *Kelo v. City of New London*, 545 U.S. 469 (2005). On freedom of speech, majorities struck down legislation banning flag burning in *Texas v. Johnson*, 491 U.S. 397 (1989) and *United States v. Eichman*, 496 U.S. 310 (1990), cross burning in *R.A.V. v. City of St. Paul*, 505 U.S. 377 (1992) and *Virginia v. Black*, 538 U.S. 343 (2003), and pornography in *Reno v. ACLU*, 521 U.S. 844 (1997) and *Ashcroft v. Free Speech Coalition*, 535 U.S. 234 (2002). On the freedom of religion, the Court continued its assault on prayer at school-related events such as graduation ceremonies and football games in *Lee v. Weisman*, 505 U.S. 577 (1992) and *Santa Fe Independent School District v. Doe*, 530 U.S. 290 (2005); forbade the use of certain religious symbols at public buildings in *Allegheny County v. ACLU*, 492 U.S. 573 (1989) and *McCreary County v. ACLU*, 545 U.S. 844 (2005); approved the use of vouchers for schools with religious affiliations in *Zelman v. Simmons-Harris*, 536 U.S. 639 (2002); and rejected the idea that religious behavior was immune from the requirements of secular laws in *Employment Division v. Smith*, 536 U.S. 639 (1990).

The Court was no less active on issues touching on the personal matters of life and death. On the "right to die," it acknowledged the existence of a right to refuse lifesaving medical treatment—but only if the patient was competent enough to exercise the right—in *Cruzan v. Director, Missouri Department of Health*, 497 U.S. 261 (1990) but then later distinguished between a physician allowing death and actively causing death (even if for noble reasons) in upholding state bans on physician-assisted suicide in *Vacco v. Quill*, 521 U.S. 793 (1997) and *Washington v. Glucksberg*, 521 U.S. 702 (1997). On abortion, the Court decided a series of high-profile cases that had the effect of limiting abortion without wholly proscribing it. In *Webster v. Reproductive Health Services*, 492 U.S. 490 (1989), it upheld a series of challenged provisions in a Missouri law, including prohibitions on government doctors performing abortions on viable fetuses and the use of public funds to counsel abortion, without

reconsidering the central holding of *Roe v. Wade*, 410 U.S. 113 (1973). In *Planned Parenthood of Southeastern Pennsylvania v. Casey*, 505 U.S. 833 (1992), three justices—O'Connor, Kennedy, and Souter—jointly authored a majority opinion that continued to operate at the margins of *Roe*, striking down one Pennsylvania provision (requiring married women seeking abortions to notify their husbands beforehand) as an "undue burden" on the woman's right to choose but upholding four others, including parental consent for minors to obtain an abortion and a 24-hour waiting period for all abortions. In *Stenberg v. Carhart*, 530 U.S. 914 (2000), Justice O'Connor joined the Court's liberal wing to strike down a state ban on late-term abortion because it lacked an exception for the health of the mother, an issue that would return to the Roberts Court—and emerge with a different resolution—in 2007.

Perhaps most important, the Rehnquist Court demonstrated that it was unafraid to assert judicial prerogatives either against other political actors or in highly controversial situations. The former was made clear in *Boerne v. Flores*, 521 U.S. 507 (1997), which, though ostensibly a religious exercise case, saw the Court declare its constitutional interpretations supreme vis-à-vis the other branches of government. The latter occurred in the case with the odd distinction of being simultaneously one of the most politically consequential and one of the most jurisprudentially insignificant judgments in Supreme Court history: *Bush v. Gore*, 531 U.S. 98 (2000). Ending the recount ordered by Florida law, the decision effectively ended the near-deadlocked presidential election in favor of George W. Bush. Finding that the Florida supreme court's method for recounting ballots represented a violation of the equal protection clause of Amendment XIV, the unsigned opinion was a source of great national intrigue, with many assuming—correctly, it turned out—that the five Republican-leaning justices (Rehnquist, O'Connor, Scalia, Kennedy, and Thomas) had voted to stop the recount while the four Democratic-leaning justices (Stevens, Souter, Ginsburg, and Breyer) had voted to let it continue. This decision, of course, not only placed a Republican in the White House for the first time in eight years but also placed in the White House the president who would, albeit after a successful reelection effort in 2004, make the next pair of appointments to the Court.

The Roberts Court, Beginning in 2005

After more than a decade of operating with no personnel changes, 2005 brought new blood to the Court. Justice O'Connor's retirement announcement in July of that year signaled the end of a "natural Court" on which the justices had grown quite accustomed to one another, and Chief Justice Rehnquist's death two months later signaled the formal end of Rehnquist Court. At first, George W. Bush nominated federal appellate judge John Roberts to replace O'Connor, but once Rehnquist died from complications related to thyroid cancer, the president withdrew Roberts's nomination as an associate justice and resubmitted it for the center seat. Although Roberts, a former Rehnquist clerk, sparked some opposition among Democrats, he was confirmed easily. With O'Connor's seat still vacant, Bush initially turned to his White House counsel Harriet Miers. When members of both parties suggested that Miers was not a suitable or distinguished enough nominee, however, the president—supposedly at Miers's request—withdrew her name from consideration, offering federal appellate judge Samuel Alito in her place only days later. Presumably because the ideological difference between the conservative Alito and the moderate O'Connor was perceived to be much greater than the ideological difference between the conservative Roberts and the conservative Rehnquist, Alito faced strong opposition from Democrats but was ultimately confirmed by a 16-vote margin. With Roberts keeping the chief justiceship in the hands of a conservative and Alito actually moving the median vote on the Court rightward (at least on certain issues) from O'Connor to Kennedy, Republicans both maintained the strong representation on the Court they had worked for in the 1980s and 1990s as well as extended their control of the Supreme Court into the twenty-first century with two new, young, and seemingly dependable conservative justices.

Although the first few years of the Roberts Court certainly witnessed significant decisions, it is difficult to assess exactly what those decisions add up to or to

determine exactly what type of tribunal the Court will be under new leadership. What is clear from its high-profile decisions is that the Roberts Court is—and will presumably continue to be—predominantly conservative. In *Gonzales v. Carhart*, 550 U.S. 124 (2007), the Court, without Justice O'Connor's vote to strike down any abortion restriction that did not include an exception for the health of the mother, effectively overturned *Stenberg* by upholding a federal ban on late-term abortion. In *Parents Involved in Community Schools v. Seattle School District No. 1*, 551 U.S. 701 (2007), the Court, without Justice O'Connor's attachment to her judicial idol Lewis Powell's *Bakke* construction, asserted that the logic of *Gratz* and *Grutter* did not apply to public high school students and applied strict scrutiny in striking down an attempt to gain greater racial diversity in public school as a violation of the equal protection clause. In *Crawford v. Marion County Election Board*, 553 U.S. ___ (2008), the justices upheld an Indiana law requiring photo identification in order to vote, raising concerns about precisely the types of discriminatory treatment in the democratic process that the Warren Court had sought to rectify in the 1960s. Finally, in *District of Columbia v. Heller*, 554 U.S. ___ (2008), the Court—in the first significant Amendment II case in almost seventy years—held that the "right to bear arms" was, indeed, an individual, as opposed to solely a collective, right.

In a regime that displayed largely conservative tendencies, issues surrounding terrorism and national security proved to be one surprising area of victories for liberals during the early years of the Roberts Court. Going further than the Rehnquist Court had gone in *Hamdi v. Rumsfeld*, 542 U.S. 507 (2004), which determined that American citizens deemed "enemy combatants" must be accorded basic due process rights, the

Roberts Court declared in *Hamdan v. Rumsfeld*, 548 U.S. 557 (2006) that military commissions could not be used to try suspected terrorists unless designed in accordance with the Geneva Conventions and the Uniform Code of Military Justice. Two years later, in *Boumediene v. Bush*, 553 U.S. ___ (2008), a bare five-justice majority of the Court's four traditional liberal votes and Justice Kennedy held that the Military Commissions Act of 2006 unconstitutionally deprived detainees of their right to habeas corpus. While this represented only one jurisprudential area, the lingering cloud of the War on Terror made issues of security and liberty an increasingly important area in an increasingly unpredictable—and dangerous—world.

Although the last quarter of the twentieth century and the early years of the twenty-first likely did not yield the wholesale transformation of American constitutional law for which conservatives had hoped, they did witness an indisputable and momentous shift in the character of the Supreme Court and its rulings. With Republicans winning five of eight presidential elections from 1976 to 2004, and with Republican presidents appointing 8 of 10 justices (even if they did not all turn out to be conservatives) from 1976 to 2006, the liberal Warren Court icons—Earl Warren, Hugo Black, William O. Douglas, William Brennan, and Thurgood Marshall—seemed but vestiges of a bygone era. With the Court growing both more conservative and more aggressive with each new chief justice, the liberal legacy of the Warren Court on issues such as racial equality and criminal procedure seem but a distant memory.

Bibliography and Further Reading

Belsky, Martin H., ed. *The Rehnquist Court: A Retrospective.* New York: Oxford University Press, 1996.

Blasi, Vincent. *The Burger Court: The Counter-Revolution That Wasn't.* New Haven, CT: Yale University Press, 1983.

Greenburg, Jan Crawford. *Supreme Conflict: The Inside Story of the Struggle for Control of the United States Supreme Court.* New York: Penguin, 2007.

Kahn, Ronald. *The Supreme Court and Constitutional Theory, 1953–1993.* Lawrence: University Press of Kansas, 1994.

Keck, Thomas M. *The Most Activist Supreme Court in History: The Road to Modern Judicial Conservatism.* Chicago: University of Chicago Press, 2004.

Lazarus, Edward. *Closed Chambers: The Rise, Fall, and Future of the Modern Supreme Court.* New York: Penguin, 1999.

Maltz, Earl, ed. *Rehnquist Justice: Understanding the Court Dynamic.* Lawrence: University Press of Kansas, 2003.

Savage, David G. *Turning Right: The Making of the Rehnquist Court.* New York: Wiley, 1992.

Toobin, Jeffrey. *The Nine: Inside the Secret World of the Supreme Court.* New York: Doubleday, 2007.

Tushnet, Mark. *A Court Divided: The Rehnquist Court and the Future of Constitutional Law.* New York: W. W. Norton, 2005.

Woodward, Bob, and Scott Armstrong. *The Brethren: Inside the Supreme Court.* New York: Simon & Schuster, 1979.

Justin Crowe

TAX POLICY

Tax policy is one of the fundamental issues dividing the conservative and liberal viewpoints, and thus it has played a vital role in American political history. Conservatives generally hold a negative view of taxation as the confiscation of private property, and they typically advocate a small government, with taxes being used only to finance essential government services such as national defense, a court system, and police protection. Liberals, meanwhile, see taxation as an important tool of public policy to influence behavior and redistribute income toward the poor. Yet despite these two distinct philosophies, both views have been repeatedly obscured as politicians from both parties have used tax incentives and government spending to win the support of influential interest groups and voters.

The Purposes of Taxation

In the postwar period, tax policy in the United States has been directed toward five general purposes. First, the traditional purpose of taxation is for the government to raise revenues in order to finance its expenditures, such as for military, infrastructure, or social services. Second, since the development of Keynesian economics during the Great Depression, taxation has been viewed as a tool of fiscal policy to manipulate demand in the economy in order to smooth business cycles. Third, tax policy has been used as a means to redistribute income between various groups of Americans. A fourth purpose of tax policy, which developed after World War II, is to use tax incentives in order to promote or discourage certain behaviors. For example, in describing some tax regulations in the mid-1980s, the economist Alan Blinder notes that one could pay less federal income tax by owning rather than renting a home, by borrowing rather than lending, by living in exclusive neighborhoods with high property taxes, by investing in municipal rather than corporate bonds, by receiving more fringe benefits such as health insurance in place of income, by saving for retirement, by investing in natural resources, by receiving capital gains rather than interest income, and so on. However, many of these benefits would only be available to those who itemize their deductions rather than taking the standard deduction. Finally, an unfortunate fifth purpose of tax policy has been for politicians to gain votes and campaign contributions by inserting modifications into the tax code to bring special rewards for their constituents, to appease lobbyists, and to provide favors to important political donors. The final two reasons have contributed to the massively complex tax system that exists in the United States today.

The Amount and Distribution of Federal Taxation

As a percentage of the gross domestic product (GDP), the amount of tax revenues collected since 1976 has been relatively consistent. The U.S. Office of Management and Budget (OMB) reports that total tax collections as a percentage of GDP rose from 17.2 percent in 1976 to 18.8 percent in 2007. The highest year for tax revenues occurred in 2000, when it stood at 20.9 percent of GDP, and the low point was in 2004, when it was 16.4 percent. Budget deficits were a feature of this time period because taxes collected were less than expenditures from 1976 to 1997, and again from 2002 to the present.

As for the percentage breakdown among various tax categories, the OMB indicates that in 1976, 44.2 percent of government revenues came from individual income taxes, 30.5 percent from social insurance and retirement receipts, 13.9 percent from corporate income taxes, 5.7 from excise taxes, and 5.8 percent from other sources. Over time, these sources remained relatively stable: by 2007, 45.3 percent of revenues came from individual taxes, followed by 33.9 percent from social insurance and retirement receipts, 14.4 percent from corporate income taxes, 2.5 percent from excise taxes, and 3.9 percent from other sources. Nonetheless, this stability masks a great deal of change in tax laws and tax rates during this time period. On some occasions, tax rates were increased to raise additional revenues or make the tax system more progressive; at other times, tax rates were reduced in order to promote economic efficiency or simplify the tax code.

Tax Policy in the Late 1970s and Early 1980s

By the late 1970s, opposition to high taxes grew considerably in the United States. In 1978, a taxpayer revolt in California limited how much local property taxes could be raised. The Revenue Act of 1978 reduced capital gains taxes, which propelled the growth of the venture capital industry. A remaining problem was that high inflation and a lack of indexing in the tax system meant that people were being pushed into higher tax brackets. Inflation also unfairly impacted the taxation of interest and capital gains. To see why, consider the case of capital gains. If the value of an investment doubles but also coincides with a doubling of prices in the economy, then the investment has not increased in real terms, as it will only be able to purchase the same amount of goods and services as before. However, the tax system of the 1970s would treat the nominal increase in the value of the investment as taxable capital gains.

President Ronald Reagan supported the Economic Recovery Tax Act of 1981, which lowered tax rates by 25 percent, bringing the highest tax bracket down to 50 percent. The legislation ended the "bracket creep" problem of inflation pushing people into higher tax brackets, and it made some initial attempts to correct the inflation problem for investment income. But the legislation created many special incentives and loopholes, leading to an increased use of tax shelters and a perception among Americans that the rich were able to avoid paying taxes by hiring accountants and lawyers to find tax loopholes. The legislation also significantly reduced corporate income taxes, in effect creating subsidies for certain business investments. Once Congress realized how much revenue was being lost as a result of the corporate tax revisions, they were repealed.

Other tax changes were made to influence behavior during this time, including the creation of Individual Retirement Accounts (IRAs) in 1974 as a way to promote retirement savings by deferring taxes on contributions until retirement is reached. The Earned-Income Tax Credit, created in 1975, encourages work among low-income people by providing a tax credit on income earned. For sufficiently low incomes, this credit acts as a negative income tax by subsidizing work effort. In 1978, 401(k) retirement accounts were created as a way for employers and employees to provide tax-deferred retirement savings.

The Tax Reform Act of 1986

Though it did not completely simplify the tax process, the Tax Reform Act of 1986 provides a rare instance of success for politicians in designing a fair and sensible tax policy and confronting the special interest groups that had made taxes so complicated. The tax reform cut marginal income tax rates and closed thousands of tax deductions and loopholes. The top marginal tax rates on income decreased from 50 percent to 28 percent. The standard deduction and personal exemptions increased, which helped low-income people and increased the threshold before which middle-income people needed to worry about whether they had to itemize their deductions in order to minimize their tax bill. Corporate tax rates also fell, with the top rate decreasing from 46 percent to 34 percent. Some of the significant tax loopholes were eliminated or reduced, including the exclusion for long-term capital gains, the investment tax credit, deductions for state and local sales taxes, and deductions for credit card interest, medical expenses, and business meals and entertainment. Though beneficiaries of these deductions were not pleased about the changes, this process helped to expand the tax base, which is what allowed for tax rates to decrease without losing revenues for the government. Nonetheless, many deductions remained because they were too politically sensitive, including those for employer-provided fringe benefits, state and local income taxes, and mortgage interest payments. The reform also kept the complicated Alternative Minimum Tax, which provides a separate way to calculate federal income taxes owed to ensure that wealthy individuals cannot avoid paying tax through the use of many tax credits and exemptions, and which is presently affecting more and more Americans because it is not adjusted for inflation.

Several important factors contributed to this legislation's success. First, the act was maintained as a unified whole, with most people kept in the same boat of losing special advantages but also gaining lower tax rates. Marketing the highest marginal tax rate as 28 percent undoubtedly made the legislation more palatable to those standing to lose special favors. Amendments to the legislation were also required to be revenue neutral, so that a politician who asked for an additional tax break would also have to find a way to increase taxes elsewhere. This made it harder for special interests to complain and get their way.

Tax Reform in the 1990s and 2000s

Many of the simplifications created by the 1986 Tax Reform Act would not survive for long. By the 1990s, tax rates were again increasing, and politicians began creating more special tax incentives and exclusions to appease special interests. Between 1987 and 2005, almost fifteen thousand changes were made to the federal tax code. The 1990s witnessed the introduction of more tax incentives to promote various types of sav-

RELATED ENTRIES

THIS VOLUME
Economic Policy, Fiscal and Budgetary Policy

OTHER VOLUMES
Tax Policy (vols. 5 & 6)

ings, such as for medical costs in 1996 (Medical Savings Accounts) and education expenses (Education IRAs and the Section 529 Qualified Tuition Program). The Roth IRA was introduced in 1997 as another retirement savings option in which after-tax contributions could be made and the investment returns could be distributed tax-free. The Earned-Income Tax Credit for low-income workers was also expanded. At the same time, the taxation for Social Security benefits was increased in order to discourage continued part-time work after retirement. In 1996, Steve Forbes ran an unsuccessful but noteworthy presidential campaign that mainly centered on introducing a vastly simplified flat tax to the United States, and the publicity garnished by his campaign demonstrated the desire Americans feel for a simpler tax system.

The Economic Growth and Tax Relief Reconciliation Act of 2001 and the Jobs and Growth Tax Relief Reconciliation Act of 2003 lowered tax rates on income, dividends, and capital gains, raised limits for retirement plan contributions, increased child tax credits, and provided other changes. But these changes will expire at the end of 2010 and without political action, the tax system will revert to its 2000 form. In 2005, Pres. George W. Bush's Advisory Panel on Federal Tax Reform proposed a number of changes to make the tax system simpler, fairer, and less distortionary, but serious legislative action was not taken on these recommendations.

The U.S. tax system remains complex. Simplifying it is difficult because although society as a whole would benefit from the removal of various special deductions, the gains to each individual would be too small to entice them to political action, while the losses to those receiving the special benefits would be large, leading them to lobby and plead with politicians for continued favor. Alan Blinder argues that, for this reason, tax policy that would make good economic sense by improving both efficiency and equity often makes for bad politics. Nonetheless, the Tax Reform Act of 1986 does show the potential for successful reform. Tax policy will certainly continue to play a pivotal role in American politics.

Bibliography and Further Reading

Blinder, Alan S. *Hard Heads, Soft Hearts: Tough Minded Economics for a Just Society*. Cambridge, MA: Perseus, 1987.

Birnbaum, Jeffrey H., and Alan S. Murray. *Showdown at Gucci Gulch: Lawmakers, Lobbyists, and the Unlikely Triumph of Tax Reform*. New York: Random House, 1987.

Gordon, John Steele. *An Empire of Wealth: The Epic History of American Power*. New York: HarperCollins, 2004.

Gruber, Jonathan. *Public Finance and Public Policy*, 2nd edition. New York: Worth Publishers, 2007.

Heilbroner, Robert L., and Aaron Singer. *The Economic Transformation of America: 1600 to the Present*, 4th edition. Fort Worth, TX: Harcourt Brace College Publishers, 1999.

President's Advisory Panel on Federal Tax Reform. *Simple, Fair, and Pro-Growth: Proposals to Fix America's Tax System*. Washington, D.C.: President's Advisory Panel on Federal Tax Reform, 2005.

Rosen, Harvey S., and Ted Gayer. *Public Finance*, 8th edition. New York: McGraw-Hill, 2008.

U.S. Office of Management and Budget. *Historical Tables, Budget of the United States Government, Fiscal Year 2009*. Washington, D.C.: U.S. Government Printing Office, 2008. http://www.whitehouse.gov/omb/budget/fy2009/pdf/hist.pdf (accessed January 24, 2009).

Wade Donald Pfau

TELEVISION

See Cable Television and Talk Radio; Network Television and Newspapers

THIRD PARTIES

Between 1976 and 2008, new political parties in the United States were launched at a rate not seen since the 1890s. Also, in the period starting in 1976, the United States saw a new phenomenon, the rise of the prominent independent presidential candidate.

The immediate cause for these developments was the Watergate scandal of 1973–1974, when a massive number of voters who usually had full confidence in the integrity of high officials in the government lost that confidence. The Republican Party's share of the vote cast for elections to the U.S. House in 1974 was the lowest in that party's history, even lower than the party's earlier nadir in 1934 and 1936. The number of new parties continued to grow in the 1980s and 1990s. The post–Cold War world has presented the United States with many perplexing problems, and there is no consensus on how to solve many of them. Also, the nation is more diverse than it has ever been, with a substantial proportion of the U.S. population adhering to religions other than Christianity and Judaism. Increasingly, the United States is a nation far too diverse to expect all its political life to fit into just two political parties.

The Rise of Independent Presidential Candidates

In 1974, in a little-noticed U.S. Supreme Court decision (*Storer v. Brown*, 415 U.S. 724), the U.S. Supreme Court said it is unconstitutional for states to have no procedures for independent candidates to get on the ballot. A former U.S. senator from Minnesota, Eugene McCarthy, noticed this decision, and in December 1974 he announced that he would be an independent presidential candidate in 1976. He also said that he would sue the 12 states that didn't permit independent presidential candidates to get on the ballot. McCarthy was a well-known figure in the 1970s. Virtually everyone remembered that he had challenged Pres. Lyndon Johnson in the Democratic presidential primary in New Hampshire in March 1968, on a platform of ending U.S. military involvement in Vietnam. After McCarthy almost won that presidential primary, President Johnson announced on March 31, 1968 that he would not run for reelection, which was one of the most surprising developments in U.S. political history. McCarthy did not receive the Democratic nomination in 1968, but he was widely credited with altering the outcome.

McCarthy did run as an independent for president in 1976, making him the first actual independent presidential candidate in U.S. history, unless one considers George Washington to have been an independent candidate. Previously, candidates who ran for president in the general election outside the two major parties had always been nominees of a new political party, or of an existing minor political party, because the ballot access laws (which came into existence in the 1890s) required presidential candidates to be political party nominees.

McCarthy gained a spot on the ballot in 29 states. Generally, he did not qualify in the other 21 states because they required too many signatures, and McCarthy's campaign funds were so limited that he could not afford to hire paid petitioners. He polled 756,691 votes, which was .93 percent of the total vote cast. In California, where he wasn't able to get on the ballot, he still polled 58,412 write-in votes, a record (for write-ins) for any presidential candidate in any state in a general election.

McCarthy's legal victories in 1976, which forced all the states to permit independent presidential candidates, opened the door for a more successful independent presidential candidate in 1980. John B. Anderson of Illinois, a Republican leader in the U.S. House of Representatives, was considered to be a liberal Republican. He ran in the Republican 1980 presidential primaries in February, March, and early April, doing well but not winning any. By mid-March 1980, it was clear that Ronald Reagan was going to be the Republican presidential nominee. Anderson, at the urging of his supporters, dropped out of the Republican race on April 24 and declared that he would instead be an independent candidate for president. Anderson drew support from Republicans who believed that Reagan was too conservative, and he also drew support from Democrats who were disenchanted with Pres. Jimmy Carter, who was running for reelection. Anderson got on the ballot in all 50 states and the District of Columbia, and he polled 5,720,060 votes, or 6.61 percent of the total.

Anderson succeeded in getting on the ballots of all the states only because he won a number of ballot access lawsuits. By the time he had announced in April 1980, the deadline for filing as an independent presidential candidate had passed in five states. But Anderson sued those states (Kentucky, Maine, Maryland, Ohio, and New Mexico), and he won all five lawsuits. The federal courts noted that throughout U.S. history, many new and minor party presidential candidates had only emerged after the two major parties had made their choices. The courts said that voters had a right to vote for someone who might only get into the race in the middle of an election year. The U.S. Supreme Court decision that affirmed this principle was *Anderson v. Celebrezze*, 460 US 780 (1983), which addressed the filing deadline in Ohio.

Just as McCarthy's legal victories had cleared the way for the Anderson campaign, the Anderson campaign cleared the way for a still bigger independent presidential campaign, that of Ross Perot in 1992. Perot had never run for elected public office, but he was well known to the public for his business success, and for his daring rescue of his own company's employees from Iran in the tumultuous period in 1980 when U.S. diplomats in Iran were held hostage. He had also won many friends by championing the interests of U.S. military personnel held prisoner in Vietnam. When Perot was a guest on the Larry King TV interview show on February 20, King asked him, "Can you give me a scenario in which you'd say, 'OK, I'm in?'" Perot said he would run as an independent if people got him on the ballot in all 50 states. And people did. Perot set up campaign offices in hundreds of cities across the nation and supplied volunteers with blank petition forms. The first poll that mentioned Perot showed him at 9 percent, but by early June the polls showed him narrowly winning the election against Pres. George H. W. Bush, with the Democratic nominee, Bill Clinton, far behind in third place (in June, Clinton hadn't been nominated yet, but it was well known he would be nominated the following month).

Once the major parties realized that Perot had the potential to win the election, they started campaigning against him, pointing out his personal characteristics that seemed to show he wasn't completely in touch with reality. He was ridiculed for seeming to believe that armed black militants had once jumped the fence around his home in Dallas, and also because he seemed to believe that Republican campaign consultants were doctoring photos to make it appear that one of his daughters was a lesbian. The pressure of these attempts seemed to diminish his enthusiasm for running, and on July 16, in the middle of the Democratic National Convention, Perot said he was withdrawing from the race. However, in the handful of states in which his petitions were still circulating, they continued to circulate. On October 1, Perot reentered the race. The first poll held after he came back in to the race showed him at 7 percent. But, because he was invited into all three presidential debates and because he did well in all of them, his support rose again. He was especially effective when he argued that the national debt was dangerously large and that budget deficits must be curtailed. He appeared on the ballot in all states and the District of Columbia, and he polled 19,741,657 votes, or 18.91 percent. In Maine, he came in second, ahead of President Bush; in Utah, he came in second, ahead of Bill Clinton.

After the election, Perot formed a nonpartisan group called United We Stand America. In the 1994 midterm elections, the Republicans made a deliberate

Independent candidate Ross Perot answers a question at the second presidential debate as incumbent Pres. George H. W. Bush and Democratic contender Bill Clinton, then the governor of Arkansas, look on. Perot was invited to participate in all three presidential debates, and his solid performance in each of them, in which he focused on the dangers of the increasing national debt and budget deficits, bolstered his support and garnered him nearly 19 percent of the vote nationally. (Cynthia Johnson/Time Life Pictures/Getty Images)

attempt to woo the Perot voters, by emphasizing that if Republicans won a majority in Congress, they would work to pass a constitutional amendment to balance the budget, except in times of national emergency. The Republicans did win control of both houses of Congress, for the first time since 1952, but they were unable to pass the proposed constitutional amendment because they lacked a two-thirds majority and very few Democrats in Congress voted for the proposal. In September 1995, when the reputation of the new Republican Congress was at a low ebb because the budget stalemate had led to a partial shutdown of the federal government, Perot announced that he was launching a new political party, the Independence Party. A few weeks later, he announced that because some states wouldn't permit a party to use that name (because it would confuse the voters by its similarity to "independent candidate"), he changed the name to the Reform Party.

The Reform Party

Perot's new Reform Party began circulating petitions and conducting registration drives to get itself on the ballot in as many states as possible. At first, Perot said he was not interested in being the party's candidate for president in 1996. He said the party would choose a presidential candidate via an all-mail ballot, and that any voter who wished to vote in that process was free to do so. He hinted that Colin Powell would be a good presidential candidate for the Reform Party, but Powell wasn't interested in running for office under any banner. On July 9, 1996, former Colorado governor Richard Lamm, who had been a Democrat, announced that he would seek the Reform Party's nomination. Shortly afterwards, Perot said that he, also, wanted the nomination. The Perot-Lamm contest was settled in August. Perot received 32,145 votes, and Lamm received 17,121. Lamm beat Perot only in Alaska, Colorado, Minnesota, and the District of Columbia.

The Reform Party qualified for the ballot in most states, and Perot qualified as an independent candidate in the remaining states so that he again appeared on the ballot in all 50 states and the District of Columbia. This time the major parties excluded him from the presidential debates, and his support was lower than it had been in 1992. He received 8,085,402 votes, or 8.40 percent. The Reform Party was the first non-major party in U.S. history to have its presidential candidate poll over 5 percent of the vote in every state.

The Reform Party also ran candidates for the U.S. House in 13 states. Perot never seemed interested in helping his party recruit candidates for office other than president, and the party did not win any partisan races in 1996. However, in 1998, the Reform Party of Minnesota recruited Jesse Ventura, a former professional wrestler, to be its gubernatorial candidate. After months of persuasion, Ventura finally agreed. He was permitted to participate in all the gubernatorial debates, and his party did receive some public funding, and he won the election, with 37 percent of the vote.

Governor Ventura took an interest in the national affairs of the Reform Party and endorsed Jack Gargan of Florida to be the party's next National Chair. Gargan was elected. Perot, who didn't approve of Ventura, used his influence to remove Gargan at a special national convention of the Reform Party called for that purpose. Because the federal law on public funding for presidential campaigns meant that the Reform Party presidential campaign of 2000 would be eligible for $16,000,000 in federal funding, and because Perot expressed disinterest in running in 2000, an intense fight began for the Reform Party's 2000 presidential nomination. As in 1996, the nomination was to be decided by a mail ballot, with the proviso that two-thirds of the convention delegates could override the mail ballot results. John Hagelin, the presidential candidate of the Natural Law Party, jumped into the race. In addition, Pat Buchanan, who had been seeking the Republican nomination in 2000, left the Republican race in late 1999 and also declared for the Reform Party nomination. The party's national convention in Long Beach, California, in August 2000 was unruly. The mail ballot results were announced, with 49,529 votes going to Buchanan and 28,539 to Hagelin, but the results were disputed. The delegates pledged to Hagelin left the convention hall and set up their own meeting in a nearby building, and court battles were launched in many states over the true identity of the Reform Party presidential nominee. Generally, Buchanan won those battles, and he appeared on the ballot in 49 states, all but Michigan, where the secretary of state refused to list any Reform Party presidential candidate because she said she could not figure out which one to list. Buchanan, whose campaign was set back because he fell ill during September, only polled 449,077 votes, or .43 percent. This result marked the end of the Reform Party as an effective force.

The Libertarian Party

The Libertarian Party was founded in December 1971. It only appeared on the ballot in two states in 1972, but it grew rapidly, especially after David Koch, a multimillionaire, started making contributions to the party in 1978. The party was not ballot-qualified at the time in California, but it placed its gubernatorial candidate, Edward Clark, on the ballot as an independent, and he polled 5.46 percent of the vote. Also in 1978, the party elected its first state legislator, Dick Randolph, in Fairbanks, Alaska. In 1980, the party nominated Clark for president and Koch for vice president. The U.S. Supreme Court had ruled in *Buckley v. Valeo*, 424 U.S. 1 (1976) that the Constitution protects the right of a candidate to spend his or her own money on his or her own campaign, and Koch was able to spend $3 million on his campaign for vice president. This money enabled the Libertarian Party to place its national ticket on the ballot in all 50 states and the District of Columbia and made it possible for the party to buy network TV ads. The ticket polled 921,299 votes, or 1.06 percent.

Koch grew disenchanted with the Libertarian Party in 1983, when the candidate he preferred for the presidential nomination, Prof. Earl Ravenal, was defeated for the nomination by David Bergland. The party has never been able to duplicate its presidential showing of 1980. Its notable campaigns since then include 1988, 1996, and 2008. In 1988, the former Republican congressman Ron Paul (who was to return to Congress again some years after the 1988 campaign) received the party's presidential nomination. He polled 432,179 votes, or .47 percent. In 1996, the noted author Harry Browne polled 485,798 votes, or .50 percent. In 2008, the former Republican congressman Bob Barr of Georgia received 523,715 votes, or .40 percent.

Libertarian Party nominees have been elected to the state legislature of three states. In Alaska, one was elected in 1978, two in 1980, and one in 1984. In Vermont, one was elected in 1998. In New Hampshire, four were elected in 1992, two in 1994, and one in 2000. The best showing any Libertarian nominee for Congress has made was in Mississippi in 1998, when the party's nominee, William Chipman, carried Warren County in a two-party race and polled 28.84 percent in the 2nd district. In 2000, the party's candidates for the U.S. House of Representatives polled 1.77 percent of the entire national vote cast in U.S. House races. It was the first time a party other than the Democratic or Republican Parties had polled more than 1 percent of the U.S. House vote since 1948, when the nominees of Henry Wallace's Progressive Party polled 1.89 percent of the House vote.

The Green Party

Green parties in Europe were founded in the 1980s, and in many nations they did well. Thus, the idea caught hold in the United States. The first Green Party candidate who appeared on a statewide ballot with the Green Party label in the United States was Derrick Grimmer, who polled 1.17 percent in the race for Minnesota attorney general in 1986. After that, Green parties came into existence in various states, but there was no presidential candidate for the Green Party until 1996, when the party persuaded Ralph Nader to be its candidate. He was a reluctant candidate and refused to spend as much as $5,000 on the campaign, because he did not wish to be subject to Federal Election Commission campaign reporting requirements. The state Green parties did the work of petitioning for a place on the ballot, and they succeeded in placing Nader on the ballot in 23 states. He polled 685,040 votes, or .71 percent, a very impressive showing for a candidate who had refused to do much campaigning.

In 2000, the Green Party nominated Nader again, and this time he put his heart into the campaign. He appeared on the ballot in 43 states and the District of Columbia (the states in which he failed to get on the ballot, due to high petitioning requirements, were Georgia, Indiana, North Carolina, Oklahoma, Idaho, Wyoming, and South Dakota). He attracted tens of thousands to some indoor rallies during the campaign, and he polled 2,882,738 votes, or 2.74 percent, in the election. Although Nader received more votes in Florida than the margin between George W. Bush and Al Gore, and was thus accused of altering the outcome of the 2000 election, it should be noted that all eight of the minor party candidates on the Florida ballot received more than this margin as well.

Nader, somewhat uncomfortable with the Green Party, never officially joined it (or any political party). He decided to run for president in 2004, but as an independent candidate. He did not ask the Green Party for its 2004 presidential nomination, and he did not attend the national convention that year. Still, he hoped that the Green Party would draft him. But the Greens nominated David Cobb instead. Cobb only received 119,859 votes, or .10 percent. In 2008, the Greens nominated former Georgia congresswoman Cynthia McKinney, but she only polled 161,797 votes, or .12 percent.

The Green Party's most impressive showing in U.S. Senate races that had both a Democrat and a Republican in the race were in Hawaii in 1992, when Linda Martin polled 13.73 percent, and in Alaska in 1996, when Jed Whittaker outpolled the Democratic nominee and polled 12.58 percent. The party's best showing in a U.S. House race that also included both a Democrat and a Republican was in a special election in New Mexico in 1997, when Carol Miller polled 16.78 percent. The Green Party elected a state legislator in a special California election in 1999. It also elected a state legislator in Maine in 2002 and reelected him in 2004. It also elected a state legislator in Arkansas in 2008, although after his first year in office he switched his membership to the Democratic Party.

Nader's Independent Runs for the Presidency

Ralph Nader's independent candidacy in 2004 was hampered by Democratic Party attempts to keep him off the ballot. He only appeared on the ballot in 34 states, and they tended to be smaller states, so that only 50.1 percent of U.S. voters saw a ballot with Nader's name on it. He polled 465,650 votes, or .38 percent. In 2008, Nader again ran as an independent candidate. This time the Democrats did not try to keep him off

any ballots, and he ended up on the ballot in 45 states and the District of Columbia (the states that kept him off were Georgia, Indiana, North Carolina, Oklahoma, and Texas). He polled 739,034 votes, or .56 percent.

Other Minor Parties that Won Congressional or State Office

Besides the Libertarian and Green parties, a few other parties have won elections for state office since 1976. In Congressional elections since 1976, however, no party other than the Democratic and Republican Parties won any seats, unless one considers Joe Lieberman's "Connecticut for Lieberman Party" to be a real political party. It is more accurate to say that Lieberman was reelected to the U.S. Senate in 2006 as an independent candidate with the ballot label "Connecticut for Lieberman." Lieberman did not register as a member of his own party and showed no interest in holding a party meeting to select party officers, but under Connecticut election law it is a political party, with automatic ballot access for 2010 for the U.S. Senate race.

Vermont's Bernie Sanders was elected to the U.S. House in all elections from 1990 through 2004, but his ballot label was always "independent." He was elected to the U.S. Senate in 2006, again with the ballot label "independent." The Constitution Party elected a state legislator in Montana in 2006, Rick Jore. He had previously served in the Montana legislature as a Republican. The Vermont Progressive Party has been electing state legislators ever since 2000, with six being elected in 2008.

Former Republican senator Lowell Weicker was elected governor of Connecticut in 1990, on a party he created, "A Connecticut Party." He did not run for reelection in 1994, but his party's gubernatorial nominee in 1994, Eunice Groark, polled 18.88 percent. However, the party faded away after the 1996 election.

Third parties and independent presidential candidates have enjoyed just enough support in the period since 1976 to remind us that one cannot always assume with certainty that only the Democratic and Republican parties matter in U.S. elections. For this, we should be grateful. The United States is far too large and varied to fit everyone into just two political parties.

Bibliography and Further Reading

Bisnow, Mark. *Diary of a Dark Horse: the 1980 Anderson Campaign*. Carbondale: Southern Illinois University Press, 1983.

Doherty, Brian. *Radicals for Capitalism: A Freewheeling History of the American Libertarian Movement*. Cambridge, MA: Perseus, 2007.

Hawkins, Howie. *Independent Politics: The Green Party Strategy Debate*. Chicago: Haymarket Books, 1996.

Herrnson, Paul S., and John C. Green. *Multiparty Politics in America*. Lanham, MD: Rowman & Littlefield, 1997.

Martin, Justin. *Nader: Crusader, Spoiler, Icon*. Cambridge, MA, Perseus, 2002.

McCarthy, Eugene. *The Hard Years: A Look at Contemporary America and American Institutions*. New York: Viking, 1975.

Ness, Immanuel, and James Ciment. *Encyclopedia of Third Parties in America*. New York: Sharpe Reference, 2000.

Posner, Gerald. *Citizen Perot, His Life and Times*. New York: Random House, 1996.

Roth, Robert. *The Natural Law Party: A Reason to Vote*. New York: St. Martin's, 1998.

Richard Winger

TOBACCO SETTLEMENT

From 1994 to 2008, in a concerted wave of litigation, a number of private lawsuits were decided against the tobacco industry using new legal theories of torts, fraud, conspiracy, misrepresentation, breach of warranty, breach of product liability, and negligent failure to inform. Mississippi also initiated a lawsuit in 1994, eventually followed by the 49 other states and the District of Columbia. In 1998, 46 states negotiated a Master Settlement Agreement with the tobacco industry, which agreed to provide monetary damages. Due to the financial and litigation pressure of the state lawsuits the tobacco industry also made an unsuccessful attempt to negotiate a federal Global Settlement in

1997 with five state attorneys general, trial lawyers specializing in product liability, and the Campaign for Tobacco-Free Kids.

In 1994, Mississippi, Florida, Minnesota, and Texas filed lawsuits against the tobacco industry, using a new legal theory that included class action lawsuits in which statistical evidence of death and disease among a large number of smokers was utilized. This allowed the states to seek higher monetary damages, due to the larger number of plaintiffs. The new legal theory was different from the one previously used, which required direct evidence of a connection between smoking and disease or death in individual cases, often many years after an individual began using tobacco.

In the next several years, the rest of the states and the District of Columbia also filed lawsuits to recoup taxpayer-paid Medicaid costs for sick and dying smokers. By 1998, Mississippi, Texas, Florida, and Minnesota had individually settled their cases with the tobacco industry. These settlements collectively resulted in the tobacco industry paying these states $40 billion dollars over the next 25 years, restricting outdoor tobacco advertising aimed at minors, and financing anti-tobacco marketing and education efforts.

In November 1998, the other 46 states and the District of Columbia settled their lawsuits through the Master Settlement Agreement. Under the agreement, the tobacco industry agreed to pay $206 billion in monetary damages over the next 25 years. There were no requirements in the Master Settlement Agreement on how the states should spend their settlement money. In addition, the tobacco industry agreed to pay tobacco farmers an additional $5–14 billion to counter any economic hardships due to reduced tobacco use. The agreement also contained weak tobacco advertising and promotion restrictions.

The Master Settlement Agreement was publicly supported as a historic event that would curb tobacco use, but in reality this did not occur. By the middle of the first decade of the 2000s, the Master Settlement Agreement had had no significant impact in reducing tobacco sales and profits. In addition, due to the lack of funding requirements, very few states had funded state tobacco control programs from Master Settlement Agreement funds and other

Olympic figure skater and spokesperson for the Campaign For Tobacco Free Kids Tara Lipinski shakes hands with Republican senator John McCain at a rally in Washington, D.C., on May 20, 1998. McCain was the chief architect of a Senate bill that would ratify the Global Settlement as well as increase the tax on cigarettes. The bill received much opposition from within the Republican Party, and although McCain insisted a bill following the framework of his proposal would pass, it was ultimately killed thanks to the successful lobbying efforts of the tobacco industry. (Karin Cooper/Getty Images)

state funding sources at suggested minimum U.S. Centers for Disease Control and Prevention levels for tobacco control programs. Instead, most of the Master Settlement Agreement funding was merged with state revenues to fund a variety of state programs, such as public works and health care.

Due to the litigation and financial pressure from the state lawsuits, an attempted federal Global Settlement was negotiated in 1998. This proposed agreement included federal regulation of tobacco marketing and promotion, U.S. Food and Drug Administration regulation of tobacco products, a national anti-tobacco education campaign, and large monetary settlement payments to the states and private litigants. In return, the tobacco industry would receive litigation relief, including a ban on future legal punitive damages and litigation. The agreement called for the Global Settlement to be enacted into federal legislation.

The proposed settlement was controversial among public health advocates, however. Proponents of the settlement thought it would allow for considerable progress at the federal level in regulating tobacco use, while opponents believed that the legal immunity afforded the tobacco industry would halt efforts at enacting stronger future tobacco control legislation.

Greatly complicating this bitter division among public health advocates was the secret negotiation participation of the Campaign for Tobacco-Free Kids without the participation of other major health organizations.

In 1998, Sen. John McCain (R–AZ) introduced legislation to ratify the Global Settlement. However, on April 2, 1998, the Senate Commerce Committee significantly amended the original McCain bill. The amended legislation increased tobacco industry monetary settlement payments from $368.5 to $516 billion, required stricter tobacco advertising restrictions, exacted greater monetary penalties on the tobacco industry for not reducing teen smoking rates, and ended tobacco industry immunity from future class-action lawsuits. The new version of the bill was unacceptable to the tobacco industry, which successfully lobbied to kill it on June 17, 1998.

Bibliography and Further Reading

Givel, Michael. "Punctuated Equilibrium in Limbo: The Tobacco Lobby and U.S. State Policymaking From 1990 to 2003." *Policy Studies Journal* 34, no. 3 (2006): 405–418.

Givel, Michael, and Stanton A. Glantz, "The 'Global Settlement' With the Tobacco Industry: 6 Years Later." *American Journal of Public Health* 94, no. 2 (2004): 218–224.

Shatenstein, Stan. "Smoke in Their Eyes." *Tobacco Control* 10 (2001): 238.

Sloan, F., C. A. Mathews, and J. Trogdon. "Impacts of the Master Settlement Agreement on the Tobacco Industry." *Tobacco Control* 13 (2005): 356–361.

Michael Givel

TRADE POLICY

After 1976, the United States continued to set international trade policy chiefly through negotiations with other nations. While increasing trade stimulated mutually opposing forces in U.S. politics, the side favoring more liberalization tended to dominate its critics through the mid-1990s. The United States increasingly opened its market, with some exceptions, and strengthened the international rules that helped keep trade open. Trade policy expanded to cover instruments besides tariffs. During the 1990s, however, public concerns over the social consequences of globalization, or at least the way it was being managed, increased domestic resistance to any further liberalization that ignored these concerns. In the 1990s, the two parties in Congress polarized over trade more than they had in several decades. Yet trade policy remained largely open.

Setting Policy through International Negotiation

Throughout this period, the U.S. government continued to use international negotiations as the most comprehensive means for setting trade policy. Under the legal umbrella of the 1947 General Agreement on Tariffs and Trade (GATT), Washington induced other signatory nations to lower barriers facing U.S. goods by offering to cut barriers against their goods in the huge U.S. market. This reciprocal process, through a sequence of multilateral rounds, had reduced the average U.S. tariff on industrial goods from around 40 percent in 1947 to about 5 percent by the late 1980s. World trade expanded several-fold in many directions.

One of these rounds was the so-called Tokyo Round, which began in 1973. A key goal was to extend the common rules to discipline governments' use of nontariff barriers, including quotas and national purchasing programs that discriminated against foreign goods. President Carter completed this round with a 1979 agreement that cut tariffs further and disciplined nontariff barriers for the first time.

Opposing Domestic Forces and Liberal Policy, with Exceptions

Increasing trade and investment always stimulates opposing forces in U.S. politics. In this period too, as before, international trade and investment made a majority of Americans better off but a minority suffered in the short term. Those who suffered organized and expressed their opinions more intensely than those who were gaining.

Traditionally, trade politics have been dominated by organized groups and their Washington representatives battling one another, often beneath the radar of the mass media. The pro-liberalization side, which included the White House and a bipartisan coalition in Congress, won the big battles, until things changed in the 1990s. Before then, certain industries organized pressures to retard liberalization or raise barriers. Congressional sympathizers complained that other countries, especially Japan in the 1980s, were guilty of unfair practices. During the 1970s and 1980s, Washington responded by limiting trade in special cases. The government added quotas on apparel, shoes, and color television sets, as well as antidumping duties on steel imports, and demanded that other countries hold back some exports—such as cars from Japan in 1981.

More generally, some scholars also objected that international trade and investment were undermining U.S. workers and unions to the benefit of corporate owners, and in the process shredding the domestic social compact that had supported open trade in the 1940s and 1950s. In a major reversal, the AFL-CIO after the 1960s began opposing almost every initiative to liberalize trade.

At the same time, however, economic forces were generating countervailing pressures from other Americans to keep trade free from new restrictions. Most Americans did not work in manufacturing, where the AFL-CIO was strong, and some of those who did produced goods for export. The more the economy became dependent on trade, the more Americans had a stake in keeping it open. Average U.S. living standards had risen smartly while average import barriers were falling. Many leaders, including members of Congress, had concluded from the Great Depression that raising barriers can be harmful to the home economy and to international relations. Large multinational firms, meanwhile, generally lobbied for policies that would promote trade and investment. The 1970s and 1980s also saw a rise in organized political effort by particular industries to oppose new protection, such as retailers and producers who depended on imports of apparel, automobiles, sugar, copper, and steel. Each Democratic and Republican president in this era, representing the entire population, favored liberalizing trade further.

Large Deficits, Japan, and a New Round in the 1980s

The 1980s brought stronger international competition and unprecedented external trade deficits. With

imports surging, political pressure to restrict them reached new highs and broke into television news shows. The Reagan administration responded with several moves, including the special protections mentioned above. In 1985, the administration also dropped its laissez faire policy regarding the high value of the dollar abroad and took steps that moved it down, which helped narrow the deficit. In September 1985, President Reagan threatened to raise barriers to the exports of four countries deemed to be unfair traders if they did not give what was demanded. The most popular target was Japan, which had the largest trade surplus with the United States and was seen as vigorously on the rise. In 1987, Reagan slapped Japan with the first economic sanctions since World War II, in a dispute over semiconductor trade. An unusually activist Congress initiated the 1988 Omnibus Trade and Competitiveness Act, which increased the executive's authority to impose trade restrictions but did not impose any by statute.

Despite some protectionist exceptions, the Reagan administration also remained dedicated to the postwar policy of attempting to lower barriers in general through multilateral negotiations. In 1986, Washington and Brussels led GATT nations to launch the Uruguay Round. The key objectives were to expand the world rules to liberalize trade in services as well as goods, to deal with the growing issue of protecting U.S. intellectual property rights, and to lower European Community and Japanese barriers and subsidies on agricultural goods. Policy makers hoped that achieving agreements that benefited these sectors would strengthen the domestic political constituency for trade.

In 1994, the GATT nations finally reached a complex new pact that opened more trade than any previous agreement in history. It cut U.S. industrial tariffs from a weighted average of 5.4 to 3.6 percent after full implementation, phased out quantitative restrictions on textiles and clothing, and included new agreements on agriculture, services, and intellectual property rights. It also created the World Trade Organization (WTO), which incorporated GATT and governed world trade thereafter.

NAFTA and Increasing Resistance to Pure Liberalization

As globalization deepened without generous compensatory programs for workers who had suffered from the trend, growing public concerns in the 1990s over its social consequences—especially pollution and the erosion of labor unions' bargaining position at home—increased domestic resistance to further liberalization that ignored these concerns. Organized labor objected strenuously to competing against imports from countries that denied workers the right to organize and other internationally recognized labor rights. Labor also asked the question, "If trade policy can be used to enforce property rights, then why not use it to enforce workers' rights?" The AFL-CIO began to oppose all new liberalizing measures unless they included authority for sanctions against the trade of a country that violated workers' rights. In the 1988 act, Congress added workers' rights as an objective of trade policy.

In addition, average U.S. household living standards did not rise as fast after the early 1970s as they had before. Income stagnation, plus a sense of greater economic insecurity that came with corporate restructuring and many layoffs in the 1980s, may have made it harder to persuade average citizens to support a deeper opening of markets.

The 1992 North American Free Trade Agreement (NAFTA) catalyzed powerful opposition that drew mass public attention to trade. This pact eliminated most trade barriers among Canada, Mexico and the United States. Initially, reflecting the preferences of U.S. industry and the Republican Bush administration, it did not include measures to compensate for environmental strains or labor adjustment costs that this market opening would generate. The independent presidential candidate Ross Perot and labor unions attacked NAFTA. The Democratic candidate, Bill Clinton, straddled division within his own party by saying he would support NAFTA, but only if Mexico accepted additional side agreements on workers' rights and environmental protection.

Environmental organizations entered trade politics forcefully during the 1993 NAFTA ratification fight. Some opposed free trade for stimulating unsustainable industrial development, pointing to Mexico's badly polluted border zone. Some feared that lower standards in developing countries were enticing U.S. firms to move there, creating an incentive to lower standards at home to keep them from leaving. Many objected to being excluded from trade policy making. Some groups opposed NAFTA outright, and others sought to use it to leverage environmental gains.

After Mexico accepted the side agreements, Clinton still had to mount an extensive political campaign to win congressional ratification, which he did by a narrow margin. In 1994, opponents put up a weaker fight against ratification of the WTO (which lacked such side agreements) and lost again.

Polarization, Backlash, and China

The year 1994 proved to be a high watermark for U.S. trade liberalization. Subsequently, trade politics only became further polarized. After the Republican Party took full control of Congress in 1995, business interests and Republicans rejected social provisions, while many labor, environmental, and Democratic leaders resisted further trade liberalization without them. Those who supported trade liberalization without social or environmental concessions achieved a few more victories, but opponents claimed as many for their side. In 1997, WTO member states signed deals to open markets for basic telecommunications services and financial services. In 1999, the Clinton administration completed an agreement with China, the rapidly rising trade power of the twenty-first century, that would grant China membership in the WTO and permanent normal trade relations with the United States, in return for a long list of concessions to open and deregulate Chinese markets, although none of these concessions concerned labor standards or the environment. Clinton and U.S. business won another tough fight in Congress to ratify this deal in 2000. Meanwhile, however, in 1997, a host of nongovernmental organizations, including Public Citizen, Oxfam, and Friends of the Earth, used the Internet to blast the proposed Multilateral Agreement on Investment, which was favorable to multinational corporations. Government negotiators soon abandoned the agreement. That same year, Congress also rejected Clinton's request for renewed authority to negotiate more liberalizing pacts.

In the late 1990s, liberalizers tried to start another new round of WTO talks, but they ran into frustrations. The years 1998–2000 witnessed several large street mobilizations against the neoliberal version of globalization. In 1999, labor and environmental critics marched in Seattle to protest a WTO ministerial conference called to launch another round of talks. That meeting collapsed without agreement, though largely because of international disagreements. In 2001, the Bush administration and the other member governments did launch the so-called Doha Round. But no agreement was reached in its first eight years. In view of this stalemate, the United States negotiated bilateral free trade agreements with several, mostly small, trading countries.

In the 2000s, the U.S. external deficit became much larger even than in the 1980s, yet it generated little business pressure for traditional protection. Imposing new protection was costly because of WTO rules and the risk of foreign retaliation, and businesses were adapting to globalization. Steel remained an exception. Farmers also continued to demand and receive large federal subsidies as well as tariff and quota protection for a few commodities. Other nations' demands that the United States give up these deviations from free trade in agriculture, and Washington's reluctance to do so, were central reasons why the Doha Round stalemated for so long.

In the 2000s, China succeeded Japan as the leading target of political attack. Angry at China's persistent trade surplus, senators Charles Schumer (D–NY) and Lindsay Graham (R–SC) introduced a bill in 2003 that would slap a surcharge on all imports from China. But the bill would have violated WTO rules and Congress did not pass it.

In conclusion, as earlier U.S. trade policy succeeded in integrating the U.S. economy more deeply into the world economy, this success generated economic gains and political support, but also great political stress at home during certain episodes. Trade politics broke into television news and the top of the political agenda in the mid-1980s, early 1990s, and late 1990s. Occasionally, the party out of power in the White House used trade problems to attack the incumbents.

RELATED ENTRIES

THIS VOLUME
Free Trade Agreements, Rise of; Globalization

OTHER VOLUMES
Tariff and Trade Policy (vols. 4 & 5); Tariffs (vols. 2 & 3); Trade Policy (vol. 6)

On the other hand, both parties remained generally committed to the internationalism that had marked U.S. trade policy in earlier eras. In the early twenty-first century, few interest groups were placing a high priority on additional liberalization, but voters never elected a presidential candidate who opposed liberal trade, either. In the 1990s, the ideological middle ground in Congress became nearly empty and partisan polarization deepened in general, which contributed to stalemates on trade as well as other issues. Yet at the time of this writing, despite controversy, the status quo in trade policy remained fairly stable.

Bibliography and Further Reading

Aaronson, Susan Ariel. *Trade and the American Dream: A Social History of Postwar Trade Policy.* Lexington: University Press of Kentucky, 1996.

Destler, I. M. *American Trade Politics.* 4th ed. Washington, D.C.: Institute for International Economics, 2005.

Destler, I. M., and John S. Odell. *Anti-Protection: Changing Forces in United States Trade Politics.* Washington, D.C.: Institute for International Economics, 1987.

Devereaux, Charan, Robert Z. Lawrence, and Michael D. Watkins. *Case Studies in US Trade Negotiation.* 2 vols. Washington, D.C.: Institute for International Economics, 2006.

Hocking, Brian, and Steven McGuire, eds. *Trade Politics.* 2nd edition. London: Routledge, 2004.

Pearson, Charles. *United States Trade Policy: A Work in Progress.* New York: John Wiley, 2004.

Rodrik, Dani. *Has Globalization Gone Too Far?* Washington, D.C.: Institute for International Economics, 1997.

John S. Odell

URBANIZATION AND SUBURBANIZATION

The terms *urbanization* and *suburbanization* refer to the development of cities and their surrounding suburbs, respectively, as well as more contemporary "exurbs" and "edge cities" beyond the boundaries of older suburbs. Issues related to land use, social goods and services, and economics highlight the fragmented nature of urban and suburban governments. Federal, state, and local bodies have differing responsibilities, and local governments can take the form of counties, municipalities, townships, school districts, and other special districts. Such political fragmentation has facilitated the separation of suburbs from cities. Still, cities and suburbs are inextricably linked politically, economically, culturally, and geographically.

Since 1976, three trends have shaped patterns of urbanization and suburbanization in American regions: segregation, the concentration of poverty, and suburban sprawl. As a result, increased social inequality in metropolitan regions has characterized the politics of land use, political participation, and voting patterns.

A Brief History of American Urbanization and Suburbanization

Throughout the twentieth century, federal, state, and local policies encouraged the development of suburbs through the uneven availability of mortgages and mortgage insurance, highway construction, and other incentives for people to move from central cities to sur-

rounding suburbs. At the same time, American cities underwent tremendous economic, social, and spatial transformations. For example, urban renewal programs designed to redevelop aging "slums" and the construction of America's highway system displaced thousands of poor residents from urban neighborhoods.

Suburban homes were denied to the urban poor, who were disproportionately people of color. As a result of this set of policy decisions and the unprecedented construction of public housing in many urban neighborhoods in the 1950s and 1960s, metropolitan areas in the United States were severely segregated by 1976. Increasing pockets of poverty characterized many cities, and suburbs were thought of as safe havens that would protect the white middle class from the "problems" of the city.

Segregation and the Concentration of Poverty

Segregation continued to shape urbanization and suburbanization after 1976. Contemporary patterns of segregation in America's cities and suburbs have been maintained by personal preference and discrimination on the part of landlords, the real estate industry, and mortgage lenders. Deindustrialization and the upsurge in the construction of public housing paved the way for the massive concentration of poverty in many of America's cities during the 1970s and beyond, particularly for cities in the North and Midwest. The decline in job opportunities, the deplorable conditions of most public housing projects and private housing stock, and massive disinvestment in central cities combined to form what many scholars have called the "urban crisis." In the year 2000, African Americans remained extremely segregated from whites in metropolitan areas, and Latino and Asian segregation from whites increased.

The social, economic, and political consequences of residential segregation are many and varied. Where a family lives determines access to wealth appreciation, good schools, jobs, groceries, health care, and a variety of other goods and services. Many urban neighborhoods lack basic social services and opportunities for jobs in the formal economy, and crime, gang activity, drug use, and the attendant distrust of neighbors have flourished. Such conditions have not typically been conducive to the unification of residents to fight their common problems.

Suburban Sprawl

The dominant form of metropolitan settlement in American history is sprawl—the outward expansion of low-density structures from central cities. In the 1990s and 2000s, increasing attention has been brought to the phenomena of "exurbs" and "edge cities," usually defined as incorporated settlements beyond the confines of traditional inner-ring suburbs on the immediate borders of urban municipalities.

By 2006, the majority of Americans lived in suburbs. While suburbs were previously characterized as havens for the white middle and upper classes, they are increasingly diverse, both racially and economically. Inner-ring, older suburbs have become much more diverse in the 1990s and 2000s. It remains to be seen how these demographic changes will influence suburban politics.

Urban Politics

The increasing number of minority mayors voted into office since the 1970s has often been used to represent the gains that disadvantaged groups have made in urban politics. Some of America's largest cities—such as New York, Chicago, Los Angeles, Detroit, and Atlanta—had elected mayors of color by 1974. Scholars continue to debate the extent to which minority mayors

effectively serve poor and segregated communities. Decentralized metropolitan regions, the primacy of local authority, weak political organization, and the pressure to revitalize urban economies limit mayors' ability to alleviate the social problems related to pockets of concentrated poverty in urban areas.

Especially since the 1970s, community organizations have emerged as an alternative to the electoral system as a means of seeking political change. These organizations address issues of poverty, disinvestment, job training, education, and crime, and they often provide the goods and services that have increasingly become unavailable from local, state, and federal government. However, while community organizations and community development corporations can increase the political participation of urban residents, they can only rarely effect major changes in public policy. More importantly, neither formal elections nor the rise of community organizations have fully succeeded in politically incorporating the urban poor in meaningful ways.

Many researchers note that the urban communities that suffer most from large-scale public policy decisions (such as the concentration of public housing in particular neighborhoods and deindustrialization) and their attendant social problems (such as the increasing involvement of residents in the drug economy, and increasing violence) have little influence on city and metropolitan politics, or on the organizations that attempt to provide social services.

Redistricting remains a complicating factor in the ability of segregated communities and communities with high levels of concentrated poverty to fully participate in the electoral process. Redistricting is the process by which new congressional and local political boundaries are drawn for electoral purposes, and it occurs on a regular basis in America's political system. It can, however, have the intended or unintended consequence of dividing segregated or poor communities so that their political power becomes less influential.

Finally, a major overarching shift to the privatization of what were public functions during the late 1970s through the 2000s has generally functioned to decrease the amount and quality of social services in urban areas. The federal government left state and local governments—which are fragmented in nature—

to attempt to solve the crises of the inner city. Left with little financial support, most local governments began to partner with private corporations through redevelopment schemes and support services. The shift toward the privatization of services has not meaningfully reduced the level of segregation or the concentration of poverty in most American cities.

Suburban Politics

A number of factors have dominated suburban politics since 1976. Suburban residents have focused on tax reduction and fiscal responsibility, struggled to check their growth for environmental and social reasons, and used the political influence of homeowners' associations and other privatized forms of security to maintain racial and economic homogeneity. Suburbs also continue to use exclusionary zoning practices to prevent multifamily units and affordable housing from being built in their communities.

On the national level, the suburban vote became increasingly important to electing conservatives into national offices. By 1992, suburban votes "outnumbered urban and rural votes combined." (Kruse 261) Southern suburban voters in particular helped to elect Republican figures like Newt Gingrich and George W. Bush. They were attracted to the conservative ideologies of smaller government, lower taxes, and increased privatization—ideologies that helped to build and sustain suburbs as homogenous communities at the local level. Suburbanites also helped Bill Clinton win the presidency in 1992 and 1996.

The urban electorate, on the other hand, tends to consistently vote for Democrats. However, city voters are less influential because of the tremendous growth of suburbia, low voter turnout, and disfranchisement. Still, the urban vote has been a key element in Democratic presidential victories. In the 2008 presidential elections, however, Barack Obama won 50 percent of the suburban vote, "the most by a Democrat since exit polling began in 1972." (MacGillis and Cohen A1)

Regional Politics

Since the 1960s, scholars have noted the difficulties of governing efficiently, due to the plethora of districts, municipalities, boroughs, townships, and other politi-cally bounded spaces in metropolitan areas, including cities and surrounding suburbs. By the 1990s, an approach called "regionalism" had gained popularity as a potential policy that would link cities and suburbs institutionally, alleviating economic disparities between cities and suburbs and allowing them to combine their strengths. Such an approach illuminates the inextricable links between urban and suburban economies, political systems, and social services. The urban policy expert David Rusk famously introduced the idea of "elastic" and "inelastic" cities. In the postindustrial economy, cities and regions compete for business, industry, and residents. "Elastic" cities have the potential to encapsulate suburban growth, lessen racial and economic segregation, and increase educational equality between school districts by annexing outlying land and making use of vacant land.

Newer cities, particularly in the South and West, have been more successful at becoming "elastic." For example, Houston and Albuquerque increased their city areas by more than 400 square miles and more than 100 square miles, respectively. Older cities like Detroit, Cleveland, and many others are "inelastic," meaning they have not been able to expand their city limits. The inability of some cities to use vacant land to their advantage and to annex outlying property can be attributed to state laws, municipalities that are annexation-proof, and resident protest. Resident protest can come from suburbs who wish to keep their political affairs separate from central cities as much as possible; protest can also come from minority city residents who feel they will lose the little control they have over local politics should their cities join with surrounding suburbs.

Bibliography and Further Reading

Carr, James H., and Nandinee K. Kutty, eds. *Segregation: The Rising Costs for America*. New York: Routledge, 2008.

Judd, Dennis R., and Paul Kantor, eds. *The Politics of Urban America: a Reader*. New York: Longman, 2001.

Kruse, Kevin. *White Flight: Atlanta and the Making of Modern Conservatism*. Princeton, NJ: Princeton University Press, 2005.

Kruse, Kevin M., and Thomas J. Sugrue, eds. *The New
Suburban History.* Chicago: University of Chicago Press,
2006.

MacGillis, Alec, and Jon Cohen. "Democrats Add Suburbs
to Their Growing Coalition." *Washington Post,*
November 8, 2008.

Rusk, David. *Cities Without Suburbs: A Census 2000
update.* Washington, D.C.: Woodrow Wilson Center
Press, 2003.

Saerzopf, Richard, and Todd Swanstrom. "The Urban
Electorate in Presidential Elections, 1920–1996."
Urban Affairs Review 35, no. 1 (1999): 72–91.

Savitch, H. V., and Ronald K. Vogel. *Regional Politics:
America in a Post-City Age.* Thousand Oaks, CA: Sage,
1996.

Squires, Gregory D., and Charis E. Kubrin. *Privileged
Places: Race, Residence, and the Structure of Opportunity.*
Boulder, CO: Lynne Rienner, 2006.

Vogel, Ronald K., ed. *Handbook of Research on Urban
Politics and Policy in the United States.* Westport, CT:
Greenwood Press, 1997.

Emily T. Molina

USA PATRIOT ACT

2001

The Patriot Act (officially the Uniting and
Strengthening America by Providing Appropriate
Tools Required to Intercept and Obstruct
Terrorism Act—or USA PATRIOT Act—of 2001)
was signed into law by Pres. George W. Bush on
October 26, 2001. This controversial law was
passed in the wake of the September 11, 2001, terrorist attacks, and it significantly expanded the
powers of law enforcement to obtain personal
records and conduct surveillance and searches. It
also served as a lightning rod for activism by civil
libertarians and a rallying point for supporters of
the "war on terror," becoming a focal point of

debate around the balance between liberty and
security in the post–9/11 era.

Provisions

The Patriot Act made several amendments to the
Foreign Intelligence Surveillance Act (FISA) of
1978. FISA allowed federal agents to conduct
searches and surveillance against "foreign agents,"
using methods they could not use against
Americans due to the "probable cause" standard of
Amendment IV. The act expanded the scope of
FISA, allowing surveillance to be conducted not
only against "foreign agents" but against "any U.S.
person" in a terrorism-related investigation.

The Patriot Act also authorized the expanded use of
undisclosed searches of homes and businesses (known
as "sneak and peek" searches). It expanded the power of
federal agents to seize records about a person from a
third party, such as an Internet service provider or a
library, and to require the third party to keep the seizure
secret. It allowed agencies to share intelligence with law
enforcement officials for purposes of investigations as
well as prosecutions. The act also permitted the indefi-
nite detention of aliens without criminal charges.

At the beginning, the Patriot Act enjoyed bipartisan support. During deliberations, Democrats
secured a number of amendments for the purpose of
protecting civil liberties. The House voted 357–66,
and the Senate 98–1, in favor of the act (Senator Russ
Feingold [D–WI] was the sole opponent in the
Senate). Its supporters argued that, before the act, the
tools available to fight organized crime and drug trafficking were more extensive than those available to
fight terrorism. Referring to reports that greater
interagency cooperation within the federal government might have thwarted the 9/11 hijackings, supporters touted the act's provisions that encourage
information sharing among government agencies.

Criticism

The USA PATRIOT Act drew instant criticism from the
American Civil Liberties Union and other civil liberties
groups, who used the act to argue that the Bush administration was using the 9/11 attacks as an excuse to take
away the liberties of the American people. Many on the

Protesters hold up signs outside of Federal Hall during a demonstration against U.S. Attorney Gen. John Ashcroft and the Patriot Act on September 9, 2003, in New York City. The Patriot Act was signed into law by George W. Bush on October 26, 2001, and enjoyed bipartisan support in the wake of the attacks on 9/11, but it drew increasing criticism from activists on both the left and the right for its expansion of government power and for its perceived intrusion into the private lives of American citizens. Despite the controversy surrounding it, the Patriot Act was reauthorized on March 9, 2006. (Spencer Platt/Getty Images)

right supported this view as well, including William Safire of the *New York Times*, Grover Norquist of Americans for Tax Reform, the conservative activist Phyllis Schlafly, Timothy Lynch of the Cato Institute, and David Keene of the American Conservative Union. Even Republican representatives who voted for the act, including Bob Barr of Georgia and Dick Armey of Texas, raised opposition. Many legislators who voted for the act claimed that they passed the bill in haste, without actually reading it.

Meanwhile, supporters of the so-called War on Terror tried to use liberal opposition against the Patriot Act to show that Democrats were soft on ter-

rorism. In December 2001, Attorney Gen. John Ashcroft said during Senate testimony that opponents who scared people with "phantoms of lost liberty" were aiding terrorists and eroding national unity. Speaking before supportive audiences, he asserted that the act gave the government the technological tools it needed to fight terrorists.

The Patriot Act continued to be a divisive issue, and civil liberties groups maintained their opposition to it. In November 2003, former vice president Al Gore used the Patriot Act to attack the Bush administration, asserting that it was undermining civil liberties and leading the country down the road to an intrusive, "Big Brother" style of government. By February 2004, 240 local governments and three states had passed resolutions against the Patriot Act.

Opponents of the act concentrated their criticism on Section 215, which they said would allow federal agents to access the library records of ordinary Americans, and Section 213, which they said would allow federal agents to search Americans' homes without informing the occupant that the search took place. Supporters of the act responded that ordinary Americans had nothing to fear from the Patriot Act. Library records, they said, could only be searched after persuading a judge that foreign intelligence, international terrorism, or clandestine intelligence activities were involved. They also dismissed objections to the "sneak and peek" provisions of the act, noting that federal courts had long approved such investigative methods.

Using Section 505 of the act, the government expanded its use of National Security Letters, which allow government agents to obtain information about an individual from financial institutions, telephone companies, and Internet service providers, while imposing a "gag order" on the recipient. In 2004, a federal court found that the FBI's use of National Security Letters under the Patriot Act violated Amendment I of the Constitution. In 2007, the Office of the Inspector General of the Department of Justice found that the FBI had abused its power to issue National Security Letters.

In 2003, federal prosecutors in Idaho charged Sami Omar Al-Hussayen, a computer science Ph.D. student, under Section 805 of the Patriot Act, for providing "expert advice or assistance" to terrorists. Al-Hussayen had created a Web site to which fatwas were posted. Prosecutors charged that he used his computer skills to aid a terrorist network. He was acquitted of terrorism charges, however, and the Patriot Act provision under which he was charged was ruled unconstitutionally vague by a federal court in Los Angeles.

Attempts at Limitation

Legislative attempts to limit the Patriot Act have not been successful. In February 2003, Rep. Bernie Sanders (D–VT) introduced a bill that would limit the ability of federal officials to obtain library records, but the bill stalled in committee. A bill introduced by Rep. C. L. "Butch" Otter (D–ID) to withhold funding for "sneak and peek" searches of private property under section 213 of the Patriot Act passed the House but died in the Senate. Other legislative attempts have also failed to pass both houses of Congress.

Many provisions of the Patriot Act were due to "sunset" in 2005, but the act was reauthorized through the USA PATRIOT and Terrorism Prevention Reauthorization Act of 2005 and the USA PATRIOT Act Additional Reauthorizing Amendments Act of 2006. These reauthorization acts made only minor changes to the controversial provisions of the original, and critics charged that the reauthorization process did not pay sufficient attention to civil liberties concerns.

The Patriot Act's ultimate impact on civil liberties is difficult to determine, given the lack of public records of searches and subpoenas. It is also difficult to determine whether the Patriot Act has significantly improved the ability of the federal government to combat terrorism, given that many of the methods the Patriot Act encouraged were already available before the act was passed. In politics, the Patriot Act served as a focal point of the claim that the Bush administration was using the 9/11 attacks as an excuse to expand government power and curtail civil liberties. Yet despite intense criticism of the act from the left and certain segments of the right, no effort to reverse it has been successful.

One reason for the lack of support for efforts to repeal the Patriot Act has been a lack of understanding about what it actually does. Surveys found that Americans, while having an opinion about the Patriot Act, did not really understand the changes it made to existing law. The act became a catchall for criticisms of the Bush administration's response to terrorism. Another reason is that there was little popular support for Ben Franklin's proposition, "They who can give up essential liberty to obtain a little temporary safety, deserve neither liberty nor safety." In American politics and culture, there was widespread agreement that something had to change after 9/11.

Bibliography and Further Reading

Baker, Stewart A., and John Kavanagh, eds. *Patriot Debates: Experts Debate the USA Patriot Act.* Chicago: American Bar Association, 2005.

Cole, David, and James X. Dempsey. *Terrorism and the Constitution: Sacrificing Civil Liberties in the Name of National Security.* New York: New Press, 2006.

Michaels, C. William. *No Greater Threat: American After September 11 and the Rise of a National Security State—With a Detailed Analysis of the USA Patriot Act.* New York: Algora, 2002.

Jonathan H. Pyle

WAR ON TERROR

President Ronald Reagan used the phrase "war on terrorism" in the 1980s, but the term "war on terror" is commonly associated with the struggle against Islamic terrorism in the wake of the September 11, 2001, attacks against the United States. The term encompasses military actions in Afghanistan and Iraq, foreign policy initiatives, and domestic initiatives ostensibly aimed at preventing or preparing for future terrorist attacks. The administration of George W. Bush frequently used the term as a means to justify the president's controversial actions abroad and at home. The use of the term had the result that the president's opponents, who could not feasibly oppose the war on terror itself, were forced to present their opposition as criticism of the president's means rather than his ends.

Initiatives of the War on Terror

As a political concept, the War on Terror came into being soon after the 9/11 attacks. On September 18, 2001, Congress passed the Authorization for Use of Military Force (AUMF), a joint resolution empowering the executive to use the U.S. armed forces against "those responsible for the recent attacks launched against the United States." Two days later, President Bush announced a more generalized "global war on terrorism" to a joint session of Congress. "Our war on terror begins with al Qaeda," he said, "but it does not end there. It will not end until every terrorist group of global reach has been found, stopped, and

defeated." This war would be fought not only with military weapons, but with "every instrument of law enforcement" and "every financial influence."

Less than a week after the attacks, President Bush secretly authorized the Central Intelligence Agency (CIA) to kidnap suspected terrorists from foreign countries and deliver them for interrogation to foreign regimes known to use torture, a practice that became known as "extraordinary rendition." The same order authorized the Central Intelligence Agency to operate numerous secret "black site" prisons for suspected terrorists in Eastern Europe, Thailand, and elsewhere. President Bush would not acknowledge the existence of these secret prisons until September 2006.

A month after the attacks, the president sent the U.S. military to remove the Taliban regime from power in Afghanistan. U.S. forces captured thousands of suspected terrorists and brought more than 750 of them to the U.S. naval base in Guantanamo Bay, Cuba. The president issued an executive order for the creation of military commissions to try these suspected terrorists. These commissions were authorized to admit any evidence that the presiding officer considered "probative," including hearsay and statements obtained by torture. They could also conduct secret proceedings and convict prisoners (even of capital crimes) on a two-thirds vote. No appeals to independent civilian courts were allowed, and prisoners were denied the right to challenge the legality of their detentions and treatment by petitioning civilian courts for writs of habeas corpus.

Plans for an invasion of Iraq, which had been underway during the 1990s, came to fruition under the rubric of the "war on terror." In his January 2002 State of the Union Address, President Bush articulated the notion that the "Axis of Evil" of Iraq, Iran, and North Korea constituted a terrorist-type threat to the United States. Although intelligence clearly indicated no links between Iraqi president Saddam Hussein and the al Qaeda network blamed for the September 11 attacks, opinion polls showed that almost half of Americans believed that such links existed. The 2003 invasion and subsequent occupation of Iraq were portrayed by the administration as a part of the war on terror.

Changes to domestic policy were also brought under the umbrella of the War on Terror. Concurrent with his announcement of this "war," President Bush created the Office of Homeland Security, which Congress expanded in 2002 into the Department of Homeland Security (DHS). The DHS absorbed 22 other agencies, including the Immigration and Nationalization Service (INS), to become the third largest executive office. In October 2001, Congress passed, and President Bush signed, the USA PATRIOT Act, which significantly expanded the executive's power to gather intelligence on suspected terrorists and others without judicial supervision. Around the same time, the president also issued a secret executive order authorizing the National Security Agency (NSA) to monitor telephone calls between the United States and other countries without first obtaining warrants, as required by the 1978 Foreign Intelligence Surveillance Act (FISA). Part of this program involved a massive data-mining of fiber optic telecommunications, including phone calls, faxes, and e-mails. The president also authorized a secret program for obtaining databases from telecommunications companies that contained all the telephone numbers dialed by customers of the companies.

The administration, particularly through the Department of Homeland Security, promoted alertness to terrorist activity. DHS created a color-coded "Threat Level" system, which from 2002 was set either at "Elevated" (yellow) or "High" (orange). In a program known as Operation TIPS, the administra-tion encouraged cable installers and telephone repair workers to report to the government anything "suspicious" they saw in other people's homes during the course of their work. After opposition from the U.S. Postal Service and bipartisan opposition in Congress, the program was abandoned.

The Justice Department used mass detentions in an unsuccessful attempt to identify terrorists among resident aliens. By November 2001, some 1,182 people had been secretly detained, and by September 2003 more than 5,000 had been imprisoned. The inspector general of the Justice Department later found that many of these prisoners had been abused, and none were convicted of a terrorist-related crime.

While the USA PATRIOT Act (commonly called the Patriot Act) attempted to dismantle institutional barriers separating intelligence operations from law enforcement operations, the administration also took steps to repeal the Posse Comitatus Act of 1878, which prohibits military forces from participating in domestic law enforcement. Over the objections of liberal and libertarian interest groups, the Department of Defense (DoD) in 2008 placed a Brigade Combat Team on call to assist law enforcement authorities with "civil unrest and crowd control or to deal with potentially horrific scenarios" such as terrorist attacks. The DoD planned to commit twenty thousand uniformed troops within the United States for such purposes by 2011.

Responses to the Initiatives

In the immediate aftermath of the 9/11 attacks, many interest groups opposed to the expansion of executive power held back, given that the political environment was one in which feelings of patriotism were strong and the public widely adopted the view that U.S. policy needed to change in order to prevent other terrorist attacks. But when the administration began to threaten war with Iraq, its critics did not hold back any longer.

The most salient argument from the mainstream political left alleged that the president's actions abroad showed a lack of concern for international law, and that his actions on the domestic front demonstrated a lack of respect for the principles of separation of power and civil liberties. From the mainstream political right, the response was that the 9/11 attacks necessitated going after terrorists, being proactive about eliminating terrorist threats, and sacrificing some amount of liberty in order to have increased security. Around the issue of domestic surveillance and the Patriot Act, civil libertarians on the mainstream left found allies among conservatives who believed in limiting executive power. Agreement could also be found between the extreme political left and the extreme political right, both of which alleged that the war on terror was an effort by the United States to crush resistance to American and Israeli imperialism.

Perhaps the strongest criticisms concerned the initiation of the Iraq War. After using the fear of "weapons of mass destruction," or "WMD," as the primary argument for beginning the war, the administration later admitted that no such weapons had been found. They then substituted the argument of "spreading democracy" as the primary reason for the war. Kofi Annan, the secretary-general of the United Nations, said in 2004 that the war violated the U.N. Charter because it was a unilateral act of aggression conducted without the approval of the U.N. Security Council. The Bush administration insisted that the war was authorized by preexisting U.N. resolutions (such as Resolution 1441) passed at the time of the Gulf War, and that it was an act of preemptive self-defense. Even supporters of the war understood that its justifications under international law were weak. The British attorney general, Lord Goldsmith, advised Prime Minister Tony Blair that "regime change cannot be the objective of military action." Richard Perle, a member and former chairman of the Pentagon's Defense Policy Board, admitted in 2003 that international law prohibited the invasion of Iraq. Meanwhile, the law professor and former Bush administration lawyer John Yoo argued that international law can and should be disregarded by the president in the exercise of his executive powers.

Despite heavy criticism of the war, as well as allegations that his administration was responsible for the torture and humiliation of Iraqi prisoners at Abu Ghraib and condoned torture at Guantanamo, President Bush was reelected in 2004. The Iraq War became more unpopular during his second term, but the concept of the War on Terror did not become unpopular. In 2008, Sen. Barack Obama, who had voted against the Iraq War, was elected president by a significant margin over Sen. John McCain, a decorated war veteran who supported the war. During the campaign, Senator Obama referred to the Iraq War as a "dangerous distraction" from what he thought was the proper target of the war on terror, namely going after al Qaeda in Afghanistan and Pakistan.

Lawyers went to court to challenge the administration's initiatives on foreign detainees. In *Rasul v. Bush*, 542 U.S. 466 (2004) and *Hamdi v. Rumsfeld*, 542 U.S. 507 (2004), the Supreme Court rejected the administration's claim that prisoners at Guantanamo Bay were not entitled to due process under the Constitution. As a result, teams of attorneys filed habeas corpus petitions on behalf of many Guantanamo Bay prisoners. In 2005, a Republican-led Congress tried to block these legal challenges by passing the Detainee Treatment Act (DTA) of 2005, which purported to strip the prisoners of all statutory rights to habeas corpus.

In *Hamdan v. Rumsfeld*, 548 U.S. 557 (2006), the Supreme Court held that the president's military commissions violated the Uniform Code of Military Justice and the Geneva Conventions, and that the Detainee Treatment Act did not prevent courts from exercising jurisdiction over habeas petitions pending at the time of the enactment of the DTA. In September 2006, however, the Republican Congress passed the Military Commissions Act, which authorized new military commissions, granted the administration and its interrogators amnesty for the torture of prisoners, gave the president exclusive power to decide what the Geneva Convention's ban on "cruel, inhuman and degrading treatment" of prisoners meant, and amended the habeas corpus statute to provide that statutory habeas corpus rights do not extend to any "alien detained by the United States who has been determined by the United States to have been properly detained as an enemy combatant or is awaiting such determination."

The administration's domestic initiatives were also challenged in court. In 2006, a U.S. District Court found that the secret "terrorist surveillance program" violated both the Omnibus Crime Control and Safe Streets Act of 1968 and FISA, which together regulate all government interception of telecommunications. Several appellate courts also ruled that the executive does not have the authority to hold citizens or lawful resident aliens in military custody. In December 2003, the U.S. Court of Appeals for the Second Circuit held in *Padilla v. Rumsfeld* that the executive lacked the authority, despite the AUMF, to detain in military custody a U.S. citizen arrested at a Chicago airport on suspicion of being associated with al Qaeda. (The Supreme Court reversed this decision on procedural grounds.) In June 2007, in *Al-Marri v. Berman*, the Court of Appeals for the Fourth Circuit held, despite its reputation for supporting presidential authority, that the AUMF did not authorize the president to detain indefinitely a resident alien suspected of being an al Qaeda "sleeper agent."

A Metaphorical War

The so-called War on Terror is not a declared war in the sense of Article I, Section 8 of the Constitution. Its al Qaeda component, at least, is more of a metaphorical war, like the "war on crime" or the "war on drugs." The invasions of Afghanistan and Iraq, on the other hand, were congressionally authorized conflicts with foreign states, but they have been rhetorically, and in some ways actually, blurred into the war on terror.

The label "war" carried a number of politically useful connotations for the Bush administration, including faith in executive power, patriotic identification with official action, the stifling of debate, the appropriateness of executive secrecy, the relaxation of limits on executive power, the supremacy of the executive branch over the judicial and legislative branches of government, fear of loss of sovereignty, and the equation of current initiatives with the objectives of historical wars.

By declaring a "global war on terrorism," the Bush administration could link its initiatives to measures undertaken by the Clinton administration, including its Antiterrorism and Effective Death Penalty Act of 1996, its bombing of Iraq, and its destruction with cruise missiles of a pharmaceutical factory in the Sudan, while simultaneously claiming that it was giving more attention to the problem of terrorism than the Democrats had.

The War on Terror led the Bush administration into making some highly debatable claims about presidential power. It also tempted it to stain the office of the presidency with involvement in torture of detainees. Proponents of harsh interrogation practices argued that longstanding Army doctrines against coercive interrogation, grounded in both the Geneva Conventions and the Uniform Code of Military Justice, had to be disregarded because 9/11 required that the "gloves come off." While Vice Pres. Dick Cheney, with support from many conservatives, continued to defend torture, both presidential candidates in 2008 (senators John McCain and Barack Obama) openly criticized the policy of torture and promised to end it.

In the years after the 9/11 attack, the anti-libertarian implications of the War on Terror have become openly debated and rolled back. Whether a subsequent, even more devastating attack inside the United States would reopen all of the stresses on American democracy that appeared soon after 9/11 remains an open question.

Bibliography and Further Reading

Bamford, James. *A Pretext for War: 9/11, Iraq, and the Abuse of America's Intelligence Agencies.* New York: Doubleday, 2004.

Clarke, Richard. *Against All Enemies: Inside America's War on Terror.* New York: The Free Press, 2004.

Fisher, Louis. *Military Tribunals And Presidential Power: American Revolution To The War On Terrorism.* Lawrence: University Press of Kansas, 2005.

Hersh, Seymour M. *Chain of Command: The Road from 9/11 to Abu Ghraib.* New York: HarperCollins, 2004.

Kuypers, Jim A. *Bush's War: Media Bias and Justifications for War in a Terrorist Age.* New York: Rowman & Littlefield, 2006.

Ricks, Thomas E. *Fiasco: The American Military Adventure in Iraq.* New York: Penguin, 2006.

Risen, James. *State of War: The Secret History of the CIA and the Bush Administration.* New York: The Free Press, 2006.

Yoo, John. *The Powers of War and Peace: The Constitution and Foreign Affairs after 9/11.* Chicago: University of Chicago Press, 2005.

Jonathan H. Pyle

WELFARE REFORM

Aid to Families with Dependent Children (AFDC) was the main federal program providing income to the poor for almost 60 years. Never popular, always controversial, and of debatable effectiveness, AFDC was terminated in 1996 by a Republican Congress and a Democratic president. It was replaced by the Temporary Assistance for Needy Families (TANF) program. While AFDC guaranteed eligible families some money, without requiring much in return, TANF expects recipients to work but promises them nothing.

Background

AFDC was created as a minor and uncontroversial element of the Social Security Act of 1935, with the intention that it would be a temporary program to provide income support to widows and their families. It did not turn out that way, however. By the late 1960s, AFDC was providing assistance to millions of Americans. Most AFDC parents were not widows but mothers who were divorced, separated, or had never married. Few AFDC recipients had paid employment. Nearly two-thirds of adults receiving AFDC had been out of work for eight or more years. Finally, almost two-thirds of the recipients were nonwhite minorities. Consequently, AFDC came to be seen as a program that discouraged marriage and work, encouraged out-of wedlock childbearing and dependency, and primarily served people of color.

Although AFDC was established, designed, and largely funded by the federal government (the states never paid more than half the cost, and most paid much less), the states set eligibility and payment standards and actually administered the program. Consequently, eligibility, participation, and benefits varied widely across the states, even though the federal government assured people that anyone eligible for benefits was entitled to receive them. Over time, a broad consensus arose within the states and the federal government (who wrestled over control), among Republicans and Democrats (who tussled over priorities), amid liberals as well as conservatives (who disagreed about the program's generosity and its "entitlement" status), that AFDC was broken and had to be replaced.

Presidents and Welfare Reform

No president after John F. Kennedy defended AFDC. Instead, Republican and Democratic presidents alike treated the program with contempt. Richard Nixon, Jimmy Carter, Ronald Reagan, and Bill Clinton all insisted that welfare was a dismal failure and that the AFDC program should, one way or another, be killed.

President Richard Nixon was the first president who sought to eliminate AFDC altogether. As he told the Congress:

> *[T]he present welfare system has to be judged a colossal failure. Our states and cities find themselves sinking in a welfare quagmire as caseloads increase, as costs escalate and as the welfare system stagnates enterprise and perpetuates dependency...It breaks up homes. It often penalizes work. It robs recipients of dignity. And it grows...[Welfare] has become unfair to the welfare recipient, unfair to the working poor and unfair to the taxpayer.* (Congressional Quarterly Almanac 1969, 75A)

Nixon's proposed Family Assistance Plan (FAP) called for replacing the decentralized AFDC program with one of nationally standardized benefits, eligibility, and administration. Although his plan was widely billed as a guaranteed annual income (in fact, it would have been), Nixon insisted that "no able-bodied person will have a 'free ride' [with FAP] . . . This transformation of the welfare system will lessen dependency rather than perpetuate and enlarge it." (*Congressional Quarterly Almanac* 1969, 71A)

President Carter spoke almost from the same page, proposing a clean break with the past. Carter's Program for Better Jobs and Income (PBJI) was to be a fully federal program that would help those who could work find jobs and provide those who could not with nationally uniform, adequate, cash assistance. President Reagan came to political prominence, in part, through his attacks on the welfare state and "welfare queens." Once in office, he proposed transferring full responsibility for the AFDC program to the states in exchange for the federal government's full financing of Medicaid (the federal health insurance program for the poor). This would have ended the federal entitlement and allowed the states to design their welfare programs as they chose.

When Clinton ran for office, one of his most popular promises was to "end welfare as we know it," adding, "welfare should be a second chance, not a way of life." (*Congressional Quarterly Almanac* 1992, 56A, 61A). Once in office, Clinton originally hoped to transform welfare by expanding it and broadening the services it offered, while at the same time limiting its duration:

> *I want to offer the people on welfare the education, the training, the child care, the health care they need to get back on their feet, but say after two years they must get back to work, too, in private business if possible, in public service if necessary. We have to end welfare as a way of life and make it a path to independence and dignity. (Congressional Quarterly Almanac 1993, 9D)*

After the Republicans took control of Congress in 1994, Clinton reversed course, at least rhetorically (as he had not promoted a specific plan), to emphasize that AFDC was "a broken system that traps too many people in a cycle of dependence," and that "the current welfare system undermines the basic values of work, responsibility and family, trapping generation after generation in dependency and hurting the very people it was designed to help." (*Congressional Quarterly Almanac* 1996, D17)

Congress and Welfare Reform

The president proposes, and the Congress disposes. At least that has been the pattern in welfare policy. Since 1968, the president has helped push welfare reform into the congressional agenda, but Congress most often has then given the president something far different than he requested, if it gives him anything at all.

Nixon introduced his FAP proposal to the Congress in 1969, and it passed the House easily the next year. But then it stalled in the Senate Finance Committee, where conservatives thought it too generous and liberals found it too stingy. The bill was beaten in committee, and attempts to revive it on the floor were decisively rejected. The next year, Nixon again introduced the FAP (now appropriately labeled HR 1), declaring that it would remain "White House priority number one until it is enacted." (*Congressional Quarterly Almanac* 1971, 520) Once again, the bill swept through the House, but this time the Senate Finance Committee did not even bring it up for a vote. After that, Nixon lost his enthusiasm for this priority and no longer pushed for it. President Carter had even less luck with his welfare reform proposals. Carter's PBJI failed even to make it out of committee in the House in 1978, and although a modified proposal was adopted in 1979, it too stalled in the Senate Finance Committee.

Congress acquiesced to Reagan's efforts to lower welfare benefits and tighten eligibility in 1982, but it rejected his proposals to turn AFDC entirely over to the states (in fact, legislation to do this was never even submitted). Congress ultimately did enact major welfare reform (the Family Support Act of 1988) during his administration, but it was hardly what he had proposed. Rather than turning AFDC over to the states, the FSA expanded the program while also imposing new standards on the states regarding two-parent families in AFDC, child support and child-care benefits, and health insurance. The act also decreed that the states establish and operate a new Job Opportunities and Basic Skills (JOBS) program designed to give welfare recipients education, training, and work experiences.

Congress, preoccupied with other Clinton initiatives, took no action on welfare reform until after the Republicans gained control of the House in 1994. Then, seizing the political momentum to enact the Republican platform (which stated, "[Welfare] cannot be merely tinkered with by Congress; it must be re-created by states and localities" [*Congressional Quarterly*

Almanac 1992 83A]), the Congress approved the Personal Responsibility and Work Opportunity Reconciliation Act, which terminated AFDC and replaced it with TANF. President Clinton was torn on whether to sign the bill: some advisors thought it both good policy and good politics, while others believed that it meant abandoning the poor. Those advocating for the bill prevailed, and several officials opposed to the bill resigned in protest.

TANF represented profound change, in that it ended the federal entitlement to welfare. Now, a state could deny benefits to eligible individuals at its discretion. It limited benefits to any individual to a maximum of five years; no longer could individuals stay in the program indefinitely. It substantially increased the work requirements for those receiving benefits, but it transformed extensive authority to the states regarding how to meet these requirements. Finally, it fundamentally changed the goals of welfare. Whereas AFDC mainly provided cash benefits to poor families, TANF's goals were to: (a) provide assistance to needy families so that their children could be raised at home; (b) promote (or require) work, so families would not need to depend on the government; (c) reduce the number of out-of-wedlock pregnancies; (d) encourage the formation and maintenance of two-parent families.

TANF remains controversial among policy scholars who seek to assess the true impact of the program on America's poor. The political controversies are over, however. First, the public and politicians continue to agree that "welfare" should not be a way of life, and that it should promote work first. Second, welfare caseloads have dropped by over 75 percent since TANF was enacted, from over 12 million recipients to less than 3 million. Welfare has not disappeared entirely, but it has vanished from the public agenda.

Bibliography and Further Reading

Congressional Quarterly Almanac. Volumes 25, 26, 27, 33, 34, 44, 48, 49, 52. Washington, D.C.: Congressional Quarterly, 1969, 1970, 1971, 1977, 1978, 1988, 1992, 1993, 1996.

Gilens, Martin. *Why Americans Hate Welfare: Race, Media, and the Politics of Antipoverty Policy.* Chicago: Chicago University Press, 1999.

RELATED ENTRIES

THIS VOLUME
Income Inequality

OTHER VOLUMES
Social Welfare Policy (vols. 5 & 6)

Rom, Mark Carl. "The Family Support Act of 1988: Federalism, Developmental Policy, and Welfare Reform." *Publius* 19, no. 3 (1989): 57–73.

U.S. House of Representatives, Committee on Ways and Means. *The Green Book, 1996.* Washington, D.C.: U.S. Government Printing Office, 1996.

Mark Carl Rom

WOMEN

By the mid-1970s, the manner in which women participated in and related to politics continued to evolve in four interconnected ways: (1) they became more politically active, eventually making up a powerful political constituency; (2) women's issues found a prominent place on the national agenda; (3) the two main political parties repolarized on the subject of feminist issues; and (4) women were elected to public office in unprecedented numbers, inhabiting increasingly powerful positions.

During this period, women capitalized on the gains that had been made in the 1960s and early 1970s. By 1960, they made up one-third of the workforce. Empowered by this expanded participation in the labor force and spurred by the civil rights movement that was also gaining momentum in the 1960s, women began to engage more regularly in political behavior. In the decades that followed, those changes were expanded and consolidated as women heightened their challenges to male dominance in political participation.

Women in the Electorate

The impact of women on politics was particularly evident in their role as voters. By the early 1990s, women had become one of the country's most influential constituencies. This impact can be traced, first, to the size of the female electorate, and second, to what is known as the "gender gap." Beginning in 1964, women voted in larger numbers than men, though a larger percentage of eligible males cast their ballots in each election for the next 16 years. Since 1980, however, the proportion of eligible female voters who cast ballots has been higher than the proportion of eligible male voters who cast ballots. As the country's largest body of voters, women often cast the majority of votes in elections, and as a result, they could significantly affect electoral outcomes. Women's votes were credited with shifting the outcome of the 1992 presidential election in favor of the Democratic candidates Bill Clinton and Al Gore. In 2000, they made the difference in 16 of the 20 states that Al Gore carried in his bid for the presidency.

This sizable clout was amplified by the gender gap, which refers to differences between women and men in political attitudes and voting choices. The gender gap in voting refers to gender-based disparities in levels of support for a candidate—usually the winning candidate. Even when the majority of men and women support the same candidate, they have tended to do so by different margins. Eleanor Smeal, the former president of the National Organization for Women (NOW), first identified the gender gap in the 1980 presidential election, noting that women were less likely than men to vote for Ronald Reagan. From 1980 to 2008, the

Vice presidential candidate Geraldine Ferraro sits next to presidential candidate Walter Mondale at a rally in Portland, Oregon, on October 1, 1984. As the primaries wound down and Mondale became the likely Democratic Party nominee, women's groups such as The National Organization for Women, the National Women's Political Caucus, the Women's Presidential Project, and the Gender Gap Action Campaign lobbied Mondale and the Democratic Party successfully to exploit the sizeable female electorate and the so-called gender gap that had first been identified in the 1980 presidential election by nominating a woman to be his running mate. As a result of their efforts, Ferraro became the first woman to be nominated by a major party for vice president. (Diana Walker/Time & Life Pictures/Getty Images)

gender gap was noted in every presidential election. It averaged 7.5 percentage points over the eight elections held in that period, from a low of 4 percentage points in 1992 to a high of 11 percentage points in 1996.

Furthermore, the gender gap in voting tends to break along partisan lines. Since 1992 women have been more likely to support and vote for Democratic Party candidates over their Republican Party opponents. In each presidential election from 1980 to 2008, the Democratic candidate received support from a greater proportion of women compared to the proportion of men voting for the same candidate. Thus, the gap in party identification parallels the gap in voting choices.

However, the gender gap in voting must be carefully interpreted, as it is actually an aggregation of factors rather than an automatic result of gender. Ideological positions are particularly important—women are more likely than men to adopt liberal political attitudes and support liberal policies. Thus, higher levels of support among women for the Democratic Party and its candidates reflect the greater number of women with liberal views. These ideological tendencies were heightened in 1980, as two complementary processes commenced. First, while women tended to become more liberal, men tended to become more conservative. At the same time, the Republican Party, influenced by the growing power of its more conservative members, shifted further to the right. These processes contribute to the observed differences in party identification and voting behavior among men and women.

The importance of the gender gap for politics in the United States has been contested. Yet the notion that women and men tend to vote differently has had important consequences for candidates and for women's groups. For candidates, it has underscored the need to court female voters by appealing to those issues that are most important to them: education, child care, and other social programs, in addition to women's rights issues. Moreover, this urgency to appeal to women is not restricted to a single political party. In 1992 and 1996, the Clinton-Gore campaign sought the support of "Soccer Moms," while the Bush-Cheney campaign pursued "Security Moms" in 2004.

Furthermore, the gender gap became an area of strategic interest for activists in the women's movement immediately after it was identified. These individuals believed that the gender gap, coupled with the size of the female electorate, could be exploited in order to advance their agenda. Women's groups successfully used it to press the Democratic Party to nominate a woman as vice president during the 1984 campaign. Hoping to unseat Republican incumbent Ronald Reagan, Walter Mondale selected Geraldine Ferraro to be his running mate, making her the first woman to run on a major party's national ticket.

Women's Issues Find a Prominent Place on the National Agenda

As women gradually wielded greater influence as voters, and as the women's movement gained momentum, greater attention was paid to issues affecting the rights and interests of women. Moreover, these issues were granted increasingly prominent places on the national agenda. Though some women's rights legislation was passed in the 1960s, the women's movement began to focus on more sweeping change in the form of a constitutional amendment known as the Equal Rights Amendment (ERA). Passed by Congress in 1972, the ERA sought to guarantee that the equality of rights would not be denied on the basis of sex. The ratification of the ERA by the necessary number of states dominated the agendas of women's groups until its ultimate defeat in 1982.

The demise of the ERA had a significant impact upon the women's movement, as one of their main targets for mobilization disintegrated. This spurred many groups to turn their attention to other goals. In particular, they focused their attention on litigation and legislation that would improve economic circumstances and expand opportunities for women. In order to force the courts to fill the perceived gaps in antidiscrimination protections left by the failure of the ERA, women's groups sued under Amendment XIV of the Constitution, Title VII of the 1964 Civil Rights Act (which prohibited discrimination on the basis of sex), and Title IX of the 1972 Educational Amendments Act (which prohibited discrimination against women in federally funded educational institutions). For instance, in *United States v. Virginia*, 518 U.S. 515 (1996), women won the right to attend the all-male Virginia Military Institute. They also pressed Congress to adopt protective legislation, eventually securing passage of the Lilly Ledbetter Fair Pay Act (2009), which expanded workers' rights to sue in cases of wage discrimination by relaxing the statute of limitations on such claims. Others sought to improve women's lives through legislation that would expand social welfare benefits, such as the Family and Medical Leave Act of 1993.

Though women experienced key judicial and legislative victories, not all efforts were successful. In *Grove City College v. Bell*, 465 U.S. 555 (1984), the Supreme Court limited Title IX by finding that it only applied to certain programs that received federal aid. President George H. W. Bush vetoed the Civil Rights Act of 1990, arguing that it would introduce quotas into the workplace. Women's groups, however, viewed the veto as killing legislation that would have made it easier for women to sue employers for discrimination. Women were also disproportionately affected by welfare reform passed in 1996, which limited the number of years that individuals were eligible for welfare benefits. Single mothers, in particular, were often faced with having to reenter the workplace while simultaneously caring for their children.

As the failure of the ERA caused women's groups to focus their mobilization efforts elsewhere, an increasingly powerful conservative constituency caused some to turn their attention toward protecting the abortion rights that had been granted by the Supreme Court in *Roe v. Wade*, 410 U.S. 113 (1973) and *Doe v. Bolton*, 410 U.S. 179 (1973). Coinciding with the election of Ronald Reagan in 1980, the rise of the New Right marked a resurgence of conservative activism and altered the political landscape. The New Right was a movement made up of various conservative secular, religious, and social groups. Beginning with grassroots organizing in the years leading up to the 1964 presidential election, the movement built a powerful network of organizations dedicated to advancing conservative causes. With their emphasis on traditional values, they considered feminism a threat to the American family and to society as a whole. In particular, they directed many of their attacks toward the issue of abortion. By the mid-1980s, the protection of abortion rights had become one of the defining issues of the women's rights movement. The issue was considered so critical that women's groups used views on abortion as a litmus test to oppose judicial nominations that might threaten to overturn key abortion rights legislation (they helped to defeat Robert Bork's nomination to the Supreme Court in 1987, for example). Most important, however, the growing influence of conservatives within the Republican Party and the emergence of abortion as a central issue set the party and women's groups on a path of opposition that endured into the twenty-first century.

The Consolidation of Party Polarization

The divide between the women's movement and conservatives in the New Right that characterized the Reagan presidency is indicative of a larger process of polarization, consensus, and realignment that had been occurring between the two major political parties in regard to the issue of women's rights. In 1940, the Republican Party inserted a pro-ERA plank into its platform and supported granting women legal equality. The Democratic Party, however, did not add the pro-ERA plank until 1944, and due to the influence of labor unions, the Democrats preferred to grant women specific legal protections rather than equality. By the 1960s and 1970s, the parties had reached a consensus, with women's rights increasingly linked with civil rights. In 1980, as the debate became centered upon issues like abortion, the parties became polarized again. This time, however, the polarization was characterized by realignment. The Republican Party moved away from feminist issues and associations with feminist organizations as its more conservative factions grew in power; that year, they removed the pro-ERA plank from the party platform. At the same time, the Democratic Party retained the pro-ERA plank and became more likely to support feminist issues. As the Republican Party shifted toward a more conservative ideological position in the late 1980s and early 1990s, the polarization that began with the rise of the New Right not only endured, it also became more pronounced. By 2009, the party positions on feminist issues were consolidated.

Expanded Roles for Women in Public Office

Efforts to install more women in the political elite had begun by the early 1970s. Yet women inhabiting these roles were still rare. By 1979, only 3 percent of congressional seats were held by women. There was not a woman on the Supreme Court until 1981, when Sandra Day O'Connor was appointed, and few women had held high-ranking positions in the executive, such as Cabinet-level appointments. Not only did existing groups, such as NOW and the League of Women Voters, shift significant attention to this goal, but a number of groups were founded specifically for this purpose, such as the National Women's Political Caucus (NWPC) in 1971 and the Fund for the Feminist Majority in 1987. Moreover, the defeat of the ERA spurred even greater numbers of women's groups to focus on recruiting, funding, and supporting female candidates as an alternate route to advancing the women's agenda.

Some focused on increasing the number of women appointed to decision-making positions. The NWPC convened the Coalition for Women's Appointments (CWA), which identified qualified female candidates for federal policy-making jobs; once candidates were identified, the CWA delivered their resumes to the White House and lobbied for their appointment. The NWPC was also instrumental in securing an expanded role for women in the party hierarchy, as it convinced the Democratic National Committee to pass a resolution requiring that 50 percent of delegates at Democratic conventions be women.

Efforts to elect more women to public office were also increased during this period. In addition to recruiting qualified individuals to run for office, women's groups raised money to fund them. As a result of changes to campaign finance reform laws in the early 1970s, several women's organizations created political action committees (PACs) to raise money for candidates of both major political parties who supported women's rights issues. The Women's Campaign Fund was founded in 1974 to support the election of pro-choice women, WISH List (Women In the Senate and House) was founded in 1992 to fund Republican women who supported abortion rights, and EMILY's List (derived from the saying, "Early

Money Is Like Yeast: It Makes the Dough Rise"), the largest of the women's PACs, was founded in 1985 to support pro-choice Democratic women. By 1997, there were more than 50 women's PACs registered.

Despite these efforts, women did not make significant gains until the 1992 election. Dubbed in the media as the "Year of the Woman," 1992 represented a watershed moment for women in politics, as female candidates competed for political office in unprecedented numbers. Over 100 women ran for the U.S. House of Representatives and 11 for positions in the U.S. Senate. At the state level, 2,375 women ran for legislative posts. Even more important, more women won seats in the House and Senate than in previous elections. In the Senate, victories by Barbara Boxer (D–CA), Dianne Feinstein (D–CA), Carol Moseley-Braun (D–IL), and Patty Murray (D–WA) tripled the number of women in that body from two to six, while 24 first-term women were elected to the House.

These results were attributed to a number of factors that converged to create unusual electoral circumstances. That election year saw an abnormally large number of open seats due to reapportionment and retirement, a situation that was exploited by the emerging fund-raising network for female candidates. EMILY's List alone supported more than 50 female candidates with over $6 million in 1992, making it the largest PAC supporting congressional candidates, regardless of gender. A House banking scandal contributed to an anti-incumbent mood, and an unprecedented sexual harassment allegation brought against Supreme Court nominee Clarence Thomas energized the women's movement while underscoring the lack of representation for women in Congress. The sight of law professor Anita Hill explaining her story to an all-male Senate Judiciary Committee on national television was credited with encouraging many women to run for office that year. The Thomas-Hill hearings also succeeded in drawing attention to the issue of sexual harassment, raising the profile of yet another women's issue on the national agenda.

The magnitude of the gains from the "Year of the Woman" slowed considerably in following electoral cycles. Yet women continued to experience absolute growth in their numbers at all levels of government.

By 2009, women held 93 of the 535 House and Senate seats. At the beginning of 2009, seven women—Jan Brewer (R–AZ), Jennifer Granholm (D–MI), Christine Gregoire (D–WA), Linda Lingle (R–HI), Sarah Palin (R–AK), Beverly M. Perdue (D–NC), and M. Jodi Rell (R–CT)—were state governors, though Sarah Palin would resign later that year. At that time, eight more women were lieutenant governors, and women held just over 24 percent of the seats in state legislatures.

Though parity was not achieved, the impact and visibility of women in government grew as they attained increasingly powerful positions in all branches of government. In the judiciary, Ruth Bader Ginsburg joined O'Connor on the Supreme Court in 1993, and Sonia Sotomayor was appointed to the Court by President Obama in 2009. In 2007, Nancy Pelosi (D–CA) became the first woman to serve as Speaker of the House, placing her second in the line of succession to the presidency. During the 2008 presidential campaign, Hillary Rodham Clinton became the first woman to win a major party's presidential primary, and she was also the first to be a presidential candidate in every primary and caucus in every state. In the same election, Gov. Sarah Palin of Alaska was selected by Sen. John McCain as his vice presidential running mate, making her the first woman to appear on a national Republican Party ticket.

Furthermore, women nominated for key executive branch posts in the latter part of this historical period—during the Bush, Clinton, and Obama administrations, in particular—were placed in roles overseeing diplomacy and national security, policy areas traditionally reserved for men. In 1997, Madeline Albright became the first female U.S. secretary of state. President George W. Bush named Condoleezza Rice as the first female national security advisor in 2000, and she became secretary of state in 2005. President Obama named women to head the Department of State, Department of Homeland Security, Department of Health and Human Services, Department of Labor, and as ambassador to the United Nations. The selection of women for these posts is indicative of the degree to which women have been challenging the male monopoly on political power.

Conclusion

Though barriers still remain to entry into the highest political offices, women have significantly altered how they relate to politics and how politics relates to them. Since the country's founding, women have moved from outright exclusion to becoming an influential political constituency and members of the political elite. As a result, women now routinely impact politics in profound ways.

Bibliography and Further Reading

Center for American Women and Politics, Eagleton Institute of Politics at Rutgers, the State University of New Jersey. http://www.cawp.rutgers.edu/index.php (accessed July 20, 2009).

Ferguson, Michaele L., and Lori Jo Marso, eds. *W Stands for Women: How the George W. Bush Presidency Shaped a New Politics of Gender*. Durham, NC: Duke University Press, 2007.

Gutgold, Nichola D. *Paving the Way for Madam President*. Lanham, MD: Lexington Books, 2006.

Haussman, Melissa H. "The Personal Is Constitutional: Feminist Struggles for Equality Rights in the United States and Canada." In *Women Transforming Politics: Worldwide Strategies for Empowerment*, edited by Jill M. Bystydzienski. Bloomington: Indiana University Press, 1992.

McGlen, Nancy E., Karen O'Connor, Laura van Assendelft, and Wendy Gunther-Canada. *Women, Politics, and American Society*, 4th edition. Upper Saddle River, NJ: Pearson Education, 2004.

Rymph, Catherine E. *Republican Women: Feminism and Conservatism from Suffrage through the Rise of the New Right*. Chapel Hill: University of North Carolina Press, 2006.

Swers, Michele L. *The Difference Women Make: The Policy Impact of Women in Congress*. Chicago: University of Chicago Press, 2002.

Wolbrecht, Christina. *The Politics of Women's Rights: Parties, Positions and Change.* Princeton, NJ: Princeton University Press, 2000.

Wolbrecht, Christina, Karen Beckwith, and Lisa Baldez, eds. *Political Women and American Democracy.* New York: Cambridge University Press, 2008.

Alison M. Uzdella

WORK, CHANGING NATURE OF

The employment system and its norms that dominated the U.S. economy from the 1950s through the 1970s collapsed in succeeding decades under the weight of deregulation, technological change (computers and communications in particular), globalization of product markets, and intense short-term pressure from capital markets. The ultimate characteristics of the new labor market remain unclear, but changes since the late 1970s have had significant political ramifications at the local, regional, and national levels.

Key work and labor market trends include: the decline of manufacturing (from about one-third of all employment in 1946 to just over one-tenth in 2000) and the rise of services; the collapse of internal labor markets within large firms and the increased importance of skills, education, and credentials to career advancement; increased employment volatility and shorter job tenure, particularly for male workers; a rise in temporary work and other forms of contingent labor; and a steady erosion of union representation in the nation's largest and highest-growth industries. In 1983, one in five American workers was a union member; in 2006, only one in eight (12 percent) was. Since the 1950s, the percentage of the workforce employed part-time almost doubled, reaching 19 percent in the 1990s. In the 1960s, unionized General Motors, which paid middle-class wages and provided generous health and pension benefits, was the nation's largest employer; in 2000, nonunion Wal-Mart, paying much lower average wages, employing more part-time workers, and providing limited benefits only to some employees, has that distinction.

Income inequality has risen as jobs at both the low and high ends of the economy have grown faster than those in the middle. About 20 percent of workers saw their earnings rise in the 1980s and 1990s. At the same time, though, a larger number of workers lost ground. Low-paying, low-skill jobs have attracted a flood of immigrants, further reducing any pressure to raise wages in those jobs. The failure to adjust the federal minimum wage for inflation led to a 30 percent fall in its real value from 1979 to 2006. The rising education and skill requirements of service jobs have driven many low-skill workers, particularly black males, out of the labor force altogether, while enabling workers with advanced degrees to pull away from other groups in annual income growth.

Perhaps more important, rising economic *inequality* has been accompanied by a dramatic increase in economic *insecurity*. The security that came from long-term full-time employment with generous benefits, which had characterized the core of the U.S. economy, has been replaced by a pattern of employment in which individuals are on their own in the labor market and their advancement is determined not by seniority but by their flexibility, mobility, and level of skill and education.

The varying realities and self-interests of workers who succeed in the new economy versus those stuck at the bottom have weakened traditional national Democratic coalitions, particularly as labor union membership and political power declined. Employers' decreased commitment to their employees and communities both accelerated and reinforced the dominance of the antigovernment, hyper-individualistic political ideology that triumphed in national politics from the 1980s on. After heated national political battles in the 1980s over industrial policy, trade, and regulatory intervention that might help slow or cushion the negative impacts of economic change on American workers, the ideology of individual risk and responsibility captured the political pinnacle by the opening years of the twenty-first century and met with little resistance. President George W. Bush tapped this sentiment by representing his efforts to reform Social Security through privatization as a move toward an "ownership society."

The salience of the issues of inequality and insecurity has tended to rise and recede in different electoral cycles, often losing out to other priorities, such as war, terrorism fears, or social issues. Whether the pendulum swings away from the current, almost exclusive, emphasis on individual risk and responsibility—in the workplace, the economy, and the political arena—to a greater balance between social democratic and market ideologies, will be an important variable in twenty-first-century U.S. politics.

Bibliography and Further Reading

Applebaum, Eileen, and Rosemary Batt. *The New American Workplace*. Ithaca, NY: Cornell University Press, 1994.

Beauregard, Robert A., ed. *Economic Restructuring and Political Response*. Urban Affairs Annual Reviews 34. Newbury Park, CA: Sage Publications, 1989.

Hacker, Jacob S. *The Great Risk Shift*. New York: Oxford University Press, 2006.

Herzenberg, Stephen, John Alic, and Howard Wial. *New Rules for a New Economy: Employment and Opportunity in Postindustrial America*. Ithaca, NY: ILR Press, 1998.

Osterman, Paul. *Securing Prosperity*. Princeton, NJ: Princeton University Press, 1999.

Richard Kazis

Cumulative Index

Page numbers in **boldface** type indicate articles on subject. Page numbers in *italic* type indicate illustrations or other graphics.

immigration policy and, **7:**215, 218

judiciary and, **7:**15, 44, 258, 347

liberalism attacks by, **7:**253

NAFTA and, **7:**42, 177

NEH appointment and, **7:**267

neoconservative critique of, **7:**271

nuclear weapons and, **7:**281

pollster for, **7:**312

popularity rise/decline of, **7:**105, 125

presidency assessment of, **7:**42–43

racialized politics and, **7:**23

savings and loan crisis and, **7:**353

son George W. and, **7:**43–44

space policy and, **7:**356, 357, 368

tax pledge reversal by, **7:**7, 8, 42, 82, 96, 171

vice presidency and, **7:**40, 43

on "voodoo economics," **7:**6

women's rights and, **7:**414

See also election of 1988; election of 1992; Persian Gulf War

Bush, George W., **6:**68, 393; **7:**26, **43–48,** 89, 97

antiabortion policies and, **7:**15, 101–2

antigovernment policies and, **7:**6, 44–45

"axis of evil" speech of, **7:**46, 382, 406

Cheney vice presidency and, **7:**45, 67, 68–69

climate change and, **7:**79, 142, 357

conservatism and, **7:**5, 43, 101–2, 131, 175

deregulation and, **7:**108

domestic agenda of, **7:**44–45, 97

drug policy and, **7:**113

education policy and, **7:**119–20

environmental policy and, **7:**141–42

executive orders and, **4:**286

executive power claims and, **7:**348

FEMA and, **7:**159–60

financial crisis (2008) and, **7:**47, 48, 166, 167

Hispanics and, **7:**200

homeland security and, **7:**204–5, 206

human rights abuses and, **7:**210–11, 212

Hurricane Katrina and, **7:**107, 151

immigration policy and, **7:**217

income inequality and, **7:**223

judiciary and, **7:**15–16, 47, 52, 133, 334, 346, 379

mistakes of, **7:**287

9/11 Commission and, **7:**65, 276, 277–78, 279

NEH budget and, **7:**268

neoconservatives and, **6:**22; **7:**239, 272

nuclear weapons and, **7:**281

"ownership society" and, **7:**10, 44, 45, 417

Patriot Act and, **7:**400, 402, 406

popularity decline of, **6:**377; **7:**46–47, 48, 50, 106, 107, 138, 285, 287, 365

presidency assessment of, **7:**47–48, 345

public opinion polling by, **7:**312

Reagan presidency contrasted with, **7:**345

reasons for presidential wins of, **7:**130–31, 133–34

Religious Right and, **7:**226, 334–35, 339–40, 344

science and technology and, **7:**357–58

September 11 attacks and, **7:**106, 131, 277–78, 360, 361, *362*

social policy and, **7:**7, 10, 44–45, 106–7, 110

Social Security privatization proposal and, **7:**6, 44, 45, 97, 106–7, 110, 117, 365, 417

space policy and, **7:**358, 366, 368–69

state-federal relations and, **7:**372–73

steel import quotas and, **4:**126

suburban voters and, **7:**399

tax cuts and, **7:**7, 10, 44, 45, 47, 68, 97, 101, 131, 168, 171, 345, 383

torture and, **7:**66

trade policy and, **7:**177

voter backlash against, **7:**285, 287, 288

war on terror and, **7:**43, 45, 46, 48, 66, 91, 150, 212, 363, 405–8

See also election of 2000; election of 2004; Iraq War

Bush, Vannevar, **6:**341–42, 343, 344

Bush Doctrine, **7:**45, 240, 272

Bushnell, Asa, **4:**166

Bush v. Gore (2000), **7:**106, 129, 222, 332, 372, 378

business. *See* corporations

Business Industry Political Action Committee, **7:**301

Business Roundtable, **7:**248

busing and anti-busing movement, **6:**69–73, 90, 95, 130, 291; **7:**20, 21, 118

Court rulings and, **6:**68, 86; **7:**37

labor unions and, **6:**248

legacy of, **6:**72–73

political backlash and, **6:**71, 400; **7:**269, 318

public opinion and, **6:**313

Butler, Andrew P., **3:**56, 97, 133, 332

Butler, Benjamin F., **3:**107, 195, 219, 245, 267; **4:**367

Grant administration scandals and, **3:**304, 305

Greenback-Labor Party and, **3:**360

Butler, Edward, **4:**376

Butler, John M., **6:**254

Butler, Marion, **4:**284

Butler, Pierce, **5:**105

Butler, Smedley, **5:**36

Butler's Rangers, **1:**198

Butz, Earl, **6:**21–22

Byllynge, Edward, **1:**242, 279

Byrd, Harry Flood, **5:**35, 94–95, 112

Byrd family, **1:**374

Byrnes, James F., **5:**82; **6:**96, 310

Byrnes, John W., **6:**263, 264

Byrns, Joseph W., **5:**23, 82

Cabinet

Articles of Confederation and, **1:**16

executive branch and, **2:**144

executive branch reorganization and, **6:**197

expansion of, **4:**138, 346

homeland security and, **7:**204, 205–10

Jackson and, **2:**119–21, 188, 377

new departments and, **6:**157

presidency and, **2:**291, 292

Tenure of Office Act and, **3:**192, 194–95, 203

Washington and, **2:**379

women members of, **5:**263–66; **6:**410, 413; **7:**415, 416

Cable Act (1922), **4:**48; **5:**413

Cable News Network. *See* CNN

cable television, **7:**49–51, 272, 273–74

deregulation and, **7:**109

Persian Gulf War and, **7:**49, 273, 298

political influence of, **7:**50

presidential image and, **7:**307

sex scandals and, **7:**145

Cabot, George, **2:**337

Cabot, John, **1:**97, 233

Caddell, Patrick, **7:**312

Cadore Letter, **2:**269

Calder v. Bull (1798), **2:**340

Calhoun, Floride, **2:**119, 121, 377

Calhoun, John C., **1:**350; **2:**73–76, 91, 107, 130, 134; **3:**63–66, 96

Bank of the United States and, **2:**60–61, 131

Compromise of 1850 and, **3:**64, 86

Eaton Affair and, **2:**119, 120, 121, 189

election of 1824 withdrawal by, **2:**282

election of 1844 and, **2:**76; **3:**64, 378

gag rules and, **2:**157

Indian policy and, **2:**48, 177

internal improvements and, **2:**74, 184

Irish immigrants and, **3:**250–51

Jackson and, **2:**75, 108, 119, 120, 121, 188

land policy and, **2:**227

Panic of 1819 and, **2:**286

slavery and, **2:**368, 388; **3:**52, 63, 64–65, 72, 86, 96, 110, 130, 243, 270, 286, 317, 318

tariff and, **2:**27, 182, 277, 346, 347, 386

Texas annexation and, **3:**317, 357, 368

vice presidency of, **2:**132

as War Hawk, **2:**73–74, 242, 254

See also nullification; Nullification Crisis

California, **1:**137, 352; **3:**38, 96; **4:**305

abortion reform and, **7:**13

Cigar Makers' International Union, **4:**31, 158

Cincinnati, New Orleans and Texas Pacific Railway Company v. ICC (1896), **4:**347

CIO. *See* AFL-CIO; Congress of Industrial Organizations

CIO-PAC, **5:**4, 31, 88–89, 113, 210, 424; **6:**301; **7:**301

circuit court system, **2:**218, 340, 341

Cisneros, Henry, **7:**198

CISPES (El Salvador), **7:**154

cities. *See* urbanization; *specific cities*

Citizen Labor Energy Coalition, **7:**249, 254

Citizens Against Government Waste, **7:**146

Citizens' Commission to Investigate the FBI, **6:**168

citizenship, **2:**173, 174; **5:**46, 47, 186, 187, 189; **6:**192

African Americans and, **2:**16, 29; **3:**10.3.193, 202, 230, 327, 336, 337

Alien Acts and, **2:**33–34, 111, 154, 207

Amendment XIV and, **4:**274, 390–91, 404

American Indians and, **4:**36, 37, 108; **7:**28

Asian restrictions and, **3:**191; **4:**46, 48, 188, 189; **5:**46, 47, 49, 187

children of undocumented mothers and, **7:**217, 218

congressional regulation of, **3:**188–89

Cuban Americans and, **6:**194; **7:**196

Dred Scott ruling and, **3:**275, 326, 336

executive branch and, **4:**139

Federalist vs. Republican policy on, **2:**263–64

full civil rights and, **4:**79, 174

Louisiana Purchase and, **2:**236

as male only, **1:**401

nativist restrictive policy and, **3:**208, 211, 247

Puerto Ricans and, **4:**340; **6:**194; **7:**196

requirements for, **4:**182, 188

Square Deal and, **4:**344

state vs. federal policy and, **3:**337–38

U.S. territories and, **4:**64

woman suffrage denial and, **4:**390–91, 404, 408

women's claim to, **3:**309, 388

Citizens United v. Federal Election Commission (2009), **7:**53

City of God, The (Augustine), **1:**284

City of New York v. Miln (1837), **2:**174

City of Renton v. Playtime Theatres (1896), **7:**70

"City upon a Hill" (Winthrop vision), **1:**398, 399

Civil Aeronautics Board, **5:**285, 289; **6:**197, 325

end of, **7:**109, 148, 192, 326

civil defense, **7:**157–58, 275, 281

Civilian Conservation Corps, **5:**63–66, 92, 147, 159, 252–53, 305, 326, 327, 376; **7:**3

African Americans and, **5:**19, 65

Perkins and, **5:**264

program of, **5:**294

Roosevelt (Eleanor) and, **5:**301

termination of, **5:**9, 65, 139, 271, 328

women's exclusion from, **5:**255

Civilian Conservation Corps Reforestation Relief Act (1933), **5:**124

civil liberties, **2:**11–12, 76–79; **3:**71–77; **4:**58, 69–74; **5:**8, 66–71, 343–45; **6:**82–87; **7:**70–74

African Americans and, **2:**78–79, 324

British antecedents of, **2:**77, 215

Burger and, **7:**36–37

conservative-backed types of, **7:**73–74

Court rulings and, **4:**69–72, 353–54, 396–97; **5:**67, 68–70, 339–40; **6:**58, 64, 66, 68, 82, 357–58, 403; **7:**70

Declaration of Independence and, **1:**16

definition of, **2:**76

Democratic Societies and, **2:**7, 116

enemy combatants and, **7:**46, 378–79

executive branch and, **4:**141–42

FBI violations of, **5:**141; **6:**168, 169, 200–201; **7:**153, 154, 156

freedom of conscience and, **2:**365–66

gag rules vs., **2:**158–59

homeland security and, **7:**45, 309, 362, 363

HUAC hearings and, **6:**2032–34

immigrants and, **3:**252

Jefferson and, **2:**78, 205, 210

liberal organizations and, **7:**251

of Loyalists, **1:**197

Marshall (Thurgood) and, **7:**259–60

national security vs., **4:**186, 189, 219, 294, 347–48, 353, 401, 412; **5:**41, 67, 68, 70, 198, 422–23; **6:**83–84, 355–56, 394, 395, 396

Northwest Ordinance and, **2:**271

peace movement and, **4:**227, 272, 273

personal liberty laws and, **3:**260–62

public opinion and, **6:**313–14

Red Scare and, **4:**61, 185, 219, 310–11

Taney and, **3:**344

USA PATRIOT Act and, **7:**400–403, 406, 407

See also Alien and Sedition Acts; Bill of Rights; Japanese-American relocation

Civil Liberties Act (1988), **6:**51

civil rights, **2:**79–82; **3:**10, 12, 71–77; **4:**11, 19, 74–79, 349–50; **5:**7–8, 71–75, 190; **6:**87–91; **7:**74–78

affirmative action and, **7:**16–19, 17, 19, 21, 75, 291

African Americans and, **3:**23, 25, 74–75, 76, 98–99, 100, 160, 161, 178; **4:**74–79, 150

Amendment XIV and, **3:**10, 220, 337

American Indians and, **2:**49, 107, 343–44

American Revolution's language of, **1:**46

Burger and, **6:**68, 359; **7:**37

busing controversy and, **6:**69–73, 90

Civil War Republicans and, **3:**298

colonial restrictions on, **1:**6, 375–76

Communists and, **5:**19, 76

conservatives and, **7:**101

Court rulings and, **3:**335, 337–38; **5:**13, 14, 20, 72–73, 75, 180, 182, 242, 319–21, 339, 343–45, 424

definition of, **7:**74

Democrats and, **6:**120, 122, 137, 164, 209

disabled people and, **7;** **7:**42

District of Columbia representation and, **6:**24–25

education access and, **4:**169; **6:**130–31

Edwards (Jonathan) and, **1:**120

Eisenhower and, **6:**133, 136, 306, 351

employment access and, **6:**145, 246, 275

expansion of, **6:**11–12, 14, 15

FBI and, **5:**144; **6:**169

federal intervention and, **6:**352

first era of, **7:**74–75

Freedmen's Bureau and, **3:**160, 161

gag rules and, **3:**21–22

gays and lesbians and, **7:**179–82

Gingrich defense of, **7:**183, 184

Hayes and, **4:**173, 174, 175, 177

housing and, **6:**207–8

Humphrey and, **6:**209

immigrant groups and, **4:**189

Jeffersonian democracy and, **2:**213

Jim Crow vs. *See* Jim Crow

Johnson (Andrew) vetoes and, **3:**192, 193–94, 202, 291

Johnson (Lyndon B.) and, **6:**5, 120, 142, 225, 228, 307

Kennedy (John) and, **6:**26, 89, 94, 230, 232–33, 235, 236, 307, 351

liberalism and, **7:**251, 253

Lincoln and, **3:**229

Manhattan Project and, **5:**232

Marshall (Thurgood) and, **7:**257, 258–59

NAACP and, **4:**12, 15, 16, 17, 79, 254–57; **5:**243, 320

Nixon and, **6:**291

poll tax ban and, **6:**25–27

post–1970s extension of, **7:**75–78

post–World War II pressures and, **6:**1, 2, 15

private vs. state infringement of, **4:**150, 206, 207, 274, 275; **7:**15

Progressive Party and, **4:**296, 302

state-federal relations and, **3:**326–27

states' rights and, **2:**335

Stevens and, **3:**329–30

tariffs and, **3:**8, 346

Tubman and, **3:**363

Uncle Tom's Cabin and, **3:**371, 372, 392

See also Confederate States of America; Copperheads; Emancipation Proclamation; Reconstruction; secession crisis; Union Army

Civil War amendments. *See* Amendment XIII, Amendment XIV, Amendment XV

Civil Works Administration, **5:**136–37, 253, 294, 377

Claflin, Tennessee, **6:**336

Claiborne, William, **1:**177, 201, 202, 203

Clapp, Moses, **4:**262

Clapper, Raymond, **5:**85, 273

Clark, Champ, **5:**35

Clark, Dick, **7:**14

Clark, Edward, **7:**388

Clark, George Rogers, **1:**141, 161, 385–86; **2:**267

Clark, Grenville, **5:**89

Clark, James Beauchamp ("Champ"), **4:**8, 131–32

Clark, J. Bennett, **5:**150

Clark, Jim, **6:**236

Clark, J. Reuben, **5:**153

Clark, Septima, **6:**295

Clark, Tom, **6:**355, 395, 416

Clark, William, **2:**228, 229, 231, 290

Clarke, Edward Young, **5:**203

Clarke, John, **1:**100, 101, 310

Clarke, Richard (counterterrorism chief), **7:**277, 278

Clarke, Walter, **1:**71

Clarke-McNary Act (1924), **5:**91

Clarkson, Thomas, **1:**52

class action suits, **7:**390

classical economics, **7:**115–16

classified advertising, **7:**274

Clay, Henry, **2:**82–86, 91, 120, 135, 170, 257, 281; **3:**82–85, 103, 186, 274

Adams (John Q.) and, **2:**27, 75, 132, 133, 187; **3:**377

Bank of the United States and, **2:**61, 94, 189, 288, 387

Benton and, **3:**50–51

black colonization and, **2:**43, 83; **3:**15, 84

Blaine policy parallels with, **4:**54

compromises of, **2:**11, 75, 83, 84, 85, 93, 249, 251, 277, 311, 312, 332

economic policy and, **2:**124–25, 287

election of 1844 and, **3:**83, 110, 129, 131

executive branch and, **3:**151, 152

Fillmore and, **3:**84, 157

Fugitive Slave Act and, **3:**84, 86, 165, 166, 168

internal improvements and. *See* American System

Jackson censure and, **2:**296

land policy and, **2:**227–28

Mexican War opposition by, **2:**392

nationalism and, **2:**331

political outlook of, **2:**52, 112, 136

Polk defeat of, **3:**268

presidential bids of, **2:**50, 53, 83, 131–32, 137, 189, 282, 391; **3:**3, 58, 83, 248, 267, 268, 351, 357, 368, 382

slavery and, **2:**388; **3:**84, 131

tariff and, **2:**84, 85, 197, 277, 312, 332, 335, 346, 348

Texas annexation and, **2:**235–36, 391; **3:**130, 131, 357, 378

Tyler and, **3:**316, 317, 356

as War Hawk, **2:**73–74, 82, 92, 168, 242, 254

See also Whig Party

Claybrook, Joan, **6:**112

Clayton, John, **3:**85, 86

Clayton Antitrust Act (1914), **4:**9, 32, 98, 116, 297; **5:**287, 342

exemptions to, **4:**9, 43, 125, 202, 218, 303

Federal Trade Commission and, **4:**315

legal challenges to, **4:**264

specific enumerations of, **4:**125

Wilson signing of, **4:**263, 399

Clayton-Bulwer Treaty (1850), **2:**259; **3:**349

Clean Air Act (1955), **6:**153

Clean Air Act (1963), **6:**153

Clean Air Act (1970), **6:**9, 149, 154, 324; **7:**80, 140

Clean Air Amendments (1990), **7:**42, 96, 140, 142, 327

Clean Water Act (1972), **6:**9, 149, 154, 374; **7:**96, 227

Clean Water Restoration Act (1966), **6:**153

"clear and present danger" test, **4:**71, 179, 353, 412

Clear Channel, **7:**273

Clearwater, Frank, **6:**32

Cleburne, Patrick, **3:**94, 251

Clemenceau, Georges, **4:**384, 402

Cleveland (Ohio)

black mayor of, **6:**18; **7:**22, 316

executive orders and, **4:**286

Hanna and, **4:**165

suburbs of, **4:**380

tariffs and, **4:**360

Cleveland, Grover, **3:**126, 306, 359; **4:**4, 57, 62, 63, 85–90, 166, 170, 173, 191, 192, 242, 345; **5:**32, 185

civil service reform and, **4:**80, 83–84, 87, 140, 286, 287

Cuban revolution and, **4:**337–38, 340

depression of 1890s and, **4:**89, 90, 114, 118–21, 126, 127, 236, 270

judiciary and, **4:**87, 152, 395

monetary policy and, **4:**4, 85, 89, 114, 115, 121, 124, 127

outlook of, **4:**85, 86, 87, 90, 96, 112, 113

presidency assessment of, **4:**85, 87, 90

Pullman Strike and, **4:**3, 89–90, 110, 124, 126, 222, 270, 306

Republican divisions and, **4:**86, 140, 249–50, 286, 322

veto use by, **4:**86–87, 113, 119, 169

Cleveland Foundation, **5:**58

Clifford, Clark, **6:**376

climate change, **7:**78–81, 139, 141, 142, 189, 356, 357, 358

Gore focus on, **7:**357

Clinton, Bill, **6:**101, 173, 184, 393; **7:**9, 81–87, 155

abortion and, **7:**15

balanced budget and, **7:**8, 10, 81, 83, 84, 97, 105, 171, 185–86

Balkan wars and, **7:**65, 81, 86, 212, 239

centrism of, **6:**211; **7:**101, 105, 124, 125, 127, 151, 252, 344, 371

climate change and, **7:**79

Congress and, **7:**84, 96–97, 306

culture wars and, **7:**271

drug policy and, **7:**113

economic policy and, **7:**42, 116–17, 164, 166–67

education policy and, **7:**119

environmental policy and, **7:**141

ethics reform and, **7:**144

executive branch makeover and, **7:**149–50, 308, 309

executive orders and, **7:**306

FEMA reorganization and, **7:**158

fiscal policy and, **7:**81, 82, 84, 86, 97, 105, 170

foreign policy and, **7:**45, 48, 82, 86, 239

gays in military and, **7:**181

Gingrich standoff of, **7:**186

Gore presidential campaign and, **7:**129

health care and, **7:**3, 8, 83–84, 89, 194

Hispanics and, **7:**198

immigration policy and, **7:**217, 218

income inequality and, **7:**223

Indian policy and, **7:**26

international agreements and, **7:**212

Internet use and, **7:**228

Iraq policy and, **7:**221, 239, 408

judiciary and, **7:**71, 377

liberal goals and, **7:**253

media and, **7:**50, 145

9/11 Commission and, **7:**277, 278

NAFTA and, **7:**394

NEH programs and, **7:**267

neoconservative critique of, **7:**271–72

New Democrats and, **6:**211

pardon controversy and, **7:**87

pollsters for, **7:**312

popularity of, **7:**84, 106, 131, 145, 221

post–presidency of, **7:**87

presidency assessment of, **7:**87

public image of, **7:**307

regulation and, **7:**327

scandals and, **7:**82, 84, 86, 88, 89, 94, 98, 105, 125, 145, 220, 230, 234, 344

property tax revolts and, **7:**6, 382

public opinion and, **6:**315; **7:**9

Reagan tax-increasing programs and, **7:**169–70

reform proposals, **4:**282, 324

Regulator opposition to, **1:**293

Republicans and, **7:**7, 8, 381

Roosevelt (Franklin D.) and, **5:**147, 148, 254, 271, 355–57

Seven Years' War and, **1:**330, 365, 366

supply-side economics and, **7:**6–7, 22–23, 169

three-fifths clause and, **2:**310

Treasury Department and, **1:**224, 367

urban decreased base and, **7:**22

Virginia Resolves and, **1:**62, 354

See also excise tax; income tax, federal; tariffs

tax rebellions, **6:**161–62. *See also* Fries's Rebellion; Shays's Rebellion; Whiskey Rebellion

Tax Reform Act (1986), **5:**357; **7:**169, 382–83, 384

Taylor, Alan, **1:**192

Taylor, Glen, **6:**311, 312

Taylor, John, **2:**22, 112, 249–50, 251, 331, 364; **3:**51

Taylor, Nick, **5:**418

Taylor, Recy, **6:**295

Taylor, Zachary, **2:**85, 392; **3:**313, **347–50,** 379, 386

Compromise of 1850 and, **3:**274, 317–18, 347, 349

conspiracy theories and, **3:**349

Davis (Jefferson) and, **3:**106

death in office of, **3:**84, 87, 157, 274, 318, 347, 349

executive branch and, **3:**152

Grant and, **3:**175

Mexican War command and, **3:**175, 241, 243, 244, 269, 347, 348, 349

slavery and, **3:**86

Webster and, **3:**382–83

See also election of 1848

Taylor rule, **7:**164

Tea Act (1773), **1:**14, 24, 157, 240, 371

colonist response to, **1:**53–54, 79, 210, 319, 345–46

teach-ins, **6:**40

TEAM Act, **7:**249–50

Teamsters Union, **5:**213, 310, 372, 423; **6:**247, 380

Teapot Dome Affair, **4:**227; **5:**4, 80, 91, 267, 296, **358–61; 6:**79, 199; **7:**153

Coolidge and, **5:**97–98, 360

FBI and, **5:**141

Interior Department and, **5:**166, 273, 358

press coverage of, **5:**273

technology. *See* science and technology policy

Tecumseh, **2:**10, 48, 243, 312, 313, 314, 372; **3:**184, 185

Teeter, Robert, **6:**320; **7:**312

Teheran Conference (1943), **5:**308

Telecommunications Act (1996), **7:**109, 272–73

telecommunications databases, **7:**406, 408

telegraph

Interstate Commerce Commission and, **4:**357

news transmission by, **3:**280

significance of, **4:**287, 289

transatlantic, **3:**313, 315

telemarketing, **7:**311

telephones, **5:**286

deregulation of, **7:**116

Interstate Commerce Commission and, **4:**357

secret database program, **7:**406

telephone surveys, **6:**320, 321; **7:**311–12

televangelists, **7:**333, 339

television, **6:**257–61; **7:272–75**

Army-McCarthy hearings and, **6:**132–33, 255, 258

campaign advertising and, **7:**53, 272, 273

campaign financing and, **6:**76

civil rights violence and, **6:**259–60

FBI portrayals by, **6:**169

Hurricane Katrina coverage and, **7:**50, 160

Iran Hostage Crisis and, **7:**236

Kennedy (John) use of, **6:**230, 282, 289, 306

McCarthy's (Joseph) downfall and, **6:**255–56, 258

network channels and, **6:**258; **7:**272–75

Nixon and, **6:**289

political ads and, **6:**120, 142, 147, 183, 261

presidential debates and, **6:**259, 289

sexually explicit speech and, **7:**70

Vietnam War and, **6:**260–61

See also cable television

Telfair, Edward, **2:**36–37

Teller, Edward, **6:**134

Teller, Henry M., **4:**34, 238, 242

Teller Amendment (1898), **4:**191, 238, 339, 340

Telles, Raymond L., **6:**192

temperance and prohibition, **2:**15, 107, 175; **3:**230; **4:**10, **362–65,** 381

Amendment XVIII and, **4:**11, 26–28, 30

Anthony and, **3:**42

background of, **4:**26–27, 362–63

Benezet and, **1:**52

Democratic vs. Republican view of, **4:**113, 319

Edwards (Jonathan) and, **1:**120

Farmers' Alliance women and, **4:**144

Garrison and, **3:**170

immigrants and, **2:**266; **3:**187–88, 248, 249–50; **4:**11, 27, 283, 363; **5:**186

labor groups and, **3:**217

Populist non-endorsement of, **4:**283

progressive reform and, **4:**302

Quakers and, **1:**302

voluntary associations and, **2:**368

woman suffrage linked with, **4:**11, 30, 134, 364, 408

women's movement and, **3:**323, 387, 390, 391, 393

See also Anti-Saloon League; Prohibition; Prohibition Party

Temporary Assistance for Needy Families, **7:**8, 371, 409, 411

Temporary Emergency Relief Administration (N.Y.), **5:**292, 376

tenant farmers, **1:**192–93; **3:**218; **5:**18, 158, 322, 371

Agricultural Adjustment Act and, **5:**19, 23–24, 253, 293

Anti-Rent War and, **3:**44–45

Ten Commandments display, **7:**72

Tenet, George, **7:**63, 277, 278

ten-hour workday, **3:**217–18, 219; **4:**40

Tennessee, **1:**139, 140; **3:**153

Amendment XXIV ratification and, **6:**26

black boycotts in, **4:**75

black disenfranchisement in, **4:**77

Confederacy and, **3:**89, 91, 94

election of 1860 and, **3:**119

Emancipation Proclamation and, **3:**148

Klan strength in, **3:**212, 213, 293

readmittance of, **3:**327

secession of, **3:**306, 315

slavery and, **2:**309

woman suffrage ratification in, **4:**11, 30, 408

Tennessee Coal & Iron Co., **4:**130, 358

Tennessee Valley Authority, **5:**82, 94, 124, 253, 305, **361–64; 6:**158–59, 165, 183, 286

competitors of, **5:**299, 363–64, 405

conservation policy and, **5:**65, 93

Manhattan Project and, **5:**231

Moley and, **5:**59

overview of, **5:**293

Tenskwatawa (the Prophet), **2:**48, 312, 313, 314; **3:**184, 378

Tenth Amendment. *See* Amendment X

Tenure of Office Act (1820), **2:**326

Tenure of Office Act (1867), **3:**99, 154, 192, 194–95, 203, 273, 277, 292; **4:**81, 83, 87; **7:**219

repeal (1887) of, **4:**87

Ten Year's War (Cuba), **4:**337

term limits, **6:**1; **7:**2

House committee chairs and, **7:**94

presidency and, **6:**1, 23–25; **7:**128, 135

Terrell, Mary Church, **4:**16

territorial expansion, **2:349–52;** **3:**150, **350–54**

Adams (John Q.) belief in, **2:**25, 26, 27

British restrictions on, **1:**389, 391

Buchanan and, **3:**58, 59, 60

constitutionality of, **2:**234–35

Cuban annexation initiative and, **3:**238, 239, 240, 265

Democratic advocacy of, **2:**107; **3:**95, 109, 110, 113

Douglas and, **3:**116

election of 1844 and, **2:**391

executive branch and, **2:**145, 147

Grant Dominican Republic plan and, **3:**278–79, 305, 333

Homestead Act and, **3:**190

immigrants and, **3:**187, 190–91